THE WHOLE
INTERNET
THE NEXT GENERATION

A Completely New Edition of the First
—and Best—
User's Guide to the Internet

THE WHOLE INTERNET
THE NEXT GENERATION

*A Completely New Edition of the First
—and Best—
User's Guide to the Internet*

KIERSTEN CONNER-SAX AND ED KROL

O'REILLY®

Beijing • Cambridge • Farnham • Köln • Paris • Sebastopol • Taipei • Tokyo

The Whole Internet: The Next Generation

by Kiersten Conner-Sax and Ed Krol

Inc., 101 Morris Street, Sebastopol, CA 95472.

October 1999:   First Edition.

TABLE OF CONTENTS

PREFACE _____ *ix*

CHAPTER ONE

WHAT YOU WILL LEARN _____ *1*

What This Book Is About   1
History   3
What's Allowed on the Internet?   11
How the Internet Works   13

CHAPTER TWO

EMAIL AND NEWS _____ *20*

When Is Internet Communication Useful?   20
An Email Primer   22
Choosing a Communications (Mostly Email) Package   26
Composing Messages: A Netiquette Primer   32
Handling Incoming Messages   38
Configuration Tips for Users   40
When Email Gets Returned   41
Email on the PalmPilot   44
Mailing Lists   47
Usenet   53

CHAPTER THREE

CONQUERING EMAIL _____ *66*

Conquering Common Email Problems   66
Using Filters   67
Mailer Configuration   71
Handling File Attachments   82
Traveling with Email   85
Free Accounts   92
Other Internet Communications Tools   96
Spam Busting   100

CHAPTER FOUR

WORLD WIDE WEB BROWSING _____ *107*

A Browsing Primer	108
Document Management	113
Security	123
Plug-Ins	124
Speeding Things Up	126
Alternative Browsers	130
PalmPilot Browsing	138

CHAPTER FIVE

PRIVACY AND SECURITY _____ *144*

Privacy	145
What Information About Me Exists on the Net?	152
Children and Privacy	154
Protecting Yourself	154
Software for Increased Privacy	159
World Wide Web Browsing	171
Fighting CyberCrime	173

CHAPTER SIX

BUYING AND SELLING _____ *175*

The Basics of Buying Merchandise Online	176
Safe Shopping	183
Buying Products	184
Books, Music, and the Amazonian Revolution	184
Food	194
Computer Equipment	196
Big Ticket Items	199
General Shopping	206
Buying from Individuals	207
Selling	211
The Future	220

CHAPTER SEVEN

BANKING AND PERSONAL FINANCE _____ *221*

Internet Banking	221
Online Investing	231

Filing Your Taxes   244
Student Loans   249
Digital Cash   249

CHAPTER EIGHT

ONLINE GAMES _____ *251*

The History and Culture of Internet Gaming   251
World Wide Web Games   253
Internet (Non-Web) Games   264

CHAPTER NINE

CREATING WEB PAGES _____ *297*

Web Publishing Basics   297
Getting Started   299
Creating a Page of Your Own   303
Specialized Text: Tables and Lists   315
Specialized Images and Links   318
Creating Graphics   321
HTML Coding: Don't Be Afraid   324
Publishing to the World Wide Web   331

CHAPTER TEN

ESOTERIC AND EMERGING TECHNOLOGIES _____ *340*

Interactive Communications   341
Streaming   355
High-Quality Audio with MP3   360
Push Technologies   366
Futures   372

CHAPTER ELEVEN

CONNECTION STRATEGIES _____ *379*

The Ground Rules   380
Gathering Baseline Information   382
The Battle Plan   384
Talking to Operations Personnel   393
Upgrading Your Connection   394
Home Internetworking   401
Non-Ethernet Solutions   410

CHAPTER TWELVE

SEARCHING AND FINDING _____ 412

Searching for Geniuses	412
Finding People	421
Finding Places	425
Archaic Search Technologies	430

CHAPTER THIRTEEN

DOWNLOADING AND INSTALLING FILES _____ 433

Downloading Files with a Web Browser	433
File Transfer Protocol Is Your Friend	434
Installing Files	436

CHAPTER FOURTEEN

RESOURCE CATALOG: BEST OF THE WEB _____ 440

CHAPTER FIFTEEN

COMMERCIAL AND FINANCIAL RESOURCES _____ 502

Buying Stuff	502
Commercial Resources	503
Selling Stuff	507
Brokerage Companies	512

APPENDIX: THE PREVIOUS GENERATION _____ 515

INDEX _____ 521

PREFACE

This is a book about the world's largest computer network: the Internet. It's aimed at the garden-variety computer user: someone with a job to get done, who isn't yet an expert or aficionado. It's also aimed at the user who has spent a lot of time in that garden; someone with a green thumb who's seen the roses and azaleas get out of control.

To those of us who have been using the Internet for a long time, some of what we discuss has become commonplace. Consequently, we envisioned a new class of Internet user, in which you might find computer-savvy people who nonetheless find themselves overwhelmed by email, unsure of online banking, dumbstruck in a chat room, or dead on the floor in an online game.

Since *The Whole Internet User's Guide & Catalog* was published, the whole Internet has changed. We've seen the growth of web-based "applications": using the Web to file taxes or order books may now involve as much knowledge as using Telnet or FTP did ten years ago.

When personal computers became common, people used them as glorified typewriters or adding machines: a little help doing budget planning, a nice word processor for writing letters, and they were satisfied. Some visionaries talked about computers as information appliances: you could use your home or office computer to connect to the national news services, get stock reports, do library searches, even read professional journals or literary classics—but, at the time, these were far-reaching ideas.

Time has passed since computers first moved into our offices and homes. In those dozen or so years, another revolution, perhaps even more important than the first, took place when the computers were networked to each other. Personal computers are great, but computers become something special when they're connected.

With the Internet, networking came of age. The information resources that visionaries discussed in the early 80s are not just research topics that a few advanced thinkers can play with in a lab—they're realities that you can tap into from your home. Once you're connected to the Internet, you have instant access to an almost indescribable wealth of information. You have to pay for some of it, sure—but most of it is available for free. Through electronic mail and newsgroups, you can use a different kind of access: a worldwide supply of knowledgeable people, some of whom are certain to share your interests, no matter how obscure. It's easy to find a discussion group on almost any topic, or to find people interested in forming a new discussion group. While free advice is often worth what you pay for it, there are also lots of well-informed experts who are more than willing to be helpful.

The challenge today lies in separating the signal from the noise.

In the almost seven years since the first edition of the Unix version of this book appeared, the Internet has become an even richer place. It has surpassed critical mass largely because of the World Wide Web, which made the Internet friendly for the average computer user. When we first wrote, the Web was a promising experiment; since then, it has completely changed the face of the Internet. People are getting online to avoid waiting in line, to look for bargains, and, not least, because they are expected to be.

Today, we constantly hear about the Internet: in newspapers and magazines, in Tom Hanks movies, on television shows. Many advertisements today provide electronic mail and World Wide Web addresses for more information. There are also more (and better) resources: there's a whole world of multimedia resources, including museums, exhibitions, art galleries, and shopping malls, that didn't exist six years ago. Even the visionaries would be astonished by what we've achieved.*

Well, then, where do you start? Getting a handle on the Internet is something like grabbing a handful of Jell-O—the firmer your grasp is, the more it oozes down your arm. Of course, you don't deal with Jell-O in this manner. To eat it, you need the right tool: a spoon.

The same is true of the Internet. You don't need to be an expert in telephone lines, data communications, and network protocols for it to be useful. You just need to know which tools to use, and how to use them.

As for uses, we've got millions of them. They range from the scholarly (you can read works analyzing Dante's *Divine Comedy*) to the factual (you can look at agricultural market reports) to the recreational (you can get ski reports for Aspen) to the humorous ("How do I cook Jell-O?"). It is also an amazing tool for collaboration: you can work with other individuals via email or upload your *magnum opus* to a web site specializing in your field to an international audience.

In a sense, the existence of almost every O'Reilly & Associates title is a tribute to the power and usefulness of the Internet. The original book in this series, *The Whole Internet User's Guide & Catalog*, is a good example. Mike Loukides, the editor of the *Whole*

---

* With the possible exception of the Victoria's Secret online fashion show.

Internet series, and Ed Krol, the original author, met via electronic mail. Network users were clamoring for Ed to update his Internet help guide, *The Hitchhiker's Guide to the Internet*. He was about to volunteer when Mike sent him an electronic mail message and asked, "How about doing it as a book?" This spurred a number of messages about outlines and time frames until both were finalized. The legalities and contracts were handled by the U.S. Postal Service; electronic contracts were too commercial for the Internet at the time, and they still are.

Shortly thereafter, via the Net, O'Reilly's tools department sent Ed macro libraries to use in the production of the book. Ed then began sending chapters to Mike, all by email. Mike would annotate, change, and send them back to Ed by the same means. Occasionally, everyone would trade file directories, screen images, and illustrations. Except for the final review copies and illustrations, everything was handled via the Internet. The whole process was accomplished with fewer than ten telephone calls.

Later titles and editions involved Paula Ferguson, in Colorado, and Kiersten Conner-Sax, in O'Reilly's Cambridge office. Since Mike works from his office in Connecticut, however, even complicated editorial discussions took place electronically.

Think for a minute about what this means. Traditional postal service between Illinois (where Ed lives) and Connecticut (where Mike lives) takes three days. If you want to pay extra, you can use a courier service and cut the time down to one day. But the entire book can be sent to Mike over the Internet in a matter of minutes. Additional "copies" are made available easily to various O'Reilly departments on the company's FTP server.

The Whole Internet and Windows 95

Concurrent with the release of Microsoft's Windows 95, O'Reilly released a new *Whole Internet* title: *The Whole Internet for Windows 95*. Microsoft, up to that point, had largely ignored the Internet. With Windows 95, however, Microsoft released a new web browser, Internet Explorer, to compete directly with Netscape Navigator. It was time for us to update *The Whole Internet User's Guide & Catalog*, and we thought that a slant toward the integration of the Internet with Microsoft's popular operating system would be worthwhile. At that time, the Web was already beginning to dominate the Internet, although you'd still come across the occasional gopher server. Amazon, Quake, and Java were still nouns that had only one meaning.

The Internet, and particularly the Web, has changed by leaps and bounds since then. Technologies like archie and gopher, to which we dedicated entire chapters in past books, are now mere footnotes. Meanwhile, we had to change the organization of the book: instead of chapters about different Internet technologies—email, the Web, FTP—we now write about different uses for those technologies. How we use the Web includes many different activities that involve more than clicking forward and back buttons on a browser. The Web has become the way we buy goods and services, read the newspaper, play games, find directions, look up old friends, and much more.

Audience

This book is intended for anyone who wants access to the Internet's tremendous resources. It's a book for both the computer neophyte and the computer professional.

Those new to the Internet need to know how to use it. We'll teach you the basics of reading email and using a web browser. We'll also tell you about what's safe, how to keep personal information private, and how to keep your kids out of the darkest thickets of the Internet woods.

Those who already know how to use the Internet may find the Internet even more daunting than those who don't. Know how to read email? Great. Know how to keep 350 newly arrived messages organized so that you can read them and still do your job? Many people don't. We'll tell you how to get the most out of the Internet efficiently.

Once we've covered that territory, we'll point you toward web sites and other Internet resources that we consider worthwhile.

We assume that you know how to turn your computer on, that you have an Internet connection, and that you are familiar with your computer's operating system, to the extent that you can launch programs, save files, and copy and paste text. Most of the book's examples presume a user operating with Windows 95/98 or Windows NT, but we've tried to make the examples as easily extensible as possible; Mac users shouldn't have a problem at all, and Unix users probably have enough knowledge anyway.

How to Approach This Book

As we stated previously, we've written this book with two different readers in mind. Why? Well, at least in part because if you're new to the Internet you may become proficient without your noticing.

If you are an Internet neophyte, start with Chapter 1, *What You Will Learn*, and Chapter 2, *Email and News*. These two chapters give you a solid grounding in the background and context of the Internet and in its most essential application. Next, take a look at Chapter 4, *World Wide Web Browsing*, and Chapter 5, *Privacy and Security*. These chapters teach you about what you can do and how to do it with a measure of security. Next, page through the Resource Catalog (Chapter 14), and look at web sites that interest you. Then you can skip around, learning about games or shopping or banking.

If you're an experienced Internet user, this book is a less linear experience. Chapter 3, *Conquering Email*, probably contains tips that you'll find useful. If you're not happy with your Internet connection or want to create a network within your own home, take a look at Chapter 11, *Connection Strategies*. From there, pick and choose the topics that you'd like to know more about. We've tried to cover each topic in as much detail as possible. Page through the Resource Catalog as well, since we've tried to select the best and brightest of what the Internet has to offer.

Conventions

The following typographic conventions are used in this book:

- *Italic* is used for filenames, pathnames, URLs, commands, and to introduce new terms.

- **Bold** is used for things you click on, such as buttons, menus, and icons.

- `Constant width` is used to indicate text that you type literally.

- `Constant width italic` is used for variables that you enter.

We'd Like to Hear From You

We have tested and verified all of the information in this book to the best of our ability, but you may find that features have changed (or that we have made mistakes). Please let O'Reilly know about any errors you find by writing:

O'Reilly & Associates, Inc.
101 Morris Street
Sebastopol, CA 95472
800-998-9938 (in U.S. or Canada)
707-829-0515 (international/local)
707-829-0104 (fax)

You can also send us messages electronically. To be put on the mailing list or request a catalog, send email to:

nuts@oreilly.com

To ask technical questions or comment on the book, send email to:

bookquestions@oreilly.com

Acknowledgments

From Kiersten:

This book is dedicated to the memory of my grandfather, Arthur B. Conner, Jr.

Many people deserve my thanks for their support while I was writing *TWING*, as we affectionately called it. My now-husband, Adam Conner-Sax, is foremost among them. I am profoundly grateful for his love, insight, and belief in me, through this and sundry other trials. My friend and colleague Steven Abrams refuted more than one statement that I couldn't possibly finish this book. He also introduced me to the joys of

Carmageddon. Finally, my friend Seth Pinsky proposed my favorite possible title, which is unfortunately too obscene to be printed here.

Alyson Berliner, Ingrid Berendt, Melissa Bramblett, and Jennifer Friedman were the most supportive gaggle of bridesmaids a postmodern bride could ask for.

I'd also like to thank my family, specifically my mother, Mary Ann Conner, and my sister, Wendy Nauman, for encouraging me to be a writer and for not encouraging me to go to law school.

I am deeply indebted to many people at O'Reilly. Frank Willison promoted me from editorial assistant to staff writer despite my lack of experience and indulged more than one of my Ideas. Valerie Quercia supplied guidance, support, and unswerving affection. And Mike Loukides presented me with the opportunity to write this book, based only on my copyedit of *The Whole Internet for Windows 95*. I owe him a debt of gratitude. Mike is a talented editor, and this is a much better book for his care. He is remarkably good at discerning what a chapter needs, while being open to suggestion and argument.

Other people contributed to this book as well. Robert Eckstein and Valerie Quercia collaborated on Chapter 7, *Banking and Personal Finance*. Jon Cooper and Stephen Spainhour contributed material on MP3 to Chapter 10, *Esoteric and Emerging Technologies*. Steven Abrams, Maureen Dempsey, and Christien Shangraw provided invaluable editorial support, checking references, printing copies, and formatting text. Pouya Shahdodaghi reviewed Chapter 8, *Online Games*. Paula Ferguson, and David Foster Wallace, should they ever read this preface, won't know why I'm thanking them, but each one provided me with guidance and inspiration in terms of the overall style of the prose. Finally, Colleen Gorman and Jane Ellin did a great job as production editors, cleaning up the text and getting it ready for the printer.

From Ed:

Thanks to my wife Margaret, who gave me the time to work on this book. My daughter Molly, who wrote a sidebar on using the Internet to choose a college, is now finishing her freshman year. And thanks to Bob Penka and the Computing and Communications Services Office of the University of Illinois, without whose permission and connectivity I couldn't have participated in writing this book.

Thanks also go to the many people who have written the sidebars scattered throughout the book: Tim O'Reilly, my daughter Molly (who I've already mentioned), Andy Oram, Val Quercia, Bill Rosenblatt, Keith Wessel, and Jon Cooper. Jon's sidebar turned out to be so important that we assimilated it into the body of the book.

And I'd like to join in Kiersten's thanks for all the staff at O'Reilly who made this book, and its predecessors, a reality.

CHAPTER ONE

WHAT YOU WILL LEARN

This is a book for people who love the Internet. Or for people who hate the Internet but can't live without it. Or for people who have known the Internet since it was a cute toddler and don't like the cranky, hormone-crazed adolescent that it's become.

In short, it's a book about making the Internet work for you and not the other way around. The thrill of browsing has worn off—now you just want to buy a sweater and don't want to spend the next month looking at online catalogs, knitting discussion groups, "design-a-sweater-online," the "sweaters of the rich and famous," and so on. A few years ago, you may have thought this was cool; now you just want your sweater. Or, you want to exchange email with your kids in college or your brother in Belgium; you don't want to be deluged with junk mail offering you lists of email addresses (so you can send your own junk email), bogus driver's licenses, and pornography.

You just want to use the Internet to get things done.

What This Book Is About

We wrote this book for network users who want to spend their time on the Internet more effectively. There's no need to waste time with aimless browsing or ineffective searches. If you pay attention to what your needs are, you can make the Internet a custom-tailored tool for gathering information; if you know what to expect, it's a lot easier to know when you've found what you want and what to do with it. At the same time, we show you how to keep the Internet from becoming a pain; for example, how to avoid getting junk email (commonly called *spam*), and how to protect yourself against fraud and intrusions on your privacy.

Parts of the book discuss the Internet's technology itself: how to add features to your browser, how to read email more efficiently, and so on. But this book isn't just about technology. There's a decidedly human side to the Internet. Therefore, we have asked some people to share their experiences about how they have planned a trip, played games, and chosen a college over the Internet. People are doing these things today, and you can do so as well.

Audience

Throughout the book, we assume that you already have a computer and an Internet connection (though not necessarily a connection you're satisfied with—we'll talk a little bit about how to evaluate Internet providers). You should be able to use either Netscape or Internet Explorer, but you certainly don't need to be an expert. If you know how to move from page to page and to enter web addresses that you get off the sides of trucks, business cards, or TV, you will be just fine.

In particular, we will cover topics like:

- *Managing email effectively.* Which is the best email client for your needs? What can you do about unwanted email? How can you protect your privacy. What are your rights? What to do if you need to change email providers?

- *Using a web browser.* Which is the best browser for you? Which plug-ins do you need? For that matter, what is a plug-in? How do you make your browser run most efficiently?

- *Ensuring your privacy and security.* How much can people learn about you because you use the Internet? How can you stop them? Is that kind of research legal? Can that information be sold?

- *Transacting business on the Net.* How can you shop safely? What can you buy or sell? Can you do so safely? How do you evaluate a buyer?

- *Managing your money online.* Are pay-per-service financial web sites worth the subscription cost? We'll teach you how to manage your accounts, buy and sell stocks, and more.

- *Playing games.* What games can you play? Why do you always get killed? How can you configure your computer to give you an advantage?

- *Creating web pages of your own.* Learn how to make a web page that others can access. We'll cover the tools you'll need, the techniques to use, and the servers that will display your page for free.

- *Using newer technologies.* What are Internet telephones, electronic books, streaming technologies, and desktop conferencing? Should you be using them? How do you use them?

- *Managing your computer for optimal network access.* How do you handle network slowdowns, bounced email, and other problems? How do you create an effective network and maximize the resources you use at home?

- *Finding what you need on the Net.* How can you use a search engine to find information quickly and effectively? Learn to find files, phone numbers, old friends, email addresses, driving directions, and more.

- *Downloading and installing files.* Find the applications you need, and learn how to download, decompress, and install them to your computer.

We've also included our list of favorite resources. Our Resource Catalog does try to be not exhaustive, like Yahoo!'s; we've picked sites that we think are the best on a particular topic; that are particularly useful, helpful, or at least interesting; and that we think are reasonably stable (that is, likely to be around a year from now). We have also asked some famous people who use the Net to share their hotlists.

Most of the examples in this book use one of the Microsoft operating systems: Windows NT or Windows 95/98. But it shouldn't matter all that much. What we talk about are techniques for using applications. The applications are similar on all operating systems. If there is a special directory where you put plug-ins on Windows 95, then there is probably a similar directory for Unix or the Macintosh. Don't be afraid to poke around.

We'll tell you whether something is dangerous to you or your machine. As you move around the Internet, things will change on your computer. You may not know what they are, but they're changing anyway. Part of making your Internet experience all that it can be is taking charge of your computer and configuring it to serve you the best way possible.

History

To most people, the Internet seems to have sprung fully formed on the world sometime after 1990. That is not the case. Nor has the Internet come into being like a car on an assembly line, engineered to exacting specifications for reliability and design features. It is more like a living organism that evolved over time—actually, quite a long time, in engineering terms. Along the way, the Internet has had some engineering, but the evolutionary process has had a bigger effect on what it is. So, let's go back and see just how the Internet became the incredibly complex thing we have today.

What Does "The Internet" Mean?

If you're connected to the Internet, you can access all sorts of resources (software, encyclopedias, magazines, and more) that others have provided. Likewise, you can "publish" your own material (software, documents, and so on) so that others can use them. Obviously, there are other ways to get software or publish your ideas, but your computer becomes a much more useful tool when you can trade files with people around the world. The Internet makes it a lot easier to play with new software, collaborate on projects, or keep in touch with friends. A lot of people who never write letters have no trouble sending email or setting up a video conference with their friends or children in college. Ultimately, the Internet breaks down barriers between you and other computer users: not only barriers that were created by operating systems, traditional network services, and hardware, but barriers of time and distance.

Perhaps the most important barrier that the Internet breaks is the barrier between different kinds of computers. Most computer networks are proprietary: you buy a bunch of similar computers, and you buy a software package that lets computers talk to each other. In the past, all the computers had to be more or less the same, and they certainly all had to run software from the same vendor. For example, you may have bought hundreds of PCs and installed Novell Netware on them. If you did, your PCs couldn't talk to computers that didn't run Novell software.

The Internet is completely different. It is based on standard protocols rather than on particular software products. The protocols for the Internet are a set of standards that allow them to communicate with each other, even if they are using software from different vendors. No one, not even Microsoft, can say, "You can't join the Internet because you didn't buy your software from me." A PC running Windows can download web pages from a Macintosh, from a computer running some version of Unix, or even an old IBM mainframe. They don't all use the same software; they don't all run Windows; they weren't all developed by Microsoft; but they do use the same protocols, which are implemented by different software packages developed by different vendors. In other words, all the computers speak the same language. It's not that different from real life: a Nigerian can converse with a Russian if they both speak English.

For the Internet, the most important protocols are called TCP (Transmission Control Protocol) and IP (Internet Protocol); they are the glue that connects local networks of computers. HTTP (Hypertext Transfer Protocol) is the protocol that carries web pages between a web server and your browser. Another standard protocol, called PPP (Point-to-Point Protocol), lets home users take part.

The Internet's standards (and its culture) began in the research and Unix communities during the 1970s and 1980s. To understand the Internet, it helps to have a sense of how it developed.

How Did the Internet Get Started?

The Internet was born around 1965 in an effort to connect a U.S. Defense Department network called the ARPAnet with various radio and satellite networks. The ARPAnet was an experimental network designed to support military research—in particular, research about how to build networks that could withstand partial outages (like bomb attacks) and still function. In the ARPAnet model, communication always occurred between a source computer and a destination computer. The network itself was assumed to be unreliable; any portion of the network could disappear at any moment (pick your favorite catastrophe—these days, backhoes cutting cables are more of a threat than bombs falling). ARPAnet was designed to require the minimum amount of information from the computer clients. To send a message on the network, a computer had to put its data in an "envelope," called an Internet Protocol packet, and "address" the packets correctly. The communicating computers—not the network itself—were also given the responsibility for ensuring that communication. The philosophy was that every computer on the network could talk, as a peer, with any other computer.

These decisions, like the assumption of an unreliable network, may sound odd, but history has proven that most of them were correct. Using these assumptions, the U.S. was able to develop a working network (the ancestor of the current Internet), and the academic and research users who had access to it were soon addicted. Sharing data, drafts of articles, and other information became much easier once they had email and file transfer capabilities. Collaborative research involving participants scattered all over the U.S. was much easier and cheaper when they could communicate through email, rather than scheduling travel for a meeting. Demand for networking quickly spread. Internet developers in the U.S., the U.K., and Scandinavia, responding to market pressures, began to put their IP software on every conceivable type of computer. The network became the only practical method for computers from different manufacturers to communicate. This method was attractive to the governments and universities, which didn't have policies saying that all computers must be bought from the same vendor. Everyone bought whichever computer they liked, and expected the computers to work together over the network.

Access to the early Internet and its predecessors (like the ARPAnet) was limited to researchers in computer science, to government employees, and to government contractors. In the late 1980s, the U.S. National Science Foundation (NSF) was looking for a way to share supercomputer access to all researchers at colleges and universities. It settled on Internet technology and promoted universal educational access by funding a campus connection *only* if the campus had a plan to spread the access around. That way, anyone attending a four-year college could become an Internet user.

In 1992, those students who had emailed their college chums became graduates and entered the work force. When their companies were looking for technologies to support the problems of a fast-paced, information-hungry, distributed worldwide corporate environment, they suggested an answer: the Internet. It quickly became clear that email was a better way to disseminate ideas within a company than traditional typed memos. It also became clear that email was much better for tasks like customer support. After all, customers would much rather send an email message than hold on the telephone. And the people answering the questions could take time to think about them without worrying about the customer waiting on the other end of the line. It turned out that other technologies, like Usenet newsgroups, were important both within companies and for helping companies deal with their customers.

But the Internet of the late 80s and early 90s was hard to use. Sending an email message or posting a thought to a newsgroup was fairly simple for the computer literate, but doing anything else required a hefty knowledge of commands and options—well beyond the understanding of many managers. The Internet would have stopped there if it hadn't been for the World Wide Web, invented by Tim Berners-Lee at CERN

(European Organization for Nuclear Research), a European center for research in particle physics in Switzerland.

Berners-Lee created a way for computers in various locations to display text that contained links to other files. The centerpiece of his work was a language called HTML (Hypertext Markup Language), which provided a very general way to tell a computer how to display a document. HTML lets you say, "This is a title," and lets the reader's computer worry about the font, size of the document, position of the document, and so on. HTML has become much more complicated since the early days, but it still holds to the same principle: documents should tell you what their various parts (like headings) are, not how they should be displayed. Again, the motivating factor was to define something that could work on any computer, regardless of its maker and regardless of whether it had a fancy display with lots of fonts or just a primitive terminal. But what really caught people's imagination was the idea of a *link*. Now, documents could embed relationships; you could jump from one document to another, make lists of your favorite web sites, and even build some simple games. The Internet was no longer a bunch of separate islands; it became a web of interconnected servers. Berners-Lee also had the idea that this system could be used to embed graphics in the text. The first web browsers were rather crude and couldn't do much besides display fixed-width (a typewriter-style font) text without graphics. Soon, however, other browsers were developed that used point-and-click user interfaces and graphical displays.

However, this early generation of browsers ran only on Unix systems. PC and Mac users were out of luck. The next step in the Internet evolution occurred at the University of Illinois, when the National Center for Supercomputing Applications integrated the ability to display pictures into a browser. Perhaps more importantly, they made their browser, Mosaic, compatible with Unix, Windows, *and* Macintosh computers. The combination of easy-to-read displays with the millions of PC users triggered the explosive growth that has made the Internet what it is today. Marc Andreessen, one of the original programmers as an undergraduate, formed a company to commercialize the Mosaic browser. That company, and, at least colloquially, its new browser, was called Netscape.*

Within two years after the birth of Netscape, Microsoft had created a browser similar to Netscape's known as Internet Explorer (IE). Since that time, Netscape and Microsoft have been adding features to their browsers to compete with each other: we've seen lots of extensions to HTML, more plug-ins, and all sorts of multimedia support, as the browser giants play a game of one-upmanship. These days, the browsers' capabilities are pretty similar, though Microsoft has been peddling the rather bizarre idea that you can't use Windows without Internet Explorer. If you read the papers, you know that the courts are having their say about this. (If you don't read the papers, see "America Online, Microsoft, and the Justice Department" later in this chapter.)

---

* The browser is more properly called Netscape Navigator, but most people use the company name to refer to the browser.

Easy-to-use browsers, a new crop of users from the PC and Macintosh worlds, and an explosion of corporate interest caused Internet traffic to skyrocket. Browsing became "cool." Eventually both the computers controlling the network and the telephone lines connecting them were overloaded. Some said the Internet was doomed; a network with no central control could not change fast enough to avoid collapsing under its own success. Such claims have been prevalent since 1987 and have always proved false.

Who Governs the Internet?

There may be no central control, but there is certainly a group dedicated to overseeing the Internet's evolution and planning for the future. This group, the Internet Engineering Task Force (IETF; for more information, see *http://www.ietf.org*) is a volunteer organization consisting of "network designers, operators, vendors, and researchers concerned with the evolution of the Internet architecture and the smooth operation of the Internet." Almost every company that derives income (or expects to derive income) from the Internet sends representatives to attend IETF meetings, where these representatives worry about current problems, standards, and future concerns. IETF is responsible for defining standards in a way that allows computers and software from different vendors to cooperate without problem.

The Internet's stability and ability to grow is rooted, paradoxically, in the assumption that networks are inherently unreliable. In some ways, this is a no-brainer: we've all heard static on our telephone lines and watched sporting events on TV that were interrupted because of a satellite problem. But designing a network with the built-in assumption that it's unreliable, yet has to work anyway, has big implications. It means that little bits of static on telephone lines won't bother you—but if that were the whole story, it wouldn't be very interesting. On a larger scale, someone can "break" a large chunk of the Internet without affecting its users. In fact, this happens frequently if not all the time: someone at a construction site or on a road crew accidentally damages some of the telephone wires carrying Internet traffic. Internet traffic doesn't flow as well until the damage is repaired, but you can still get work done. An important consequence is that portions of the Net may be upgraded at any time without significantly disturbing the people who are using it. While parts of the Net are unavailable, traffic finds other ways to get to its destination. You won't go to your office, log in to your computer, and find a message saying that the Internet is inaccessible for the next six months because of improvements. Perhaps more importantly, the process of improving the Internet has created a technology that's extremely mature and practical. The ideas have been tested; problems have appeared and consequently solved. Despite all the growth, the reliability of the Internet as a whole is actually much better than it was five or ten years ago.

The Commercial Era

Big corporations have been on the Internet since its inception. Their participation was originally limited to their research and engineering departments. Those same corporations usually used a private network for their business communications. Marketing via computer network was unheard of. You weren't allowed to use the Internet for commercial purposes. And even if you could, who would design a market strategy around twenty thousand people? So a noncommercial, noninvasive, communal culture developed in the early years of the Net.

Two things happened that opened the Internet to commerce. First, a prohibition against commercial activity, which stemmed from U.S. government funding, was lifted. Essentially, the government had said, "If we're paying for a research network, we want it to be used for research. If you want to build a network for commerce, do it with your own money." But in the early 90s, the government gradually got out of the Internet business—and as their money disappeared so did the restrictions. These days, schools may be able to get government funding for Internet connections, but most of the high-speed data lines that compose the Internet are privately owned. To get an Internet connection, you don't call the government—you call a business (often, a small local business) that doesn't receive government subsidies. Currently, the federal government funds only a few major connection points for the Internet to ensure competition among Internet service providers (ISPs). These are likely to be transferred to a public corporation on the model of the Corporation for Public Broadcasting: existing for the good of the Internet but funded by fees.

Additionally, the Internet started growing at incredible rates (as much as ten percent per month), and people started to envision ways of making money. Suddenly, there were retail catalogs all over the Web, and people started using HTML forms to buy products. (O'Reilly & Associates had one of the first commercial web sites, GNN.) Everybody was developing software for the Internet, hoping that his or her product would be the next Netscape. Some of these ideas had merit and others were half-baked, but they were all pitched to the Internet user. Scams, electronic stalking, junk mail, and all of the other perversions of real society invaded. All of this happened, and continues to happen, at a pace too fast for the legal system to react to. Often, the legal community doesn't even understand the problems. Even the IETF, which engineered change for the better part of the Internet's life, is now merely trying to herd changes in the right general direction, with success similar to that of attempting to herd cats.

Today, the Internet's commercial growth is largely governed by the invisible hand of the free market. Most people think that's beneficial, though there are some disadvantages. It really isn't anything new: the U.S. government never really played a significant role in governing the Internet. Mostly, it made sure the phone bill got paid.

If you don't believe that a loosely organized, rather chaotic group of people cooperating for fun and profit can work better than a large corporation with central control, just think back a few years. The chaotic Internet proved much more successful than the centrally organized proprietary network services. In 1992, home networking was dominated by companies like CompuServe, America Online (AOL), Prodigy, and a few other large corporations. The Internet was a small, sort of weird thing that a few nerds played with. These days, CompuServe and Prodigy still exist, but they're shadows of their former selves. America Online is still doing reasonably well, but that's because they realized that the big opportunity was in connecting people to the public Internet, not providing a private network. In other words, AOL really isn't a private network; it's a very large Internet service provider. In 1995, Microsoft tried creating their own network (MSN) along the private network model. They'd connect you to the Internet, but of course, any sane person would want their nicely organized content rather than the Internet's seething mass of bits. Microsoft soon discovered what people really wanted; as a private network, MSN went absolutely nowhere.

What does this mean to you as an Internet user? There are some lessons we can learn from history. No one owns the Internet, even though some large corporations would like you to think otherwise. The Internet really was created through the cooperation of thousands of widely separated people, with completely different interests, most of whom had never met. For the most part, members of this community did things because they were fun or interesting and not necessarily to make money. One example: lots of software is now available for free. And not only is it free, it's often better than the commercial competition. For the Internet to continue thriving, it has to stay fun, and it has to remain a loose community of individuals who cooperate for each other's good. The moment someone says, "I'm the Internet; I'll plan it and I'll regulate it; buy my software or go away," either they're wrong, or the Internet is dead. For the moment, they're wrong.

America Online, Microsoft, and the Justice Department

That's not to say that all's well in paradise. When Windows 95 was released, there was an outcry from America Online founder Steven Case and other ISPs about the Microsoft Network icon appearing on the desktop. Each Windows 95 system that shipped displayed the MSN logo from day one—and you couldn't delete it. The AOL brass thought this was just lovely: virtually every computer sold to their core market came with a built-in advertisement for a potential competitor. Then Microsoft gave AOL Internet Explorer, and Steven Case changed his mind. The Microsoft Network was a failure anyway; people wanted the real Internet, not a cheap imitation. But that was just the beginning of the story.

All along, Microsoft's strategy has been to force people to use its software by creating problems in the interactions between its software and other computers. We've just said that the radical idea behind the Internet was that computers and software from different manufacturers could co-exist. One important example is Java™, a programming language that lets you write software that runs correctly on any computer, regardless of its type. Java programs can be downloaded over the Web and run inside browsers. Documents recently released by the courts show that Microsoft's executives found this idea terrifying: in the long run, if the same program could run on any computer, operating systems like Windows 95 or 98 could become irrelevant. At the same time, Java was too popular to ignore. Their solution was to release a version of Internet Explorer that incorporated Java, but it had a number of significant changes, omitted a few major pieces, and added some nonstandard extensions. The result? If you used any of

Microsoft's extensions in your Java program, your program would run only on Internet Explorer. If you used some features of standard Java that Microsoft decided didn't include in its set, your program wouldn't run on Internet Explorer. Although people are still fighting over this in the courts,* the prospect of a universal programming language, which could transform the Internet into something we can only begin to imagine, is unlikely.

Unfortunately, the Java development example is the rule rather than the exception. Microsoft has told lots of companies that they can give away Internet Explorer, but only if they don't give away Netscape. (When the courts challenged this, Microsoft said, Sorry, we didn't know this was against the law.) There's an important feature in PPP (the software that connects home users to the Internet) called *authentication*, which prevents other people from gaining access to your account. There's a standard way to do authentication, and then there's Microsoft's way. Initially, Windows 95 provided only Microsoft's version, which meant that if you turned on authentication, the machine on the other end of the connection had to be running Windows NT. Microsoft has added a standard implementation since. Microsoft's email programs have lots of nice features—but a lot of them only work if the person who receives the mail also uses Microsoft software. For a while, RealPlayer (an application you'll read about later) stopped working if you installed Microsoft's competing product. This problem has been fixed, but you get the idea. Microsoft's strategy has consistently been to introduce incompatibilities that make it inconvenient to use other people's software.

Windows 98 opened another can of worms. In Windows 98, Internet Explorer is the user interface. Everything you do, you do through Internet Explorer, whether or not it involves the Internet: for example, you use IE to browse files on your disk and launch applications like Microsoft Word. This understandably enraged Netscape, and it was the starting point for an antitrust suit that will probably fester for years. Even if the Netscape browser is free, why would anyone bother to install it? You're forced to use Internet Explorer from the start. And you can't delete IE without breaking Windows 98.†

Was this really a feature that Windows users wanted or just Microsoft's attempt to trash a competitor? Pleasant as browsing may be, it's really difficult to believe that the browser model is appropriate for everything. Again, Microsoft's strategy has been to deny their users the right to choose. Integrating the Internet with its product is a great idea, but preventing Microsoft users from considering alternatives is contrary to the spirit on which the Internet is based. (Whether it's against the law is something we won't learn for a few years.) And enticing the Internet's web authors to use features that only work on Internet Explorer, running under Windows, is a serious threat to the Internet's universality.

---

* Microsoft lost the first round of this battle fairly decisively, but may have won the second; there are bound to be many more rounds.

† Department of Justice or not, Microsoft's strategy appears to be working. As we were finishing this book, the Netscape company ceased to exist. It was bought out by America Online in a joint deal with Sun Microsystems. It's not at all clear where things will go from here, though the Netscape browser will certainly be around for the immediate future.

We're not for a moment saying that you shouldn't use Microsoft's software. Far from it—some of it is pretty good, and it's certainly widely available and easier to get your hands on than anything else. But we are saying that you should keep your eyes open. You should be aware that there are alternatives; Microsoft's products are rarely the best available, and the competition is often free. If you're writing your own web pages, remember that there are a lot of people using Macs, Unix systems, Linux systems, and so on. And the next generation of cell phones, pagers, and other hand-held devices is starting to include Internet access. Will these support proprietary Microsoft features? I doubt it.

A year ago, most of us had written Apple off. Surprise—their newest machine, the iMAC, is a big hit. It's a powerful and genuinely innovative network-centric computer. If you stick to standards, users of all these platforms will be able to read your stuff. If you use Microsoft's proprietary features, you're limiting your audience, and in the long run, limiting the extent to which the Internet can develop. After all, the Internet is an extraordinary model of cooperation between many people, institutions, and companies. If it had been up to Microsoft or IBM or Apple to build the Internet, it just wouldn't exist.

The Future

The U.S. government has not become completely disinterested in the Internet's development. It views the transition from research tool to useful production environment to overloaded frustrating environment as a natural progression. The government sees a chicken and egg problem: the next generation of Internet applications will require speeds and facilities that the current Internet cannot provide, but there is little motivation to develop applications for a network that won't run them. To spur this development, they are actively promoting the Internet2 initiative.

Internet2 is a research network, just like the original Internet. Anyone who pays the price of participation may join. The research happens on a variety of levels: increasing transmission speeds, making the network easy to use by software developers, and developing those software applications. These applications include real-time full motion video and remote surgery. The goal is that after the seed has been planted, Internet2 will take off and become commercialized just like the current Internet. For up to date information on Internet2, see *http://www.internet2.org*.

What's Allowed on the Internet?

Enough about the Internet's chaotic means of self-government and the companies that would like to stage a coup. What about the real governments? The ones with laws, police departments, and jails?

Longtime users of the Internet have always liked to think of it as an anarchy that exists apart from the legal system. Whether that's a good idea or not, it's clear that it's more fantasy than reality. Sooner or later, governments and the courts are going to have their say about what is and isn't allowed.

The problem is that the Internet crosses so many boundaries, whether social, technical, and political, that it's very hard to tell who governs what. Can you prosecute someone in Kentucky for looking at pornography posted to a web site in Denmark, where it's perfectly legal? Can you prosecute an adult child molester for pretending to be ten years old and participating in children's chat groups, even if the actual children are hundreds of miles away? Are you breaking the law if you participate in one of many online gambling sites, most of which are based off-shore? And if you buy something online, and the vendor turns out to be a scam artist, what protection do you have? You don't even know which Better Business Bureau to call.

No one really knows the answers to these questions. Problems with jurisdiction, applicability of existing case law, and constitutionality of new laws all need to be solved. In one current case, Canada is trying to prosecute a Nazi sympathizer living in Toronto under their laws against hate crimes. But the web site on which he publishes his material is located in the U.S., where his content is protected as free speech. Whose laws count? Can Canada prevent someone from doing something electronically in the U.S.? Nobody knows. Similarly, the German government has been in court with CompuServe over what it considers to be pornography distributed via their network. Unfortunately, a breast cancer newsgroup fit Germany's definition of pornography. But the legal nightmare CompuServe faced was even worse than trying to decipher the bizarre consequences of obscenity laws. CompuServe wanted to be considered a "common carrier" in the U.S., like the telephone companies. Being a common carrier means that you carry data, and have no responsibility for what's in the data; common carriers can't be sued for the contents of the data on their networks. But in return, they can't do anything to control the contents of the data on their networks. CompuServe's big problem was that censoring certain Internet traffic (even in Germany) would leave them liable for all sorts of legal problems in the U.S.; once you've started restricting what people can say, you can't stop. For example, if CompuServe were not considered a common carrier, they could conceivably be sued for carrying libelous email. After all, if they stopped some traffic because it was objectionable to some people, they could legally end up with the responsibility to stop any traffic that could be considered objectionable, regardless of its nature. Even if that were desirable, it would be both humanly and technically impossible.

Additionally, there are all sorts of problems associated with export laws, patents, copyrights, and other issues. Phil Zimmerman, the author of a popular encryption package called PGP, found himself the subject of a federal investigation because people outside the U.S. had been downloading PGP from the Internet, arguably a violation of U.S. restrictions against exporting cryptographic software. The government ultimately dropped the case—which was really more about harassing someone who had done something they didn't like than about a serious legal issue—but only after Zimmerman had incurred huge legal expenses. This isn't to say that you should be afraid of using the Internet because a U.S. Marshal will come knocking on your door to seize your computer. But you should be aware that the Internet is not an anarchy beyond the reach of the law. The legal community is currently in the process of figuring out how to deal with the Internet.* In the meantime, "what's allowed" will remain a difficult question to answer, but not a question that can be ignored.

How the Internet Works

It's nice to know a little about how the Internet works. Having some background knowledge allows you to make sense out of some of the hints you'll see in this book, so they don't seem like capricious rules to be learned by rote. We will explore the guts of the Internet with a maximum amount of hand-waving. We'll never say something like "This field is three bits long. If you want to know more, several books on the Internet's implementation are available."

Modern networking is built around the concept of *service layers*. There are multiple layers. You start out trying to move bits from here to there, losing some along the way. This level consists of wires and hardware, although not necessarily good wires. Then, you add a layer of basic software to make it easier to work with the hardware. You add another layer of software to give the basic software some desirable features. You continue to add functionality and smarts to the network, one layer at a time, until you have something that's sophisticated and user-friendly. Let's start at the bottom and work our way up.

Packet Switching and the Internet Protocol (IP)

When you try to imagine what the Internet is and how it operates, it is natural to think of the telephone system. After all, both are electronic, both let you open a connection and transfer information, and both are primarily composed of dedicated telephone lines. Unfortunately, this is the wrong picture, and it causes many misunderstandings about how the Internet operates. The telephone network is a circuit-switched network. When you make a call, you get a piece of the network dedicated to you. Even if you aren't using it (for example, if you are put on hold), your piece of the network is unavailable to others. This leads to the underutilization of a very expensive resource— the network itself.

A better model for the Internet, strangely enough, is the U.S. Postal Service. The Postal Service is a packet-switched network. You have no dedicated piece of the network. What you want to send is mixed together with everyone else's stuff, put in a pipeline, transferred to another post office, and sorted out again. Although the technologies are completely different, the Postal Service is a surprisingly accurate analogy; we'll continue to use it throughout this section.

---

* In May 1999, an appeals court ruled that export restrictions on cryptography were unconstitutional. This decision will certainly be appealed, and the problem probably won't be resolved for some time. And even when it is, the larger issue remains: it's unclear how the Internet relates to current legal institutions.

A wire can transport data from one place to another. However, you already know that the Internet can transport data to many different places, distributed all over the world. How does this happen? The different pieces of the Internet are connected by a set of computers called *routers*, which connect networks together. What's more, the different pieces that make up the Internet have many different types—just like the computers themselves. Some parts are regular phone lines, some are special high-speed data lines, and still others are local networks, like those that exist in most offices (Ethernet cables and token rings). Figure 1-1 shows how routers stitch the Internet together.

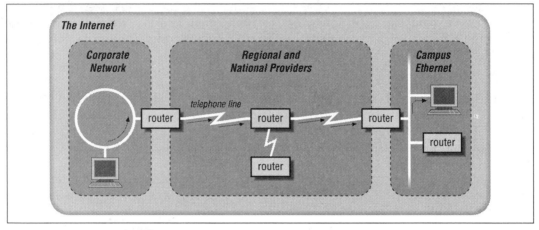

Figure 1-1. Internet hardware

The telephone lines and Ethernet cables are equivalent to the trucks and planes of the Postal Service. They are the means by which mail is moved from place to place. The routers are postal substations; they make decisions about how to route data (or packets), just like a postal substation decides how to route envelopes containing mail. Each substation or router does not have a connection to every other one. If you put an envelope in the mail in Dixville Notch, New Hampshire, addressed to Boonville, California, the post office doesn't reserve a plane from New Hampshire to California to carry it. The local post office sends the envelope to a substation, the substation sends it to another substation, and so on, until it reaches the destination. Each substation only needs to know which connections are available, and what is the best "next hop" to get a packet closer to its destination. The Internet works in a similar manner: a router looks at where your data is going, decides which of the routers it is directly connected to will get it most efficiently closer to its destination, and sends it down the pipeline to that router.

How does the Net know where your data is going? If you want to send a letter, you can't just fold it up, drop it into the mailbox, and expect delivery. You need to put the letter into an envelope, address it, and stamp it. Just as the post office has rules that define how its network works, there are rules that govern how the Internet operates. The rules are called *protocols*. The Internet Protocol takes care of addressing—they make sure that the routers know what to do with your data when it arrives. Sticking with our post office analogy, the Internet Protocol works just like an envelope (see Figure 1-2). Some addressing information appears at the beginning of your message; this information gives the network enough information to deliver the packet of data.

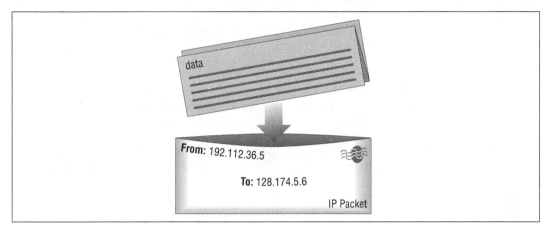

Figure 1-2. IP envelopes

Internet addresses consist of four numbers, each less than 256. When written out, the numbers are separated by periods, like this:

192.112.36.5
128.174.5.6

The address consists of multiple parts. Since the Internet is a network of networks, the beginning of the address tells the Internet routers which network you are part of. The right end of the address tells that network which computer or host should receive the data. Where the network portion ends and the host portion begins is a bit complicated. It varies from address to address, based on agreements between adjacent routers. Fortunately, as a user you'll never need to worry about how this works. It is part of the magic information (probably called the subnet mask) your Internet service provider gives you to configure your computer to use the Internet, but even that is becoming more automatic every day.

Every computer on the Internet has a unique address under this scheme. Again, the Postal Service provides a good analogy. Consider the address "50 Kelly Road, Hamden, CT." The "Hamden, CT" portion is like a network address; it gets the envelope to the correct local post office—the one that knows about streets in a certain area. The address "50 Kelly Road" is like the host address; it identifies a particular mailbox within the post office's service area. The Postal Service has done its job when it has delivered the mail to the right local office, and when that local office has put it into the right mailbox. Similarly, the Internet has done its job when its routers have gotten data to the right network, and when that local network has given the data to the right computer, or host, on the network.

For a lot of practical reasons (hardware limitations, in particular), information sent across IP networks is broken up into bite-sized pieces called *packets*. The information within a packet is usually between 1 and (approximately) 1,500 characters long. This prevents any one user of the network from monopolizing it, allowing everyone equal access. It also means that when the network is overloaded, its behavior becomes slightly worse for everyone; it doesn't stop dead while a few heavy users monopolize it.

One of the amazing things about the Internet is that on a basic level, IP is all you need to participate. It wouldn't be very friendly, but you could get work done if you were clever enough. As long as your data is put in an IP envelope, the network has all the information it needs to get your packet from your computer to its destination. That's a start. But if all you had was IP, you'd be faced with several problems:

- Most information transfers are longer than 1,500 characters. You would be disappointed if the Postal Service carried postcards, but refused anything larger.

- Things can go wrong. The Postal Service occasionally loses a letter; networks sometimes lose packets or damage them in transit.

- Packets may arrive out of sequence. If you mail two letters to the same place on successive days, there's no guarantee that they will take the same route or arrive in order. The same is true of the Internet.

So, the next layer of the network will give us a way to transfer bigger chunks of information and will take care of the many distortions that can creep in.

The Transmission Control Protocol (TCP)

TCP is the protocol, frequently mentioned in the same breath as IP, that is used to get around the problems we just described. What would happen if you wanted to send a book to someone, but the Postal Service accepted only letters? What could you do? You could rip each page out of the book, put each page in a separate envelope, and dump all the envelopes in a mailbox. The recipient would then have to make sure all the pages arrived and paste them together in the right order. On the Internet, TCP rips up the book and then pastes it back together for you.

So, to continue the metaphor, TCP takes the information you want to transmit and breaks it into pieces. It numbers each piece so you can verify receipt and the data can be put back in the proper order. To pass this sequence number across the network, it has an envelope of its own which has the information it requires "written" on it. A piece of your data is placed in a TCP envelope. The TCP envelope is, in turn, placed inside an IP envelope and given to the network (see Figure 1-3). Once you have something in an IP envelope, the network can carry it.

On the receiving side, the TCP protocol collects the envelopes, extracts the data, and puts it in the proper order. If some envelopes are missing, it asks the sender to retransmit them. Once it has all the information in the proper order, it passes the data

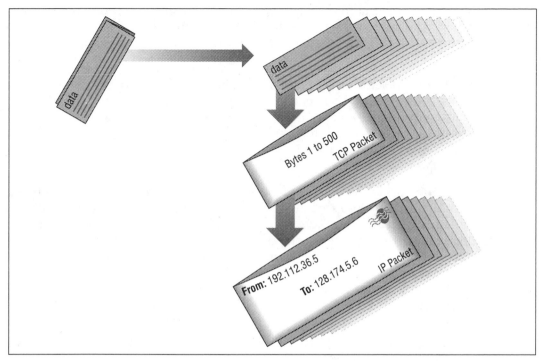

Figure 1-3. TCP packet encapsulation

to whatever application program is using its services. The application could be an email client, a newsreader, a browser—anything that transmits and displays information on the Internet.

TCP and IP were designed back when computers were big and expensive. Once you connected a computer to the Net, it stayed connected and stayed in the same place. Now computers are cheap and portable. People want to use the Internet from wherever they happen to be and connect when they are using it. They also want to use a regular modem that can work over a standard telephone line. To make this type of use possible, a set of protocols was developed to allow IP connections out through the serial port of a computer. This protocol is called *Point-to-Point Protocol* or *PPP*.

The Domain Name System

Fairly early on, people realized that numerical addresses were fine for machines communicating with machines, but human beings preferred names. Therefore, computers on the Internet were given names for the convenience of their human users. After all, *www.whitehouse.gov* is much easier to remember than 128.102.252.1. Every contemporary Internet application lets you use system names instead of host addresses. Likewise, every application lets you use a host address if you insist, but you'll rarely need to. Numeric addresses are useful when you're debugging, and somebody occasionally gives out an address rather than a name for a web site, though this is usually an indication that something fishy is going on. (For example, the site may contain bootleg material.)

Naming introduces problems of its own. For one thing, you have to make sure that no two computers connected to the Internet have the same name. You also have to provide a way to convert names into numerical host addresses. You can use a computer name where an address is called for, but a program needs some way to look that name up and convert it into an address. (You do the same thing whenever you look someone up in the phone book.)

The *Domain Name System* is a method of administering names by giving different groups responsibility for subsets of the names. Each level in this system is called a *domain*. In the name *ux.cso.uiuc.edu, ux* is the name of a host, a real computer with an IP address. The name for that computer is created and maintained by the *cso* group, which happens to be the department where the computer resides. The department *cso* is a part of the University of Illinois at Urbana Champaign (*uiuc*). *uiuc* is a portion of the national group of educational institutions (*edu*). So the domain *edu* contains all computers in all U.S. educational institutions, the domain *uiuc.edu* contains all computers at the University of Illinois, and so on (see Figure 1-4).

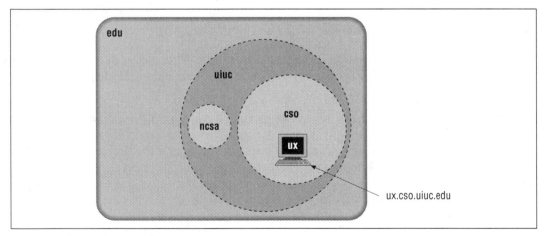

Figure 1-4. Domain authority

Originally there were six "top-level" domains (*.org, .com, .edu, .mil, .net,* and *.gov*) and all computers were named within one of these domains. When the Internet became truly international, additional top-level domains were added. These new domains corresponded to the two-character ISO country codes (*.ca* for Canada, and so on), and allowed countries to control their own domains. This all worked fairly well until names in the *.com* domain got valuable. Names had traditionally been given out on a first-come, first-served basis, but this approach ran into problems when someone had a prior claim to a particular name. What if McDonald's Computer Consulting applied for the domain name *mcdonalds.com* before the fast-food chain did? There's no good way to take a name back (although some people have bought and sold names that were already taken). Furthermore, although McDonald's (the restaurant) has had their trademark since the 1950s, it's not really clear that their trademark should take precedence in the online world. What if there's a McDonald's distillery in Scotland that has been distilling since the 1700s? Shouldn't they have first dibs? In the real world, trademarks are defined by industry and geography. On the Internet, these distinctions don't work.

As a result, we are now running out of desirable names in the *.com* domains. This controversy is still being played out, both in committee work and in fights over the names that already exist. Some people are getting around the problem by registering their domain under *.net* or *.org*. That's a good trick, but it's not really legitimate, since *.net* and *.org* are reserved for networking organizations (like Internet service providers) and nonprofit organizations. We're also seeing an explosion of extremely long names (as a hypothetical example, *mcdonalds-distillery-scotland.com*). A committee has suggested adding additional top-level domains, like *.nom* for personal names and *.store* for retailers. Although this would help, it certainly doesn't solve the problem. Whatever McDonald owned *mcdonalds.com* would probably also grab *mcdonalds.store* and we would be no better off than we are now. A few countries with rare domains have started generating extra income by letting outsiders register in their domains—for example, you could register Ford Hair Oil Products in the *.tg* (Tonga) domain, thereby improving the economy of the South Pacific and avoiding a conflict with Ford Motor Company. Keep watching the business section of your newspaper to find out how this is playing out.

The Domain Name System may sound complicated, but it's one of the things that makes the Internet a comfortable place to live. Pretty soon, you'll start realizing, "Yes, this is the University of Virginia's web server; this person works for IBM in Germany; this is the address for reporting bugs in Nutshell Handbooks (*nuts@ora.com*)," and so on. The real advantage of the domain system is that it breaks the gigantic worldwide Internet into a bunch of manageable pieces. Although hundreds of thousands of computers are "on the Net," they're all named, and the names are organized in a convenient—perhaps even rational—way, making it easier for you to remember the ones you need.

That's a very brief tour of the essentials. If you know roughly what's going on, you'll find day-to-day work on the Internet a lot more pleasant, and you may even be able to fix problems when something is broken. We'll give you some help on troubleshooting later in the book. In the meantime, let's look at how you can make email more effective.

CHAPTER TWO

EMAIL AND NEWS

Communications in the late 20th century have taken a giant leap backwards. Suddenly, everything epistolary is new again: while it was once thought that the telephone would make letter writing obsolete, electronic mail has taken business and personal communication by storm. Once people become comfortable with email, they realize that it means much more than lightning-fast memos. You can communicate with a broad range of individuals, both those you know and those you don't, with alacrity and precision. You're not limited to short, typed memos, either: you can include pictures, audio files, software, almost anything you can imagine.

Communicating via the Internet doesn't just mean sending email, either. Usenet newsgroups allow you to communicate with thousands of other enthusiasts on virtually any topic. And mailing lists are something of a fusion between the two: broad discussions are delivered directly to your mailbox, sometimes with editorial influence over the content or the participants.

In this chapter, we'll discuss the various methods for communicating over the Internet. What are email, newsgroups, and mailing lists? How do you use them? How do they differ?

When Is Internet Communication Useful?

Communicating via electronic messages offers a few advantages over more traditional forms: speed, low cost, and the potential for a wide broadcast. Of course, such communication has inherent weaknesses.

For communication between individuals, using email is faster than sending paper letters, and more formal than a telephone call. It's wonderful for keeping in touch, brief exchanges, inquiries, and the like. However, it's much easier to convey one's meaning over the telephone, primarily through tone of voice, than it is in a briefly written message. And because of the anonymity of typed messages, many people feel less responsible for what they write.

One really useful application of Internet communication is letting people conduct group discussions. This may simply involve sending messages to a bunch of your friends, your department at work, or an entire school. The term *mailing list* is used to refer to a list of people to whom mail from other people on the list is sent. Many mail programs let you create an alias for a list of email recipients. When group discussions via email have many participants, a more formal mailing list becomes necessary, often with automated distribution, subscription, and so on. There are literally thousands of such mailing lists currently in operation on a wide range of topics.

Usenet news is another service that allows for distributed discussion. Posting to Usenet is useful when you want to discuss esoteric or difficult topics. If you've never encountered Usenet, it's hard to appreciate what it's like. Basically, Usenet is comprised of thousands of groups of people who share ideas online. These newsgroups are organized by subject. Each newsgroup is run similarly to a bulletin board service (BBS), with people posting messages that everyone who subscribes to the group can read and respond to. Subscribing is a very loose business; basically, it just involves telling your newsreading program that you want to see that group.

Some newsgroups conduct very professional and formal discussions of serious topics; others are like online clubs of people with the same hobby or passion. There's a lot of enthusiasm, sharing of valuable help and ideas, and unexpected camaraderie. There's also a lot of confusion, controversy, and downright belligerence. You really have to experience Usenet for a while—and sample different groups—to get a full picture.

While email and news frequently use the same software, the truth is that they are different services. They're also very different in character. You probably know—at least superficially—most of the people with whom you exchange email (unless you're sending it to a very large mailing list). In Usenet newsgroups, people initially know only superficial details about each other: names, email addresses, organizations, and so on. They have to rely on the content of news postings to get an idea of what the people behind them are like. The facelessness of Usenet sometimes encourages people to say things they might otherwise think better of. In many groups, in fact, it's a free-for-all.

What email and news do have in common is that they both let you communicate with other people online. In both cases, you can compose and send messages. Email is delivered to one or more recipients. News messages are posted so that anyone who subscribes to the group can read them. Both mail and news also allow you to read messages sent by other people. Thus, many of the features you need in an email program, you also want in a news program.

This logic is not lost on Internet software developers. Both Netscape Messenger and Microsoft Outlook Express come with modules that let you participate in email *and* Usenet news. Posting a message to a newsgroup and writing an email message to a person (or group) have become the same function: you click the same **New Message** button, compose in the same composition window, and so on. Certain menu items, buttons, and other controls are limited to one or the other application, but there is more overlap than not.

An Email Primer

The ins and outs of sending and receiving email are just about second nature to anyone who's done so for a while. If you're new to email, there are a few nuances you should know about.

Email Addresses

Email addresses commonly take the following form:

> *username@hostname.domain*

Here are some typical email addresses:

> *Walter_Cronkite@cbs.com*
> *president@whitehouse.gov*
> *princewilliam@buckingham.org*
> *einstein@princeton.edu*
> *bridgetjones@aol.com*

Not all hostnames are this simple; a few smaller networks require a syntax other than the *name@address* format. If the intended recipient gets mail on one of these networks, you'll have to work a little harder to learn the exact address. Sometimes, the person puts this information in his signature file, described later.

When you choose a login name for email purposes, you may want to pick a "portable" name; that is, a name that you're likely to be able to use if you move your email account to another host. For example, "mary" is probably already taken at most hosts. You may want to consider using your last name, a first initial and last name, or even just initials.

How do you find an individual's email address? The best and easiest way is to ask that person directly. If you'd like to use email to make an initial contact, you may search for an email address via a people-finding service on the Web (see Chapter 12). Or, if someone sends you a message and you'd like to record that email address for future reference, most mailers have a "make alias" feature that performs the action for you semi-automatically.*

---

* We'll discuss specific mailers later in the chapter, but a note should be included here. Outlook 98's version of this feature is an email option that automatically creates entries for individuals to whom you've replied and places them in the Contacts folder. When I tried it, the result was that I frequently had to clean out my contacts list for people I'd never heard of. You may want to turn this feature off.

Composing Messages

You have a few options as to how you send your messages. Generally, you can specify the recipients by entering their email addresses in the proper fields of the message header. Typically, all messages have a To: field where you enter the email addresses of the primary recipients. With some email programs, you can separate multiple names with a space or a comma, while Microsoft favors a semicolon; check your mailer's documentation.

When you fill out the address fields of your messages, keep in mind that almost every mailer has an *address book* feature. An address book, shown in Figure 2-1, is basically a file where you can store frequently used email addresses, along with abbreviated versions of them (known as *aliases* or *nicknames*). Once you've created an address book, you should be able to fill in the various email addresses in a message header by selecting the addresses from an address book dialog box, or from a drop-down list that appears automatically. If you define aliases in your address book, you can enter them in the header instead of typing the full addresses. Your mailer expands the aliases before it sends the message.

Figure 2-1. Eudora's Address book

Carbon copies

It's easy to send email to more than one recipient. In the To:, CC:, and BCC: fields, enter the addresses (or aliases), separated by commas, of the people who should receive the mail. Post to multiple newsgroups the same way. Place the names of the primary recipients in the To: field. These are the people to whom the message is most important.

Generally, the carbon-copy feature (often abbreviated cc) is used to send copies of messages to people who aren't among the primary recipients—they are people whom you'd like to make aware of the message's contents. People sometimes copy themselves on messages as well, to keep a record of their communications. In general, this isn't necessary, since most mailers provide a setting to keep copies of all your outgoing messages in a particular folder.

When you send mail to a group of people, each of their addresses usually appears in the message's *header* (special lines telling the email system how to handle the message). So, everybody who gets the mail knows who else received it (see Figure 2-2).

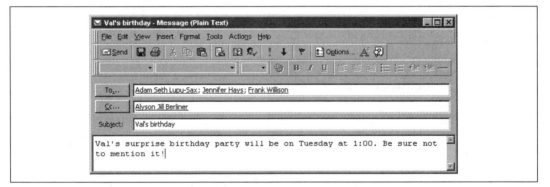

Figure 2-2. A message regarding a surprise party

However, some mailers provide an extra copy feature called *blind carbon copy* (abbreviated bcc). When you send a blind carbon to someone, that recipient's address doesn't appear in the message headers sent to the other recipients. They don't know about the person who got the blind copy—and that's the idea. (As Figure 2-2 shows, many mailers don't automatically display the BCC: field. If you're using Outlook, you'll need to select **BCC field** from the **View** menu to access the field. Note that this option is only available on the **View** menu *after* you've opened a message for composition.)

The subject line

Next in the header, you'll usually find a Subject: line, the contents of which are entirely up to you. It's polite to jot down a phrase that will clue recipients into the message's content. Some people ignore messages without a subject line—many unsolicited messages (spam) have no subject. And some mailers will warn you if you try to send a message without a subject—though they usually let you do it anyway.

Once you've addressed your message and provided a subject line, write the body of the message itself. When you're finished, click the **Send** button.

Replying to and forwarding messages

You'll frequently find yourself using a message you've received as the content of a new message by including it as a reply, forwarding, or redirecting it to another address. These terms refer to differing, but related, actions:

- *Replying* to a message means sending a message back to the original sender (and, possibly, any other recipients of the message).

- *Forwarding* a message means sending the message on to a new person or persons.

- *Redirecting* a message also means sending the message on to a new person or persons, but the *original* sender's name appears in the From: field.

To forward a message, for example, you would click the **Forward** button or select a **Forward** item from a menu. This generally opens up another window, in which the text of the forwarded message appears. Most mailers somehow tell recipients that a message is being forwarded. Messenger and Outlook forward messages as attachments. Other mailers forward messages as text and identify the message as such in the header. The text of the forwarded message may also be preceded by a line that identifies it, as in Figure 2-3.

```
Floyd-

Get a look at this!

-----Original Message-----
From: "coyote" [mailto:coyote@likeminds.com]
Sent: Monday, April 13, 1998 7:07 PM
To: ora@ora.com
Cc: jenni@domestic.org
Subject: Inflatable underpants


AP STORY OF THE WEEK
Tokyo commuter Katsuo Katugoru caused havoc on a crowded
tube train when his inflatable underpants unexpectedly
went off.
```

Figure 2-3. Outlook's forwarding attribution

More commonly, especially in replies, the text of an included message is indented or preceded by right-angle brackets. The source may also be identified, as in Figure 2-4.

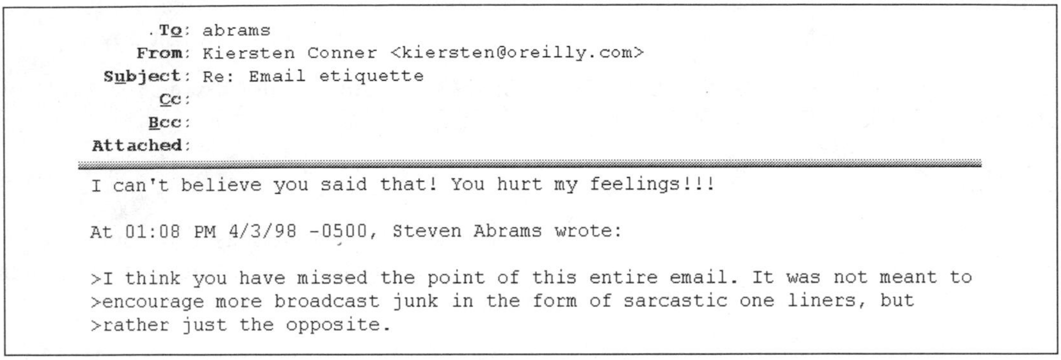

```
        .To: abrams
       From: Kiersten Conner <kiersten@oreilly.com>
    Subject: Re: Email etiquette
         Cc:
        Bcc:
   Attached:
===============================================================
I can't believe you said that! You hurt my feelings!!!

At 01:08 PM 4/3/98 -0500, Steven Abrams wrote:

>I think you have missed the point of this entire email. It was not meant to
>encourage more broadcast junk in the form of sarcastic one liners, but
>rather just the opposite.
```

Figure 2-4. Reply attribution in Eudora

(It's not practical—or considerate—to quote an entire, long message using angle brackets. Use only pithy excerpts.) Once you have an included message in a composition window, you can type in the address, edit the message, and so on, before sending. Keep in mind that things get complicated when you reply to groups of people, especially when you reply to an individual who sent mail to a group.

Your mailer's commands or buttons let you choose whether you want to reply only to the sender, or to the sender and all recipients. Naturally, however, you can then edit the header lines to send your reply to anyone you like. You may, for example, want to reply to a partial list of the original recipients.

Check your mailer's options to see whether the default reply option is set to "Reply to sender" or "Reply to all." You'd be surprised how often people send sensitive information to their entire company because they didn't check the distribution list before clicking Send.*

One more important note: if you reply to a message with attachments, the attachments aren't sent when you send the reply. (The mailer logically assumes that the people you're replying to already have the attachment.) But if you *forward* a message with attachments, the attachments *are* sent.

Choosing a Communications (Mostly Email) Package

Odds are that you read, compose, and send email more often than you read and post to newsgroups. Moreover, most newsreaders are currently very similar in operation.

---

* Outlook 98 is particularly troublesome on this count. Outlook includes forwarded messages as attachments. If you double-click the attachment to read it, then click the **Reply** button, the reply goes to the *author* of the forwarded message, not to the person who *forwarded* the message to you. As a result of this kind of mishap, I once sent a rather strange missive to a gentleman who was about to interview my fiancé for a job.

So, when you're choosing a communications package, you'll want to focus on what kind of mailer best suits your needs:

- On what platform will you be reading mail or news: on a PC, a Macintosh, or in a Unix environment? Would it be easier for you to communicate via the World Wide Web?

- How will you be storing your messages? Personal hard drive, web server, or a computer in the workplace?

- Will you be downloading your mail to a PalmPilot or some other handheld computer?

- With whom will you be exchanging mail? How closely are you tied to them? You're more likely to need to exchange formatted files with co-workers than with friends.

- What do you need in a user interface?

- How often do you travel?

- Do you need to send formatted text or images?

- How robust does your address book need to be: do you need a simple catalog of aliases or a full-featured personal information manager?

- How much filtering do you need?

One of the most important questions you need to ask is where your mail will be stored, locally or on the mail server. If your mail is stored locally, it's on the hard drive of your machine. Mail stored on the server is kept on the machine from which you download your mail. The advantages of local storage include increased privacy, easy search capabilities, and increased opportunities for customization. However, locally stored mail may not be as private as you think, and is hard to access from any other machine. Mail stored on the server can be quite easy to access, but is frequently subject to small space allowances.

Microsoft's Outlook, Qualcomm's Eudora, and Netscape's Messenger all store mail messages on a local hard drive. They operate according to the *POP3* protocol. *POP* stands for Post Office Protocol, which is currently in its third iteration, and describes the "dialog" between two computers. POP clients don't transfer email to other Internet hosts directly; they let some larger computer with a full-time, dedicated connection act as their Internet mail server. This means that your machine is not required to be available for email transfers all the time. You can have a dialup Internet connection, or you can turn off the computer when you're done working. Whenever you ask for email, your computer contacts the server and downloads all the mail that has accumulated for you.

If you always use a particular computer to check your mail, a POP mailer will be suitable for your needs. POP was designed for people who use one computer exclusively and who connect to the Internet only occasionally. If you don't want to maintain a constant connection to the Internet, you can connect, download your messages, and disconnect. You can then read your mail, write replies or new messages, and queue those messages to be sent, all while disconnected from the network. The next time you connect to the Net, the queued mail is sent. This minimizes the amount of time you are actually connected to the email server, and therefore tends to lower connection costs. For the traveler, POP also lets you dial into your ISP while you're in Chicago, download twenty messages, and then disconnect. You may then read and send the queued mail, and pick up a new batch when you arrive in Washington, D.C. Your mail goes with you on your personal computer.

What happens, though, when you get back to Chicago? If you've saved messages on your laptop, but usually work on a desktop machine, coordinating messages can be a chore. Many POP clients allow you to operate in *remote mode*. This allows you to leave message you don't want to deal with immediately on your mail service computer. Eudora and Outlook may both be configured in this manner.

Even so, POP clients can be frustrating. If you work in remote mode, you have to either leave *all* of your mail in your inbox or only have full access to your saved mail from one location. Additionally, if you don't have a portable computer of your own, you'll find yourself downloading messages to someone else's POP client—almost certainly something you don't want.

Clients that store mail remotely include the IMAP-based mailers Pine and Mulberry, server-based Pine, and WWW-based packages, such as HotMail or RocketMail.

Thus, in certain situations, using an email package that lets you contact the server directly and manipulate your messages there is more appropriate. Using IMAP (*Internet Message Access Protocol*) instead of POP is one such solution. IMAP allows you to use a pretty, graphical mailer on a PC to access messages on the server, manipulate them, and save them in folders there. This allows you to access those folders easily from other locations. Unfortunately, IMAP is more complex than POP, slower, and not as widely used. Additionally, certain mailers, including Outlook, can only search through folders saved on the local machine—a fairly large handicap, given the necessity of using email as a reference. (A mailer called Mulberry *can* search through folders on the server; see the "Pine/Mulberry" section in this chapter.)

Other server-based options essentially bypass your PC. You can use a Telnet session to run Pine directly on the server. You may also want to consider a WWW-based email package. In that case, the only software you need is a web browser, and messages are saved on the Web, not on a local PC. See Chapter 3, for more on WWW-based mailers.

Another consideration in choosing an email package is the interface you'll be using. Graphical interfaces may look nice and be easy to navigate with the mouse, but you may have other considerations that are more important. Keystrokes are often more efficient and less hard on the hands than mouse strokes, and Pine is a good option in this situation.

Many features are common to all mailers. Other features (such as digitized pictures and voice plug-ins) can be used only when the sender and recipient both use similar mail software and operating system utilities. If your goal is to transfer all kinds of files between a small circle of friends or co-workers with as little trouble as possible, then you and your friends (or system administrators) should agree on a single mail system and use it. If that is not a big concern, then you should pick the email software that you find the easiest to use and with which you feel comfortable.

What follows are very brief descriptions of some of the most popular mailers. With the exception of Eudora Pro and Outlook 98, each mailer is free.

Eudora Pro and Eudora Lite

Qualcomm's Eudora is the favorite email application for many people. With good reason: the package is one of the most robust available, with excellent filtering capability and an intuitive interface, along with features like a spellchecker and HTML formatting. Eudora's HTML display is somewhat lacking, however, since it requires Internet Explorer (IE) to be on your machine. It then uses IE as a plug-in to view HTML messages. The integration is seamless, but if IE isn't your web browser, this configuration requires you to keep an extra browser around—which takes up an extra chunk of hard-drive space.

Eudora's main flaw used to be its search feature, since the application returned only one message at a time instead of a list of messages containing the desired string. As of release 4.2, that feature had been much improved. In fact, Eudora's search tool is now one of the best. Moreover, Eudora 4.2 is the only mailer to support an excellent feature: if you highlight the text of a message and click **Reply**, only the highlighted text is included in the resulting message.

While Eudora Lite is free, the Eudora Pro package supports additional filtering, and provides tech support. Note that Eudora is the only package we discuss here that doesn't provide a newsreader. Eudora Pro's filtering and stationery features are far and away the best of the bunch, however, including features the others conspicuously lack.

Outlook 98 and Outlook Express

Microsoft now ships Windows 98 with both Internet Explorer and Outlook Express. Outlook Express provides basic mail functions, including an address book, HTML formatting and display, multiple accounts, stationery, filtering, and a newsreader. If you'll be sending basic email to friends and family, Outlook Express will suit you fine.

Outlook 98 provides a veritable cornucopia of additional functions. Aside from the mailer, which supports all of the Outlook Express functions, along with multiple pane displays, signature options, and filtering wizards, you'll find a fully functional Personal

Information Manager (PIM). You can coordinate this PIM, which features a calendar, contacts file, journal of interactions with an individual, and notes for tasks to do, with your email in surprising, but frankly daunting, ways. The Find feature is the best in the pack of mailers we discuss here.

Note, however, that Outlook 98 *doesn't* include the newsreader that's built into Outlook Express. Therefore, you can't throw Outlook Express off your drive just because you're now using Outlook 98, unless you're also using a completely separate newsreader. This is intensely irritating. If you choose to continue using both Outlook 98 (as a mailer) and Outlook Express (as a newsreader), you'll want to set Express to work offline (in the **File** menu) to avoid having your mail downloaded to the wrong application. One plus is that the applications share the same address book file, so modifications made to one Outlook address book do in fact appear in the other.

One big minus to Outlook is something that Microsoft claims is a feature: its integration with the rest of the Office suite of applications. The now-infamous Melissa virus spread, in part, because of its ability to be opened as an application in Word, from which it would then access the Outlook address book. Many people have recommended against using Outlook as a result of this debacle.

Netscape Messenger

Netscape built its mailer, Messenger, into the 4.0 release of Communicator, which is the umbrella term for the browser (Navigator) and its attendant parts. With release 4.5, the newsreader was incorporated into Messenger as well, a sound decision since the newsreader, formerly called Collabra, was part of the "Message Center," sharing some mailer functions, and was thus quite confusing to use.

Currently, Messenger supports IMAP, filtering, spellcheck, HTML formatting and display, and an address book, all in a three-pane display that's more intuitive than Outlook's. Netscape's threaded message display, which organizes messages by subject, is a favorite with some users. Message filtering isn't as strong as it should be, however. Messenger also lacks stationery and multiple mailbox features. It's a solid mailer and newsreader, but it lacks some of the fancy features you'll find in the others.

Pine/Mulberry

If you're interested in using either IMAP or a less mouse-intensive mailer, take a look at Pine or Mulberry. These not-very-graphical mailers are not for the faint of heart. Until version 4.0, Pine, which was created for the Unix operating system, supported *only* IMAP.

Mulberry is a graphical IMAP mailer that works on the Mac, Windows, and Unix. While not widely known, it's a powerful tool, and the only graphical mailer really designed around IMAP. The price is approximately the same as that of Eudora Pro; see *http://www.cyrusoft.com/mulberry* for more information.

Pine is a freely available mailer and newsreader that works on Windows and Unix systems. It's available from *http://www.washington.edu/pine/*. Compared to Eudora, Messenger, and Outlook, it's somewhat limited, but it performs all the important functions, including handling MIME messages, and you can configure it extensively—a major plus for power users. The big advantage of Pine is that it requires no mousing at all and less typing than with any other mailer we know. If you have problems with carpal tunnel syndrome or tendinitis, it can be a real help. Obviously, you have to type any messages you want to send, but you can read all your mail using nothing but the spacebar. Although it doesn't have a friendly graphical interface, Pine is surprisingly easy to use; it always displays a list of commands at the bottom of the screen, and it was designed so that you could learn to use it without reading a manual.

America Online

In AOL version 4.0, America Online has made some improvements to its mailer: a spellchecker, the ability to send image files, and an alphabetized address book. However, any image files included appear only when sent to other AOL subscribers; if you want to send a photo to someone with a non-AOL address, you'll have to attach the file instead. All in all, AOL's mailer is pretty bad, and the improvements don't bring it up to snuff. Thus, we wanted to include a section in this chapter about configuring AOL to work with a POP mailer. Unfortunately, AOL doesn't support such an option. There are services that provide a workaround for a yearly fee; see *http://www. emailman.com/aol/index.html* for further information.

Configuring Your Mailer/Newsreader

Once you've selected a communications package, which may consist of a mailer/ newsreader combination (Netscape Communicator or Outlook Express) or one of each (Eudora, Outlook 98, or something else entirely), you'll need to install the package on your computer. To do so, follow the instructions provided by the manufacturer.

Next, you'll need to configure the application(s) to access messages from the Internet—contact your Internet service provider for information. However, the odds are good that your options will look something like those pictured in Figure 2-5 (for Eudora) or Figure 2-6 (for Outlook Express's newsreader).

Note that the reply address we list in Outlook for the newsreading program in Figure 2-6 is different from the actual email address. Why? Well, posting to Usenet frequently results in a good deal of junk email, or spam, being sent to the poster. Therefore, it's a good idea to use a fake address for replies or a separate account dedicated solely to Usenet. See Chapter 5 for more information.

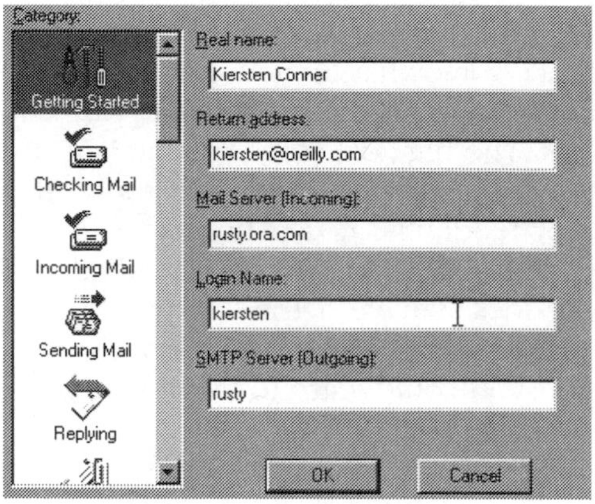

Figure 2-5. Eudora configuration options

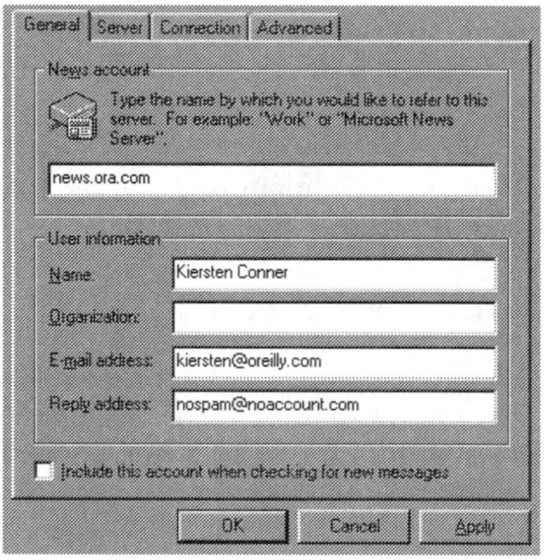

Figure 2-6. Outlook Express configuration options

Composing Messages: A Netiquette Primer

Now that you're ready to send some mail, you should know that there is some basic etiquette to communicating on the Internet. Be polite, to the point, and don't engage in insults just because you won't see the hurt look on someone's face when you do so.

It's not that difficult to write email messages and Usenet posts that don't cause misunderstandings or come back to haunt you. But it does take a little effort. Here are some guidelines that should help:

- Be polite. Address people in an appropriate and respectful manner. Take the time to say please and thank you. Don't take liberties, and observe common courtesy.

- Sign your name (or screen name).

- Don't nest tons of other messages in a single message. Cut quoted material down to the relevant parts, and edit out broken lines or multiple brackets. Figure 2-7 is a good example.

```
At 01:36 PM 3/11/99 -0500, you wrote:
>
>
>>>>A priest, a
>>>>rabbi, and a minister walk into a bar. The bartender looks up and
says
>>>>what is this, some kind of a joke?
>
>I don't get it.
>-Tina
>>
>>
How dull it is to pause, to make an end,
      To rust unburnish'd, not to shine in use,--
      As tho' to breathe were life!
Tennyson, Ulysses
```

Figure 2-7. A difficult-to-read message

- Consider your audience. In messages to strangers, acquaintances, or large groups, spell things out. If you know someone well, you have more latitude.

- Re-read your messages to make sure they make sense. It's a good idea to pay some attention to grammar and spelling, too.

- Unless you know your recipients can view complex formatting, use only ASCII (plain text) characters. Many mailers still don't support HTML formatting. Set your preferences (which some mailers, including Outlook and Eudora, support on an address-by-address basis) to send plain text only.

- Don't write anything you want to keep private. Once a mail message is out there, system administrators have access to it, and savvy hacker types can get at it, too. Some companies may monitor employees' email. Even a company with a stated privacy policy may read your mail and legally use it against you. See Chapter 5 for more information.

- Don't fan the "flames" other people start—that is, don't let yourself get dragged into an online brawl. If you feel inclined to write something in the heat of the moment, cool off for a while before you post.

- If you're not sure whether a question is appropriate to a particular newsgroup, consult the group's FAQ (Frequently Asked Questions list), if there is one, before posting.

- Don't post the same message to multiple groups (called *cross-posting*) without a good reason. Remember that some people will be reading multiple groups about the same subject—and they don't want to read your message over and over again.

- If you must get into a dispute with someone else on a mailing list or in a newsgroup, take the discussion out of the group and into email.

Even if you follow these guidelines, it can be tough to convey your meaning. If you try telling a friend a funny story in email, you'll quickly appreciate some of the limitations of communicating in type. The most obvious one is that you can't use any vocal inflection to indicate that this part is suspenseful, that this is a surprise, that somebody's mad, there are two voices here, this is the silly part, and so on. And you can't indicate any of this by shrugging your shoulders, raising an eyebrow, smiling, or clapping a hand to your forehead, either. All of the nonverbal clues we employ readily in other forms of communication are missing.

The result is that miscommunications abound online. Naturally, it's easier when you know the other person well, but that isn't always the case. Even when you know someone, it's difficult to convey humor, irony, or other subtle emotions. Simple brevity can be mistaken for rudeness or even anger. Some people think of email as a casual statement that doesn't commit them to anything, while others think it's been typed in stone.

Things are even worse in Usenet news, where the relative anonymity of participants encourages missed meanings and liberates people to be a lot nastier than they would be in person.

Sounds kind of hopeless, doesn't it?

Well, things aren't really all that bad. Communicating over the Internet involves a few shorthand forms that help to clarify meaning: smileys, abbreviations, signatures, and formatting conventions.

Smileys :-)

A simple way you can clarify your meaning in email is to use so-called *smileys* (also known as emoticons). A smiley is a little picture created with a few ASCII characters depicting a smiling face turned on its side. There are actually a huge number of variations on the basic smiley, to suggest all kinds of different emotions. Here are a few popular ones:

    :-) smile
    :-(frown
    ;-) wink
    :-| straight face
    :-o surprise!

Smileys are a concrete way of saying "I'm kidding," "I'm sad," or whatever—without coming out and saying it. Certainly a well-placed winking smiley can let someone know you're joking, though they seem rather banal to the Internet cognoscenti.

Abbreviations

Abbreviations are another widely used way to clarify your meaning. Like a smiley, an abbreviation can quickly indicate your true feelings. For example, IMHO stands for "in my humble opinion," which gives your statement a different tenor than IMHO's cousin, IMO, "in my opinion." Here are some commonly used acronyms:

Acronym	Meaning
BRB	Be Right Back
BTW	By The Way
GMTA	Great Minds Think Alike
IMHO	In My Humble Opinion
IMO	In My Opinion
IMNSHO	In My Not So Humble Opinion
LOL	Laugh Out Loud
OTF	On The Floor (laughing)
OMG	Oh My Gosh/God
ROTFL	Rolling On The Floor Laughing
ROTFLMAO	Rolling on the Floor Laughing My Ass Off
TTFN	Ta Ta For Now
TTYL	Talk to You Later
WB	Welcome Back
WTG	Way To Go

Signature Files

When you receive an email message, you should find the person's proper email address among the message's header lines. Here's a sample header:

```
Date: Fri, 29 May 1999 11:37:55 -0400
To: kiersten@oreilly.com
From: "Floyd Goodbody" <floydg@erols.com>
Subject: Mugsy report
```

There may be no Floyd Goodbody, but if there were, it would be easy to see that his[*] email address is *floydg@erols.com.*

---

[*] Or her; if you don't know the person, don't assume.

Unfortunately, some message headers get garbled en route, as the message is passed among different servers. That's why including a signature file is a good idea. A *signature file* is a short text file your mailer appends automatically to mail messages and Usenet news posts to let people know something about you. Often, this information is limited to basic facts, such as your email address, full name, and business phone number, but you could include your business title, work address, fax number, and so on.

Putting your email address in a signature file ensures that people you send messages to can reach you. For business purposes, it's nice to be able to give people some relevant phone numbers and addresses, as well. While many people include their home address or phone number, I wouldn't recommend it; see Chapter 5 for more information.

Signature files were devised for practical purposes, but they've also taken on an element of fun. Many people include quotations or art drawn using ASCII characters. However, netiquette dictates that signature files should be kept to a few lines. Long *sig* files (as they're called) waste time, disk space, and money, since many people pay for their connection time.

So, supply your name and email address, but keep the sig short and to the point, at no more than four lines of text:

```
Wendy Nauman
wendyn@earthlink.net
Better to have loved and lost a short person than never
to have loved a tall.
```

To create a signature file, check your mailer's help files. Most allow you to browse for this file, so if you've already saved a signature in one mail program, it's easy to use in another. Once you've created that file, you may want to change your option settings to append it automatically to outgoing mail messages.

Outlook and Eudora allow you to create multiple signature files. You may want to use one signature for business contacts, another for Usenet posts (since this is a case in which you probably want to scramble your signature; see Chapter 5 for more information), and still another for personal mail. To append these signatures, click the **Signature** button on the mailer's toolbar.[*]

When (and How) to Use Formatting

As mentioned earlier, many mailers *don't* support HTML formatting. Thus, unless you know your recipient can handle formatting, (for example, Outlook, Netscape, or AOL users), use the ASCII character set.

---

[*] If you're using multiple signatures with Outlook, you'll want to turn off the "automatically include your signature" function, under **Options**. Since Outlook appends the signature before you start writing the message, selecting a signature from the drop-down list in the composition window simply pastes in a second signature instead of replacing the first.

There is some formatting you can—and even *should*—perform on your messages, however.

Set your mailer to wrap long lines after 72 characters at the most. Many people advocate wrapping long lines after 60 to 65 characters. Since some mailers wrap lines according to the size of the window in which the message was composed, make sure that your window is reasonably small, or insert hard-carriage returns by pressing the Enter key at the end of each line.

You can still convey some meaning using only the ASCII character set. Asterisks or underscore characters around words indicate italics:

```
Have you read _War and Peace_?
```

Be aware that using all uppercase letters is considered shouting and is discouraged.

Creating and using stationery

Some mailers also allow you to create *stationery*, or preformatted text files you can use in mail messages. You create the file and save it. Later, you can open the file in your mailer and either make changes or send it as is. Eudora even allows you to create filters that respond with stationery, so that automated replies are a snap.

To create stationery in Eudora, simply create a new mail message. Type the subject line and body that you want, and append a signature file you consider appropriate. Then, instead of sending the message, choose **Save As Stationery** from the **File** menu. The stationery now appears in the **New Message With**, **Reply With**, and **Reply to All With** drop-down menus in the **Message** menu. When you select it, the message opens, and you can edit it as you like.

Outlook claims to support stationery, but I found the results remarkably unsatisfying. Outlook 98 ships with a number of preformatted stationery files included. To use them, select **New Mail Message Using...** from the **Action** menu, then select **More Stationery...** from the drop-down menu. From there, you may select from such stationery options as For Sale and Tiki Lounge (see Figure 2-8). Stationery may be sent only in Rich HTML format, and when I tried to save stationery of my own (open a message, compose it, and choose **Save stationery** from the **File** menu, as described previously for Eudora), nothing was preserved. The chosen title appeared, but not the content or format of the message.

If you have a use for Outlook's standard stationery (for example, frequent yard sales or luaus), and if you only plan to communicate with people who also use Outlook, you'll appreciate this feature. If you need to create your own pre-formatted files for a specific purpose, you're better off using Eudora.

Figure 2-8. If only you could see that the text is orange

Handling Incoming Messages

Email programs give you the option of handling your incoming mail in a number of ways. Each of the mailers we discuss allows you to create different folders or mailboxes in which you can store both incoming and outgoing messages. You should also be able to save messages to files elsewhere on your system, and send messages directly to the printer.

POP clients should check for new mail when you open the application. After that time, the mailer checks the server periodically to see whether new mail has arrived. Set the interval in your preferences settings. To check for new mail between sessions, click the **Check mail** or **Send and receive** button. Server-based mailers alert you as soon as mail arrives.

Once that mail does arrive, you'll probably want to read it. Then, reply to it or forward it to someone else. Once that's done, move it to a folder. Each of the graphical mailers supports drag and drop; just "grab" the message's header by clicking it with the mouse, and drag it to a folder. You should also be able to click a **Move folder** or analogous button in just about any mailer. For example, Eudora lets you drag and drop a message into a mail folder, as shown in Figure 2-9.

To move multiple messages to the same folder, select their headers while you hold down the Shift key, then drag the headers to the folder of choice.

Folders may seem like a hassle at first, since you won't have that many messages. Your inbox fills up quickly, however, and once it does, you'll have a hard time finding the information you need in your saved messages. See Chapter 3 for more information on folder organization.

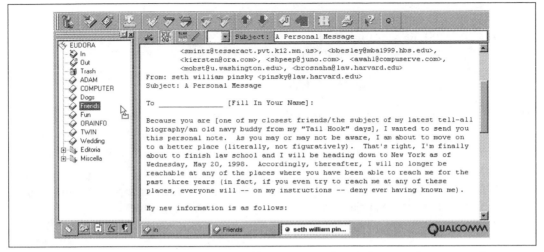

Figure 2-9. When using Eudora, you can file a message by clicking on the tow truck icon, then dragging the message to the appropriate folder

Filtering

One way to make organizing your incoming mail easier is to set up mail filters. With mail filtering, you tell the mailer what to do with incoming messages that match certain criteria. For example, you could create a filter that deletes all the messages with the words "you're fired" in the Subject line (probably a bad idea). Or, you can specify that messages from your mother are automatically saved in a particular folder. See Chapter 3 for more information.

Notification

Most mailers play a sound and place an icon in the taskbar alerting you to the arrival of new mail. Sounds simple enough. However, things quickly become complicated: multiple accounts may be hard to keep track of, and some people, who receive hundreds of messages a day, don't need to be alerted as each arrives: your boss's message, yes, but not new mail from the Frequent Mailer's mailing list.

Only Eudora handles audio alerts the way a mailer should: by allowing you to assign a specific alert noise to certain messages. You can create filters so that certain messages have special sounds, general messages have a default sound, and messages from a mailing list don't have an associated sound at all. The other mailers allow you to turn audio and visual alerts on or off.

If you love Outlook or Messenger, but want more notification options, or you're checking multiple accounts, try a mail plug-in, such as the Ristra Mail Monitor, or an email service, such as Bigfoot's Notification. See Chapter 3 for more information. Ristra, for example, checks your web-based freemail accounts at specified intervals and then plays a choice of alert sounds; it then launches your browser to the freemail accounts login page. Bigfoot's service can be even more helpful: route multiple accounts through its consolidation service, and it will filter out duplicate messages, and reroute the remaining messages to your primary account.

How to Handle Formatted Mail

Many of the popular PC mailers currently allow you to format your messages in ways you never could before. The result is that people with older mailers, or mailers that don't support formatting, display these messages as barely readable gobbledygook.

The standard adopted is a familiar one: HTML. If you receive a file that appears to have HTML tags (see below) or seems to be missing information, open the file in your browser. If you're using an older version of Eudora, right-click the message and select **Send to Browser** from the drop-down list. If you're using another mailer, save the message as text with the *.htm* extension. Then use the **Open** command in your browser to see the contents as they were meant to be seen. Don't forget to flame the sender and tell him that not everyone uses HTML-compatible mailers.

Folders, and How to Organize Them

There are three general ways to organize folders: by topic, by sender, or by date. What works for you is largely a matter of personal preference. Regardless of your choice, you can always create a filter to route mail to the appropriate folder automatically. You can always search for the information you need, or, if you're really neurotic, save an extra copy of a message to another folder (for example, one into the folder where you keep messages from your boss and one into the folder for a specific project).

At this point, we've covered the very basics of using email: composing, reading, and storing messages. But there's a lot more to know. To learn about viewing and sending attachments, free email services, handling email on the road, using filters to route mail, and managing multiple email accounts, see Chapter 3.

Configuration Tips for Users

Mailers are steadily becoming more and more complex. Since the number of options now available to the average user boggles the mind, we've assembled some tips here that should help your mailer run smoothly.

No matter which mailer you're using, keep the following tips in mind:

- Be sure to check periodically for updates. Take a look at the manufacturer's web site every few months to see whether there are any new software patches or upgrades. Installing these upgrades is a snap; just follow the instructions at the web site. (See Chapter 13 for more information.)

- In virtually every graphical mailer, click the headings (Date, Sender, Priority, and so on) at the top of the message pane to sort messages according to various criteria.

- Right-click a message in the inbox for quick access to functions.

- Most mailers don't *really* delete your messages unless you ask them to. Instead, deleted messages are transferred to a Trash or Deleted items directory. To save disk space, empty the trash occasionally (in most mailers, this is a command found in the **File** menu).

- Set your preferences to send plain-text messages by default.

See Chapter 3 for specific tips for individual mailers.

When Email Gets Returned

When email cannot be delivered, you usually receive a message telling you why. This takes the format of a really ugly, strange message from something called the Mail Delivery Subsystem with the subject "Returned mail," as shown in Figure 2-10.

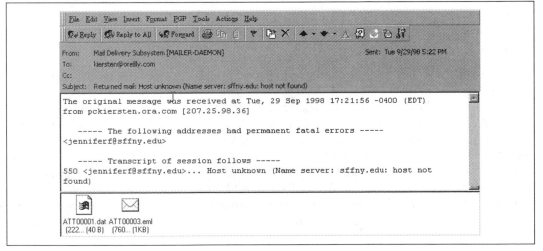

Figure 2-10. Returned email

At this point, all you know is that your mail didn't go through; you have no idea why. To find out, you have to wade through the cryptic message that has been returned, and look for clues.

There are three common reasons why email may not reach its destination:

- The mail system can't find the recipient's machine.

- The recipient is unknown at that machine.

- The mail system can find the machine, but the machine isn't accepting mail.

Unknown Hosts

When you send a message to someone, the network tries to make some sense out of the stuff to the right of the "at" symbol (@). If it can't make sense of it, or if it can't look up the address of the named machine, the mailer that gives up sends you a message stating that the host is unknown. Let's assume we were trying to send a message to *JenniferF@sffny.org*, but incorrectly typed the computer host name as *sffny.edu*. Our first indication that something was wrong would be a "Returned mail" message. We can read it as we would any other message. As a message travels to its destination, it passes through a number of mail handlers. One of these intermediate handlers didn't like the message we sent. Since users have no control over the intermediate computers, the messages you see may differ from what is shown in Figure 2-10. The wording will usually be similar. In this case, we're in luck: the mail forwarder generated a Subject: header that tells you fairly explicitly that the name server could not find *sffny.edu*.

Had this intermediate host not been so nice, the next place to look would be the text of the message. Look for the section marked "Transcript of session." Here, you find a message that the host *sffny.edu* is not found on the network. Sometimes the wording "Host Unknown" is used.

After this text, you'll usually find the text of the unsent message itself. This mailer wrapped it up as a MIME attachment, but didn't provide the subject line as the attachment name (which some will).

What should you do when something like this happens? First, check the address. Is *sffny.edu* correct? In this case, it isn't. It should be *sffny.org*. Second, check whether the address is complete. When presented with an incomplete name like *JenniferF*, many mailers assume it is an address book alias and, if the alias isn't there, either display an error message or append a default domain. However, if you are replying to a message, the mailer may assume that the return address is correct, which is not always the case. It passes the message to the mail server, which will notice the incomplete name and (most likely) assume the suffix should be the same as its own. While this is sometimes a good assumption, (for example, much of the mail originating within a university will be going to another address within the university), if the mail came from outside, it will not reach its destination.

If your mail appears to have been correctly addressed, you'll have to use an ancient technology: the telephone. Call the intended recipient and make sure you have the correct address.

Unknown Recipients

Now, let's assume that your mail made its way to the correct host. Eventually, a machine forwarding your mail makes contact with the destination machine and tells it the recipient's name. What happens if the destination machine hasn't heard of the message's addressee? In this case, the returned message will have a subject like this:

```
Subject: Returned mail: User unknown Status: RO
```

and a session transcript similar to this:

```
        —— Transcript of session follows ——
While talking to oreilly.com:
>>> RCPT To:speke@oreilly.com
<<< 550 speke@oreilly.com. . . User unknown
550 speke@oreilly.com. . .User unknown
```

This failure is frequently caused by mistyping the username in the address. (That's what happened here. I mistyped "spike.") It is also possible that the username is correct and that the hostname is incorrect, but legal. For example, if you address a message to *spike@rocky.oreilly.com* instead of *spike@rusty.oreilly.com*, you may get a "User unknown" message. The machine *rusty* exists, but there is no user spike on it. (In the worst case, the wrong person may receive your mail: some spike that you've never met, but who happens to have an account on rusty.[*])

Invalid Return Addresses

Occasionally, an individual's mailer or mail server may be misconfigured, so that the return address is invalid. Inexperienced users frequently enter erroneous addresses in the Reply to: field (usually a simple misspelling or typo) or don't enter anything at all (for example, leaving only a domain name in this field). While mail that is sent from such an address usually arrives intact, it may eventually get bounced. More frequently, however, people to whom the mail was sent will try to reply to it. If users tell you they've been unable to reply to your mail, examine your Reply to: field and make sure it matches your correct email address.

From AOL

America Online can pose problems even for those who don't subscribe to their services.[†] Frequently, you'll send mail to an address with an *aol.com* domain, and, a few hours later, receive an error message in return, shown in Figure 2-11.

What can you do? If you have an AOL account or the AOL instant messaging software, you can check to see if the person you sent the mail to is online. If they are,

---

[*] This actually happened to me once. My mother had an account at Earthlink, and I sent her a very chatty message. The reply I received indicated that a certain Michael Conner was *not* my mummy and wasn't interested in the stuffed chicken breasts I was making for dinner (mconner, it seemed, was this gentleman, not Mary Conner, my mother).

[†] Actually, the same may be true of other ISPs. Since AOL is one of the largest, however, and its email service is proprietary, you're more likely to see this kind of message regarding an AOL account.

```
The original message was received at Mon, 9 Feb 1998 16:45:45 -0500 (EST)
from ruby.ora.com [207.25.98.2]

Your mail is being returned due to one or more non-delivery conditions
listed below:

(Refer to the "  ----- Transcript of session follows -----  " section)
1: SMTP 550 .... User Unknown
     Your recipient no longer exists on AOL.

2: SMTP 550 .... Mailbox Full
     Your recipient's mailbox is full.

3: SMTP 550 .... is not accepting mail from this sender
     Your recipient has blocked mail from you.

4: SMTP 550 ... Delivery not authorized
     Your site has been blocked from sending mail to AOL.

     -AOL Postmaster
```

Figure 2-11. The myriad reasons for returned mail to an AOL address

send an instant message. They may not know that their mailbox is full. Otherwise, once again, break out the telephone.

Email on the PalmPilot

If you need to read mail on the go, the PalmPilot[*] is an excellent mechanism for doing so. Why drag a 10-pound laptop on a trip, when you can carry a PalmPilot in your shirt pocket?

There are two ways you can transmit email and news to your PalmPilot: by HotSync-ing with your PC or Mac or by connecting directly to your ISP via modem.

If you use the HotSync method, mail that's been downloaded to your PC is trans-ferred to the PalmPilot, and is coordinated easily between the two machines. Your PC does all the work of downloading, sending, copying, and archiving mail. Two pro-grams let you interface with the PalmPilot and PC in this manner: PalmPilot Mail (built in to the PalmPilot Professional and later models) and Palmeta Mail, available via shareware (and which works on every PalmPilot).

If you use a modem with your PalmPilot, you'll need one of the programs designed to handle mail directly from the Internet: HandStamp (available from *http://www. smartcodesoft.com*), MultiMail (available from *http://www.actualsoft.com)*, or Postman (available from various shareware archives). Downloading your mail in this manner is more efficient for frequent travelers, but it means you have two mailboxes. If you download mail to two mailboxes, how do you know where a specific message is at

---

[*] We use PalmPilot as a generic term for a family of products, starting with the Palm 1000, continuing with the PalmPilot itself (now obsolete), and continuing further with the Palm III, V, and VII. Even though the name "PalmPilot" only refers to a particularly out-of-date product, it's the term most people use for the whole series.

any given time? Odds are, you'll want to leave messages on the server and download a copy to your PalmPilot.

In the following paragraphs, we'll be discussing PalmPilot Mail, the program that comes built in on the current crop of PalmPilots. We also assume you'll be downloading mail from your desktop PC, not using a modem connected directly to your PalmPilot.[*]

Setting Up PalmPilot Mail

Setup is fairly straightforward. The Palm Mail Setup program runs automatically when you install your PalmPilot and allows you to designate your desktop email program from a drop-down list. You can select from Microsoft Exchange 4.0+, Microsoft Windows Messaging 4.0, Microsoft Outlook 97, Microsoft Outlook Express, Eudora 3.03+, Lotus cc:Mail 2.5, Lotus cc:Mail 6.0, and Lotus cc:Mail 7.0. Outlook 98 users should use the Outlook 97 setting, and Eudora 3.03 users should access the **MAPI options** menu and turn on the options called **Use Eudora MAPI Server** and **When Eudora is running**. The next time you perform a HotSync, the PalmPilot downloads copies of your mail.

Reading and Answering Mail

To read your mail, turn the PalmPilot on, tap the **Applications** button, and tap **Mail**. The list of waiting mail appears (see Figure 2-12).

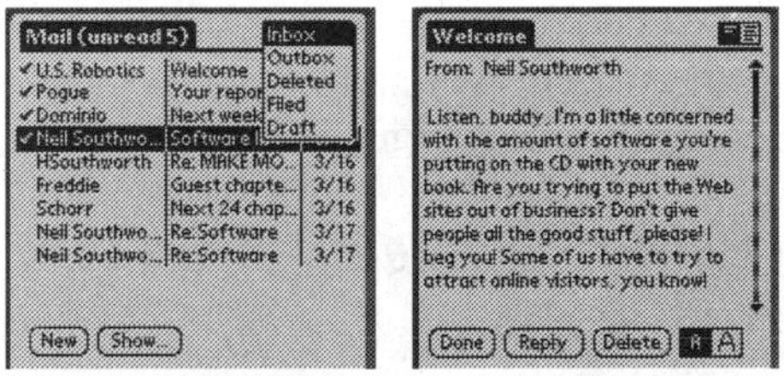

Figure 2-12. Available mail appears on the left; tap a message's name to view its contents (right)

Tap the triangle in the upper-right corner to access the folder pop-up menu, listing your Inbox, Outbox, and Deleted mailbox. The icons in the upper right corner are the Hide Headers/Show Headers icons.

To begin reading your mail, tap a message's summary line. The message opens. Use the scrollbar to navigate through the message: tap a lower or higher portion for page down or page up; drag for smooth scrolling.

---

[*] Of course, we can't go into the depth that this topic deserves in this chapter. For a fuller explanation, see David Pogue's *PalmPilot: The Ultimate Guide*, Second Edition (O'Reilly & Associates) or the eMailman section on Palm-Pilots at *http://www.emailman.com/palmpilot/index.html.*

When you're finished reading a message, you can tap one of these three buttons:

- Tap **Done** to return to the main index screen. The message you've just read remains there, but a check mark appears to indicate that you've read it.

- Tap **Reply** to reply to the sender, reply to all recipients, or forward the message to others. The PalmPilot will include the message you've just read in standard commented format.

- Tap **Delete** to delete the mail.

Deleting PalmPilot Mail

With most PalmPilot data, you're offered the opportunity to archive deleted memos or addresses on your desktop machine when you HotSync. In this case, the deleted message is simply moved to the Deleted folder. At this point, you may view the message again (by choosing **Deleted** from the **Folder** menu). You can even move the message back out of the Deleted folder.

If you want to restore a deleted message, however, *be sure to do so before your next HotSync*. When you HotSync, the message is deleted from both your PalmPilot and your desktop, irretrievably.

If even that amount of deleting power seems wimpy to you, you can purge your PalmPilot of deleted mail *before* your next HotSync, removing it permanently from the PalmPilot's memory. You may want to do this if you've just deleted a good deal of spam, for example. The purged mail will still be deleted from your desktop machine. To purge mail, tap **Menu → Options → Purge Deleted**.

Composing a New Email Message

To open a new, blank email message, tap **New** on the main index screen, or choose **New** from the **Message** menu from anywhere in the program. The form shown in Figure 2-13 should look familiar.

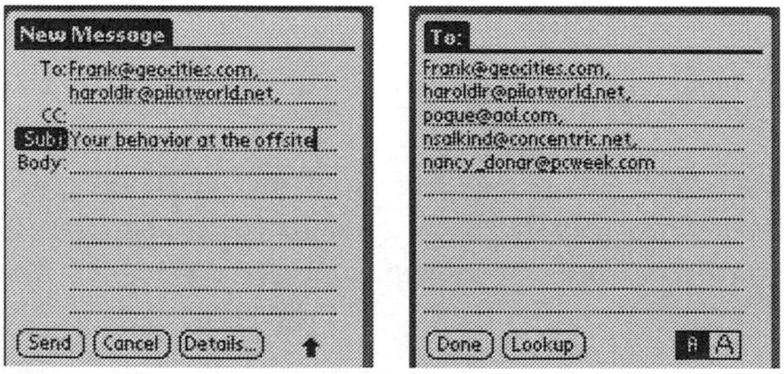

Figure 2-13. Composing a message on a PalmPilot

Put the recipient's address in the To: field, a brief summary in the Subject: field, and the actual message in the Body: field. Conveniently, tapping the To: field allows you to access the **Lookup** button. Tap it, and you may scroll through, and select addresses from, your PalmPilot's Address Book program. Tap the correct individual's name, then tap **Add**. You return to the message in progress, with the correct address inserted in the To: field (see Figure 2-14).

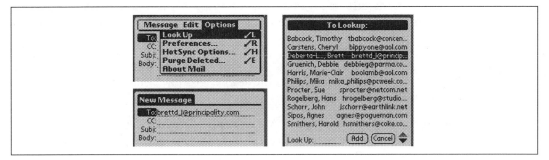

Figure 2-14. Inserting addresses

The same method may be used to fill in the CC: field. Multiple addresses may be separated by commas.

Once you've finished composing the message, tap **Send**. The message is placed in the Outbox folder. The next time you HotSync, all messages in the Outbox are transferred to your PC mailer's Outbox. Before you HotSync, however, any messages in the Outbox may be read, edited, deleted, etc.

This concludes our brief discussion of PalmPilot mail. It should be enough to get you started. Keep in mind, however, that there are a number of other options and features, and you should examine the appropriate documentation to learn more about signatures, filters, and HotSync settings.

Mailing Lists

Up to this point, we've been talking primarily about one-to-one communications: sending a letter to a friend, or, at most, a group of friends. But many other communications models are possible: addressing a large group, or broadcasting something to anyone who's interested. The rest of this chapter will discuss two technologies for one-to-many communications: *mailing lists*, which are email addresses that serve as aliases to many other email addresses, and *Usenet* (the name is a contraction of "User's Networks"), a distributed bulletin board system of servers that adhere to a set of voluntary rules for passing and maintaining newsgroups. First, let's look at mailing lists.

Publicly accessible mailing lists allow people with common interests to receive and share information via electronic mail. While some mailing lists exist simply to disseminate information on a particular topic, most lists allow people to conduct a group discussion about the subject in question.

How do mailing lists work? First, you subscribe to one by sending a fairly simple email message to an address set up for list administration. This may be the address of a program (if the list is automated) or a person (if it's not). Some mailing lists now have their own web sites; those that do frequently allow you to subscribe by filling out a form at the site.

Once you're subscribed, you participate in the discussion by sending messages to a second address, set up to forward mail to the entire group. You'll also receive email messages from other list participants via this address.

While many lists require you to subscribe before sending mail to the group, some will distribute messages from nonsubscribers. Also, some lists require you to have certain professional credentials or affiliations in order to subscribe, although these are in the minority. The sources you use to find out about the mailing list (some of which are covered later in this chapter) will include information about any requirements.

For each mailing list, there is generally an owner (sometimes more than one), who is responsible for managing the list. This owner may also moderate the discussion, as is done in certain Usenet newsgroups. A moderator reviews messages sent to the list and may choose to exclude messages that seem to be outside the list's stated focus. If the number of subscribers to a mailing list gets so large that disseminating the discussion by email becomes impractical, the subscribers may try to launch a Usenet newsgroup instead.

There are a few commonly used list-management programs. The ways you manage your subscription vary slightly, depending on the administration program. However, there are also many similarities among programs. Whether a mailing list is managed by a program or a person, subscribing and participating tends to be very simple. As a matter of fact, with more than 7,500 available mailing lists (and counting), the hardest part may be determining which lists suit your interests.

Finding the Right List

Mailing lists are like Usenet newsgroups in more than one respect: not only do they provide a means for discussions to take place online, the subject matter runs the gamut from the banal to the incredibly esoteric. In fact, pinpointing the list or lists you want could easily be a nightmare. There is a fairly comprehensive list of all the groups, called the PAML (for Publicly Accessible Mailing Lists). It's maintained by Stephanie da Silva and may be found on the Web at *http://www.NeoSoft.com/internet/paml/*.

(You may also want to take a look at ONElist, at *http://www.onelist.com*; at the time of this writing, I found a number of groups there that weren't listed at PAML.) Click on the **Search** link at the bottom of the page to access a search engine for the list. There's also an Index link, which lets you choose between an index organized by mailing list name and an index organized by subject.

Mailing List Basics

There are three important things to know in order to participate in a mailing list:

- How to subscribe

- How to send messages to and receive messages from the list

- How to get off the list

Subscribing to a mailing list

Whatever source you consult to find out about mailing lists—be it the PAML information page, the list's web page, or a forwarded message from a friend—there ought to be some basic information about the list, usually including information on how to subscribe. This information is important. Although there are some fairly common ways to deal with mailing lists of different kinds, there are also a number of exceptions. So, the first guideline is to depend on whatever information the list owners are distributing about their list.

If the basic information you find about a list doesn't include instructions on subscribing, it will include an email address you can write to for information. Generally, the word "help" in the subject or body of the message is sufficient to get you a substantial reply with all of the instructions you'll need.

With just about everything in the world moving onto the Web, it's no surprise that a lot of mailing lists are getting their own web pages. Whether a list has a web page is the kind of information you can get from the PAML list. If a mailing list is on the Web, there's a good chance that you can actually subscribe from there by filling out a form. However, for lists that don't support this kind of interface or for those who prefer to work entirely through email, the current section explains what you'll need to know.

Many of the publicly available mailing lists are managed by programs, which are referred to generically as list servers or *listservs*. The generic name listserv is actually taken from the specific name of one of the more popular programs. Other popular programs include listproc and majordomo.

A listserv program responds to a discrete set of commands that you send to the list's administrative (admin) mailing address. You use these commands to manage your subscription. Though you'll often be sending a single command to a list's admin address, keep in mind that you can send multiple commands in one message when necessary. You'll find examples of such cases in the next section. Because list servers process multiple commands, it's a good idea to turn off your signature (i.e., tell your mailer not to add your signature to the message) before sending a message. Otherwise, the server may try to interpret your signature as commands.

With automated lists, generally the email address where you send your subscription request from is the address to which the messages from the mailing list are sent. It's also the only address from which the list will accept your mail. (Lists run by the major-domo program are an exception—rather than relying on the header of your message to get your email address, majordomo lets you specify an address within your subscription request.)

When a person is running a mailing list (which is becoming very, very rare), the admin address may be just about anything, but in many cases it takes this form:

    listname-request@hostname

For example:

    fun-talk-request@greattime.org

When a listserv program is running the list, the administrative email address takes the form:

    listserv_program@hostname

where *listserv_program* is the admin software (for example, listserv, listproc, major-domo), and *hostname* is the computer from which the list is run.

To subscribe to a mailing list, you need to send the request to the admin email address. For lists that are run by people, you should consult any information you have about the list for subscription guidelines. Since it's hard to tell which lists are run by people and which lists are run by programs, always try to follow guidelines to the letter.

Most lists, including, ironically enough, the Deviants list ("Purpose: The workings of the Great Wok and all things deviant from accepted social norm") still ask you to follow a certain syntax. To subscribe to this list, you'd send a message to the address *majordomo@mousetrap.net* and put the words "subscribe deviants" in the body of the message.

However, you can subscribe to many of the lists run by people just by sending a polite note like this one:

    From: dudley@oreilly.com
    To: jokeaday@jokeaday.com
    Subject: Subscription request for Joke A Day
    Hi. Would you please add my name to the Joke A Day mailing list?
    Thanks!
    Dudley D.

For lists that are run by programs, commands (such as subscription requests) need to follow a syntax specific to the program. As a general rule, you should place commands in the body of the message and leave the subject line blank. Some listserv programs will choke on a subject line.

To subscribe to a mailing list run by listserv or listproc, send a message with the body text:

```
SUBSCRIBE [ listname ]  your_first_name your_last_name
```

Since some servers will run more than one list on a particular host, it's a good idea to name the list in your subscription request. A mailing list called kitchen (which serves as a recipe exchange) is run by listserv. The following message requests a subscription for renowned chef Julia Child:

```
From: julia@world.std.com
To: listserv@lombardia.com
Subject:
SUBSCRIBE kitchen
```

For listproc, the command to subscribe is the same. Here's a request to subscribe to the WWW publishing and design mailing list:

```
From: floydg@erols.com
To: listproc@listserver.com
Subject: subscribe advanced-web
```

For lists run by majordomo, you may optionally include the email address at which you want to receive list mail. The following message requests a subscription to the list service-dogs (discussion of working dogs for disabled people):

```
From: wendyn@aol.com
To: majordomo@acpub.duke.edu
Subject:
subscribe service-dogs wendyn@aol.com
```

When you request a subscription (or actually issue any request to the admin address), you'll probably receive a message requesting authentication of the subscription. Once you follow the instructions in the message (which generally involve a simple reply or a reply containing a specified string), you should receive a confirmation message back. This message generally includes all you'll need to know to manage your subscription and participate in the discussion, often including guidelines for what's appropriate. Save this message for future reference.

Sending and receiving list mail

Every mailing list has an address that serves, in effect, as the list's mailbox. When you send a message to this address, the message is forwarded to the entire list of subscribers. The address generally takes this form:

```
listname@hostname
```

Thus, to send mail to the *Law & Order* discussion list, address it to:

    LAW-AND-ORDER@LISTSERV.AOL.COM

If you think that's easy, receiving mail from the list is even easier. Your mailbox simply fills up with it. Therein lies a potential problem. Some of these lists generate an incredible amount of traffic.

If your mailbox brims with mailing list messages, check the initial message you received from the list to see if the list offers a digest option. Some lists will save up messages and send you a bunch, merged into a single message that is commonly known as a *digest*.* Some digests are compiled weekly and some daily, depending on the nature and amount of information involved.

If your list offers a digest form, you can send a message to the admin address requesting to receive your mail that way. For listserv, mail the following line to the admin address to turn on the digest option:

    SET [*listname*] DIGEST

Turn off the digest option as follows:

    SET [*listname*] NODIGEST

For listproc, you can receive your mail in digest form by sending the message:

    SET [*listname*] MAIL DIGEST

and turn off digest form by sending the message:

    SET [*listname*] MAIL ACK

The majordomo program treats the digest form and the regular form of a mailing list as separate lists. So, in addition to subscribing to the digest form, you also need to unsubscribe to the regular list:

    To: majordomo@*thathost.com*
    Subject:
    subscribe *myfavelist*-digest
    unsubscribe *myfavelist*

Getting off a mailing list

If you decide you no longer want to be included on a mailing list, it's simple to get your email address off the list. For person-run lists, check the documentation on the list. Some may require a message with the body "unsubscribe." But many will happily remove your name if you simply write, "Please take me off the list. Thanks a lot."

---

* Depending on your mailer, these messages will appear as a single, lengthy message, or as a number of attachments that you may read independently.

For automated lists, the command to keep in mind is also unsubscribe. For listserv and listproc, send a message to the list's admin address, and put the following in the body of the message:

```
unsubscribe [ listname ]
```

The same line should work for *majordomo*, unless you subscribed under a different email address. In that case, you'll need to tell the program that address:

```
unsubscribe [ listname ] [ email_address ]
```

listserv alternately accepts the following:

```
signoff [ listname ]
```

Some automated list processors will only accept commands from an email address that has subscribed to the list. Therefore, if you are changing email accounts, unsubscribe from your old account before it is deactivated. Then subscribe from your new account.

Every time you make a change to your mailing list subscription, you should receive an acknowledgment by email. Thus, when you unsubscribe, you should get a message confirming that you're off the list.

Usenet

Mailing lists, as we just described, let you communicate with a closed group of people: those who subscribe to the list. Usenet, however, lets you communicate with an open group. Subscribing to a Usenet group is much simpler than subscribing to a mailing list; if you read Usenet articles at a WWW Usenet archive site, you don't have to subscribe at all. Usenet is a little more anonymous than a mailing list. Messages are posted and may or may not be noticed, rather than being delivered to a user's mailbox, where they must be dealt with in some manner—even if it's only the user glancing at the content while pressing the Delete key.

Usenet is not a network in the sense that the Internet is. It's actually a part of the traffic that occurs over the Internet. Usenet is like a worldwide conversation, or more accurately, thousands of conversations that take place among online users, in the context of groups of users interested in the same subject. There are literally thousands of these newsgroups accessible via the Internet.

You participate in a newsgroup by sending (or "posting") messages (or "articles"), and by reading other people's posts. These posts happen sequentially—as on an electronic bulletin board or an AOL message board—not all at once, as in a real conversation.

When a series of posts ensue from an initial one, the particular sequence is known as a message *thread*. There are newsgroups for people interested in just about anything, including various types of hardware and software, branches of science, sports, the arts, travel, health, or whatever. Each newsgroup is named to identify the subject area of its discussion, using a hierarchical naming scheme.

Getting Oriented

Most news servers limit the size of the "newsfeed" they receive (that is, they make only certain groups available or expire articles quickly). The sheer (and ever-growing) number of groups necessitates this. However, highly trafficked groups—those with a lot of posts—are generally available. And, while you used to be limited to the newsgroups your ISP provided, virtually every group may now be found and read on the World Wide Web, via Deja.com (*http://www.deja.com*) or Talkway (*http://www.talkway.com*).

Some newsgroups have one or more moderators who judge whether posts are appropriate to the group. Moderators can exclude postings at their discretion. They may also maintain one or more files of frequently asked questions, though these so-called *FAQs* (pronounced "F-A-Qs" or "fax") may also be maintained by other interested group participants. In unmoderated newsgroups, anything goes—at least in theory. However, as in any social context, if you act rudely or inappropriately, you may be called on it.

Of course, you don't have to be out of line to get into a Usenet conflict. Misunderstandings and simple disagreements can—and do—flare up all the time.

Sometimes, newsgroups aren't what they seem—or they are what they seem, but not what they were intended to be. Occasionally, a group has been hijacked, either by well-meaning people who misunderstand what the group is about, and happen to outnumber the people who started it, or by hostile newcomers. Don't be surprised, then, if a group you join has a different tenor than you expected: you may, for example, come across a good deal of feminist bashing at *soc.feminism*.

In fact, the difficulties you might experience while communicating via email—the inexpressiveness of words without vocal or facial expression—may be ten times more severe with news. Why? Well, partly because it's a free-for-all. Anyone can respond to anyone else. The sheer number of participants who don't know each other from a hole in the wall (at least initially) can exacerbate the problem.

A disagreement that escalates into the Usenet equivalent of a brawl is generally called a *flame war*. The nasty messages that compose it are called *flames*. When you send one, you're flaming the recipient. To complicate matters further, the facelessness of news seems to breed tactlessness and rudeness, even from people who may be quite agreeable in person.

Using the netiquette described earlier in the chapter should minimize difficulties you may have. For the most part, netiquette isn't much more than common courtesy. But, in addition to being polite in your communications, avoid computer-related rudeness, such as including long signature files or posting binary files to groups other than *alt. binary* and its subgroups.

It's appropriate to read a group for a while to understand the tenor and scope of the conversations before you contribute—some groups welcome novices, and other groups can be downright hostile. You should always read the group's FAQ before posting. Most groups post the FAQ from time to time, or you can find the FAQ file at the web site All the FAQs, at *http://www.arc.nasa.gov/enhanced/faq/index.html*.

Newsgroup Naming Scheme

Usenet uses a hierarchical naming scheme, not unlike that used for Internet domain names. Newsgroups have a name composed of at least two parts, divided by periods (or "dots"); the first part generally classifies the group's interest by type or geographic location. For example, groups beginning with the syllable *rec* deal with subjects that are generally considered recreational; groups beginning with *comp* discuss computer-related topics; the *alt* hierarchy encompasses a wide range of "alternative" news-groups. There are also prefixes to distinguish groups geared toward a particular city, region, or country. For example, *boulder* introduces groups focusing on the Colorado city, *ba* refers to the San Francisco Bay area, *ne* is New England, and *de* refers to groups originating in Germany. Some institutions even have their own groups: *ucsc* refers to the University of California, Santa Cruz, and *ora* refers to O'Reilly & Associates, the publisher of this book. While regional groups are usually available outside the region, organizational groups aren't usually propogated outside the intended organization.

Table 2-1 gives descriptions of some of the most common top-level newsgroup hierarchies and the types of groups you're likely to find in them.

Table 2-1. Top-Level Newsgroup Names

Group	Type	Description
biz	Business-related topics	This part of the Usenet tree includes groups interested in business in general, company-specific groups, and groups relating to employment. Groups that begin with *biz* allow advertising within the group, while the rest of Usenet frowns on it.
comp	Computer- and engineering-related topics	There are hundreds of groups under the *comp* hierarchy. Among the subhierarchies are *ai* (artificial intelligence), *data-bases*, *infosystems*, *lang* (programming languages), *mail* (email applications), *os* (operating systems), *protocols*, *society* (social repercussions of computers), *sys* (hundreds of groups covering most computer systems), and so on.
misc	Miscellaneous groups	This part of the hierarchy is an umbrella for whatever groups don't really fit elsewhere. While some of these groups cover topics that are unique newsgroup (for example, *misc.kids*), some merely offer a different slant on subjects dealt with in other newsgroups, or even overlap with them. For example, while the *comp* branch of news includes *comp.forsale.computers*, *misc* offers *misc.forsale.computers*.

Table 2-1. Top-Level Newsgroup Names (continued)

Group	Type	Description
news	Topics relating to Usenet and the newsgroups	While many of these groups simply distribute facts and statistics about news, this is the home of the important group *news. newusers.questions*, which helps new Usenet participants get oriented. The group *news.software* discusses news-reading programs.
rec	Recreational interests and hobbies	Among the larger subhierarchies are *rec.sport*, *rec.music*, and *rec.arts*. Beyond these parts of the tree are groups dealing with a wide variety of hobbies and interests, such as bicycles, woodworking, travel, boats, pets, bird watching, and even beer.
sci	Topics relating science	Groups in the *sci* branch range from weird science to science in education to the most arcane technical pursuits.
soc	Topics relating society, social life, and so on	This is a fairly diverse hierarchy, encompassing groups focused on social issues and society, cultures of the world, and general socializing. The huge *soc.culture* subhierarchy has 111 branches and counting.
talk	Chat-type groups	A free exchange of ideas is the general spirit of the *talk* hierarchy. Flames abound here. *talk.politics* has a number of branches.
alt	Alternative newsgroups	Alternative groups are actually considered to exist outside the realm of Usenet proper. While you must follow a strict set of guidelines to create a newsgroup under the Usenet umbrella, group creation under the *alt* hierarchy is a free-for-all. Thus, there are many oddball groups, as well as many specious or just plain stupid ones. There are also plenty of legitimate groups who want a different venue or who don't have the readership to merit a full-fledged Usenet group.

The first part of each newsgroup name lets you quickly classify it under a general subject area. Additional name components more clearly define the newsgroup. In some cases, the second name component represents a subcategory of the first component. For example, under *rec* is a category called *pets,* as shown in Figure 2-15. Then, under *pets*, are five groups concerned with various types of pets. *rec.pets.ferrets* is a group for people interested in having a ferret as a pet, while *rec.pets.herp* provides a forum for those who like to snuggle up with reptiles and amphibians. Both groups fall under the top-level category *rec* and the second-level category *pets*.

Advocacy groups deserve a special mention. Advocacy groups are really designed to separate arguments from technical discussions and questions. For example, *comp.os. linux.advocacy* would discuss questions like "Is Linux better than Windows NT?" while *comp.os.linux* would discuss questions like "I changed something in the path file, and now my mailer won't work. How do I fix this?"

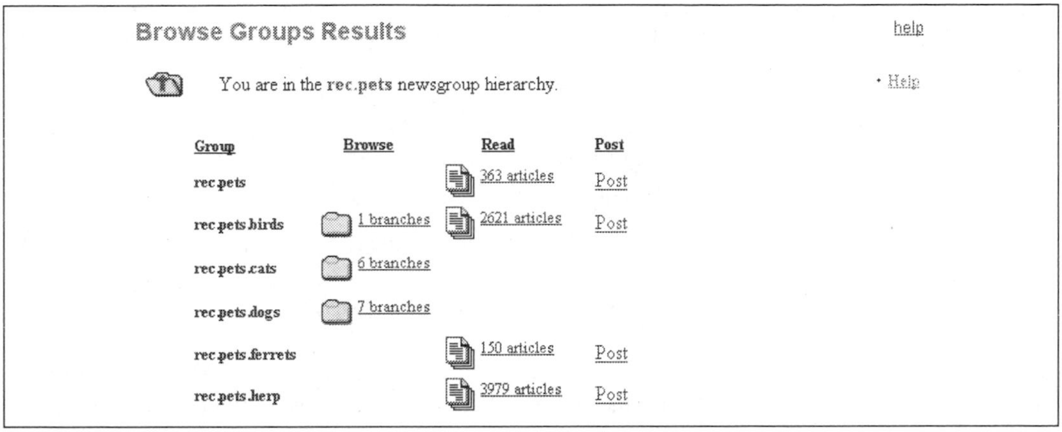

Figure 2-15. The rec.pets hierarchy

Along similar lines, there are "discuss" groups that parallel some of the binary groups. The binary groups are supposed to be kept clear for binaries (that is, software, or for that matter, dirty pictures); the discuss groups are for arguments about the same ("Are the software or the dirty pictures any good?").

Just the FAQs

Many newsgroups maintain a list of frequently asked questions in a file called a FAQ. Some groups will even have multiple FAQs, each with a different focus. For example, the newsgroup dealing with reptile and amphibian pets has FAQs about Uromastyx, iguanas, herp net resources, and more.

Some FAQs present helpful information concisely, while others are long and full of arcane detail. You should always at least scan the FAQ before posting to a group, however, as it can help you in a few different ways. First, it can give you some insight into the atmosphere within the group, the level of discussion, and so on. Second, it can stop you from posting a question that's been asked, well, frequently; sometimes, hundreds of times before. If you have a question, it can only work in your favor to check the FAQ before posting. Some groups take the reposting of a commonly asked question lightly, and participants answer it happily no matter how often it crops up. In some groups, however, participants may bark, "Read the FAQ!"

FAQs are usually posted to the newsgroup periodically, but you don't have to wait. Use one of the following URLs to access the FAQ archives: *http://www.lib.ox.ac.uk/search/search_faqs.html* or *http://www.faqs.org/faqs/*.

Popular Newsreaders

Even if you've never read a single news post, you almost undoubtedly have a newsreader on your PC. As we mentioned earlier, Windows 95/98 and Windows NT come with Outlook Express pre-installed, and Netscape Communicator's Messenger component includes a newsreader. Both are free, and either one is perfectly adequate for the average user.

If you want a more serious newsreader, with more features, Gravity from Microplanet, Inc., is a popular choice. The program supports advanced filtering and display properties. A 30-day free trial is available for download from *http://www.microplanet.com.*

Throughout this chapter, however, we'll continue to discuss Outlook and Messenger.

Subscribing to Newsgroups via a Newsreader

Choosing **Subscribe** from Messenger's **File** menu or (more esoterically) **Newsgroups** from Outlook Express' **Tools** menu, opens a dialog box in which you can subscribe and unsubscribe to Usenet newsgroups. The basic concept for each dialog box is the same: highlight the name of the group to which you want to subscribe, and click the **Subscribe** button (see Figure 2-16). If you don't want to scroll through an entire hierarchy of newsgroups, enter your search string in the text box, use **Messenger's Search** tab, or search for the newsgroup via Deja.com or another search engine.

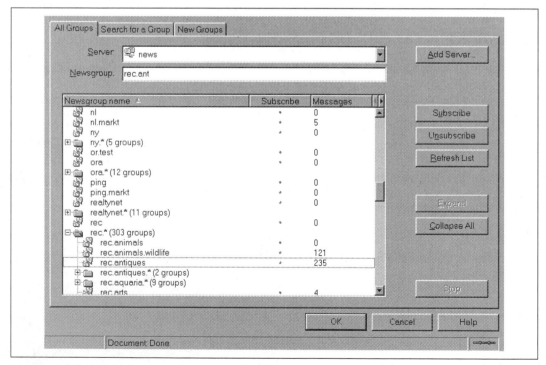

Figure 2-16. Subscribing to newsgroups in Messenger

There are a few ways to unsubscribe from a group. The simplest way is to delete the group name from the list of folders/groups in the lefthand pane. If you have the Subscription dialog box open, you can unsubscribe from a group by clicking the **Unsubscribe** button.

Whatever you do in the Subscribe/Unsubscribe dialog box, you'll have to click the **OK** button to save your changes.

Reading Usenet Newsgroups

Outlook Express and Netscape Messenger work in a similar way when it comes to reading news. Consequently, we'll describe generic newsreading in the following section.

To start reading news, open your newsreading application, and click on the newsgroup you wish to read in the leftmost pane. In Figure 2-17, we're reading *comp.mail. eudora.ms-windows*.

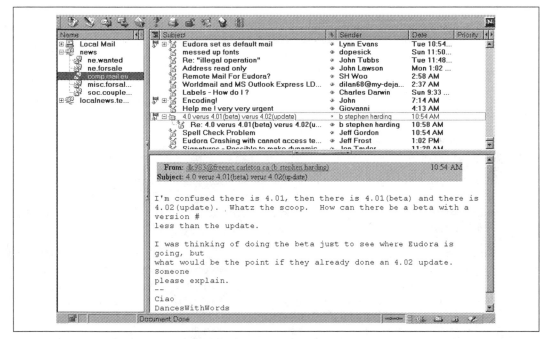

Figure 2-17. Reading news via Messenger

Once you've selected the newsgroup, the application contacts the server and downloads the number of headers specified in the Preferences section. You'll want to keep this number fairly low (say, 250), depending on the frequency of the group; otherwise, you'll frequently download outdated headers. The application then displays the first unread message. Click on it, and the contents are displayed in the bottom pane, as in Figure 2-17.

The Telltale (Usenet) Heart

—by Valerie Quercia

Usenet can be a scary virtual place. Every time you get into a new newsgroup, you have to assess the territory. What's appropriate for this discussion? What are the people like? If I ask such-and-such, how will people react? Will I get flamed?

Whether you're walking for the first time into a new crowd, a new neighborhood, or a new newsgroup, it's smart to scope things out before you start shooting your mouth off. Different newsgroups have climates almost as diverse as the different neighborhoods of New York City. Some are almost as dangerous to the sensitive of heart.

Here's a lousy case scenario. You jump into a new newsgroup. You quickly decide to post a question or comment. A number of other participants view your remarks as, um, well, stupid. They post flames telling you what a jerk you are. You apologize profusely. But it's too late. You slink away into Usenet oblivion, to live a lonely, miserable existence, with only flesh-and-blood friends who show up in person and no electronic friends at all. Boo hoo. You also can't get the information you asked about in the first place.

If you're new to Usenet or to a particular group, here are some steps to take that should help you get your feet wet (rather than drown in the process):

1. Read a group for a while before posting anything. Get to know the scope and tenor of the discussion, so you can gauge what's appropriate.

2. If you're not sure what's appropriate, post your questions to the group *news. newusers.answers.* This is a calm, understanding, and supportive environment where you can basically ask any dumb question you have and get a reasonable answer. This group is intended primarily for Usenet newbies.

3. Find out if the group you're interested in has an FAQ (Frequently Asked Questions) list. The FAQ is intended to answer the most common queries posted to the group. Reading the FAQ up front will save you from posting one of these questions and being told to go and read the FAQ. (Not that that's such a terrible thing.)

4. Once you start participating, use reasonable netiquette. Most of that is no more than common sense, but read the section called "Composing Messages: A Netiquette Primer" earlier in this chapter.

Threads

The concept of a thread is important when reading newsgroups. A *thread* is a group of messages on the same topic. You may set your newsreader to view threaded discussions. Figure 2-18 shows a threaded discussion of recipes for soup, specifically tomato bisque.

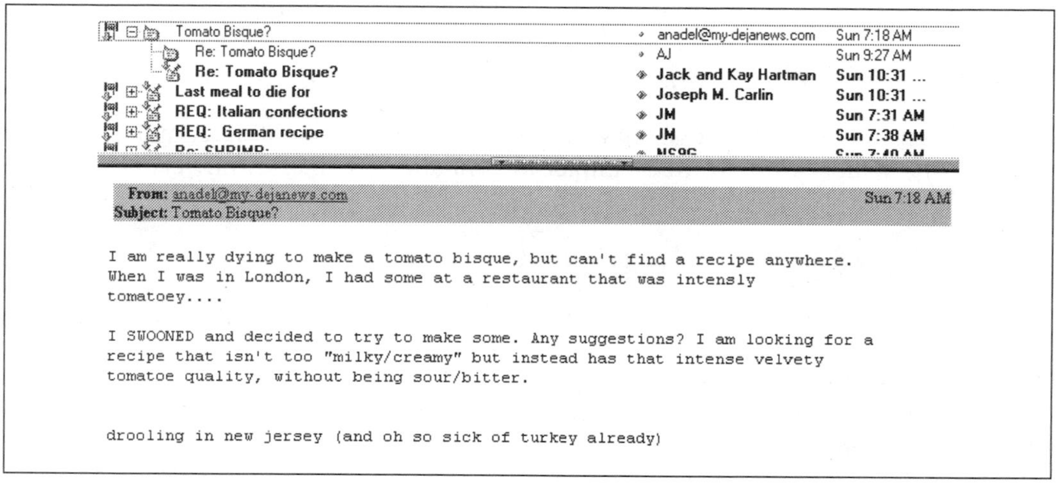

Tomato Bisque?	anadel@my-dejanews.com	Sun 7:18 AM
Re: Tomato Bisque?	AJ	Sun 9:27 AM
Re: Tomato Bisque?	Jack and Kay Hartman	Sun 10:31 ...
Last meal to die for	Joseph M. Carlin	Sun 10:31 ...
REQ: Italian confections	JM	Sun 7:31 AM
REQ: German recipe	JM	Sun 7:38 AM
Re: SHRIMP	NSQG	Sun 7:40 AM

From: anadel@my-dejanews.com   Sun 7:18 AM
Subject: Tomato Bisque?

```
I am really dying to make a tomato bisque, but can't find a recipe anywhere.
When I was in London, I had some at a restaurant that was intensly
tomatoey....

I SWOONED and decided to try to make some. Any suggestions? I am looking for a
recipe that isn't too "milky/creamy" but instead has that intense velvety
tomatoe quality, without being sour/bitter.


drooling in new jersey (and oh so sick of turkey already)
```

Figure 2-18. A threaded discussion of tomato bisque

As you can see, Messenger displays a threaded discussion by listing the first message in the thread, with a plus sign to the left of the message subject. Clicking on the plus sign displays the message tree of replies on the same thread. This can be a more efficient way to read newsgroups, as you don't need to read or scroll through multiple subject headers on the same ho-hum topic.

Handling Usenet messages

Once you've finished reading mail, you have a few options. You can reply to individual messages or post to the newsgroup by clicking the **Post** button, which spawns the Composition window we described in the section "An Email Primer." You may also, as with mail, move the message to a folder, save the message to a file, or forward the message to someone else.

Messages may also be *marked* and threads *ignored* or *watched*. What does this mean? Once you've clicked on a message to view it, your newsreader considers it read and indicates as such by de-bolding it. You may change the marking of messages in a number of different ways:

- Mark all messages as read.

- Mark messages as read up to a certain date.

- Mark a message you've read as unread.

- Mark an entire thread as read.

To do any of these, select the messages you wish to act upon, and then select the appropriate option from your newsreader's **View** menu. Watching and ignoring threads is largely a matter of symbolism: icons appear next to a thread indicating how you feel about it, but you may manipulate the message as usual.

News Configuration Tips

Outlook Express and Messenger have not yet attained the stunning complexity of the mainstream mailers, and are thus simpler to configure. There are, however, a few tips you may want to keep in mind.

Filters and kill files

The most important news configuration tool is the *filter*. As with email, you use news filters to specify certain actions. When it comes to news, however, the most common action is to block postings from particular individuals. As a result, you'll sometimes see these filters referred to as *kill files*, as they permanently remove an individual from your Usenet world.

To turn on a filter, open **Edit → Message Filters...** in Messenger, or **Tools → Newsgroup Filters** in Outlook Express. Set the options as desired. You can filter messages by sender or subject.

General tips

A few more things to think about:

- Use your kill file liberally. You'll find plenty of spam, porn solicitations, and ridiculous flame wars on Usenet.

- Usenet is a rowdy place, and some groups have a gigantic signal-to-noise ratio. Even with a gigantic kill file, you may have to wade through too much junk to make the group worth your while. Don't read it.

- If you're looking for specific answers, or feel overwhelmed with posts, use the tools your newsreader provides. Messenger allows you to mark specific threads to watch (select **Watch Thread** from the **Message** menu), and Outlook Express supports a number of options under the **View → Current View** menu, including the ability to view replies only to your own posts.

- If your ISP's news server doesn't carry groups that interest you, search for them on Deja.com, Talkway, or RemarQ, via a web browser (see the next section).

- If you find a group you like, but would prefer to read it in a newsreader, take a look at Yahoo!'s list of publicly accessible news servers (*http://dir.yahoo.com/*

Computers_and_Internet/Internet/Usenet/Public_Access_Usenet_Sites/). If you're browsing the list with Netscape, adding a server is as simple as clicking a link to it; with Outlook Express, use the **Tools** → **Accounts** → **Add wizard** to add the server.

- Spam abounds on Usenet, and spammers use Usenet postings to garner email addresses for mass postings. Thus, you may want to scramble your return address, or use an additional account just for posting. See Chapter 5 to learn how.

- By the same token, turn off your signature file (or use an alternate; see "Signature Files" earlier in this chapter) before posting, and don't reveal any personal information.

- Deja.com (and other Usenet-focused web sites) archive Usenet postings, so bear in mind that what you post will be accessible to the general public for years to come. To avoid near immortality (this trick may not work for other archives), place the following line at the top of your post, before any other text:

```
x-no-archive: yes
```

Web-Based Newsreading

There are a number of Usenet archive sites on the World Wide Web. These sites, which include Deja.com (*http://www.deja.com*), Talkway (*http://talkway.com*) and RemarQ (*http://www.remarq.com*), are remarkable resources for anyone interested in Usenet. These sites are the only places to find *all* the newsgroups on Usenet, archives of posts, and comprehensive, powerful search engines.

These sites are great for finding newsgroups or searching for information, but they can also be used to read news. Why might you want to read news on the Web? Reading groups via a standard newsreader is more efficient: it's easier to download messages, view the headers, and save messages—it's just plain easier all around. But if your server doesn't carry certain groups, and you don't want to connect to a public domain server, then Deja.com is the way to go. Now, let's take a look at searching and reading newsgroups at Deja.com.

Subscribing to groups

Perhaps you've heard about a group that your server doesn't support. In this case, use the **Browse Groups** link to find it. Either enter the group's name in the dialog box, or click on the links to **Popular Top Level Groups** to locate it. If you're not sure about what groups cover a certain topic, however, use the **Interest Finder** link. This time, you'll enter the topic you're looking for—say, rutabagas—and click the **Find Forums** link, as shown in Figure 2-19.

Not exactly the results we were expecting. Clicking on the links to the group doesn't help much, since the message containing the term "rutabaga" could have appeared some time ago. (If you *really* want to find information about rutabagas, use the Power Search feature. We'll discuss this further in Chapter 12.)

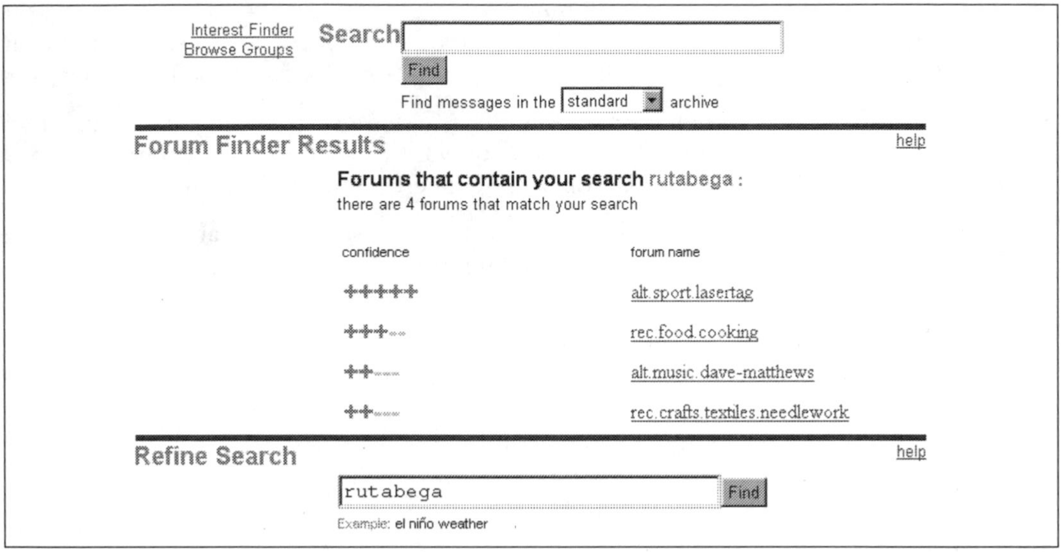

Figure 2-19. Searching Usenet with Deja.com by subject

For now, let's say we go out on a limb and take a look at *rec.food.cooking* (see Figure 2-20). The results are initially organized by date; if we click the **Subject** link, at the top of the screen, they're now sorted by subject.

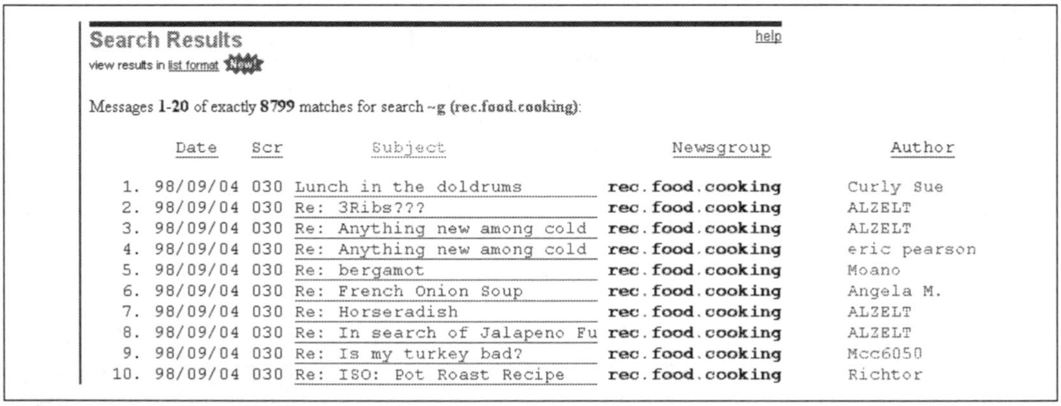

Figure 2-20. Organizing newsgroup results

Unfortunately, even in list format, Deja.com doesn't thread the results for us in this view—and there still isn't anything about rutabagas. If we were interested in French Onion Soup, however, we could click on the sixth message shown in the example, with the subject "Re: French Onion Soup."

It's only from the resulting screen that we can perform some vital functions, including subscribing to the group, viewing an author's profile, posting a message (or replying to this one), or viewing the thread of messages together. To perform any of these functions, simply click the links.

Reading news

Now that we've subscribed to some newsgroups, how do we read them in the future?

First, connect to the Deja home page. Now, click the link to My Deja. The resulting screen, in Figure 2-21, shows the groups you currently subscribe to.

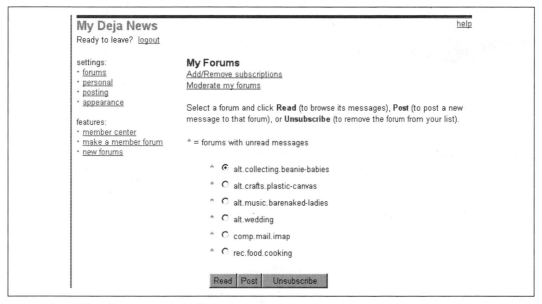

Figure 2-21. Reading groups via Deja.com

As you can see, you can also adjust various options from this page. If you'd like to read news postings, click the **Read** button, and prepare to engage in a frank exchange of opinions and ideas.

CHAPTER THREE

CONQUERING EMAIL

When I first heard about email, a friend described it to me as "free long distance." Obviously, that's not quite accurate. Users type instead of speak, and while transmission of messages is quick, it's not instantaneous. Email was more complicated when I first learned about it than it is today. Nonetheless, the tantalizing promise of a means of fast, essentially free communication across vast distances proved true. Soon, it seemed that everyone I knew had an email account.

A few months later, I spoke with my uncle, who was then an executive at Apple, during Thanksgiving dinner. As I passed the cranberries, he mentioned receiving email from an old friend.

"Don't you love email?" I asked. "It's so efficient."

He grimaced. "I get so many messages that I have my secretary print them out. Then I take them home and read them after work."

These stories cover the range of the electronic mail experience: it's a cheap, convenient, paperless medium that is also easy to abuse. As email becomes more and more of a prerequisite for doing business and keeping in touch, the question becomes, how do you keep it organized, and under control?

Conquering Common Email Problems

You know how to use email. You've mastered composing, sending, and replying; you've even learned how to use Reply to sender instead of Reply to all and stopped sending your payroll information to the entire office. Nonetheless, email can overwhelm even the seasoned technical professional. If you don't want to let email rule your work day, you may decide to respond only to crucial messages. Unfortunately, you could miss the "get here or you're fired" message from your boss if you don't notice it among the glut of solicitations, mailing lists, jokes, and treatises that deluge your mailbox.

Common problems contributing to email deluge include spam, or junk email; mailing lists that flood your mailbox; and just the large volume of regular mail you receive each day. Some people have been so traumatized by this kind of inundation that they've cancelled their email accounts entirely. This isn't the answer, and this chapter will tell you how to avoid spam, organize the mailing lists, and prioritize the rest of your mail.

More advanced users may encounter other problems: managing multiple accounts, sending and decoding readable file attachments, reading and saving mail while traveling (or using more than one machine), and configuring a mailer to support features that may not be obvious from the user interface. Easy solutions and configuration techniques are just a few pages away.

Using Filters

One of the most overlooked email tools is already built in to most mailers: the filter. Most popular email packages support filters, and most work in a similar manner. These include Netscape, Eudora, Microsoft Outlook, and others. Filters are a good way of making email clutter more organized by automatically moving some messages into folders and automatically deleting others.

How Can Filters Help?

Filters allow you to specify automatic actions the mailer must take when it receives email that meets certain criteria. Here are some of the ways you can use filters to make you more efficient:

- Move repetitive or annoying messages directly into your Trash folder, so that you never have to read them.

- Automatically sort messages from mailing lists into designated folders, instead of leaving them scattered about your inbox.

- Have your mailer affix a certain label or play a certain sound for an incoming message, depending on the sender. A dog barking could mean another message from your dog lovers' mailing list, while an exclamatory "Oh my god!" could indicate a message from the company president. This way, you won't necessarily stop whatever other work you're doing to read the update on your officemate's kittens.

Turning filters on

You'll generally find filter settings under your mailer's **Edit**, **Tools**, or **Special** menus, or in the Preferences section. There, you can create a new filter by setting certain conditions. If an incoming or outgoing message meets those conditions, the mailer takes the actions you specify. We can use Netscape's filters as an example.

Let's say you work for a firm that sends out recycling reminders to all employees once a week. Let's also say that you're an evil-hearted person who finds these messages tedious. You decide to create a filter that automatically deletes them.

First, select **Mail Filters**... from the **Edit** menu. Click the **New** button in the resulting Mail Filters dialog box. This spawns the Filter Rules dialog box, pictured in Figure 3-1.

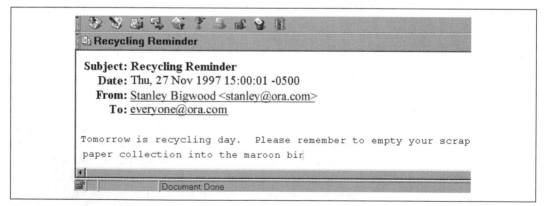

Figure 3-1. Netscape's Filter Rules dialog box

Name the filter "Recycling." Next, decide on the selection criteria. Think about what makes recycling messages different from all other messages. You don't want to delete every message with the word "recycle" in the subject line, since you would then lose messages like "Warning: Recycle Bin virus" or "Your job is about to be recycled." Make it too specific, though, and your filter won't filt. Take a good look at the recycling message you receive each week, as shown in Figure 3-2.

Subject: Recycling Reminder
Date: Thu, 27 Nov 1997 15:00:01 -0500
From: Stanley Bigwood <stanley@ora.com>
To: everyone@ora.com

```
Tomorrow is recycling day.  Please remember to empty your scrap
paper collection into the maroon bin
```

Figure 3-2. A sample recycling reminder

Based on this message, and the fact that you receive an identical message each week, we can set the options detailed in Figure 3-3. Notice that we've set the subject line to "is" rather than "contains."

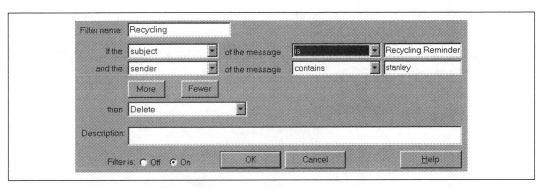

Figure 3-3. A filter to remove recycling messages

As we discussed, a rule specifying the deletion of all messages in which the subject line *contains* the word "recycling" would be too general. Try a few test messages to make sure the filter works the way you'd like. If your mailer logs filter actions, you may want to take a look at the log files, to see precisely what's happening. Look for such files in the same directory as your email client. Netscape calls this file *mailfilt*, and specifies it as a log file, as displayed in Figure 3-4.

```
mailbox:/C|/Program Files/Netscape/Users/kiersten/mail/Spam I Am?id=
Applied filter "Smut" to message from 80511921@aol.com - HOT BABES GO
LIVE! HOT STUDS TOO! ADULTS ONLY! at 11/21/97 22:05
Action = Move to folder /C|/Program
Files/Netscape/Users/kiersten/mail/Spam I Am

mailbox:/C|/Program
Files/Netscape/Users/kiersten/mail/Trash?id=199711241412.JAA27323@admin.co
n2.com
Applied filter "Scarlett" to message from Alicia & Derek Chmielarski
<adchmiel@SENTEX.NET> - Re: [SHIHTZU-L] Gina, Judy, Alicia, Alice, David,
Scarlett, all at 11/25/97 1:20
Action = Move to folder /C|/Program
Files/Netscape/Users/kiersten/mail/Trash

mailbox:/C|/Program
Files/Netscape/Users/kiersten/mail/Trash?id=01bcf96a$32ea5980$264ddece@ari
es-tower
Applied filter "Recycling" to message from Stanley Bigwood <stanley@ora.com>-
Recycling Reminder at 11/27/97 15:00
Action = Delete
```

Figure 3-4. Netscape's mail filter log

Similarly, you may want to filter a mailing list into its own folder. To do so, simply set the sender criteria to the name of the mailing list sender. Be sure you know how your mailer indicates new mail, so that you'll know when messages arrive. If the list is particularly active—I've been on some *digests* that send 10 to 15 messages per day—make sure you delete the folder's content occasionally, to keep your mailer running smoothly.

It's also good to set up a few basic spam filters, to reduce random smut. Figure 3-5 illustrates one possible smut filter.

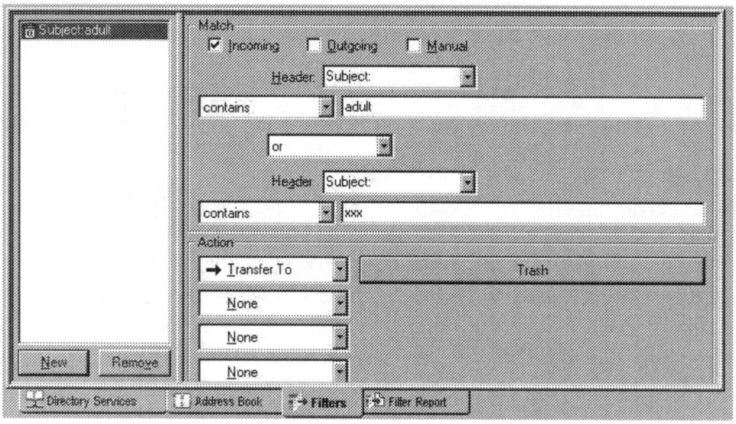

Figure 3-5. A smut filter

Another good idea is to assign a higher priority to messages that meet certain criteria. This way, important messages stand out in your inbox (Figure 3-6).

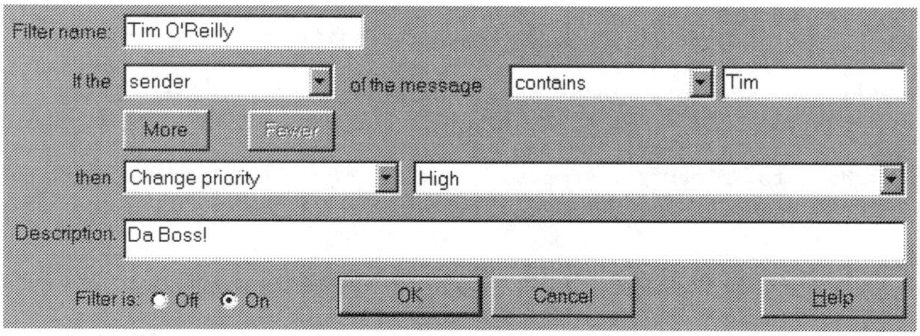

Figure 3-6. A boss filter

Unfortunately, Netscape doesn't support audio alerts. If you'd like your mailer to play a special alert noise, think about using Eudora, or take a look at the email plug-ins described later in the chapter.

Filter order

Since your mail program filters messages in the sequence you specify, you need to be careful of the order of your filters. Take a look at the mail filter window in Figure 3-7.

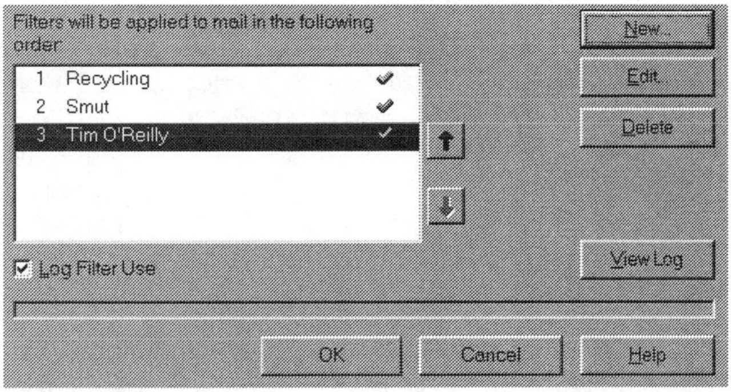

Figure 3-7. Netscape's mail filter window

Hypothetically, a message could arrive from Tim O'Reilly with the subject line "Stamp out live adult sites." Under the current configuration, Netscape would move that message to the Spam directory. While that directory would appear in bold because it contained new messages, the odds are that you would never check the message. To avoid such mishaps, use the arrow keys to move the most important filter up to the top. That way, future messages from Tim O'Reilly would immediately be given highest priority and wouldn't be put through the other filters.

Mailer Configuration

Today's mailers support a mind-boggling array of options. Sometimes, even the manuals don't list every setting or describe how to change them. Even if you know how to set the Advanced options under your mailer's **Preferences** or toolbar menu, there may be more settings for you to customize. Some applications let you manipulate the mailer's initialization file (commonly referred to by its file extension, *.ini*), change the Reply-to indicator, alter annoying settings, or customize reply lines. Additionally, separate helper applications, called *plug-ins* (just as they are for browsers), can customize or extend your mailer's capabilities.

Eudora Configuration Tips

Eudora may be the mailer that lets you get the most down and dirty with the configuration options, thanks to its easy-to-modify initialization file. If you're looking for even more tweaks, take a look on the Web or at *comp.mail.eudora*; Eudora's dedicated group of fans are always ready to provide customization insight or at least some new mail alert sounds.

.ini files

It's actually easy to muck around with initialization files. Many Windows 95 programs use these files—which are merely text files with a special file extension—to maintain user settings. Changing the settings is as easy as opening the file with a text editor, changing a line of text, and saving the file. Initialization files are usually found in the same directory as the application; the icon appears as a notepad with a yellow gear on the front.

First, be sure to save a backup copy of your *.ini* file before making any changes!

If Eudora is open, close it. Open the *.ini* file by double-clicking on it. Notepad opens the file.* Scroll down through the text until you reach the [Settings] section, as in Figure 3-8.

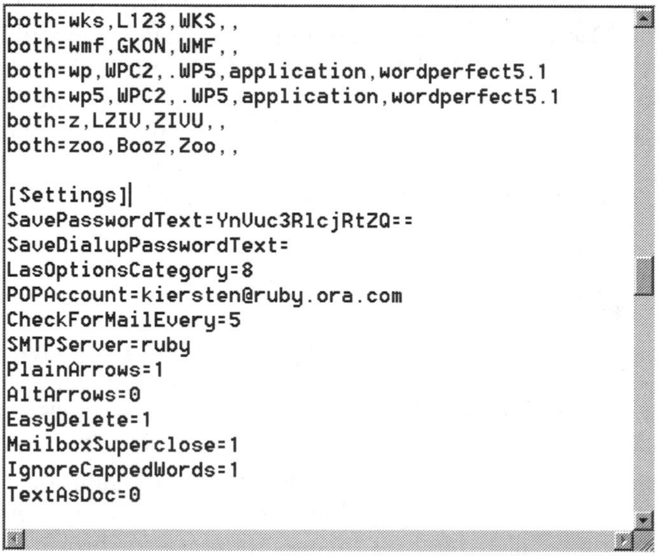

```
both=wks,L123,WKS,,
both=wmf,GKON,WMF,,
both=wp,WPC2,.WP5,application,wordperfect5.1
both=wp5,WPC2,.WP5,application,wordperfect5.1
both=z,LZIV,ZIVU,,
both=zoo,Booz,Zoo,,

[Settings]
SavePasswordText=YnVuc3R1cjRtZQ==
SaveDialupPasswordText=
LasOptionsCategory=8
POPAccount=kiersten@ruby.ora.com
CheckForMailEvery=5
SMTPServer=ruby
PlainArrows=1
AltArrows=0
EasyDelete=1
MailboxSuperclose=1
IgnoreCappedWords=1
TextAsDoc=0
```

Figure 3-8. Eudora.ini settings section

Now, you can simply add a few lines to implement your changes.

To remove the splash screen that appears when you open Eudora, add the following line to the [Settings] section:

```
NoSplashScreen=1
```

If the line already exists with a value of 0, change it to 1.

---

* Be sure to use Notepad or WordPad to open initialization files. Microsoft Word will try to attach file extensions that will cause the file to cease working.

To change the Reply Attribution line, which appears before quoted text in replies, add the following line:

    ReplyAttribution=*your message*

You can use the variable %1 to insert the time and date of the original message, and %2 to insert the sender's name. For example, the line:

    ReplyAttribution=***At %1, %2 had the gall to write:***

would cause your reply messages to appear as in Figure 3-9.

```
***At 02:01 PM 12/9/97 -0500, Kiersten Conner had the gall to write:***

|You big weenie!
|
```

Figure 3-9. A ReplyAttribution example

Similarly, adding the line:

    ReplyAllAttribution=*your message*

changes the Reply-to-All attribution line.

To change the character that appears before quoted text in replies (an exclamation point or vertical line might be a good choice), add the following line:

    ReplyPrefix=*your prefix*

To change the character that appears before quoted text in forwarded messages, add the following line:

    QuotePrefix=*your prefix*

When you're done, save the file. Be sure to check that your changes worked before sending any mail. Sending mail to yourself, and then replying to it, is one good testing technique.

Changing the layout

Eudora opens in a three-pane layout. If you don't like the preview pane, which appears below the listing in the inbox, open **Tools** → **Options** → **Viewing Mail**, and clear the checkbox next to "Show message preview pane."

If you like the preview pane in general, but get tired of it when you're viewing a particular message, press F7 to make it disappear automatically.

Sending mail to multiple addressees in the address book

To send mail to multiple addresses in the address book, hold down the control key while selecting names, then click the **To** button.

Automatic Netscape/Eudora coordination

To have Netscape launch Eudora to send mail messages, select the checkbox next to "Intercept Netscape mailto: URLs" in the Miscellaneous section of the Options dialog box.

Faking IMAP

If you check mail from multiple machines, don't mind a full inbox, and don't want to use IMAP, try this trick. On each machine, access Checking Mail from the Options dialog box in the **Tools** menu; then select the Leave mail on server and Delete from server after X days checkboxes. Set X to a number greater than the usual number of days between when you check mail on each machine.

Netscape Messenger Configuration Tips

Messenger is a solid but uninspiring email client. There isn't a wealth of information about it on the Web, but there are a few tricks worth knowing about.

Hard delete

If you want to truly delete messages, rather than transferring them to your trash directory, hold down the Shift key as you press **Delete**.

Faster searching

Messenger searches through folders alphabetically. If you have old or archived mail and want to avoid waiting for Messenger to sort through it, give the folder a name beginning with a letter late in the alphabet. Ze Olde Mail will be searched after About Work, Best of Steve, Concerning Wendy, and the rest of your current folders.

Automatic expansion

To expand collapsed threads, press the asterisk (*) key.

Automatic mail notification

You don't have to be running Netscape to be notified of new mail. Just run the Netscape Mail Notification utility, which you'll find in Netscape's folder in the **Start** menu. If you'd like this utility to launch automatically, drag the icon to your Startup folder.

Making your mail more irritating

I don't know why I'm telling you this, but to add a background image, color, or animated GIF to your Messenger Mail message, choose **Page Colors and Properties** from the **Format** menu. Set the text and background colors as you wish, or add an extra-annoying image file to use as a background pattern.

Drag and drop

If you want to send someone a URL, drag the hyperlink from Navigator into an open email composition window. Actually, you can drag and drop all sorts of elements throughout Communicator, including images or URLs, into email messages. You can also drop them into web pages you're creating in Composer.

Outlook Configuration Tips

Using Outlook is a wonderful and horrible experience. Outlook has so many complicated features that it pays to probe its nooks and crannies. Take a look at the newsgroup *microsoft.public.outlook.usage* for more information.

Changing reply attribution

Outlook's standard reply attribution is rather baroque:

```
-----Original Message-----
From: Floyd Goodbody [mailto:floydg@erols.com]
Sent: Tuesday, September 21, 1999 10:15 AM
To: kiersten@oreilly.com
Subject: Go Niners
```

You may not want or need this much information to preface every reply (or forwarded message) you send out. To change it requires a bit of work.

First, open the *Program Files\Microsoft Office\Office\Headers* directory on your hard drive. The directory should look something like Figure 3-10.

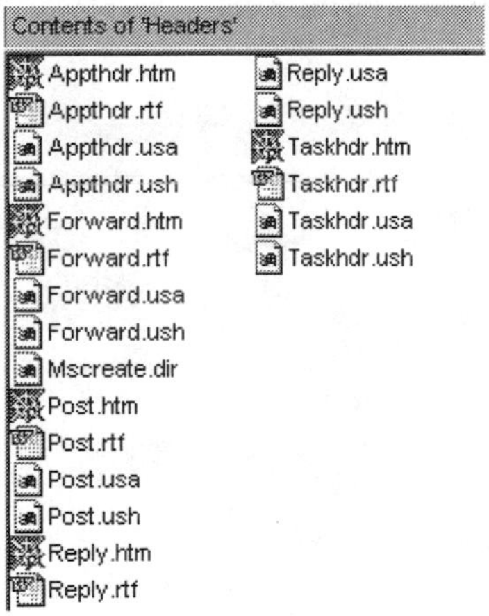

Figure 3-10. Contents of the Headers directory

To change your reply attribution, you'll need to change the following text files: *Reply. htm, Reply.rtf, Reply.usa*, and *Reply.ush*. Make backup copies of all four files, saving them in another directory.

You'll need to open each file in a text editor, such as WordPad. *Reply.rtf* and *Reply.usa* are different only in font, and look like Figure 3-11.

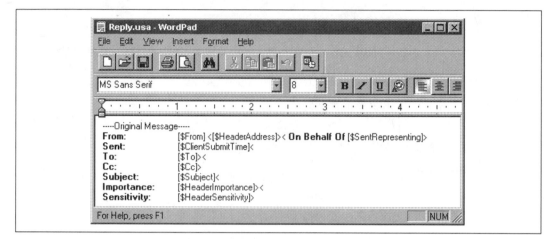

Figure 3-11. A Microsoft mail header file

Change both files so that replies appear the way you'd like. Figure 3-12 shows one possibility. As you can see, you want to keep individual units of code intact. However, you may then string those units together into a format you prefer. *Reply.htm* (Figure 3-13) and *Reply.ush* are also very similar. Change them so that the output matches that of *Reply.usa* and *Reply.rtf*. The edited file appears in Figure 3-14.

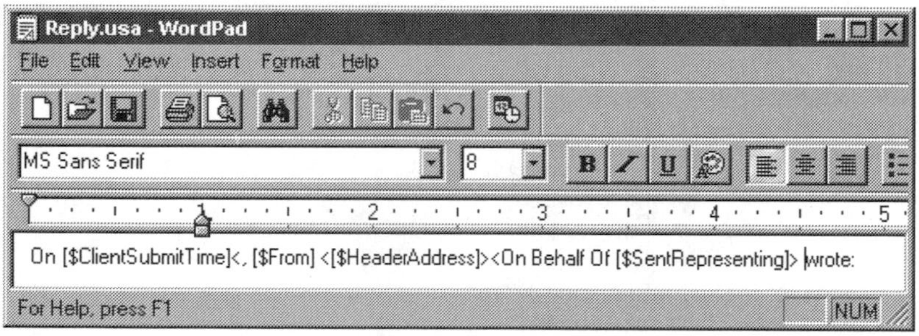

Figure 3-12. A new mail header file

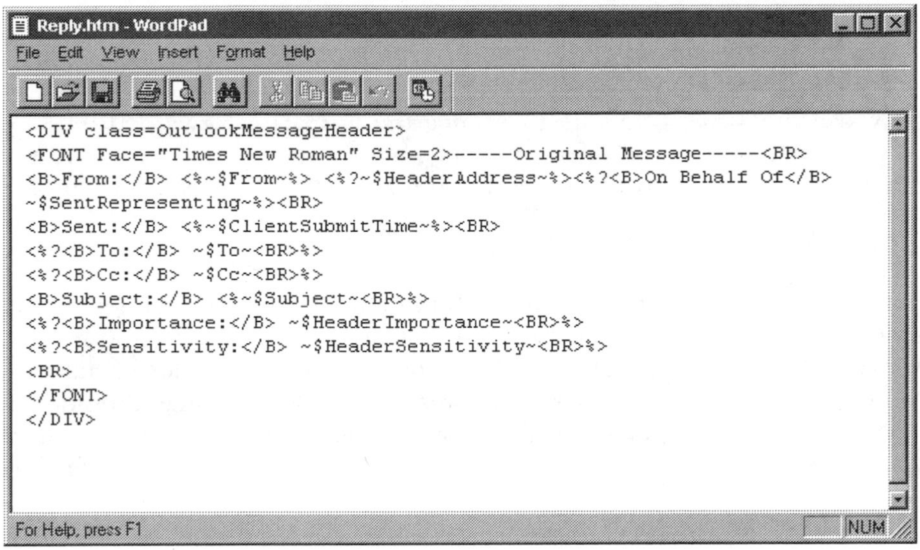

```
Reply.htm - WordPad
File  Edit  View  Insert  Format  Help

<DIV class=OutlookMessageHeader>
<FONT Face="Times New Roman" Size=2>-----Original Message-----<BR>
<B>From:</B> <%~$From~%> <%?~$HeaderAddress~%><%?<B>On Behalf Of</B>
~$SentRepresenting~%><BR>
<B>Sent:</B> <%~$ClientSubmitTime~%><BR>
<%?<B>To:</B> ~$To~<BR>%>
<%?<B>Cc:</B> ~$Cc~<BR>%>
<B>Subject:</B> <%~$Subject~<BR>%>
<%?<B>Importance:</B> ~$HeaderImportance~<BR>%>
<%?<B>Sensitivity:</B> ~$HeaderSensitivity~<BR>%>
<BR>
</FONT>
</DIV>

For Help, press F1                                    NUM
```

Figure 3-13. Reply.htm

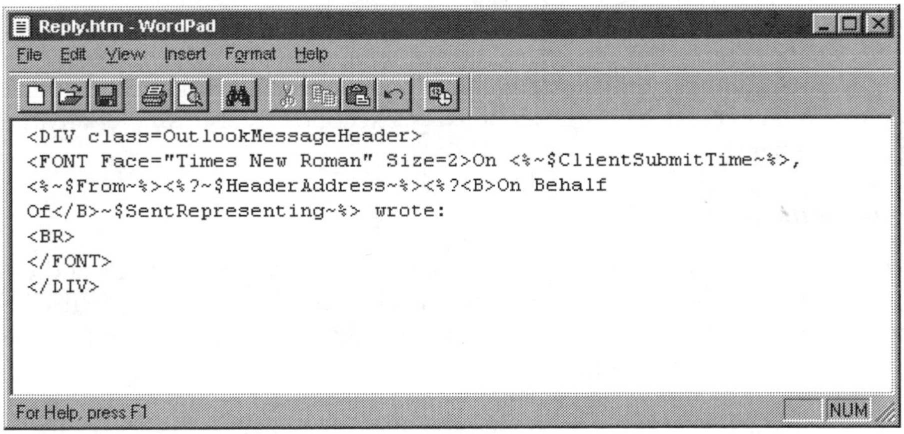

```
Reply.htm - WordPad
File  Edit  View  Insert  Format  Help

<DIV class=OutlookMessageHeader>
<FONT Face="Times New Roman" Size=2>On <%~$ClientSubmitTime~%>,
<%~$From~%><%?~$HeaderAddress~%><%?<B>On Behalf
Of</B>~$SentRepresenting~%> wrote:
<BR>
</FONT>
</DIV>

For Help, press F1                                    NUM
```

Figure 3-14. New Reply.htm

Now, my Outlook reply attribution looks like this:

```
> On Wednesday, September 23, 1998 11:59 AM, Floyd Goodbody
> [mailto:floydg@erols.com] wrote:
```

You may use the same technique to change the format of forwarded messages and Usenet posts. The files you'll need to change are located in the same directory, and are called *Forward.rtf, Forward.usa, Forward.ush, Post.rtf, Post.usa,* and *Post.ush.*

Adding new features

Microsoft is constantly adding new features to Outlook. To add features not included in the original installation (especially if you took advantage of the free download), use the Add/Remove Programs utility in the Control Panel. First, close Outlook. Then, open the Control Panel (either from Explorer, or from the **Settings** drop-down menu on the **Start** button) and launch Add/Remove Programs. On the **Install/Uninstall** tab, select **Outlook 98** and click the **Add/Remove** button. The resulting Maintenance Wizard walks you through the process of downloading components from Microsoft's site.

Avoiding the hazards of the junk email filter

You may not want to turn on the junk email filter. Why? Microsoft, in all its wisdom, created a text-based filter that marks as spam any message that contains an exclamation point and question mark in the subject line, as well as such words or phrases as "for free!" and "removal instructions" in the body. Unfortunately, you can't modify the automatic filters. You'll want to either create your own filters, specify that the junk email filter can't automatically delete messages, or keep a careful eye on your Deleted Items folder. You'll also want to create a list of exceptions; for example, anything from your boss's domain.

Configuring the filters

If you do want to use the junk email filters, it's easy to add a spammer's address to the list. When you receive mail from a spammer, click on the message, then click **Organize** and choose **Junk E-mail**. Or, you can right-click the message and choose **Junk E-mail** from the drop-down menu.

Although you'll find both settings in the **Organize** section under Junk E-mail, Outlook provides the option of specifying different actions for junk email and adult content email. Keep in mind that Outlook's rules for the spam filters are faulty and, if you're using the filters to move messages, move them to a junk email file instead of the Trash folder.

Avoiding address corruption pitfalls

If you send a message to multiple recipients, but even one address is corrupted, Outlook won't send the message to anyone. Be sure to send the message again to the other recipients.

Text scrolling

Pressing the spacebar brings up the next page of text in the preview pane. (For some reason, this doesn't work in a standard message window.)

Preview pane options

To change the preview pane options, right-click the gray header immediately above the pane. You can select font options and decide whether you want to view the pane at all, whether you want to view header information, and whether to mark messages as read.

Drag and drop

You can drag and drop items throughout Outlook 98, which makes it easy to convert one kind of item into another. If you received mail from your boss with an assignment, just drag the message onto the calendar icon under Outlook shortcuts. Outlook creates an appointment, with the message text as a note; the message subject becomes the appointment subject.

Pine Configuration

Using Pine is fairly straightforward, but it's not your standard graphical user interface experience. Inexperienced users who are interested in the mailer should take heart: using Pine is really easier than using Outlook, in spite of its more daunting interface.

Using Telnet

If you don't want to use Pine with IMAP, it's usually easy to start a Telnet session and work with Pine directly on the server. Make sure that your ISP supports Pine and will allow you to access it via a Telnet session.

First, you'll need a Telnet client. Windows 95/98 comes with a Telnet client that you'll find in the Program Files directory. Your ISP may recommend a client; there are many freeware clients you can download. Once you've installed the Telnet client, launch it and choose **Remote System...** from the **Connect** menu. You'll need to find out the hostname, port, and TermType settings from your ISP. Once they're entered, click the **Connect** button (see Figure 3-15).

Enter your login and password as directed. Once you've logged in, you'll see a prompt that looks something like this:

```
Sun Microsystems Inc.    SunOS 5.6      Generic August 1997
TERM=(ansi)
Erase is delete.
Kill is control-U (^U).
Interrupt is control-C (^C).
kiersten(kiersten) 1%
```

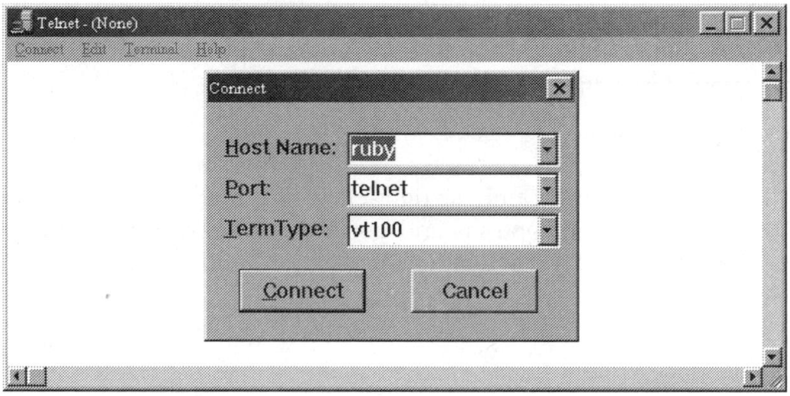

Figure 3-15. Telnet settings

Type the word "pine" at the prompt (after the 1%, in this case), and press Enter. Pine launches, and you can use it as usual.

The following sections give some additional tips for using Pine.

Automatic alias creation

You can create aliases automatically via the *Take Address* command. When viewing a message from an address you wish to alias, press "t" and enter a nickname as prompted. Ctrl-X exits the address book.

Accessing the BCC field

To access the BCC field, you'll need to open a message composition window first. Press "c" to do so, then Ctrl-R. The resulting Rich Header includes the "BCC" option.

Easy deletion

To delete a full line of text, place the cursor on the appropriate line and press Ctrl-K.

Searching

Search for messages using the *whereis* command. First, enter your mail index by pressing "i", then press "w" (for whereis). Enter the string of characters you wish to find in the subject or sender fields of the message.

Suspend composition

Use Pine's *postpone* command to switch between composing a message and other tasks. Ctrl-O pauses message composition. The next time you press "c" (for compose), Pine asks whether you want to continue the postponed composition.

Turn off confirmation requests

Pine, constantly seeking validation, frequently asks the user to confirm actions. By going to Pine's extensive configuration menu, you can turn off most (but not all) of these confirmation requests.

Minimize typing

To minimize the amount you have to type while reading mail, turn on the enable-cruise-mode option on the configuration menu. You may also want to turn on enable-cruise-mode-delete, which deletes messages as soon as you've read them, although this can be dangerous.

Easier saving

You can make saving messages easier by associating the email addresses of people you correspond with to folder names; you do this in Pine's address book. The only problem is that some people use multiple email addresses. Just add an entry to the address book for each address the person uses. You don't have to assign a nickname to each address, and it's not worth bothering to assign nicknames to addresses that you probably won't use.

Plug-Ins

Just as a wealth of helper applications exist to modify or customize your web browser, a broad range of plug-ins exist to streamline your email. Both Eudora (*http://www.eudora.com/central/plugins/*) and Outlook (*http://www.microsoft.com*) support a broad range of commercial programs.

Email plug-ins tend to fall into the categories listed below. Most are available as shareware. If you'd like to download these plug-ins, visit one of the shareware sites listed in the Resource Catalog and look at the site's "email" section. Note that some of the plug-ins' functions can be performed through the built-in filters that are included in most mailers.

- *Voice.* Would you like to send a recording of your voice instead of a text message? Then try a voice plug-in. Some allow for playback via standard email programs; others require the recipient to download the voice plug-in themselves.

- *Greeting cards/animation.* If plain text just isn't enough for you, you can send animations, graphics files, or amusing noises, many in the form of pre-made greeting cards. Some of them bark.

- *Encryption.* These helper applications encode your email to increase privacy. For more information, see Chapter 5.

- *Spam killers.* Various programs scan for addresses of known spammers and automatically filter mail from them into the trash. The programs have varying degrees of complexity. Some support retributive actions, such as automatically mailing the spammers' ISP.

- *Signature handlers.* These are utilities to help manage multiple or random signature attachments to your outgoing messages.

- *List managers.* Overwhelmed by mailing lists? These applications promise to help manage them.

- *Bulk emailers.* Don't use these. They're wrong.

- *Notifiers.* If your mailer doesn't alert you to new mail, these programs play a sound or display an icon, usually in the taskbar tray.

- *Multiple account managers.* If you have multiple POP3 accounts, these programs can help check and consolidate them.

- *Spellcheckers.* If your mailer doesn't have a spellchecker built-in, these small plug-ins may be useful.

- *Converters.* Moving from one mailer to another? Don't want to re-type your entire address book? Many utilities exist to convert stored messages or address books from one email program to another.

Handling File Attachments

Some of the greatest confusion surrounding email comes from the problems with file attachments. You have a document your friend needs. You send her a message that says, "Here's the file," click the **Attach** icon, browse for the file on your system, and click **Send**. She gets a file that looks like it was written by a bunch of monkeys trying to pound out the works of Shakespeare on multiple typewriters. What happened?

Unfortunately, there's no clear answer. Some possibilities include:

- You and your friend are using two different word processors. The file transmitted fine, but is incompatible with your friend's program.

- You and your friend are using the same word processor on two different platforms. Again, the file could transmit perfectly and still appear to be garbled.

- If the file was large, your mailer probably compressed it. Your friend's mailer may not have recognized the compression scheme and tried to use a different program to decompress it.

Sending Attachments

What's the best way to guarantee the safe arrival of an email attachment? Well, there are no guarantees. However, you can take steps to improve the odds of your file making it through unscathed.

To transmit a message over the Internet, your mailer converts both your message and its attachment into ASCII text and sends them as a single unit. When that unit arrives, the recipient's mailer reconfigures the information it receives into the original text message and (hopefully) its original attachment.

Unfortunately, there are currently not one but three Internet encoding "standards." These standards are incompatible and vary by platform. The most popular standard is called MIME encoding, for *Multipurpose Internet Mail Extensions*; it is also the standard of choice on the Windows platform. The Macintosh platform generally uses BinHex encoding, identified with the extension *.hqx*. Finally, uuencode is an older standard, still seen on rare occasions. All modern mail programs support MIME, but you may occasionally see the other formats. One final complication: it is notoriously difficult to send attachments to users with accounts on online services, as many don't support the encoding standards. Be doubly sure to check with these users before sending an attached file.

Here are some general tips on sending file attachments:

- Check with the recipient in advance, to find out whether he has the software to handle the file you're sending. For example, say your friend Bob needs a carefully formatted press release from you pretty darn quick. Instead of just sending Bob the file, call and find out which word processor he uses and on which platform he uses it. If you're both using Word for Windows on Windows 95, great. If you're using Word for Windows and he's using Word for the Mac (or WordPerfect, etc.), check the Save As... dialog box to see whether you can save the file in a more appropriate format for Bob's needs.

- Bob, however, may be running Emacs on a Linux box and may not have Word. Check to see if he has any of a number of programs that claim to accept Word documents. (You may have more luck if you save the file in *Rich Text Format*— RTF). If Bob can't find any software capable of reading the file on Bob's end, MIME isn't going to help. To send a file as plain text, copy the contents of the file onto the clipboard, and paste it into the body of the mail message itself—in other words, don't send an attachment at all. Then fax Bob the original for reference.

- If you're using Windows 95, set your mailer's options to send attachments using the MIME format.

- If you're using a Mac, MIME encoding is still a good choice. However, some Mac mailers still aren't MIME compliant, so your recipient may still have trouble decoding it. If you're unsure, send the file using *both* MIME and BinHex (in other words, send two attachments).

Certain file formats are more standard for certain types of files. If you aren't sure what kind of platform your recipient is using, or if you have to send a file to a different platform, here are your best bets:

audio
> AIFF (Audio Interchange File Format), WAV (a Microsoft standard that to my knowledge isn't an acronym, but, hey, sound travels in waves), or AU (audio) files.

drawings
> EPS (Encapsulated PostScript).

graphics
> GIF (Graphics Interchange Format), BMP (bitmap), JPEG (Joint Photographic Experts Group).

spreadsheets
> Text. To send a spreadsheet file as text, use the spreadsheet application's **Save As** command to save the file as tab-delimited or comma-delimited text. Other spreadsheet applications can then easily import and rebuild the file.

text files
> RTF (Rich Text Format).

video
> QuickTime, MPEG (Motion Picture Experts Group), or AVI.

One note: merely knowing that you and your recipient are both using Microsoft Word is not enough. In fact, using Microsoft Word on the same *platform* isn't enough. Word 97 isn't compatible with Word 6, although there are tools for making the two recognize each other's files. Either send RTF files, or check to see if you have a compatible **Save as** option.

Finally, if you're sending large files, you'll want to use a file compression utility to make the file smaller and thus easier to transmit. Once again, different operating systems use different compression standards. The most standard file extensions are *.zip*, for PKZIP files on Windows; *.sit*, for StuffIt files on the Mac; and *.tar*, for GZIP files on Unix. It's a good idea to compress word-processing files (including RTF files) and bitmap images, which may shrink to one percent of their original size. Compressing GIF or JPEG graphics files won't help much, however, since they've already been compressed. See Chapter 13 for more information.

Receiving and Reading Attachments

Most current mailers make reading attachments simple. A message that has an attachment included displays an icon, frequently involving a paper clip, with the attached file's name. The user clicks or double-clicks the icon to read the attachment, which generally launches the appropriate viewing software. The attached file itself is usually deposited in an Attachments directory, separate from the mail directory.

What if your computer doesn't recognize the file?

First, try to determine the type of file you were sent. The computer may not recognize the file type with a handy icon, but there may be a file extension that gives you a clue. If the file is called *Dec01.puz*, and your friend's message reads, "Here's a crossword puzzle for you to try," you probably want to try to open the file with your crossword puzzle program. If the file extension isn't immediately apparent, try to look at the file's **Properties** or **Info**; you can usually find a clue there, under **File type** or **MS-DOS name**.

If you see the following extensions, here are the applications you'll need to open them:

.doc	Microsoft Word
.gif	Graphics program or browser
.htm	Browser
.jpg	Graphics program or browser
.mpg	MPEG video player
.pdf	Adobe Acrobat reader
.ps	Postscript reader

If you don't have any luck, try to open the attachment with a text editor. Locate the file, launch the text editor, and try to open the file with the **Open** command. If you don't see the file at first, change the List Files of Type: checkbox to "All Files (*.*)." Even if the file turns out not to be a text file, you may get a clue as to what it is; HTML files, for example, should be easy to recognize as such from the line <HTML> up at the top of the document.

Traveling with Email

Anyone who frequently travels on business, or has taken a few weeks off, can find email especially frustrating: if you read email on the road, it's easy to lose messages between your desktop and your laptop; if you simply don't read email for a few weeks, you face the daunting task of sorting through a deluge of email upon return.

Reading Mail on the Road

Many people use more than one computer to read their email, whether it's from home or from a laptop while traveling. Coordinating mail files between more than one computer may be a frustrating task: if you're using a POP account, you end up with messages stored in different locations, which are usually hard to access if you're not right there. This can create a difficult situation if, for example, you're home with a cold and need to quote a message from a co-worker, but the message is saved on the hard drive of your PC at the office. Since you can't access your PC at work from your PC at home, you might as well succumb to the cold and binge on Sudafed.

I'd like to tell you there's a better way, but there isn't much you can do to solve this problem (except convince your company or ISP to use IMAP). There are, however, two ways to minimize it: use an email account on a different platform, or set your POP accounts to leave messages on the server.

Using non-POP accounts

If you travel frequently, consider using an email account that doesn't operate via the Post Office Protocol. That way, you simply won't store the messages on your PC at all. They'll remain on the Unix or World Wide Web–based server where you read your mail.

The disadvantages to reading your mail this way are actually fairly few. You'll need more connection time, since you can't download your messages and read them offline. If you'll be reading a Unix mail account from a PC, you'll most likely need to use a Telnet client to access it, but these are simple to use (see the appendix). Most Unix platforms support the Pine mailer, which is fairly uncomplicated, even for graphical user interface diehards (see Figure 3-16). You can even use a POP mailer at work (or wherever you maintain your primary computer) and read messages at home or on the road directly from the server, using Pine.

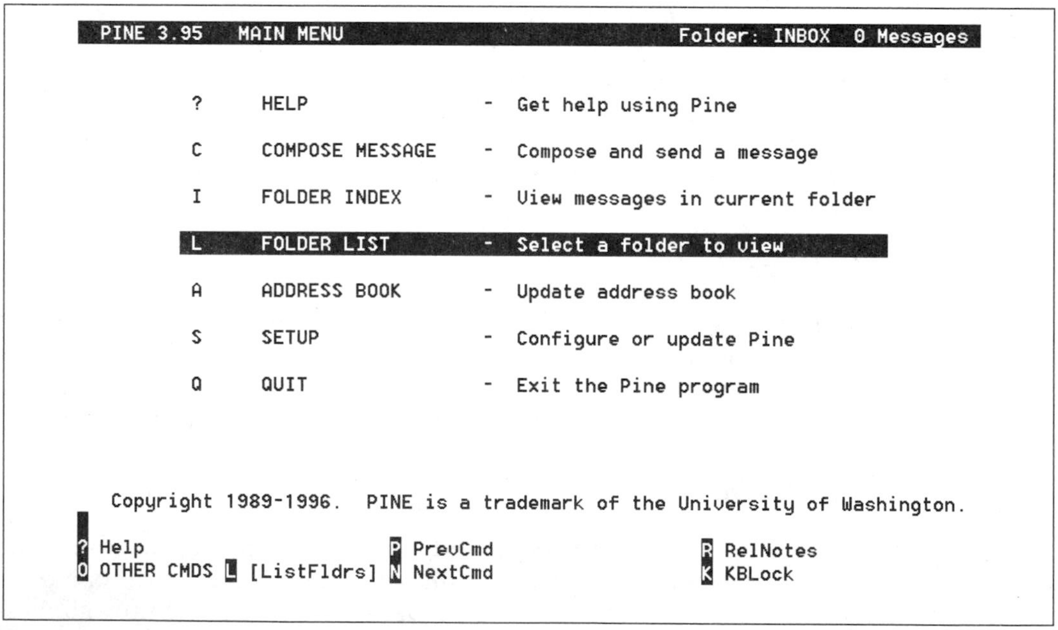

```
 PINE 3.95    MAIN MENU                          Folder: INBOX  0 Messages


          ?     HELP              -  Get help using Pine

          C     COMPOSE MESSAGE   -  Compose and send a message

          I     FOLDER INDEX      -  View messages in current folder

          L     FOLDER LIST       -  Select a folder to view

          A     ADDRESS BOOK      -  Update address book

          S     SETUP             -  Configure or update Pine

          Q     QUIT              -  Exit the Pine program




      Copyright 1989-1996.  PINE is a trademark of the University of Washington.

 ? Help                   P PrevCmd                 R RelNotes
 O OTHER CMDS L [ListFldrs] N NextCmd               K KBLock
```

Figure 3-16. Using Pine

Dealing with attachments can be a problem. If you telnet into some mainframe to read mail, and then receive a message with an attachment, the attachment will be stuck on the mainframe, where it won't do you much good. You'll have to FTP to the main-frame, download the attachment, and then open it.

If you use an email account that's based on the Web, there are privacy issues to think about; see "Free Accounts," later in this chapter, for a full discussion.

Leaving Messages on a POP server

If you absolutely must use your POP account at all times, set your email clients to leave messages on the server until you delete them. You'll end up with multiple cop-ies of the mail you receive, but you won't be without it. When using Eudora, select the "Leave mail on server" checkbox by accessing the **Incoming Mail** option, in the Tools window (**Tools** → **Options** → **Incoming Mail**). If you're using Microsoft Outlook, change the setting by accessing **Accounts...** in the **Tools** menu. Select your mail account and click the **Properties** button. Select the **Advanced** tab, and change the settings accord-ingly. Figure 3-17 shows some possible settings.

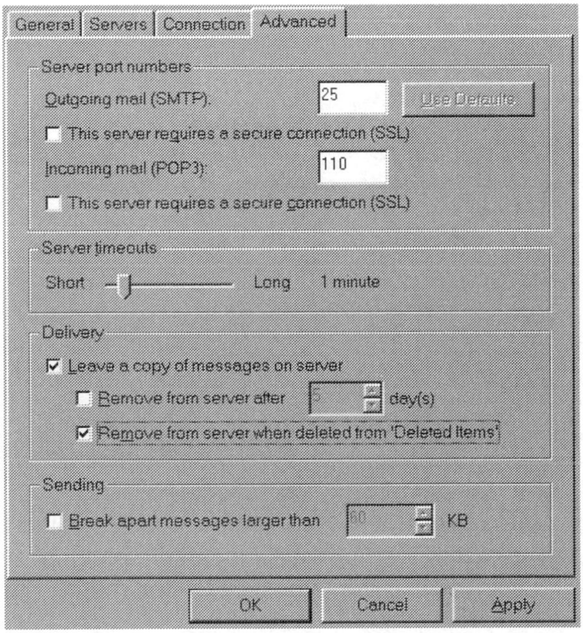

Figure 3-17. Outlook options

Depending on the mailer you're using, you may then specify how the messages should be deleted from the server. Outlook lets you specify certain conditions under which the mail is deleted. Eudora allows you to essentially delete the mail twice: once from the mailer and once from the server. If you click the button to delete the mail from the server, it will be deleted the next time you download new messages.

Using Vacation Programs

If you'll be away from your mail for a few weeks, you can take a few steps before your departure to stem the tide of email. Some mailers allow you to create a filter that sends an automatic response to anyone who writes you, telling them you won't be reading your mail. If your mailer doesn't support this feature, many Unix platforms support a program called "vacation" which serves the same purpose. Many of the free-mail accounts, described later, also support this feature. And it's a good idea to suspend (or even cancel) mail from automated mailing lists while you're away.

Creating vacation filters

One of Eudora's filter actions is Reply With, which makes creating a vacation filter easy:

1. Create the message you'll send as a reply to people who send you mail. To do so, create a new message, leaving the To: field blank, as in Figure 3-18.

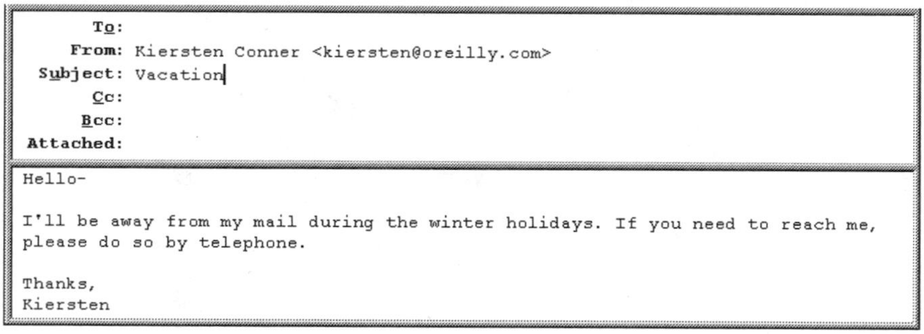

```
        To:
      From: Kiersten Conner <kiersten@oreilly.com>
   Subject: Vacation
        Cc:
       Bcc:
  Attached:

Hello-

I'll be away from my mail during the winter holidays. If you need to reach me,
please do so by telephone.

Thanks,
Kiersten
```

Figure 3-18. Creating a Eudora stationery file

2. Use the Save As... command to save the message as a stationery file in Eudora's stationery directory.

3. Select **Filters** from the **Tools** menu. You want to create a filter that responds to any message you receive while you're away. Our filter, pictured in Figure 3-19, specifies any incoming message that contains a "12" (for the month of December) anywhere in the header.

4. For the action, specify **Reply With**. Choose the appropriate reply from those saved in your Stationery directory.

If I sent myself mail while I was away, I would receive the response shown in Figure 3-20.

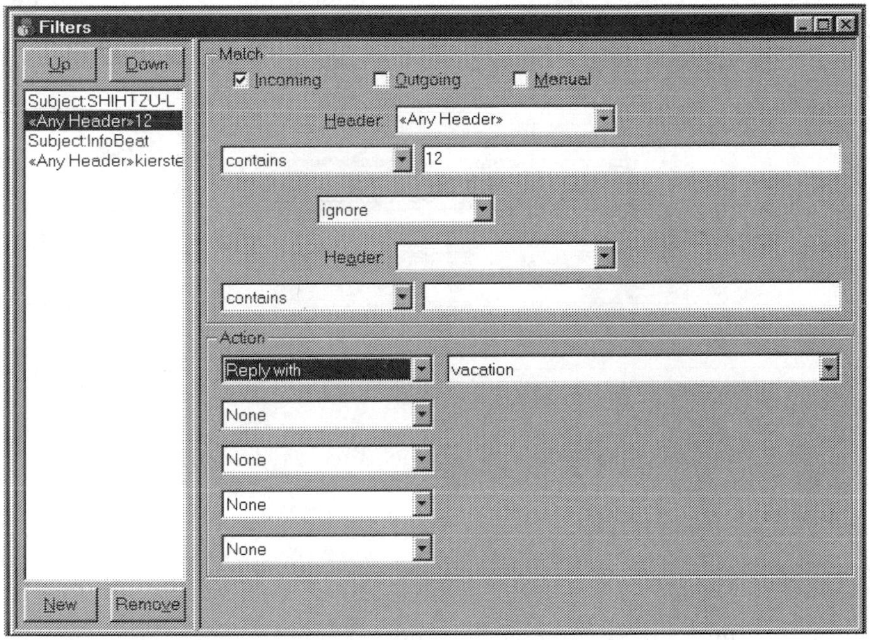

Figure 3-19. A vacation filter

```
X-Sender: kiersten@ruby.ora.com
X-Mailer: QUALCOMM Windows Eudora Pro Version 3.0.5 (32)
Date: Mon, 08 Dec 1997 12:46:40 -0500
To: Kiersten Conner <kiersten@oreilly.com>
From: Kiersten Conner <kiersten@oreilly.com>
Subject: Away from my mail (was Re: Meaningless task)

At 12:46 PM 12/8/97 -0500, Kiersten Conner wrote:
:Can you please do a repetitive, uninteresting task for the next few weeks?
:
:Kiersten Conner                      kiersten@oreilly.com
:O'Reilly, Cambridge                  (617) 354-5800
:
Hello-

I'll be away from my mail during the winter holidays. If you need to reach
me, please do so by telephone.

Thanks,
Kiersten

Kiersten Conner                      kiersten@oreilly.com
O'Reilly, Cambridge                  (617) 354-5800
```

Figure 3-20. Automatic reply

If you want this filter to send a reply to every piece of mail you receive while you're gone, be sure to move it to the top of your filter list. Think carefully about this, however. If you don't suspend your mailing lists, you're likely to end up with a chain reaction of bounced replies when the vacation filter sends a response to the mailing list's server, which sends back an error message, to which the vacation filter sends a reply. A better filter order might place this filter last, allowing mailing list messages to be filed before activating the vacation reply, as shown in Figure 3-21.

Figure 3-21. Non-bounce-inducing filter order

Keep in mind that to use this option, you'll need to leave your computer running and connected to the Internet, with Eudora open. Only do so if your computer is located in a *very* secure place.

On a Unix server

If you're using a PC to read your email, odds are that you're using an account that downloads your mail from a Unix server and displays it according to the Post Office Protocol (POP). Thus, if you're using a mailer with filter capacities less advanced than Eudora's—Messenger, for example—you may want to enable the vacation program at the server level if you'll be away from your mail.

You'll need to know how to log in to your Unix account, and how to use a text editor on that platform. If you don't know how to do those things, you may still be able to find a kindly system administrator willing to help you.

Log in to your account, and type "vacation" at the command line. The program determines whether you have a message to send in response to incoming mail. If you don't, it launches your text editor, with a sample message already loaded, as in Figure 3-22.

The variable $SUBJECT will be replaced with the incoming message's subject line in the reply. Edit this message as you wish and save the file. You're automatically returned to the vacation program. When it asks whether you would like to create a *.forward* file and enable the vacation feature, answer "yes," as in Figure 3-23.

Upon your return, run the vacation program again. This time, the program will ask whether you would like to disable the vacation feature. Once again, answer "yes."

The vacation program supports a wider array of options than those discussed here. To learn about them, type "man vacation" at the Unix prompt.

```
Buffers Files Tools Edit Search Help
From: kiersten (via the vacation program)
Subject: away from my mail

I will not be reading my mail for a while.
Your mail regarding "$SUBJECT" will be read when I return.




-----Emacs: .vacation.msg      (Fundamental)--L1--All----------
█                    done
```

Figure 3-22. The Unix vacation program

```
kiersten(kiersten) 9% vacation
This program can be used to answer your mail automatically
when you go away on vacation.
You have a message file in /ruby/home/kiersten/.vacation.msg.
Would you like to see it? n
Would you like to edit it? n
To enable the vacation feature a ".forward" file is created.
Would you like to enable the vacation feature? y
Vacation feature ENABLED. Please remember to turn it off when
you get back from vacation. Bon voyage.
kiersten(kiersten) 10% █
```

Figure 3-23. Enabling the vacation feature

Suspending Mailing Lists

If you'd like to suspend mailing lists while you're away, it's easy to do. If your list uses the listserv program (which it does if you see the word "listserv" in the address), send a message to the listserv address to suspend receiving messages from the list. The sole content of the message should be the command and the name of the list, as in Figure 3-24.

```
        To: To: listserv@listserv.aol.com
      From: Kiersten Conner <kiersten@oreilly.com>
   Subject:
        Cc:
       Bcc:
  Attached:

SET law-and-order nomail
```

Figure 3-24. Suspending the Law & Order mailing list

This suspends mail delivery without unsubscribing you from the list. To resume mail delivery, send the command:

```
set law-and-order mail
```

in the same manner.

If you subscribe to a majordomo list, it may be easiest to unsubscribe for a little while. Send a message like the one in Figure 3-25.

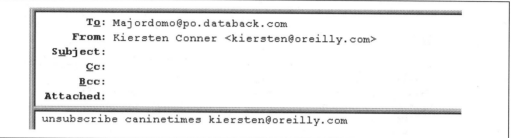

```
         To: Majordomo@po.databack.com
       From: Kiersten Conner <kiersten@oreilly.com>
    Subject:
         Cc:
        Bcc:
   Attached:

unsubscribe caninetimes kiersten@oreilly.com
```

Figure 3-25. Unsubscribing from Canine Times

Simply re-subscribe when you return.

If you're looking for a list of available commands, send the single word "HELP" to the list's command address.

Free Accounts

Many people have lamented the exclusivity of the computer age. Even as the Internet made the world a much smaller place, it did so only for those wealthy enough to afford computers. Now, the freedom of email is available to everyone.

A few years ago, many people signed on with America Online or other online services mainly to get an email account and the software to use the account from home. No more. Now, a growing number of services provide free email accounts, and many of them are web-based. Thus, you won't need any software besides a browser to read your mail. For that matter, you won't even need a computer. You can read your mail anywhere you can access the Web: school, work, cafés, or libraries.

While many of these burgeoning services are still somewhat clunky in operation, they offer distinct benefits, even if you already have an email account. With growing privacy concerns, many people welcome the idea of a separate, private account their bosses can't read. Some of these accounts even allow you to forward mail from one address to another, so that you can read your mail from a single location. Further, many offer anti-spam policies that include built-in filters. Most promise an address for life, intending that once you register an email address with them, you can keep it in perpetuity, and thus be able to print it out on business cards, résumés, and presumably your forehead—but keep in mind that one of these services has already folded. A growing number also allow you to receive HTML documents instead of straight text (though email in general seems to be moving in this—in my opinion unfortunate—direction). Others allow you to forward or consolidate your mail over various accounts. Finally, while reading your mail over the Web is rather slow, it's great for the frequent traveler.

Why are these accounts free? The answer incorporates a broad range of Internet money-making attempts, from generating advertising revenues to sucking you into services that do cost money. The No Such Thing as a Free Lunch rule does apply. Most sites have advertising on their login pages, and some attach a small plug at the end of every message you send. Others offer an account for free, but added whiz-bang features, such as consolidation, forwarding, or POP access, are available only for a fee. Finally, most require that you fill out an extensive demographic questionnaire when signing up. Some users may see this as a way to create a target for spam, in spite of the services' declared anti-spam policies; however, it seems perfectly logical to me that a computer would need to know whether you are 18–25 or 26–39 before automatically creating your account.

Features

There are two different kinds of freemail accounts currently available: what we'll call forwarding accounts and web-based accounts. The pros and cons of individual services are discussed in this section. A forwarding account, such as Bigfoot or NetAccess, provides you with an email address; you then set preferences to indicate where mail sent to that account should be forwarded. A web-based account, on the other hand, provides an address and a fully functional mailer, available on the Web. If you'd like to use your own mailer—say, Eudora or Netscape—a few also provide POP3 access to their servers, allowing you to download messages as you normally would from an ISP.

One word of caution regarding web-based accounts: privacy is a concern, due to the way that browsers store web pages on users' machines. The browser's cache is an archive of recently accessed documents on a user's hard drive, kept there to reduce download time for frequently accessed files. A typical cache may look like Figure 3-26.

While the file names aren't easily recognizable, it's easy to open the hypertext documents and take a quick tour of recent web browsing. Moreover, if you've just read your mail and walked away from your computer, anyone could click the **Back** button a few times to join in your epistolary adventures. Therefore, if you access your email through the Web, you're likely to end up with copies of your correspondence resting neatly on whichever computer you just used.

To avoid these problems, be sure to log out of the email site instead of just clicking away. Logging out disables the **Back** button from being able to access your account to

Contents of 'cache'

M03nnvef	M07q4bvn	M0cji7s2	M0gpt5oq	M0lkfr0j
M03pcgqg	M07q8t4f	M0ck7nqb	M0gqo0n4	M0ltiuu1
M03qpa1t	M085n6bp	M0cke1i3	M0gujtir	M0lumceu
M03t262v	M08eblhg	M0ckt6oi	M0h32ohb	M0m3ij9f
M03ue359	M08j66v6	M0com2ss.coo	M0hdb2v8	M0mfhp38
M03v78ie	M08oogol	M0d8mvbc	M0hkoafp	M0mge6a7
M0428ii9	M08qfg59	M0db59dc	M0hljpg5	M0mi48sh
M04g8oa8	M08qub9p	M0dbsbcs	M0i6fuc7	M0mkli46
M04igf2d	M08ucb27	M0ddgn5q	M0ic8oga	M0n0iikj
M055t8co	M092q25s	M0dh3o1e	M0ip8b6k	M0n2src8
M05erhqc	M093srhf	M0dhh4fh	M0ipq3pf	M0n39ss8
M05jt15t	M094nema	M0dp8cq6	M0iqj804	M0n6f6kd
M05jtsp8	M099ggg4	M0e91ebd	M0ir1n5j	M0nc70m7
M05nva9s	M0a1aa30	M0ea3fa8	M0j9fdqd	M0ncs4p0
M05rieaf	M0afb5m1	M0eaas4q	M0ja3c5a	M0nf94ed
M05vohav	M0aqqf99	M0ei0b76	M0jf0b1a	M0nq4hbp
M06619dm	M0atrfhg	M0ei3nv2	M0jgbchm	M0nvstsn
M06h1qfv	M0b02966	M0eqv8f9	M0jgtj1i	M0o24akf
M06k47v0	M0b3prbk	M0er4emk	M0jv4j85	M0o25pkk
M06qo33g	M0b5n1ia	M0fl63du	M0k73l29	M0o5epjd
M06ts75h	M0b7ittp	M0flsj5d	M0k9mqru	M0o66mbh
M070032v	M0b8tslu	M0ftkueu	M0kc1ktd	M0o7k8fg
M072gm20	M0b9rvok	M0g67m5n	M0kdc2cs	M0o8bsog
M075cfe8	M0bdea9j	M0g7mt2n	M0kfs567	M0of3lr4
M07682ma	M0btlj6d	M0g85utc	M0kndn6d	M0oknams
M079f51v	M0btmo2q	M0gb1h25	M0kt0hmv	M0oufeuv
M07fj37u	M0ccr1fq	M0gp478l	M0kusfrq	M0pbmc7h
M07kb4pb	M0chocmi	M0gphaso	M0lhst5q	M0pc5mff

Figure 3-26. Contents of a cache folder

send or receive mail, though not from being able to display the mail you just read. The only way to do that is to completely quit the browser when you're through. Unfortunately, this doesn't clear the cache. To do so, select **Clear Disk Cache** (for Netscape) or **Empty Temporary Internet Settings** (for Internet Explorer),* or simply find the cache directory on the hard drive and delete the contents manually.

If you have your own computer, you'll most likely want to avoid reading mail on the Web on a regular basis, and you'll want to set up a POP3 account. Services that provide POP access supply the server name and brief instructions. Hotmail already charges for POP access, and other services are likely to do so in the future.

Freemail Accounts

A representative sampling of freemail sites appears in this section. As always, the Web changes minute by minute, so the information provided here is almost certain to be inaccurate. Netscape's WebMail is currently the best of the bunch. Also, don't overlook alumni associations and other organizations—they may also provide freemail accounts.

---

* On IE 5, clear the cache with **Tools** → **Internet Options** → **General** → **Temporary Internet Files** → **Delete**.

Bigfoot (http://www.bigfoot.com)

Founded in 1995, Bigfoot boasts the most features available in a forwarding account. You can't read your mail from Bigfoot's site. However, along with your address for life, your options range from simple forwarding of your Bigfoot mail to your main account, distribution over multiple accounts, or advanced filtering, to the Premium services: consolidation, reminders, anti-spam, virus protection, an auto-responder—even wireless email to alphanumeric pagers. Many of the premium services are currently free, though that may soon change. Additional features include a large searchable directory, classifieds, and "Bigfoot privacy."

Bigfoot does have a few glitches, however. I couldn't get my account up and running for more than a week, even after calling the support center. Additionally, the consolidation feature was somewhat inconsistent, though useful if you have an AOL account.

GoPlay (http://www.goplay.com)

GoPlay email is another web-based email account, with all the features of Hotmail (see below), but much quicker loading times and a more streamlined interface.

Hotmail (http://www.hotmail.com)

This web-based email account boasts all the features of a standard email client, including filters, folders, and HTML support. Unfortunately, it's also slow, and heavy on the hard sell. Hotmail allows you to load mail from a POP account to your Hotmail account (great if you're traveling), but the feature won't work if your POP account is behind a firewall.

Netscape WebMail (http://webmail.netscape.com)

As part of Netscape's Netcenter on the Web, Netscape offers web-based email accounts that are the best of the bunch. The interface is quick and intuitive, and you'll find features that some full-fledged POP mailers don't support. You'll find folders, address books, import utilities, stationery, HTML formatting, automatic responders, vacation replies, junk mail blockers, and more. Netscape even offers a free collection service, so that you can read all of your POP3 mail at their site—fantastic for travelers. This is the freemail account to beat.

RocketMail (http://www.rocketmail.com)

RocketMail's web-based email is highly recommended by some reliable sources. Features include filters, folders, rich multimedia support, and customized signatures. The site is supported by personalized advertising.

NetForward (http://www.netforward.com)

Unsurprisingly, NetForward supplies forwarding accounts. While it lacks the fancy features you'll find at Bigfoot, NetForward does allow you to choose your own address *and* domain name. Thus, you could be *cutie@pie.com*, for example. Additionally, all demographic information is optional, and more features are promised soon. Strangely, the password fields aren't protected, so you'll want to be very careful when using this service in public.

5Star Communications (http://www.5star.net)

5Star Communications offers graphically simple and thus refreshingly quick email accounts. You won't spend a lot of time on the sign-up process, either. My account was up and running within a matter of minutes. Netscape's Messenger interfaces with 5Star.

Juno (http://www.juno.com)

Juno is accessible with a personal computer and a modem, as well as with a copy of Juno's downloadable, free software. You'll also find Juno Gold and Juno Web for sending and receiving attachments and Internet access, respectively.

Net@ddress (http://www.netaddress.com)

This another graphically rich, slow-moving web-based email client. It provides a reminder service, so that you may send yourself messages as reminders for important events.

MailCity (http://www.mailexcite.com)

The sheer number of blinking ads may send you into a seizure, but otherwise this web-based email client is fairly quick moving. Features include signatures, POP settings, filters, and vacation reply. All messages include a tag line directing people to the service.

MailCity also offers something called "Bonusmail," where you reply to commercial email to win prizes. Be suspicious of such a messenger from spam heaven.

Other Internet Communications Tools

Email has become a ubiquitous means of business communication. However, it's not the only way to communicate via the Internet. Many people have turned to "chat" to keep in touch with loved ones or talk with others who share a special interest, like stalking David Duchovny. Somewhere in between lies instant messaging. Originated by the Unix program called "talk" and popularized by America Online, instant messaging allows people to write back and forth to each other instantaneously.

How is this different from sending email back and forth? It isn't, really. Most instant messaging programs open up a pane for each party to write in, easing the tremendous burden of opening and addressing new messages; the programs also alert you when a friend logs on so that you may pester that person immediately (see Figures 3-27 and 3-28).

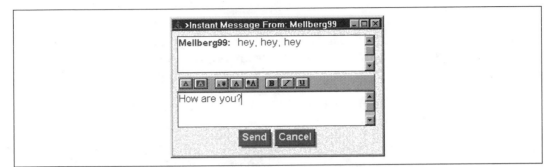

Figure 3-27. Communicating via instant messages using America Online

Figure 3-28. I have no friends

The problem with such programs is that they're still proprietary. In other words, you're only alerted about, and can only converse with, people using the same service.* AOL's seems to be the emerging standard; they even have two separate instant messaging programs: the one that is built-in to the online service, and a separate, standalone client for Internet users.

Many people work around the proprietary issue by subscribing to multiple services, using everything from AOL to ICQ to Unix *talk*. *talk* is, in many ways, the simplest application of the bunch. To begin speaking to another user, simply enter the command "talk," followed by the user's email address, at the prompt:

```
talk mugsy@ora.com
```

The program spawns a text window, and you and the other user can talk away. Use the command Ctrl-Z to return to the Unix prompt.

---

* At the time of this writing, a number of services either plan to allow users to converse with users on other services, or are suing for the right to do so.

Surviving Chat

—by Valerie Quercia

Facilities like email and Usenet news let people communicate asynchronously, which basically means there's waiting time involved. I send you a message, I wait, you read it, then you send me one, you wait, and so on. These kinds of exchanges have some obvious disadvantages, notably the delay involved and a lack of intimacy (somewhat related to the inexpressiveness of written communication in general).

But there are also a number of advantages, some obvious—it's cheap, you can talk to people between other tasks—and some more subtle: you can think about what you want to say, and think about it some more; you can keep records of what everyone is saying and trace the history of events; and messages are good reminders for what you are supposed to do.

In some cases, it's better for communications to happen in a more immediate fashion. The nerd classification for such interchanges is "real time." Online chat is not a new phenomenon or even a particularly original one. There have long been utilities that allow people to communicate with one another over a network in real time. Many Unix users are veterans of the *talk* program, which lets two people have a real-time conversation in a divided terminal window.

Internet Relay Chat (IRC) ups the ante to multiple people involved in a conversation in a virtual room known as a *channel*. There are thousands of chat channels out there, distributed on a variety of servers. Some have staying power, with a core of loyal participants, but many exist for only a few or even a single session.

Among serious computer users, chat gets little respect because it tends to attract people inclined toward sophomoric chatter rather than meaningful conversation. This is actually a polite characterization of the bulk of chat, which seems dominated by pornography pushers and (what a coincidence!) sex-obsessed teenagers.

To make matters worse, chat developers have gone the way of web developers in general. They've added graphical elements to chat programs simply because the Web supports such applications. Thus, there are a number of chat programs where participants are represented by a cartoon-like image of their own choosing. And because this is the computer world, such an image has to have a special name, which in this case is an *avatar*.

(The term "avatar" long precedes all things chatty. The meaning that most likely inspired this particular connotation is "an incarnation in human form" or possibly "an embodiment (as of a concept or philosophy) in a person.")

—continued—

A chat with these graphical elements looks entirely different than a conventional chat. In the latter, the text you enter is broadcast line by line, something like a teletype. In a more graphically based chat room, an image corresponds to each participant and what he says appears next to his avatar, often in a cartoon-style dialog bubble.

Now some people may be more inclined to have an online chat because they can be represented by a cartoon image, of say Dudley Doright, or maybe Cruella DeVil, or possibly an aardvark—but I am not one of them.

So, obviously, I am simply a trasher of chat, a buttoned-up, avatar-challenged square who would rather pick up the phone and call someone I know than trade online innuendoes with high school freshmen masquerading as Donald Duck.

But not so fast. Not only do I see value in chat, I am a regular participant. The sick-to-silly part of the chat spectrum gets the press, but in reality there are plenty of online chats in which the talk's the thing.

More and more commercial sites are sponsoring chats for people with real things to say. Many media entities are going this route. For instance, it's common for sports sites to run chat sessions with famous columnists or athletes. Chat is a cheap way for a bunch of fans to get together and share insights. Avatars generally play no part in such sessions.

You also don't have to rely on being on the receiving end of a chat session. IRC allows pretty much anyone to open a chat channel almost any time. While much of this is done in a free-for-all fashion, if you want to do some organizing, a chat session is an economical way to communicate with friends in distant places. It's not quite as good as being there or as using the phone—but at least you can get something of a party-line effect. Most any IRC server can provide the forum for one of these meetings. I must confess that I would be more inclined to run up my long-distance phone bill than go to the trouble of arranging a chat. But in leaner circumstances, a chat can definitely come in handy.

If you check out some of the channels active on a particular chat server at any given time, you may feel like you're drowning in a caldron of indigestible pabulum. It takes a little more boiling to find what's palatable in chat. Truth be told, you can actually be a thoughtful person with a heart and mind and soul and still get something out of chat. You just can't go dressed as a duck.[a]

---

[a] To learn more about IRC, see "A Short IRC Primer" at *http://www.irchelp.org/irchelp/ircprimer.html*. To learn more about web-based chat, see ZDNet's Chat 101 at *http://www.zdnet.com/products/chatuser/chat101.html*.

The catch, of course, is that your friend has to be sitting at a Unix machine when you try to reach him. This is the problem with most of these programs.

If you're interested in instant messaging, you'll probably want to use the same client used by the majority of your friends. Here are a few to check out. Since each is trying to become the dominant standard, most are free.

Netscape AOL Instant Messager
   http://www.newaol.com/aim/netscape/adb00.html

Yahoo! Pager
   http://pager.yahoo.com/pager/

ICQ
   http://www.icq.com/icqhomepage.html

PAL: Personal Access List
   http://talk.excite.com/communities/excite/pal/

Infoseek Instant Messaging
   http://www.peoplelink.com/v1/down_infoseek/

Spam Busting

Have you ever received an email message that looked like this?

```
*******************************************************************
Natural Alternative to Dangerous Weight Loss Drugs
*******************************************************************


Recent reports about serious side-effects and even deaths resulting from the use of the
latest "fad" weight loss prescription drugs are alarming. But many people want and need
help in dealing with unwanted extra pounds.
Now you can choose program that meets your weight loss goals, choose from an intensive or
gradual weight loss program that is as effective as the prescription drug regimens..
without any of the side effects. Weight loss proceeds naturally, without feelings of
depravation, depression and loss, increasing energy (without feeling the "jitters"),
increasing positive mood and self confidence, while naturally changing your appetite for
more healthy foods.

These are Homeopathic Medicinal Nutraceuticals, with ingredients that are registered with
the FDA, that work for you around the clock (24 hours), and have been used by thousands
of satisfied customers. All this with a no-risk money-back guarantee.
```

Perhaps you've been looking for some medicinal nutraceuticals, and would like to buy medical supplies from a company incapable of correct grammar. It's much more likely, however, that you find such missives tedious. Wading through five to ten per day becomes exceedingly time-consuming, and, if you're paying for connection time, expensive.

Such messages promoting weight loss, get-rich-quick schemes, and adult web sites are referred to on the Internet as *spam*, after a Monty Python skit in which a woman in a restaurant wants to order a dish without Spam, the food product, but can't. The characters end up singing in four-part harmony about Spam, as follows: "spam, spam, spam, spam." In other words, spam is ubiquitous and repetitive; you don't want it, but you can't not have it, much like unsolicited commercial email sent over the Internet.

Unfortunately, it's hard to stop spam. Email is a remarkably cheap way to advertise to a mass audience, as evidenced by the sheer amount of spam that sells means of spamming others. However, steps are being taken to combat spam. Congress is considering banning Internet junk mail, just as junk faxes were outlawed some years ago. Legislators are also considering forcing the spammers to label their messages as advertising, thus making them easy to filter out. While government intervention may seem appealing on the face of it, enforcement would be difficult. Moreover, most freespeech advocates don't want the U.S. government getting anywhere near the slippery slope of controlling content sent over the Internet.

Some, perhaps naively, believe that spammers are merely confused souls who think you really *want* to read their mail and send it to you not knowing any better. They have created opt-out lists on the Web, where you can sign up to not receive spam. One case in point is the Internet Email Marketing Council, or IEMMC, which was created in May 1997. The IEMMC's web site provided a "global remove list," which some of the most notorious spammers, including Cyber Promotions, Cybertize Email, Integrated Media Promotions Corp., Internet Savings Group, Quantum Communications, and Apex Global Internet Services, were to use to remove addresses from their databases. Unfortunately, those who participated received *more* spam, not less. By September of 1997, the IEMMC's web site barely functioned, and the group seems to have disbanded.

One popular reaction is to spam the spammers. Some techies will trace a message back to its source, then mail bomb the sender with messages every minute. While turnabout certainly feels like fair play, vigilantism in some sense adds to the problem of Internet junk mail, by increasing the amount of null traffic on the Net. However, some ISPs have been forced into anti-spam measures by such tactics.

Spam Avoidance

Keep in mind this simple rule: there's a fine line between clever and stupid. If you don't want unsolicited email, don't give out your email address! Many spammers buy lists of addresses from companies that use software robots to collect them from Usenet posts, mailing lists, web directories, and Internet access providers' member databases. You'll avoid a good deal of spam if you simply don't fill out web registration forms, surveys, etc., which seek to garner demographic data. If you do supply your address, read the fine print and look for an option not to receive mail as a result of the form submission. Select this option.*

---

* Unfortunately, doing so may have little or no effect. Many companies provide the option, but sell the marketing information anyway.

User profiles are another source for email addresses—particularly for America Online users (who should be sure to go to AOL keyword: marketing prefs, and instruct AOL not to send you marketing materials). Delete any information you may have there. Similarly, take a look at any email directories or white pages listings on the Internet (see Chapter 12 for a list). Request that they remove your information from their databases, then check back a week or so later to see that they actually did so. You may be surprised at how much of your personal information is available on the Net.

Mailing lists and Usenet postings are another treasure trove of addresses for the potential spammer. Check with your list administrator to make sure that anti-spamming policies are in place. When posting to newsgroups, alter your reply-to address, or use one of the software programs discussed later to disguise your address entirely.

Finally, never, never ever buy anything advertised in unsolicited commercial email. You're only encouraging the marketers to generate more junk mail.

Avoiding spam when posting to newsgroups and mailing lists

If you don't post articles to Usenet very often, there probably won't be too many spammers gleaning your address from this source. If you'd like to disguise your address so that robots can't figure it out, but people can, simply add a few nonsense symbols:

```
wendy@@ollie.com
```

Another method to avoid Usenet spammers is to post articles from a separate account or identity. Simply create a separate account and use that account only for posting to Usenet or mailing lists. Create a separate account by using one of the freemail accounts described previously, a separate AOL screen name, or a different Eudora "personality." Then, you can either never check mail from that address or automatically filter it into the trash.

Using an anonymous remailer is another solution. Anonymous remailers are the Witness Protection Program of the Internet: these organizations receive your mail, strip off any headers that reveal your identity, and forward the mail to the intended recipient. The remailer's return address is substituted for yours. Remailers offer various features, such as time delays, to further disguise the location of the original sender. To learn the latest news about anonymous remailers, take a look at the *alt.privacy.anon-server* newsgroup. The canonical list of anonymous remailers may be found at *http://www.cs. berkeley.edu/~raph/remailer-list.html*. See Chapter 5 for more information.

Rejecting spam

You may not be able to keep unsolicited mail from coming your way, but that doesn't mean you have to read it. In fact, you don't need to deal with it at all.

The first step is to talk to your system administrator or ISP. Find out whether anti-spam measures are already in place. Most big ISPs have some form of spam filter to at least cut down on the volume. Find out what your options are, and use what you can. If you're using AOL, be sure to turn on Preferred Mail, to filter out a list of blocked sites.

One note: while researching this book, I set up more than 10 different email accounts. About 90 percent of the unsolicited commercial mail I received came to the AOL address. If you dislike spam, or you're particularly disturbed by mail regarding adult sites, consider using a different ISP.

AOL is currently part of the problem when it comes to spam. They regularly sell subscriber information, and user profiles are a rich source for email addresses. However, they are taking steps to eradicate the problem. Recently, AOL actually took a spammer to court after receiving tens of thousands of complaints from users. Over the Air Equipment, Inc. sent these AOL users email advertising pornographic sites that included the AOL trademark and appeared to come from the online service itself. The company has threatened similar actions against other spammers.

One of the major problems with spam is the increased traffic it places on the Internet backbone, which is rapidly becoming overburdened. Moreover, once spam reaches its destination, the junk mail takes up server space and work time. Thus, you'll want to delete spam at the earliest point possible—preferably before it reaches your server. Good system administrators will use a set of filters with sendmail to reject spam before it even reaches the server. sendmail rejects mail that doesn't have a verifiable domain name or IP address; since many spammers use falsified addresses that can't be verified, this mail is rejected.

sendmail is notoriously complicated, however, and configuring should be left to system administrators. If you have access to a Unix mail server, you may be able to use a program called procmail to filter out spam before it reaches your machine. A discussion of procmail is beyond the scope of this book, but if you're desperate you might persuade a friendly sysadmin to help out.

When spam finds you

Even if you've taken all these precautions, spam may still reach you. What should you do? And how can you reduce spam on the Internet?

First, make sure that your mail client supports filters (discussed previously), and use them accordingly. Whenever you receive unwanted mail, place the sender's name in a filter that sends such mail to the trash. Whenever new spam arrives, add the sender's address to the filter rule. Take a look at the Netizens Against Gratuitous Spamming site (*http://www.nags.org*) for a list of frequent offenders. You may find, however, that entering all of these addresses is more trouble than simply deleting the spam as it arrives.

Next, forward the mail to your system administrator or ISP (usually, *postmaster@wherever.com*), and request that the address be placed in the system-wide filters. Additionally, look at the address's domain name and forward it to the spammer's ISP. If it comes from *aol.com*, forward the mail to *TOSspam@aol.com* (if the mailbox is full, try *TOSspam1@aol.com*, *TOSspam2@aol.com*, *TOSspam3@aol.com*, *TOSspam4@aol.com*, *TOSspam5@aol.com*, *TOSspam6@aol.com*, or *TOSspam7@aol.com*); from *compuserv.com*, mail it to *abuse@compuserv.com*. Also, take a look at the Anti-Spam Network at *http://www.tntcomtec.com/SPAM/*; a form on this site allows for spam submissions.

If you want to trace the message and send further complaints to the spammer's ISP, set your email client to show the message's full headers. The Reply-to address probably won't help you; spammers anticipate that you'll try to send them nasty replies. However, you can glean useful information from the postmarks in the headers. Take a look at the full header information on the following piece of spam:

```
Return-Path: ued9s7yg@fastgrowth.com
Received:  from rock.west.ora.com (rock.west.ora.com [207.25.97.8]) by rusty.ora.com (8.
6.13/8.6.11) with ESMTP id RAA26222 for <kiersten@rusty.ora.com>; Fri, 19 Sep 1997
17:43:44 -0400
From: ued9s7yg@fastgrowth.com
Received: from bftoemail3 (bftoemail3.bigfoot.com [209.1.135.193]) by rock.west.ora.com
(8.6.13/8.6.11) with SMTP id OAA11550 for <kiersten@oreilly.com>; Fri, 19 Sep 1997
14:44:02 -0700
Received: from bfmail2 (206.156.198.172) by bftoemail6.bigfoot.com (Bigfoot Toe Mail v1.
0) with message handle 970919_174343_2_bftoemail6_smtp; Fri,19 Sep 1997 17:43:43 Eastern
Daylight Time for kiersten@bigfoot.com
Received: from bfcons.bigfoot.com (209.1.135.132) by bfmail2.bigfoot.com (Bigfoot Toe
Mail v1.0) with message handle 970919_174330_0_bfmail2_smtp; Fri, 19 Sep 1997 17:43:30
Eastern Daylight Time for kiersten@bigfoot.com
Received: from americaonline.aol.com [198.81.28.20] by bfcons.bigfoot.com with Bigfoot
for <kiersten@bigfoot.com>; Fri, 19 Sep 97 21:35:39 -000
Received: from mrin39.mail.aol.com (mrin39.mx.aol.com [198.81.19.149]) by air01.mx.aol.
com (V32) with SMTP; Sat, 06 Sep 1997 16:25:18 -0400
Received: from eighteen86andfifty ([208.18.86.50]) by mrin39.mail.aol.com (8.8.5/8.8.5/
AOL-4.0.0) with SMTP id QAA22128; Sat, 6 Sep 1997 16:22:14 -0400 (EDT)
Date: Sat, 6 Sep 1997 16:22:14 -0400 (EDT)
Message-ID: <199709062022.QAA22128@mrin39.mail.aol.com>
To:                kierstie@aol.com
Subject:           The Clock is Ticking......
 X-Bigfoot-Message: 22002738-38
Status:
X-Mozilla-Status: 2001
45,000,000+ EMAIL ADDRESSES
                    ******* $279.00 *******
*** See below on how to get'm for FREE if you act now!! But  hurry, the clock is ticking.
....
MILLIONS AND MILLIONS OF EMAIL ADDRESSES
```

If you send a reply to *ued9s7yg@fastgrowth.com*, the message bounces back and only increases everyone's annoyance. However, if you read through the "received" headers from top to bottom, it's easy to determine that the message actually came from an AOL address. Take a look:

The message from:

```
ued9s7yg@fastgrowth.com
```

was delivered to:

```
rock.west.ora.com by rusty.ora.com  for
<kiersten@rusty.ora.com>
```

and received:

```
from bftoemail3  by
rock.west.ora.com for
<kiersten@oreilly.com>
```

and received:

```
from bfmail2  by bftoemail6.bigfoot.com for kiersten@bigfoot.com
```

and received:

```
from bfcons.bigfoot.com  by bfmail2.bigfoot.com
```

and received:

```
from americaonline.aol.com by bfcons.bigfoot.com with
Bigfoot for <kiersten@bigfoot.com>
```

and received:

```
from mrin39.mail.aol.com by
air01.mx.aol.com (V32) with SMTP
```

and received:

```
from eighteen86andfifty ([208.18.86.50]) by mrin39.mail.aol.com with SMTP
Message-ID: <199709062022.QAA22128@mrin39.mail.aol.com>
To: kierstie@aol.com
Subject: The Clock is Ticking......
```

The mail was sent from *mrin39.mail.aol.com* to *kierstie@aol.com*. It was picked up from AOL via my Bigfoot account, which then forwarded the mail to my O'Reilly address. The spam thus made it through a total of four filters (AOL's, Bigfoot's, O'Reilly's, and my PC's) intact. Now, however, I know to forward the message, and a complaint, to AOL.

One more thing about the previous example: had you been willing to wade through the promises of unforeseen riches, you'd find the following at the end:

```
NOTE: We have many products and services in which we think you
might have an interest.  However, if you never want to hear from us
again, send an email to:  REMOVE@MAILOUT.COM  and you will
promptly be removed. *DO NOT REPLY* to this email to get removed
as the system cannot remove you.
```

Whether taking this action will reduce your portion of junk email is unclear. Responding to such offers from unreliable sources has never been shown to prevent your inclusion on spammers' address lists. Notice that the message actually offers to remove you—not to remove your address from a mailing list.

Finally, use your Delete key liberally! It's generally easy to recognize spam from the sender and subject line of the message (see Figure 3-29).

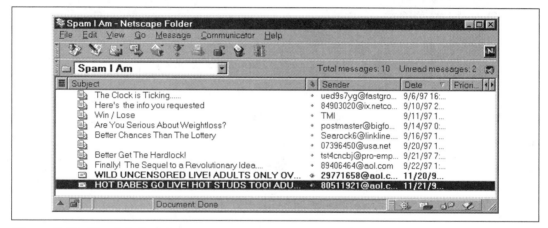

Figure 3-29. Chock full o' spam

Spam-fighting software

A number of shareware and freeware tools exist to help in the fight against spam, particularly for those using POP clients. Some of the most useful tools come with lists of known spammers and check your incoming mail against them. They also save you time and money by downloading only the headers to your machine, and allowing you to delete the mail from the server there, instead of after you've downloaded the entire message. Tools to fight back also exist, in the form of automatic responders, utilities to fake bounced messages, and anonymous remailers to keep your address private. See the Resource Catalog for a listing of sites from which software may be downloaded.

CHAPTER FOUR

WORLD WIDE WEB
BROWSING

The World Wide Web, or WWW, is the most popular, powerful, and easily navigable portion of the Internet. The Web is based on a technology called *hypertext*, which allows documents to be connected, or linked, to one another. When you are viewing a document that contains these links, you can view any of the connected documents simply by clicking the appropriate link. Linked documents on the Web are stored on host computers spread throughout the Internet; the Web lets you navigate the Internet by following such links.

The Web is also the fastest growing information service on the Internet. Since the first publicly available web servers appeared in early 1993, the number of sites providing information over the Web has grown exponentially. In October 1993, there were just over 500 WWW sites; today, there are over two million.

The World Wide Web originated at CERN, the European Particle Physics Laboratory, but it would be a mistake to see the Web as a tool designed by and for physicists. Tim Berners-Lee, an Oxford University graduate who came to CERN with a background in text processing and real-time communications, wanted to create a new kind of information system with which researchers could collaborate and exchange information during the course of a project. Berners-Lee used hypertext technology to link together a web of documents that could be traversed in any manner to seek out information. This web does not imply a hierarchical tree, which is the structure of most books, nor a simple ordered list. In essence, it allows many possible relations between any individual document and others. Berners-Lee implemented hypertext as a navigation system, allowing users to move freely from one document to another on the Net, regardless of where the documents are located.

There were many implementations of hypertext systems before the World Wide Web. What Berners-Lee did, in cooperation with others at CERN, was define an Internet-based architecture using open, public specifications and free sample implementations. Because the specifications are public, anyone can build a web client or server. Because there are sample implementations and the code can be obtained for free, developers can choose to build or refine parts of the system. Both factors encourage other people to contribute to the project, and as is true of many things on the Internet, the WWW effort has turned into a collaborative project involving people and organizations from around the world. Netscape's decision, in 1998, to open up its code has continued this trend.

To navigate the Web, you need a web client (more commonly called a browser). A WWW browser interprets and displays hypertext documents; it knows how to find and display a document pointed to by a link. The first WWW browser was a line-mode browser implemented by the team at CERN. However, it was Mosaic, a browser developed at the National Center for Supercomputing Applications (NCSA), located at the University of Illinois at Urbana-Champaign, that took the Internet community by storm, and is in large part responsible for the tremendous initial growth of the Web. Mosaic is the direct ancestor of both Netscape Navigator and Microsoft Internet Explorer.

A Browsing Primer

Today, a browser lets you access different sites on the Net and display their offerings on your own computer. You visit a site by supplying the browser with an address, or *uniform resource locator* (URL). At that address is a file, or document, that you can view in the browser's main window. For you to see the document, the browser makes a copy of it on your local computer by *downloading* the file.

Browsers are intended primarily to allow you access to resources on the World Wide Web—the hypertext files discussed earlier. However, you can, and frequently will, use a browser to access other types of file systems. The Internet (and browser technology) has progressed to the point that you're unlikely to realize when you've left the WWW.

The two most well-known browsers, Netscape Navigator (properly called Navigator, but more frequently referred to as Netscape) and Microsoft Internet Explorer (frequently referred to as MSIE, IE, or Explorer), are a little bit like Pepsi and Coke: they dominate the market, but actually aren't your only choices. However, both are free and packed with features. Most computers come with a browser already installed: the iMac ships with both Navigator and IE, and you'll find IE bundled with Windows 95/98 and Windows NT. So, if you're just starting out on the Web, don't worry about which browser you're using. Try whatever you have around.

Every browser displays a document from the Internet on your computer screen in a similar manner. Like any window-based program, a browser has a number of features—buttons, menus, scrollbars, etc.—that let you control its operation. Depending on the browser you choose, there may be superficial differences in the way displayed documents look. Having a more recent version of a browser is much more significant than the particular browser you choose. Since the technologies involved in publishing information over the Net are constantly changing, your browser has to keep pace.

So double-click that browser icon, and we'll get started.*

Home Pages

The first time you open your browser, you see your current *home page*. A home page (or *start page,* as some sites have begun to call them) is the hypertext document that your browser specifies as the first to load when the application is launched. (The term "home page" is also used to refer to the primary document about any subject or person.) Explorer is frequently set to display Microsoft's home page, shown in Figure 4-1.

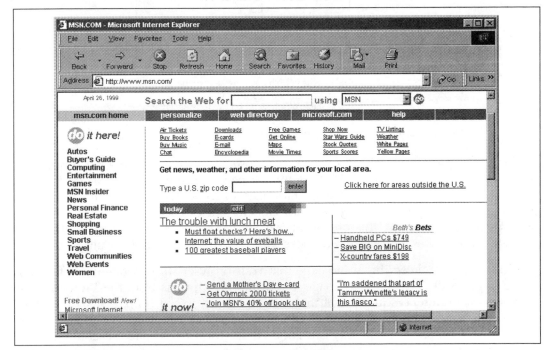

Figure 4-1. The Microsoft home page

The underlined text provides links to other hypertext documents. To distinguish textual links from plain text, the browser highlights the text by underlining it (or, in other cases, making it a different color). More tellingly, when you pass the cursor over a

---

* If you've never used the Internet before, you may need to buy and install a modem, and then create an account with an Internet service provider. This book presumes that you're already connected. However, if you're sitting in front of a brand-new computer, we'll say this: the iMac ships with an Ethernet card and Earthlink (a popular ISP) software built-in, and most PCs ship with internal modems and Internet software (Windows 98 has a folder called Online Services that contains software for AOL, ATT Worldnet Service, CompuServe, Prodigy Internet, and the Microsoft Network). These programs should contain enough information to get you started.

link, it becomes a hand and the URL that the text links to is displayed in the bottom pane of the browser. Click the link, and your browser displays the indicated page. Images may be used as links, as well. As you can see, it's easy to navigate from one page to another by clicking the links. Use the browser's **Back** button, in the upper left-hand corner, to return to pages you saw before.

As an example, let's look at Microsoft's home page (*http://www.microsoft.com*). When you place the cursor over the **Edit** buttons, a message pops up, as in Figure 4-2. These pop-up messages are called *mouse-overs* and are frequently used to help navigation.

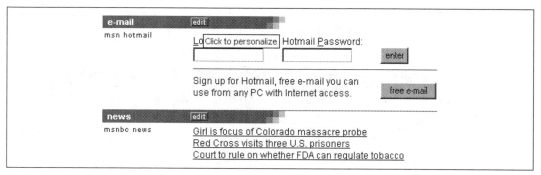

Figure 4-2. Personalizing Microsoft's home page

Clicking this specialized link allows you to choose a Zip Code for weather reports and move the location of that report up or down the page. Once you do so, Microsoft's web site places a *cookie*—a small packet of information accessible by Microsoft's server—on your hard drive. That way, whenever you launch your browser, it checks the information you're interested in ("this user wants box scores for these teams, weather for this Zip Code, and prices on these three stocks") and downloads it automatically.

You don't have to keep the home page that your browser ships with—or, in fact, any home page at all. To change the page, open **Internet Options** from the **View** menu in Explorer, or **Preferences** in the **Edit** menu in Navigator. Excite (*http://www.excite.com*) and Yahoo! (*http://www.yahoo.com*) both support home pages that you can customize. Any page you visit frequently is a good choice for a home page. It could even be a page on your local hard drive. See Chapter 9 for information on creating your own home page.

Entering URLs by Hand

Just as you need an email address so that people can communicate with you, files on the Internet need an address so that people can access them. A file's address is more formally known as its URL (Universal Resource Locator). While this is not the friendliest name, the Internet addressing system is simpler than the term suggests.

Even if you're a complete computer novice, you've undoubtedly seen some Internet addresses on billboards, in print ads, and on television. Many organizations, especially in the media, make themselves accessible via email and the Web. As a matter of fact, if you've seen a television program recently, they've probably closed with an arcane list of symbols beginning with the letters "http://www." This is the address of their web site; "http" stands for "hypertext transfer protocol," the technology behind the Web. The "www" is obvious. A TV show's web address would probably then give the name of its program, followed by the suffix ".com"—which indicates that they are a commercial enterprise.

This sort of naming scheme may sound complicated, but it quickly becomes second nature. Any time you see a URL you want to access, simply enter it in the text box on your browser labeled Netsite (Navigator) or Address (Explorer). You don't even need to enter the "http://"; your browser assumes it. After you type in the address, press Enter, and your browser accesses the page.

Hypertext URLs are the most common, but there are other types you can enter. If you'd like to use your browser as an anonymous FTP client, enter the address of the FTP site, preceded by the string "ftp://". For example, to access the popular shareware site Walnut Creek CD-ROM, you would enter the following line in the Address box:

```
ftp://ftp.cdrom.com/
```

As you start to enter a URL into the location bar, the browser tries to complete it for you. Netscape highlights what it thinks the URL will be, while Explorer provides a drop-down list of possible matches. Either press the Enter key (Netscape) or select a URL from the list (Explorer) to complete the URL and save yourself some typing.

If you enter a string that isn't a URL into the location box, one of two things can happen. Netscape automatically appends "www." on one end, and ".com" on the other. Explorer, however, transfers the term to the Microsoft Network's Autosearch feature and displays the results in the left-hand pane. You can turn this feature off, or tinker with it, by accessing **Tools** → **Internet Options...** → **Advanced** → **Search** from the address bar. On its face, this is a handy feature and you probably want to keep it, but if you like quick shortcuts, Netscape's solution is a time saver. The choice depends on your browsing style.

One more thing to keep in mind: while an address ending in *.com, .edu,* or *.org* is probably safe, there are some URLs you *don't* want to enter manually. If the URL has the term "cgi" at the end, it accesses a *Common Gateway Interface*, and is probably used to transmit a form that you have filled out to a server. Entering it in the address bar will likely result in an error.

Frames

Sometimes, web pages are actually comprised of two, three, or four documents laid out side by side. Each individual document, since each has its own URL, is called a *frame*. Frames may be used to create a table of contents effect, so that a list of links remains visible while other page content changes, or as a link to the referring site.

The URL that you see in the location box in Figure 4-3 actually refers to neither frame. Instead, it refers to a separate HTML document that loads both frames, but doesn't appear, per se, in the browser window. If you'd like to bookmark a specific portion of the content (in this example, the glossary term), place the cursor within that frame, right-click, and choose **Add Bookmark** from the pop-up menu.

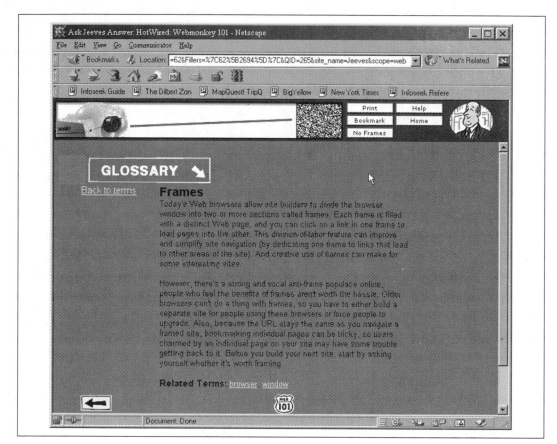

Figure 4-3. A document that uses frames

Channels

Some web sites or content providers organize their information into subject areas that they call *channels*. The concept can be confusing, since the push technologies generally use the term to describe their content, and much of the hype around channels implies that they are more fixed than standard web pages.* Channels are merely subject

---

* In my opinion, channels are merely another attempt by marketing departments to morph the Web into something it's not, but *is* something that the supposedly dumb-as-a-post American public will better understand and therefore throw money at. So, what do the marketers try to make the Web look like? Television!

areas. Don't think that a browser, search engine, or online service provides something special if it comes in a channel (or a "zone" or a "web guide," for that matter).

So, if you come across information in a channel, access it the way you normally would, by clicking links and reading documents.

Document Management

Now that you've clicked around and explored a little, you may be wondering how to manage all the information that is at your fingertips. Literally billions of documents exist on the Web, many of which contain information you want or need. Pages full of vital information are much more useful when they're organized and easily accessible. Thus, in the coming pages you'll find information on bookmarking, searching, saving, printing, and editing the documents you find on the Web.

Bookmarking Documents

A link that you want to catalog for future reference is called a *bookmark*. Once you've found a document you might want to view again, bookmark it by choosing **Add Bookmark** from the **Bookmarks** menu (Netscape), or **Add to Favorites...** from the **Favorites** menu (Explorer), as shown in Figure 4-4.

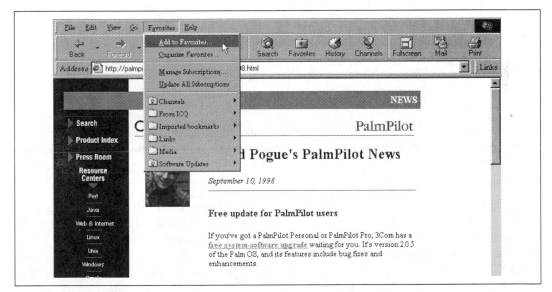

Figure 4-4. Adding a bookmark to the Favorites menu

Once you've added the bookmark, it appears at the bottom of the **Bookmarks** or **Favorites** menu. To return to a bookmarked page, simply click on its entry in the menu.

If you're using Explorer, there's an additional feature you should be aware of. If you click the **Favorites** icon on the toolbar, the Favorites folders are listed in the browser's left-hand pane, while the page content appears on the right (see Figure 4-5). This may be useful if you spend a lot of time bouncing between pages.

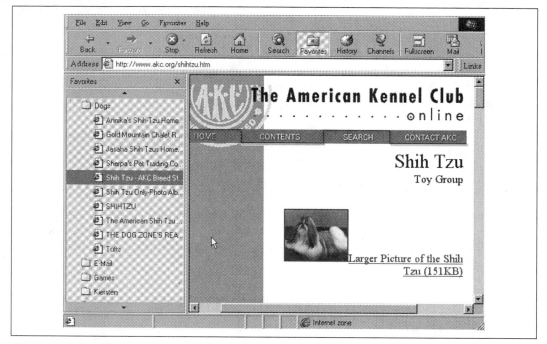

Figure 4-5. Another way to access bookmarks

Editing bookmarks

As you can imagine, adding bookmarks to an unorganized list becomes unwieldy pretty quickly. Thankfully, you can edit your bookmarks so that they're filed neatly into folders. To do so, select **Edit Bookmarks** from the **Bookmarks** menu, or **Organize Favorites** from the **Favorites** menu. You'll see a window like the one in Figure 4-6.

If you're using Netscape, you can create new folders, name them, and drag your bookmarks into them. You can also import bookmarks from another user or program. Should a bookmark change, select it in the Edit Bookmarks window, then choose **Bookmark Properties** from the **Edit** menu. Change the URL in the dialog box. Any changes you make are saved to a file on your hard drive called *C:\Program Files\ netscape\users\your_name\bookmark.htm*.

Explorer's Organize Favorites window offers fewer options. You can move, rename, or delete files. You can also create a new folder by clicking the **Create New Folder** icon in the upper right of the window.

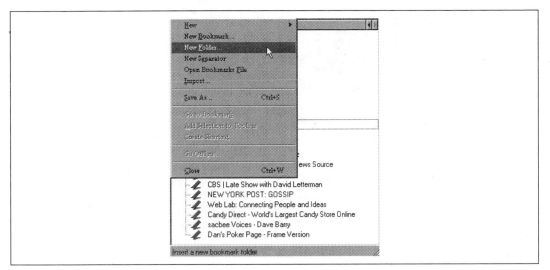

Figure 4-6. Navigator's window for editing bookmarks

Filing bookmarks

When you add a bookmark, you don't have to do so indiscriminately. Instead of adding the link to your general bookmarks, you can file it directly to the folder in which you'd like to keep it.

If you're using Netscape, load the page you want to bookmark, select **File Bookmark** from the **Bookmarks** menu, and choose the appropriate folder from the drop-down list. (If you want to file the bookmark in a new folder, you'll need to use the **Edit Bookmarks** feature first.)

If you're using Explorer, select **Add to Favorites**, then click the **Create in>>** button, as in Figure 4-7.

In the Create in: field, you see a list of folders, and you can double-click the folder when you want to file the bookmark. You can also click the **New Folder** button to file the bookmark into a new directory. Ignore the "Make available offline" option right now; we'll discuss it later in the chapter. When you install IE, the installation wizard gives you the option of importing bookmarks, but you don't have that opportunity once installation is complete. If you'd like to import bookmarks from Netscape or another program, you'll have to open the file *C:\windows\favorites* on your hard drive and muck around with it by hand.

Netscape's Personal Toolbar folder

Netscape Navigator offers one further bookmarking option: the Personal Toolbar. This is a list of links that appear just above the main browser window, ready for easy access, as shown in Figure 4-8.

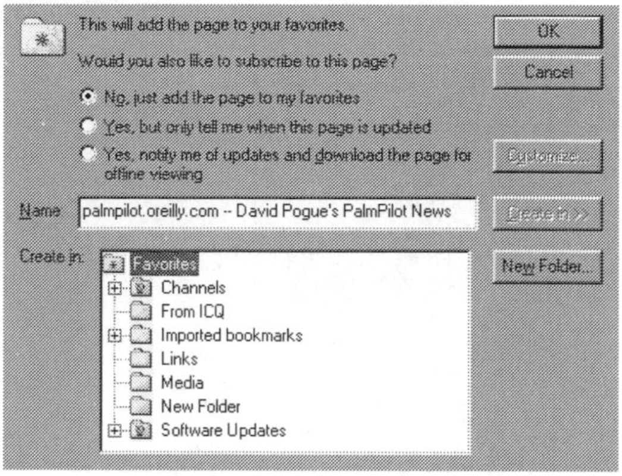

Figure 4-7. Filing bookmarks in Explorer

Figure 4-8. Netscape's personal bookmarks

If you'd like bookmarks to appear in this toolbar, file them in the Personal Toolbar folder. Netscape ships with this folder pre-installed. You can also delete or rename bookmarks that are already in this file at your discretion.

Updating bookmarks

If you browse frequently, you may end up with tons of bookmarks nested in multiple folders. If you don't want to view those web sites until the content there has changed, your browser can check the site for you so you don't have to wait for the entire page to load.

To update bookmarks using Netscape, choose **Edit Bookmarks** from the **Bookmarks** menu. Then, select **Update Bookmarks** from the **View** menu. Netscape quickly scans for updated bookmarks, indicating sites that have changed with an equals sign. Unreachable sites are indicated with a question mark. (The bookmarks aren't actually modified, so the menu is misnamed.)

Explorer version 5.0 lacks an updating feature. If you're using Explorer version 4.*x*, however, click the **Subscribe** button when adding a Favorite, as in Figure 4-9.

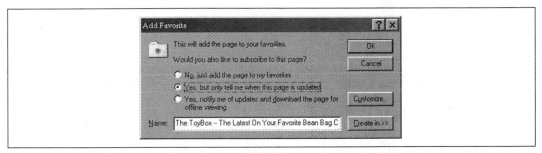

Figure 4-9. Subscribing to a web site

Now, when the site is modified, IE alerts you, either by adding a red "gleam" to the site's icon, or by sending you an email message (select which one by clicking the **Customize...** button). You may also update all of your subscribed sites by selecting **Update All Subscriptions** from the **Favorites** menu.

Viewing and Using the History List

A browser's history file is a listing of every document visited over a specified interval (usually the last 10 to 20 days). You can view this file by selecting **Tools** from Netscape's **Communicator** menu, or by pressing Explorer's **History** button on the toolbar. Explorer's history file, shown in Figure 4-10, is easier to access, as the browser places it in the left-hand pane and organizes the resources by week. Both Netscape version 4.5 and Explorer version 5.0 vastly improved their history lists by making them searchable, allowing you to find cached documents quickly.*

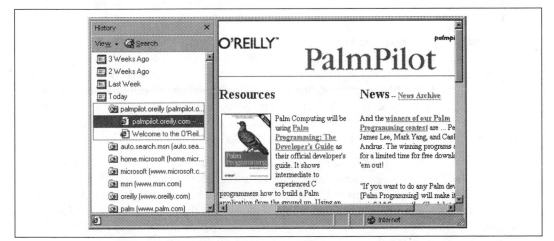

Figure 4-10. Explorer's history file

---

* Searchable history lists are a particularly valuable tool for anxious parents. If you aren't sure what your kid is doing online, browse the history list, or search for the specific term you're concerned about.

How I Chose a College Online

—by Molly Krol

There are about 2,800 four-year colleges in the United States. I took the PSAT and the PLAN tests early in my junior year and was flooded with information from what seemed like everyone. I needed to cut the number down and, eventually, get accepted to at least one college. I used the Internet to do this.

My use of the Internet started not with looking for colleges, but looking at the SAT and ACT tests. Most high schools offer you a chance to take the tests once, but if you either can't make the date or want to take them a second time, you're on your own. The testing organizations let you find test dates and locations, and sign up over the Internet. All you have to do is go to their web sites at *http:// www.collegeboard.org* for the SAT and *http://www.act.org* for the ACT.

I decided that I probably wanted to attend a smaller, private liberal arts school. My father suggested using the Internet to find the college I wanted. I first tried using Yahoo!, which divides web sites by simple categories. I clicked on **Education**, then **Universities**, then **United States** and got a listing of hundreds of schools. This is a great place to start if you don't really know what you want or if you already have particular colleges in mind. If you want to find schools that meet your specific criteria, try College Edge at *http://www.collegeedge.com*. College Edge is a web site that offers a chance to search for the best colleges for you, based on information that you give. All it asks you to do is register with a name and password, and you have free access to its services. I could enter information about the location, size, majors offered, and extracurricular activities offered for the type of college I wanted to attend.

From that information, the site gave me a list of about 75 colleges that met my criteria with links to their web sites and a brief overview of each. From that list, I narrowed my choices down to about 10 schools. I visited their web sites and even emailed some of the admissions offices. I also received email from students at various schools. One reason I chose to go to a small school was because I wanted to participate in intercollegiate athletics. Many of the schools offered rosters, schedules, and other information about their sports teams on their web sites.

College web sites often offer other information about topics such as student life, financial aid, admissions, news and events, email address locators, and departmental information. Sometimes these web sites also have virtual tours that show you around the campus and have lots of pictures, so that you get a good feel for the place. Some schools I visited gave you the chance to apply over the Internet. I used the service offered by Washington University in St. Louis (*http://www.wustl. edu*). That school allowed me to submit the first part of my application online. The admissions office then mailed the second part to my house through the mail.

—*continued*—

Once I chose Luther College (*http://www.luther.edu/luther.htm*) as my number one choice, my parents, having never heard of it, checked out Luther's web site. They looked at faculty web pages and found information about programs of study. When I decided to make that all-important college visit, we made some of the arrangements through email. My parents used an Internet map service (*http://www.mapquest.com*) to plan the trip and another web site, *http://www.switchboard.com,* to look for hotels in the area, because they assumed a town the size of Decorah, IA (population 8,000) would not have its own web page. Little did they know that while I was looking at Luther's web site to see what was happening during the time I planned to be there, I found a link to a Decorah home page.

I guess I'd have to say my experience was typical. If you start at the school you should be able to find web sites with information about the surrounding community as well. When I started talking private school, my parents started worrying about financial aid. Most of the college web pages I looked at had sections on Financing Your Education that had links to all the right places. The two that seemed most useful and were the FAFSA and the FinAid sites. You can find the FAFSA application (Free Application For Federal Student Aid), which you used to have to file on paper, but can now be filed over the Web, at *http://www.fafsa.ed.gov*. This web site is the starting point for getting any kind of federal aid you might qualify for. The other site is FinAid (*http://www.finaid.org*), which has links to other scholarship opportunities and calculation programs.

Once I was accepted to Luther and had made campus visits, I emailed the basketball coach to let her know that I was interested in playing there. I could also email the admissions office or student ambassadors to discuss any questions or concerns I had about Luther. Most schools have people willing to talk to you through email. Many schools have general email directories available from their web pages. This way, if you know someone attending the school, you can look up her address and get the inside story. The Internet helped me narrow down the choices and find the college that was right for me. It also allowed my parents to see where they were sending me to spend the next four years of my life. I recommend looking for colleges over the Internet. Now, if only high school were over . . .

Forward and Back buttons

Here's something I swore I'd never do: tell people how to use the **Back** button on their browsers. But, if you'd like to access the document you accessed prior to the one you're currently viewing, click the **Back** button! Once you've gone back, if you'd like to move forward again, click the **Forward** button! Using this method is a lot faster than re-entering the URL.

Now, here's the tricky part: the **Forward** and **Back** buttons have hidden features! If you click the small arrow to the right of the **Back** (or **Forward**) button on Explorer, or you hold down Netscape's **Back** (or **Forward**) button without releasing the mouse button, a list of the documents you've visited drops down. Select the document you want from the list.

Searching Within a Document

Some documents may be quite long, and sometimes you're searching for a very specific piece of information. As with a word processor, you can use the **Find** command to ferret out specific strings of text. Both Netscape and Explorer include the **Find** command in the **Edit** menu.

After you select the **Find** command, type the text string you're looking for into the text box. No matter where you place the cursor, you have two options for a starting point: the top of the page, or the bottom. Select the check box that indicates your preference. If capitalization is important, select the "Match Case" checkbox. If you're using Explorer, you can also choose to search for the entire word. (If you'd like to search for an entire word with Netscape, enter a space before and after the word.) Click the **Find Next** button once you've chosen the correct options. The browser locates your string and highlights it. To continue searching, press **Find Next** again.

Once you've finished the search, you can use Netscape's **Find Again** command to automatically perform a search for the same string.

Saving and Printing

There may be pages that you access frequently and take a long time to load, or pages that you want to save for future reference—a newspaper article, for example, that may not be accessible after a few days. Therefore, you may want to save them to your hard drive for easier access. Saving a web page to your system is as easy as selecting **Save As** from the **File** menu. Explorer gives you the option of saving the document as text or HTML; Netscape saves only HTML. Performing this kind of save preserves *only* the HTML content of a page, however; if you want to view the images later, you'll need to right-click (see the next section) each one and save those, too.

To print a file, choose **Print** from the **File** menu. Selecting **Page Setup** from the **File** menu allows you to specify a few additional printing options, including margins, orientation, and the inclusion of such information as URL and page numbering in headers and footers. In general, if you're printing a page that includes frames, the entire document will print. In some cases, however, you need to click within a particular frame to print it. If you're using Netscape, and you'd like to see how many pages are in a document and how they'll print, select **Print Preview** from the **File** menu.

Editing

Sometimes, you'll want to use the information you find on a web page. You can perform the following editing functions:

- Select text with the cursor for copying.

- Choose **Select All** from the **File** menu for copying.

- Choose **Edit Page** from the **File** menu (Netscape) or **Page** from the **Edit** menu (Explorer) to edit the entire document in an HTML editor. See Chapter 9 for more information.

Note that you can't edit a web page from within a browser window. You'll have to open the page in an HTML editor, or copy the information to a text or graphics editor, before you can modify it.

The Right-Click Menu

If you want quick access to many of the functions described in this section, Netscape and Explorer provide pop-up menus that you can access by right-clicking a document or image. Figures 4-11 and 4-12 show these menus.

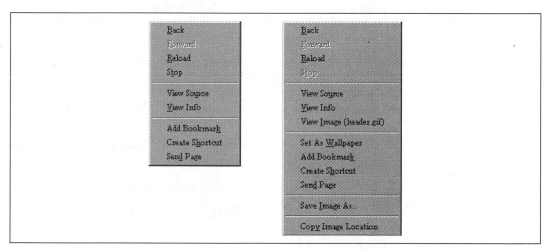

Figure 4-11. Netscape's right-click document menu and right-click image menu

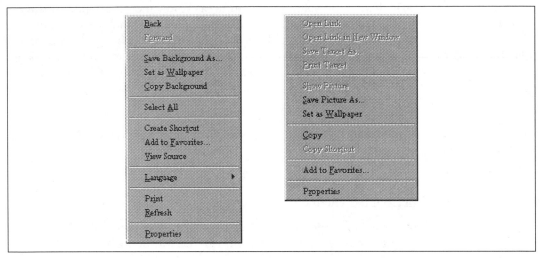

Figure 4-12. Explorer's right-click document menu and right-click image menu

A few notes on right-click menu options:

- If you right-click on a document within a frame, the pop-up menu will also provide the option of viewing the frame in a new window. Frames are sometimes easier to view *without* their surrounding frames. To do so, place the cursor within the frame you want to view, and select **View Frame in New Window**.

- Reload a document whenever you think its contents may have changed, after a server error, or when an image was unable to load.

- IE's **Create Shortcut** is distinct from Netscape's **Add Bookmark** in that it creates a shortcut on your desktop. When you double-click that shortcut, it launches your default browser and loads the page you've specified.

- The **Set as Wallpaper** option allows you to specify the image you're viewing as the background for your Windows desktop.

- Netscape's **Copy Image Location** and IE's **Copy Shortcut** options mean that the browser copies the URL of the image, rather than the image itself.

- Netscape's **Send Page** option opens a mail composition window with the URL of the current page pasted into the body of the message.

By this point, you know how to browse the Web. It's pretty simple, really, but there's more to browsing the Web than simple navigation.

Security

Security is an issue when browsing the Web. There are two important categories for security settings on your browser: settings for cookies, which are a potential security *threat*, and settings for certificates, which are meant to increase your *sense* of security.

Cookies

A *cookie* is a small piece of information shared between your browser and the server that placed the information on your hard drive. Basically, a cookie retains information about how you feel about the particular site you're visiting: whether you've specified any special settings, security features, saved your username or password, or shopping options. Each time you visit a site after specifying options, your browser sends the cookie back to the site's server.

For the most part, the use of cookies is relatively harmless. They're used to make your browsing more efficient. However, if you're concerned about someone keeping tabs on you via accessible information on your hard drive, you can either turn off cookies entirely, or delete selected cookies from your cookies file. You can also use software tools to accept or reject specified cookies.

Specify your cookie options in either the Preferences or Internet Options dialog box. The setting I'd recommend is "Accept only cookies that get sent back to the originating server" on Netscape and "Prompt before accepting cookies" on IE. See Chapter 5 for a more thorough discussion of the topic.

Certificates

Recently, encrypted web sites have begun using certificates to verify themselves as genuine. A certificate is a digital identification document that includes a public key, the name of the entity it identifies, an expiration date, the name of the Certificate Authority (CA) that issued the certificate, the digital signature of the CA, and a serial number.

When you enter a secure web page, as indicated by the padlock in the lower left corner of your browser, the server sends its certificate to you. The browser displays the certificate and asks for your approval. Most users just click **OK**. That's pretty safe if you're familiar with the site. If you are using some strange site for the first time, make sure that the name on the certificate is what you think it should be, and that the certificate authority is one of the well-known authorities (like VeriSign or Thawte). If it doesn't check out, think twice about giving the site any sensitive information.

If you'd like to get fancy, you can specify providers to accept content from without seeing a warning. If you're using Netscape, access that provider's certificate (**Communicator → Tools → Security Info**). Next, select the appropriate certificate, and click the

Edit button. You may now specify whether you want to always accept the certificate provider for:

- Accessing network sites
- Certifying email users
- Certifying software developers
- Be warned before sending data to the provider

Microsoft provides an "Always trust content from" check box when it displays a security warning (see below). Unfortunately, you can only access this option when that warning is displayed.

Plug-Ins

A number of new tools have emerged to make browsing a safer, faster experience than may be offered by browsers alone. As we described earlier, browsers were originally designed to display two types of files: text and graphics. Today, browsers can access and display every file type an overpaid software engineer can dream up. As a result, helper applications have been designed to work with your browser, running so that, for example, you can view a streaming media file within a web page, instead of having to download the media file and launch a separate application to view it.

The terminology of plug-ins may be a little confusing. Netscape calls helper applications *plug-ins*, and this has become the most frequently used term. Microsoft, however, used to call helper applications *ActiveX controls* for reasons I don't think anyone was ever entirely clear on. ActiveX fell by the wayside, partially because of potentially disastrous security concerns. Now, Microsoft seems to have decided that helper applications are *just* applications, since they want Internet Explorer to take over the computer's operating system, anyway. Although Microsoft appears to have dropped the ActiveX name, the technology remains the same.

Perhaps as a result of this confusion, many people fear plug-ins. How do you use them? What do they do, where do you find them, and if they don't work, how do you uninstall them?

Plug-ins are nothing to get excited about. They're just software applications, like any other you might use on your computer. It just so happens that some—like the Real-Player, for example—open automatically when you click a link to an appropriate file and display that file without (necessarily) launching another application for you to control. To find out which Netscape plug-ins you have installed, select **About Plug-ins** from the **Help** menu. Selecting **Internet Options...** from the **View** menu allows you to set a few specifications in IE.

Thus, installing, removing, and paying for helper applications takes place on a case-by-case basis. Some require payment, others don't. Some spawn a separate user interface, others don't. You don't need to worry about finding plug-ins, either: plug-ins will find you. When you access a web page or file that requires a plug-in, your browser displays a message telling you which application you need and asks whether you'd like to download it. Follow the instructions on your screen to do so. (See Chapter 13 for more information.) If, later, you decide you don't want the plug-in, uninstall it. Use the Windows Uninstall feature, just as you would any other application.

Three Plug-Ins You Need

As I just said, you don't need to run right out and install a bunch of plug-ins as soon as you've finished installing your browser. Nonetheless, let's take a look at three of the most popular plug-ins and where to find them. Each one makes a large contribution to the accessibility of information you'll find on the Web.

The RealPlayer from Progressive Networks (*http://www.real.com/products/playerplus/index.html*) plays live audio and video files with near-CD quality sound. This is one of the most prevalent sound formats on the Internet.

Macromedia's Shockwave player allows you to see complicated animations and to play games within the browser window. Visit *http://www.macromedia.com/shockwave/download/* to download it.

The Adobe Acrobat reader is the preferred format for all sorts of formatted files on the Web, including IRS forms, newspaper front pages, and more. See *http://www.adobe.com/supportservice/custsupport/download.html* to download the program.

... and One You Don't

You probably don't want to install the Windows Media Player. Why? Well, let me tell you a little story.

If you spend any time at Microsoft's web site, you'll receive a number of messages like the one in Figure 4-13. In general, you want to say "no" to most of these offers. Random Microsoft bashing? No, although the "Always trust content from Microsoft Corporation" option gave me a good laugh. When I installed the Windows Media Player, it *uninstalled the RealPlayer currently on my system without alerting me.* Such practices make me want to give Janet Reno a great big hug.

Since a plug-in could potentially do disastrous things to your system (as ActiveX has proven), you don't want to be loading a plug-in from just anywhere. This window means that the plug-in comes with a certificate that proves the plug-in actually came from Microsoft, and not Joe Hacker. It wants you to say "Not only do I trust this certified Microsoft plug-in, but I'll trust anything else in the future that presents a Microsoft certificate. Because this has proven it's from Microsoft, I trust it." Of course, uninstalling your software without warning is just the sort of thing Joe Cracker would get arrested for, so it's important not to confuse the notions of certificates and trust.

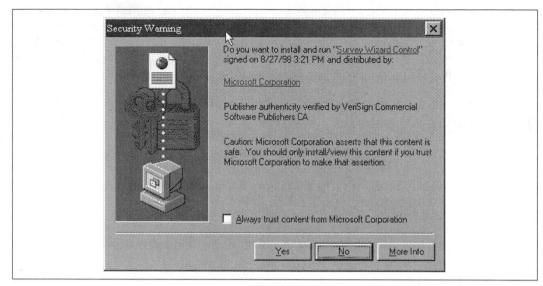

Figure 4-13. A security warning about a Microsoft download

Speeding Things Up

No matter how fast your Internet connection is, browsing can often seem slow. Before you rush out and buy that cable modem, however, there are some steps you can take to speed up your browser's performance.

Tweaking Preferences

Some elements of web pages take longer to download than others. Those elements may be extraneous, however, and you can actually view a page *first*, and then decide whether you really want to see the fancy images and Java applets.

Automatically loading images

One way to speed up page loading is to turn off the **Automatically Load Images** option. Without images, the home page for the *New York Times* looks like Figure 4-14.

Notice that Netscape's toolbar now displays a new icon, which looks like a picture hanging on a wall. If you click this icon, the page's images load. (On a page with frames, like this one, you'll need to place the cursor over each frame and click the **Display Images** icon to load the images). To turn off automatic image loading, deselect it in the Netscape Preferences dialog box (access this dialog box in the **Edit** menu, then click the **Advanced** section, as shown in Figure 4-15). If you're using IE, access **Internet Options** in the **View** menu, then change the Multimedia settings on the **Advanced** tab.

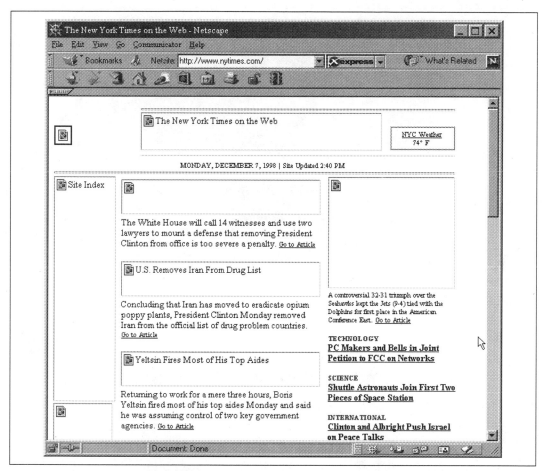

Figure 4-14. The New York Times without images

Turning off Java/JavaScript

If you disable Java or JavaScript, you're telling your browser not to load Java applets or execute JavaScript programs. Java and JavaScript are actually completely different programming languages with vastly different applications. Java applets tend to be fun, slow, and extraneous, while JavaScript programs may be important for the functioning of complex web pages. If you want to save page loading time, my recommendation is to turn off Java applets. JavaScript, however, probably isn't slowing things down too much and is more important to the proper viewing of pages on which it resides.

However, a **Load Java** icon doesn't appear when you turn these options off. So, if you spot a Java applet you'd like to access, you'll need to turn Java back on, and reload the page. Not a big deal, but something to be aware of.

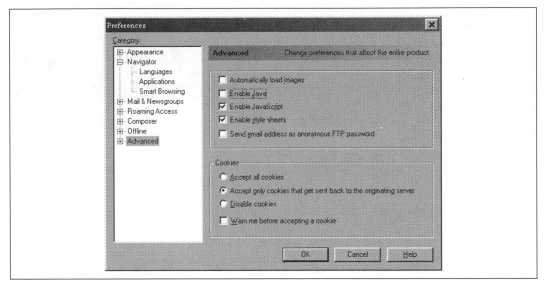

Figure 4-15. Netscape's advanced preferences

To disable Java or JavaScript, access Netscape's advanced preferences, or Explorer's **Advanced Internet Options** tab (see Figure 4-16).

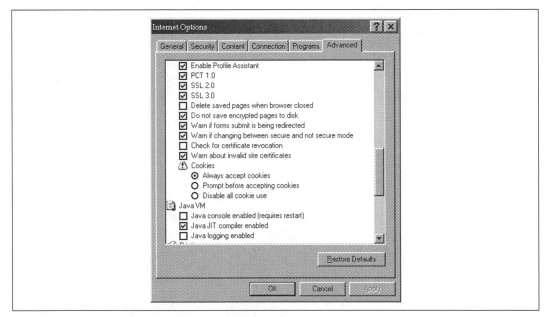

Figure 4-16. IE's Advanced Internet Options tab

Blank start page

If you'd like to speed up the rate at which your browser opens, nix the home page. Without a first page to download, you'll be able to download the page you do want much more quickly—just enter the URL in the address field, and press Enter. (Note that Netscape and IE both use "smart" URLs, and they fill in the most recent address that starts with the letter you've specified. So, if I entered "www.o" the browser would fill in the address *http://www.oreilly.com.*)

Optimizing the Cache

Another way of speeding up your browser is to tinker with your *cache*, the copies of Internet files that the browser keeps on your hard drive for easy access. Set the cache size (usually found in Preferences and sometimes Advanced settings) to about 5% of your hard drive. If performance (of either the browser or your computer) starts to slow down, clear both the disk and memory caches. To do so, access **Tools** → **Internet Options** → **General** → **Temporary Internet Files** (IE) and click the **Delete Files...** button, or access **Edit** → **Preferences** → **Advanced** → **Cache** (Netscape) and click the appropriate button.

A software tool called Surf Express actually replaces your browser's cache with an entirely different caching technology, called FASTore. The software also updates frequently visited pages automatically.

Browsing offline

A number of software tools speed up web browsing by making page downloading a background process. While you do other things, the browser or tool busily downloads the pages you want to view. When you access the pages later on, you'll essentially be surfing the cache. While this seems like much more trouble than it's worth, and perhaps needlessly increases Net traffic since many of the tools download entire sites so that you don't have to wait even a minute to see that picture of a prize Pekingese, many people use them and enjoy them. See the section "Offline Browsing" for more information.

Content Aggregators

Other tools, like the NeoPlanet browser described later, are *content aggregators*. What this fancy term means is that they notice and evaluate the kind of site you're looking at, provide information about it, and suggest other sites like it. Manufacturers claim these tools speed up browsing by directing you to the information you're looking for more efficiently. You may save a moment here or there, but these tools are probably gimmicks rather than anything else: they're essentially search engines that take up extra screen space and computer memory while you browse.

To find a list of content aggregators available for download, try looking in the "Browsing Companions" section of any shareware archive.

Alexa and archiving the Web

We'll describe one tool, Alexa, from Alexa Internet (*http://www.alexa.com*), a little more fully. Alexa is both an emblematic content aggregator and a tool with a potentially large impact on the Web.

Alexa works by placing a toolbar on your screen along with your browser. As you visit different sites, relevant information appears on the toolbar: in Figure 4-17, O'Reilly's web site shows up, along with other pages that a user visiting this site might be interested in; an ad; an archive link; and other tools.

Figure 4-17. Information relevant to the O'Reilly home page

Alexa's archive is one of the most interesting, and dangerous, options that it features. The company boasts an archive of more than 500,000 documents. In 1998, Alexa Internet donated a two-terabyte copy of the Web to the Library of Congress.

Thus, if you visit a page that you can't reach or is no longer available, you may access Alexa's archive by clicking a link in the **Stats** tab. Your browser then displays a copy of the page from Alexa's archives. Unfortunately, you can't reach most pages for a reason. Information may have changed. For example, clicking the archive button while visiting the O'Reilly page displays the home page of a gentleman named Jim O'Reilly, who used to own the *oreilly.com* name. Use this feature at your own risk.

Alternative Browsers

The vast majority of people reading this book will be using one of two browsers, Microsoft's Internet Explorer or Netscape's Navigator. Either one is a valid lifestyle choice. Each tends to be about as good as the other in terms of features, speed, and so on. Since they're both free, you can't beat the price. I described them earlier as being like Coke and Pepsi: minor differences, but pretty much the same thing.

But what if you like RC Cola?

Well, you're probably obstinate, and may want to be different just to be different. However, when it comes to browsing, Netscape and Microsoft have created browsers that are bloated with features. You may not need Java, JavaScript, frames, tables, and the latest in "push" technology that eats up memory and takes over your hard drive. If so, try one of the alternative browsers discussed next.

Online Browsers

The browsers listed here are generally similar in function to Netscape and IE, though each differs in its specific features.

Opera

What makes Opera different? Well, it's 1 MB in size, for starters. Yes, 1 MB total. While it costs $35 (or about half that for students), it has a sleek, no-nonsense interface that you can customize extensively, including settings for sound, JPEG images, font size, and window settings. Moreover, the application is lightning fast, loading pages a blink more quickly than Navigator on a contemporary system, but much more quickly on older systems (such as Windows 3.1 on a 386 chip, and no, that's not a mistake). Simple mail and news readers are included in that 1 MB application. Visit the home page at *http://www.operasoftware.com* to download a 30-day free trial copy.

NeoPlanet

Bigfoot, the people who bring you email addresses for life, present this content aggregator/lightweight browser. The program works either as an interface on top of Explorer or Netscape, directing you to additional content with recommendations at the top of the screen, or as a lightweight browser on its own. Free, and, at 800K, even smaller than Opera. You can find it at *http://www.neoplanet.com.*

Mosaic

Ah, it's sad. The granddaddy of all web browsers, the web browser that made us love the Web, is now an "alternative." Even so, it's fairly small, well-maintained, and free. Look for the well-maintained part to fall by the wayside, since the NCSA recently suspended support for the package. Other features include the AutoSurf crawler, which automatically retrieves specified pages for offline viewing, and an option to reload text only while pulling images straight from the cache. Don't look for Java applets, JavaScript support, or frames here, however. Download it from *http://www.ncsa.uiuc.edu/ SDG/Software/WinMosaic/HomePage.html.*

Opera Lover

—by Jessica Perry Hekman

One of Webster's Ninth New Collegiate Dictionary's definitions for "alternative" is "existing or functioning outside the established cultural, social, or economic system," and it provides "alternative newspaper" as an example. When people call Opera "the alternative browser," I don't think they mean exactly that, but the connotation's there. Netscape and Internet Explorer are the two obvious choices in browsers. Or you could try Opera, if neither of the Big Two work for you.

It's funny, though. Opera may be younger than Netscape and IE, but it's finally caught up with them. Now that you can run Sun's Java plug-in with it, Opera supports pretty much everything Netscape and IE do: JavaScript, secure server connections, cascading style sheets. It's smaller (under 2 MB—phew) and faster, to boot. So why's it the third choice?

For one thing, Opera Software is a significantly smaller company than Netscape (or maybe I should say AOL now) or Microsoft. Opera Software can't always keep up with the latest innovations but tends to wait until a new technology is proven before investing time in it. This can be obnoxious for web developers who need a browser that lets them play with the latest thing, but, in my experience, tends not to interfere with the experience of the average user too much. There's a definite up side to the small size of the Opera Software company, though: damn, it's responsive. When I wrote them to complain that a new hotlist feature interacted poorly with my speech recognition software, they provided an option to use the old method of presenting the hotlist, and they did so within a week. Gosh.

This focus on accessibility issues is typical of Opera Software. The company is the absolute leader in accessible browser design. Opera was the first browser you could navigate solely by keyboard, quite a few months before Netscape and IE began to let you tab between hyperlinks. Opera's list of keyboard alternatives is still at least three times as long as IE's. Opera also has this neat zoom feature— you can increase font and image size by up to 1000%, in case your eyesight isn't what it used to be. (You can also decrease the size, in case you've got a lot of browser windows open and your screen real estate has become more valuable.)

Did I mention a lot of browser windows? That's another one of Opera's unique features. You can open multiple windows within one Opera window, you can size and place them as your heart desires, and then minimize them all at once, hiding your multiple Dilbert windows when your boss walks in. Tell Opera to save its current state, and all those windows reappear when you boot your machine up and restart Opera the next morning. Tell it to ignore its most recent state, and it brings up those windows that you start with every day—your stocks, *news.com, slashdot.org*.

—*continued*—

Being a huge Opera fan for all the reasons I've listed here, I've been recommending it to friends. And I've been asked: Does it run under Unix? So, finally, I think I know what keeps Opera so firmly in third place. The promised Linux version is still under development, and Opera for Mac OS isn't on the radar screen yet. And that's a big deal. To be loyal to Opera Software, I should point out that they know that their lack of support for non-Windows OS's is a big issue for their customers and that they definitely are working on porting their browser. (It already runs under OS/2.) However, to be honest to you, gentle reader, I should add that, since they haven't set a date yet for the release of their Linux version, you shouldn't hold your breath; and, though porting from Linux to other Unix systems is generally a snap, they haven't mentioned any intention of attempting to do so, so don't wait for a Solaris version, either. I guess the Unix junkies among us just need to watch and be patient. But those of you who use Windows—what are you waiting for?

Lynx

Lynx is a text-based browser for those who find pictures too darn distracting or simply have a slow connection. It's free and lightning fast. Download it from *http://www.fdisk.com/doslynx/lynxport.htm.*

HotJava

HotJava is a full-featured browser from Sun. Programmed in Java, the browser is secure, platform independent, easily customized, and painfully slow. You can specify everything from menu items to graphics in the user interface. It's free for individual use from *http://java.sun.com/products/hotjava/3.0/.*

TOBE

This so-called The Other Browser-Emailer is another new, free browser. The fully-featured browser supports Netscape plug-ins and features a permanent log that provides users with information about incoming data and visited sites. A folder manager centralizes files for easy access, and the browser creates a map of your path that you can click while you surf. TOBE is available from *http://www.pixelogic.com.*

Arachne

Arachne is a browser with a graphical user interface that runs under DOS. Arachne's makers, xChaos, *do* recommend a 386 or better. The software includes a freeware PPP dialer along with MPEG and WAV players. It also supports most of the basic toolbar functions found in Netscape and Explorer. The browser is free, but certain features are disabled until you register, and pay for, the software. Download it from *http://www.naf.cz/arachne/.*

Cyberdog

Unfortunately, Apple stopped development on this very nice browser for Macintosh. Based on Apple's OpenDoc document architecture, the browser is actually faster than Netscape or Explorer on the Mac, and supports tables, frames, and forms, along with a number of popular plug-ins. Email, FTP, news, and Telnet clients are included in the 2 MB package. Use it now, before the standards pass it by. Free, from *http://cyberdog. apple.com.*

ChiBrow

This "web browser designed for children" only displays sites that have been specifically approved. See Chapter 5 for more information on filtering software. The browser is shareware and is available from *http://www.chibrow.com.* Be sure to check out the picture of the scary Stepford family that created it.

Offline Browsing

Believe it or not, some people prefer to browse the Web without being connected to the Internet. How? Well, instead of randomly clicking links, you specify the content that you're interested in and the format in which you'd like to view it. The application you're using then downloads the information, and you browse through it at your leisure. People choose to do so for different reasons: sometimes, you just want to speed up the browsing process, and pages load more quickly when they've already been downloaded to your hard drive. You might also want to browse the Web on your PalmPilot, which, given its portability, is probably easier offline. Finally, so-called push channels, such as Pointcast or Windows 98's active desktop, work in this manner as well.

There's a wider range of application choices when it comes to offline browsers. Some try to guess which pages you'll be interested in based on your browsing choices; others use timers or special caching technology.

BlackWidow

This offline browser scans web sites and lists the files in a Windows Explorer–style interface. Features include resumable downloads and site-mapping tools. Download it from *http://www.softbytelabs.com/BlackWidow/.*

Grab-A-Site

Enter a URL, or list of URLs, and this offline browser downloads the entire site—text, images, the whole shebang—for your offline browsing pleasure. The frightening thing about this package is that it will follow as many links from those pages as you specify. Download Grab-A-Site from *http://www.bluesquirrel.com/grabasite/.*

Internet Angel

Another offline browser that downloads web sites, but this one has a timer. Download it from *http://www.download.com.*

Speed Surfer

Speed Surfer is an offline browser on, well, speed. Using what manufacturer Kiss Software calls special "smart agent" technology, Speed Surfer loads the next level of links on a page into your cache before you get there, particularly for sites you visit frequently. Order it online at *http://www.speedsurfer.com.*

Web Turbo

Web Turbo is an offline browser that presents web page summaries in outline format. And, it's free. Download it from *http://www.download.com.*

NetSonic

Web 3000's NetSonic uses intelligent pre-caching to speed offline browsing. You can download it from *http://www.download.com.*

Windows 98 Active Channels

First, let's address the most salient question about active channels: what the heck are they?

Turns out that an active channel is . . . HTML content in a *really* big window. Hence, we include them in this section on alternative browsers.

Many users may be wondering not only what I'm talking about, but why I'm talking about it. A little background: over the last few years, there's been a lot of talk about so-called "push" technologies. Two of the biggest names involved are Pointcast and Marimba; we cover them in Chapter 10. Push technology basically involves a browser, running in the background of whatever other programs you have running. At specified intervals, new content downloads automatically from the content providers a user has indicated.

Microsoft has bundled so-called active channels into Windows 98 and plunked them right down on the desktop. Or in the desktop, depending on your configuration. If your desktop properties are set to view your desktop as a web page, some channels could actually be planted right there. Here are a few of the news-ticker style channels you could plant within your desktop:

- Sports scores from ESPN
- ·A news ticker from the *New York Times*
- A search box from Snap! Online

- Instant access to news, information, clips, and pictures from Paramount Pictures' television shows, movies, and video releases

- Market news and analysis from *Fortune* magazine

So, active channels can actually be broken into two categories: active channels and active desktop items. Channels remain in a browser window (although Windows 98 blows Explorer up *really big* so that it looks like you're watching television, as shown in Figure 4-18) and while they are occasionally refreshed without your having to hit the **Reload** button, they're otherwise just like web pages, with links, text, pictures, and so on. You can even open the URLs in Netscape, if you want to.

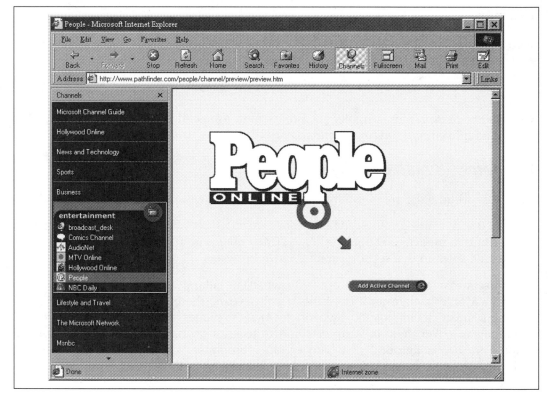

Figure 4-18. Windows 98's active channels in a more manageable form

Active desktop items, however, nest within your desktop and slow down your computer.

So, here is what you need to know about active channels:

- To subscribe to a channel, click the **Add Active Channel** button in the right window pane. The only change this makes is that when you double-click Explorer's **Channels** button or click the **View Channels** icon in the Windows 98 access tray, a small red asterisk appears next to channels with new content.

- As far as I can determine, the content—the active, animated frontend that links you to a standard web site—isn't updated on anything approaching a consistent or frequent basis.

- You can't delete channels, nor can you unsubscribe from them. However, it doesn't matter. If you don't want to see a channel, don't click on it.

- To navigate within a channel, use the **Forward** and **Back** buttons, as you normally would.

- If you click the **Fullscreen** button, the channel condenses into the standard IE browser view.

- To add an active desktop item to your desktop, click the **Add to Active Desktop** button.

- To remove an Active Desktop item, select **Settings** from the **Start** menu. Select **Active Desktop**, and either deselect "View As web page" or select "Customize My Desktop..." From there, first select "View As web page," then select the active desktop item you want to remove, and click the **Delete** button (see Figure 4-19).

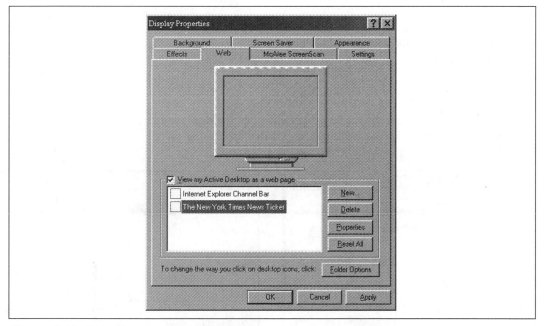

Figure 4-19. Removing an active desktop item

I'd advocate removing active desktop items, as there was not a single active desktop item that didn't strike me as more than a passive performance retardant.

Using active channels with a modem actually isn't much different from normal browsing. Connect to your ISP, then double-click the **View Channels** icon. If you've subscribed to a channel, IE checks with that channel's server to see if there's been an update. When you click on the appropriate channel, that content is downloaded and displayed. When you click links within the channel, you're browsing normally.

Active desktop items are a bit different. When you subscribe, be sure to click the **Customize Settings…** button to specify how often you want the ticker to update, and thus how often you need to connect.

PalmPilot Browsing

Yes, you can browse the Web from your PalmPilot. You don't even need a modem, so long as your computer (to which you've connected the PalmPilot via the cradle) has one. As you might expect, PalmPilot web browsing is heavily cache-dependent.

Online Browsing

If you'll be browsing in the traditional, connected-to-the-Internet sense, you'll need to have your PalmPilot connected to the Internet, which means that you'll need to have a modem connected to your PalmPilot. You can use the snap-on PalmPilot modem (which has its own batteries), or you can connect the PalmPilot to any external modem via a PalmPilot modem cable. The Novatel wireless modem is an option for the financially flush.

Setting up your PalmPilot for browsing

To prepare your PalmPilot, open up **Preferences**, under **Applications**. From the upper-right pop-up menu, choose **Network**, as shown in Figure 4-20.

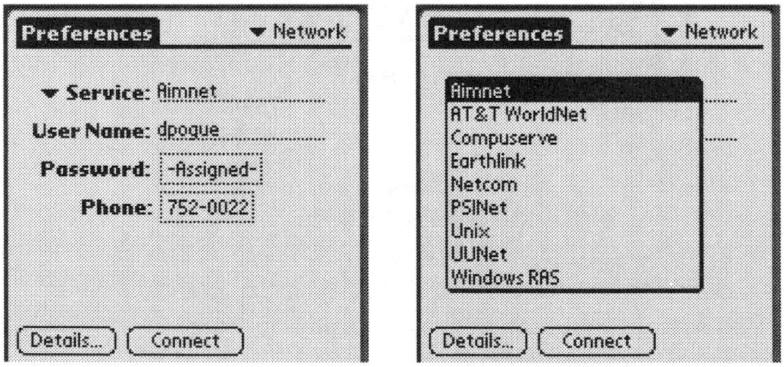

Figure 4-20. The Network Preferences screen lets you select an ISP

If you see your ISP on the list, tap it; if not, tap **Menu** → **Service** → **New**, and write the name of your ISP into the Service dialog box. Enter your username into the second blank. Enter your password into the password blank, and, finally, tap the **Phone** box and enter the local phone number you use to access your ISP.

ProxiWeb

ProxiWeb* is the only PalmPilot browser that can display mixed text and graphics from the Web. As it is also free, it's the only PalmPilot web browser that we'll cover in any depth here.

To install ProxiWeb, you'll first need to download it from *http://www.proxiweb.com/ proxiweb/download/*. Following the instructions on the screen, download the file to the add-on folder on your PC (most likely *C:\Program Files\Palm\add-on*). Extract the files (with WinZip or an analogous utility; see Chapter 13) to the same directory. Now, launch the Palm Desktop application and click the **Install** button. In the resulting dialog box, click the **Add...** button, and double-click on the **ProxiWeb** icon. Click **Done**. The next time you HotSync your PalmPilot, ProxiWeb will be installed to the Applications section.

When you launch ProxiWeb, a welcome screen appears. At this point, you have a choice of two buttons: **Load Page** and **Offline Viewing**. If you tap the **Load Page** option, you can write in the URL of the web page you're looking for; a pop-up menu of canned web address pieces (such as "http://", "www.", ".com", and so on) saves you a lot of writing. Just choose one to insert into the address you're entering.

More often, however, you'll probably want to tap **Offline Viewing**. By accessing the **Edit Bookmarks** option (from the **Save** menu), you'll see ProxiWeb's list of starter bookmarks, as shown in Figure 4-21. To add URLs of your own, tap **New**. Any bookmarks that appear in bold type are those that have been cached—which means that you can view those pages without being connected to the Web.

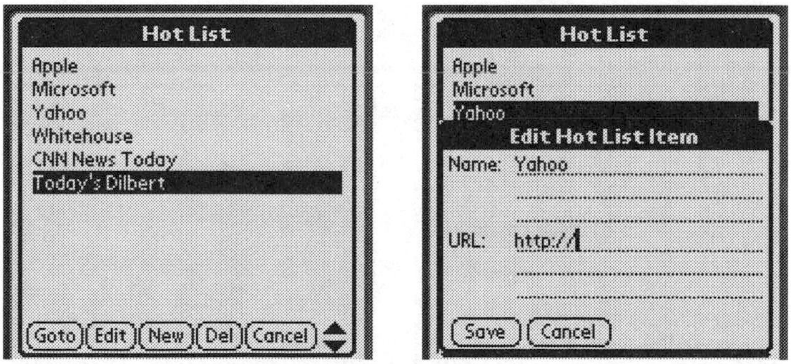

Figure 4-21. Adding new bookmarks

---

* The ProxiWeb browser was known as Top Gun Wingman until 1998; versions of it still float around the Web. Much as with the morphing of Mosaic into Netscape, ProxiWeb is the version you want.

To access a web page, tap the name of a bookmark and then tap **Goto**. The message shown in Figure 4-22 appears, reminding you that this page has not yet been stored on the PalmPilot; tap **Yes**. Now, your PalmPilot dials; a progress bar appears, followed by, finally, an actual, miniature web page.

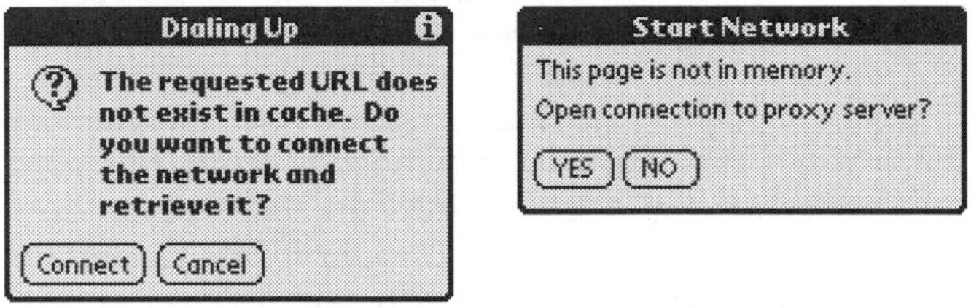

Figure 4-22. Opening a connection to the server

Whenever you see a dotted line under text, you're looking at a link, much like in your standard desktop browser. Tap the link to access the indicated page. You can even fill in web-based forms by tapping the dialog box and entering the data via the Graffiti area.

The easiest way to scroll through a page isn't by using the tiny scrollbar on the right, but by dragging your stylus down the middle of the page. Since the PalmPilot screen is so small, you won't find a toolbar; the **Back**, **Forward**, **Reload**, and **Cancel** commands are in the **Go** menu.

In its attempt to represent the web page proportionally (the way it would look on a desktop browser), the PalmPilot makes the graphics appear quite small. That's why, if you tap a graphic, the pop-up menu shown in Figure 4-23 appears. Tap **View Full Size** to view a bigger version of the image. If the image is an image map, containing a link, the blown-up graphic functions as you would expect, summoning other web pages when you click the appropriate area.

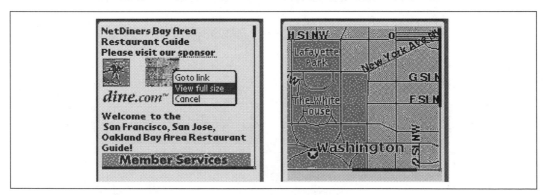

Figure 4-23. To get a better look at a graphic, tap it to enlarge it

Since you probably won't be connected all the time, you may want to save pages for later viewing. To do so, tap the **Menu** icon and choose **Lock in Cache** from the **Save** menu. To access or delete pages after that, use the **Save** menu's **Edit Cache** command to see a list of stored pages. Note that you'll probably want to set your cache size (by selecting **Prefs** in the **ProxiWeb** menu) to 100 K to keep cached pages from taking over your PalmPilot's memory.

An even more important preference to set is the "Map Phone/ToDo as Prev/Next" checkbox. When this option is selected, the plastic hardware buttons corresponding to the Address Book and To Do programs become **Previous** and **Next** page (**Forward** and **Back**) buttons. It's much easier to navigate the Web with your thumbs than with Graffiti-shortcut pen strokes.

Other PalmPilot browsers

HandWeb is a browser for the PalmPilot that is text only and costs between $60 and $70. However, bookmark access is much easier than ProxiWeb's, and the bookmarks themselves may be categorized. Additionally, web pages may be automatically saved as memos. Download HandWeb from *http://www.smartcodesoft.com/products/ showcase/showcase.html*.

The Palmscape browser is the only PalmPilot browser that is able to handle frames. It features an icon bar at the bottom of the page, a save-to-memo feature, and is available for free from *http://www.palmcentral.com*.

Offline Browsing

You don't actually need a modem to browse with your PalmPilot: let your computer do the work and push the pages to your PalmPilot during a HotSync. The AvantGo program uses desktop PC software to download and compress pages into PalmPilot-ready format.

AvantGo

You can download AvantGo, which is free for personal use, from *http://www.avantgo. com/products/download/free.html*. Download the file to the add-on folder on your PC (most likely *C:\Program Files\Palm\add-on*). Extract the files (with WinZip or an analogous utility) to the same directory. Now, launch the Palm Desktop application and click the **Install** button. In the resulting dialog box, click the **Add...** button, and double-click the **AvantGo** icon. Click **Done**. The next time you HotSync your PalmPilot, AvantGo will be installed to the applications section.

AvantGo comes with the AvantGo update channel pre-installed. Access AvantGo from the Applications screen. When you tap it, you'll see a list of stored pages, ready for viewing. The AvantGo update page may not give you a full sense of the program's possibilities, however, since it's pretty dry material. You'll want to add web pages (which AvantGo calls channels) of your own.

You can add channels in one of two ways: by visiting AvantGo's Subscription page at *http://www.avantgo.com/webtogo/subscribe/* or by specifying channel selections of your own.

First let's take a look at AvantGo's page, which appears in Figure 4-24.

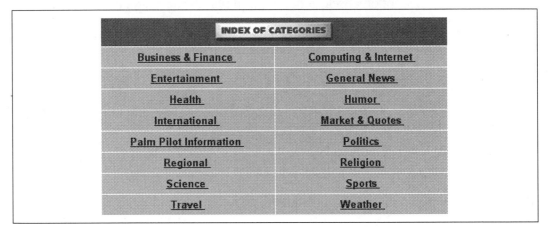

Figure 4-24. AvantGo's list of channel categories

When you choose a category, you have two options: optimized corporate sites, or sites submitted by users.

Click on a link to an optimized channel, and a new browser window pops up, describing that channel. If you click the **Subscribe to AvantGo Channel** button, yet another window opens, asking whether you want to open the file or save it to disk. Choose **Open**, and AvantGo Desktop launches and adds the channel to your list. (You can ignore the warning about AvantGo Desktop only allowing a link depth of 1.) Subscribe to the user-submitted channels by selecting the checkbox next to those you want to add and then clicking the **Subscribe** button.

You can also create a channel of your own by pasting in the URL of the desired page.

Once you've chosen a channel, you need to set a few options, including the page URL and title (see Figure 4-25). The size limit can be no larger than 256 KB. The Link Depth indicates how many pages AvantGo should pursue: in this case, it downloads the front page of the *New York Times* and the stories that that page links to. However, it doesn't download the pages that *those* pages link to. Specifying a username and password allows you to download web sites at which authentication is required.

Decide whether you want to include images in the pages you download, and whether you want AvantGo to download links to other sites, or merely to those within the

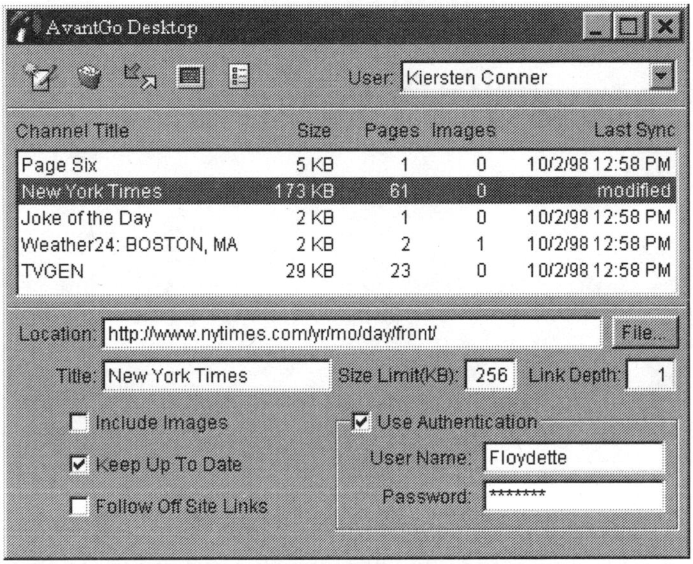

Figure 4-25. Setting AvantGo options

same domain—in this example, other pages within the *New York Times* site. If you select the "Keep Up To Date" checkbox, AvantGo downloads new versions of the page each time you HotSync.

Once you finish setting the options, do a HotSync. The pages will be loaded into AvantGo. Note that the greater the number of pages and the more links they have, the longer HotSync will take.

Browsing in AvantGo is easy. Links appear as text with dotted lines beneath them. Furthermore, AvantGo supports only two buttons: **Back**, which appears as an arrow at the top of the screen, pointing to the left, and **Home**, which takes you back to AvantGo's list of documents. If you want to perform some document management, tap the **Details** button on the home page. From the Details screen, you can delete channels you no longer want or see information about the total pages downloaded for each channel. Deleted channels will be removed from your AvantGo desktop the next time you HotSync.

AvantGo does have a few quirks. Be sure to access the **Preferences** in the **Options** menu and turn on **Show Tables** and, optionally, **Show Images** (actually, these are the only options you have). For some reason, AvantGo ships with **Show Tables** turned off, which means that any content in a table is not displayed. Additionally, the **Use Authentication** feature seems to work only sporadically.

CHAPTER FIVE

PRIVACY AND SECURITY

If you've ever visited New York City, you may have run across a gentleman selling usually high-priced watches for only a few dollars. The gentleman doesn't appear to have bathed and is selling his wares out of a suitcase. What a bargain! What a lucky day for you! The watches must be real, so you give the gentleman your credit card number.

Sounds nuts, right? It is. Yet many people believe information and divulge facts on the Internet that they would never communicate to a stranger in-person. We still haven't gotten over the miracle of Gutenberg: if a document appears in print, we tend to assign it authenticity.

Would you ever leave an outgoing message like this on your answering machine? "You've reached Ben. I'll be out of the office from June 12th through June 30th while taking a family vacation to Florida. My social security number is 222-34-9834, and my computer password is 'testing.'"

Let's take a look at another hypothetical situation: After getting chewed out by your boss, you complain to a co-worker: "That slime-sucking windbag would be toast if it weren't for me. Good thing he doesn't know 'working at home' means sleeping off a hangover." Turns out your boss was standing outside your office and heard every word. You lose your job.

These examples are implausible, but they provide a good illustration of some basic concepts for maintaining privacy and security while using the Internet. Don't believe everything you read, don't reveal sensitive information indiscriminately, and be aware that someone may be listening.

Is the Internet a dangerous place? No. In fact, it's not a place at all—it's a network of computers that allows sometimes dangerous people to communicate. The only way to get hurt is by making yourself vulnerable.

Therein lies the problem: when using a new medium, many people don't realize what's safe and what isn't. Should you have a web page? Sure. Should it list your home address? Probably not. Once you know your rights online and in the workplace, and the means used to garner information about yourself, you'll be able to use the Internet with relative confidence.

Privacy

Computers are funny things. Even as you sit in front of a terminal, alone, fragmented from society, you reach out to other, lonely souls and form a community.

How might others invade your online privacy? Methods fall into two broad categories:

- Cyberstalking
- Information mining

Cyberstalkers are individuals who pursue you via email, in a chat forum, or through instant messages. They can be very unsettling and make you feel quite threatened. Fortunately, you can avoid cyberstalkers by changing your screen name, turning off your machine, or taking various other actions. Some basic avoidance techniques will dissuade others from irritating you in the first place.

Information mining is less obviously creepy but potentially much more threatening. What's the big deal, you may think, if someone knows my name and address? Or my email address? Or my occupation, interests, and how much money I make per year? It can be a very big deal. Abuses range from spam in your mailbox to faked email to identity snatching, where someone applies for credit cards and identification using your name and social security number. Furthermore, any number of *legal* methods of gaining information could get you into a lot of trouble. Again, knowing your rights and taking a few precautionary steps can prevent a world of worries.

Try c|net's privacy test at *http://www.cnet.com/Content/Features/Dlife/Privacy2/ss01. html* to see how much information about you exists on the World Wide Web.*

---

* Note that c|net's search only skims the surface. The information you can search on the Web doesn't include information companies have gleaned from cookies and registration forms.

Private and Public

—by Andy Oram

What's private has become a very public issue. In recent months, international negotiations and even threats of sanctions—usually associated with weapons of mass destruction—have highlighted the campaign to keep computers from invading your personal space. The drama is all rather novel and perplexing to the U.S. public (although the press has started reporting developments fairly often, which is gratifying to privacy activists) but shows that a debate going on in Europe, Australia, and other parts of the world for two and a half decades is finally having an impact on North America.

Public concern about computer data started in the mid-70s, when mainframe computers became vast storage-and-retrieval devices with fast access to hundreds of tapes. Remembering the Nazis, who cataloged and tracked everybody under their rule, many Europeans asked what such machinery could do in the hands of a maleficent government. They clamored for laws restricting the collection and dissemination of data, first as a brake on the power of the state. Later, when it became clear that businesses were collecting and collating large amounts of data, laws were passed to cover them, too.

Thus it came to be that Europe led the way in the 1980s for what is known as "omnibus" laws protecting every type of data that can be collected about individuals. The campaign for privacy took on new momentum with an international directive calling for such laws, issued by the Organization for Economic Co-operation and Development in 1980 (*http://www.oecd.org/dsti/sti/it/secur/prod/PRIV-EN. HTM*). Few Americans have heard of the OECD, which grew out of the Marshall plan after World War II, but the U.S. is a member. By ignoring the directive on privacy, therefore, we are technically in violation of an international agreement.

Well, nobody is quaking in their boots over the OECD. But a more radical European initiative is heading our way. The impetus is a directive from the governing bodies of the European Union declared in October 1995 (*http://aspe.os.dhhs.gov/ datacncl/eudirect.htm*). While reiterating the call for its member countries to pass laws along lines laid down by the OECD, it added a clause forbidding "the transfer of personal data to a third country that does not ensure an adequate level of protection." If the U.S. lags behind international standards, you may find that you can't use a credit card in Europe or book a seat on a flight on an airline there.

—continued—

What's in the privacy laws? The goals are straightforward; they enforce such elementary rights as:

■ Knowing who's looking at your data

■ Getting a request before your data is used for any purpose other than the one for which it was collected

■ Being able to review and correct your data

You might think that setting and following a policy of respect for privacy would be a simple task. But the details get sticky. For instance, should a law give organizations a right to share data so long as the individual fails to opt out? Or should they prohibit dissemination until the individual opts in? (Most laws lean toward the latter principle.) When should data be destroyed if it is no longer needed for its original purpose? Who is responsible if leaks occur?

Furthermore, to ensure that all parts of a large organization understand and adhere to the policy, you need bureaucratic support. Germany, for instance, requires large institutions to employ a privacy regulator who remains relatively separate from the main hierarchy of decision making. The law covers the federal government, the local (Land) governments, and even corporations above a certain size.

Few laws are currently in place in the United States. Legislatures tend to respond in narrow fashion to particular incidents, as when a law protecting the privacy of video rentals was passed after Robert Bork's video preferences were leaked. Congress has passed a law requiring web sites to get parental permission before collecting personal data from children, and some other laws are being considered—but American businesses keep promising they'll fix the problem through self-regulation, and the administration brings this position into its negotiations with the European Union.

Medical privacy is making slow progress. The Secretary of Health and Human Services, Donna E. Shalala, called for legislation in September 1997, and a couple bills have been introduced over the years but not passed into law. The most recent bill is the 1997 Medical Information Privacy and Security Act (S. 1368).

Other countries are passing omnibus laws under pressure from the European Community. Canada is reportedly close to passing a Personal Information Protection and Electronic Documents Act. Australia has a comprehensive law regarding government-held data, although a proposed law covering corporate-held data is stalled. Hong Kong and Taiwan have strong laws; Japan and South Korea are seriously considering them.

—continued—

Will the United States step up to take its place in the new culture of privacy? For the first time, our government has lifted its bulky carcass and started to survey the privacy scene. Still, it's way behind other governments in thinking about privacy; expertise on the subject is rare and tends to be shunted from place to place. When it comes to data-sharing issues, the U.S. government listens mostly to credit collection and reporting agencies—and you can guess what position they take.

Despite stated intransigence on the part of the European Council, it's hard to believe that Europe will actually enforce the laws against data sharing. The impact would hurt its member nations economically in grievous ways. Still, courts may be forced to apply sanctions by individual or class-action suits. In any case, the conflict is leading to some interesting pressure in the Unites States and other countries affected by the directive.

Some U.S. companies may do what some Japanese companies are doing, which is to submit their own policies for approval so that they can do business in Europe. European Union negotiators are keeping up pressure. As of this writing, it's not clear whether European governments will enforce the draconian provision against data sharing. But they shouldn't be put in the position of doing so. Polls show that Americans themselves are afraid of losing privacy through the Internet, and data travels so easily that only comprehensive laws can hold back the flood.

Your Rights

Many Americans feel, and mistakenly believe, that email messages are a form of communication protected by the Constitutional right to privacy. Unfortunately, there is no such right; some people have inferred it from the Fourth Amendment to the Constitution, which protects against unreasonable search and seizure by the *government*. While some state constitutions do explicitly grant a right to privacy, that right has frequently been construed as pertaining to personal matters, not those in the workplace, and it doesn't apply to email. Moreover, court findings in California have held that email doesn't fall under the wiretapping statutes that apply to telephone conversations, and maintained an employer's right to intercept and read employees' email messages. The 1986 Electronic Communications Privacy Act restricts the ability of law enforcement agencies to intercept oral, wire, and electronic communications; unfortunately, it also provides an exception for the provider of the communications service—including employers.

This issue continues to evolve in the courts.

Workplace Rights

Employers continue to see the benefit of electronically monitoring their employees. In some ways, the boss keeping an eye on Internet usage is the least of your worries:

many workplaces now monitor everything from the number of keystrokes per hour to an employee's location within the building. Most companies that monitor web and email usage don't inform employees, and aren't required by law to do so.

Roughly one-quarter to one-third of businesses using email maintain written policies governing employees' proper use of the Internet. Unfortunately, even policies that support employees' private use of email are no protection. Courts have upheld an employer's right to intercept and read employees' email, even in the face of such a stated policy.

Your employer can legally do the following:

- Intercept and read your email

- Keep copies of that mail indefinitely

- Fire you based on the content of that mail

- Monitor your World Wide Web usage

Consumer Rights

Caveat emptor, baby.

This may seem strange, but there is no protection against companies or individuals gleaning information about you from your Internet activities. Furthermore, they can acquire that information not only from forms that you submit but from cookies placed *on your computer*, tracking your web usage—you may not even know exactly what you're revealing. That information may then be filed in a database, used to target advertising directly to you, or sold to other organizations.

What Kind of Information Can People Learn About Me?

People can document, archive, and sell anything you tell them. If you fill out a form that asks for your name, age, bank account number, social security number, and mother's maiden name, that information may be legally bought, sold, posted, or traded. A piece of "freeware" that requires such information before you download it probably isn't worth it.

You may think that once you've stopped browsing the Web, the possibility of anyone learning about you stops as well. Unfortunately, that's not true.

Online profiles are a source used by many marketers to gain email addresses and preferences for online marketing. Delete any information from such profiles that could be insecure. See Chapter 3 for a fuller discussion.

Similarly, information you record on browser and email preference pages may be recorded. Even if you don't submit the information to a particular site, it's easy for servers to record it.

Finally, browsers leave trails of information across the Web and on your computer.* Servers may leave cookies, or settings files, on your computer, which record pertinent information about what you've done on the Web. Some of these cookies keep track of the URL from which you came, which pages you visit in a site, in what order you visit them, and which links you visit while you're there. Finally, certain seemingly innocuous files on your computer keep a very accurate record of where you've been. The files in your history or cache directories record the web sites you've visited and could be used by a boss or co-worker to document your Internet activities.

A cache of cookies, with history on the side

If you're concerned about privacy, you probably know enough not to have a "porn" file in your Bookmarks folder. You may not realize, however, the data that lurks behind the scenes.

The history file is exactly what it sounds like: a listing of all the web sites you've visited over a period of time—the default is a few weeks. Access it from within your browser with the **History** command.

The browser's cache contains copies of recently downloaded text and image files. (For more information, see Chapter 4.) You can access it by opening the cache file(s) in the browser's directory.†

The term "cookies" describes a kind of technology that allows you to set preferences for the web pages you visit. When you customize such a page, the information you've submitted (frames or no-frames? Java or not?) is stored in your browser directory for the server to access each time you visit that page. To view your own cookies file, take a look in your browser directory for a text file with the word "cookies" in the name and open it with a text editor, as shown in Figure 5-1.

Notice that most of this information seems harmless, mostly URLs and Boolean statements.

What may make you uncomfortable are entries like this:

```
thegiftgallery.web2010.comTRUE/cgibin/shopFALSE887587132orderid596353297
```

That orderid number could contain all sorts of information in encoded form: what you bought, your address, name—even your credit card number.

---

* IE version 5.0 is particularly bad for web privacy. In early 1999, it was revealed that numerous Microsoft products, including the Windows Media Player, embed identifying numbers in their transmissions, so that user actions on the Web can be traced. IE 5.0 contains just such a "loophole": when a user bookmarks a site, that information is transmitted back to the site owner. For these reasons, I wouldn't advocate using IE 5.0.

† In the case of IE 4.0+, the cookies directory may be in the Windows directory instead of directly beneath the Explorer directory. This seems to be because of Microsoft's intended blend of browser and operating system. In any event, you may need to search your hard drive to find cache and cookie files.

```
cookies.txt - Notepad                                                    _|&|X
File   Edit   Search   Help
# Netscape HTTP Cookie File
# http://www.netscape.com/newsref/std/cookie_spec.html
# This is a generated file!  Do not edit.

www.godiva.com   FALSE   /godiva FALSE   944035310       SHOPPERMANAGER%2FGODIVA PERU1U0L9XSH2JMM06
.linkexchange.com        TRUE    /       FALSE   942192188       SAFE_COOKIE     3527c1ce02106a75
www.lendingtree.com      FALSE   /       FALSE   1293753789      EGSOFT_ID       140.247.46.148-106
.mrshowbiz.com   TRUE    /       FALSE   1522499800      SWID    AF380E56-CCB6-11D1-ADF9-00A0C9713E
.movielink.com   TRUE    /       FALSE   958496106       CookInfo        +FP:Purchase+FR:2+MID:NY+2
ads.softbank.net         TRUE    /       FALSE   1893456412      uid     0x0.0x8cF72F75
.pathfinder.com  TRUE    /       FALSE   2051222604      PFUID   cc47F21d353178e22e431000ffffff9d
.focalink.com    TRUE    /       FALSE   946641807       SB_ID   0892511400000878594092276483
.preferences.com         TRUE    /       FALSE   1182140628      PreferencesID   JSzQZpW4jeadCPxT24
marktwain.miningco.com   FALSE   /       FALSE   942188431       NGUserID        d18fd433-280-89251
marktwain.tqn.com        FALSE   /       FALSE   942188432       NGUserID        d18fd433-280-89251
www.americancentury.com  TRUE    /       FALSE   2137622890      USERID  199841319225 0%2E25187307
mutualfunds.miningco.com         FALSE   /       FALSE   942188432       NGUserID        a010026-85
mutualfunds.tqn.com      FALSE   /       FALSE   942188437       NGUserID        a010026-85-8925139
search.miningco.com      FALSE   /       FALSE   942188438       NGUserID        a010010-176-892514
www.wallstreetcity.com   FALSE   /       FALSE   1293753819      EGSOFT_ID       140.247.41.115-154
.jwtt3.com       TRUE    /       FALSE   942250800       NGUserID        cffc0566-25711-898300778-1
.gamecenter.com  TRUE    /       FALSE   946685005       u_vid_0_0       0000810a
.shareware.com   TRUE    /       FALSE   946685034       u_vid_1_0       00201be4
.computers.com   TRUE    /       FALSE   946685007       u_vid_0_0       00007874
www.nec-now.com  FALSE   /       FALSE   1293753788      EGSOFT_ID       140.247.47.126-3897320496.
194.207.162.129  FALSE   /       FALSE   1293753826      EGSOFT_ID       140.247.47.142-763478704.2
.zdnet.com       TRUE    /       FALSE   946659644       browser 9925833537176082
.nytimes.com     TRUE    /       FALSE   946685041       RMID    8cF72F8d35488F50
.nytimes.com     TRUE    /       FALSE   946685040       PW      '90:992B
.nytimes.com     TRUE    /       FALSE   946685040       ID      <)0+*9,B
.nytimes.com     TRUE    /       FALSE   946685040       RDB     C80200085C0000555300002000000000010(
www.BeanieBabyOfficialClub.com   FALSE   /       FALSE   1293753766      EGSOFT_ID       140.247.47
www.wld.com      FALSE   /       FALSE   942189311       NGUserID        ac10031e-161-894482186-1
.hotbot.com      TRUE    /       FALSE   946738928       p_uniqid        1UFxCOrsqFQFTK6nnA
```

Figure 5-1. A cookies file

Should you immediately delete *cookies.txt*? Maybe not. The people who invented this technology weren't total boneheads. Only the site that creates a cookie may access that cookie once it's set. In other words, continuing with the example above, even though all these cookies are part of the same text file, Mplayer, Infoseek, and Netscape couldn't access the orderid cookie left by the Gift Gallery—which, furthermore, appears to be encoded.

Sounds safe, right? Well, remember that you connect to a lot more sites than you're typically aware of, via banner ads. So, if Mplayer, Infoseek, and Netscape all have an ad on their pages from the same advertiser, that advertiser could create a separate cookie for itself. Then, whenever you encounter one of their ads they could tell where else you've seen their ads and build a dossier of your habits. You can blissfully ignore those ads at the top of the page, but every time one in loaded it can tell the company what page you are displaying.

Cookie busters

If you don't feel comfortable with people storing information about you on your machine, the first step is to change your browser's preferences so that it will not accept cookies (Netscape: **Edit → Preferences → Advanced → Disable cookies**; IE: **View**

→ **Internet** → **Options** → **Advanced** → **Cookies** → **Disable all cookie use**). Then, delete your cookie file or directory.

You may also want to use some software tools to make accepting, rejecting, or deleting cookies from your system a more informed process. Try Anonymous Cookie from Luckman Interactive, which may be downloaded from *http://www.luckman.com/anon-cookie/index.html*.

What Information About Me Exists on the Net?

Even if you've never created a profile, submitted a form, or bought anything online, information about you may already exist on the Internet. Companies glean this information from myriad sources: phone books, Internet service providers, and others. Here are a few online sources you might check.

People Finders

A number of web directories let you search for email addresses, telephone numbers, home pages, or home addresses of individuals. Some even provide a map to a "found" individual's house. You may not want this information publicized, especially considering that these databases may be accessed from virtually anywhere in the world. If so, contact the services and request that any information about you be removed. Be sure to check back a week or so later; sometimes, you'll need to make more than one request. Take a look at *http://www.yahoo.com/Reference/White_Pages/Individuals/* to find a current listing of people finders.

Removing your listing

Persistence is the key to having your vital information removed from a people-finding service's database. First, locate the service's FAQ to find out how to have information about you removed. Start with a simple email message to the appropriate person.* Check back in a week. If the information hasn't been removed, call the proprietors of the site, ask for the name of the person with whom you're speaking, and state that you are unhappy and don't want to be listed. Check back in another week. If your information is still there, call back and ask for the same person who helped you originally. This time, mention that you are unstable and that their service provides a map to *that person's own house*.

---

* If no such path for the redress of grievances is listed, start with whatever email address you can find.

Online Services

Many online services allow you to create an online profile that may be accessed by anyone within the service. These profiles are optional, and as has been stated many times throughout this book, profiles are generally a bad idea. It's the unstated policies of these networks that are dangerous: first, many sell their subscriber lists to marketers and bulk emailers; second, many (AOL in particular), *keep a copy of every outgoing message you send and willingly turn those copies over to law enforcement agencies.**

If you are concerned about privacy, AOL is probably a poor choice for a service provider. While the company claims not to release subscriber information without a court order, a search warrant, or a subpoena, a case from January of 1998 would seem to indicate otherwise. At that time, the Navy discharged the unfortunately named Chief Petty Officer Timothy McVeigh because he indicated his marital status as "gay" in his personal AOL user profile, which the Navy deemed not in accordance with its "Don't ask, don't tell" policy. Controversy stemmed from the incident because McVeigh's profile did not identify him as a member of the Navy, and because transcripts from the discharge hearing indicated that AOL violated its stated policy of anonymity by readily providing the billing address for the screen name. A U.S. District Court judge eventually reinstated McVeigh, and issued a permanent injunction banning the Navy from discharging him. A series of desk jobs quickly forced him into retirement, though he did reach court settlements with both the Navy and AOL.

Usenet Posts

When you post a message to a Usenet group, it seems to have a pretty short lifespan. People read the message, and while there's always a possibility that they save it or forward it, odds are that you won't be seeing it again. However, search services, including Excite, AltaVista, and Deja.com, now archive Usenet posts and allow them to be searched. While Excite and AltaVista keep the posts for only a few weeks, Deja.com keeps the posts indefinitely.

Preventing archiving of posts

You can prevent the inclusion of your posts in Deja.com and AltaVista's archives by inserting the phrase:

```
x-no-archive: yes
```

at the beginning of each post. Additionally, you may send email to *comment@deja.com* to request that any old posts be deleted. Nevertheless, it's best to either take responsibility for your Usenet posts or submit them anonymously.

---

* Be sure to mention this the next time your mail gets wiped out and they refuse to restore it.

Children and Privacy

The Internet is not a place for children.

People rave about the educational opportunities on the Net—the pen pals, web sites, interactive games, etc. None of them are worth the risk that either your child learns information objectionable to you, or that someone objectionable finds your child. If you feel that there is an Internet resource so valuable it is not to be missed, explore it together, but be warned that children are inquisitive little buggers and once they realize they have Net access, they'll probably explore it when you're not there. If you're looking for an electronic baby-sitter, stick to the television.

Nonetheless, opportunities to explore the Internet are everywhere, from friend's houses to schools to libraries and cafés. Teach your children that the same rules about safety and strangers apply in *every* situation. While online, children should never reveal their real name, age, phone number, or address, and should be suspect of anyone who asks. If someone online says something strange or requests that a child keep a secret, the child should immediately contact a trusted flesh-and-blood adult.

Keep in mind that checking a site's content once is not enough. The Internet changes on a minute-by-minute basis, so you'll never really know what's there. Moreover, in an October 1997 study the Federal Trade Commission found that 86% of the children's web sites they surveyed were collecting personally identifiable information from children—most without requiring parental permission. The information included names, email addresses, postal addresses, and telephone numbers. Only about a quarter of those sites posted a privacy policy or confidentiality statement regarding their intentions to the information. While the result of such data collection is probably just junk mail addressed to your child, there are plenty of examples of unscrupulous people preying on children via the Internet.

Protecting Yourself

Now that you're thoroughly terrified, let's take a look at what you can do to protect yourself. First, you should know your legal rights. You don't want to create a personal home page only to find yourself sued for libel or shut down for copyright infringement. Anytime you think about online security, you need to think about viruses and what you can do to protect your computer from them. We'll also discuss the best ways to protect your identity online and preserve the integrity of your email account. Finally, we'll take a look at so-called "nanny" software to block web sites you don't want children to see.

What's Legal on the Net?

Lawmakers aren't entirely sure of how to legislate the Internet, since by definition it spans a number of jurisdictions. To be safe, however, there's an easy test. If it's legal to publish the information in your country or state, you can be fairly certain that it's legal to post it online. In other words, follow the current legal guidelines regarding trademark, copyright, libel, slander, etc. Parody is a protected form of free speech, and many states protect news, commentary, and satire as well.

Protect Your Identity While Chatting

To protect your identity and keep harassment to a minimum while chatting online, take the following steps:

- Don't use your real name. Create a screen name that doesn't bear any resemblance to your own.

- Don't reveal your gender. Many people seek out women online and harass them.

- Either delete or don't create a user profile.

- Create a fictitious email account and use it while chatting. People can't harass you if they don't know how to reach you. Either list a completely fake account, or create a free account (see Chapter 3) that you never need check.

- Use the /ignore feature. Most chat clients or rooms allow you to issue the *ignore* command by typing:

  `/ignore username`

  at the prompt.

Shopping Securely Online

Many people are quite fearful of shopping online. Believe it or not, the instant you hit the **Submit** button, your credit card number is not sent to Thieves 'R' Us for worldwide distribution. The odds of a break-in are about the same as when you call in a catalog order. Here are a few guidelines for secure shopping:

- Buy only from a reputable source. Is the web site that of a nationally known chain with a good reputation? If it is, the odds are good that you'll receive your merchandise in working order.

- Look for a secure site. Most browsers have an indicator that displays whether the information being sent is encrypted against theft. For example, both Explorer and Netscape use a padlock. If the padlock is locked, then you're data is transmitted securely.

- Use a special credit card with a low credit limit. One Sacramento, California banker supplies her clients with credit cards especially for web use. Since this card has a $500 credit limit, it ensures that even if the number is stolen, the hacker's spending spree isn't going to last very long.

See Chapter 6 for further information.

Viruses

Many neophyte users have an overblown fear of computer viruses. Some don't want to turn the computer on at all, let alone connect to the Internet.

Unfortunately, as the old saying goes, even paranoids have enemies. While most computer viruses are more annoying than destructive, they present an increasing threat. To protect your computer, you'll need to be ever vigilant: install a good-quality virus checker, and update and run it frequently. Any approaching viruses will be quickly found and eradicated. You can also take some simple steps, like not opening unknown email attachments, to keep viruses away from your computer in the first place. And don't panic—most of the viruses you hear about via email are hoaxes, and those described in the media are almost never as dangerous as reported.

A computer virus is much like a biological virus. Computer viruses are computer programs that infect other programs, so that those programs continue to spread the virus, just as biological viruses infect cells. A small percentage of viruses also contain a *payload*, or a set of instructions for the virus to damage the infected computer—sometimes by erasing sections of the hard drive. More often, viruses simply replicate, flash messages, send email, and the like.

Viruses, then, tend to be more annoying than harmful. The now-infamous Melissa virus, which struck in the spring of 1999 and made the front page of the *New York Times*, was harmful only in the sense that it slowed down servers and system performance by sending multiple, unwanted email messages.

How viruses work

A virus cannot infect your computer unless you run the program that contains it. Thus, you can receive email and read messages or load a floppy disk and view the file directory without worry. It's only when you read the email attachment or open the spreadsheet that your computer becomes infected.

Most viruses infect one of three types of files: boot-sector files, executable files, or the template files that applications (almost always Microsoft applications) use to create documents or spreadsheets.

- *Boot-sector viruses* are found on floppy disks, and copy themselves into the boot sector of the hard drive when the computer is restarted; since most computers aren't booted from floppies anymore, boot sector viruses are dying out.

- Viruses that infect executable files are called *program viruses*. When you run a program that contains such a virus, it loads itself into your computer's memory and copies itself into other files.

- *Macro viruses* are the most prevalent viruses today. Once a macro virus alters (most frequently) Microsoft Word's *normal.dot* file, every file modified with MS Word after that is infected. Macro viruses tend to be less destructive than program viruses, but are harder to detect.

When people discuss types of viruses, you'll also hear them discuss entities called "worms" and "Trojan horses" in the same breath. A *worm* is a program that exists only to propagate itself, instead of to alter files on the host computer. Worms infect a computer's memory and send copies of themselves to other computers on the same network. A *Trojan horse* is a term for a computer program that disguises its true purpose from the computer user. Happy99, another virus prevalent in early 1999, was actually a Trojan horse: the program attached an executable program to outgoing email messages. When users double-clicked the attachment, it launched an application that presented a small fireworks display. While users watched the fireworks, Happy99 modified the user's system to automatically and secretly send out just that attachment to future email messages.

Though not technically viruses, worms and Trojan horses are transmitted in the same manner and may be detected and eradicated by virus-checking software.

There's one more important virus category to be aware of: the hoax. Well-meaning users forward descriptions of viruses to everyone they can think of, but these viruses almost never exist. The most famous example is the Goodtimes virus. The message warns against a dastardly virus called Goodtimes, and tells readers that they should automatically delete any message that contains the term "Goodtimes" in the subject line—as does the very message they're reading. The reader is then instructed to forward the message to everyone he can think of. The virus, in effect, causes millions of silly messages to be sent every year, probably more than Melissa generated in its short life span. Hoaxes like Goodtimes, then, are something of a postmodern form of virus.

Avoiding viruses

For your computer to be infected with a virus, you have to take a specific action: namely, run the program that contains it.

Viruses are frequently contained in the following types of files:

- *Microsoft Word templates.* Almost every known macro virus came from a Microsoft Word file, although a few have been found, or shown to be possible, in Excel, Ami Pro, or Lotus 1-2-3 documents. Word documents can't contain macro viruses, only Word templates can; the infected files are usually templates with *.doc* extensions, allowing them to mask themselves as documents. Although Microsoft has taken little action against viruses, Word 97 warns you if a file you're opening contains macros and asks whether you want to load them. Respond negatively and scan the file with a virus checker. More importantly, don't open Word documents you don't trust.

- *Email attachments.* Email is the favored virus-delivery mechanism of the moment. Email attachments are what you have to worry about, however; merely reading an email message doesn't execute any programs, and therefore cannot launch a virus onto your computer. The Melissa virus was so effective because it sent itself to everyone in the Address Book of the recipient. So once someone got infected, the infection soon spread to her co-workers. Recently, Windows applications have been the favorite target of viruses spread by email attachments.

- *Shared files.* You might assume that applications or documents on a local network or from your co-workers would be safe, but you'd be wrong. Files in this environment are sort of like toddlers at nursery school: they're at ground zero of the breeding ground for viruses.

- *Downloaded software.* Files you find at software archives on the Internet— *Download.com,* for example—are actually *less* likely to have a virus than those you'd find on a local network. Why? Because *Download.com* knows that they wouldn't have very many visitors if they transmitted viruses with their files, whereas Joe Co-Worker doesn't mind if the system administrators have a few more chores each day. Even so, you should scan every file you load onto your computer before you run it.

Occasionally, you'll even find viruses contained in commercially shipped, shrink-wrapped software. It's ugly out there.

If you're really concerned about viruses, consider an alternate operating system like Linux. It is (by nature) invulnerable to Windows viruses, and has rarely (if ever) been attacked in its own right.

Increasing Email Security

While most people should probably worry less about online shopping, they should probably worry more about the security of their email account. Apart from the dangers of your email being read by others, email forgery is a very real and dangerous problem. While email lacks the authenticity that handwriting lends a written message, people take its authorship for granted. Consequently, someone who has gained access to your account can send offensive messages under your name, sign you up for unwanted mailings, post bizarre messages to newsgroups, etc.

Here are some tips to follow to maintain email privacy:

- Never save your password. Many mailers have an option that allows you to set your server password and then save it so that you don't have to use it every time you launch the application or every time it checks for mail. Don't use it.

- Once you've read your mail, delete it. Mail that isn't sitting in your inbox is that much harder to snoop through. (Keep in mind that a sysadmin or dedicated sneaky person may still be able to unearth the messages from your hard drive, server, or backup tapes.) If you're using a POP client, be sure that your options are set to delete mail from the server as well.

- Before you close your mailer, *truly* delete your unwanted mail by emptying the trash (or Deleted Items) folder.

- Never open email attachments you aren't expecting. They may contain viruses (and are usually annoying). Melissa and Happy99 proved that even attachments from someone you know aren't always safe.

- If you're reading email via the Web, clean up when you're done. Log out, close the browser, and empty the cache file. (See Chapter 3 for more information.)

- Encrypt or digitally sign your messages. Using applications like Pretty Good Privacy or VeriSign (see the next section) allows you to ensure that the proper recipient of your mail is the only one who'll be able to read it.

- If you ever check mail from an insecure terminal (e.g., a public terminal at a library or conference), consider changing your password as soon as you get back to your home or office.

A few more tips for using email in the workplace:

- Most importantly, remember that even when a company has a stated policy that employee email is private, U.S. courts have upheld a company's right to fire you for the content of messages sent via that system.

- Don't write anything incriminating in an email message—like corporate secrets. Think Richard Nixon; you don't want to record for posterity your unscrupulous dealings.

- Don't libel your boss in a message. In 1997, a Pennsylvania court upheld the Pillsbury Company's right to fire an executive for calling his bosses "backstabbing bastards" in an email message.

- Create and use a separate account for personal mail. If possible, access this account on a computer other than the one you use at work. Your employer may still have a legal right to read that mail if you're using company equipment to read it. See Chapter 3 for more information.

Software for Increased Privacy

Nothing's foolproof, but there are methods for avoiding prying eyes and slippery fingers. Email messages may be encrypted to maintain privacy and signed to prove their integrity. You may even want to use an anonymous remailer service to keep your email address secret.

Pretty Good Privacy (PGP)

PGP and programs like it encrypt email messages (or any file) into gibberish that is unintelligible to anyone other than the intended recipient. Philip Zimmermann invented PGP in 1991, and the program has been so successful that the U.S. government won't allow its export, because it considers the encryption quality a security threat. You can use PGP to encrypt and sign email messages or other files.

To use PGP, you create a *key pair*, which consists of a private key, to which only you have access, and a public key, to which, well, only the public has access. To send someone an encrypted file, you use her public key to encrypt the file. When she receives it, she uses her private key to decrypt it.

PGP is freely available on the Internet. Visit *http://www.pgp.com/products/pgpfreeware. cgi* to download the latest version of PGPfreeware for Windows 95, Windows NT, or the Macintosh. Follow the instructions on your screen to download and install the software.

Creating a key pair

Once you've restarted your machine, you'll notice a new icon in the Windows system tray. Click the icon, and select **Launch PGPtools** from the pop-up menu (see Figure 5-2).

Figure 5-2. PGPtools

The first step is to create a new key pair. Click the **Launch PGPkeys** icon on the left. The PGPkeys window opens. If necessary, select **New Key...** from the **Keys** menu. Follow the instructions in the Key Generation Wizard, entering your name and email address, and choosing a size for the new keys. The larger the key, the more difficult it is to break, but this also makes encryption and decryption take longer. The recommended sizes work fine. (In fact, if you don't choose one of the default values, generating the key pair could take hours.) Next, the wizard asks when you would like the key pair to expire. Choose **Never** unless certain strange conditions exist under which you wish the key to expire.*

Enter a password for the Passphrase field; as with all good passwords, try to include a smattering of upper- and lower-case letters, numbers, punctuation marks, etc. PGP warns you if your password isn't secure.

Once you've generated a key pair, the Wizard presents the screen in Figure 5-3. Send your key to the server. That way, people can access your key when you send them encrypted documents.

When the key generation wizard has finished, be sure to back up your key rings. First, save both public and private rings to a disk other than your hard drive, as recommended. Next, think about moving your private key ring out of the default PGP

---

* If you do set the keys to expire, you'll still be able to decrypt files and verify signatures with them once the expiration date passes; you just won't be able to encrypt or sign new files.

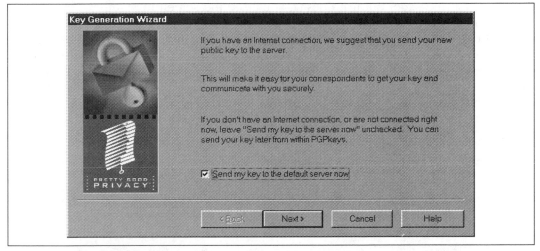

Figure 5-3. Sending your key to a server

directory and renaming the file. If it's easy for that sneaky someone to access your private key ring, it doesn't do much good to encrypt your files.

Using PGP to encrypt and sign email

PGP is remarkably easy to use with Eudora, Outlook, or any email client that supports PGP/MIME. These mailers seamlessly integrate PGP as a plug-in. To use PGP to encrypt messages, write the message as you normally would, then click the **PGP Encrypt** button on the toolbar (see Figure 5-4). Click the **Send** button when you're finished.

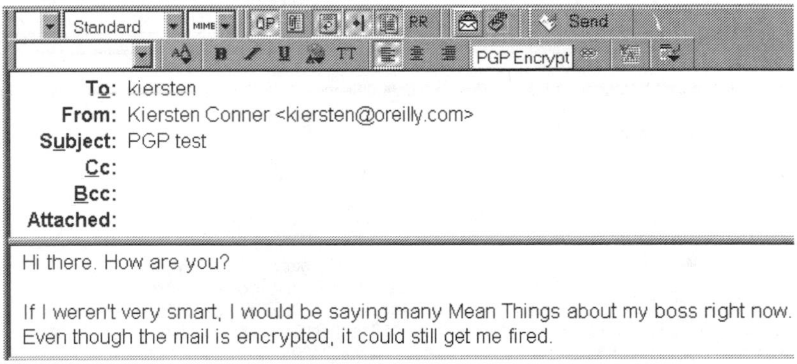

```
┌──────────────────────────────────────────────────────────────────┐
│ ▼│ Standard ▼│MIME▼│ QP ▓ ▓ ↗│ ▓ RR │ ✉ ✂ │ ❖ Send │       │
│        ▼│ AA  B / U ↗ TT │≡ ≡ ≡│PGP Encrypt│∞│ ▓ ▓          │
│     To: kiersten                                                   │
│   From: Kiersten Conner <kiersten@oreilly.com>                     │
│ Subject: PGP test                                                  │
│     Cc:                                                            │
│    Bcc:                                                            │
│ Attached:                                                          │
│────────────────────────────────────────────────────────────────── │
│ Hi there. How are you?                                             │
│                                                                    │
│ If I weren't very smart, I would be saying many Mean Things about my boss right now. │
│ Even though the mail is encrypted, it could still get me fired.    │
└──────────────────────────────────────────────────────────────────┘
```

Figure 5-4. Encrypting email with PGP

PGP then tries to locate the public key of your intended recipients by matching their addresses to addresses in a key repository. If it finds matches for all the recipients, it just sends the message. But if it doesn't, you'll see the screen in Figure 5-5 asking you to pick the intended recipient. If your recipient appears in the top pane, select the listing and drag it into the bottom pane. If it doesn't, search for the address by double-clicking the address you listed (with the line through it) in the bottom pane. While the Key server is pretty good at finding matches, one more problem may arise. Users with older versions of PGP freeware for Unix may have keys that are incompatible with PGP freeware version 5.5. If it's essential that you encrypt correspondence with this person, he or she will have to upgrade, or the two of you will need to find another solution.

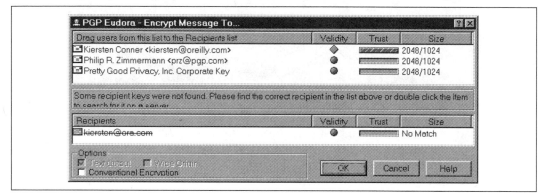

Figure 5-5. The Encrypt Message dialog box

Signing messages works similarly; just click the **PGP Sign** button on the toolbar.

Decrypting email and verifying signatures

When the mail I sent arrives, it looks like Figure 5-6.

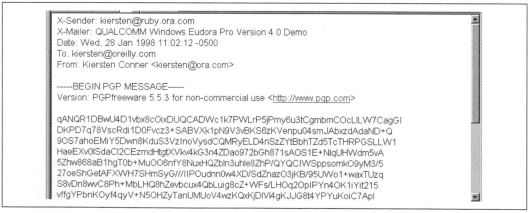

Figure 5-6. Encrypted mail message

To decrypt, click the **PGP Decrypt Verify** button and enter your password in the resulting dialog box. The message becomes legible. If a signature were attached, it would be verified at the same time.

Using PGP with unsupported mailers

Encrypting email with unsupported mailers is a similar process. First, write your message as usual. Then select the text you wish to encrypt and use the **Copy** command to copy it to the clipboard. Next, click the **PGP** icon in the system tray, and choose **Encrypt Clipboard**, **Sign Clipboard**, or **Encrypt And Sign Clipboard** from the pop-up menu. Figure 5-7 shows one way of doing this.

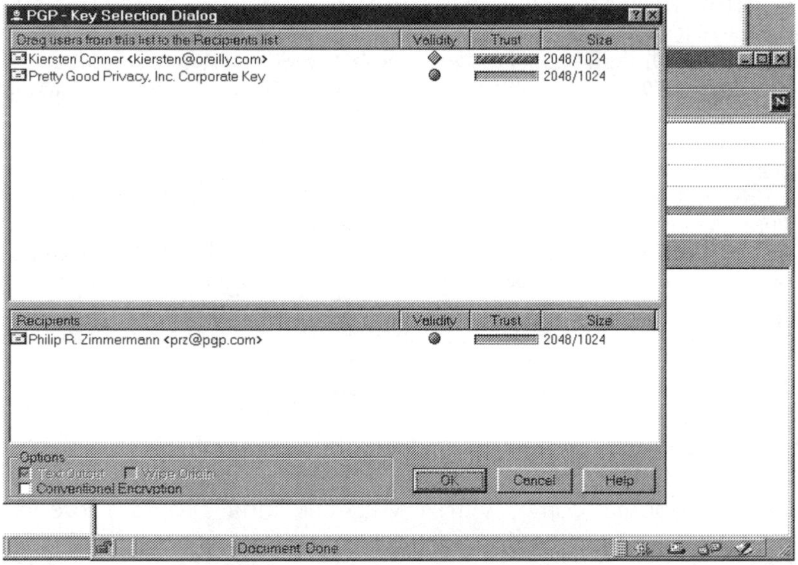

Figure 5-7. Signing a message in an unsupported application

Select the recipient of the message and drag the appropriate public key for those who are to receive a copy of the encrypted email message into the bottom pane. Return to your email application, and paste the clipboard's contents back into the message.You may now send your encrypted email.

If you need to read PGP mail sent by an unsupported mailer, as in Figure 5-8, the process is reversed: open the encrypted message, copy it to the clipboard, click the **PGP** icon, and select **Decrypt Message**.

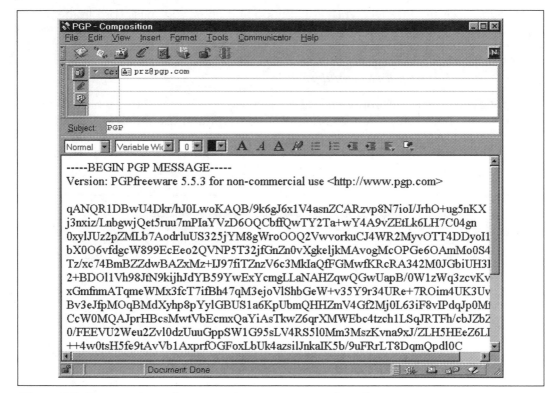

Figure 5-8. Encrypted email message in an unsupported mailer

Virus Checkers

If your computer doesn't come with a virus-checking program pre-installed, you should install one as soon as your computer is out of the box. Once you have, you should update your virus data files on a regular basis. New viruses are released almost daily; if you don't update the virus definitions, your virus checker will be almost worthless. Once your virus checker is installed and up to date, use it to scan every file on your computer.

How to determine whether you have a virus

If you haven't yet installed a virus checker—and sometimes, even when you have—your computer might become infected with a virus. Here are some indications that you might have an infected computer:

- Scanning your files with a virus checker reveals a virus. Viruses may be lurking that haven't yet started to do damage. Never leave a "benign" virus on your machine; it may well be lying in wait before taking destructive action.

- People tell you they received something from you that you didn't send. I learned I was infected with Happy99* when a friend told me how nice it was to start the day with fireworks. While my virus checker didn't yet have an upgrade against Happy99, a quick net search told me what was wrong and pointed toward a demo version of a virus checker that would clean my files.

- Performance slow-downs. Destructive viruses, and even viruses that merely send extra mail messages, need to work in the background so that you won't notice and eradicate them. So, if your computer or Internet connection slows down for unaccountable reasons, run a virus scan.

- The media. Viruses have been big news recently, but the media frequently blows the threat of viruses all out of proportion. Take a look at the Computer Virus Myths home page (*http://kumite.com/myths/*) for a more thorough discussion.

How to remove viruses

If you think your computer might be infected, don't panic. Removing viruses is fairly straightforward. Just to be on the safe side, be sure to take the precautionary measures described here—and most importantly, back up your files on a regular basis. And save your old backups—a backup after you've received the virus will be infected, and restoring files from that backup won't help.

The first step, of course, is to install a high-quality virus program. That program should have two components: a virus shield, which runs in the background and scans the files you load onto your computer, and a virus checker or scanner, a program that scans your computer for viruses, then alerts you to the infected files, and, if possible, removes the virus. The virus program should also support updates over the Internet. If you don't have the most recent virus definitions, scanning becomes largely worthless.

Three popular retail virus suites are McAfee VirusScan, Norton AntiVirus, and DataFellows F-Secure. Each supplies a virus shield and scanner. Each one is also available as a limited-time demo. Downloading a demo may come in handy if, for example, you don't currently have a virus checker installed, or if one of the companies has a virus definition you need before the other. To install a demo, see Chapter 13. To install from a retail package, follow the enclosed instructions.

Next, make absolutely certain to update the virus data files to the most recent version. We'll take a look at VirusScan as an example. The initial window appears in Figure 5-9.

---

* Since I'm giving out all this helpful advice, you might be wondering how I came to be infected with Happy99. The answer is that I was being really stupid: I received email from someone I wanted to trade merchandise with. The message had an attachment, which I thought might contain a list of references, so I double-clicked it. Fireworks and infection resulted.

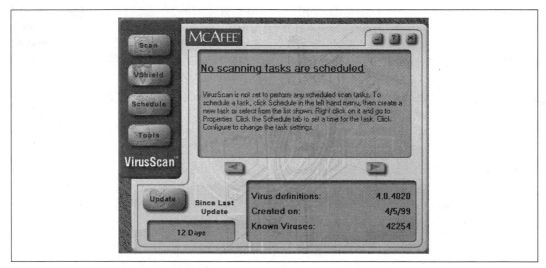

Figure 5-9. Using McAfee VirusScan

We can tell from this screen that the last time the virus definitions were updated was 12 days ago, and that the virus definition files were created on April 5, 1999. If we were running a scan because we suspected a virus, we should update the definitions first.

So, click the **Update** button and follow the screen prompts. VirusScan connects to the McAfee server to see whether a more recent virus definition file has been created. If a newer file is available, the program downloads it and asks whether you'd like to install it. Follow the prompts to do so, and reboot your machine.

Running VirusScan and the other virus programs couldn't be simpler.

Launch the scanner, and click the **Scan** button. From the resulting screen, browse to the drive or files you wish to scan, and click the **Scan Now** button (see Figure 5-10). Be sure to scan all your files, not just program files, and be sure to scan each drive on your machine (especially if you have more than one hard drive). Follow the prompts to clean or remove files.

Configuring your computer against viruses

The best way to deal with viruses is not to be infected with them in the first place. By taking the following steps, you'll avoid the hassle of infected files and the embarrassment of sending them to others.

The most important configuration you can set is that of your virus shield. This program scans incoming files for viruses, but you'll miss some unless you have the shield configured properly. If you were using VirusScan, you would set those options by launching the application, and clicking the **VShield** button, as shown in Figure 5-11.

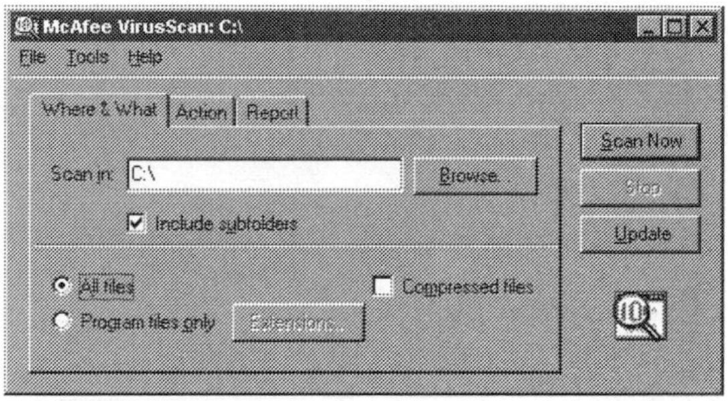

Figure 5-10. Selecting drives to scan

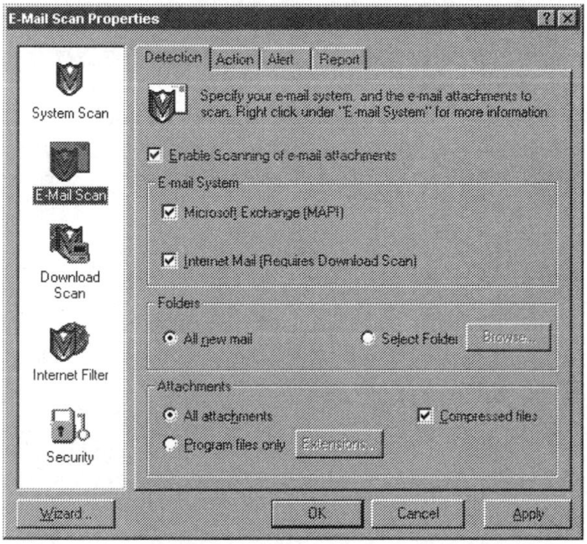

Figure 5-11. Virus shield configuration settings

Go through each tab and set the options so that the shield program scans every possible type of file: all types of files (not just program files), email attachments, Java applets, ActiveX controls, etc. Make sure that each **Action** tab is set to "Prompt for user action," and make sure that each **Alert** tab is set to "Sound audible alert."

When VShield is running, you'll see its icon in the Windows taskbar.

Macro viruses present another configuration issue. To avoid them, open Word 97, and on the **General Preferences** tab (**Tools** → **Options** → **General**) select the "Macro virus protection" checkbox.

Doing so will only help you avoid some older macro viruses. One of Melissa's more clever features was to turn this option off, making Word more vulnerable to generalized virus attack. To really protect yourself against macro viruses, consider the following options:

- Word 6.0 is more prone to macro viruses than Word 97. Consider upgrading. Or, conversely, downgrade to Word 1.0 or 2.0.

- Similarly, use WordPerfect or another word processor. The vast majority of macro viruses are written for Microsoft Word.

- Save any files you plan to share with others in RTF or ASCII format. Since no macros are used, you're inuvnerable to macro viruses.

- On the same note, use the Notepad or WordPad text editors instead of Word; they don't support macros and thus can't be infected.

- Make regular and comprehensive backups of your files.

Email Plug-Ins for Increased Privacy and Security

While PGP is the most prevalent encryption and verification technology, there are a number of other such products, many of which provide plug-ins for various mailers. VeriSign is the most well known. Table 5-1 describes security plug-ins that may be of interest.

Table 5-1. Mailer Security Plug-Ins

Name	Maker	Supported Mailers	Features
ArmorMail	LJL Enterprises, Inc. *http://www.ljl.com*	Microsoft email clients cc:Mail Lotus Notes client Eudora Light/Pro	■ Digital signatures and encryption ■ Interoperable between all major ■ Macintosh and PC mail clients
PGPmail	Pretty Good Privacy *http://www.pgp.com*	Eudora Light/Pro Microsoft Outlook/Outlook Express	■ Digital signatures and encryption
Secure Messenger	Worldtalk Corporation *http://www.worldtalk.com*	Microsoft email clients Eudora Pro	■ Digital signatures and encryption ■ Supports VeriSign ■ Digital IDs
Ultimate Privacy	Ultimate Privacy Corporation *http://www.ultimateprivacy.com*	Eudora Light/Pro	■ Encryption ■ "One-time pad" algorithm

Table 5-1. Mailer Security Plug-Ins (continued)

Name	Maker	Supported Mailers	Features
Steganos for Windows 95/NT 4.0	Deus Ex Machina Communications *http://www.steganography.com/ english/steganos*		■ Encryption ■ Hides files within image, sound, or ASCII files
RPK InvisiMail	RPK New Zealand Ltd *http://www.InvisiMail.com*		■ Digital signatures and encryption ■ Not subject to U.S. export restrictions ■ Transparent to the user
VeriSign	VeriSign *http://www.verisign.com*	Outlook Express Netscape Messenger Deming Frontier Premail Opensoft Connectsoft Eudora Light/Pro	■ Digital signatures and encryption ■ Transparent to the user

Anonymous Remailers

If you really, really don't want to be held responsible for your electronic communications, use an anonymous remailer. These free services conceal your email address, even from the recipient. The remailer (usually) strips your name and email address from the message, encodes it, and transmits it to the sender. Remember, though, that if you send a message to a remailer, the message could still be intercepted between your computer and the server.

Since anonymous remailers operate for free—how would they charge you?—changes are frequent. The Usenet group *alt.privacy.anon-server* will keep you up to date, and is a good place to ask questions.

Generally, there are two kinds of anonymous remailers. The first, in the parlance of the paranoid community, is considered a *pseudo-anonymous remailer*. Pseudo-anonymous remailers operate by giving you an account with a password on their server; whoever runs the server knows your actual email address and identity. *Truly anonymous remailers* provide more privacy, but are much more difficult to use. These may be further broken down into *Cypherpunk remailers* and *Mixmaster remailers,* and for absolute privacy you should send an encoded message via at least two of each kind of truly anonymous remailers. However, you'll probably be too busy tending your 57 cats to send the message through more than five or six servers.

Using an anonymous remailer

First, take a look at the reliable remailer list at *http://anon.efga.org/anon/rlist.html.* Figure 5-12 shows a recent snapshot.

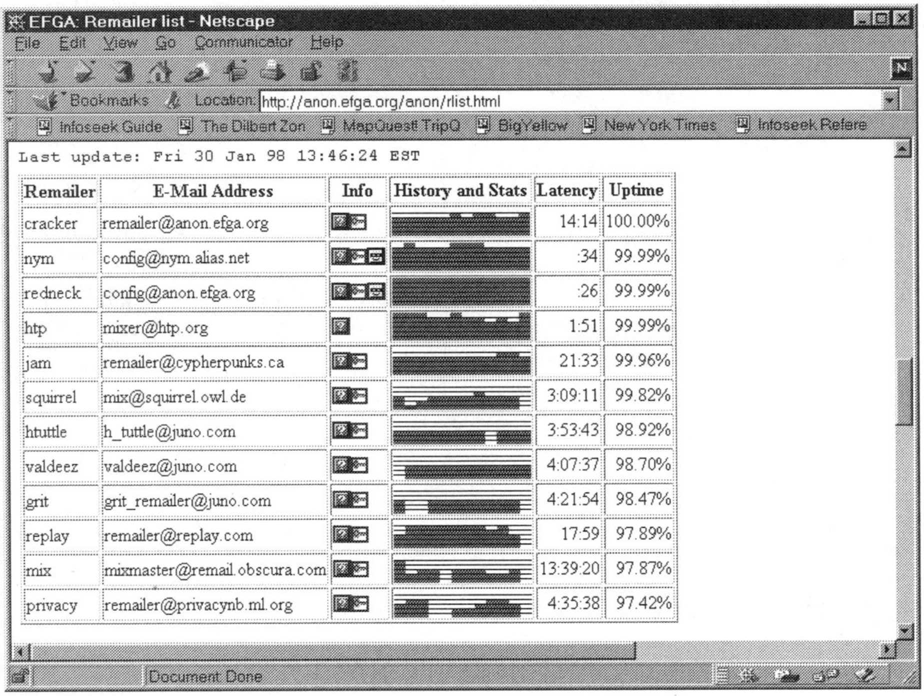

Remailer	E-Mail Address	Info	History and Stats	Latency	Uptime
cracker	remailer@anon.efga.org			14:14	100.00%
nym	config@nym.alias.net			:34	99.99%
redneck	config@anon.efga.org			:26	99.99%
htp	mixer@htp.org			1:51	99.99%
jam	remailer@cypherpunks.ca			21:33	99.96%
squirrel	mix@squirrel.owl.de			3:09:11	99.82%
htuttle	h_tuttle@juno.com			3:53:43	98.92%
valdeez	valdeez@juno.com			4:07:37	98.70%
grit	grit_remailer@juno.com			4:21:54	98.47%
replay	remailer@replay.com			17:59	97.89%
mix	mixmaster@remail.obscura.com			13:39:20	97.87%
privacy	remailer@privacynb.ml.org			4:35:38	97.42%

Figure 5-12. List of reliable anonymous remailers

By clicking on the question mark icon to the right of the remailer's email address, you're provided with a help file that tells you how to send anonymous email via that server. In general, you'll need to create a reply block using a PGP key. The technique is fairly easy to use. Most of these servers support freemail frontends called premail, for Unix, and Private Idaho, for Windows. You can find premail at *http://atropos.c2.net/~raph/premail.html*, and Private Idaho at *http://www.eskimo.com/~joelm/pi.html.* While I would normally cover Private Idaho here, it isn't compatible with PGP freeware 5.5, and was also a little too buggy to recommend.

For ease of use, WWW interfaces to anonymous remailers can't be beat. Take a look at *http://www.stack.nl/~galactus/remailers/index-www.html* for a current list. The W3 anonymous remailer at *http://www.gilc.org/speech/anonymous/remailer.html* is also a good choice. Keep in mind that you will lose some amount of security when you use them, since your message is first transmitted across the Web before it's encoded.

World Wide Web Browsing

There are software tools you can use to increase your privacy and protect your loved ones while browsing online. So-called nanny software lets you create a list of filters to block out web sites you think might be harmful to your unsupervised children while they sit alone in front of a computer. Other services allow you to mask your web browsing, making it difficult for others to force you to take responsibility for your actions.

Nanny Software

A number of software packages work as the V-chip is intended to work on a television set, allowing parents to block out content they don't want their children to see. Different programs have different features; most come with password protection and pre-installed filters with a basic list of sites and content to block. Keep in mind that a child may find "objectionable" content via other Internet services, such as FTP or online gaming forums. Content-filtering software should block access to these services, as well.

Many people feel that these tools espouse censorship, especially since they are more and more frequently used in public schools and libraries. Concern is understandable, but keep in mind that while filter updates from the software companies are a great help, *you* set the filters yourself and may block or unblock sites or concepts as you see fit. Additionally, if you feel that a site is blocked in error, write to the software company. They should take a second look at the site and may change their minds.

It's a good idea to make up your own mind about what constitutes objectionable content. HateWatch (*http://hatewatch.org/index.html*), for example, provides a good list of sites that foster hate speech on the Web—ironically, with links to the sites so that you can examine them yourself.

Table 5-2 presents a list of content-filtering software packages. None of them are a substitute for supervising your children.

Table 5-2. Content-Filtering Software Packages

Name	Maker	Features
SurfWatch	SurfWatch Software *http://www.surfwatch.com*	Blocks 16 topics across four core categories: sexually explicit material, violence/hate speech, gambling, and drugs and alcohol; automatic daily filter updates; restricts searching for objectionable material in all search engines; blocks access to web-based chat sites and all IRC servers; limits access to Yahoo!'s kid-appropriate online environment and sites that you choose.

Table 5-2. Content-Filtering Software Packages (continued)

Name	Maker	Features
CyberPatrol	The Learning Company	Large number of filter categories; multiple-user support; precise control of filtering options; keep in mind that manual weekly filter updates cost $29.95 per year, which seems a bit steep.
Cybersitter	Solid Oak *http://www.solidoak.com*	Automatic filter updates; third-party filter files available; transparent operation; full support for PICS content rating; context-sensitive filtering
NetShepherd	NetShepherd Inc.	Still in beta; creates filters based on democratic tabulation of data from the NetShepherd community.
WinGuardian	Webroot Software *http://www.webroot.com/chap1.htm*	Transparent operation; doesn't block sites, merely logs them; blocks running unwanted executables; posts Acceptable Use Policy that user must agree to before accessing Internet.
WebChaperone	WebCo International *http://www.webchaperone.com*	Supports different filters for multiple users; pre-scans each site; offers alternatives to blocked pages.
NetNanny	Trove Investment *http://www.netnanny.com*	Prevents personal information from going out; blocks inappropriate images and executables as well; transparent operation.

Anonymizers

When searching the Web for software to filter Internet content, I found at least five shareware applications devoted exclusively to monitoring employee Internet usage. If you're concerned about someone monitoring your online habits, take the steps described previously, and try to browse as anonymously as possible.

The Anonymizer home page, shown in Figure 5-13, is a good privacy resource that also provides a means of anonymous browsing (*http://www.anonymizer.com/surf_free.html*). Simply type the URL you'd like to visit into the dialog box, or use the provided list of links.

Unless you sign up for the Anonymizer service, there will be a noticeable delay in connecting to your desired site. For the occasional visit to the Playboy site, however, this is a good solution.

The Crowds home page provides another free solution, utilizing Perl scripts (*http://www.research.att.com/projects/crowds/*). Based on the idea of blending into a crowd, Crowds operates by grouping users into a large, geographically diverse group. When a

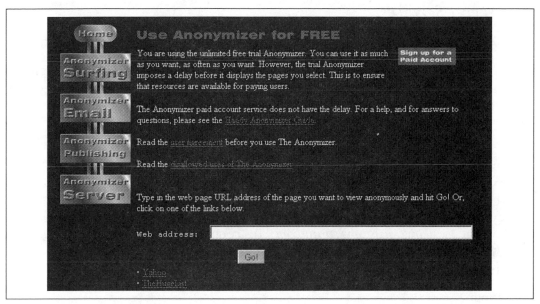

Figure 5-13. Anonymous browsing

user makes a request of a web server, that request is passed to a random member of the group, who then either issues the request (via a proxy on that user's local machine) or passes it along to yet another member. Crowds requires Perl version 5. 0004 or later, and it may be run under either Windows 95/98/NT or Unix.

To keep abreast of current privacy and anonymity issues, consult the newsgroup *alt. privacy* or the Technology and the Law page at *http://www.urich.edu/~lta/techlaw.html*.

Fighting CyberCrime

What happens if you are wronged while online? You aren't entirely on your own. The following law enforcement agencies can help. One note of caution: don't send these agencies any "evidence" you may have found over the Internet. Doing so could be a crime unto itself. Talk to them first and ask for instructions.

The Federal Bureau of Investigation

If you find a child pornographer online, contact your local FBI field office. You should also contact the FBI if you think you've found a hacker or terrorist. The FBI has computer-crime squads in San Francisco (415-553-7400), Washington, D.C. (703-762-3160), and New York City (212-384-1000). You can also reach them via email at *citacwatch@fbi.gov*. Further information may be found at the FBI web site at *http:// www.fbi.gov/fo/fo.htm*.

The Secret Service

As a division of the U.S. Treasury Department, the Secret Service is interested in more than protecting the president and watching Clint Eastwood movies. Fraud, one of the most popular Internet crimes, seems to be their specialty, especially bank fraud, credit card fraud, telecommunications fraud, and financial fraud. Contact the Secret Service at your local field office (see *http://www.treas.gov/usss/location/* to find one). The Headquarters for the Secret Service's Financial Crimes division may be reached at Room 942, 1800 G St. NW, Washington, D.C., 20223, or at (202) 435-5850.

U.S. Customs

The U.S. Customs office specializes in pornography, theft of intellectual property, money laundering, and smuggling. If you suspect someone of child pornography, send email to *icpicc@customs.sprint.com*. To contact the Customs office regarding child pornography or other crimes, first call 1-800-BE-ALERT. You may also contact your local U.S. Customs field office. You'll find more information at the Customs' web site (*http://www.customs.ustreas.gov/index.htm*), not to mention the Detector Dog of the Month.

Police agencies

Some local police agencies have special computer-crime units:

- The San Jose Police Department High-Technology Crimes Unit may be reached at (408) 277-4521 or via email at *sjpdhitek@aol.com*. Visit its web site at *http://www.sjpd.org/hitech.html.*

- The Houston Police Computer-Crimes/Forensic Unit may be reached at (281) 405-5870 or via email at *ccfu@hal-pc.org.*

- The New York City Police Department Computer Investigations and Technology Unit may be reached at (212) 374-4247.

CHAPTER SIX

BUYING AND SELLING

Do sane people really buy things over the Internet?

Absolutely. People use the Internet to buy everything from dog bones to books to groceries, and even to shop for homes and cars. More importantly, their credit cards aren't immediately maxed out, their credit rating isn't destroyed, and their bank accounts aren't raided. Why not? Because shopping online hasn't, thus far, proved to be more dangerous than shopping at a mall.

As soon as the World Wide Web soared in popularity and legitimized the Internet for the nontechnical crowd, retailers envisioned the Internet as a marvelous combination of advertising and direct-sales medium. Savvy catalog-retailers focused on the Web to increase existing sales, as L.L. Bean did, offering secure online ordering via their web sites. Others created innovative sales models that took advantage of the Web's accessibility: the creators of Amazon.com realized that a *virtual* storefront was all they needed. With only a small warehouse, and *without* an actual bookstore, they could sell books cheaper than the competition.

Amazon competes against other big bookstores, but when you're buying books, you have other options. If you're looking for a Hemingway first edition, for example, it may be easier to find the book for sale by an individual seller—a collector in another state, perhaps, who is selling off his collection and advertising on the Internet.

The Internet has always been a haven for the esoteric and the strange, and that doesn't change when it comes to shopping. Looking for something unusual or one-of-a-kind? Try Usenet newsgroups, web rings, or collector's sites. Newsgroups like *misc. forsale* function as 24-hour virtual flea markets. Looking all over the world becomes as easy as looking down the street. The Internet also provides a convenient means for selling goods and services for the individual crafter or collector.

The Internet is a useful tool even if you don't complete the transaction online. Before you make that major purchase, you'll probably want to do a little research. Choosing between jobs in different cities? Take a look at housing prices, school reports, pollution rates, tax rates, and more. Thinking about buying a used car? Check out the virtual paper trail a dealer's left with Usenet messages, or write to an auto club for a recommendation.

What if you do want to buy something over the Web—are such transactions safe? Do you want to be transmitting your credit card number, social security number, and address over the Internet? As with most things in life involving money, you'll need to take some basic precautions. Once you do, however, you'll probably be fairly well protected. In fact, using the Internet *increases* the security of some of your transactions—your tax return won't get lost in the mail, and how well do you know that waiter who just disappeared with your credit card?—and the added convenience can be tremendous.

Just think: you could buy a car without ever having to speak to a car salesman. That's progress.

The Basics of Buying Merchandise Online

Why would you want to shop on the Internet? You'll miss many of the advantages of shopping in person: the social milieu of the mall, the conspicuous consuming, meeting your mother for lunch and hoping that, even though you're well into your mid-20s, she'll still buy you that suede jacket you'll be able to wear maybe two or three days out of every year.

Well, Internet shopping does have some advantages—great advantages, depending on what you're buying. Unique items, such as antiques, handmade crafts, or a mint-condition Libearty Beanie Baby, are more easily located via a search engine than a phone book. Similarly, if you know what you want and don't mind paying shipping charges (keep in mind the gas you'll expend driving to the mall, the value of your time, and the cost of having your bumper repaired after you finally find a parking space and someone cuts you off and you consequently accidentally nick his fender), it's much easier to order specialized items—a book from the bestseller list, say, or a SuperVGA3DxQuadspeedhypno card for your monitor—and have them sent to your home. My uncle swears by the site for Cuban cigars.

In this chapter, we'll describe four paradigms for how people buy and sell things. If you understand the paradigm and know how to find the marketplace you want, you've learned what the chapter has to offer.

There are several different models for buying and selling things:

- *The store*. Web stores are generally large-scale retail establishments that use a shopping-cart sales model and accept credit cards via a secure server. Examples include Amazon.com, J.Crew, and Microsoft's Expedia travel service.

- *The auction.* Auctions make person-to-person sales easier and provide a forum for feedback. Examples include Up4Sale and eBay.

- *The want ads.* The want ad model is fairly straightforward, including classified advertising listings on the Web and postings of items for sale on Usenet. You'll also find classified advertising listings on individual hobbyist's web pages.

- *The convention.* The convention model is our most abstract: a group of users communicating via newsgroup or mailing list, for example. Just like a real-life convention, our online convention paradigm focuses on communication and research more than straightforward sales.

These are important to different extents, depending on what you're interested in. If you're buying a ticket, you're probably interested in a store, though the convention might help if you want to find out about upcoming events or if the event you want is sold out. If you're buying an item from an individual, such as a Beanie Baby, you're probably interested in an auction, want ad, or a convention. As you can see, the models overlap, and you'll frequently find the item you want in more than one setting. Thus, understanding the differences between them becomes even more important.

The Shopping-Cart Model

Web pages are becoming increasingly more like applications: you use them to do things, buy things, or view things. One of the most popular applications is for shopping, and this application is frequently implemented via what we call the shopping cart model.

When shopping for products in the stores of the World Wide Web, you'll find that most web sites use the metaphor of a shopping cart to guide your selection and payment. To begin shopping, browse the web site for products. If you find one you like, there will usually be a button labeled "Buy," "Purchase," or "Add to Cart." Once you've clicked that button, most sites display a page listing the current contents of your cart. You may then continue shopping (either by clicking a link or clicking the **Back** button), add or remove items from your cart, or pay for your selections. To do so, click the appropriate link, which in this case is usually labeled "Check Out." At this point, you'll be asked for credit card and shipping information.

Not every web retailer follows this model, but many do. A good web site dedicated to shopping will be well organized, present product and price information clearly, and provide both a good search facility and a secure server.

One-click ordering

Another popular web shopping option is commonly referred to as and one-click ordering. This model allows you to enter billing and shipping information only once, after which time the data is stored on your computer as a cookie. When you return to the web site in the future, you won't need to enter the information again.

What Makes Shopping on the Internet a Good Idea?

The Internet is an invaluable tool for the smart shopper, even if you never close a deal via email or transmit a credit card number via a secure link. Why? Because you can research scads of information easily and quickly, and some of that information may not be available in other media. Research the product you're planning to buy by examining consumer literature, product descriptions, and price comparisons. Then, research the seller the same way. You can glean additional information, however, by joining mailing lists on the topic, contacting other users via email, looking at Usenet posts by or about the seller, or consulting informational web pages about the individuals in that community.

The Internet also allows you to contact a broad range of buyers and sellers. You can use it to read and post advertisements to everyone with Internet access around the world. Thus, you can learn about esoteric or hard-to-find items relatively easily, and can also compare a greater range of prices. Instead of only your local newspaper's classifieds, you suddenly have worldwide classifieds.

The Internet's search functions also make it a good shopping tool. While your local paper probably doesn't have a listing of four-bedroom houses in Boston in the $150–$200,000 price range, it's easy to use the Internet to review a list of just those kinds of houses. Moreover, if you're moving across the country, you can use the Internet to do a lot of your research in advance. You'll save yourself a fair amount of aggravation by determining the neighborhood you want to live in by researching schools and crime levels via the Internet instead of by word of mouth or the local paper. That way, you'll be prepared when you arrive in the new town.

Similarly, if you know the exact item you're looking for—the latest *New York Times* bestseller, say, or a CD that's about to come out—you may prefer to order the item over the Internet rather than visit a store. Such purchases are especially good when you have a long list of similar items (and thus can save on shipping costs).

One nice feature of online specialty stores is the ability to notify you when something you are interested in becomes available. Stores like Amazon.com and CDNOW.com allow you to request email alerts, such as, "Send me an email when any Mrs. Polifax novels are released" or "Send me a weekly update of new folk music recordings."

One-click ordering is another Internet plus. Moreover, if you frequently order from catalogs, you may prefer to enter ordering information via a keyboard than relay it verbally to a telephone operator, who could ask you to spell your name, verify everything three times and still enter the wrong size. While you may have to enter a lot of information the first time you make a purchase (name, address, phone number, credit card number, passwords, etc.), many sites will save this information for you as a cookie, so that you don't have to enter it the next time you order. We'll discuss further whether you actually *want* to save such information later in this chapter.

What Makes Shopping on the Internet a Bad Idea?

The main problem with shopping over the Internet is that it's virtual. You can't drive the car, squeeze the melons, or look into the seller's eyes. You'll also have to pay a (usually small) surcharge for shipping and handling and wait for the item to arrive. Perhaps more importantly, if you need to return whatever you ordered, you'll have to pay to ship it back.

Another problem, though one that has been vastly exaggerated, is the possibility of fraud or theft. The Internet's low cost of entry and ease of achieving anonymity allows scam artists to proliferate. Spotting such people is simple if you take a few precautions, but the risk is still there.

If you don't like receiving junk mail, electronic or otherwise, buying on the Internet may not be for you. The forms you have to fill out to have merchandise sent contain all the information marketers need to send you reams of unsolicited mail. While many reputable retailers will provide an option to not receive unsolicited information, many do not, and selling lists of names and addresses is a valuable source of revenue to many firms.

Password insecurity is another problem with Internet shopping. Many sites, particularly those that provide one-click ordering, require a password. If you do a lot of shopping online, you can end up with literally dozens of passwords. To be safe, you'll want to have a different, non-English word for each account, and not write that password down anywhere. Short of CIA training, it's unlikely that this is a possibility for you, and you'll probably use two or three passwords, at most, and become a security risk to yourself. While this is a problem with Internet use in general, shopping sites exacerbate it.

The Credit Card Myth

To many people, their greatest fear about shopping directly over the Internet is transmitting a credit card number to a retailer. Thus far, however, using a credit card over the Web has proved no more risky than using it in person or over the telephone. Even though many retailers support secure online ordering, there is a fear that a dedicated hacker will steal credit card numbers, break into bank accounts, set fire to your house, and steal your dog. In fact, people aren't entirely sure of what they're afraid of when it comes to the Internet, as the email I received recently illustrates:

```
IMPORTANT VIRUS NOTICE

If you see a message on the boards with a subject line of "Badtimes," delete
it immediately WITHOUT reading it.  This is the most dangerous virus yet.

It will re-write your hard drive.  Not only that, but it will scramble any
disks that are even close to your computer (20' range at 72 Fahrenheit).   It
will recalibrate your refrigerator's coolness setting so all your ice cream
```

```
melts and milk curdles.  It will demagnetize the strips on all your credit
cards, reprogram your ATM access code, screw up the tracking on your VCR and
use subspace field harmonics to scratch any CDs you try to play.

It will give your ex-boy/girlfriend your new phone number.  It will program
your phone auto-dial to call only your mother's number.

It will give you nightmares about circus midgets. It will replace your shampoo with Nair
and your Nair with Rogaine, all while dating your current
boy/girlfriend behind your back and billing their hotel rendezvous to your Visa card.

It will seduce your grandmother. It does not matter if she is dead. Such is
the power of "Badtimes" it reaches out beyond the grave to sully those things
we hold most dear.

It will rewrite your back-up files, changing all your active verbs to passive
tense and incorporating undetectable misspellings which grossly change the
interpretation of key sentences.

"Badtimes" will give you Dutch Elm disease. It will leave the toilet seat
up and leave the hairdryer plugged in dangerously close to a full bathtub.

It will wantonly remove the forbidden tags from your mattresses and pillows,
and refill your skim milk with whole. It is insidious and subtle. It is
dangerous and terrifying to behold.

It is also a rather interesting shade of mauve.

These are just a few signs. Be very, very afraid. PLEASE FORWARD THIS MESSAGE
TO EVERYONE YOU KNOW!!!
```

Could a virus do all these things? No, it couldn't. Similarly, transmitting your credit card number via a secure server that uses encryption is, in my opinion, safer than handing that credit card to a waiter, for example, who disappears with the card and returns a few minutes later. With Internet transmission, the number is encoded and no one ever sees it; in a restaurant, a perhaps surly, underpaid individual has unrestricted access to that number.

More tellingly, there have been very few examples of financial abuse as a result of shopping online.

Is Shopping on AOL Different Than Shopping on the Web?

Shopping on America Online is not safer than shopping on the Web, and doesn't provide better deals.

It seems that every time I log on to AOL, I'm greeted with an invitation to buy something. Recently, I was greeted with two sales solicitations even before that soothing male voice so warmly welcomed me.

About half of the AOL welcome screen is dedicated to shopping and products (see Figure 6-1).

Figure 6-1. Opportunities to purchase ham, picture frames, and more

Even my new mail was clogged with offers (see Figure 6-2).

Figure 6-2. Where else could I find arthritis relief, insurance, and flowers, all in one place?

The point I'm trying to make is that if you use AOL, it's hard *not* to shop online.

The actual shopping experience is largely similar to shopping on the Web—the same shopping-cart model, the same input of credit card information. I had hoped that since AOL already had all my credit card information, one-click ordering might be an option,* but such was not the case. In fact, many of AOL's shopping links are merely links to the merchandiser's site on the World Wide Web. Don't think that you'll make up the cost of AOL subscription fees in special AOL "member's only" deals, either; those I checked out were all identical to deals available to any other consumer.

AOL does offer an "increased" level of security over shopping on the Web. AOL requires a certification process of the merchants they list and vows to "protect you" should credit card fraud occur. The fine print reveals that this protection ranges to that normally afforded by your credit card, plus fifty bucks (see Figure 6-3).

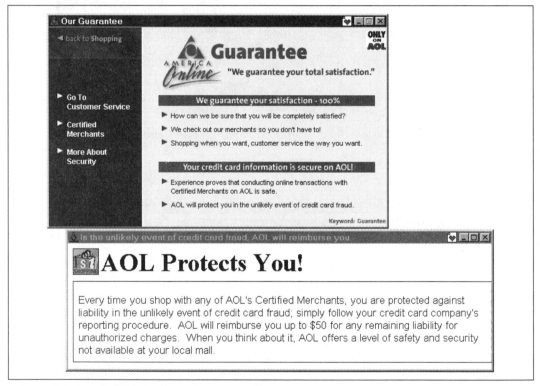

Figure 6-3. Big Brother with exclamation points

The upshot? America Online does have substantial shopper's resources, but it doesn't offer anything you won't be likely to find on the Internet.

---

* Particularly since the relevant credit card information directs the billing to O'Reilly & Associates and one-click ordering might have resulted in the entirely *accidental* delivery of a five-pound box of chocolate truffles to my office.

Safe Shopping

Throughout this chapter, I try to cover the safest, most convenient means of exchanging money online. Here are some general tips for safely conducting business on the Internet.

Things to Remember When Trading Online

The wild-west nature of the World Wide Web is appealing to people who seek the thrill of the deal. If you plan to trade online regularly, however, a reputation as a scoundrel will only prove a hindrance. Be sure to learn about the community you're trading within, and remember the following (throughout this chapter, "sellers" refers to individuals selling goods, while "vendors" refers to corporations):

- Don't be a chump—never give out your credit card number for free merchandise.

- Before buying from individual sellers, try to find out whether there is a "good traders" list on the topic. These lists are generally created by groups of users and may contain detailed information about individuals who buy or sell goods on the Net. Pay attention to warnings about bad sellers.

- Determine the seller's refund and return policies before you place an order.

- If you're interested in trying a new vendor, one that you are not familiar with, ask the vendor for its physical location (address and phone number) so that you can check on its reliability with outside organizations, such as the Better Business Bureau and other consumer agencies.

- If you're buying from a vendor with a web site, pay attention to the site's URL. If it doesn't look legitimate (legitimate J. Crew clothes probably won't be found at *http://www.screwme.com/~floyd/00000877.htm*), don't buy from this vendor. (One hint: be suspicious of any commercial web site with a URL that contains a ~.)

- Print out a copy of your order (including any confirmation numbers), and save it until the merchandise arrives.

- If you're sending an individual a check, print out a copy of the agreement the two of you made and send that along with the payment.

- The same laws apply to online vendors as to real-world vendors. By law, a vendor must ship your order within the time stated in its ads (30 days if no time is stated). The Fair Credit Billing Act protects credit card transactions.

- If you're paranoid about your credit card number, phone the vendor directly, or use an application to encrypt the number with PGP.

- If you really don't feel good about buying directly over the Internet, you may want to check out Trade-direct at *http://www.trade-direct.com*. This service will act as a broker between you and another party, and allows you to pay by check instead of credit card.

Consumer-information web sites

If you'd like to register a complaint about a user or learn more about a merchant on the Web, here are a few good places to start. Cybercop (*http://www.cybercops.org*) bills itself as "a place for consumers to gripe about their bad experiences, vent their frustrations, or just report suspicious online activity." The site maintains archives of complaints, with a section on consumer "success stories" about people who've resolved consumer disputes. The Internet ScamBusters site (*http://www.scambusters.org/index.html*) focuses on email abuse and Internet fraud and explains the reality behind many nefarious Internet offers. The old standbys, the Better Business Bureau (*http://www.bbb.org*), National Consumer Complaint Center (*http://www.alexanderlaw.com/nccc/cb-intro.html*), and the Federal Trade Commission (*http://www.ftc.gov*), all maintain web sites with pages dedicated to online concerns. Most offer information in a newsletter-style format.

Buying Products

When buying products online, there are a number of paradigmatic activities that are repeated in lots of different contexts. Once you know how to buy a book online, you already know all you need to know to buy a CD online, or a sweater, or a plane ticket.

The different kinds of shopping activities appear to be:

- Buying a "generic" product, such as a book, CD, or item of clothing. You'll usually find these items in online "stores."

- Buying a generic product that requires local delivery, such as groceries or meals. Again, you'll usually find such items in the storefront format.

- Buying a one-of-a-kind product or collector's item. These items are more likely to be found via conventions, auctions, or want ads.

- General "fan" activity, which is often mixed with buying and selling fan paraphernalia, such as concert tickets or bootlegged recordings. This is more suited to a convention.

In the following sections, we'll discuss how to find and secure books, music, tickets, new and used cars, houses, apartments, computer equipment, groceries, and meals online. We'll also discuss the intricacies of buying from individual sellers.

Books, Music, and the Amazonian Revolution

In 1994, a young investment banker name Jeff Bezos quit his Wall Street job to open a bookstore. The bookstore was Amazon.com, and it changed the way people bought books.

Bezos wasn't necessarily a bibliophile—after noticing the manic growth of the Web, he chose books from a list of twenty products he thought could be sold successfully online. Why books? For one thing, because there are a lot of titles out there for consumers to choose from. Bezos' philosophy ("Our goal is that if it's in print, it's in stock"), appealed to consumers who could search for specific books they might not find at the local bookstore. With a database of more than two and a half million books both in and out of print, Amazon presented a wide range of choices.

The 10 to 40 percent discounts appealed to consumers, as well. Amazon sells its books more cheaply than other retailers, since it doesn't have a storefront and maintains very little inventory. Once customers have ordered their books (or, now, music, toys, and other products) via a secure server on the Web, Amazon then requests the purchase directly from a publisher or distributor. Amazon's other advantage lies in its marketing. Customers can search for books, for example, by keyword, author, title, or subject. Amazon can then recommend other books customers might be interested in, track their preferences, and send them email when a book they've been looking for arrives. The site also provides links to reviews in popular publications and allows readers to review books online.

So what? Well, Bezos and Amazon created the classic web store, and people who've never used the Internet before are now flocking to the site. Booksellers Barnes & Noble and Borders have both followed suit and opened up web sites hawking books at deep discounts. For the first time, a large number of people feel confident buying nongeeky consumer products on the Web. Amazon isn't the only—or even the best—place to buy books or music online, but it has changed the way people think about the Web.

Books

Buying books online has certain advantages over buying them at a bookstore. If you're researching a specific or esoteric topic, such as a travel destination, wedding vows, or John Quincy Adams, the Web is a great place to get recommendations for titles. Once you've found the books you're looking for, even the local superstore may not have all of the titles you want. Moreover, books are fairly safe to buy online: books don't really vary in production quality, since the bindings shouldn't be cracked, the pages shouldn't fall out, and the text *really* shouldn't vary from copy to copy. Finally, many web sites offer discounts over local bookstores.

There are a few disadvantages, as well. For all the recommendations you get online, you can't pick up the book and browse through it, looking over the table of contents or scanning the index. Additionally, you'll have to pay shipping charges and wait a few days for the books to arrive.

One of the Web's best book-related features is the research you can do on the books beforehand. You can solicit recommendations from:

- Newsgroups, on a specific topic
- Special-interest web sites

- Literary magazines and newspapers

- Bookseller's web sites

You'll find plenty of recommendations, particularly from the booksellers, who frequently provide comment pages for readers.

When shopping for books online, keep in mind that while Amazon is the most famous, it isn't the only site that sells books. Both Borders (*http://borders.com*) and Barnes & Noble (*http://www.bn.com*) have web sites that sell books at a discount. Acses (*http://www.acses.com*) searches for books at over 25 online bookstores, including Amazon, and returns results in order of price, including shipping. Publishers' web sites are another option. Most provide information about their books and authors, and many allow you to order their books directly. You're unlikely to find discounts at these sites, however, since such a practice would (understandably) annoy retail booksellers.

Book purchasing walkthrough

When might you use the Web to purchase a book? Perhaps you have a specific task to research. You're getting married and don't know what kind of ceremony to have. Where to start?

First, take a look on the Web. The newsgroup *soc.couples.wedding* seems like a good place to start. The FAQ post has a section that's just what we need, as shown in Figure 6-4.

```
2) Recommended Reading

2.1) For those who want to save money:

"Bridal Bargains", Denise and Alan Fields.  Windsor Peak Press, 1996.
"How to Have a Big Wedding on a Small Budget", Diane Warner.
Writer's Digest Books, 1992.

2.2) For those interested in writing their own vows/ceremony:

"Wedding Vows" by Peg Kehret.  Meriwether, 1989.
"For as Long as we Both Shall Live" by Roger Fritts.  Avon, 1993.
"Weddings from the Heart" by Daphne Rose Kingma.  Conari press, 1991
"With these words...I thee wed", Barbara Eklof.  B. Adams, 1989.
"I Do" Sydney Barbara Metrick.  Celestial Arts, Berkeley, 1992.  ISBN
     0-89087-679-7
"Wedding Readings: Centuries of Writing and Rituals for Love and Marriage"
     Eleanor Munro ed.  Viking, 1989.
```

Figure 6-4. Finding books about sincerity

At this point, you may want to post to the newsgroup to find out what other people think of these titles. What kind of people have used them? Do they seem to have tastes similar to yours? Similarly, you may want to look the titles up at Amazon.com and see whether other book buyers have had positive or negative things to say about each book.* For example, take a look at Amazon's entry on wedding vows, by Peg Kehret, which appears in Figure 6-5. Unfortunately, there's only one customer review. However, between the publisher's synopsis and the comments from "A reader from united states," we now have a much better idea of what the book is about.

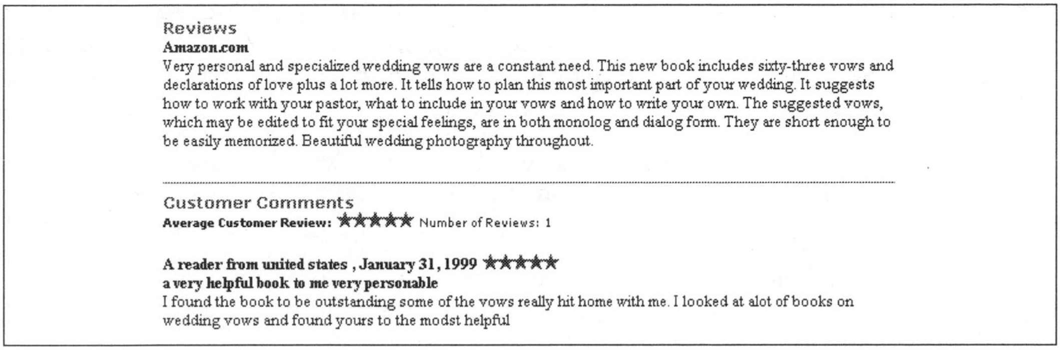

Reviews
Amazon.com
Very personal and specialized wedding vows are a constant need. This new book includes sixty-three vows and declarations of love plus a lot more. It tells how to plan this most important part of your wedding. It suggests how to work with your pastor, what to include in your vows and how to write your own. The suggested vows, which may be edited to fit your special feelings, are in both monolog and dialog form. They are short enough to be easily memorized. Beautiful wedding photography throughout.

Customer Comments
Average Customer Review: ★★★★★ Number of Reviews: 1

A reader from united states , January 31, 1999 ★★★★★
a very helpful book to me very personable
I found the book to be outstanding some of the vows really hit home with me. I looked at alot of books on wedding vows and found yours to the modst helpful

Figure 6-5. Additional information about a book on wedding vows

For the sake of argument, let's assume that we want to buy all six books listed in the FAQ. Let's take a look at Acses, a book "supersite" that searches through a list of online bookstores for the best prices. When we visit the home page, we click on the **ISBN Search** link, to search for the lowest prices on multiple titles, as in Figure 6-6.

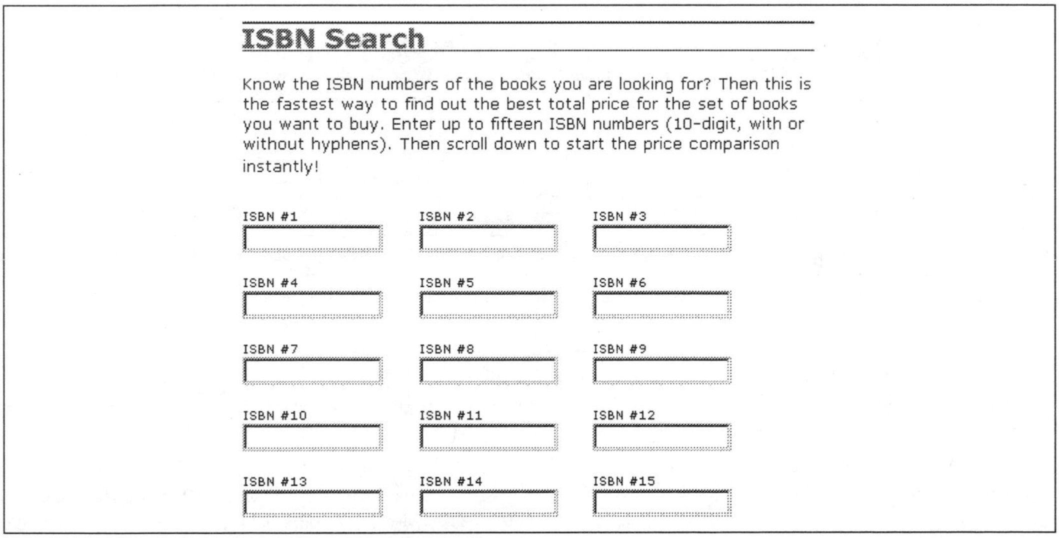

ISBN Search

Know the ISBN numbers of the books you are looking for? Then this is the fastest way to find out the best total price for the set of books you want to buy. Enter up to fifteen ISBN numbers (10-digit, with or without hyphens). Then scroll down to start the price comparison instantly!

ISBN #1	ISBN #2	ISBN #3
ISBN #4	ISBN #5	ISBN #6
ISBN #7	ISBN #8	ISBN #9
ISBN #10	ISBN #11	ISBN #12
ISBN #13	ISBN #14	ISBN #15

Figure 6-6. Using Acses to find books for cheap

---

* Take the words of these book buyers with a grain of salt. There have been numerous accounts of authors posing as readers and uploading glowing reviews of their own works. More importantly, in 1999, it was revealed that Amazon was selling spots on their book recommendations list.

ISBN stands for *International Standard Book Number,* and that number is the social security number of the publishing world. Keep in mind that different editions have different ISBNs, as do paperback and hardback editions. Since we only have the ISBN number for one title, *I Do,* we'll have to search for the rest. To do so, follow Acses' instructions and perform a standard search by author, title, or keyword. You can search for each individual title or enter a keyword, like "wedding vows," and see whether the titles you want turn up in the resulting list. If a title has two ISBNs, try the most recent publication first. If the book's not out yet, however, and the older title is still in stock, you may be better off going with that.

It's easiest to open up a second browser window to perform this research. That way, when you find the ISBN number, you can copy and paste it into the Advanced Search window.

Once you've found all the ISBN numbers, choose your location and preferred currency from the drop-down menus, and click the **Search** button.

The Acses results page (Figure 6-7) shows us how much the books will cost from different vendors and how its research progressed. Click the **Total Price** link, in the lefthand column, to order the books from the appropriate shop.

Click on one offer (1st column) to proceed to the respective shop!

For more info about a Multi-Shop Offer, click on the respective link (2nd column).

Displaying Top Ten offers:

Total Price	Shop	Item Price	US Sales Tax	Shipping Costs	Shipping Time	Shipping Service	Delivery Time
US$ 49.09	alphaCraze.com, USA, NY/CA	US$ 39.75	US$ 1.59	US$ 7.75	3-7 days	UPS Regular Mail	n/a
US$ 55.19	Amazon.com, USA, WA/NV	US$ 47.44	US$ 0.00	US$ 7.75	3-7 days	USPS Priority Mail	4-8 days
US$ 55.84	Bookbuyer's Outlet, USA, NY	US$ 47.44	US$ 1.90	US$ 6.50	2-7 days	Standard	n/a
US$ 56.09	alphaCraze.com, USA, NY/CA	US$ 39.75	US$ 1.59	US$ 14.75	2 days	UPS 2nd Day Air	n/a
US$ 56.93	Borders.com, USA, TN/MI	US$ 49.43	US$ 0.00	US$ 7.50	3-7 days	Standard	31-49 days
US$ 63.07	WordsWorth, USA, MA	US$ 55.57	US$ 0.00	US$ 7.50	3-7 days	UPS Standard	n/a
US$ 63.09	alphaCraze.com, USA, NY/CA	US$ 39.75	US$ 1.59	US$ 21.75	1 day	UPS Next Day Air	n/a
US$ 63.15	Books.com, USA, OH	US$ 59.30	US$ 0.00	US$ 3.85	14-42 days	USPS Book Rate	n/a

Figure 6-7. The Acses results page

Acses does have a few flaws, however: clicking the link to alphaCraze.com doesn't transmit the entire order. You'll have to click on each and add it to your virtual shopping cart.

Paying for the books

If this is the first time you've bought books online, things bog down at this point. As mentioned earlier, you have to click on each title to add it to your order, a process that quickly becomes painful on a slow connection. Once you're ready to check out, you'll need to enter a wealth of information: billing address, home and daytime phone numbers, shipping address, email address, and credit card number. You'll also need to choose a shipping method and specify any special instructions.

Once that's done, however, many sites support one-click ordering, so that shopping at them becomes a much more streamlined experience (see Figure 6-8).

Figure 6-8. One-click experience

If you click Amazon's **Buy 1 Now** button, you won't even have to confirm the order. All your shipping and billing information is saved as a cookie on your hard drive, and the book is sent to your default shipping address.

Music

The Web is changing the way music is sold. As with books, music is well suited to the online store paradigm: there is a wide selection of products to choose from, and, when purchasing music on compact disc, the quality is uniform. Even better, you can try before you buy, by listening to audio selections from the music online. SonicNet (*http://www.sonicnet.com*) offers a wide selection of clips. The new Liquid Audio technology even allows you to buy music by downloading it. And, increasingly, web sites allow you to create your own compilations of music for cassette tape or CD.

Buying albums over the Web is very similar to buying books, with one important exception. While you can't pick a book up and leaf through it, you *can* perform the virtual equivalent on an album. Many music sellers, including Amazon, CD World, CD Now, Tower Records, and others, provide links to audio files containing clips from the album in question. These files are usually in RealAudio format, though you'll sometimes find WAV or AU files as well. You're likely to find audio clips at web sites for individual record labels. Individual web pages or newsgroups are another option. You may find more sound clips here, though they probably won't be in RealAudio format and may be posted illegally.

Finding music on the Web

Where to find music on the Web? If you're looking to buy, try Amazon.com, Tower Records, CD Universe, or CDNOW. If you'd like to find information or fan pages about a band, try the All-Music Guide (*http://www.allmusic.com*) or the Ultimate Band List (*http://www.ubl.com*); you might also search a Usenet archive site to learn about music newsgroups. Band labels are also online, and these present one of the more interesting phenomena in buying music online.

Some independent labels have shifted their distribution almost entirely to the Internet, allowing customers to place orders for albums via the Web, and, eventually, to download albums in the same manner. Distributing records over the Internet has the same advantages as distributing books: low overhead. For a small record label, low overhead can translate into a profit margin. If you're interested in finding such labels, take a look at the Partial Guide at *http://www3.sympatico.ca/partialguide/indie.html*.

Compiling your own CD

Many web sites are springing up to create the CDs for you. Sites such as CustomDisc. com and SuperSonic Boom (see the Resource Catalog for a more comprehensive list) allow you to pick and choose music tracks for inclusion on a CD that they'll then send you, for a price (see Figure 6-9). Although it's improving rapidly, the selection of music at these sites isn't comprehensive enough to make them really worthwhile, probably due to copyright restrictions. Even such seemingly public-domain friendly genres as folk and Christmas songs lacked selection breadth. I was excited to find Ella Fitzgerald listed as an artist at one site, only to see such song selections as, "I Want the Waiter with the Water" (lyrics: "I want the waiter with the water for my daughter"). Additionally, most were slow and lacked adequate search features.

Another, better option is to compile songs on your computer and transfer them to compact disc or MP3 player. Unfortunately, you'll need access to a writable CD-ROM drive. A burgeoning number of sites, including Billboard and Music Boulevard, support the Liquid Audio format. This technology provides CD quality audio more quickly and reliably than RealAudio, and is designed to allow you to download singles (usually at a cost of a dollar or two) to your computer; from there, you may do with them as you wish: use your computer as a stereo or burn the songs to a writable CD. To learn more about Liquid Audio, take a look at its web site: *http://www.liquidaudio. com.* You may also want to check out the MP3 format. To learn more about MP3, see Chapter 10.

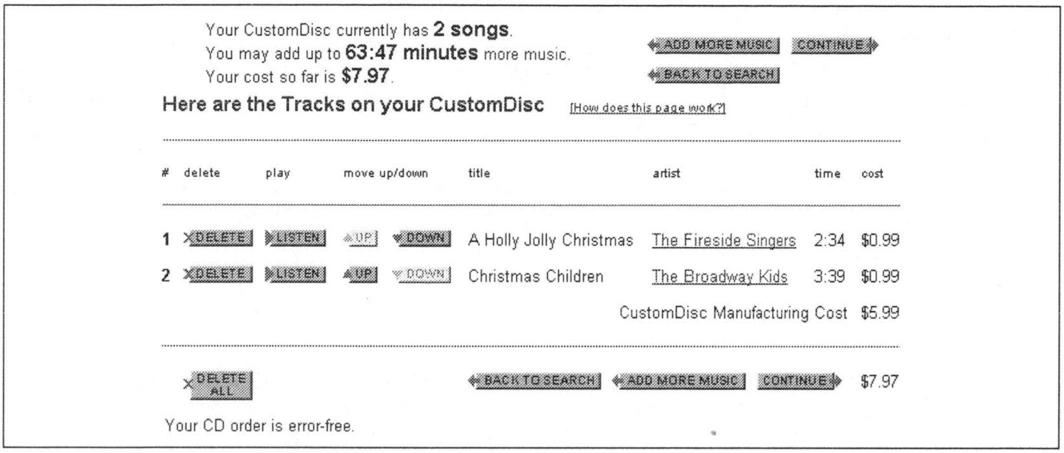

Figure 6-9. Creating a CD of Christmas songs

Musical trading

What if you want to find music that money can't buy? Finding music on the Internet also leads you into our convention paradigm. The Web is a great means of finding the bootleg cassette and videotapes that fans make at concerts. To do so, take a look at newsgroups, web pages, and mailing lists related to the group you're interested in. You're likely to find listings of people interested in trading or copying such tapes. For example, clicking the Bootlegs link at a Barenaked Ladies fan site eventually took us to the page in Figure 6-10.

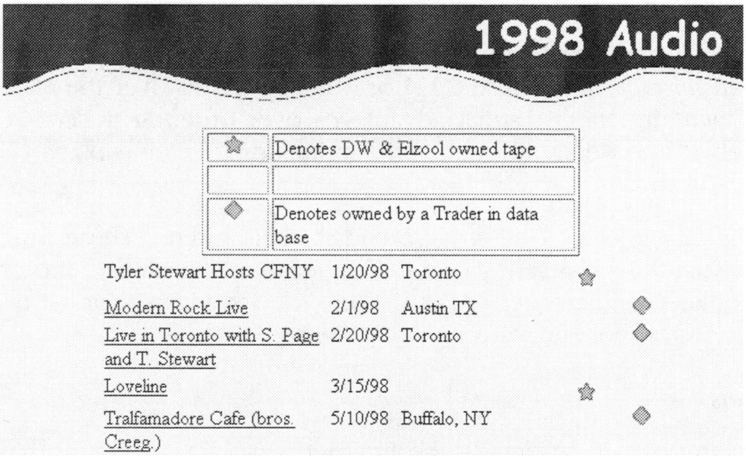

Figure 6-10. Obtaining copies of Barenaked Ladies bootlegs

By clicking the links to the shows that were taped, you can obtain additional information about the recording and how to get it. The best way to reach someone is usually via email; the person making the request generally sends an audio tape for the show to be copied on or trades a bootleg tape of her own. Be sure to follow any rules listed, and be polite.

Such web sites are usually a good source of information about bands or musicians, especially for concert schedules—you'll often find information there well in advance of professional sites, such as TicketMaster.

Tickets

Selling tickets is another burgeoning commercial enterprise occurring via our online store model. You can find tickets for everything from movies to concerts to sporting events, not to mention airline tickets that are often substantially discounted. Most of these tickets can be found at commercial sites—a concert hall or theater's web site, for example—but you can frequently find substantially discounted tickets to upcoming events at the various for-sale newsgroups.

Event tickets

One web site, MovieLink (*http://www.movielink.com*), uses an innovative ticket purchasing model. When you visit the site, you can view trailers of the movie, read descriptions, and visit links to the official movie site or to gossip pages about the stars. If you choose to buy tickets, you enter your credit card information via a secure server. Then, when you reach the theater, you insert your credit card in a machine in the lobby, which spits out your tickets. You'll pay a small premium (usually a dollar or so per ticket) for the convenience.

Additionally, you can buy tickets to just about any event from TicketMaster (*http://www.ticketmaster.com;* see Figure 6-11) or a ticket broker over the Web. Buying tickets this way actually offers distinct advantages over ordering tickets over the phone, since the web site presents all your options, including seating plans (Figure 6-12), in an easy-to-read format.

Ticket brokers are another option for buying tickets online. These businesses, which are illegal in some areas, resell tickets for higher than face value, and often have tickets to events that are otherwise sold out. There are too many regional ticket brokers to cover here; search for one in your area that seems reputable.

Airline tickets

If you're looking for airline tickets, the Internet is a bargain-hunting haven. American Airlines (*http://www.americanair.com*) and US Airways (*http://www.usairways.com*) both offer web site sections and mailing lists that allow users to receive news of discounted tickets a week or so before the departure date. Additionally, airline web sites

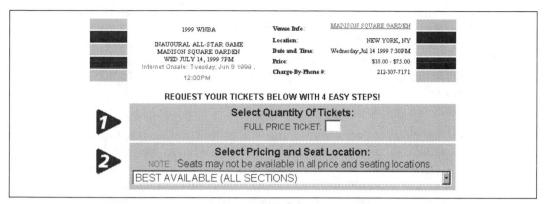

Figure 6-11. *Online ticket ordering with TicketMaster*

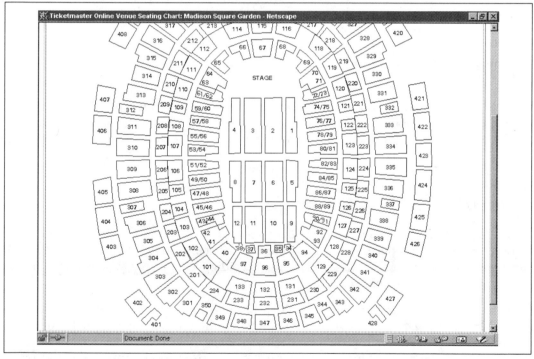

Figure 6-12. *Madison Square Garden seating plan*

frequently describe other special offers, such as bonus frequent flyer promotions and credit card offers.

Microsoft's travel web site, Expedia (*http://expedia.msn.com*), is usually a convenient source for good deals. Clicking the **Travel Agent** link is the first step in finding low-cost airline tickets. The site also offers hotel and car rental reservations. Enter your itinerary information via Microsoft's secure server, wait a few minutes, and Expedia searches its database. Select a flight from the returned listing, enter your credit card number, and make the purchase. You may then use either a standard, paper ticket or an electronic, paperless ticket. Standard tickets are sent through the mail and should arrive within five days. I've used both methods without problem. In fact, I once had to give a travel agent a confirmation number before she could find a bargain flight turned up by Expedia.

The Priceline web site was recently granted a patent for its manner of doing business—a Web first. As ubiquitously advertised by William Shatner, the site uses a "reverse auction" format to sell airline tickets and other high-priced goods. Potential passengers name the amount they're willing to pay, and the airlines decide whether they're willing to sell a ticket for that amount. To use the site, you'll need to input more than the usual amount of information (I had to input nine separate pages worth), since Priceline checks on fares from various airports at various times. Once you've submitted your request (*including* your credit card number), Priceline gets back to you within the hour about a fare.

Food

Increasingly, you can use the Web to order groceries or dinner and have either one delivered to your door. The general model seems to be that of the store that delivers: the web site contracts with local vendors, who receive the order and deliver the goods. So don't worry—that cucumber came from your local grocery, not a central processing center in Cleveland.

Groceries

The idea of buying groceries online may seem a little strange at first. Shopping for food, particularly produce, is a very tactile experience. You're taking a risk when you grocery shop online; however, you're also avoiding crowded aisles, waiting in line, and the sound of screaming children.

The national online grocery services, Peapod (*http://www.peapod.com*) and Net Grocer (*http://www.netgrocer.com*), each contract with a local supermarket. After you transmit your order, the local market delivers your food either the same day or the next day. Temperature-controlled containers keep frozen foods frozen. Peapod promises that produce specialists hand-pick fresh produce according to Produce Marketing Association standards.

What are the advantages to buying groceries online? If you need a lot of staples, such as canned food or dry goods, there's really nothing to lose. You'll automatically receive the market's preferred customer savings, and you can submit coupons as you normally would. Peapod saves your last three grocery orders, so that you don't have to make another grocery list from scratch. Delivery is free for orders over $60. So go ahead, look up recipes on the Web, make a shopping list, buy the groceries online, and have them arrive after you get home from work.

Peapod's software, which I used to conduct this research, made the task simple (though the Java-based programming also made it somewhat slow). It's thorough, however, and for most products, you can even read the nutritional information on the labels.

Once you've filled your shopping cart, click the **Check Out** button (see Figure 6-13). You'll have to enter your delivery and credit card information the first time you shop with Peapod. If you need to stop shopping and resume later, Peapod saves your order for future reference.

Figure 6-13. Grocery shopping via Peapod

Restaurant Delivery

If you'd like to avoid the pesky human interaction that comes with ordering food over the phone, you can do so over the Web. While I only found two nationwide delivery services available at the time of this writing, Cybermeals (*http://www.cybermeals.com*) and Cyberchefs (*http://www.cyberchefs.com*), take a look at *http://www.yahoo.com/ Business_and_Economy/Companies/Restaurants/Delivery_Services/* to see whether others have become available. Unsurprisingly, more than a few service Silicon Valley. The nationwide services contract with local restaurants to deliver meals.

Ordering is easy. Input your address and state whether you'd prefer take out or delivery, and Cybermeals provides a listing of restaurants that service your area, including the restaurant's hours and whether they are open. Clicking on a restaurant's link takes you to a detailed menu that allows you to choose details down to the last anchovy.

Cyberchefs, in Figure 6-14, works in the same manner.

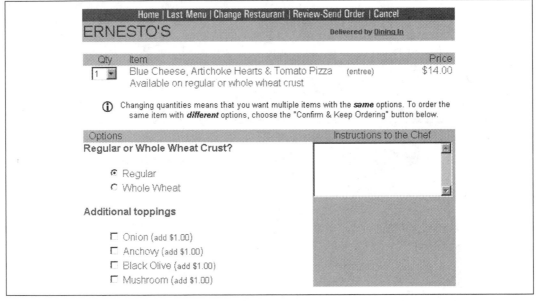

Figure 6-14. Mmm, pizza from Cyberchefs

Name a delivery time and complete the transaction as you would any other online purchase.

Computer Equipment

While I doubt that this will come as a surprise, the Internet is a great place to buy computer equipment. Moreover, computer equipment may be bought in forums spanning three of our paradigms: stores, auctions, and want ads. New and used hardware, software, and peripherals are easy to find. In fact, a number of software retailers have shut down their storefronts and now operate solely via catalogs and web sites. The great advantage to shopping for computer equipment online is the ability to compare prices easily.

Before you buy, be sure to research your product first. Many products have confusing names and configuration options, and returns can be a hassle when shipping is involved. You'll also want to shop around for the best price.

Such prices do range wildly. The digital camera market, which is admittedly volatile, sees prices for the same camera range by three to four *hundred* dollars. Obviously, calling multiple electronic/computer stores would be a hassle, but typing a query into the PriceWatch (*http://www.pricewatch.com*) search engine takes only seconds.

See the Resource Catalog for a listing of computing equipment retailers on the Web. The Insight web site (*http://www.insight.com*) deserves special mention. This site provides a plug-in that will test your computer specifications and make recommendations as to whether software and peripherals will work adequately on your system.

Hardware

Many retailers, including Dell, Gateway, and PC's for Everyone, sell entire desktop and notebook computers online. They allow you to configure a computer exactly as you see fit, including any cards or peripherals you desire. Since looking at a floor model computer in a show room can't tell you much more than reading a computer's specifications online, you have very little to lose in shopping this way.

How might you go about buying a new computer? First, do some research. c | net's Computers.com (*http://www.computers.com*) presents reviews of hardware in categories including desktop configurations, monitors, scanners, storage, notebooks, modems, cameras, memory, servers, printers, hand-helds, and graphics and sound. Let's say we wanted to find a very thin notebook computer, so we click the **Notebook** link, as in Figure 6-15.

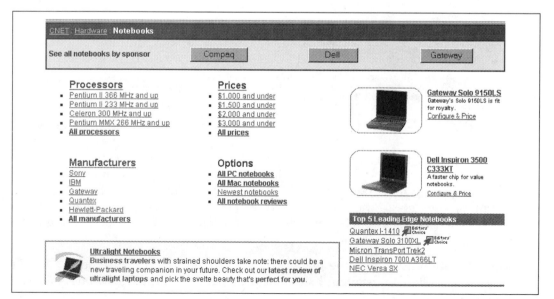

Figure 6-15. Computers.com's notebooks page

The page is broken down nicely for our needs. There's a link to Ultralight notebooks and various feature articles. After doing some research here, and at a few other web sites that review computers, we decide to go with the Hitachi VisionBook Traveler.

The next step is to find a good price for the VisionBook. At the top of c|net's review is a link labeled **Latest Prices**. Clicking the link returns a list of prices, the lowest being $1,446.28 from a vendor called Hardware Street. Just to be safe, let's try another price comparison. The PriceWatch site has a low price of $1623, so it seems like a good idea to go with the Hardware Street price.

Or is it? How much do we know about Hardware Street? According to Computers.com, we know that they offer an extended warranty and a return policy for 30 days. We can take a look at the Hardware Street web site; their home page confirms the 30-day return policy and adds that when you place an order, they plant a tree. That's all well and good. Do a little research of your own, as we've discussed previously: a search on Infoseek for information about the company turned up a web site called Reseller-Ratings.com (*http://www.sysopt.com/vendsurv.html*) that had a section on buyer comments, shown in Figure 6-16, that was somewhat mixed.

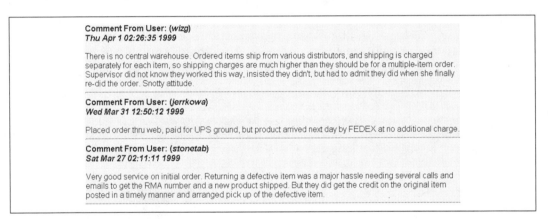

Figure 6-16. User comments

A search at Deja.com revealed the interesting story that appears in Figure 6-17. A few other messages confirm the fact that buying via Shopper.com is cheaper than buying directly from Hardware Street. All in all, Hardware Street looks like an okay place to buy from, so let's go to Shopper.com and go ahead. (In case you haven't noticed, we're now back in a store.) When we click the **Buy Info** button, we see a listing of the specifications of the VisionBook.

Be sure to confirm that this is the model you're looking for. Click the **Add to Cart** button, and you'll follow the standard shopping-cart purchasing model to buy your new computer.

And what about used hardware? Computer equipment, which usually doesn't have moving parts to wear out, is actively sold by individuals in both the auction and

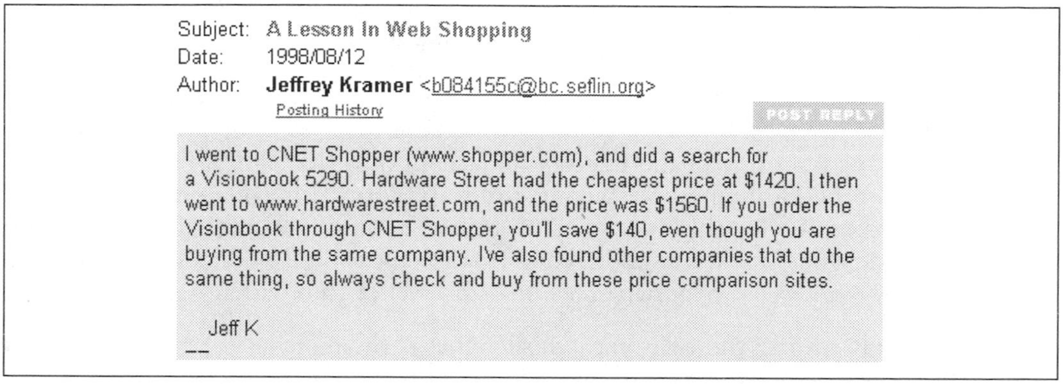

Subject: A Lesson In Web Shopping
Date: 1998/08/12
Author: **Jeffrey Kramer** <b084155c@bc.seflin.org>
Posting History

POST REPLY

I went to CNET Shopper (www.shopper.com), and did a search for
a Visionbook 5290. Hardware Street had the cheapest price at $1420. I then
went to www.hardwarestreet.com, and the price was $1560. If you order the
Visionbook through CNET Shopper, you'll save $140, even though you are
buying from the same company. I've also found other companies that do the
same thing, so always check and buy from these price comparison sites.

Jeff K
--

Figure 6-17. Cheaper prices

want-ad format. CPUs may become out of date quickly, but they also seem to work forever; disk drives and monitors will eventually fail, but may take five to six years to do so. Take a look at web-based classified ads, Internet auctions, and for-sale newsgroups if you're interested in buying such equipment. Similarly, many of the online auction sites do a big business in peripherals. See the section "Buying from Individuals," later in this chapter, for tips on this kind of transaction.

Software

Software is another excellent online buy, again, because it's a standardized product. Some manufacturers even allow you to download the software directly, allowing for near-instant gratification (depending on your modem speed). Purchase the software with a credit card, and they'll mail you the manuals or send them as Adobe Acrobat files. Take a look at Beyond.com (*http://www.beyond.com*) for a list of downloadable software.

Of course, many people download software without paying for it—in the form of shareware. There are a number of excellent shareware archives on the Web (see the Resource Catalog for a complete list), and there's very little risk to buying software in this manner (so long as you can have an up-to-date virus checker installed). Once you've found a software package you'd like to try, follow the instructions to download and install the files to your computer. If you'd like to keep the software, remit payment to the makers. This may take the form of a secure credit card transaction or a check to a snail-mail address. Some software developers take payment in beer, but that seems unwieldy for most transactions.

Big Ticket Items

Some purchases are just too big and can't be delivered to your door. However, you can use the Internet to research everything about your prospective car or house.

Additionally, you can apply for financing online and use that knowledge to weigh your options. Think of the Web as a tool for facilitating such purchases.

Cars

The idea of buying a car over the Internet may seem quite strange. A car is something you need to be quite careful about buying and to perform a thorough physical inspection on. However, the Internet is a wonderful place to start: you probably have a very specific idea of what you want, and it may be difficult to find within your local area. Moreover, since prices are negotiable, it's probably better to broaden your search.

Of course, even with all the bells and whistles that car makers are currently adding to their WWW sites, you still can't test drive a car over the Web.

The first step is to decide on the car you want. Do research on the Web and via actual tactile experiences. Then use Internet dealer or locator services to find that car at the best price. You can even use services like CarFinance.com to set up an auto loan ahead of time. While many web sites are devoted to locating specific cars for consumers, you can also look at auto enthusiasts' web pages, which frequently have classified or bulletin board listings of cars for sale, or for-sale newsgroups in your area.

Here's a real-life example. Last year, my fiancé and I realized we needed a car, since the lease on our reliable, yet microscopically small, Honda Civic was about to run out. We decided that a used Audi 4000 was the way to go, based on our desire for all-wheel drive coupled with abject poverty. After looking at *ne.forsale* and an Audi club web site, we found a 1985 Audi 4000S Quattro for sale from a guy in New Hampshire. My uncle, my friend who lives in Idaho, and my fiancé's mother all told us not to buy it. We drove to New Hampshire for a test drive. It was manufactured while I was still in high school, had 98,000 miles on the odometer (which we learned later was stuck), and the rear doors didn't open from the inside.

"We'll take it!" we told the guy from New Hampshire. After all, it had a sunroof.*

Since the odds are high that you're a somewhat more rational person, let's take a look at how you might go about using the Internet to buy a car.

Researching a car purchase

First, decide on the car you want. The informational conventions about automobiles on the Internet are legion. To get started, you might visit a few auto maker web sites. Or, if you have a few different models in mind, you might want to compare them. Microsoft's CarPoint (*http://carpoint.msn.com*) is a good place to begin. Click on the **Prices & Reviews** link to get started (see Figure 6-18).

---

* I didn't say it was a good example.

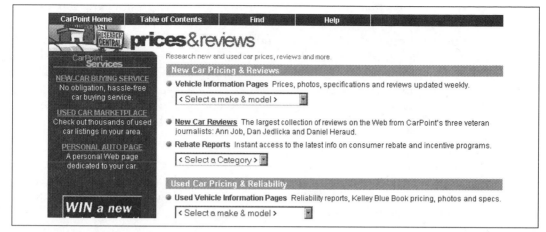

Figure 6-18. Microsoft's CarPoint reviews

The resources you'll find here make it easy to compare the value of various cars on a point-by-point basis. Let's say we're interested in the Volkswagen Beetle, and select it from the new car reviews section. Clicking the **Compare** link takes us to a page that compares the Beetle with other cars in the same price range, as shown in Figure 6-19.

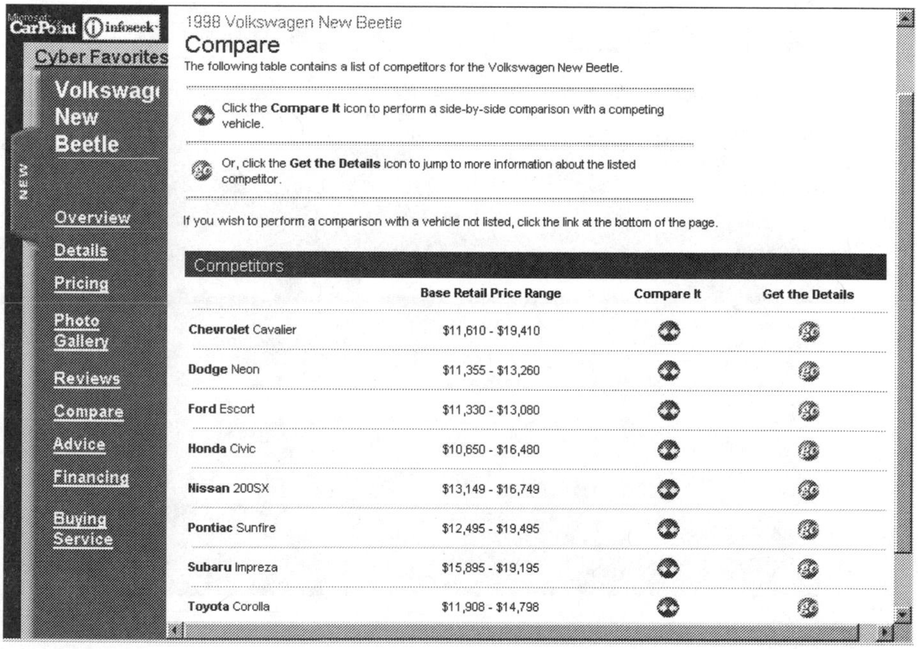

Figure 6-19. Comparing car prices

At $16,000 or more, the Beetle seems pretty pricey. What makes it so special? Visiting The Bubble Car (*http://spyder.tcn.net/beetle/*) links to a movie of a Beetle in a head-on crash (the dummy bounced right off the airbag) and describes an article from CNN that "everybody" should read. Since the article states that the new Beetle involved "a massive data-center migration to client/server Unix systems, Oracle Corp. databases and SAP AG software" for Volkswagen factories, the car starts to seem like a better buy. If we wanted more information, however, we could take a look at Car Talk's test-drive notebook (*http://cartalk.cars.com/Info/Testdrive/*) or the newsgroup *rec.autos. makers.vw.*

We decide we want the Beetle despite its exorbitant price. Since we're taking the leather seats, we'll need financing, and try CarPoint's **Financing** link. Turns out, however, that CarPoint provides only advice, not actual money, so click the **Back** button a few times to get back to the Automotive channel.

Look at Infoseek's web sites listing and click the **Finance your car** link. From there, it's easy to reach CarFinance.com and apply for a loan online (see Figure 6-20). Before doing so, however, be sure to check the Bank Rate Monitor at *http://www.bankrate. com/brm/rate/auto_home.asp*, to make sure you're getting a good deal. This site compares the interest rates for auto loans at banks in individual states.

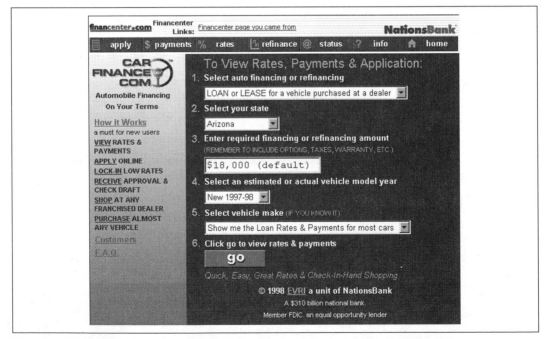

Figure 6-20. Applying for a car loan online

Now that we've got the financing, all we need to do is find the actual car. Again, from Infoseek's Automotive channel, enter Volkswagen and your Zip Code under the "Buy a car online" heading. (Yes, we're heading back to an auto store.) You're taken directly to Auto-By-Tel's FasTrak* page, where you select the make of Volkswagen you wish to buy, and its condition (new or used). Choose how soon you plan to buy the car, and click **Continue**. Fill in a form with the features and colors you want in the car, along with your name, address, and phone number. Auto-By-Tel promises you'll be contacted by a dealer within 24 hours "with a low, no-hassle, no-haggle, up-front price quote." Since there are no obligations or fees for filling out the form, there's very little risk to the consumer. You'll then visit the dealership that returns the quote and purchase the car.

There are other web-based options. Do you want an unusual or complex combination of options? Do you hate haggling? If so, Auto-By-Tel is probably a good choice. You may want to compare the price online with one you can get at a dealer. At the very least, you can get a quote online, take it to a dealer, and ask him to match it. Use the Web as a tool to make the right choice, not just as a conduit to a purchase.

After all, Auto-By-Tel isn't the only way to go, and their dealers may not have the car you're looking for, particularly if you want an older, used model.

Used cars

What if we decide the new Beetle really is too much? Maybe we should look for a used Beetle.

The Web is a fantastic place to research used cars. Informational resources like the Kelley Blue Book (*http://www.kbb.com*) and Edmund's Automobile Buyer's Guide (*http://www.edmunds.com*) make it easy to find used cars online. Once you've settled on a model, check out fan pages and/or newsgroups for classified listings. If you decide to buy from an individual seller, be sure to check that person out, using the methods we discuss later.

The web sites listed in Resource Catalog provide model searches, financing, or both.

Car rentals

Is buying too much of a commitment? You can also *rent* a car via the Internet, again according to the store paradigm. Hertz, Avis, and other car rental agencies both provide online reservations and discounts, while Microsoft's Expedia, mentioned earlier, includes car rental reservations in its Travel Agent wizard. Once you've logged into Expedia, click the **Car Wizard** link and start filling in your pertinent information (see Figure 6-21).

Expedia searches its database and returns a list of rental cars at the airport of your choice. Click the link next to the car of your choice, and Expedia provides more

---

* Why smashing words together and misspelling them is considered a sound marketing ploy is beyond me. Why would anyone prefer to buy anything from a hurried illiterate?

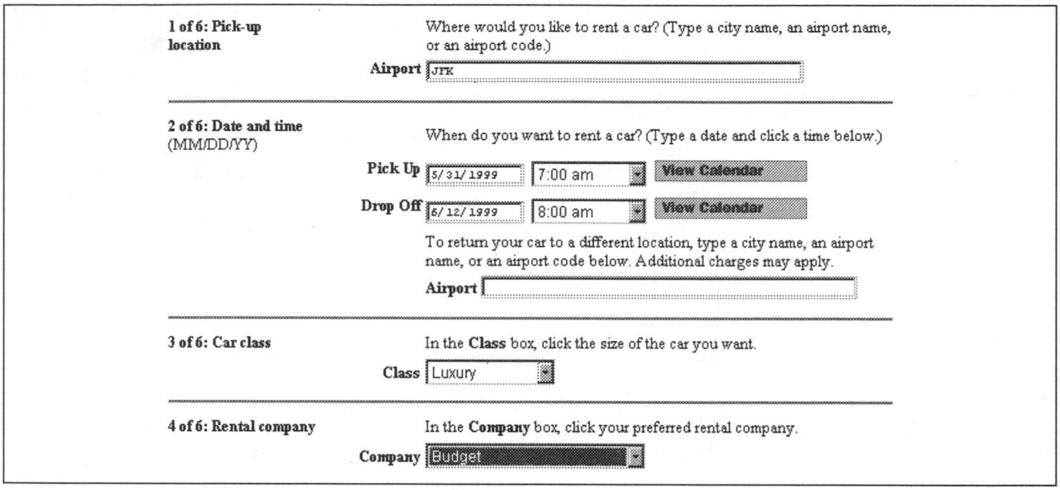

1 of 6: Pick-up location	Where would you like to rent a car? (Type a city name, an airport name, or an airport code.)
	Airport [JFK]

2 of 6: Date and time (MM/DD/YY)	When do you want to rent a car? (Type a date and click a time below.)
Pick Up	[5/31/1999] [7:00 am ▾] **View Calendar**
Drop Off	[6/12/1999] [8:00 am ▾] **View Calendar**
	To return your car to a different location, type a city name, an airport name, or an airport code below. Additional charges may apply.
	Airport [ ]

3 of 6: Car class	In the **Class** box, click the size of the car you want.
Class	[Luxury ▾]

4 of 6: Rental company	In the **Company** box, click your preferred rental company.
Company	[Budget ▾]

Figure 6-21. Reserving a car via Expedia

details about that car (location of the rental agency, hours of operation, etc.); the following page allows you to request further specifications, including bicycle rack, mobile phone, ski rack, or car seat. You'll also be able to enter any frequent traveler plan numbers if you wish. Finally, enter your credit card information, and the car will be waiting for you at the airport.

Take a look at the sites in Chapter 15 for a more complete listing of rental car services on the World Wide Web.

Finding a Home

Finding a home is a complex process, and the Web can be a good place to start. Most people have some basic criteria: price range, number of bedrooms, number of bathrooms, specific amenities, distance from in-laws, etc. Various house and apartment search facilities can narrow down listings according to these needs. Some also help you look for current mortgage rates, calculate your monthly payments, and assess your credit rating.

Researching a neighborhood

First, follow the convention paradigm and use the Web as a tool to figure out where you want to live. If you're really unclear about where you're going, look at *Money* magazine's online Best Places Finder (*http://pathfinder.com/money/bestplaces/*). You can plug in answers to 63 questions, and the engine will return the best place for you to live. The International Salary Calculator (*http://www2.homefair.com/calc/salcalc.html*) helps you compare the cost of living in hundreds of cities, while the Moving Cost Calculator (*http://homefair.com/late96/movecalc/movecalcin.html*) will help you estimate the cost of moving between U.S. cities.

Most people, however, will already know which city they're moving to; they'll need to choose a neighborhood. Many local publications publish a guide similar to *Money's*. Check the web sites for local newspapers and magazines, or post a few questions to local newsgroups. You might also try a search on the name of a particular town. Looking up "San Anselmo" led me to the page in Figure 6-22.

Figure 6-22. Learning about San Anselmo, California

Scrolling down this page takes us to a link to a site about Marin County, where San Anselmo is located. From there, we can learn about the county's various communities, schools, and services.

Such locally-created sites are often largely promotional, however. You'll want to check web sites of watchdog groups or newspapers for statistics on crime, taxes, education, and pollution. The Environmental Protection Agency sponsors a web site (*http://www. epa.gov*) that has a convenient Zip Code search. Enter a Zip Code, and find out about concerns in that area: pollution, hazardous waste sites and other regulatory information, environmental conditions and trends in that county and its watershed, and computer-generated maps of regulated sites.

Finding and buying a home

Once you've chosen a neighborhood, switch to the want-ads paradigm and start looking for actual houses. There is a wealth of real estate agencies and newspaper listings available on the Web; most search engines and start pages support a real estate channel that should start you off. Many of the sites feature pictures of the properties, and they're a good source for a ballpark sense of housing prices. Of course, the most current listings for homes and apartments will probably still be in your local Sunday newspaper.

Once you've found a property that looks promising, use one of the map tools on the Web (see Chapter 12) to get directions to it and a sense of a neighborhood. You may also want to look at public transportation routes and schedules nearby. If you have a portable or handheld computer with a mobile phone link, you might be able to save yourself hours otherwise spent lost, looking in the wrong neighborhood.

Another smart use of the Web is to compare mortgage rates, and perhaps even to apply online. Most of the real estate channels will have a section on finding and applying for a mortgage. Most mortgage sites switch back to the store paradigm. HomePath, from Fannie Mae (*http://www.homepath.com*), has good sections for people who know very little about buying a house, with calculators to help you compare renting with owning, to see how much house you can afford, to learn how to shop for a lender, to see what it means to close on a loan, and to get information on when to refinance. You'll also find a glossary of mortgage and finance terms. Once you feel comfortable in the mortgage world, take a look at the Mortgage Mart (*http://www.mortgagemart.com*), Infoseek's Homeshark Rate Shopper (*http://rateshop.homeshark.com/scripts/crateshop.dll?center=infoseek*), or Microsurf's Mortgage Quotes (*http://www.mortgagequotes.com*) to compare rates and monthly payments. Many sites allow you to begin the qualification process online or over the phone. For more information on mortgages and how they may be linked with other accounts, see Chapter 7.

General Shopping

Obviously, you can buy just about anything you want over the Internet. Most catalog retailers have web sites (i.e., J. Crew and L.L. Bean), and even some department stores are joining the online fray. Check the Resource Catalog for shopping sites that display some distinguishing feature: they provide links to the best or most popular shopping sites, have added security features, provide otherwise difficult to obtain merchandise, or are simply well organized and easy to search.

Certain sites provide specialized services. Wedding registries put the store paradigm to good use, since people shopping for wedding gifts don't need to examine the items in question and are merely choosing but just want to choose from a list. Such registries are additionally convenient when they can be accessed via the Web. And auctions, which we've mentioned throughout the chapter, are an important means of bringing buyer and seller together online.

Wedding Registries

While you might think that registering for a wedding would be fun—you are, after all, shopping with other people's money—most couples seem to come to blows over how many towels they need. Many wedding sites promise online registries, which, one would think, would at least allow the arguments to occur in the privacy of your own home. View pictures and descriptions online, fill out a form, hit **Submit**, and be done with the selections. Even better, wedding guests could order the merchandise online from anywhere they might be.

Unfortunately, only a few retailers offer such complete services. TheGift.com (*http://www.thegift.com*) does a remarkably good job with an easy-to-navigate layout and a number of retailers. It's easy for guests to find a registry and order online. Couples or customers may also register or order via phone, fax, or mail. The Wedding Network (*http://www.weddingnetwork.com*) provides a similar service but is very difficult to navigate and requires a complex registration process. Other major national retailers, including Macy's (*http://www.macysbridal.com*), J.C. Penny's (*http://www.jcpenney.com/giftreg/index.htm*), and Service Merchandise (*http://www.servicemerchandise.com*), allow guests to shop your registry online once you've registered by phone or in person. Crate & Barrel, the Mecca for the about-to-be-wed, promises an online registry in the near future.

Online Auctions

Online auction sites let sellers put all sorts of small items up for sale. Don't expect a virtual Sotheby's full of priceless paintings; most auction sites provide a far broader range of items. You'll find everything from software packages to comic books to jewelry.

Why do people shop the online auctions? First, you'll find a broad range of collectibles and antiques for sale at such sites. Prices are frequently somewhat lower than you might otherwise pay, though you'll want to be careful not to get caught up in a bidding war. Finally, buyers can learn a little bit about the people selling products at the auction sites. The site archives information about the people who sell their products there, and you can click a link to a seller's feedback page to see how many items they've sold, and what previous buyers have had to say about the transactions.

To bid on items at most sites, you'll need to register and choose a username. The site then sends you a password you can use to bid on items. The site sends you mail to confirm your bid, and also emails you if that bid has been topped by another user. If you win an auction, both you and the seller receive each other's name and email address. At that point, it's up to you to complete the transaction from that point. Keep in mind that sellers can place feedback about buyers as well, so don't renege on an auction you've won. See Chapter 15 for a list of auction sites on the Web.

Buying from Individuals

One of the best things about the Internet is the way it connects individuals. This principle holds equally true when it comes to making purchases. If you're looking for the kind of merchandise that could formerly only be found at a swap meet, yard sale, or flea market, the Internet is an invaluable resource. This is where the convention paradigm really comes into play: you'll want to learn a lot about both the item you're buying and the person from whom you're buying it. Baseball cards, Beanie Babies, handmade crafts, and all sorts of collectibles can be found in abundance in cyberspace. We'll use Beanie Babies throughout the following examples, since they're a particularly hot item being traded on the Internet right now (see Figure 6-23). The paradigm holds true for any collectible or small item being sold on a person-to-person basis.

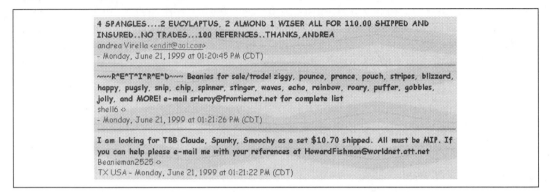

Figure 6-23. Listings of Beanie Babies for sale at the Ty, Inc. web site

Why might you want to buy from a person rather than from a reputable institution? After all, it's much easier for some guy to rip you off and skip virtual town than for, say, J. Peterman. There are, however, several reasons why you might. First, it's easier to find esoteric items for sale from an individual seller. The shop on the corner may not stock Hopi jewelry or Garcia the Retired Beanie Baby, but you can almost certainly find sellers online. Second, individual sellers are likely to have better prices than baseball card shops or antiques dealers. Finally, some individuals—mostly collectors— may be interested in *trading* goods, so that you could get what you want without any money changing hands (see Figure 6-24).

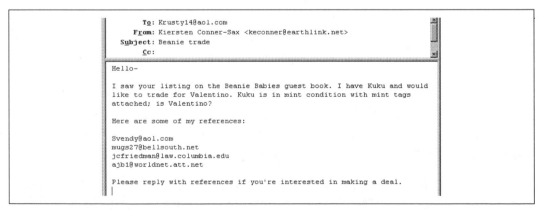

Figure 6-24. Initiating a Beanie Baby trade

Finding people selling what you're looking for is easier than you might think. Check out the want ad style forums we've discussed.

Usenet is a good place to start. Try newsgroups dedicated to the product you're interested in—say, *rec.collecting.sport.baseball*—or **.forsale* newsgroups. Web pages are another good source. Free classified advertising sites (see the Resource Catalog for a complete list) are filled to brimming with wares for sale. Manufacturer's web pages sometimes have guestbooks where sellers or traders gather to communicate. Similarly, the web page for a club may have a guestbook related to products for sale; automotive clubs, for example, frequently have a section listing cars and parts for sale. Web rings* on a certain topic are frequently a good place to find hobbyists selling their wares. Finally, online auctions (again, see the Resource Catalog) provide nicely organized listings, and a seller feedback system allows buyers to know a little bit more about who they're buying from.

Researching sellers

Even if you aren't using an intermediary, like an auction web site, it is possible to learn something about the background and business practices of a seemingly anonymous seller on the Internet. If you found this person at an auction site, check their feedback page. Are the comments generally good? Even if you didn't find this person through such a structured forum, there may be feedback about them on the Net. Ask for online references via email. References may be provided in the form of a listing at a Good Traders sight, an auction feedback page, or email addresses of people with whom they've traded.

When the seller gives you a reference, don't assume they must be honest because they provided it. Follow up with a brief, polite inquiry to that address, as in Figure 6-25.

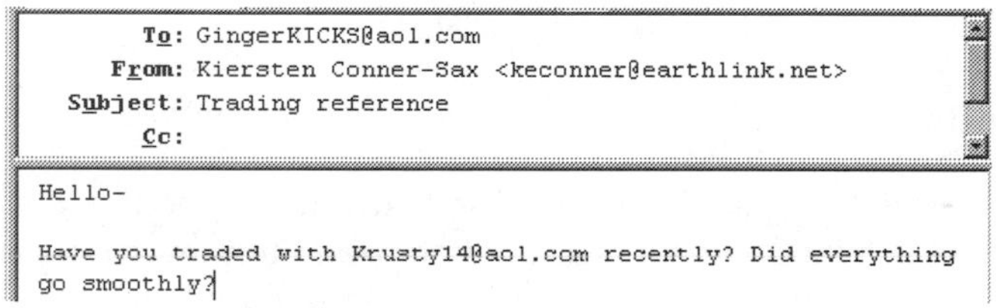

```
        To: GingerKICKS@aol.com
      From: Kiersten Conner-Sax <keconner@earthlink.net>
   Subject: Trading reference
       Cc:

Hello-

Have you traded with Krusty14@aol.com recently? Did everything
go smoothly?
```

Figure 6-25. Checking a reference

If the person at that address doesn't reply, doesn't have a working mailbox, or doesn't have anything good to say, you might not want to go through with the transaction. Or, you may want to suggest performing the trade in a safer manner: if you were trading two Beanie Babies, for example, you might ask someone with poor references to send her item first; you'll send yours upon its arrival.

---

* A *web ring* is a group of web sites about the same topic hooked together through a set of circular links. We'll discuss web rings further in "Web Pages," later in this chapter.

A sneakier method of checking up on someone is to search for the seller's name or email address at Deja.com. You may then view comments other people have made about them or posts they've made themselves.

You could also check to see whether the person has a feedback rating at one of the Internet auction sites, such as eBay or Up4Sale. Many traders also sell their wares. Check for a rating by searching for an email address, as described at the site.

Many interest groups maintain web pages with lists of reputable Internet traders. Such so-called "good trader's lists" provide a list of the names and email addresses of people who have participated honorably or (dishonorably) in online transactions (see Figure 6-26). Don't consider such a reference an ironclad guarantee, although it certainly imparts a measure of security.

GOOD TRADERS LIST A-I

For A look down below

Bears@tznet.com

Bessie7464@aol.com

Bethany@threesisters.com

Bronty1130@aol.com

Bunggie@lewiston.com

BuyBeanies@aol.com

ByDesign9@aol.com

Cbutler@weir.net

Ciao@gtii.com

Figure 6-26. This good trader's list indicates the number of references

These lists can also be a good resource for learning about the culture of whatever community you're dealing with—research you definitely want to undertake before engaging in a monetary transaction. Otherwise, you could end up with a MIP TBB Quacks on your hands, when you were looking for a non-mint wingless Quackers.* To avoid such a pitfall, take a look at Beanie Mom's web site (*http://www.beaniemom. com*) or any of the myriad web sites on the topic.

---

* Okay: Quacks and Quackers are Beanie Babies. Quackers is a full-sized retired Beanie, which means that it's out of production; the wingless model was one of the first ones made and is consequently very valuable. "Mint" refers to mint-condition. Most mint-condition Beanie Babies are MWMT, which means "mint with mint tags," which means that the Beanie is perfect and still has unmarred manufacturer's tags attached to it. Quacks, a miniature version of Quackers, is a Teenie Beanie Baby (or TBB) from a McDonald's Happy Meal promotion. "MIP" refers to "mint, in plastic," which refers to the fact that Teenie Beanie Babies are delivered to the consumer in closed plastic bags. So you can see that a TBB MIP Quacks and a non-mint wingless Quackers are two very different things, and that I've had *way* too much free time on my hands for the last six months.

Selling

One of the best things about the Web is the low cost of entry. Anyone with access to a computer can make information available to millions of other people. Consequently, the Internet is a great means for selling things.

How should you go about it? There are a number of different methods available, depending on the audience you're trying to reach and the amount of money you wish to spend. Some things you might want to think about:

- Are you trying to reach people within a specific geographic area?

- Is it more important to reach a group of people with similar interests?

- How are you pricing your item? Is it in high demand?

Depending on your answers to these questions, you may want to list your item in a classified ad on the Web or post a message to a Usenet newsgroup. You may want to create a web page describing the item or items you have for sale, submit it to search engines, and then enter the page as part of a web ring. Or, you may want to put the item up for auction.

Things to Remember When Selling Online

Once again, you'll want to follow the rules in order to sell items successfully. Be sure to learn about the community you're trading within, and remember the following:

- Be honest—all you've got is your reputation.

- Don't ignore email—if you make someone an offer, and then ignore their requests, they may blackball you.

- Don't take a personal check. Ask for a money order to ensure that you receive payment. If you do decide to accept a check, tell the buyer that you'll need to wait for the check to clear before you send the merchandise.

- Spell out the details. Make sure that the buyer knows how much the item will cost, method of payment you'll accept, how you'll be shipping the item, and when the item should reach its destination.

- If you'll be trading items with someone else, check that person's references before agreeing to the trade.

Usenet/Classifieds

Selling merchandise via classified ads on the Web or via a Usenet newsgroup is easy and quick. These methods are similar in that you post a brief message describing your item to the appropriate location. While your listing probably won't turn up on any search engines or be available for more than 30 to 60 days, the ease of use and ability to tailor the ad to your specifics make this an excellent means of selling small or single items.

Usenet

Posting a for-sale message to a newsgroup is fairly simple. First, decide to which groups you wish to post. That way, you can cross-post your message to each of the appropriate groups at the same time. Deja.com (*http://www.deja.com*) is a good place to start. From the Deja.com home page, enter a few words describing the item you wish to sell in the Find box. Then, set the archive setting to complete, select the Forums radio box, and click **Find**.

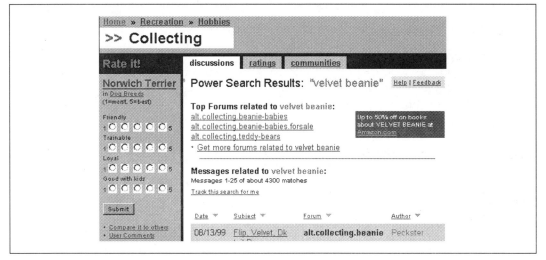

Figure 6-27. Finding newsgroups on which to sell overpriced collectibles

Notice that the results in Figure 6-27 provide a number of collecting and dolls-related sites. One site, however, is more general: *nc.charlotte.forsale*, a *general* for-sale group for Charlotte, N.C. It would be good to cross-post our listing to sites listing general merchandise for sale as well as to the more specific toy or collectibles sites. Scroll down the page to the Interest Finder: click the "Search Again" checkbox, and enter the word "forsale." The list (Figure 6-28) is much longer this time.

Some groups, like *alt.forsale*, are appropriate to our needs. Others, like *dfw.forsale*, probably aren't unless we live in Texas, since "dfw" is an abbreviation denoting a group dedicated to the Dallas-Fort Worth area. You'll probably want to check out groups pertaining to your local area, as well; see Chapter 2 for more information on finding newsgroups. Continue to narrow down your search until you've decided which groups would be right for your item. And be sure to read a selection of messages from a group before you post to it! You don't want to end up with a mailbox full of flames because, for example, a certain collecting group frowns on people selling merchandise.

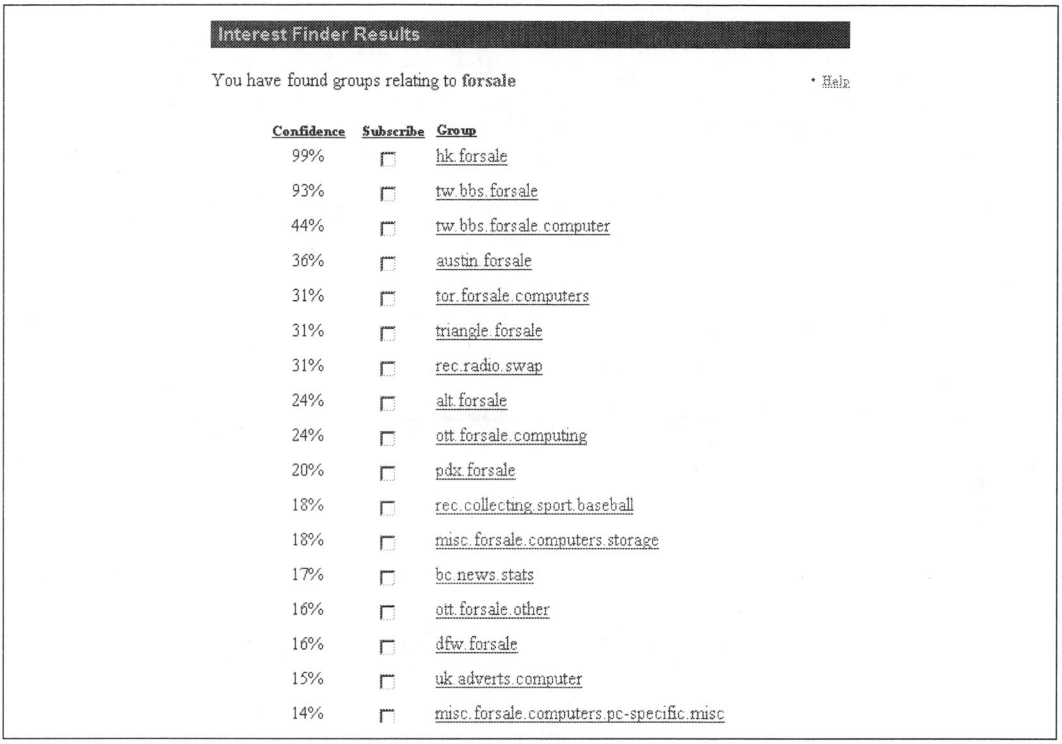

Confidence	Subscribe	Group
99%	☐	hk.forsale
93%	☐	tw.bbs.forsale
44%	☐	tw.bbs.forsale.computer
36%	☐	austin.forsale
31%	☐	tor.forsale.computers
31%	☐	triangle.forsale
31%	☐	rec.radio.swap
24%	☐	alt.forsale
24%	☐	ott.forsale.computing
20%	☐	pdx.forsale
18%	☐	rec.collecting.sport.baseball
18%	☐	misc.forsale.computers.storage
17%	☐	bc.news.stats
16%	☐	ott.forsale.other
16%	☐	dfw.forsale
15%	☐	uk.adverts.computer
14%	☐	misc.forsale.computers.pc-specific.misc

Interest Finder Results

You have found groups relating to forsale   • Help

Figure 6-28. Various newsgroups listing items for sale

Once you have your list of groups, click the **Post** button from Deja.com,* or from your own newsreader. You might want to send a message similar to the one in Figure 6-29.

A few things to keep in mind about selling items via Usenet:

- Only post to appropriate newsgroups, and don't do so more than once a week.

- Don't include your phone number unless you want all sorts of people calling you, all the time. Keep in mind that many newsgroups are now being archived, and information you give out this way may be preserved for years to come. You may need to turn off your usual signature feature if it includes too much information.

- You may want to use an email address specifically for this purpose, both to stay organized and maintain your privacy. See Chapter 3 for more information.

- Request payment in the form of a money order, so that you don't need to worry about receiving a bad check. If you do agree to take a check, wait until it clears before sending the merchandise.

---

* Since Deja.com only allows you to cross-post to four newsgroups at a time, it probably isn't the way to go; you probably want to post to as many appropriate groups as you can find.

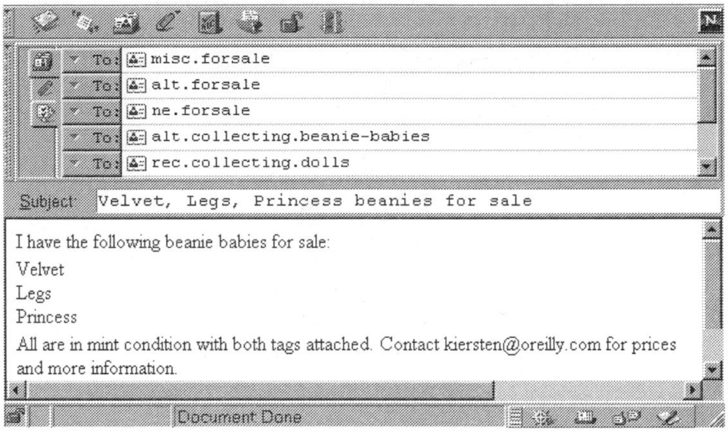

Figure 6-29. A drinking problem would be less embarrassing

Web classifieds

A number of pages sponsoring free classified advertising have sprung up on the Web. Web-based classifieds are national and some are better organized than your average newsgroup; otherwise, advantages and disadvantages of using them are very similar to placing a listing on a Usenet newsgroup. Most require some form of registration. Additionally, the web-based forms that you must fill out to submit an entry hold your hand through the process, as shown in Figure 6-30.

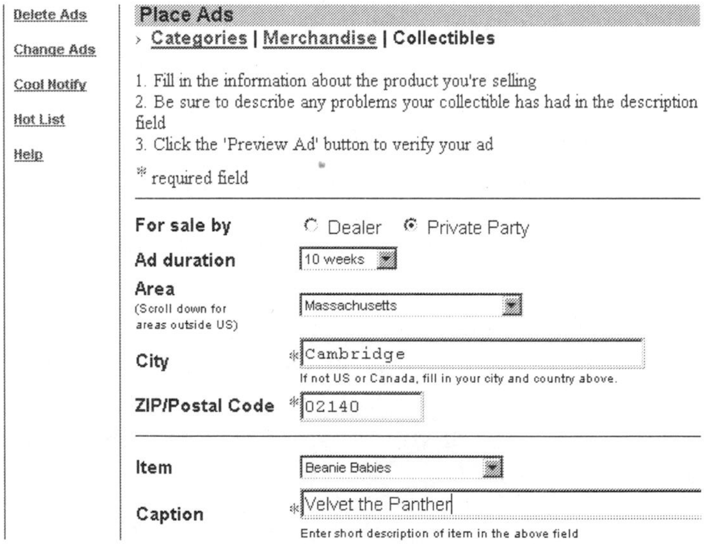

Figure 6-30. Submitting a classified ad to Classifieds2000

The sites listed in the Resource Catalog all provide World Wide Web-based classified ad listings. You'll also want to check to see whether your local newspaper lists classifieds online.

Auctions

Auctions on the Web are a great way to sell merchandise. In general, listing an item is free; some auctions take a percentage commission if you sell the merchandise, while others rely on advertising to make money. Some auction pages focus only on computer equipment or collectibles, while others are more specialized. Auctions are also buyer friendly, since most support a rating system for users to post feedback about sellers.

Let's take a look at a sample auction. We'll place our listing at Up4Sale (*http://www. up4sale.com*), which allows sellers to list items for free. Skip the New Visitors link and click the **Auction Your Item** button on the top of the page.

On the next screen, you'll need to decide how to auction your item. Choose between a standard auction, where bidding starts at the minimum you specify, and you sell to the highest bidder, or a reserve auction, where you don't have to sell your item unless a specified reserve price is met. For our example, we'll start a standard auction (see Figure 6-31).

Start a Standard Auction

Intro: Posting Tips

1. If you are a registered user, continue below...Otherwise, please **Register Now!**
2. Fields with a red * next to them are required.
3. If you are selling more than one different item (for example, a monitor and a bicycle), and you are NOT selling them together as a block, PLEASE post the items separately (go through this process twice, or more). This will reduce confusion for bidders.
4. Go to the **Power Post** page. This is a faster way to post items on the system (Only recommended for sellers who have posted at least one item using this page).
5. Note: Your post should be a true AUCTION, not a classified ad listing! This means that the posting needs to have a SPECIFIC number of items that can be bid on at Up4Sale. Otherwise, this creates confusion for bidders.
6. If you start an auction at Up4Sale, you are obligated to sell this exact item (no substitutes) to the high bidder at Up4Sale - do not list the item at other sites (unless you ask people to bid on the item at Up4Sale). Many states consider this a legal contract.

Thanks for your cooperation and good luck! Take a look at our Marketing Tips for Sellers!

Step 1: Enter your username and password

Username: [   ] * Password: [   ] * Forget Your Password?

Figure 6-31. Starting an auction

Register and fill out the form (see Figure 6-32). When answering questions about the minimum bid, payment method, and shipping options, be sure to think carefully.

Don't list a minimum bid lower that the amount you're willing to sell for. Once you've posted the listing, you've made a good-faith promise to sell the item for the highest bid. Payment method and shipping are important, as well. A prepaid money order is the safest way to receive payment, and you don't want to choose a shipping method that will be inconvenient or expensive. At the same time, services such as Federal Express, which provide superior tracking, may be a better choice for small, expensive items.

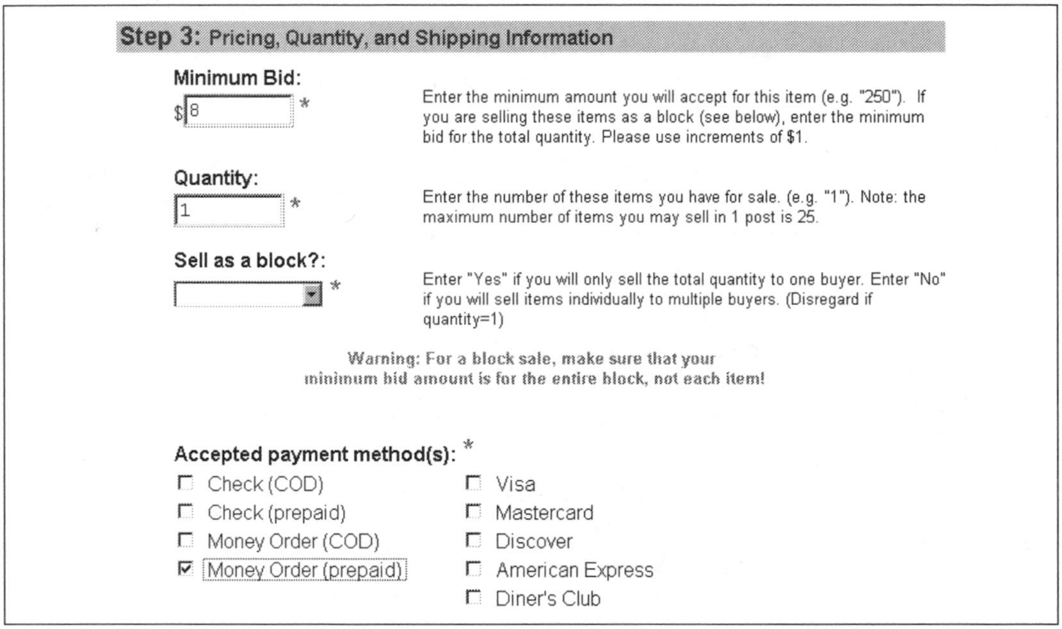

Step 3: Pricing, Quantity, and Shipping Information

Minimum Bid:

$ 8 *

Enter the minimum amount you will accept for this item (e.g. "250"). If you are selling these items as a block (see below), enter the minimum bid for the total quantity. Please use increments of $1.

Quantity:

1 *

Enter the number of these items you have for sale. (e.g. "1"). Note: the maximum number of items you may sell in 1 post is 25.

Sell as a block?:

*

Enter "Yes" if you will only sell the total quantity to one buyer. Enter "No" if you will sell items individually to multiple buyers. (Disregard if quantity=1)

Warning: For a block sale, make sure that your minimum bid amount is for the entire block, not each item!

Accepted payment method(s): *

☐ Check (COD) ☐ Visa
☐ Check (prepaid) ☐ Mastercard
☐ Money Order (COD) ☐ Discover
☑ Money Order (prepaid) ☐ American Express
☐ Diner's Club

Figure 6-32. Preparing to make a killing

Fill in all the details and click the **Submit** button. You have three choices for the post-ing duration: 3, 7, or 14 days. If you decline standard email notification of new bids, you'll receive notification only at the end of the auction, instead of every time some-one bids on your item. (When the posting duration is up, you'll receive an email mes-sage telling you who the high bidder was and how to reach that person.) You'll be able to review and change everything you've written. Click the **Post this item!** button to start the bidding.

Once you've posted your first item, you can use the Power Post link; the form you fill out skips the detailed instructions shown in Figure 6-33. See the Resource Catalog for other online auction sites.

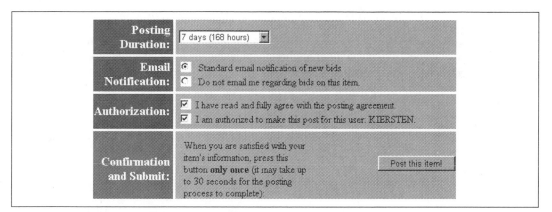

Posting Duration:	7 days (168 hours) ▾	
Email Notification:	⦿ Standard email notification of new bids ○ Do not email me regarding bids on this item.	
Authorization:	☑ I have read and fully agree with the posting agreement. ☑ I am authorized to make this post for this user: KIERSTEN.	
Confirmation and Submit:	When you are satisfied with your item's information, press this button **only once** (it may take up to 30 seconds for the posting process to complete):	[Post this item!]

Figure 6-33. The heady thrills of capitalism

Web Pages

If you're selling more than one item, or you have a continuous supply of items to sell, it may be a good idea to create a web page as a storefront on the Internet (see Figure 6-34). Your page can remain available on the Web for as long as you wish; it is indexable by search engines and you can customize and present the information as you see fit. (See Chapter 9 for information on how to create a web page and where to post it.)

Figure 6-34. A well-designed site for bichon frises

The drawback to using a web page to sell your wares is that it may be difficult to direct users to it. To increase visitors, try the following methods:

- Submit the page to search engines (see Chapter 9 to learn how to submit your web pages to search engines).

- Periodically submit classified ads and/or post to newsgroups with a pointer to your page.

- Find web pages with bulletin boards or guest books and place a pointer to your page there.

- Join a web ring.

Web rings

A *web ring* is a collection of web sites that focus on a single theme (see Figure 6-35). Each site features a banner at the bottom that provides links to other sites in the ring. Web rings focus on a wide variety of topics, from the Australia and New Zealand Fishing web ring to Zero God's Ring of Hell. Many people with wares to sell will join a web ring, so that people interested in that topic will be directed to their pages

Figure 6-35. Joining the Small Dog web ring

If you'd like to advertise your site using a web ring, the first step is to find a ring you'd like to join. Take a look at RingWorld: The WebRing Directory (*http://www.webring. org/ringworld/*) or at Yahoo!'s listing (*http://www.yahoo.com/Computers_and_Internet/*

Internet/World_Wide_Web/Searching_the_Web/Indices_to_Web_Documents/Rings/) to find a ring you'd like to join, like the Small Dog ring, shown in Figure 6-35. Frequently, the banner that appears at the bottom of pages on the ring will provide a link for people who want to join.

After you submit the form, you'll need to add the ring information to your page. In this case, the ring administrator requires only a link to the Small Dog web ring page and a link to the next site in the ring. However, you may also copy and paste the entire Small Dog banner, shown in Figure 6-36, onto your page.

Figure 6-36. The Small Dog banner

Be sure to follow the directions. You'll need to change some of the HTML code within the banner so that it reflects the particulars of your site (see Figure 6-37).

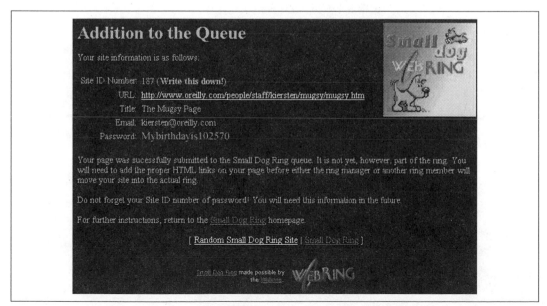

Figure 6-37. Getting in the club

To join a web ring, you'll need a site ID and password. The site ID and password are used to update your information on the web ring. For more information on creating and editing web pages, see Chapter 9.

The Future

There's no single way to do business on the Web. Shopping sites range from relatively predictable online versions of printed catalogs to shopping robots to online auctions. What you can buy ranges from the mundane things I've discussed (books, cars, houses, pets) to the exotic (rare books, musical instruments, antiques, you name it). The only thing that's a given is that more paradigms will appear. This is only a sample and there are bound to be even more paradigms in the future.

CHAPTER SEVEN

BANKING AND PERSONAL FINANCE

The Internet is a hot medium that's also making steady inroads toward some of our more staid institutions. More and more financial companies are providing services via the Net. You can check account balances, make payments, transfer funds, pay bills, research loans, file taxes, and more online. And Wall Street is already well established on the Web, making it easy to buy and sell stocks and securities from your computer.

Many of the benefits of making such transactions via the Net are obvious. You can save time and trouble by paying bills online, rather than writing out checks and mailing them yourself. The Internet lets you use a bank anywhere in the country, if that bank's services suit your needs. It's often cheaper to deal with a web site that serves as a stockbroker than to pay an actual person to make your deals. You get the idea.

This chapter discusses some of the benefits of using the Internet for banking, playing the stock market, filing your taxes, etc. It also mentions some of the potential pitfalls. The Net certainly makes doing certain kinds of business easier, but easier is not always better. When it comes to handling your finances, you want to be as comfortable and well informed as possible.

Internet Banking

Believe it or not, there was a time when you actually had to walk into a bank during regular business hours to make a deposit, pay a loan, or pick up some cash. Then came banking by mail, which at least let you deposit checks, pay loans, and make transfers, although cash remained an in-person proposition. Automated teller machines (ATMs), of course, changed all that, allowing everyone to replenish their pocket money right near the stores, restaurants, and other businesses where they were going to spend it.

Banks intended ATMs to make transactions more convenient for customers, but also to make bank operation cheaper. With automated tellers handling a sizeable percentage of business, banks could be open for fewer hours and reduce their staffing requirements.

With the advent of Internet banking, both of these objectives seem headed toward a new extreme. Internet banking allows you to transact a large portion of your banking business online, while connected to your bank's web site. Granted, your PC is not likely to spit out tens and twenties in the near future, but you can probably use it to transfer money between accounts, monitor account activity, pay bills, apply for loans, and so on.

Most Internet banks also let you download account information directly into personal finance software such as Intuit's Quicken or Microsoft's Money. (If you already use such a program, make sure the online bank you choose is compatible with it.) Once you've downloaded account info, you can dump the raw data into tax preparation software (such as TurboTax) and file your tax returns online. (Increasingly, you can perform many of these same tasks using a web browser alone, without the proprietary software and/or extra fees.)

The presence of banking services online also makes it easier to compare interest rates and opens up your options beyond your local area. The MyBank Directory (*http:// www.mybank.com*) lists online banks around the country by state. We've also included a table of current online banks, as well as the personal finance software they support, in Chapter 15.

Internet banking is the next generation of an electronic banking movement that began with direct dial-up. A number of banks that offer service via the Net began by providing customers with a direct dial-up by modem, and many still offer this option. However, since this method circumvents the Net, we're not going to deal with it here.

Currently, many banks charge additional fees for some of their online services. In most cases, you should be able to check account balances and make transfers between accounts for free. If you want to pay bills via your online account—and this is perhaps the main advantage of having one—it may cost you a nominal fee.

A friend of mine gives his bank $4.50 a month to be able to pay bills online. Now, if this activity were limited to electronic transfers, it might seem like a bit of a rip-off. In fact, however, in only a few cases are his payments made via electronic transfer—two utility bills and his credit card bill. Every other payment he makes is to a business or individual who cannot receive payments in this way. In these cases, the bank cuts a check for the amount and mails it to the correct address.

Not only does this save my friend the trouble of writing out a check (and, in some cases, addressing an envelope), he doesn't have to shell out the money for a first class stamp, either. Since it's also easy to set up recurring payments, online banking can cut the amount of time you have to spend on such tedious activities to a bare minimum.

Why Bank Over the Net?

Not everyone is comfortable with the concept of Internet banking. I have another friend who likes the tactile reality of his checkbook and doesn't at all mind writing out payments for his bills every month. He's also the kind of person who would never use a spreadsheet program or personal finance software of any kind. He's not going to be doing any Internet banking in the near future.

But I have yet another friend who already records all of his expenses and generates all of his checks using Quicken. And he still complains that this wastes too much of his time. This guy is a prime candidate for Internet banking.

Is it safe? Security issues

Now that we've covered all the advantages of banking online, we come to the most important question: is it safe?

Relatively, yes. The most persuasive argument I've heard in favor of online banking safety is that, when it comes to a vicious computer hacker, the banks have much more to lose than the individual consumer. And banks are signing up in droves. Moreover, the banks are trying to assuage consumer fears—Wells Fargo, for example, provides a guarantee against loss due to a cyber thief. In fact, the greatest threat to your online banking security is the same as the greatest threat you face when using an ATM: an insecure password.

Therefore, if you're planning to bank on the Web, be sure to use a browser with the best encryption techniques. In general, this means the latest release of Explorer or Navigator. And take the following steps with your password:

- Memorize the password immediately. Don't write it down, and don't use your birthday as did an otherwise very intelligent friend of mine in college.

- Change your password regularly.

- Remember to sign off. As with web-based email, banking by browser could leave a trail on the hard drive that you'd rather not have others see.

- Utilize the built-in security features of your browser. Turn up security options to the highest possible levels.

Browser requirements

If you'll be performing any kind of sensitive financial transaction, your browser absolutely, positively has to be equipped with Secure Sockets Layer version 2 or 3 (SSLv2 or SSLv3). This is a cryptographic protocol used to transfer information securely between your browser and your broker; it keeps others on the Internet from eavesdropping on your investments. Support for this version of SSL exists in version 4.0 (or later) of both Netscape Navigator and Microsoft Internet Explorer. If you're using something else, check with the browser manufacturer to see if they support the SSL protocol.

This presents a thorny issue. The federal government, through the efforts of the U.S. National Security Agency (NSA), classifies encryption as a nonexportable munition. Thus, only browsers with weak encryption algorithms are allowed to be downloaded outside of the United States. Netscape, for example, allows users to download a browser with 40-bit encryption by default; this is not considered safe as of the late-1990s. However, if you're inside the United States, you are allowed to download a browser with a stronger 128-bit encryption. If you're outside the United States, check with your browser company to see how it handles this issue, and see if there is any workaround.

When you first connect to a banking or brokerage site, the encryption protocols should be negotiated through the SSL protocol. Be sure that the browser indicates that encryption is active; Netscape and Internet Explorer typically use a solid lock (see Figure 7-1) or key to indicate that the transmission is encrypted if it doesn't explicitly warn you with a dialog box. Once the solid lock or key is present, you can proceed.

Figure 7-1. Secure connection icons

Online banking is relatively safe and should only get safer. Browsers and banks continue to develop better encryption technology, and both industries are committed to reassuring consumers. Wells Fargo even has wanted posters (*http://wellsfargo.com/ wanted/*).

What should I look for in an Internet bank?

Institutions that offer Internet banking are not all created equal. While one bank may offer a soup-to-nuts banking smorgasbord, another may limit you to a few different transactions.

You can shop around for an Internet bank. We'll get into the specifics of what to look for in a moment. Keep in mind that if your current bank offers online services, you might simply want to expand your account with them.

A good online bank should offer the following basic services:

- Online viewing of current balances on various accounts
- Ability to transfer money between accounts
- Bill paying
- Online viewing of cleared checks and posted deposits and withdrawals
- Service transactions, such as check reorders or change of address

Some banks also offer value-added services, such as:

■ Viewing of credit card transactions and balances

■ Loans, applications and equity buying, etc.

One important difference among Internet banks is the personal finance software with which the site is compatible. If you normally use a program such as Managing Your Money, Money, or Quicken, you should choose an Internet bank that works with your program of choice. This will enable you to download your bank account information and incorporate it into your own electronic records.

You should also think about the physical location of the bank you're using online. Internet banking makes it possible for you to bank with an institution located far away. But there are advantages in selecting a local bank, even if you're going to do most of your banking via the Net. For one thing, you probably already have an account at a local bank. If that bank has online services, it should be easy to expand your account to include them. Then you can continue to take advantage of your regular bank account privileges, such as check writing.

When you open an online account, you can do most of the work over the Net. However, you will need to fill out signature cards, and possibly some basic paperwork. Although there's no real harm in this material being sent to you from Sheboygan Falls, having a close bank means you'll be able to exchange any important correspondence more quickly.

Cost is another consideration. Different banks support different means of access, and there is usually a range of fees. Using a browser to bank is generally free, but most banks assess a per-month charge for banking via personal finance software. Note, however, that with some banks you may also perform the actual banking transaction via browser, then download and export account information into the software. Bill paying usually incurs a per-month fee.

Performing Banking Transactions

First, take a look at the various software packages available for banking over the Internet. Then, take a look at Chapter 15 for a list of banks that support PC banking.

Browser

More and more banks allow you to access your accounts and pay bills without any proprietary software whatsoever. Simply use your browser to access your accounts. Be sure to take the security precautions described earlier.

BankNOW

BankNOW, from Intuit, is a browser plug-in for use with AOL or the Web under Windows. It allows you to pay bills, transfer funds, and view balances from one screen.

Quicken/Money/Managing Your Money

The big three personal financial software packages offer similar features:

■ Online and offline account management

■ Budgeting, tax, and financial planning

■ Electronic payments and transfers

■ Expense categorization

■ Investment tracking

■ Household inventories

These features may or may not be useful to you. You don't need any of these packages to bank online.

Online banks

The information listed in Chapter 15 details Internet banks and the financial software they support. See *http://www.intuit.com/banking/participating.html* for the most recent list of Quicken-friendly banks, or the Online Banking Report at *http://www.onlinebankingreport.com/top100banks2.shtml* for the 100 largest American banks with true Internet service, or *http://www.yahoo.com/Business_and_Economy/Companies/Financial_Services/Banking/Internet_Banking/* for the most current list of Internet banks. For some reason, a disproportionate number are in Texas.

A typical day at the Internet bank

The truth is that I don't have an Internet bank account. So, in order to see what life is like in the world of banking via the Net, I had to poke my nose into the personal and private financial transactions of a good friend of mine. Luckily (at least for the purpose of this writing), neither one of us has very much money.

My friend (let's call him Joe) uses his online account mostly to pay bills. Joe has Internet banking privileges at the same bank he has always had his regular old checking and savings accounts. But now, with Internet banking, he can check his account balances simply by accessing the bank's web site and giving his account number and password. He's also set up things so that he can pay bills electronically. But we're getting ahead of ourselves.

For Joe to extend his account to include Internet banking, he simply went to the bank's web site and filled out a very short form, with his name, account number, etc. He also chose a password. The whole business took only a couple of minutes. The steps you have to go through to do the same thing vary from bank to bank. But most banks make it fairly easy for their existing customers to extend their privileges to include Internet access.

If Joe didn't have an account, he would have had to fill out longer electronic forms, and make an initial deposit. But he would have been able to make the deposit via credit card online, and he still would have been up and banking fairly quickly. If you open an account via the Net, you have to return some actual paperwork as well—a signature card, for example—but it's still fairly easy.

Being able to open an account remotely is not something I would personally choose to do, but many people would consider it to be a wonderful convenience. And for people who can't get to a bank for one reason or another, it's a godsend.

As discussed earlier in this chapter, although (hypothetically) the Net allows you to have an account at a bank anywhere in the country, there are some advantages to choosing a bank physically close to home. Any paperwork you have to exchange you can get more quickly. You might also need to physically visit the bank on occasion, to get cash, a money order, travelers checks, etc. And many merchants only take local checks; even though you live down the street, they may turn up their noses at (or at least be confused by) a check from a bank in North Dakota. But those things might not be important to you.

An important note: regardless of which bank you choose, you are going to need a browser with 128-bit encryption, in order for your transactions to be secure. If you attempt to make transactions with a nonsecure browser, in many cases the bank's web site will tell you that you need to upgrade and should also provide you with a link to an appropriate browser. Joe linked to and downloaded his upgraded browser before my very eyes, and it went fairly quickly.

Then he gave his account number and password, and he had access to his savings and checking. Figure 7-2 shows the primary screen, with menu items to access the bank's various online services.

At Joe's bank, you can check balances and transfer money between accounts without paying any fee for Internet access.

However, Joe also wants to pay his bills via the Net. That costs him a monthly fee of $4.50. Many Internet banks require a fee for bill paying. But from the snooping I did through Joe's typical month's business, these services are a bargain.

The web site for Joe's particular bank provides five menus that run across the top of virtually every window, regardless of what information he's viewing. By taking a closer look at the menu titled **Bill Payments**, we can get a better idea how Internet banking can simplify many routine financial transactions. In Figure 7-3, Joe has displayed the **Bill Payments** menu and selected the item **Make Payments**.

A series of screens walk Joe through the process of paying one or more bills. First he is asked to Select payee(s) from the displayed list, which includes his credit card companies, telephone, auto insurance, etc. Where did this list come from? Joe set it up himself using the menu item **Add/change payees** from the same **Bill Payments** menu.

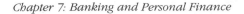

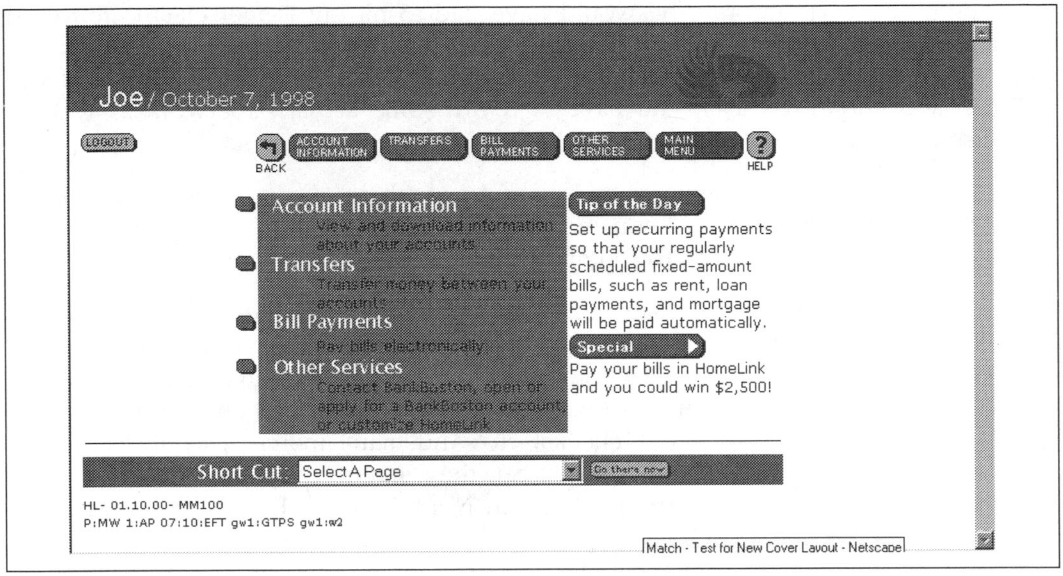

Figure 7-2. Top-level banking window

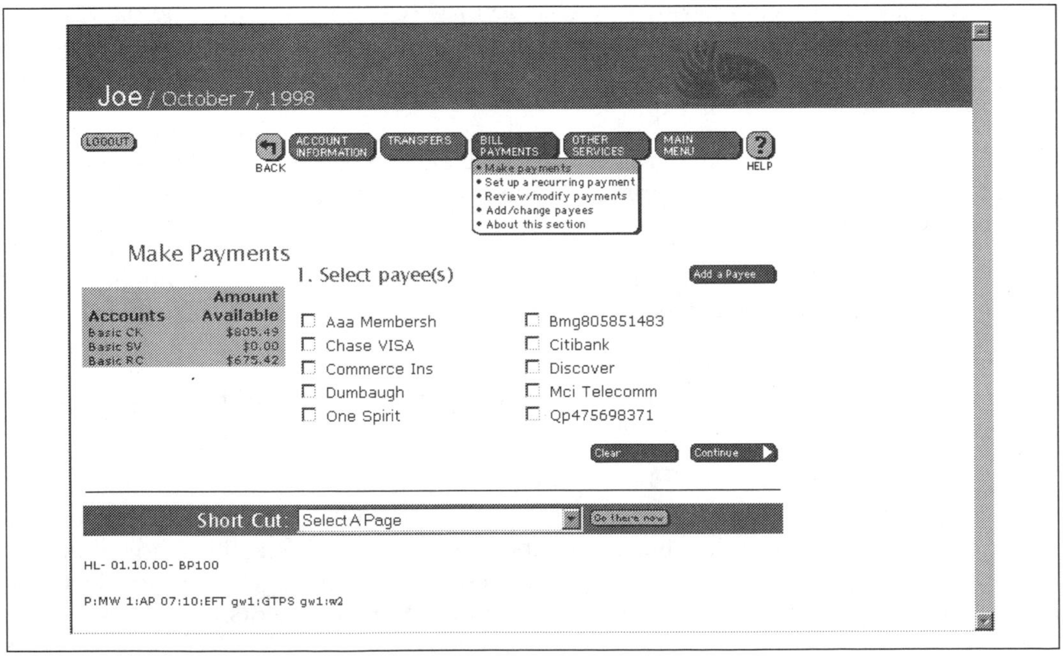

Figure 7-3. Paying bills electronically

To specify that a payment should be made, Joe clicks on the box preceding the creditor. He can request payments to multiple creditors on the same screen. Then he clicks the **Continue** button in the bottom-right corner of the screen to fill in the details of the payment.

In the second Make Payments window, Joe enters the amount of each payment he wants to make as well as the date the payment should be made (see Figure 7-4). For some creditors, payments are made electronically, by direct transfer. Joe's Citibank credit card fits into this category. No actual check is cut.

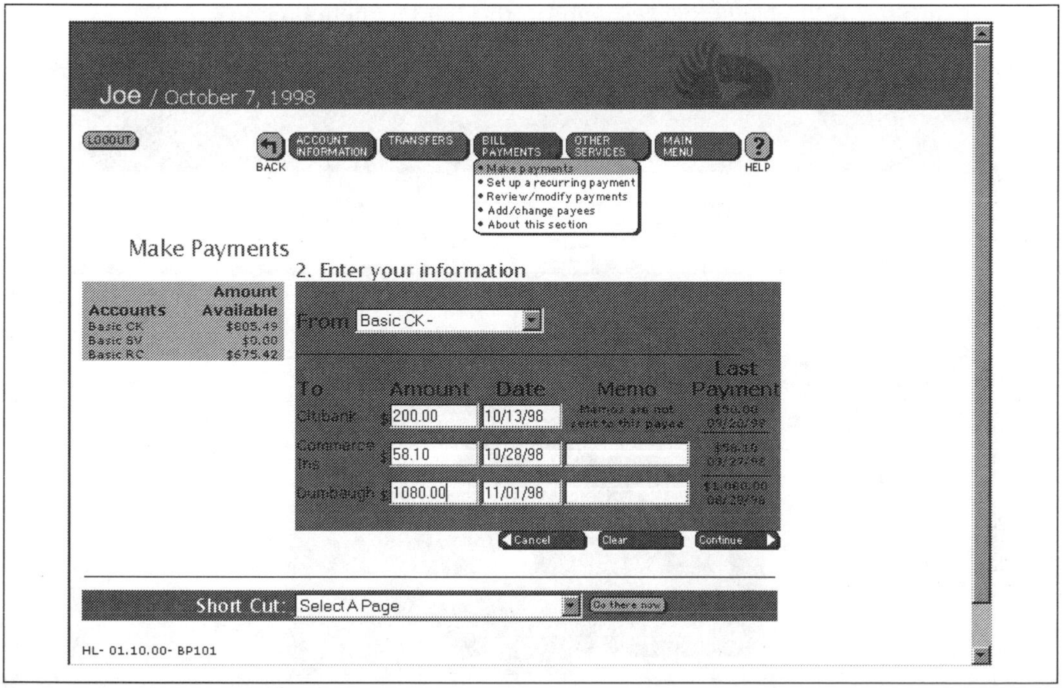

Figure 7-4. Specifying payees and amounts

But many creditors are not set up to receive electronic payments. In these cases, Joe's bank cuts a check for the amount he requests and mails it to the creditor. The bank lets you include a personal note or memo on the check, just as you would if you were writing it out yourself. For creditors who are getting electronic payments, this Memo column does not accept input.

One of the most useful services an Internet bank is likely to provide is to let you schedule recurring payments. These are the real time-saving transactions. While certain creditors allow you to pay your bills by automatic deduction from your checking account each month—many utility companies, for instance—not every creditor is set up to receive payments in this way. Certainly few landlords, and even fewer insurance companies, health clubs, etc., are equipped to deduct your payments automatically from your checking.

But with Internet banking, you can specify that a check for your rent or mortgage is written and mailed at the same time every month. You can specify that a certain number of monthly payments are made to your auto insurance company. Or you can make sure your monthly membership dues are sent to your health club on time. You get the picture.

At Joe's bank, the **Bill Payments** menu offers an item called **Set up a recurring payment**. Joe used this item to specify a series of eight monthly payments to cover his car insurance for the year. Figure 7-5 shows some of the information he needed to enter to accomplish this. (Joe had already specified the insurance company as a possible payee, using the **Add/change payees** item on the **Bill Payments** menu.)

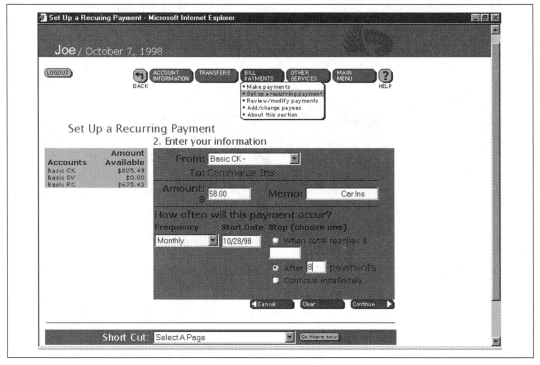

Figure 7-5. Setting up a recurring payment

And now he doesn't have to worry about insurance payments until next year. He might also do the same thing for his rent or mortgage payment. Then he doesn't have to write out checks or envelopes, or buy stamps, or even go to the post office. And all for $4.50 a month.

Online Investing

One of the newest and most exciting areas of the World Wide Web to emerge over the past year is online brokerages. The concept behind this unique form of *electronic commerce* (e-commerce) is relatively simple: replace your Armani-suited broker with your Internet browser. As you might guess, there are both pros and cons to this approach, and they typically amount to the same thing: there's no human being at the other end of the line to advise you on your stock purchases. On the other hand, online stock trading is typically cheaper than trading via broker, so if you're willing to take a little risk and you feel comfortable enough to throw your broker away, then read on!

Welcome to Wall Street

The term Wall Street has come to signify many aspects of investing in America. In reality, however, Wall Street is an actual street located at the southern end of Manhattan. It gets its claim to fame because it houses several investment brokerages as well as the major stock exchanges in America. In essence, it holds a great deal of the financial power of the nation, if not the world, in the buildings that line its curbs. Now, thanks to a swelling interest in electronic commerce, Wall Street can come right to your computer with online trading.

Let's briefly review some concepts that are vital to trading online: an *exchange* is simply a marketplace to buy and sell stocks and bonds. Companies sell shares of their stock on an exchange in order to provide themselves capital. Each share of a company's stock has a specific price associated with it, which can go up and down each day based on Wall Street's perception of that company as a whole. Exchanges are not public—in other words, you cannot buy or sell stocks at the exchange yourself. Instead, you must go through a *brokerage*, a company that specializes in investment trading and owns "seats" at the exchange. These seats allow brokerage employees access to the floor of the exchange, where they can trade stocks from each other freely. There are many brokerages throughout the United States that would love to process your orders, but they'll always charge either a flat-rate or percentage *commission* to handle your orders.

Here are the three most common stock exchanges in the United States:

New York Stock Exchange (NYSE)
> Housed in the World Trade Center in New York City, the NYSE has become the symbol of economic health in America. When it performs well, the economy is generally in good shape. When it performs poorly, the economy could be in trouble. So how do we measure its performance? Through an indicator called the *Dow Jones Industrial Average* (DJIA), or Dow Jones for short. The DJIA is essentially a composite of specific *bellwether* stocks or stocks that are indicative of how the market as a whole is doing. If you watch your nightly news, they will likely provide a summary of this indicator, including how much it went up or down during

the current trading day. The NYSE generally opens at 9:30 a.m. Eastern time and closes at 4:00 p.m. Eastern time each weekday.

American Stock Exchange (AMEX)

The American Stock Exchange is another popular stock exchange which is listed in most major newspapers. Originally called the Curb Market, the AMEX has grown to be the world's second largest equities market. The AMEX is measured by its own AMEX indicator as well as a more popular indicator called the Standard and Poor's 500 (S&P 500), which also takes in the other exchanges. The AMEX is in the process of merging with NASDAQ, and will be known afterwards as the NASDAQ/AMEX market. This does not necessarily mean that the indicators will merge.

NASDAQ

The National Associates of Securities Dealers (NASD) operates an exchange that is primarily devoted to over-the-counter (OTC) stocks. This exchange is called the NASDAQ. It differs from the other markets in that it is mostly computerized through a vast telecommunication network. The NASDAQ has its own market valuation tool, the NASDAQ index, which is usually reported in conjunction with the Dow Jones. Many technology companies are located on the NASDAQ, and they tend to form the bellwether stocks of the market. Hence, the NASDAQ is often called "tech heavy" and can have more dramatic gains and losses based on the performance of these stocks. Each stock traded on an exchange has a unique symbol to aid in unique identification and make the dissemination of information about trades easier. For example, Microsoft is MSFT, Cisco is CSCO, and Dell Computer is DELL. The NASDAQ opens at 9:30 a.m. Eastern time and closes at 4:00 p.m. Eastern time on weekdays. There are proposals for expanded hours (driven largely by online trading), that may be in place by the time you read this.

Trading Online

With online trading, a brokerage's web site relays transaction information from your browser to the floor of the exchange or through its own servers. In essence, it eliminates a middleman at the other end of the telephone line and replaces it with a high-speed networking router. You are given complete control to decide how much you wish to purchase, when, and for what price, and the market will react immediately to your purchase.

There are currently several online brokerages actively trading over the Internet. Table 7-1 lists the more popular choices, as well as their locations on the Web, in alphabetical order.

Table 7-1. Online Brokerages

Company	Web Site
Ameritrade	*http://www.ameritrade.com/*
DLJdirect	*http://www.dljdirect.com/*
Datek Online	*http://www.datek.com/*

Table 7-1. Online Brokerages (continued)

Company	Web Site
Charles Schwab	*http://www.schwab.com/*
E-Trade	*http://www.etrade.com/*
Fidelity.com	*http://www.fidelity.com/*
Suretrade	*http://www.suretrade.com/*
WellsTrade	*http://www.wellsfargo.com/wellstrade*

See Chapter 15 for a more complete listing of online brokerages.

Browser requirements

In order to trade online, your browser has to be equipped with Secure Socket Layer version 2 or 3 (SSL v2 or SSL v3). This is a cryptographic protocol used to transfer information securely between your browser and your broker; it keeps others on the Internet from eavesdropping on your investments. Support for this version of SSL exists in version 4.0 (or later) of both Netscape Navigator and Microsoft Internet Explorer. If you're using something else, check with the browser manufacturer to see if they support the SSL protocol.

This presents a thorny issue. The federal government, through the efforts of the U.S. National Security Agency (NSA), classifies encryption as a non-exportable munition. Thus, only browsers with weak encryption algorithms are allowed to be downloaded outside of the United States. Netscape, for example, allows users to download a browser with 40-bit encryption by default; this is not considered safe as of the late-1990s. However, if you're inside the United States, you are allowed to download a browser with a stronger 128-bit encryption. If you're outside the U.S., check with your browser company to see how they handle this issue, and if there is any workaround.

When you first connect to a brokerage site, the encryption protocols should be negotiated through the SSL protocol. Be sure that the browser indicates that encryption is active; Netscape and Internet Explorer typically use a solid lock or key to indicate that the transmission is encrypted, if it doesn't explicitly warn you with a dialog box. Once the solid lock or key is present, you can proceed.

Getting Set Up

The first decision you need to make when trading online is what type of account you want. There are several different types you can set up, but they fall into three main categories: *individual/joint, professional,* and *retirement* accounts. The most obvious of them will be an individual or a joint account, where you (and possibly a spouse) manage the money that has been invested solely for yourselves. A professional account represents investment assets of a business (such a corporation, partnership, or sole proprietorship) or a trust. Finally, retirement accounts deal with individual and corporate IRAs and pension accounts.

Almost all of the companies listed in Table 7-1 will allow you to apply for membership online, no matter which account you choose. This typically involves giving your name, address, and other personal data to the brokerage through an encrypted connection, depending on how you want the account set up. For example, Figure 7-6 shows an application for a joint account, which requests information about both you and the other tenant responsible for the account. Much like setting up a bank account, information such as your address, proof of residence (social security number), and employment information must be furnished. If accepted, the brokerage will mail you several agreement forms, which you must sign and return to them along with some means for an initial deposit.

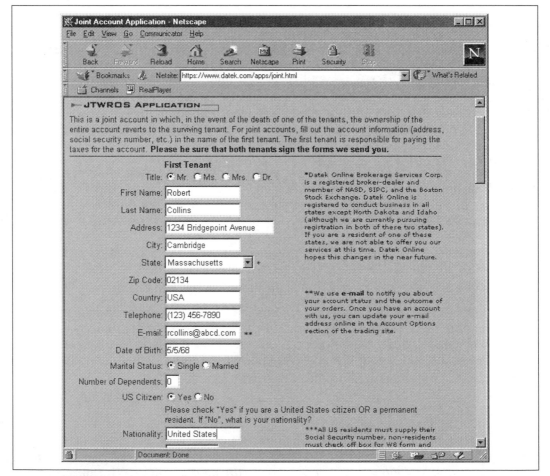

Figure 7-6. Applying for an online brokerage account

Online brokerages will subsequently issue you a user ID and a password, which you can use to access your account at any time. Your user ID and password will be transmitted to your brokerage when you first log in. A word of warning: not all web pages on your broker's site will be encrypted. You should check to see that all sensitive pages are encrypted. If you feel uncomfortable about entering any personal or financial information on a nonencrypted web site, speak with the brokerage to see if there is a more secure way to enter that information, such as through the telephone.

Once you have your account and password, you're ready to hit Wall Street! Simply go to your brokerage web site, log in with your name and password, and you're ready to view your portfolio.

How It Works (Online)

Now that you know how to open an account, let's take a look at how you go about buying and selling stocks and bonds online.

Load balancing

Your brokerage house may use more than one computer to process requests. These computers (servers) are networked together such that when you log in, you'll be assigned a server with a minimum amount of traffic. This technique is called *load balancing*, and it helps to make sure that you are not refused a connection to a server when you're trying to make a trade. For this reason, it's not a good idea to bookmark the trading server that you first encounter, but instead to log in and log out each time you want to make a trade.

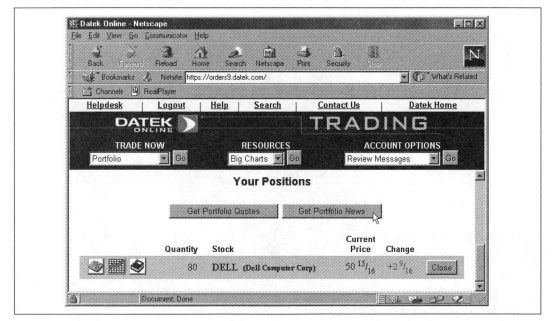

Figure 7-7. Learning about your portfolio

Your portfolio

Your portfolio represents the amount of assets that you have in your account at any given point in time (see Figure 7-7). It tells you the current value of each of your stocks and the collective amount of money that the account is worth. Better brokerages will also tell you how each of your stocks has performed during the day. If you have borrowed any money on margin, that amount will be reported as well.

Online brokerages also allow you to see your transaction history over the life of the account (see Figure 7-8). While this will not only remind you of the price you bought a particular stock at, it can also be important at tax time to determine how many shares of a particular stock you bought, when, and how they should be taxed.

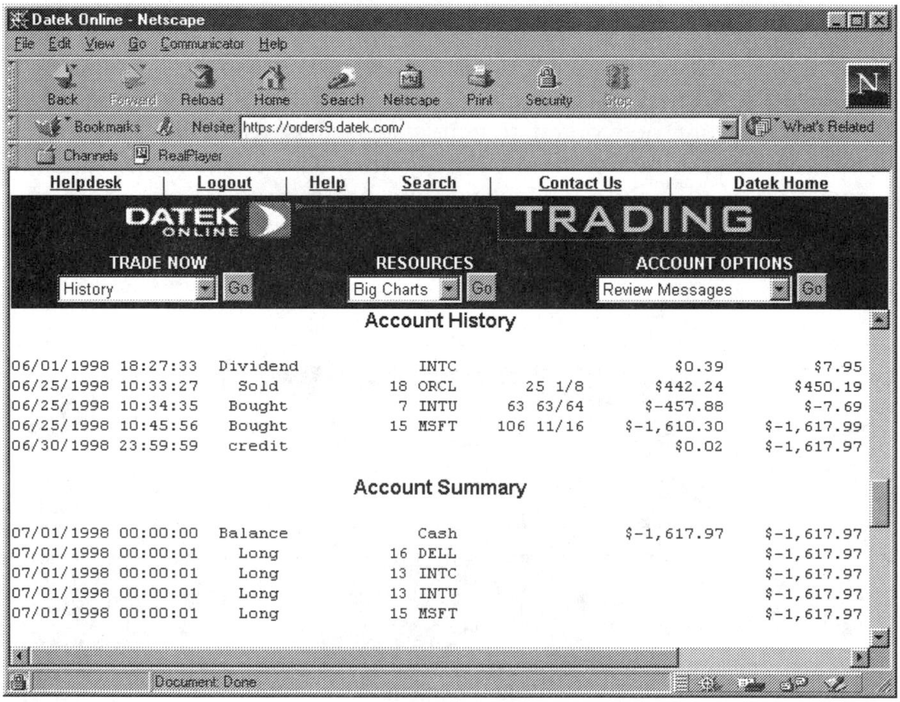

Figure 7-8. Datek's transaction history screen

Quotes: Ask, bid, last sell

Along with your portfolio, the brokerage should give you the ability to get real-time quotes for any stock. When you request a stock quote, you may be expecting a single price. However, because there is always negotiation on the floor of the exchange, there are actually three prices that a particular stock can reflect at any given point in time (see Figure 7-9):

Ask
The lowest price that sellers on the floor will sell the stock for

Bid
The highest price that buyers on the floor are willing to pay for the stock

Last Sell
The last known transaction price of the stock

These three prices come into play because you won't always buy a stock at its bidding price, nor will you always sell a stock at its asking price—brokers on the exchange floor often meet somewhere in the middle. This middle point, where a transaction finally takes place, will then be reported as the last selling price, which (based on supply and demand) may cause the stock's asking and bidding prices to again fluctuate. The difference between the bid price and the asked price is called the "spread," and is a function of the interest in trading stock.

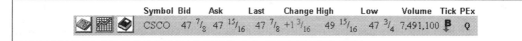

Figure 7-9. The bid, ask, and last sell prices for a stock

In addition, the following information may be displayed to you when you request a stock quote:

Change
The amount the stock has gained or lost in the current trading day

High
The highest transaction price of the stock today

Low
The lowest transaction price of the stock today

Volume
The amount of shares that have been traded today

Tick
Whether the bidding price has gone up or down since the last transaction

Types of orders

Like traditional offline brokerage houses, there are several types of online orders that you can place through your browser:

Market order
This is an order to buy and sell at the best price available on the market, based on the current asking and bidding prices.

Limit order

> This is an order to buy and sell stocks, but only at a specific price or better. The sale will not take place if the transaction price of the stock does not meet the limit specified. Note that a simple limit order does not wait for the transaction price to meet the limit; it attempts to execute the trade, if it can, at the point it was entered into the market.

Limit orders provide a safety valve, as stock transactions are not guaranteed to take place immediately after you transmit them. As you might expect, they work in your favor: if you're buying a stock, the limit order will not execute if the price is *above* the limit you specify, and if you're selling a stock, the limit order will not execute if the price is below the limit you specify. In both cases, this prevents you from losing money on a trade.

If you don't want to wait for the market to come around to your price, some brokerages will allow you to enter a *stop order*. A stop order, sometimes called an *activation order*, allows you to specify a market or limit order that is entered into the exchange only when the price of a stock reaches a preset value. It differs from a simple limit order in that if conditions are not right for the order to take place, it will simply wait until they are. At that point, the order will activate and enter itself into the exchange. However, the rules are reversed: if the order is a buy order, the activation will not take place until the price is *above* the stop limit. If the order is a sell order, the activation will not take place until the price is *below* the stop limit.

In addition, there are two types of stop orders you can enter:

Stop market order

> This is a market order to buy and sell at the best price. The order is entered into the exchange *only* when the price of a stock reaches the stop activation price you specify.[*]

Stop limit order

> This is a limit order to buy and sell only at a preset price or better. The order is entered *only* when the price of a stock reaches the activation price you specify. This may seem redundant, but you can actually use stop limit orders to define an exact price range for buying and selling. For example, let's assume you create a simple limit order that says, "Buy XYZ, but only if it is below 40." You can then create a stop order that triggers your limit order only if XYZ is above 30. Hence, once XYZ rises above 30, the order is entered into the market. However, if XYZ is skyrocketing and rises above 40 before your order is even executed, the limit portion of the order will prevent it from executing (see Figure 7-10).

It's important to note the distinction between regular orders and stop orders. You will generally be charged commission for any market or limit order, including limit orders

---

[*] For example, you can enter a stop market order to sell shares of stock only if they drop below 40. Otherwise, you will hold on to the stock.

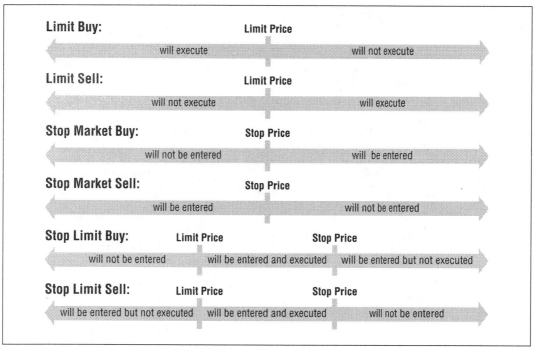

Figure 7-10. Stop orders matrix

that do not execute, because these are orders that have been entered onto the exchange. However, because stop orders do not immediately enter the exchange, you won't be charged a commission until they are activated. Also, not all brokerages will allow you to enter stop orders on all markets; check the fine print to see what your brokerage offers.

Also, you can specify the expiration policy of your order:

End of day
> If the order is not executed at the closing bell of the market, it is automatically cancelled.

GTC (Good 'Til Cancelled)
> This means that an order does not expire after a given period of time, but instead is active until it is executed or the customer cancels it.

Executing a trade

Let's put all this into practice. Let's say we want to enter a simple market order purchasing 20 shares of Dell, and we want this order to remain on the market until we cancel it, or we want to the order to be "Good 'Til Cancelled." We would enter the information in Figure 7-11, and press **Enter Order**.

Figure 7-11. Entering a Good 'Til Cancelled order

Now for a limit order. Let's say that we want to enter a limit order purchasing 20 shares of DELL, but we don't want the order to execute if the transaction price is above $55 a share. It must be below $55 a share to execute when it hits the market, otherwise, the order dies. (Again, we're charged a commission no matter what happens.) In addition, we want the order to cancel at the end of the day, if for some reason it hasn't executed by then. Figure 7-12 shows how me might accomplish this.

Figure 7-12. Entering a limit order

Finally, let's say that we wish to purchase 20 shares of Dell *only* if it rises above $55 a share, but we want to prevent the order from executing if it goes above $63 a share. This is a stop limit order, and we would enter the information in Figure 7-13.

Figure 7-13. Entering a stop limit order

Again, the order is not entered into the market until Dell rises above $55 a share. However, if, when the order executes, the price has risen above $63 a share, our limit order safety-valve kicks in and the order will not be processed. If the latter happens, however, we are still charged commission, because the order made it onto the exchange.

After we press the **Enter Order** button, the brokerage will usually confirm the order, requesting you to enter your account password again. If everything goes smoothly, the order is entered into the brokerage, and you can sit back and watch (or go do something else). Your online brokerage should notify you of the price that a transaction finally took place at, as well as send you a confirmation of the actual trade within three working days. And that's all there is to it!

Trading on Margin

Trading on margin essentially means that you are trading with borrowed money. Your online brokerage will allow you to borrow a specific amount of liquidity (charging you interest, of course), which lets you invest more in the stocks of your choosing. Hence, you stand to gain more money if your stocks gain, and vice versa. You are typically not allowed to trade on margin by default; you must instead elect this option for your account. If you do trade on margin, be aware that you can get a *margin call*, which notifies you that you are in violation of either the brokerage or the market rules. If this occurs, you should check with the online brokerage to see what corrective action is necessary.

Shorting stocks

The price of a stock does not have to go up for you to make money off of it. If you're feeling that a particular company's stock will drop over a period of time, you can *short* the stock. This essentially is a reversal of a standard trading with shares borrowed from the brokerage.

Let's look at an example. Company A's stock is valued at $10. You wish to short the stock, so you sell a share, which you borrow from the brokerage at $10. After the stock drops to $5, you buy it back, thus returning it to the brokerage. However, because you've bought it back at a lower price, you can pocket the five dollars difference. Shorting stocks is a common way of capitalizing off a bear market on Wall Street.

Monitoring the market online

Historically, stocks have an annual growth rate that averages around 11%. This is typically the rate that most people target when they invest money in the stock market—that is, they invest for the long term. On the other hand, you can also try to invest for the short term, hoping that a stock will gain a solid amount very quickly. The obvious downside is that you can lose your money just as quickly. We won't discuss investment strategies here; there are libraries of books that cover these topics in excruciating detail. However, you may want to know how you can monitor various aspects of the stock market to see if your strategies are paying off.

First things first. There are countless items that can affect the stock market as a whole. Here are some of the more common things you should always be on the lookout for:

- Large brokerage houses changing the rating of a stock
- Several companies in a sector exceeding or missing earnings targets
- Changes in foreign economies
- Governmental changes likely to affect the economy
- Actions by the United States Federal Reserve

That being said, each of the major markets has an online web site that you can use to track the indicators of the market at any given point in the day:

- *http://www.nyse.com*

- *http://www.amex.com*

- *http://www.nasdaq.com*

In addition, you can get business news that is likely to affect the stock market at the following URLs:

- *http://biz.yahoo.com*

- *http://www.thestreet.com*

- *http://cbs.marketwatch.com*

Finally, your online brokerage will likely have an endless array of news outlets for you to peruse as well.

Crashes

It happened in 1929; it happened in 1989; wise investors know that it can happen any time. The word "crash" is used to describe a stock market that loses an unusual percentage of its value, generally over the period of a single day. Crashes are not as likely to be as dramatic as the one that sparked off the Great Depression in the 1930s—primarily because more safeguards now exist to keep the market from entering a freefall. However, you should be aware that there is a significant amount of risk in investing in any stock.

Online Brokerages: Things to Watch Out For

Despite everything we've told you, online brokerages aren't necessarily a bed of roses. Here are some common issues that you should be aware of when making a choice to trade online:

Limit orders may not have the same commission as market orders.
> Just because a site advertises trades for only $5.00 may not mean that limit orders are that inexpensive—that price may only apply to market orders. Be sure to check the fine print.

How much for real-time quotes?
> This may seem like a given with trading online, but brokerages may actually charge you for providing the asking, bidding, and selling prices of a given stock in real time. Again, the key word here is "real time." Many sites on the Internet will provide stock quotes, but they will be delayed fifteen or more minutes. Again, check the brokerage's policies to be sure what you're getting, and more importantly, when.

Is the site easily overloaded?

Like it or not, even the best brokerage sites can get overloaded. The best times to check a site's capacity are exactly when the market opens or closes. If you are consistently having trouble connecting to the servers at that time, and there are no dramatic changes in the market, then your brokerage service is probably easily overloaded. It may be time to start looking for another one.

Is there a reasonable failure plan?

There will be cases when the brokerage service completely fails, and you can't even connect. Or perhaps the DJIA falls 1000 points in one day, and it triggers a massive selloff. In that case, you should check to see if you can place an order via a telephone call. Also, look for a toll-free line—you may be placed on the "Your call is very important to us..." holding queue for a while.

Be wary of fees hidden in the price.

Some online brokerages are being investigated for advertising low trading fees, but buying the shares at a higher price and getting a kickback from the seller. For example, you buy 100 shares of Cisco through your online broker for a fee of $19.95, and the order gets filled at $63.50 a share. In reality, a full service broker might have gotten the shares at $65.25, so you have essentially paid another $25.

Be wary of people hawking day trading.

Day trading, so called because you frequently buy and sell the same stock in the same day, takes advantage of the low trading cost of online brokerages. It used to be a strategy professionals used to take advantage of small price changes. Some amateurs try to emulate the professionals; most lose their shirts.

Brokerage Companies

There are many companies with an Internet presence that would love to represent you on the floors of the major stock exchanges. For a sampling of the most popular Internet brokerages, see Chapter 15.

Keep in Mind . . .

Aside from allowing you to execute trades, online brokerages provide a wealth of information. Other online resources not devoted exclusively to trading may also aid in the building of your portfolio. While some of the resources listed below don't include web sites, you should still be aware of them.

The Securities and Exchanges Commission (SEC)

The SEC is the regulatory body over the exchanges in the United States. Companies that want to publicly trade stock must file papers with the SEC, including their quarterly earnings. If these earnings meet or exceed Wall Street's expectations, the stock will generally do well. If not, the stock typically drops.

The only reason that you, the investor, would need to be concerned with the SEC is if you make a trade based on information that is not generally known to the public. This is known as *insider information,* and the SEC vigorously investigates any indication of insider trading. (Just because you're online doesn't mean you're exempt!) For example, if your friend created the product that is losing millions of dollars for a publicly traded company, and he informs you of a loss has not yet been reported to the public, you'd better think twice before selling your stock. It could be illegal.

Taxes

Sorry, but the money you earn while it is in the stock market is subject to taxes by both Uncle Sam and (possibly) your state when you take it out. This is classified as a capital gains tax, and it depends greatly on how long you've had the stock and how much has been gained. Check with your local IRS and state agency to see how capital gains taxes will affect you next April. Alternatively, you can look through IRS publication 550, which is available online from *http://www.irs.ustreas.gov,* for more information on how to report gains and losses throughout the life of your investment.

Online investment resources

Finally, here are some other online resources that may help you understand the wild world of the stock market:

- The New York Stock Exchange has an excellent introduction to the world of Wall Street entitled "You & The Investment World." It is located on its web site at *http://www.nyse.com/public/educate/6a/6aix.htm.*

- The Motley Fool Investment Guide is a wonderful online resource designed to "educate, enrich, and amuse." It appeals to the beginning investor and serves as a chatroom of sorts for people wishing to invest in particular stocks. See *http://www.motleyfool.com/.*

- The *Wall Street Journal* is the quintessential newspaper for information about the investment markets. You can visit the Wall Street Journal online at *http://www.wsj.com.*

Filing Your Taxes

Filing your taxes is actually another task you can undertake online. If you're receiving a refund, the process is almost paperless, and you'll receive those hard-earned dollars a good deal more quickly.

Otherwise, filing online is still something of a mixed bag in terms of increased efficiency. A number of states made online filing an option last year but certainly not all; odds are you'll need to print out and send your state return. If your return isn't too complicated and you qualify to file electronically, you'll still need to send the IRS a paper check[*] and Form 1040-V once your form 1040-PC has been accepted at the electronic filing center. You'll also need to send the IRS a paper copy of Form 8453-OL (the Tax Declaration for Online Filing; be sure to see the Paperwork Reduction Act Notice[†] for more information) with your Form W-2, W-2G, and/or 1099-R stapled to the front, and myriad other forms stapled to the back.[‡] See Figure 7-14 for an example. And, finally, electronic filing isn't free. The lowest rate I found was $7.99 per return.

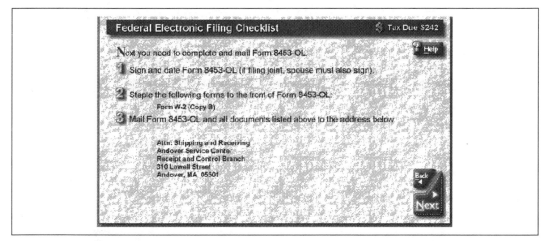

Figure 7-14. How is this filing online?

So why file online? To be honest, I don't think there's much value to it at this point. The IRS is encouraging consumers to file electronically and over the next few years the cost of doing so should decrease while the ease increases. The IRS does note that when filing electronically "you are less likely to have a problem with your tax return, thereby reducing your likelihood of receiving an error notice" due to faster processing and improved accuracy.

However, the Web is a very useful tool in *preparing* your tax returns, even if you submit those returns the old-fashioned way. If you're using personal finance software, it's often easy to port the information into tax preparation software such as TurboTax or TaxCut. These programs walk you through the process of filling out your returns, and come with almost all the forms the IRS seems to create. You can download these forms for free from the IRS web site (*http://www.irs.gov/prod/cover.html*), but if you want to avoid lengthy download times, having the forms on CD-ROM is a real convenience. There are other sites on the Web that allow you to fill out your return via a form-based question-and-answer format.

---

[*] The inability to pay by credit card saddened more than one friend of mine.

[†] I am not making this up.

[‡] These other forms include the Physician's Certificate of Blindness, and requiring that it be stapled to the back strikes me as something of a sick joke.

Internet Tax Filing

Tax preparation software helps you prepare your taxes and then transmits the returns electronically to its filing centers.

TurboTax and TaxCut

The two creme-de-la-creme tax programs, Intuit's TurboTax and Kiplinger's TaxCut, each support online tax filing. See Figures 7-15 and 7-16 to get a sense of what TurboTax is like.

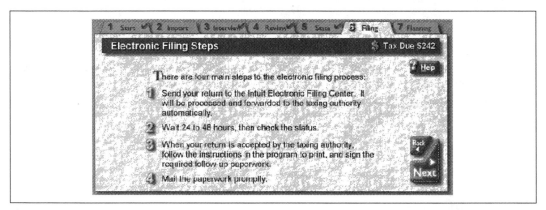

Figure 7-15. Intuit's service: a very taxing authority indeed

Using the programs to file a return is relatively inexpensive—once you've bought the software. The cost is approximately $10 per return, with a rebate card enclosed for one free return.

While you can use web-based filing centers for less overall cost, these income tax programs are a good choice if you have a complicated return or wish to file electronically without transmitting information over the Web.

Web-Based Tax Filing

If you're looking for an online tax solution without all the fuss, there are a number of sites on the Web that can fulfill your tax needs. Even Intuit and Kiplinger support web-based versions of their tax programs. If your needs are simpler, these sites are a much more affordable way to go. See *http://www.intuit.com/turbotax/ttonline/ welcome.html* or *http://www.taxcut.com/taxcut/do_taxes_online/index.html* for further details.

A number of other tax-filing web sites exist. If you plan to file online in the year 2000, take a look at Infoseek's Taxes channel for a current list. A few representative sites are listed here.

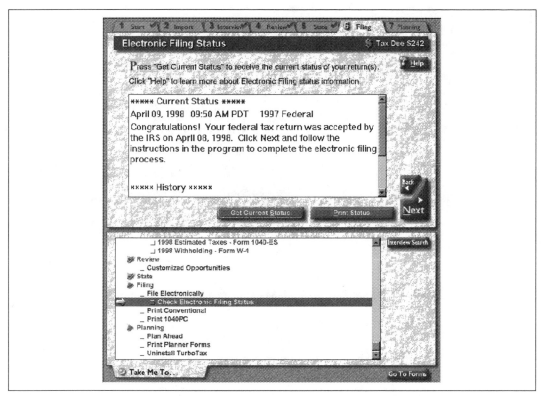

Figure 7-16. What kind of loser would wait until April 8th to file her taxes?

SecureTax (http://www.securetax.com/)

The SecureTax site is well organized, and it's easy to get started (see Figure 7-17).

Once I started filling out the return, however, things got very confusing, both in terms of navigation and entering the tax information itself. Steve's Checklist left a lot to be desired (Figure 7-18).

Electronic filing is actually free—once you pay for printing. Who they thought they were going to fool with this gambit is beyond me, but filing a 1040 (or 1040A) and state return costs $14.95. You'll need the Adobe Acrobat reader and a letter-quality printer.

Tax Systems online (http://www.filesafe.net/TaxSys/go.htm)

The Tax Systems site is much more complicated than SecureTax's, but it uses the File-Safe encryption system to boost security. Be prepared for a lot of Java/JavaScript interaction.

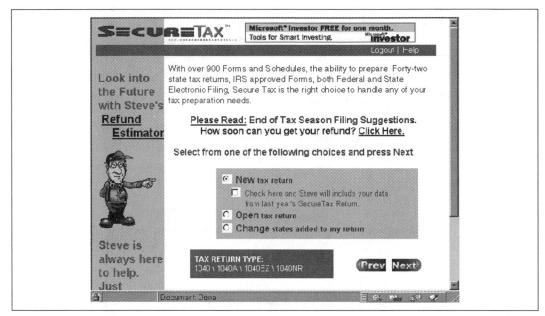

Figure 7-17. Tax filing online

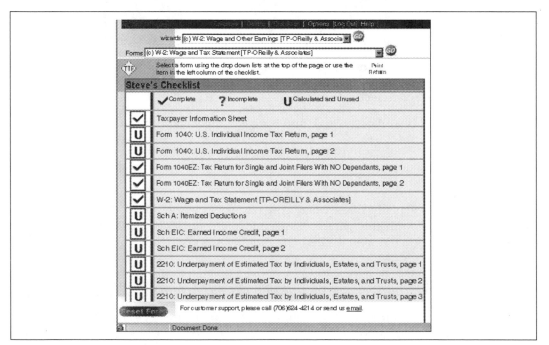

Figure 7-18. Huh?

Student Loans

Even if you have student loans, you may not realize that there's a good deal of information available to you on the Web. You can check account balances, get information about loan consolidation, and learn about debit programs that affect your interest rate, as displayed in Figure 7-19.

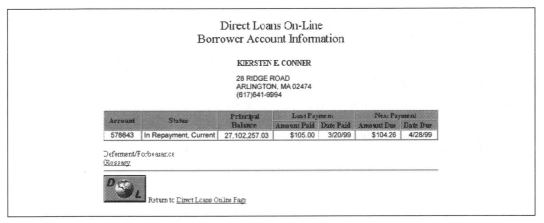

Figure 7-19. *I am so screwed*

Take a look at the following resources for more information on student loans.

Sallie Mae: Student Loan Marketing Association
  http://www.salliemae.com/home/index_e.html

FinAid's List of Lenders
  http://www.finaid.org/finaid/loans/lenders.html

Yahoo's list of lenders
  http://www.yahoo.com/Business_and_Economy/Companies/Education/Financial_Aid/Lenders/

Digital Cash

Remember when I made the joke earlier about turning your PC into an ATM? Plans are in the works to do just that.

Unfortunately, your new minitower won't come with a cache of fifties just below the DVD drive. What it might have is a smart-card reader that fits in your floppy-drive slot. These so-called smart cards are plastic cards embedded with microcircuits. The increased security built in to these cards would allow you to download cash to them from your bank. You could then use the card as you would a credit or debit card.

Why might you want to use digital cash? There aren't very many merchants who currently accept this means of payment.* However, the technology offers both portability and privacy advantages over credit cards, especially when used over the Web. Though currently in its infancy, customers can use digital cash when they want to make a purchase without revealing credit card information. And while the smart cards aren't in wide use yet, customers could put digital cash account information on a floppy and use it at any computer, anywhere in the world.

For more information, see Chapter 15.

---

* A trial program on Manhattan's upper West side failed in 1998. It's unclear whether flesh-and-blood merchants will ever be interested in smart cards, but they still hold some promise in the virtual world.

CHAPTER EIGHT

ONLINE GAMES

Did you ever stumble into an arcade and come across a machine that allowed you to match wits with poultry? When computer gaming started, it was a lot like playing tic-tac-toe with a trained chicken. The experience was novel in and of itself, but the game wasn't that fascinating and the experience quickly grew tiresome, especially for the chicken.

People eventually turned to computer networks to allow them to play these games against each other. Legend has it that the Internet was invented in part for users to play a game called NetTrek.

The History and Culture of Internet Gaming

From the beginning, the Internet was always a great place for information about games. FTP sites provided shareware and demos you could download, collected bug reports, and provided patch files. People even began to play turn-based games via email. Players would take a turn, then email the virtual game board back to the other player. Other players created text-based Multiple User Dungeons (MUDs) in order to play Dungeons and Dragons–style games over vast distances.

As computing technology advanced, artificial intelligence improved—as Garry Kasparov can attest. Computer games allowed for a wide variety of virtual experiences: you could battle Attila the Hun in (what is defined as) real time or play bridge while Omar Sharif commented over your shoulder. Many of these games were so complex or graphically rich that it was difficult to envision playing them over a network.

Today, the technologies have coalesced. Internet connection speeds are increasing and you can play more and more games over the network. Many, if not most, commercial games today come with multiplayer network options built in. Game services like the Total Entertainment Network, Battle.net, and Mplayer are creating forums for online gaming; there's even a nascent professional computer gamers' league. How do you find these games? Moreover, how do you join them, and play successfully?

This chapter is broken down into two sections: games on the Web and games on the Internet. The distinction is actually quite important. While the Web is an excellent source of player matchmaking or game support, the games you'll find there are frequently multiplayer only in the sense that your score is compared to that of others, rather than supporting a number of players going head to head. Meanwhile, connecting directly across the Internet is a better means for players to do battle.

Early Klingons

—by Ed Krol

One of the first computer games appeared online even before the existence of the Internet. As early as 1975, people would sneak onto the ARPAnet to play a text-based *Star Trek* game. The short-range scanner looked like this:

```
. . . . . . . . . .
.K. . . . . . . .
. . . . . . . .E.
. . . . . . . . . .
. . . . . . . . . .
. . . . . . . . . .
. . . . . . . . . .
..B. . . . . . .
. . . . . . . . . .
```

E represented the Enterprise, B was a starbase, and Ks represented the Klingons. The entire game consisted of about 1,600 lines of FORTRAN.

Hazards of Net Gaming

Unless you're connecting with real, breathing people you already know (and if so, why aren't you in the same room, interacting with each other in person?), be prepared for a fairly hostile environment, and don't allow children to play online unsupervised. There are some online gaming arenas that are more refined than others—online bridge players, for example, tend to be more sedate than first-person shooters. Keep in mind, though, that while some people may be online because they're just too good at Scrabble for anyone else in the neighborhood, many may have chosen to isolate themselves for a reason. There are cathartic benefits to be found in throwing grenades at exploding mutants, but don't expect to find charm school graduates sitting properly in the chat rooms.

On a more real-world note, many people are excited by the recent prospect of Las Vegas–style gambling on the Internet. American and international laws governing the Internet and World Wide Web remain unclear, although some U.S. states have already declared the practice illegal. Even so, an online casino may still operate if its server is located in a state or country where gambling is legal. Bet at your own risk.

World Wide Web Games

There are a few different categories of games on the Web. You'll find sites that support many different types of games, commercial sites presenting online versions of TV game shows, trivia games for prizes, offshore gambling, and diversions like the *New York Times* crossword puzzle. You'll also find sites that support existing games. These sites—some from the game's creators, some not—may provide hints, scenarios, or support. Often, you can find free hints that are being charged for elsewhere.

Commercial Games

In the quest for advertising revenue from the Web, some companies have fixed on games as the means to capture the consumer's attention. Perhaps as a result, some of the best games on the Web are produced by big, money-sucking organizations.

Riddler (http://www.riddler.com)

Interactive Imaginations' Riddler site sports some great games. Members (registration is free) can win cash and prizes; members and nonmembers can play other games just for fun. Registration requires a lengthy demographic interview, and the site is ad-supported—somewhat ingeniously, in that you have to scroll through an ad page to get to the game you've chosen. Loading is fairly quick; unfortunately, if you get the wrong answer in some trivia games, Riddler doesn't provide the right one. Only residents of the United States and Canada are eligible to win prizes. Since many games are Java-based, you'll do best to use Netscape Navigator 3.0 or later or Internet Explorer 3.0 or later. You're warned when a game you've selected requires Java. Games are easy to understand and run smoothly.

Games include single-player and multiplayer crosswords, single- and multiplayer trivia challenges, riddles, web-based scavenger hunts, visual palindromes, solitaire, and word searches.

It takes time to win the prizes. You accumulate *CAPS* (tokens) toward certain prizes by winning games. For example, winning Mental Floss (a trivia game) on the medium difficulty level by answering 7 out of 10 questions correctly nets you 49 Credit Card protection from Credentials CAPS. Depending on the prize you want, you may need anywhere from 2,500 to 12,500 CAPS to win. Past prizes have included a Sony Watchman, a Calypso sailboard, golf clubs, cash, vacations, modems, and Broadway tickets, but prizes change frequently. You can't choose to work toward certain prizes; according to

---

Castle Wolfenstein, Doom, and Quake

Computer games changed dramatically with the advent of seemingly three-dimensional, first-person "shooter" games. Espousing an ethic of "if it moves, shoot it; if it doesn't move, shoot it anyway," these games escalated in popularity when id software's "Doom" supported multiplayer games via LAN (Local Area Network), modem, or TCP/IP, and actually worked. Users got hooked on the shareware demo and kept coming back for more.

Doom was created by id Software, Inc., which first received worldwide notoriety with a game called Castle Wolfenstein 3D in 1992. This precursor to Doom (and, eventually, a slew of other titles, including Quake) popularized the point of view in which the player looks out over a shotgun into a Gothic, three-dimensional world full of monsters. Doom, Doom II, Quake, and Quake II extended and improved upon this basic concept. Multiplayer support, which allowed players to hunt or be hunted by their own friends, turned the game into a bonanza of bloodletting and capitalized on the Internet gaming subculture. Quake allows players to set up their own servers, and add-ons and plug-ins like QuakeWorld and QuakeSpy allow for better play and easier detection of nearby servers looking for players.

If shooting a bloody-mouthed Doberman with a nail gun isn't your idea of a pleasant afternoon, these games are not for you. The makers claim not to be Satan worshippers.

The multiplayer climate can be quite hostile to the newcomer. You'll frequently find your character dead seconds after you enter a game. If a single-player version of a game exists, be sure to play it enough to familiarize yourself with the controls and your surroundings before you venture online.

Riddler, "The sponsor pages you see are based on the interests you expressed when you first signed up for Riddler. The more you play, the more sponsor pages you'll see, which improves your chances of winning CAPS toward the prizes you want most."

You Don't Know Jack /Acrophobia/What's the Big Idea? *(http://www.bezerk.com)*

Berkeley Systems, the company that created the flying toasters screensaver, brings us the Bezerk Online Entertainment Network, which supports four games: You Don't Know Jack the Netshow, You Don't Know Jack the Sports Netshow, Acrophobia, and What's the Big Idea?. Download the plug-in software once, which takes about 15 minutes over a 28.8 Kbps connection; after that, just visit the web site with your browser and click the **Play** button, and the new episode launches automatically. The games are free, supported by ads shown twice during the game. Hit the Escape key for game controls.

The original Jack is the online version of the popular CD-ROM trivia game, and it's one of the few things on the Web that lives up to its hype. One or two players compete in a trivia contest that includes multiple-choice questions, gibberish riddles, and a matching game. The game play is quick and graphically rich, the questions are interesting and just difficult enough, and the announcer is sarcastic and funny. New episodes are released every few weeks.

You Don't Know Jack the Sports Netshow is similar to the original and features a new game every Tuesday. Additionally, Berkeley gives away prizes if you play the game on certain days, which are shown on their prize calendar.

Acrophobia is Bezerk's multiplayer word game. Download the application, then compete with 8 to 10 other people to create phrases out of acronyms on a certain topic. Like Jack, the game moves quickly and the interface is clean. A chat window allows for commentary on the game. You'll probably want to opt for the clean-language rooms to avoid incessant mentions of the male anatomy. Prizes are offered.

Finally, What's the Big Idea? was in beta at the time of this writing. It's a game about conformity. The moderator asks a multiple choice question, and the number of points you receive depends on how many players answer the question in a similar manner. It's still rough around the edges, but the graphics are cute (you're a little guy in a space suit, jumping up a pyramid).

Jeopardy/Wheel of Fortune (http://www.station.sony.com/jeopardy, http://www.station.sony.com/wheel)

Ever dreamed of appearing on *Jeopardy*? Buying a vowel? Now, you can play the games, even if you don't like Alex Trebek's snotty tone. Be prepared for Java applets and a burst of theme music when you log on. The sites are part of Sony's Station, and play requires you to create an account. Engage in multiplayer games, or play against the computer.

You'll also find a "game show" section at the Station, featuring Napoleon (described as French Poker), a few word games, and a beta of The Dating Game (sample question: "What's the noisiest part of your body?"). The SubStation section supports multiplayer war games, including a tank game called Tanarus, a fantasy/war game called Fantasy War, and a two-person strategy game called Chron X.

New York Times Crossword Puzzles (http://www.nytimes.com/diversions)

Now, crossword fanatics can get their daily fix without that pesky newspaper surrounding it. The puzzle is considered a premium service, although it's free with your AOL account or subscription to the paper edition of the *New York Times*. You'll also find a trivia quiz, and the bridge, chess, and game theory columns.

Traditional Multiplayer Games

> *http://www.playsite.com*
> *http://play.yahoo.com*

If you're looking for some of the more traditional card or strategy games, numerous sites on the Web can supply entertainment (particularly at the two sites listed here). You'll find bingo, checkers, chess, poker, blackjack, poker, and other games at Java-enabled sites.

If you're an AOL member, you'll find many of these games under the keyword: Games.

Online Gambling

Gambling in the United States has been on the rise in recent years. If setting dollar bills on fire is too messy and the local Indian reservation is too far away, you can get a fix over the Web.

Most online casinos base their servers in countries outside the United States, where gambling is legal.* While the legality of computer users participating from countries where gambling is illegal remains unclear, you can now get your gambling fix without taking off your bathrobe. Simply download the software and send out your credit-card number over a secure browser. As mentioned previously, betting may or may not be legal for U.S. residents.

One note: if the creators of a site don't know how to spell "deuces" or "roulette," don't trust them with your money.

Acropolis Casinos (http://www.acropoliscasinos.com)

Acropolis offers "elegant gaming online." Visit guest services to adjust game options, including turning off the music. Acropolis offers a choice of roulette, video poker, and blackjack, and proclaims the best odds on the Internet. You have the option to play offline, though occasional messages will pop up to remind you that you could be losing your money on the Net.

Starluck Casino (http://starluck.com)

It's easy to set up an account with Starluck, and the minimum order is $14.95, which gives you 1,495 PlayChips. Game play takes place via CGI, which has advantages and disadvantages—the games actually work, but playing is painfully slow. Games include blackjack, video poker, keno, lotto, and slots.

---

* Gambling is also legal in the state of Nevada, where gamblers have long been able to place bets by phone. A pilot program, scheduled for the summer of 1999, plans to let casinos provide smart cards and software for gamblers to place bets by PC. However, according to Nevada law, gamblers must first visit the casino to establish an account, and then dial in directly to the casino, from within the state.

CyberBookies (http://www.cyberbookies.com)

The Oasis Casino (part of CyberBookies' offerings) supports online betting not only on poker and blackjack, but on sports bets as well. Side bets, totals, parlays, teasers and more are offered on professional and college football, basketball, baseball, hockey, golf, boxing, car races, horses, and tennis. Play the Vegas line without even making a phone call.

Intercasino (http://www.intercasino.com)

This standalone software client supports blackjack, Caribbean poker, roulette, and slot machines with up to 95% payouts and up to $10,000 jackpots, and four kinds of video poker machines. The software also supports Full Sports Book with betting on football, basketball, hockey and baseball with parlay cards, teaser cards, and straight cards. There's also full electronic cash support. The site includes a link to Gamblers' Anonymous.

I-Net Casino (http://www.ibetinet.com)

Currently, blackjack, roulette, and slot machines are available to play for fun only. The interface is clean, however, and once the Java application loads, game play is very quick and smooth.

Golden Palace Online Casino (http://www.goldenpalace.com)

Play roulette, blackjack, poker, slots, keno, craps, and baccarat for money or for fun on this standalone client.

Web Sites That Support Games

Some sites support games that already exist, instead of offering a gaming environment. Some provide shareware games or playable demos that you can download. Others provide hints, cheats, scenarios, or support groups. You'll find a nice mixture of sites from the corporate and private gaming worlds with the advantages attendant to both.

Types of game help

One of the really positive attributes of the WWW culture is the belief in the open exchange of information. Many retail software games come with helpful 900 numbers that provide direct access to hint lines. However, you can find all the information you need, free of charge, on the Web. If a retail game exists, a web site undoubtedly supports it. Popular games may have dozens of web sites discussing the games merits, changes, or updates, and at least a few cheats, hints, or tips.

A *cheat* is usually a code that you enter while the game is running to give you an advantage in the game, frequently in the form of extra powers, abilities, or supplies.

Sometimes, entire menus full of cheats are provided with the game. You may need to enter the code at a designated time during the game play, however, or at the DOS command line.

Hints take the form of advice on playing the game. Veteran players may have learned that it's more effective to kill an ogre with a nail gun than a rocket launcher, or that a simulated city grows more quickly when surrounded by roads.

Tips take many forms. A *walk-through* involves a step-by-step solution to an entire game (frighteningly enough, I found not one but two walk-throughs for Riven within a week of its release date). Obviously, a game won't be much fun to play this way; if you're stuck, however, reading up to the point at which you're stuck in a walk-through may be your best hope. *Hack codes* are programming tips that detail how to alter the code of a program to make it easier to play. Finally, a *patch* is a link to a file that updates, or fixes bugs within, the original game.

GamePower (*http://www.gamepower.com*)

CMP Media's GamePower site features Hot Pages with cheats & hints, demos & patches, and desktop themes. It also breaks games down into Categories (for example, sims, role-playing games, action); go to that category for a well-organized list of almost every available computer game. For example, clicking on **SimCity 2000** links you to a page with a review from *Home PC* magazine, player comments, related downloads, and links to hints, cheats, Easter eggs, patches, demos, and walk-throughs.

Game Center (*http://www.gamecenter.com*)

c|net's game site isn't very well organized, but there's a wealth of stuff here for the gamer. Reviews and articles cover everything from input devices to equipment upgrades to games that changed history, and the search feature catalogs a wide array of files and articles.

Happy Puppy (*http://www.happypuppy.com*)

The self-proclaimed #1 game site on the Internet is eclectic, fun, and replete with links. The Multiplayer Online Game (MPOG) page has a fantastic list of multiplayer games you can download, along with comprehensive lists of game services, what they are, how much they cost, and which games they support. If you're looking for a specific game, browse through this list first.

Yahoo! games (*http://games.yahoo.com/top/review.html*)

A very well-organized site in the Yahoo! tradition (see Figure 8-1). Games are broken down into eight categories. For each category, click on reviews, demos, hints, or links for a definitive, pithy guide to what you're looking for. Unfortunately, it lacks a search feature.

Figure 8-1. Yahoo! Games

GameGirlz (http://www.gamegirlz.com)

This site is dedicated to the promotion of multiplayer online gaming for women. You won't find a million downloads here, but you will find excellent reviews, articles, news, and gaming events. There are also a number of good Quake links, the game toward which the site seems biased.

GameSpot (http://www.gamespot.com)

ZDNet's game offering includes the usual round of downloads, reviews, articles, and contests. A list of the top-ten available demos is convenient. The top-ten page features more interesting lists (although it seems unclear on the concept of "top ten"): the top-ten games by GameSpot score, top-ten Games by player score, top-20 downloads, top-ten hardware products, top-five action games, top-five adventure games, top-five driving games, top-five puzzle games, top-five role-playing games, top-five simulation games, top-five sports games, and top-five strategy games. The site seems to favor the commercial; you won't find a lot of shareware here. The guide to downloading is helpful for the novice.

Games Domain (http://www.gamesdomain.com)

The Games Domain is a comprehensive gaming site with thousands of links to everything game related: cheats, demos, downloads, freebies, and reviews from their volunteer-run computer and console magazine's the *Games Domain Review*.

Specific Game Support

Some games have created entire subcultures unto themselves. You can find a wealth of free information about them on the Web. If you don't want to spend a fortune on telephone hint lines or (Great Scott!) buy a book for help, such web sites are invaluable.

First, try the official site for a game for the latest patches and information; sometimes, you'll also find links to individual gamer's pages.

Each of the general gaming sites we mentioned previously is a good place to try next. You'll usually find cheats, hints, tips, walk-throughs, modifications, and so on. Also try personal gamers' pages. Fanatics are unreliable, but frequently prolific.

Quake III was not yet in beta at the time this book was written, but test demos had been released for the Mac and Linux platforms. A search at Yahoo! yielded two web sites, which led us to the Quake III Nation site, shown in Figure 8-2.

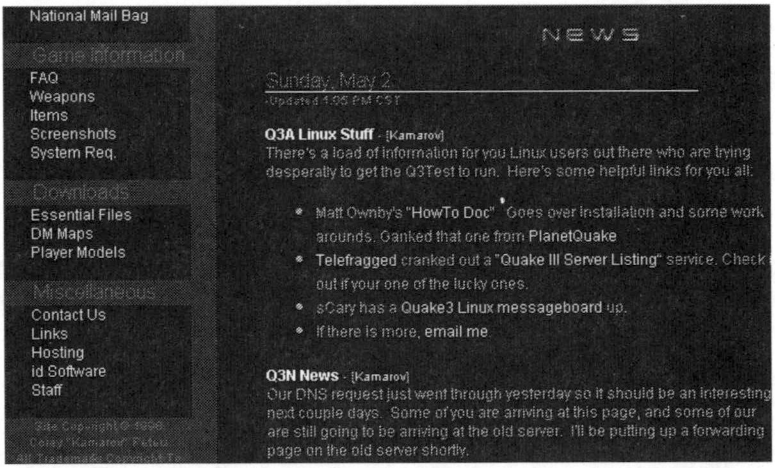

Figure 8-2. Quake III information

From this example, you can see that it's easy to find every possible aid you need to solve the game, for free—in fact, if you take advantage of walk-throughs, you don't even need to play a game to solve it!

Tutorial: Implementing Scenario Files

In computer-game parlance, a *scenario file* allows you to play the game according to certain modified criteria, such as historical or fantasy situations. You can find scenarios for a number of different games, including Quake, Civilization2, and others. Since finding and implementing a scenario can be a complicated procedure, this is a good opportunity for a small tutorial.

Civ2 is an empire-building game in which you build up a civilization and then go on to conquer others. MicroProse and a number of individual users have created scenario files for Civ2. Let's take a look at a page created by a user, Brian, to support the game. It's available at *http://www.jps.net/bmt/* (see Figure 8-3).

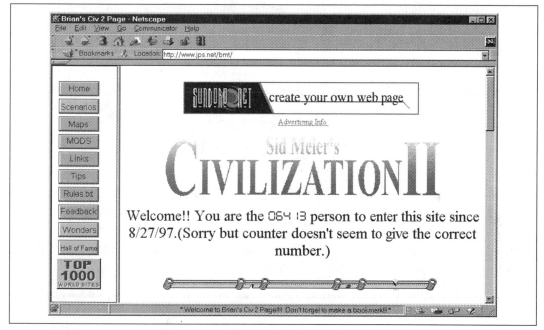

Figure 8-3. Brian's Civ2 page

Brian's page not only contains hints and strategies for winning the game, but additional files he created (or collected) himself. These other files include alternative maps on which you can play the game, scenarios in which you can take a certain side in a battle (say, Gettysburg or D-Day), and modifications that allow you to customize the game by, for example, adding a big scary monster unit.

Let's take a look at how you would modify Civ2 to play one of these scenarios.

First, find a scenario you'd like to play. Typing "civilization" into GameCenter's search feature yielded the page in Figure 8-4.

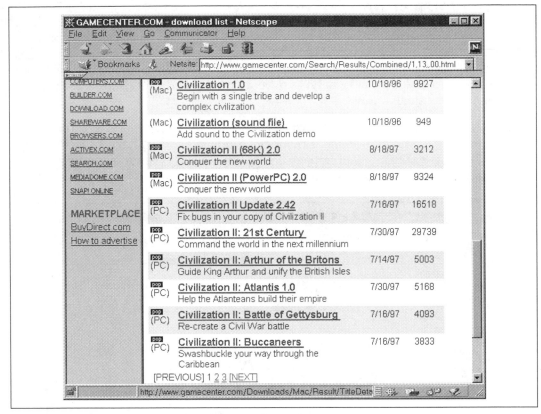

Figure 8-4. GameCenter's Civilization search results

Let's say we want to unify the British Isles. Click on **Arthur of the Britons**, and download the file. But once we've got it, what do we do with it?

Before extracting the file with WinZip or another extraction utility, be sure to read any *readme.txt* files. If there aren't any readme files, read *all* the text files. One of them ought to give you at least rudimentary instructions on installing the scenario. If you don't find such instructions, you might want to think twice about installing the files at all.

In this case, the file *Document.txt* provides extensive notes on playing the scenario, but not that much about installing it. Where might we find more? The download link provided by GameCenter was *ftp.glyphweb.com*. Let's try typing *www.glyphweb.com* into our browser's location window (see Figure 8-5).

The page doesn't look promising (for our purposes) at first, but if we scroll down to the Leisure Complex link, you'll see that we've hit paydirt.

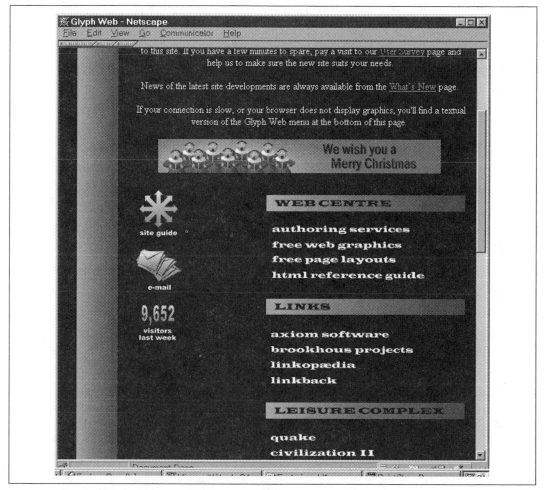

Figure 8-5. Glyph's home page

Note: This wasn't actually the first method I tried. Here are a few other techniques you could use to find out more about installing scenario files:

- Search the Web for the author's name.

- Search for the phrase "+civilization+scenario" on the Web, or at different gaming sites.

- Notice the company name that GameCenter listed? Search for that on the Web.

Scrolling down to the "Leisure Complex" section reveals a wealth of links about Civilization2. The "Scenarios" section provides detailed instructions on installing the many different files they list. The best method for installing Civ2 scenarios is the simplest:

1. First, make sure you have your original CD-ROM, or have backed up the Civ2 directory.

2. Extract the scenario file into the *Civ2* directory.

3. Move any WAV files into the *Sounds* directory.

4. Civ2 specifications are based on the *.txt* files in the Civ2 directory. To run the scenarios, you'll replace those files with the scenario files, which have their own rules, city names, and maps. Arthur of the Britons renames the necessary files for you. Other scenarios require you to rename files yourself. For example, for the Atlantis scenario, *Atlrules.txt* and *Atlcity.txt* need to be renamed *rules.txt* and *city.txt*.

Keep a few notes in mind when installing scenarios or modifications you find on the Web:

- Download files from a reputable source, and be sure to scan them for viruses before installing them.

- Read all readme files for instructions.

- Make sure that you have backup copies of all your files before installing any new game files into the same directory.

- Be flexible and don't give up! You got this stuff for free. If you can't make things work, email someone at the site you downloaded the file from, or take a look at a Usenet group for the particular game. You're almost sure to find someone there who'll be happy to help.

Internet (Non-Web) Games

The Internet is more than the World Wide Web. In fact, depending on your personal enthusiasms, you may find a more satisfying gaming experience without the Web as an impediment and without the attendant line noise. While the Web (and, to a certain extent, the gaming services described in this section) is easy to use, it can get in the way of actual game playing.

Many games support direct TCP/IP or modem connections between players, allowing for relatively smooth, quick play. Problems arise, however, when a solitary player tries to find an open game. You won't get very far rubbing your temples and saying, "I feel a game in need of a player at 206.12.54.876." That's why there are now a number of ways to find games, spanning the Web, chat clients, individual utilities, and gaming networks.

It's becoming increasingly easy to find other people who are enthusiastic about your favorite games. If you're willing to put in a little work, you'll find the more rudimentary methods of connecting (those that don't use the Web or an overly pretty graphical user interface) to be the more reliable. Kali and QuakeSpy take a little more user savvy to get up and running, but they're free (or require a one-time fee), require much less processor support and/or bandwidth, and currently have a much larger user base.

In general, you'll need a connection speed of at least 28.8 Kbps, a reasonably fast processor, and a minimum of 16 MB of memory (RAM) in order for these games to work adequately over the Internet. Direct modem-to-modem links require somewhat less firepower. Unfortunately, perhaps, as connection speeds and processor power increase, so too does the complexity of most games. The best way to speed up game play over any of these services is to upgrade your hardware—but don't expect it to make a world of difference.

Internet *lags* (as such frustrating delays are called) are merely irritating when playing games like Scrabble or Risk. For real-time multiplayer games, however, you may find yourself consistently blown to bits before you can get up off the cave floor. For a change of pace, try hosting the game yourself—this time, you'll be the one running laps with the rocket launcher. If you're a Quake player, take a look at the "Quake-World" section later in this chapter before creating an account on a gaming service.

The rest of this section describes gaming services, including a list of the games that each service supports; standalone applications to help you connect with other gamers; utilities and drivers you can use to maximize your hardware configuration; and an overview of sites that list play-by-mail games.

Games Services and Networks

Internet gaming systems currently seem to be coming into their own. Kali, the grandfather of them all, is a home-grown service that started out as shareware in the finest Internet tradition. Other services are rapidly improving and may be reaching critical mass: DWANGO recently merged with Microsoft's Internet Gaming Zone, while Mplayer and Total Entertainment Network have left the beta phase and started supporting games, rankings, and tournaments in earnest. They've also started charging users fairly substantial fees. From this viewpoint, AOL could also be considered something of a gaming system, since it supports a number of different multiplayer games and smooths the process of finding other gamers and setting up a round.

Kali

One of the cheapest, most comprehensive gaming networks actually isn't a network at all. The Kali shareware application operates on Windows 95/98, Windows NT, MS-DOS, Macintosh, and OS/2 platforms and supports dozens of games over hundreds of servers. It works by letting you use the Internet to simulate a local area network, or LAN, thus "tricking" the Internet into letting you run the IPX/SPX protocol over the

Internet's own TCP/IP protocol. All you need to do is connect to your ISP as usual, and launch the application. If a game supports multiplayer play over the Internet, you can play it on Kali.

Until you register, you'll only be able to use Kali for 15 minutes at a time. The good news is that registration involves a one-time fee of only $20. Although using Kali may be daunting at first, most gamers find it well worth the fee.

First, visit *http://www.kali.net/* and download the software appropriate to your platform. If you're using DOS or the Mac, Kali recommends that you also install the latest PPP software, to which Kali provides a link. Install the software on your machine as instructed, including any PPP utilities.

Now restart your machine and connect to the Internet. Select **Kali95** from the **Start** menu, and fill in the User information as the application requests; don't worry about the serial number for now. The About to Scan dialog box opens; answer No when it asks whether you'd like to keep your current launch and game button information. Manually add any games on your hard drive Kali doesn't automatically pick up. Game icons then appear along the bottom of the screen, as in Figure 8-6.

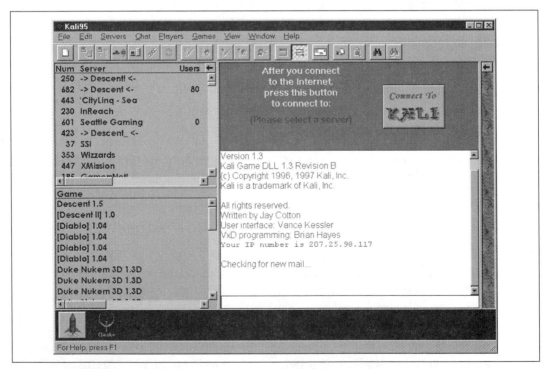

Figure 8-6. Kali95's opening screen

A standard chat pane sits on the bottom right. To the left, Kali displays a list of servers above a list of games in progress. A button reads **Connect to Kali**.

Getting started is easy. First, choose a server. Right now, you don't know much about them—in fact, you don't know anything about them but their names. Choose a server based on its *ping rate*, which describes how quickly information packets from your computer reach the desired server. Ping rates are affected by your processor and connection speeds, as well as your geographical location as related to the server, the number of players on the server, and the server's processor and connection speeds.

To learn what each server's ping rate is, grab the middle bar that separates the two panes and move it to the right until you see the Ping heading, to the right of Users. Next, click on the **Servers** menu, and select **Ping All Servers**. It may take a few moments for Kali to contact all the servers. While it does so, select **Settings...** from the **File** menu. On the **Advanced** tab, select the checkboxes next to "Ping servers on startup" and "Disable Win95 key." This way, each time you launch Kali, it checks for the closest servers. (Disabling the Win95 key prevents you from accidentally killing a game by pressing that key.) Figure 8-7 shows some typical Kali settings.

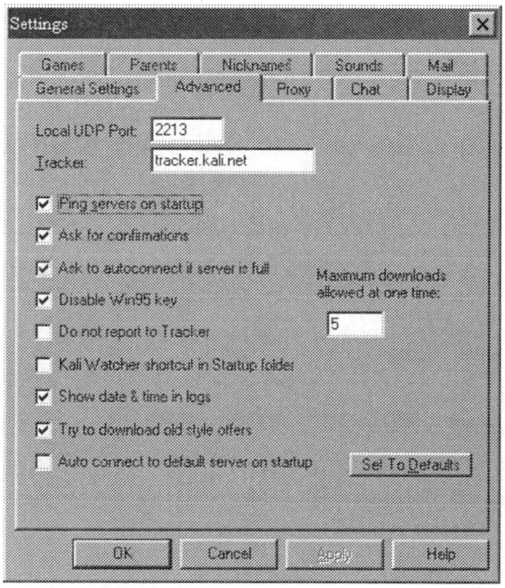

Figure 8-7. Kali settings

If you're interested in setting the parental controls, this is a good time to click on the **Parents** tab. Use this option to create a Profanity Filter to block any words you specify and block others from changing your configuration settings. A password protects your choices.*

---

* Even with this option activated, children should not be allowed to use Kali unsupervised, if at all. The vast majority of games are more violent than what you'll see on the evening news, and chat participants, while often friendly, are rarely discreet.

Let's go back to your server settings. Choose the server with the lowest ping rate from the list by double-clicking on it.

A list of games appears in the lower-left pane. The same list appears regardless of which server you've connected to. Find a game you'd like to play, and once again examine the ping rate listed next to it. (Again, you'll probably need to re-configure your windows to do so; you can also right-click on a game and select **Ping Host** from the pop-up menu.) If it's over 600 milliseconds, odds are it's not worth attempting to join the game. If you can't find a game with a low enough ping rate, try connecting to a different server. The server with the lowest ping rate may not always provide access to games with low ping rates; you may have to try a few before you get lucky. Servers closest to you geographically are usually a good place to start.

Double-click on the game you've chosen, and Kali attempts to connect you. If all goes well, the game's server accepts you and Kali launches the game. You may be rejected, however, if your ping rate is too high, or you don't have the correct version of the software. If so, try to find another game.

If you can't find another game, or you'd like to play a game not currently on the games list, launch your own. You can play any game that supports IPX networks over Kali. To launch a game, connect to a server as described earlier. Then, click on the rocket icon at the bottom of your screen. Kali opens the Game Options dialog box, shown in Figure 8-8.

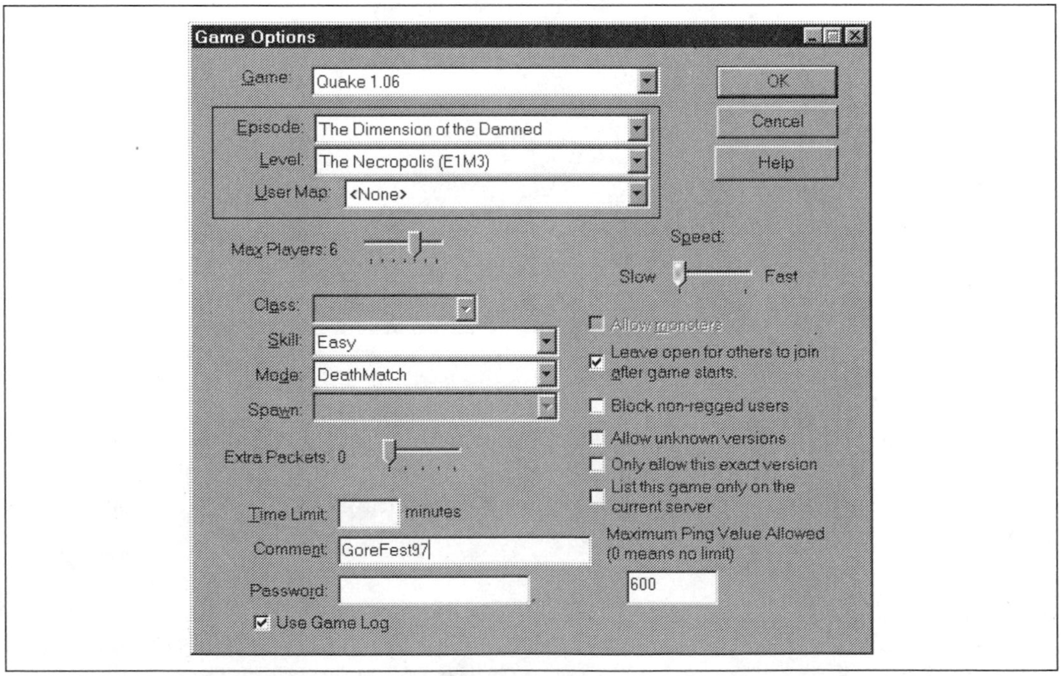

Figure 8-8. Kali's Game Options dialog box

Fill in the options you'd like. Kali opens the Launch window. Wait for at least one player to join (depending on the game) and click the **Launch** button (second from the right), and Kali automatically launches the game. If you choose not to play, click the **Disconnect** button on the right.

Kali supports a wide array of other options, including the ability to create macros and ban players, that we won't be able to discuss here. Examine the toolbars and help files to learn about the available options.

Total Entertainment Network

TEN, the Total Entertainment Network, bills itself as an "Internet entertainment service" that's by, for, and about gamers. For a fee, TEN provides software, player rankings, web access, email, and original game-related content. You don't even need an ISP: although you can use one, TEN provides dial-up access for an additional fee. Currently, TEN operates only under Windows 95/98. Four different rate plans are available (including a free account that provides access to nine popular multiplayer games and access to Excite's classic games), but you can probably expect to pay about 15 to 20 dollars a month for the service.

TEN's advantage lies in its smooth graphical interface and the latency parity that it provides for players. Here, you don't need to look at ugly menus to find the best connection. TEN provides a list of games. You select the one you want, and a character called Mr. Bandwidth appears to check the quality of your connection (see Figure 8-9). Games are then divided into arenas located in various zones, with your best zone appearing at the top of the list. If the connection's no good, Mr. Bandwidth doesn't let you play. Thus, players in real-time games find themselves on a much more even playing field than those playing via Kali or QuakeWorld.

Additionally, TEN is the host network for the Professional Gamer's League. A group of sponsors has created an online tournament for "professional" computer gamers, with prizes totaling more than $200,000. If you think you could make your fortune playing Quake or other games, take a look at the PGL site at *http://www.pgl.net*. MADCamm technology lets you watch the death matches of others.

TEN's service also has its disadvantages. Most Internet game players are die-hards who'll find the cost fairly high—and needless, since there are options that are less costly, if not free. Additionally, there aren't yet enough players using TEN; it's frequently hard to scare up a game. TEN also offers a free account; players can access about one-third of the games free of charge. These games are shareware versions of the product and can also be accessed from the manufacturer's web site.

To sign up, visit *http://signup.ten.net/signup/*. The first five hours are free. At the time of this writing, TEN announced its plan to switch to an all-Java client, doing away with the TEN frontend and presumably extending play across platforms.

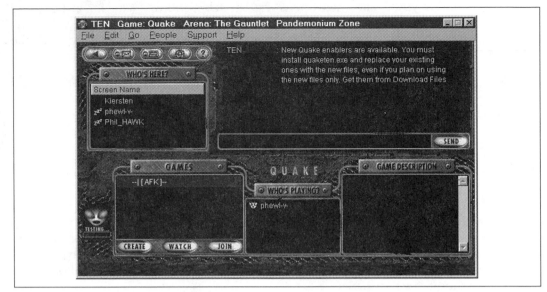

Figure 8-9. Mr. Bandwidth and friends

TEN currently supports the games listed in Table 8-1. This list is subject to change.

Table 8-1. Games Available on TEN

Name	Maker	Version	Overview
AD&D Dark Sun Online	SSI	Retail	An online Dungeons & Dragons game role-playing game. Based on TSR's DARK SUN, you can create a character, embark on quests, and cast magic spells.
ARC	HoopyEn-tertainment	Shareware	No role-playing or complex strategy here: choose a side, then shoot everything in sight.
Blood	Monolith	Retail, Shareware	First-person action game involving cultist madness. Based on the Duke Nukem 3D Build engine.
Command & Conquer: Red Alert	Westwood Studios	Retail	When merely commanding isn't enough, try this real-time action strategy game. Set in an alternate past, you fight Stalin instead of Hitler in a do-over of World War II.
Command & Conquer	Westwood Studios	Retail	The original Command & Conquer pits the Global Defense Initiative against the Brotherhood of Nod in a battle for command of the free world.

Table 8-1. Games Available on TEN (continued)

Name	Maker	Version	Overview
Deadlock	Accolade	Retail	This science fiction game lets you explore and conquer with one of seven races trying to take over the Universe.
Diablo	Blizzard	Retail	This fantasy role-playing action game lets you satisfy all your personalities at once while you combat evil.
Duke Nukem 3D	3D Realms	Atomic, Retail, and Shareware	Another first-person, real-time, 3D shoot-'em-up game.
EF2000 V2.0	Digital Image Design	Retail	A flight simulation based on the EF2000 Eurofighter.
Magic: The Gathering	MicroProse	Shareware	Computer version of the trading card strategy game.
Master of Orion II	MicroProse	Retail	What do you do when your race's home world is overpopulated? Expand or die.
Myth: The Fallen Lords	Bungie	Retail	3D realtime strategy game; up to 16 players can interact at a time.
NASCAR Racing Online Series	Papyrus	Retail	Race against up to 19 other drivers on any of the 16 NASCAR race tracks.
Panzer General	SSI	Retail	I first played this World War II turn-based war game when I was five, but my grandfather called it "checkers."
Quake/ Quake II	id Software	Retail	You should know by now. TEN provides mod files for Capture the Flag, Team Fortress, etc.
Shadow Warrior	3D Realms	Retail, Shareware	First person shooter, also based on the Duke Nukem 3D engine.
Total Annihilation	Cavedog	Retail	When you tire of partial annihilation, try this futuristic real-time strategy game.
Twilight Lands	ICE Online	Retail	First-person fantasy role-playing game allows for detailed game play with hundreds of other players.
Warcraft	Blizzard	Retail	Play as either the Orcs or the Humans in this real-time two-player strategy game that pits the Orcs against the humans.
Warheads	Ionos, Inc.	Shareware	Turn-based strategy game; player can opt for provided artillery or build his own weaponry.

Table 8-1. Games Available on TEN (continued)

Name	Maker	Version	Overview
WizWar	TEN	Shareware	Online version of the board game; wizards duke it out in a maze of dungeons.
Wulfram	Bolt Action Software	Beta, Shareware	Action-strategy game involving "hover tanks"; two opposing forces seek to destroy one another on a crowded planet.

Mplayer

Much like TEN, Mplayer sports a slick graphical user interface. The frontend, a modified version of Internet Explorer, looks something like an old-time radio crossed with some kind of command module. The service is free for some games, which are supported by advertising; others can only be played for a fee. The range of free games, however, is fairly extensive.

Also like TEN, Mplayer is encouraging the idea that the road to computer gaming is paved with gold. In December 1997, Mplayer held the ABC Sports College Football: Heroes Of The Gridiron Quest For The Best Internet Championships (ridiculous title including incorrect capitalization and all). The two finalists, of the screen appellations DA Schaffner and Jay-Bad, won 3D graphics cards, airfare to Pasadena, California, and tickets to the Rose Bowl. After the "ultimate showdown," the hero apparently walked away with $10,000.

The problem with Mplayer is the number of upgrades and installations required to play even the simplest game. Perhaps more importantly, the interface doesn't indicate the quality of your connection or your distance from the server. You're likely to try a number of different games before finding one that's viable.

What, then, does Mplayer have going for it? First, it's free, and if you have the patience, the interface is friendlier than Kali's. Additionally, Mplayer supports a good number of games (see Table 8-2), and seems to have attained a critical mass of players. Additionally, there's an excellent gimmick factor: with a microphone, sound card, and speakers, you can actually talk to other people while you're playing. Insanely irritating? You bet, but some people like it.

The Mplayer community *is* friendly. Chat rooms are kinder, and players sometimes help each other out. Mplayer is the best gaming service I found for old favorites like Checkers, Battleship, Scrabble, and Risk, alongside Tear the Zombie's Head Off.

The games in Table 8-2 are currently available on Mplayer. While we would have liked to designate games that you can play for free, this information changes frequently and sometimes varies within a single game: a shareware or demo version may be played for free, for example, while the retail version may not be.

Table 8-2. Games Supported by Mplayer

Name	Maker	Overview
@Range	S.E.A. Multimedia	Submarine shoot-'em-up.
ABC Sports College Football: Heroes of the Gridiron	ABC Interactive	Coach a college football team made up of the all time great college players, while listening to authentic school fight songs.
ABC Monday Night Football '98	ABC Interactive	Play Monday Night Football, creating teams from the National Football League's 1997 rosters, while listening to Dan Dierdorf.
Armor Command	Ronin Entertainment	The inhabitants of Earth have finally made peace, and just in time, because alien forces threaten to take over the planet in this 3D strategy game.
ATF Gold	Electronic Arts	Flight simulator that will take you right into the Danger Zone.
Battleship	Hasbro Interactive	You sunk my battleship!
Big Red Racing	Eidos Interactive	Driving simulation involving "Rock & Roll" attitude.
Blood	Monolith	First-person action game involving cultist madness. Based on the Duke Nukem 3D Build engine.
Checkers	Mplayer	The classic game, but now you can moo at your opponent.
Command & Conquer	Westwood Studios	The original Command & Conquer pits the Global Defense Initiative against the Brotherhood of Nod in a battle for command of the free world.
Commandos	Eidos Interactive	WWII rages on, and players have to not only disengage Germany's plans, but keep their own commandos in line as well.
Crush Deluxe	Megamedia	Turn-based strategy sports game, in which the objective is to locate and deliver the B.A.L.L. (Bionic Augmented Lower Life-form).
Deadlock	Accolade	This science fiction game lets you explore and conquer with one of seven races trying to take over the Universe.
Diablo	Blizzard	This fantasy role-playing action game lets you satisfy all your personalities at once while you combat evil.
East Front	TalonSoft	Tactical combat game played on the "platoon level" between German and Soviet troops during World War II.
Extreme Assault	Blue Byte Software	Wartime helicopter simulation.

Table 8-2. Games Supported by Mplayer (continued)

Name	Maker	Overview
Fighter's Anthology	Electronic Arts	Flight simulator using missions from ATF Gold and USNF'97
Hearts	Mplayer	The classic card game.
Heavy Gear	Activision	This simulation game allows the player to enter the future; the year is 6135, to be exact. The player will quickly learn that anger and vengeance still run rampant, though.
Incubation	Blue Byte Software	Mission-based strategy game in which you lead a group of space marines against—surprise!—mutant monsters.
Links LS '98	Access Software	Golf simulation.
Machine Hunter	MGM Interactive	Defend Mars against the robotic forces of an alien attack.
Mech Warrior2	Activision	3D robot battle set in the year 3057.
MechCommander	Fasa Interactive	You control a large unit of Mechs; whether they continue to fight as a large unit is up to you. Keeping track of resources and tracking the enemy keeps you and your unit strong.
Panzer General/ Panzer General II	SSI	I first played this World War II turn-based war game when I was five, but my grandfather called it "checkers."
Populous III	Electronic Arts	Enter the game as a shaman and work your way through the ranks to a god. Match wits against other minor deities.
Quake/QuakeWorld	id Software	You should know by now. Mplayer provides additional mod files.
Command & Conquer: Red Alert	Westwood Studios	When merely commanding isn't enough, try this real-time action strategy game. Set in an alternate past, you fight Stalin instead of Hitler in a do-over of World War II.
Red Alert	Westwood Studios	Players battle tanks, land mines, and a variety of spies in an attempt to crush Soviet enemies.
Risk	Hasbro Interactive	The classic board game that makes war fun!
Road Rash	Electronic Arts	Players speed through streets with the objective of destroying man and vehicle alike.
Scarab	Electronic Arts	Ancient Egyptians battle crazy mechanical Gods using mortars, lasers, and mines.
Scrabble	Hasbro Interactive	The classic board game. Remember, "qat" is a valid word.

Table 8-2. Games Supported by Mplayer (continued)

Name	Maker	Overview
Sid Meier's Gettysburg	Electronic Arts	3D real-time war game recreating the Battle of Gettysburg.
Steel Panthers III	SSI	Fifty years of warfare packed into one game. Players plan from an overhead battle map and zoom in to witness the bloodshed.
Take No Prisoners	Red Orb Entertainment	Strategy shooter game in which you fight your way through death match levels on a post-nuclear Earth.
Terminal Velocity	Terminal Reality	Flight simulator in a futuristic jet.
Total Annihilation	Cavedog	When you tire of partial annihilation, try this futuristic real-time strategy game.
US Navy Fighter '97	Electronic Arts	Flight simulator war game.
Warcraft	Blizzard	Play as either the Orcs or the Humans in this real-time two-player strategy game that pits the Orcs against the humans.
Warlords III	Red Orb Entertainment	Fantasy/strategy game in which you strive to take over the planet.
WarSport	TimeSink	Complex futuristic football.
War Wind	SSI	Real-time strategy game in which four races descended from the same guy fight for survival.
WordZap	Crick	Players attempt to form words from a shared field of twelve letters; Scrabble meets Boggle.
Y.A.R.N.	Mplayer	Players compete by adding sentences to a story in progress; the entries are voted on and the winning sentence becomes part of the story.

AOL

Of course, America Online isn't a gaming service *per se*. And technically, it's not part of the Internet, though it does connect to it. AOL does, however, support a broad range of games and is one of the few family-friendly forums that you'll find online, overtones of Orwellian niceness aside.

What kind of games will you find here? The logical place to start is the Games channel, accessible from the button on the channel menu or via keyword: Games. Once there, you'll find a wealth of trivia contests, card games, word games, board games, a few adventure games, and a version of Warcraft II optimized for AOL. Additionally, you can access games on the Web through AOL's WWW gateway.

Many of the games are designated as premium services, however, requiring an additional hourly fee. Most of these games also require lengthy downloads of additional software. While AOL purports to handle the downloading and installing for you, it took at least nine attempts to download separate Backgammon and Hearts clients. The good news is that when you reconnect, AOL picks up the download where it left off, so don't throw away those seemingly orphaned ZIP files before you resume downloading. The bad news is that you have to resume eight times.

AOL doesn't charge you premium rates while you download the clients. This is a definite benefit, since AOL promised me a download time of 28 minutes over a 14.4 Kbps modem for a file that took me five hours and a year off my life to download over a T1 line. Make sure to check the system requirements. For example, a game entitled Legends of Kesmai requires a Windows 95 DLL file that isn't found on most systems. Although most installations include whatever DLL's are needed, this one, for some reason, is separated from the rest of the download and listed in the System Requirements window. You won't find it unless you look for it there.

If you're looking for fast-paced action, this isn't the place for you. Playing even a relatively simple game like Hearts over a TCP/IP connection results in frustrating lags. Similarly, the trivia games, while offering amusing content, progress too slowly to hold my attention. Moreover, $2 per hour plus AOL's fees feels brutal when you could be playing similar games for free.

A few multiplayer action games look promising, particularly Harpoon. Unfortunately, as there were no players, it was difficult to assess the quality of multiplayer options. Other games, like Splatterball and Magestorm, hosted a wealth of players, but seem to be based on somewhat outdated game engines that are a pale imitation of the first-person-shooter gaming theory. The lag was considerable, but it seemed to be considerable across the board.

AOL's WorldPlay games offer a little more for your premium dollar. Games are speedier, and you access them through a snazzy frontend with all sorts of bells and whistles—chat windows, player avatars, game-watch features, and more. Additionally, the rules files are well written and succinct. Keep in mind, however, that WorldPlay games will soon be available through ATT WorldNet and Earthlink as well as AOL. You can find other games on the GameStorm web site at *http://www.gamestorm.com.* $9.95 a month entitles you to unlimited playing time on the GameStorm service along with a CD-ROM containing the game software.

Perhaps more frustratingly, some of the free games can be found on the Web. Virtually all of the games and content found at the Heckler's Arcade can be found at Heckler's online site, *http://www.hecklers.com/main.htm.*

On the plus side, the folks at AOL are a friendly group. Newbies joining card games find supportive players, even when they haven't bothered to read the rules before joining a table. Most games have a plethora of players waiting to join. The Gaming Forum (keyword: ogf) provides a good place to meet and discuss game trends.

Table 8-3 lists games that are currently available on AOL. Titles and prices are subject to change.

Table 8-3. Games Available on AOL

Name	Maker	Price	Overview
Air Warrior/Air Warrior II	Air Warrior/ AirWarrior II	Free	Classic flight simulation game; World War II buffs will enjoy uniting to defeat the enemy.
Antagonist Trivia	AT	Free	Multiple-choice trivia game with hints provided by a sarcastic moderator.
WorldPlay Backgammon	WorldPlay Backgam- mon	Premium: $1.99/hour	Nicely graphical backgammon game with advanced chat features.
Brainbuster Trivia	Brainbuster	Free	Another multiple-choice trivia contest with a more sober tone and a chat area.
Casino Blackjack	Blackjack	Premium: $.99/hour	Straightforward version of the classic game; enter through the gamestorm parlor lobby.
GameStorm Bridge	Classic Cards	Premium: $.99/hour	Straightforward bridge game; enter through the GameStorm parlor lobby.
WorldPlay Bridge	WorldPlay Bridge	Premium: $.99/hour	Smooth, highly graphic and reasonably quick bridge game; allows you to watch games being played.
CatchWord	CatchWord	Premium: $1.99/hour	Create words from random letter tiles in this Boggle-esque game.
GameStorm Casino Poker	Online Casino	Premium: $1.99/hour	Choose from Atlantic City, Las Vegas, or Monte Carlo styles.
Claw	Claw	Premium: $.99/hour	Arcade-style game; you, as Captain Claw, battle assorted animal villains.
Cosrin	Cosrin	Premium: $1.99/hour	Text-based role playing fantasy game; travel through the land of Cosrin in search of heroic quests.
WorldPlay Cribbage	WorldPlay Cribbage	Premium: $.99/hour	The classic game with a fancy interface and advanced chat features.
Darkness Falls	Darkness Falls	Premium: $1.99/hour	Text-based role playing fantasy game; the player assumes the role of the villain in the "gothic" game.
Destructo Discs	Destructo Discs	Premium: $.99/hour	Shuffleboard with a twist. The player uses his mouse to manipulate explosive discs into scoring areas.
Dragon's Gate	Dragon's Gate	Premium: $1.99/hour	Text-based role playing fantasy game that continues twenty-four hours a day; real-time play.

Table 8-3. Games Available on AOL (continued)

Name	Maker	Price	Overview
Games Paradise	Games Paradise	Free	Merger of AOL's Trivia Forum and AOL's Parlor Games; collection of scheduled events including word, music, and trivia games.
GameStorm Whist	Classic Cards	Premium: $.99/hour	Straightforward version of the classic card game with an attached chat window.
WorldPlay Gin	WorldPlay Gin	Premium: $.99/hour	The classic game with a fancy interface and advanced chat features.
Harpoon	Harpoon	Premium: $1.99/hour	Complex war game scenario in which NATO and the Soviet Union go to war in the Atlantic.
GameStorm Hearts	Classic Cards	Premium: $.99/hour	Straightforward version of the classic card game with an attached chat window.
WorldPlay Hearts	WorldPlay Hearts	Premium: $.99/hour	The classic game with a fancy interface and advanced chat features.
Heckler's Arcade	HO	Free	Write bad fiction and submit mock top ten lists for fun and prizes.
Jack Nicklaus Golf	Jack Nick	Premium: $.99/hour	Multiplayer online version of the series. Play against renowned golfers on famous courses.
Legends of Kesmai	Legends	Premium: $1.99/hour	D&D-esque graphical adventure game. Fairly low-tech. Note: You'll need to download *odbc32.dll* separately from the rest of the files; see the "How to Play" section on the "Legends of Kesmai" window.
MultiPlayer BattleTech	MPBT	Premium: $1.99/hour	Real-time game in which you battle other players.
NTN	NTN	Free	A variety of trivia games. Trivial Pursuit Interactive can be found here.
Out of Order	Out Of Order	Free	Game show in which you unscramble jumbled words.
WorldPlay Poker	WorldPlay Poker	Premium: $.99/hour	Classic game that features ten poker variations.
Puzzle Zone	Puzzle Zone	Free	Variety of word puzzles featuring warm-ups and challenges that change daily.
Rabbitjack's Casino	RJ	Free	Bingo. Isn't this purpose already served by religion?
Rolemaster: Magestorm	Magestorm	Premium: $1.99/hour	3D game that's something like a combination of Quake and D&D.

Table 8-3. Games Available on AOL (continued)

Name	Maker	Price	Overview
Schwa Pyramid	Schwa Pyramid	Premium: $.99/hour	Unusual graphics keep the player occupied in this pyramid-climbing strategy game.
Slingo	Slingo	Free	Wacky fun combination of Bingo and Slot machines.
GameStorm Spades	Classic Cards	Premium: $.99/hour	Straightforward version of the classic card game with an attached chat window.
WorldPlay Spades	WorldPlay Spades	Premium: $1.99/hour	The classic game with a fancy interface and advanced chat features.
Splatterball	Splatterball	Premium: $.99/hour	Essentially a kids-friendly version of Quake that's clearly based on the same game engine as Magestorm. Teams play capture-the-flag and try to avoid being hit with a paint ball.
Strike-A-Match	Strike A Match	Free	Game show in which you find similarities amongst groups of words.
USCF Chess	USCF Chess	Premium: $.99/hour	Straightforward version of the classic game; option to enter the world of rated tournament chess.
Virtual Pool	Virtual Pool	Premium: $1.99/hour	Play billiards online!
Warcraft II: Tides of Darkness	Warcraft	Premium: $1.99/hour	AOL's own version of the popular PC game pitting the humans against the evil Orcs.

SMSN Gaming Zone (http://www.zone.msn.com/)

Last year, Microsoft bought both DWANGO and the Internet Gaming Zone, two early online gaming services. At first, only IE users could access the Zone; now, a plug-in allows everyone to do so.

Installation is quick and fairly painless. The game selection is, unsurprisingly, Microsoft-focused. And while you'll find Quake II, you won't find Quake—a strange choice, given the original's unflagging popularity. But you will find a wide array of strategy, role-playing, and board games.

Unfortunately, you won't be able to find ping rates. Using and connecting is fairly simple, however, and the site does support a large number of users, so you're bound to find players for even the less heavily trafficked games. Membership to the Zone is free; premium games require a "nominal fee" of $49.95 for six months. See Table 8-4 for the games you'll find.

Table 8-4. Games Available in MSN Gaming Zone

Name	Maker	Price	Overview
Ants	MSN	Free	Players assume the role of ants within a colony that is hungry for food, power, and action, and battle against competing colonies in various theme rooms.
Axis and Allies	Hasbro Interactive	Software required	Turn-based World War II simulation based on the board game.
Checkers	MSN	Free	Straightforward version of the classic game.
Cosmo's Conundrum	MSN	Free	Trivia game with cash prizes.
Cribbage	MSN	Free	Straightforward version of the classic game.
Crossword	MSN	Free	Traditional crossword puzzles; "regular" mode provides hints.
Dominant Species	Red Storm Entertainment	Software required	Real-time strategy game in which you take on the role of a Mindlord on the planet Mur.
European Air War	Microprose	Software required	Another WWII flight simulation game offering vintage planes and air raids.
Expansion: The Rise of Rome	Microsoft	Software required; free trial version available	An extension of Age of Empires, with new scenarios, maps, and technologies.
Fighter Ace	MSN	Premium game; fee required.	WWII flight simulation.
Forsaken	Acclaim	Software required	First-person shooter on a motorcycle of the future.
Frogger	Hasbro Interactive	Software required	Updated version of the classic arcade game in which you nudge a frog across a river.
Game of LIFE	Hasbro Interactive	Software required	3D version of the classic board game.
Golf 98/99	Microsoft	Software required	Your standard golf game; players can try various courses, some of which created by famous course designers.
Hexplore	Infogrames Entertainment	Software required	Save your friends and land from the evil Garkham.
Jedi Knight: Dark Forces II	LucasArts	Software required; free trial version available	Luke, I am your father, etc.

Table 8-4. Games Available in MSN Gaming Zone (continued)

Name	Maker	Price	Overview
Kuba	Patch Products	Software required	Marble-based strategy board game.
Monster Truck Madness (I and II)	Microsoft	Software required; free trial version available	Monster Truck racing.
Mind Aerobics	MSN	Free	Word, picture, and logic puzzles.
Quake II	id	Software required; free trial version available	Kill, kill, kill.
Rainbow Six	Red Storm Entertainment	Software required	Assume the role of leader of an elite team of Special Forces members and battle various terrorists.
Reversi	MSN	Free	Straightforward version of the classic board game.
ruthless.com	Red Storm Entertainment	Software required	Role-playing game in which you embody the CEO of a successful computer corporation.
Tanarus	Adrenaline Vault	Premium game; fee required.	Multiplayer futuristic tank war.
Spades	MSN	Free	Straightforward version of the classic game.
Sports Trivia Blitz	MSN	Free	Answer ten sports questions in one minute and move on to the next level.
Stratego	Hasbro Interactive	Software required	Internet play and five game variations have modernized this classic boardgame.
UltraCorps		Premium game; fee required.	Sci-fi based strategy game.
Word Search	MSN	Free	Straightforward version of the classicgame.

Standalone Applications

You don't need a games service to play online. About half of all the traditional retail computer games (i.e., shrinkwrapped packages with a CD that you buy in a store) that ship today support multiplayer combat over the Internet. Most provide some method of connecting with other players. Some, however, seem almost willfully obscure; this section takes you through the basics you'll need to know to get online.

The first step is to read the manual that was shipped with your game. It may contain valuable clues to finding other players.

Game "lobbies"

Games that come from Westwood Studios, including Monopoly and the popular Command & Conquer line, ship with a chat client included. Once you install Westwood Chat, you may log on for free, chat with other players about the games, and launch a game from there. Westwood's chat client has become a real Internet gaming resource; many people create rooms here to play games not even associated with Westwood.

Similarly, Blizzard provides the online gaming service, Battle.net, free for customers. Players using Blizzard's popular Diablo or Starcraft may select the Battle.net option from within the game to access the service. There, players may chat and initiate multiplayer games.

Web pages/IRC

Web pages are another good place to look for game partners. Some pages devoted to games support Java chat clients, message boards, or email lists of available players. To find such pages, perform a web search for the particular game.

Another good resource is *Internet Relay Chat,* or IRC. IRC is similar in tone and use to Usenet newsgroups; however, since IRC chats are live, it's much easier to find players here. To find chat rooms and download a windows-based IRC client, see *http://www. mirc.co.uk/.*

QuakeWorld

id Software, the makers of Quake, realized shortly after its release that multiplayer options, while popular, could be much improved. Consequently, id's John Carmack created QuakeWorld, a patch that allows players to connect to special QuakeWorld servers, which use something called client-side prediction for smoother, faster Internet play. Included in the QuakeWorld download is a utility called Qspy to help you locate and connect to QuakeWorld servers on the Internet. These servers support not only Doom, Quake, and Quake II, but also Shogo, Sin, Blood 2, Hexen II, Heretic II, Half-Life, and Unreal.

QuakeWorld is available only to registered users, so you'll have to buy the retail version first. Next, download the QuakeWorld files from id (*http://www.idsoftware.com*), Frag.com (*http://www.frag.com/quakeworld/*), or many of the gaming sites discussed previously. You'll want to download both the QuakeWorld client and the Qplug browser plug-in. Extract the QuakeWorld files to the same directory where you placed Quake. Create a subdirectory called *QW,* and a subdirectory within that called *skins.* Extract the Qplug plug-in to a temporary directory and follow the installer's instructions.

To launch a game of Quake using QuakeWorld, don't double-click on the *qwcl* executable! It won't connect you to a server. If you'd like to launch a game via the Web, visit one of the QuakeWorld server index pages (*http://www.idsoftware.com/ quakeworld/index.html*). The Qplug plug-in queries a list of available servers and displays the results, as in Figure 8-10.

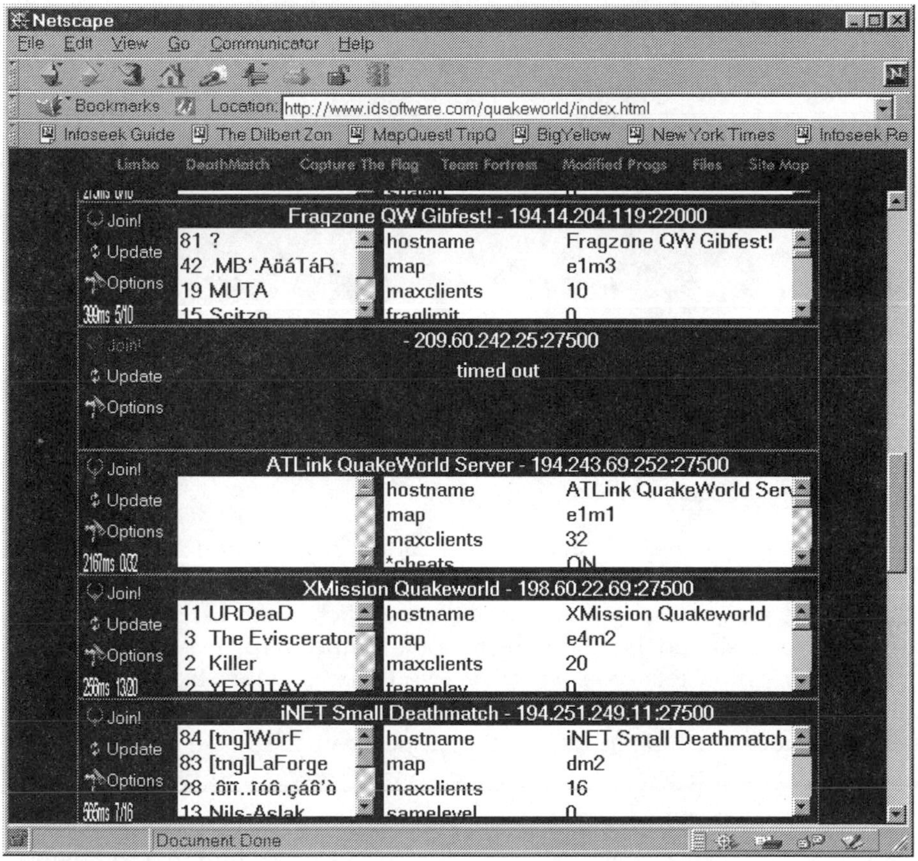

Figure 8-10. QuakeWorld server listings

Select the type of game you'd like to join from the list at the top, then scroll through the listings. The **Options** button allows you to specify your player name and any command line arguments you want to use. Click **Update** to get the most recent ping rate. Clicking **Join** connects you to the game.

If you don't want to connect through a web browser, use the GameSpy (formerly QuakeSpy) utility. Connect to the Internet and launch GameSpy. Read the installation configuration, and create a player profile, as in Figure 8-11.

Click **Continue**, and wait for GameSpy to query the servers.

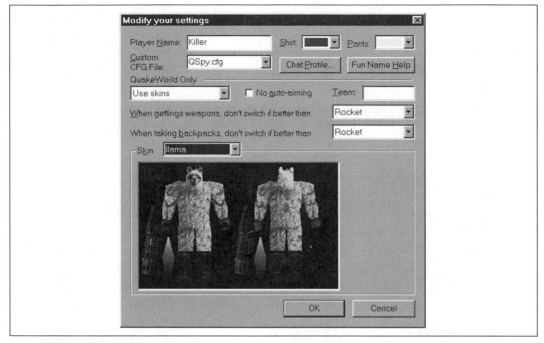

Figure 8-11. GameSpy's Player Profile dialog box

As you can see, GameSpy's interface is more complicated than QuakeWorld's (Figure 8-12). We've connected to the id DM (for Death Match) server. Servers are listed in order of ping rates, so theoretically, the higher in the list a server appears, the more responsive it should be. Be sure to look at the Map, Players, and Game columns. This information tells you what level you'll be playing, how many people are currently in the game, and what type of game it is. If you single-click on a server, a list of players and additional game information appears in the lower panes. Once you've found a game you'd like to join, double-click on the server and QuakeWorld launches automatically.

You can customize GameSpy in a number of ways, creating buddy and favorite server lists, finding players, setting up filters, etc. It's worth configuring well. Use the wizard on the **Filters** tab (**GameSpy → Games and Filters → Game Filter Settings**) to create a set of server filters, as in Figure 8-13. (Pressing the **Wizard** button creates an excellent set of filters automatically.) Once you're back on the main screen, click the **Passed Filters** button. You'll find quick-moving, playable games.

QuakeWorld supports one other feature you'll want to put to use. You can smooth out the game play even further by leveling out your latency using the */pushlatency* console command. After you join a QuakeWorld game, press **Tab** to find out your

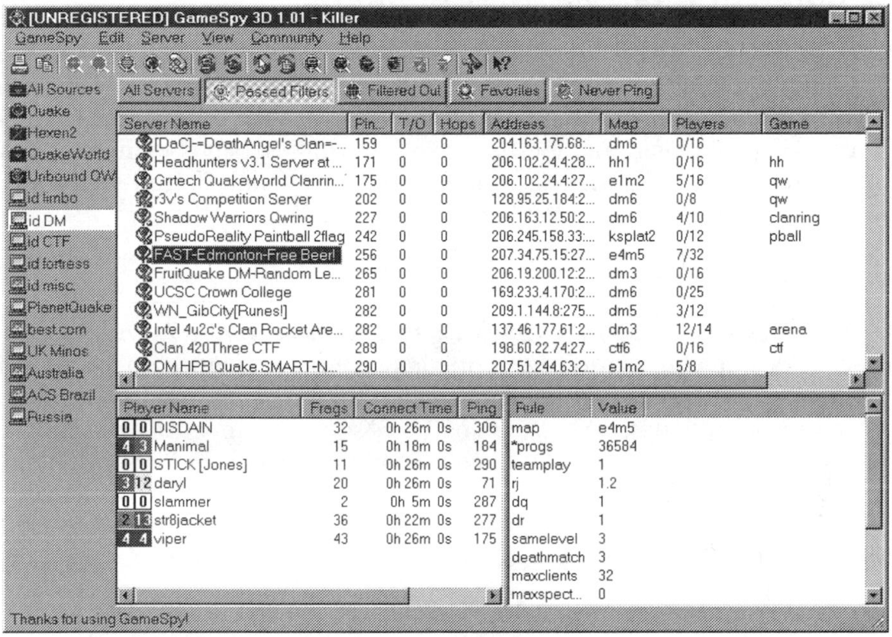

Figure 8-12. Using GameSpy

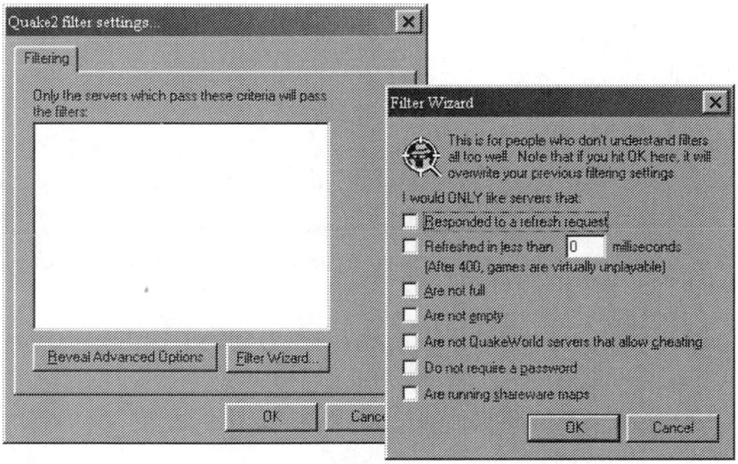

Figure 8-13. Filters tab

ping rate. Lower the console by pressing the tilde (~) key, and enter the command */pushlatency* followed by a negative number equal to your ping. So, if your ping was 237, you would enter:

```
/pushlatency -237
```

Games Configurations for Your Computer

As Internet games grow more graphically rich, they require more complex configurations. Although the following utilities and drivers aren't directly related to Internet gaming, you'll need to know about them if you play most of these games. If you don't know what you're looking for, locating these resources may begin to feel like an adventure game unto itself: messages like "Fatal error!" and "Need DirectX" start to sound like instructions to tithe to the Microsoft gods.

Display Doctor

SciTech Software's Display Doctor (*http://www.scitechsoft.com/sdd.html*) is an application that checks out your hardware configuration and maximizes it. After analyzing your graphics card, it allows you to increase the visual resolution on your screen without sacrificing application speed. Download the software and install it as instructed; it's currently free for 21 days. The Display Doctor is available for Windows, Linux, and DOS machines.

DirectX drivers

Many recent games call for Microsoft's DirectX version 6.0 video drivers. While not strictly applicable to online gaming, a discussion of the installation of this driver is relevant, in that finding and installing it can be intensely frustrating.

1. Install the game.

2. Try to launch the game.

3. Watch the game crash.

4. Make a note of the fatal exception error.

5. Log on to a chat group or IRC channel for the game to learn what the fatal exception error means.

6. Find out that it means that you need to install the appropriate Microsoft (surprise!) DirectX driver.

7. Use the system's File Search utility to see if the driver is already on your system. You almost assuredly installed this driver when you installed the game.

8. Discover that the driver is in fact on your system.

9. Restart your machine if you haven't already done so.

10. Realize that even though the machine is telling you that you need DirectX, this is not the problem. The problem is that your video card doesn't have the proper patch to work with DirectX.

11. Open the **Control Panel for the Display**, under **Settings**. Find out the name of your video card.

12. Download the proper updater file from either Microsoft or the vendor of your video card. If you're unsure, try searching the Web for a phrase like "DirectX 6.0 update Acme video card."

13. Follow the instructions to update your video drivers, and restart your computer.

Most games that require DirectX drivers should ship with the drivers on the CD-ROM. If the drivers are included, you probably want to install them—though they may throw your video configuration into disarray (see step 10). Unfortunately, there isn't really a solution to this problem. If you are a dedicated computer gamer, you're probably going to need DirectX, and the configuration issues, as with so many things Windows, will simply have to be worked out.

Play by Mail

In the early days of the Internet, email was the predominant application. Many games enthusiasts had been playing strategy games like chess or checkers via U.S. postal mail for years. With the advent of email, many of these people sped up the rate of play astronomically by playing over the Net. You'll find everything from basic strategy games to rotisserie football and baseball leagues. See the Play by Mail (PBM) Games home page at *http://www.pbm.com/~lindahl/pbm.html* for a list of all currently known play-by-mail games.

Some other sites that detail play by mail games include:

The Gamer's Den
   http://www.den.com

The Leadeater's PBEM Wargaming Club
   http://www.leadeaters.com

PBeM Directory
   http://www.geocities.com/TimesSquare/1395/

PBEM Magazine
   http://www.pbm.com/~lindahl/pbem_magazine.html

Pheonyx Play By Email Roleplaying
   http://www.phoenyx.net/index.html

VenQuest Productions
   http://www.ohio.net/~venquest/

The Future of Online Games: An Addict's Story

—by Kiersten Conner-Sax

People watch professional bowling, don't they?

Researching this chapter was an intriguing experience. I've always liked computer games, from the days when I played Breakout on the first Atari system, to blackjack on my Pcjr, through Tetris on the Mac, and on to Pipe Dream, Sim City, and finally Civilization, which crippled me forever.

Unfortunately, I'm not kidding. After buying a powerful Macintosh Performa on which to complete a thesis for my master's degree, I became addicted to Civilization, and would play for 10 to 12 hours at a stretch. My hands curled up with repetitive strain injuries, so I changed the mouse to my left hand and clutched a pen in my right, using it to press the keys. I would play until three or four in the morning, trying to eradicate the pesky Germans. My then-boyfriend contemplated support groups, and I thought I had a glimmer of what it felt like to be a substance abuser: I felt guilty for playing, then felt unworthy of others' attention and therefore continued to play in order to punish myself.

Eventually, I threw it off the hard drive. I completed my Master's degree, my fingers relaxed, and the spasm in my shoulder went away. Then Civilization II came out.

I thought I was safe. The game was available only for Windows 95, and I had refused to join the Bill Gates revolution. Of course, I had a PC at work, where I needed it to keep abreast of the technology our audience used. But that was *at work*, and I couldn't install a game on a machine in my office. Hundreds of Puritan ancestors would rise up from their graves, moaning the phrase "work ethic" over and over again. I was able to hold out until I saw the reviews, which basically said that Civ2 was the most fun anyone could have, ever.

I can play on my machine after work, I thought.

For months, I conquered the world in secret. I stayed at work until eight or nine at night. I spent my break time as Queen Shaka of the Zulus, and lived in fear and shame. Sometimes, my breaks would last for three or four hours. It was some time before my boss put me on a project with serious deadlines, and I once again threw the game off my drive. I gave the CD-ROM to a friend across the hall. When she offered to return it, I told her that that was like offering heroin to a junkie.

Eventually, I was assigned to a revision of our Internet book. There are games on the Internet, I thought. Why not a chapter on games? My boss, my editor, my co-author—they all went for it. Suddenly, I'd gone legit.

That was when I saw the press release: the Total Entertainment Network was forming a league of professional computer gamers. Good lord, I thought, maybe I do have a future. TEN and the nascent Professional Computer Gamer's League were to hold a press conference and qualifying round at San Francisco's 3Com Park. A business trip had long been a professional goal—the glory of a coach ticket, maybe even a *rental car*—and this was even applicable to my job. I sent the release to my boss, editor, and managing editor.

My boss shrugged—it sounded good to her, but she couldn't imagine the managing editor would support it. Not wanting to do any actual work, I decided to visit him myself and find out.

First, the managing editor called me a boogereater. Then he told me I could go.

Preparation

I created an account on TEN, under the screen name "Kiersten." I am nothing if not creative. The same day, I bought Command & Conquer: Red Alert, and downloaded Quake, the two games that would compose the playing field for TEN's inaugural season. After all, if I was going to interview the natives, I'd need to understand the language.

I had seen both Quake and its predecessor, Doom, before, and had not been impressed. The point seemed to be to run around and shoot things. While I appreciated the haiku-like simplicity of the theme, it didn't hold me in thrall.

Red Alert appeared more intriguing. Surprisingly, time travel was involved. According to the opening video, Albert Einstein, answering an age-old moral dilemma, went back in time and assassinated Hitler prior to World War II. Unfortunately, it didn't have the intended effect. Now, instead of the war being fought between the Axis and the Allies, the Soviet Union has risen up under Josef Stalin, and the Germans are incorporated into the Allied side. The game consists of a series of missions allowing you to either liberate Europe or conquer it. To do so, players build bases, direct spies, train troops, repair buildings, and more.

When engaging in Internet play, combatants build bases, then run around and shoot things.

The Online Experience

Wanna Play?™

Mplayer has trademarked the phrase "Wanna Play?™" Do I owe them money merely for writing those words? Every time I saw Mplayer's logo screen—and frequently, it was the only screen I saw for a long, long time, while the service tried to initialize—it made me think I should trademark a few phrases for future enrichment, phrases like "How are you?" or "Care for a beverage?"

Shortly after logging on for the first time, I encountered a player with the screen name "Pube Hair." This confused me. Why would you want your identity, even for a moment, to be tied up with pubic hair? Is it an attempt to shock people? And is anyone really shocked by a reminder that pubic hair exists? The moniker seemed an unfortunate choice, regardless.

Not wanting to spend any more time than necessary with Pube Hair, I visited the various "game arenas." The Quake players all sported violent avatars, and the chatting consisted of various threats of the "I'm gonna kick your ass" variety. After finally finding a room that wasn't locked, full, or too far away, I couldn't get Quake to execute. However, Thumper3 wanted to know how old I was.

The Scrabble arena was a little more low-key; for example, no one threatened to "scrabble the hell out of my ass" or "spell me into defrag." One Scrabble player's avatar even appeared to depict a grandmother who scanned in a photo she took by holding the camera really far away from her face. The rest of the Scrabble players were mostly involved in private games and shunned me.

After five attempts, I was able to join a game. I spelled "quiz" and my computer crashed. I restarted the machine and called the sysadmin to ask whether the new memory had arrived yet. I hated calling her; she always looked at me with contempt when she saw what I was "working" on.

Offline Experience

The week before I had to leave for San Francisco, the services were slow and the software buggy. Actually, to say that the services were slow is to imply that anything at all happened, on, say, the scale of geological time (other than my computer crashing). Not only were the online games slow, but either the services or the games or the hardware continually crashed the machine. The trip to California loomed before me, and I wanted to have played each of the games more than once before I left.

I felt a personal, palpable hatred toward Bill Gates.

Tom, the personable temporary sysadmin, attempted a system re-installation, but he couldn't get the machine to recognize the CD-ROM drive. I left the office.

It was Halloween, and the neighbors had decorated my street with pumpkins and lanterns and what appeared to be decapitated bodies. In fact, two houses displayed three headless bodies on my block alone. Consequently, as I walked the dog up the street every day, I thought about death. Isn't it strange that once a year, we encourage little children to celebrate and fetishize death? Or is the purpose of the holiday to inoculate us to the fear of nothingness via a strong sugar kick?

I was having the same reaction to these games. It wasn't the graphic death that got to me—the fireballs or spurting blood or flying limbs, the zombies that use chunks of their flesh as weapons or the ogres whose heads land face-up on the ground. Maybe the whole TV generation-inured-to-violence thing is for real, because what did bother me were the details—the whimper of the attack dog you shoot in Red Alert, and the necessary robbing of the dead bodies in Quake.

Perhaps as a reaction to all this, I decided I wanted to attend my friend David's Halloween party as a fairy princess. I bought a gold sequined crown and wand, only to realize too late that my junior prom dress no longer fit. I suppose I'm an adult, I thought, although I *was* able to make my boyfriend dress up as a pirate. He looked smashing in the hat and scabbard, not to mention the earring.

The Flight

I sat next to an older man on the plane to Chicago. He absolutely *had* to talk to me and asked whether I was from Boston or Chicago, then proceeded to tell me that he was from Milwaukee, and arose at 3:00 a.m. to fly in for an interview. A glint in his eye made me think he was either an early Alzheimer's victim or had already started drinking. I ask what he interviewed for. He replied, "a position," and continued to tell me about his brother-in-law's upcoming 40th birthday, which would involve a limousine.

I took the pillow and blanket from the seat between us and fell asleep. It isn't restful to sleep on a plane, but the time passes much more quickly.

By the time we reached Chicago, I realized I'd only seen one laptop. The legions of professional computer gamer hopefuls, I thought, must be commanding and conquering somewhere else.

I hadn't been to O'Hare for years, but I found it little changed. It's as if they put a coat of paint and a lattice of grillwork over the drabness. I especially hated the "art"-filled tunnel between concourses B and C. The neon squiggles flash on and off in a pale imitation of Tomorrowland, while United's jinglized version of "Rhapsody in Blue" plays so slowly as to be barely recognizable.

In fact, the airport seems to be owned by a combination of Michael Jordan and Starbucks. Every other shop features Bulls merchandise, from a life-size cutout of MJ (would one have to buy an extra seat for the return trip?) to a small plastic trophy bust of his head, filled with gum balls. The other store sells coffee. Next to gate and baggage information on the directional signs rests the single word "Starbucks."

Well, I thought, my first official business trip doesn't feel much different from any other cross-country flight. I've often pretended to be on business while traveling alone. The last time, I was stranded in Orlando after visiting Disney World. I was 25.

But on this trip, I sat in the Fast Lane Snack Bar (where all the food is very speedy—Deli Express, Muffins to Go, Pizza in a Hurry), and watched the planes trundle around outside and then looked at the people around me. There was a woman in hiking boots knitting nearby, and a young man in a Michigan sweatshirt, cutting his pizza neatly with a plastic knife and spork. The Label Woman, sitting with her back to me, sported a Wilson leather jacket, Coach brief case, and unfortunate haircut. I half expected the cast of "ER" to come around the corner; Anthony Edwards carrying a Tall Latte, looking worried.

A few hours later, my plane landed at the Oakland International Airport, which was quiet on a Saturday night. "I'm here," I thought, dragging my carry-on and laptop toward the rental car counter, clutching the travel agent's itinerary in my free hand.

Game Day

The Sunday before I arrived, the 49ers played the Cowboys at 3Com Stadium, formerly known as Candlestick Park. Troy Aikman played in spite of a recent concussion, though I doubt there've been many times in the last five years that Aikman has played *without* a recent concussion. Together, Aikman and 49ers quarterback Steve Young make tens of millions of dollars per year, not including endorsement contracts and appearance fees. Young, too, has played entire games with injuries that would keep a civilian in the hospital overnight.

Although the 49ers trailed the Cowboys until well into the fourth quarter, they came back to win the game. Jerry Rice, arguably the finest receiver to play professional football, paced the sidelines, out for the season with an injury to his left knee. A first-round draft pick from Mississippi Valley State college in 1988, Rice combines both tremendous talent with an unusual work ethic—his physical conditioning regimen is legendarily punishing, even during the off season, and during games he catches passes on the sidelines between plays instead of resting or watching the other players. Even that Sunday, when he was wearing street clothes and coaching the younger receivers, the cameras constantly trained on his frown.

The empty parking lot surrounding 3Com park had a distinctly post-apocalyptic feel the following morning, vast and empty and covered in beverage containers and cardboard beer cases and pizza boxes. Gulls swooped and picked among the trash.

I drove slowly through the lot, unable to see the parking lines beneath the trash, trying to find an entrance. Garth Chouteau, the public relations contact, had said that there would be signs "everywhere" that would point me toward the stadium club and the PGL press conference. One giant scoreboard told me that the early November temperature was 68 degrees and that I was welcome in the home of the Giants and the 49ers. I drove along a chain-link fence until I saw a lone person standing in a black shirt, who waved me into a small parking lot that wasn't entirely obscured by trash. I climbed out of the car, and a series of black-shirted TEN employees directed me up an asphalt hill and into the stadium. "The stadium club is around the corner," the last one told me, pointing. "You see the guy in the suit, on the phone? In there."

I went inside and a young woman in a black shirt gave me a badge. I love having a badge. To me, much of life is a quest for a really good badge that gets you into lots of cool stuff.

The stadium club was dark, draped with black curtains and gigantic portraits of the professional gamers. Most appeared to be in their (very) early twenties. Black-shirted gamers clustered around two banks of terminals: one group playing Quake and the other, Red Alert. Press people gnawed at the buffet and talked to each other. Most were from the computer press ranks—*PC World,* c|net, *PC Gamer*—but the *Sacramento Bee, San Francisco Examiner,* and KRON-TV were also present. I found myself following the lights of the television cameras like a postmodern lemming.

One of the Red Alert players, C&C_God, was a 16-year-old young man from St. Louis. He participated in a few Red Alert tournaments sponsored by TEN and rose quickly through the tournament rankings. TEN flew him to San Francisco for the press conference. He was missing school. I spoke with a few of the other Red Alert players. They were all men. One was 18; his brother was 21.

The Quake players were more social, less slope-shouldered, and had better hair. Virtually every one seemed familiar with the concept of gel, and many were gainfully employed. They bantered back and forth, both taunting and warning each other. I spoke with Sean McGrath, better known as Bitterboy, and his friend Brandon Spikes, or Alcazar. The two knew each other personally before they began playing Quake and working at their own web company. McGrath spent a number of months as Quake champion.

None of the players were happy to talk to me. Some appeared to be frightened, like zoo animals who were happily munching grass until disturbed by a loud noise. I tried to ask the hard-hitting questions, like "How old are you?" and "When did you start playing this game?" The Red Alert players shuffled their feet in response; the Quake players stared at each other's terminals.

I circulated like this for a while, and then sat down to take notes. I continually reminded myself that the people staring at my chest were doing so only to read my badge.

At this point, a few public relations people—both women, and the only women I noticed in the room—swooped over and began sucking up to me. I asked about whether there were any female gamers present. "Have you met Tonka?" each one asked with exactly the same inflection. "Let me find her for you." I told them I would find her, not to worry. Swiveling around in my chair, I still couldn't see any women at the terminals.

What I could see, however, was that the stadium club reeked of venture capital. At that point, the businessmen began to gather in front of the chairs. One of them, Nolan Bushnell, invented the first-ever video game, Pong, and is one of the founders of Atari. I had to stop myself from telling him how he saved my childhood.

The press conference started and Jack Heistand, President and CEO of TEN, dressed in a European black turtleneck and checked blazer, compared the professional gamers to professional athletes. "This property will truly be the next pro sports league," he said. I tried to picture Dennis Rodman playing Quake, or C&C_God sleeping with Madonna.

Heistand continued to explain that they expected career players to emerge, and that these players would have endorsement contracts; in fact, some already do. The PGL apparently boasts 2 million dollars in advertising support, anchored by Advanced Micro Devices. (Later, AMD gave me a keychain.) Other sponsors included USRobotics, Logitech, GTE, and Dockers. In fact, Heistand said, one day the players will probably have sporting cards. He showed us the trophy that would be given out at the end of the season—a golden joystick. "We haven't named it yet," he said sheepishly, asking Bitterboy to hold it. I refrained from suggesting "Thrustmaster."

Heistand then called the gamers to the front of the room. Of the 14 who appeared on-stage, two were women; six were Asian; none were black, Latino, or over six feet tall. Each muttered his or her name, online nickname, and where he or she was from. One mentioned his clan: "Go Postal!" When Heistand asked Dennis Fong, or Thresh, whether he wasn't the reigning Quake champion and whether he hadn't recently won a Ferrarri as such, Fong bashfully acceded.

The PGL brass then opened the floor to questions. Five or six members of the press asked variations on the theme of whether the PGL really thought people would pay to watch other people play computer games.

Various members of the PGL's Governing Board answered, "Yes, they will; yes they already do," one after another.

Finally, the demonstration started with the Red Alert players. No one watched the really big screen, though people did watch over the shoulders of the players and on the smaller screens scattered around the room. An announcer described the action as the players built bases and engaged in a tank war. The action lasted for about six or seven minutes, though no one seemed to notice when it ended.

Professional sports trappings a PGL press release described the league as including:

1. Referees/umpires/officials

2. Serious cash to players

3. Media/broadcast partners

4. Big-name sponsors

5. Sports agents

6. Player endorsements

7. Trash talking ;) (smiley theirs)

The Quake tournament garnered more interest and the announcer seemed more familiar with the game. Even so, his comments frequently ran to, "... and Tonka runs around the level. She gets the armor, and—then she runs into—oh, there's Alcazar, and the red team is way ahead, they're—well, Tonka's running around the corner . . ."

Professional sports trappings a PGL press release described the league as excluding:

1. Salary disputes

2. Player strikes

3. A salary cap

4. The Wave, The Macarena, etc.

5. Season-ending injuries

6. Boring halftime shows

7. Over-the-hill former players–turned announcers

8. TV timeouts

9. The National Anthem (yawn) (insult to American values theirs)

10. Wind-chill factors

11. Idiotic mascots

12. Idiotic Name the Mascot contests

13. Gun-toting management/coaches

14. On-field player brawls

15. Organ Music

I looked around the room at the monitors and the spectators watching. There *were* spectators, but I noticed that most of them were wearing the PGL's black shirts. Members of the press talked to each other, conducted interviews, and continued to gnaw at the buffet.

The demonstration ended. Having finally seen Tonka on stage during the introductions, I decided to approach her. Her name is Bridget Fitzgerald, and she was demure and polite in a manner I hadn't expected from her short, spiked hair and choker-style necklaces. She didn't have a lot to say about being one of the few women there, though she does engage in an all-women clan called the Psycho Men Slayers. When not dismembering fiends, she is a scholarship student at Julliard, studying the viola.

"Aren't you worried about your hands?" I asked. She smiled and shook her head.

A few months later, the 49ers would lose the NFC championship game to the Green Bay Packers at 3Com Park on a rainy Sunday. That same weekend, Thresh defeated Qboy, 29 to –6, on DM2. The PGL covered the action, and preserved the commentary as a demo available at its FTP site.

But back in November, I looked up from the computer terminals and glanced around the room. Toward the empty podium, the trophy sat forgotten. For the last year, I'd had a strange desire to shoplift things—magazines, boxes of chocolate—just to see if I could get away with it. If I had ever had the courage to do so, I would have gladly returned the items unharmed. No one noticed as I walked over and picked up the trophy. It was plastic, and it was already chipped.

CHAPTER NINE

CREATING WEB PAGES

Even if you work with the Web every day, you may not realize just how easy it is to create World Wide Web pages. You don't need programming experience, special skills, or even special software. All you need is access to a web server on the Internet and the ability to tag text files according to the *Hypertext Markup Language* (HTML) specification. Using an HTML editor makes the process even easier.

In some sense, the most important question is not *how* to create a web page, but *why*. The heart of a good page is the information you include, not the design scheme. You may want to create a web page with personal information, pointers to your work that appears elsewhere on the Web, or a storefront to sell items or services. The information you choose to present dictates the appearance of the page.

In this chapter, we'll discuss choosing an editor, using templates, creating and acquiring graphics, creating specialized text, inserting HTML code manually, and, finally, publishing your pages to the Web.

Web Publishing Basics

Right about now, you're probably thinking, "Hey! Don't I have to learn *some* hard stuff, like HTML or Java?" No, you don't. All you need to create a web page is a text file formatted according to HTML specifications. There are a number of HTML editors that hide the HTML code from you, allowing you to use a word processor–like interface to create web documents from scratch—including text, images, tables, and Java applets. While some of these tools are of professional caliber and quite pricey, others are available for free.

Professionals, however, frequently don't use HTML editors. Why not? It's fairly easy to write HTML code manually in a text editor, and in some ways, HTML editors only get in the way. Easy access to the HTML code is a feature you'll appreciate, believe it or not. Hypertext Markup Language isn't very hard to learn, and if you'd like to become a web designer, you'll need to learn it sooner or later. Additionally, there are some nifty HTML tricks that HTML editors don't provide directly. Inserting these features into the code, however, is quite simple.

In this chapter, we'll discuss both how to use an HTML editor and how to insert HTML tags by hand.

Hypertext Markup Language

HTML is a document-layout and hyperlink-specification language. It defines the syntax and placement of special, embedded directions that aren't displayed by the browser, but that tell it how to display the contents of the document, including text, images, and other support media, such as sound files or Java applets. The language also tells you how to make a document interactive through special hypertext links— when you select a link by clicking on it, the document you're viewing can connect to another HTML document or with other Internet resources linked through protocols such as FTP.

Choosing an Editor

Over the last few years, a number of HTML editors have flooded the market. Sophisticated programs, including Hot Dog Pro, WebGenie, CorelWEB.DESIGNER, Claris Home Page, and NetObjects Fusion usually support drag-and-drop page layout and advanced site-organization tools. Such programs frequently cost a bundle. For the average user who wants to put up a home page, or even a small web site, the advanced features are overkill.* Therefore, we'll be covering two free HTML editors: Microsoft FrontPage Express, and Netscape Composer. FrontPage Express comes bundled with Internet Explorer, and Composer is bundled with Communicator. As with the rest of the book, the examples come from these two tools, but the principles should be easily extensible.†

FrontPage Express features include a personal home page wizard, table creation and editing, forms, page templates and wizards, and (rather mediocre) support for Java applets, JavaScript, plug-ins, and ActiveX. The Save feature allows you to save the images in a Web document along with the HTML (although it'll take you a minute to figure out how to do so). While it's easy to edit the HTML code—a feature I consider to be of utmost importance—the file importing and pasting capabilities are both bizarre and limited. Nonetheless, this is the HTML editor I'd recommend for the advanced amateur because of the ease with which you can edit the code.

---

* Once you get the hang of web authoring, you may be interested in one of these higher-end composition tools. If so, many have excellent beta versions or limited time demos available that you can download.

† If an editor isn't specified in an example, you can assume that the example applies to both FrontPage Express and Composer.

If you find FrontPage Express's interface too confusing, Netscape's Composer works more the way you'd expect it to (more on this comparison throughout the chapter). It's also pretty tightly integrated with Navigator. You won't find FrontPage Express's fancy wizards, but the Paste feature works the way it should, it's easy to edit pages straight off the Web, and the Java console lets you tinker with applets. Composer is also better suited for uploading pages from a PC to a server. This is the editor I'd recommend for most beginners or for those who doesn't want to mess around much with HTML code or FTP clients.

Composer's only real flaw lies in its terrible code-editing interface, but this is a substantial and serious flaw. Thus, I can't wholeheartedly endorse either editor. Since both are free, I encourage you to use both and bounce between the two.*

Getting Started

We'll start by creating a *home page*. A home page is a welcome mat on the Web—usually, a screen full of information and links to other information on a subject. A personal home page represents the Web at its most basic and most eccentric. When you create a home page, you can publish anything you want: a conservative, professional-looking front door on the Net, or a creative, personal expression of your interests, hatreds, activities, etc.

It's important to think about the contents of your web page before you create it. Will you be using this page for business purposes, to make contacts, or as an online résumé? Then you'll want a formal, well-structured page with a professional-looking photograph and business-related links. You may want to use the page as your browser's start page—the page that first comes up when you start your browser. In that case, you'll probably want to include your hot list, with all your favorite links, pictures of your family or your most recent vacation, and maybe even a special section for your favorite hobby. There are many other styles of pages you can create, and the type of page you want will dictate much about the page design.

Once you're familiar with creating web pages, you can easily create a page for a product you're selling, party you're throwing, directions to your house, or whatever information people might need to access.

Using Templates

One easy way of getting started creating in web pages is by using a *template*. By using another web page as a guide, it's quite easy to create your own.

Where would you find templates? Anywhere on the Web. A template is, for our purposes, any page you like and want to use as a pattern.

---

* Keep in mind, though, that Composer might screw up a page created by FreeHand, and vice versa. It's a good idea to make a backup copy of a page before editing it.

Netscape templates

Netscape provides a number of web page templates, though the information about them hasn't been kept up to date. Anyone, including FrontPage Express users, may use them by accessing *http://home.netscape.com/browsers/templates/index.html.*

Any old web page templates

Start out by finding a web page you like. Then, replace the information in the template with your own, make a few changes, and you're done. The Well's alphabetical index of member pages (*http://www.well.com/community.html*) is a good place to start. Browse through the listed pages until you find one that suits your purposes.

Stevo's Home Spot is a good example of a solid home page, with clear headings, actual information, and a nice blend of text and graphics. Take a look at Figure 9-1.

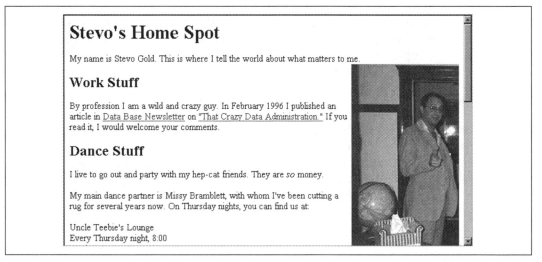

Figure 9-1. Stevo's Home Spot on the Well

Start by choosing **Edit Page** in your browser (**Edit** → **Page** in IE; **File** → **Edit Page** in Netscape Navigator), which transfers the file to your designated HTML editor. Now, save the page to your hard drive, by selecting **Save as**... from the **File** menu. If you're using FrontPage Express, click the **As File**... button to access the standard Save dialog box; otherwise, FrontPage Express tries to upload the page to a server on the Web. When FrontPage Express asks if you'd like to save the images to files, click **Yes to All**. If you're using Netscape, the Save as... dialog box works the way it should. Unfortunately, if you'd like to save the images as well, you'll need to go back to your browser and right-click each one, including the background, and use the save dialog on the right-click menu. (In this example, you'll probably only want to save the background image for later use, since you probably want pictures of yourself on your page instead of pictures of Stevo.)

Now you're ready to make some changes. Select Stevo's name with your mouse, then type in your own name. You can do the same with the rest of the text. Don't worry if you throw off the formatting. Play with the spacing, and remember the magic of the Undo command in the **Edit** menu. We'll cover how to create the web links a little later. Go through the rest of the page, replacing Stevo's information with your own. Here are a few tips:

- If you want to keep the formatting the same, highlight only one style at a time. If you want to replace "Work Stuff," for example, with another phrase, and you want to keep it bold, select only the words "Work Stuff," without spaces before or after, and not the rest of the line.

- If you scroll down to the bottom of the page, you'll find a bulleted list of Stevo's favorite things (Figure 9-2). If you want to add an item to the list, start a new paragraph by pressing Enter. The HTML editor indents the paragraph and starts it with a black bullet. If you don't want the next paragraph you enter to be part of the list, select it, then choose Normal from the Format list box.

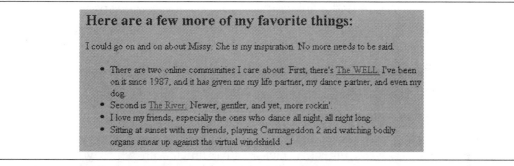

Figure 9-2. Applying paragraph styles

- If you'd like to add images of your own to replace Stevo's, first select an image by clicking on it. Then, choose **Image** from the **Insert** menu and browse for the image you'd like to display. When you click the **Open** button, your selected image replaces Stevo's. (You may want to move a copy of the image to the same directory where you are saving this page, and then re-insert it; we'll discuss this further, later in the chapter.)

- You can delete the images by selecting them and pressing either Backspace or Delete.

- You may want to play with the different formats, paragraph styles, type styles, and headings that you can find in the **Format** menu.

Be sure to save the file occasionally. Next, let's add a few links.

Creating Links

A *link* is really the most basic HTML concept. When you click on a link, it tells the browser to load the specified document and display it. Thus, related information is woven together for easy reference.

Now that you've replaced Stevo's text, you probably want to create some links of your own. Let's say you'd like to create a link to your company:

1. Select your company name within the document.

2. Choose **Insert → Link** (Composer) or **Edit → Hyperlink** (FrontPage Express).

3. Type or paste the URL in the dialog box.

You just created your first link!

You'll probably add a few more links. That way, people looking at your page can quickly learn more about your background and interests. Another way to create links is by dragging and dropping them. Here's how:

1. In a browser window, find a link you'd like to include on your page.

2. Grab that link with the mouse by clicking on it and holding down the left-mouse button.

3. Drag the link into the Editor window.

4. Release the button in the spot where you'd like the link to appear.

5. Edit the underlined link text.

Later in the chapter, we'll discuss the concept of absolute links, with which you specify the entire URL of a document, versus relative links, with which you specify only the filename of a document (which resides on the same server as the first). This concept isn't really necessary when you create freestanding web pages; it really comes into play when you create complex Web *sites*.

Hmmm. Why Does It Look Like That?

When you're done adding the text, images, and links that you'd like, you'll want to preview the page in your browser. To do so, save it, then either manually open the page in your browser (FrontPage Express) or select **Browse Page** from the **File** menu (Composer). You may notice that the page doesn't look precisely the way you thought it would—or even the way it looked in your editor.

When you create a document using HTML, you are formatting the page very generally. Instead of saying, "Put my name in 24-point, bold, Times Roman," you're saying, "Put my name in the format Heading 1."[*] Different Internet browsers may define

---

[*] Although you can format the text to appear in 24-point, bold, Times Roman, I wouldn't recommend it. Unless you're creating a very specific layout, it's best to use relative headings and text. Browser are finicky, and depending on a user's View Font settings, a 24-point, bold, Times heading may be transmuted into something you *really* don't want.

Heading 1 differently—some a little bigger, some a little smaller, some in a completely different font. All of them, however, should define Heading 1 as the biggest header they've got. Page fonts are particularly fragile: many browsers are limited to the fonts Times and Courier. If you format a page using only the Desdemona and Footlights, many users in the academic and scientific communities will be only able to view a strangely formatted version of your page. Consequently, if you open your new page in your browser, or even in different browsers, some elements may look different: your address and phone number may not be formatted the way you desired, and some of the line breaks may look strange.

So, your page may need a little fine tuning. If so, you can go back to the editor and fix things immediately. To check on your progress, save your changes, then hit your browser's **Reload** button. The revised page should appear shortly.

Starting Places on the Web for Free Design Stuff

Here are a few places to hunt for free image files that can be used for backgrounds, icons, and other applications.

Backgrounds:

> *http://www.specialweb.com/original/bgrounds.html*
> *http://www.geocities.com/SiliconValley/Heights/1272/index.html*
> *http://www.nepthys.com/textures/*

Images:

> *http://www.specialweb.com/original/*
> *http://www.yahoo.com/Computers_and_Internet/Multimedia/Pictures*
> *http://www.photolib.noaa.gov/*

Creating a Page of Your Own

At this point, you've got enough information to create basic pages on the Web. Now, however, we can move on to creating interlinked pages with more complicated elements: images, tables, icons, customized text, images, and formats, optimized to be easy to read and indexed by search engines.

Page Construction

At this point, I'm going to assume that you know how to browse, select text and apply formatting to it, and save your page. Now, by building a sample page for a family to learn about a wedding, I'll describe some more advanced web page features.

To start, open up your HTML editor of choice. As with a word processor, you start out with a new file. First, set the properties for the page, by selecting **Page Colors and Properties** from the **Format** menu (Composer) or **Page Properties** from the **File** menu (FrontPage Express). You'll see a dialog box that's similar to the properties you might set for a word processing or spreadsheet file (see Figures 9-3 and 9-4). HTML page properties are quite important, since this is the information accessed by search engines.

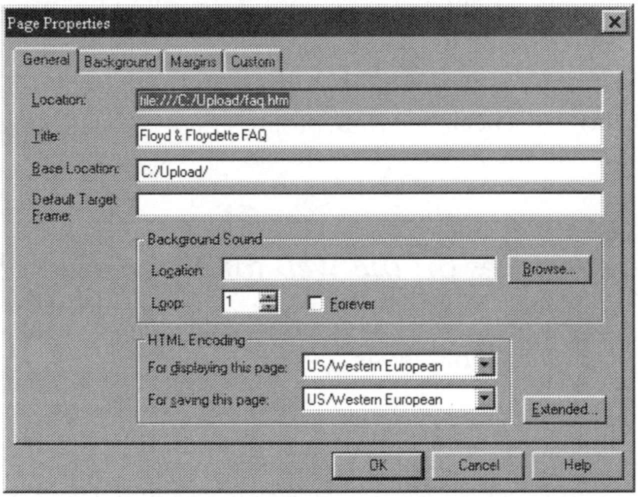

Figure 9-3. Setting page properties in FrontPage Express

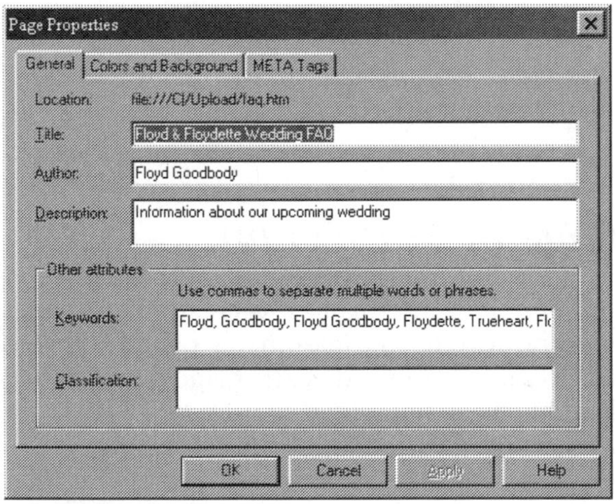

Figure 9-4. Setting page properties in Composer

First, enter a page title. Now, we'll move on to *Meta* variables, so called because they allow you to specify terms that won't appear in the browser window, but may be accessed by the server (see Figure 9-5). If you're using Composer, enter an author name, page description, and list of keywords in the appropriate boxes. If you're using FrontPage Express, you'll need to enter this information via the **Custom** tab. Select it, then click the **Add** button next to the User Variables box.

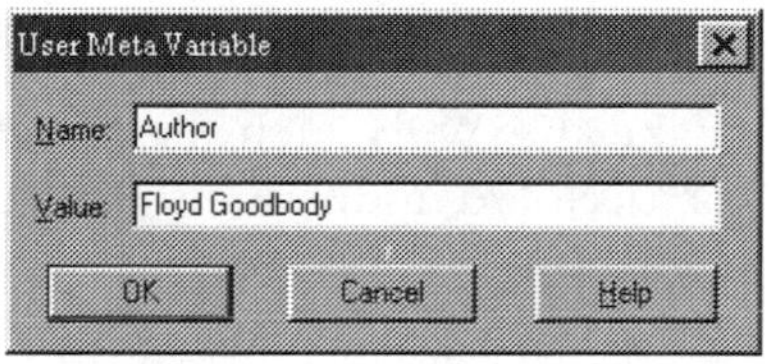

Figure 9-5. Entering variables

Adding author, description, and keyword variables to your page is a good idea if you'd like search engines to index these terms. If you'd like to enter other Meta variables, go ahead and do so; if you're using Composer, click on the **META Tags** tab and enter them there.

Now, we'll move on to some of the page properties viewers will experience directly: the background and color scheme of your page.

Backgrounds

Any image file can serve as a background, but I'd recommend one that won't distract visitors from your page's content—for example, a white background with subtle texture or a light-colored background with a contrasting bar of color running down one side of the page. Be careful with the colors you choose, since garish backgrounds can make it nearly impossible to read page text.

If you have an image file you'd like to use, great. If not, browse around the Net and find one you like—many are available to non-commercial users for free. It's best to use a JPEG file, as this type of image file loads more quickly than a GIF file.

Select a background you like and save it to your hard drive (via the right-click menu), placing it in the same directory as the page you're creating, and making sure to include the *.gif* or *.jpg* extension. Don't worry if the background appears to be only a small square—the browser tiles the image file you select to create a background as large as the page requires.

Open your editor, and click the **Background** tab of the Properties dialog box. Enter the name of the background image you selected.

Making Data Accessible for Users with Disabilities

—by Keith Wessel

When a new web page appears in your web browser, what's the first thing you notice? The pictures? The flashy colors? Perhaps the multimedia?

These elements are what make the Web such a powerful and effective form of distributing information. For disabled individuals, however, these are often the elements that put the information out of reach. "Accessibility" has become a major buzzword since the passing of the Americans with Disabilities Act. Its meaning, however, is quite broad. It can be as simple as Braille labels in an elevator, a wheelchair ramp, or a volume control on a telephone. How it applies to the accessibility of information technology, however, is somewhat vague.

Ever since the Web caught on, HTML has been expanded and made more interactive. We're now to the point where the Web does things that it was never originally intended to do. New, sometimes browser-specific changes to the Web happen at a frightening pace. Most of the time, these new changes come along so quickly that accessibility hooks can't be created for disabled users. The effect is inaccessible web pages that leave some users out in the cold.

The 1997 U.S. Census estimates report that 49 million Americans are disabled. This is nearly 20% of the population. Not all of these disabilities are severe enough to hinder access to computers and the web. Many of these individuals, however, are unable to fully access some of the information on the Web. People with visual, hearing, motor, and learning disabilities are among those effected.

As a disabled individual, I can tell you that there is nothing more frustrating than searching for information on the Web in a page that I can't read. It's like locking your keys in your car. It's right there, but you can't reach it. Instead, you have to depend on someone else to solve the problem for you. In this case, the "someone else" is the designer of the web page.

It doesn't take a lot of work to make a web page accessible. It becomes even easier if the issue of accessibility is considered during the initial design phase of the page. Furthermore, it's well worth the time. Once pages are made accessible, businesses can reach all customers who might stop by. Business on the Web increases, more than paying for the time that it took to add accessibility. Organizations and individuals with useful information on the Web can now provide that information to everyone. In some cases, the law may require pages to be accessible. If anything, it's simply an act of human kindness.

—continued—

Accessible web pages don't just help the disabled. They can also benefit users of older, slower hardware who don't want to wait for graphics to download. They can help users with the non-graphical web browser, Lynx, by offering a non-graphical representation of a page.

Accessible pages can often times be easier to understand, too. When the extra effort is put in to make a page accessible, the purpose of graphics and formatting on the page receives an extra level of clarification. Typically, there are only a few things that can make a page inaccessible. Graphics without text descriptions, tables, frames, bad color and font schemes, image maps, and cluttered pages can all be culprits. If used correctly, though, there is no need to avoid these items. It comes down to simply knowing what is good HTML and what is not.

When designing a web page, there are a few questions one should ask:

- Do all graphics have text descriptions?

- Can information on the page be accessed through means other than graphical links and image maps?

- Is the text on the page clear and well organized?

- Are color schemes and fonts reasonable and easily readable?

Of course, accessibility can't be made that simple. There are other issues involved. By asking yourself questions like those mentioned here and a little common sense, maximum accessibility can be achieved.

People who work in the area of information accessibility can't be the ones responsible for making web resources accessible. There is far too much data out there, and new web pages are always being created. The few thousand people in information accessibility can't fix the work of millions of web developers. Instead, the developers must take this responsibility. By learning about accessible hooks in HTML and using them, the Web becomes a much friendlier place for everyone.

There is a huge amount of information about accessible web design available on the Web. A good place to start is Yahoo's Disabilities page. From there, developers can read about web accessibility guidelines, the needs of disabled users, and the latest accessibility issues. Another useful site is the Trace Center for Research and Development at *http://www.trace.wisc.edu*. Trace Center has been doing work with accessibility since the early 1970s. Its site is one of the best for accessibility information. The World Wide Web Consortium's Web Accessibility Initiative (WAI) at *http://www.w3c.org/wai* is another good site. WAI provides information about the most recent guidelines and international efforts in web accessibility.

—continued—

There are also some tools on the Net that aid developers in making their sites more accessible. Among these are the Center for Applied Special Technology's Bobby at *http://www.cast.org/bobby* that detects accessibility issues in your HTML code. The National Center for Supercomputing Applications' Tom at *http://lunch. ncsa.uiuc.edu/tom* is a newer tool that actually tries to fix accessibility problems in your page, generating a new HTML document for you. Other current and future accessibility tools will teach about accessibility guidelines, create more accessible pages, and show web developers how to improve their HTML.

The information to make the web more accessible is available. Now, web developers need to use that information. By taking the time to make the web accessible, everyone benefits. The world of information becomes usable by all. The limits of a disability disappear. By taking a few minutes of time to make a web page accessible, you've eliminated the time that an inaccessible page might waste for someone else later.

Color scheme

Once you've chosen a background, you can move to another design element: the text color, and the color of visited, active, and standard hyperlinks. To do so, click on the **Colors and Background** tab (Composer) or the **Background** tab (FrontPage Express). Select custom colors by clicking on the color currently listed. Composer also provides a drop-down list of color schemes.*

Margins and background noise

FrontPage Express provides two other important settings in the Page Properties dialog: Background Sound and Margins. On the **General** tab of the Page Properties dialog box, you may enter the filename for a sound file to play once your page has finished loading. To use this feature, find a WAV, midi, AIFF, or AU file and save it to the same directory as your page. Then, enter the filename in the dialog box, and specify the number of times it should play in the Loop box. You can also select the Forever box to have the sound play continuously.† This sound will be audible only to IE users.

Clicking on the **Margins** tab allows you to specify top and left margins for the page. The content is moved the specified number of pixels away from the edge of the browser window. Note that pixels are very small, and you'll need quite a few of them to have a noticeable effect on the page position.

---

* When choosing colors, take into account computers that can only display 16 colors—they're still around. To check how your page will appear on these machines, go to the Control Panel, temporarily set the display to 16 colors, and see if you still like your page design.

† I strongly urge you not to use a background sound, and never, ever to have that sound play forever. Such bells and whistles quickly become irritating.

Text

The text you include is probably the most important element of your page, since good content is what you want to impart to your visitors. Once you have an idea of how you'd like your page to look, add some text, and include some links. In the rest of this section, we'll describe different ways of formatting your text and links.

Adding text

It seems a little strange to include a heading about how to enter text. Doing so should be simple—either type it in via the keyboard (or however you normally would) or paste it in.

If you're using Composer, entering text is that simple. FrontPage Express, however, complicates things if you're trying to paste text. This seemingly simple operation isn't simple unless you're copying text from an HTML document. For example, here's the previous sentence, when copied from Microsoft Word into FrontPage Express:

```
{\rtf1\ansi \deff8\deflang1033{\fonttbl{\f8\froman\fcharset0\fprq2 Times;}}{\colortbl;\
red0\green0\blue0;\red0\green0\blue255;\red0\green255\blue255;\
red0\green255\blue0;\red255\green0\blue255;\red255\green0\blue0; \red255\green255\blue0;\
red255\green255\blue255;\red0\green0\blue128;\red0\green128\
blue128;\red0\green128\blue0;\red128\green0\blue128;\red128\green0\blue0;\red128
\green128\blue0;\red128\green128\blue128;\red192\green192\blue192;}
{\stylesheet{ \nowidctlpar \f8\fs20 \snext0 Normal;}{\*\cs10 \additive Default Paragraph
Font;}}\widowctrl\ftnbj\aenddoc\formshade \fet0\sectd \linex0\endnhere {\*\pnseclvl1\
pnucrm\pnstart1\pnindent720\pnhang{\pntxta .}}
{\*\pnseclvl2\pnucltr\pnstart1\pnindent720\pnhang {\pntxta .}}
{\*\pnseclvl3\pndec\pnstart1\pnindent720\pnhang{\pntxta .}}
{\*\pnseclvl4\pnlcltr\pnstart1\pnindent720\pnhang{\pntxta )}}
{\*\pnseclvl5\pndec\pnstart1\pnindent720\pnhang{\pntxtb (}{\pntxta )}}
{\*\pnseclvl6\pnlcltr\pnstart1\pnindent720\pnhang {\pntxtb (}{\pntxta )}}{\*\pnseclvl7\
pnlcrm\pnstart1\pnindent720\pnhang{\pntxtb (}{\pntxta )}}{\*\pnseclvl8\pnlcltr\pnstart1\
pnindent720\pnhang{\pntxtb (}{\pntxta )}}{\*\pnseclvl9\pnlcrm\pnstart1\pnindent720\
pnhang{\pntxtb (}
{\pntxta )}}\pard\plain \nowidctlpar \f8\fs20 FrontPage Express, however,
complicates things if you\rquote re trying to paste text. This seemingly simple
operation isn\rquote t simple unless you\rquote re copying text from an HTML document.}
```

Importing files doesn't work well, either. You can use the **Insert → File...** command to import text files. When you do this, FrontPage Express asks if you'd like to insert the files as text or HTML. Unfortunately, whichever one you choose you get a mishmash of paragraph marks and text in a single, long paragraph. So, if you want to copy or insert text from a word-processor file into FrontPage Express, you have the following options:

- Save the file as HTML in your word processor, then import it into FrontPage Express (word processors usually create lousy HTML, but this will get you a lot closer).

- Save the file as text in your word processor, then open it in your browser. You'll have to set the file-type box in the browser's Open dialog box to text, but browsers can open text files. Then copy the text from your browser into FrontPage Express.

- Paste the text into FrontPage Express and delete the garbage manually. Depending on the length of your text selection, this may be the quickest, if least elegant, way to go.

Headings

A *heading* is a title or caption that you place in the text of a page. Create a heading by selecting the text you want to change, then selecting a heading from the Style dialog box (see Figure 9-6).

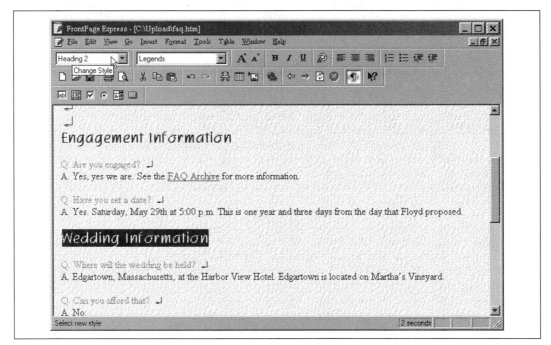

Figure 9-6. Creating headings

There are currently six different headings you can use on the Web, and their appearance ranges from larger than the text and bold (Heading 1) to smaller than the text and bold (Heading 6). In Figure 9-6, we create level 2 headings. Heading 1 should really be used only for the title of the page; headings lower than 4 are difficult to read or not substantially different from the text. Finally, don't apply headings to paragraphs. Use the other styles listed under **Format → Paragraph** (i.e., Address, Normal, BlockQuote, etc.) for this purpose.

Format menu options

FrontPage Express and Composer's **Format** menus function similarly to the **Format** menu on a word processor. The **Paragraph** menu, in the **Format** menu, features the following standard web styles:

- *Normal*: The default style for standard text. Unless you select a font, the text appears in the browser's default font, usually Times Roman. This is the best choice for body text, since virtually every browser supports the Times Roman font.

- *Address*: Address is the proper web style for entries like your name and email address.

- *Formatted*: A formatted paragraph appears in a constant-width font with all the original carriage returns and spacing; this is a good choice for things like email messages. Formatted paragraphs can also be used to introduce fixed spacing into a page, but we'll talk more about that later.

- *Block Quote*: A BlockQuote has smaller margins than the rest of the page, but otherwise appears as a normal paragraph.

- *Description Title/Description Text*: This is actually a list format, which we'll describe later.

You may also designate paragraph alignment by changing alignment in the Paragraph dialog box (FrontPage Express) or **Alignment** menu (Composer). Paragraphs may be aligned to the left, to the right, or in the center of the page.

Both Composer and FrontPage Express support a wide range of fonts, and you may also specify text color and size via the **Font**, **Color**, and **Size** menus. Keep in mind, however, that even with specific font settings, browsers may not display exactly what you intend. If you code your text to appear in the Lucinda handwriting font and a user's browser or computer doesn't support that font, the text will (likely) appear in Times Roman. Similarly, setting a font to appear in 10-point pitch is no guarantee: if a user has fonts set to Smallest, your text may be illegible. This is why HTML originally specified font size on a scale between –2 and +4: the sizes were relative, with 0 representing normal text. While Composer allows you to specify relative font size on this scale, FrontPage Express uses a scale ranging from 1 to 7; normal text seems to equate to size 3.

Adjust the type style via the **Style** menu (Composer) or the **Special Styles** tab of the Font dialog box (FrontPage Express). This is where you'll find Bold, Italic, and Underline, along with other options as Strikethrough, Superscript, Subscript, Keyboard, and Citation.

Additionally, you may combine a number of different styles. Be aware, however, that not all browsers recognize these usages, that reading on a screen is more difficult than reading on paper, and that excessive use of strange type styles, colors, and sizes is really, really annoying.

If you don't like the result, you can remove one or all of the applied styles. To undo one style from selected text, click on the style again—the check mark next to it will disappear. To undo a number of different styles all at once, select **Remove All Styles** (Composer) or **Remove Formatting** (FrontPage Express).

Images

You'll certainly want to include some images on your page, whether it's a photograph of yourself, icons, maps, or special bullets. We'll discuss how to create and acquire images of your own later. For right now, let's assume that you've already got a few saved to your hard drive or that your company's web site has a logo you'd like to drop on your page.

Once you've found the images you'd like to include, select **Image**... from the **Insert** menu, and enter the filename from your hard drive. To make transferring the site to the server easier, move a copy of each image file to the same directory as your HTML page, and insert the file from there (see the section on file management, later, for a further discussion). If you're using Composer, you don't need to worry about this problem and may insert images from anywhere on your hard drive.

Composer supports another nice image placement feature: you can drag and drop images directly from the Web. To do so, click the image in the browser window and drag it to the proper location in the Composer window. (Composer saves the image to your Temporary Internet Files directory.) Unfortunately, FrontPage Express doesn't support drag and drop, but you can copy the image's location via the right-click menu and paste it into the Image dialog box (see Figure 9-7). (Ignore FrontPage Express's **Clip Art** tab. Nothing is listed there.)

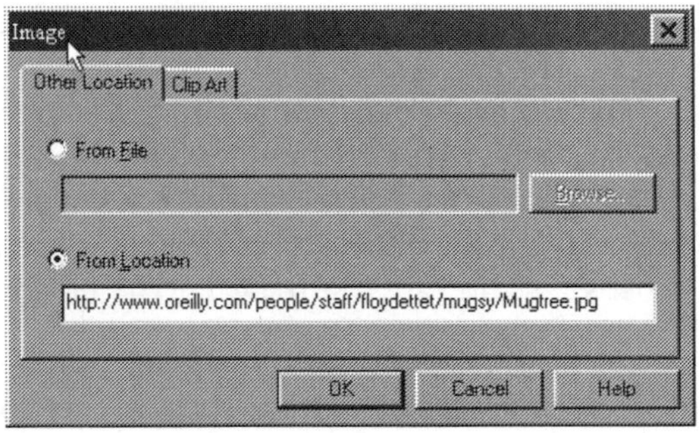

Figure 9-7. Pasting in an image from the Web

Once you've placed the image on the page, you have additional choices about placement. Double-click the image to open the Image Properties dialog box.

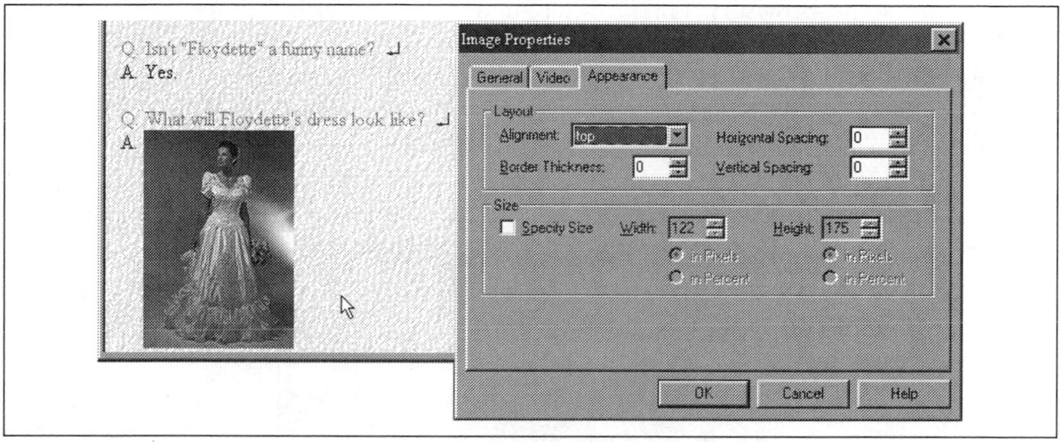

Figure 9-8. Aligning images in FrontPage Express

We chose **top** so that the top of the image would align with the text, "A." (see Figure 9-8). Other alignment options include:

- *Bottom*: The bottom of the image aligns with the bottom of a line of text; dropped characters, such as "g" or "y," appear with their tails below the image.

- *Absbottom*: The bottom of the image aligns with the bottom of a line of text; dropped characters, such as "g" or "y," appear with the end of their tails at the same level as the bottom of the image.

- *Middle*: A line running through the middle of the image would also run through the middle of a line of text.

- *Texttop* (Composer only): The top of the image is aligned with the top of the tallest text item in the current line.

- *Baseline* (Composer only): Same as bottom.

- *Absmiddle:* A line running through the middle of the image would also run along the bottom of a line of text.

- *Left*: Text flows around the image, which is aligned against the left margin.

- *Right*: Text flows around the image, which is aligned against the right margin

As you can see, the phrasing is somewhat deceptive; you're actually choosing how to align the text around the image. Right and left are the only options that allow you to wrap text around images.

The next step is important: providing a text description of the image. Non-graphical browsers show their users only text, without images, and this description provides an idea of what the graphics look like. The brackets distinguish the unseen image from the rest of the text. This description also appears while the image loads or in place of the image in some browsers. Enter a brief summary or label in the Alternative Representations/Text field (FrontPage Express; see Figure 9-9) or in the Alternate Text field (Composer). You may also want to specify a low-resolution image to load first. If you do, this presumably faster-loading image appears first, lessening viewer frustration while the higher resolution image loads (although total download time is necessarily increased).

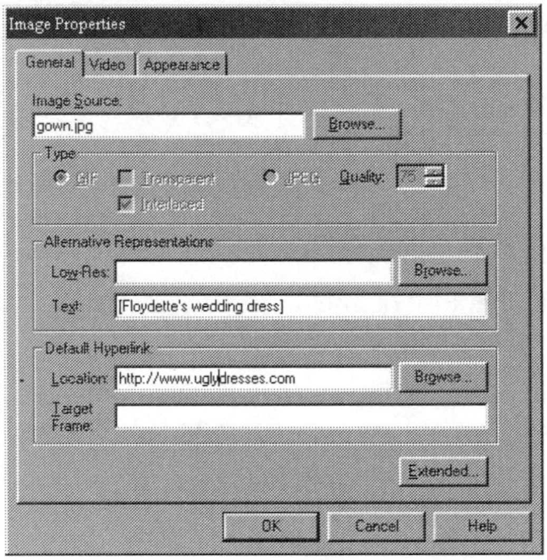

Figure 9-9. Specifying image options in FrontPage Express

Another image option is to make the image itself a hyperlink. To do so, enter a URL in the Location field (if you're using Composer, you'll need to click the **Link** tab to access it).

FrontPage Express's Type box is one that you don't want to use. It allows you to covert image compression formats on the fly, turning GIFs into JPEGs and vice versa. FrontPage Express fills in the original settings automatically when you insert the image. Leave these options as they are. If you'd like to change image options, use a graphics application, such as Paint Shop Pro, to convert the image to your desired format. We'll discuss transparent GIF images later in this chapter.

Composer provides a few additional image options. If you want to load an image from another server on the Web, instead of copying the image to your own server, select the "Leave image at original location" check box[*] and enter a URL in the Image Source box. If you wish to include whitespace around the image or a solid-color border, enter

---

[*] This is considered poor form, since you're taxing the other server every time someone accesses your page. It's best to get permission to use the image from the site's system administrator, then copy it to your own server.

the number of pixels in the appropriate boxes. Finally, Composer's **Paragraph** tab allows you to apply paragraph styles directly to an image; it's somewhat redundant, and you want your images to be in the same style as the surrounding text, anyway.

Page Layout Hints

Now that you know the basics of creating a web page, there are a few techniques you should keep in mind.

Use your spellchecker

Use your spell check; friends don't let friends publish typos. You'll find it under Composer's **Tools** menu. If you're using FrontPage Express, copy the text into a word processor and check it there.

Don't overdo the flashy elements

A lot of blinking, moving, bouncing content is incredibly frustrating to read. Sites that sport midi-jukeboxes on every page are an abomination. Keep this kind of slow-loading frippery to a minimum.

Preview the page

Always be sure to preview the page in a browser—preferably, in both Netscape and IE—before you upload it to the server. The page may look substantially different than it did in your editor.

Adding a hit counter

A counter is an image that appears on a web page, showing how many times it has been accessed. It can be useful for gauging how much interest your page receives, especially for a business trying to advertise on the Web. If you are using your page within a company, however, or just for your family to keep up with you, some people consider counters obnoxious and a waste of web resources. Use your own discretion.

There are services on the Web that will provide you with a counter for free; they make money by asking users whose pages receive a large number of hits per day (typically, 1,000 or more) to switch over to the commercial service. See *http://www.markwelch. com/bannerad/baf_counter.htm* for a listing of free web page access counters.

Specialized Text: Tables and Lists

Once you've got the basic text and images on the page, you may want to include some more complicated elements. Certain kinds of text require a little more formatting than others. Tables and lists are good ways to organize complicated information, and FrontPage Express and Composer actually make them easy to create.

Lists

HTML supports different types of lists for your formatting pleasure. To type in a list, place the cursor where you want the list to start, select **List Item** (Composer) or the type of list (FrontPage Express) from the Style box, and begin to enter the data. If you're using Composer, you specify the type of list via the **List** drop-down menu, in the **Format** menu. The text appears with whatever symbol is appropriate—bullet, numeral, etc.—to the left. Each time you press Enter, the next paragraph begins with the same symbol and formatting. To format existing text, select it and choose the list style as you normally would.

Bulleted and numbered lists

Bulleted lists appear with an indented black bullet to the left of each paragraph. Type the information that should appear next to it. When the text wraps, it aligns underneath the bullet instead of going out to the original margin. Press Enter, and a new black bullet appears below the first. A numbered list functions the same way, replacing the bullets with sequential numbers.

You've probably noticed that some web pages feature bulleted lists with customized icons. Instead of the standard black bullets, list items are denoted by a customized icon. To learn how to create such lists, see the section "Graphical Icons, Rules, and Bullets," later in this chapter.

Definition lists

A definition list, in which some term is followed by an indented definition paragraph, is more complicated. It's easiest to format this kind of list by entering a list of terms first. Then, select them and choose Desc. Title (Composer) or Defined Term (FrontPage Express) from the Style box. At the end of each line, press Enter. If you're using FrontPage Express, the next paragraph is automatically a definition paragraph; if you're using Composer, you'll need to define the paragraph as Desc. Text yourself.

Tables

Creating HTML tables is one of the few tasks for which I absolutely advocate the use of an HTML editor. Editors make creating tables very similar to doing so in a word processor (see Figure 9-10). To get started, select **Insert Table...** from the **Table** menu (FrontPage Express) or **Table** from the **Insert** menu (Composer).

Choose the number of columns and rows that you want. Table alignment places the table in the center of the page or along the left or right margin. Columns are vertical, rows are horizontal. Choose whether you want a table caption, and whether it should appear above or below the table. The border size is the width, in pixels, of the outside border of the table.

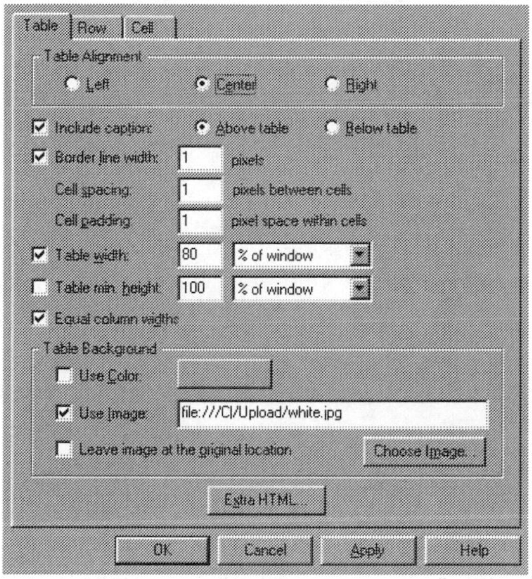

Figure 9-10. Creating tables in Composer

A table with a larger border (for example, of about 10 pixels) will look as if it were surrounded by a picture frame. The Cell padding field sets the amount of blank space, again, in pixels, between the table entry and the border around it. Similarly, the Cell spacing field sets the width of the table borders themselves. If this is too confusing, don't worry about it. The default entries for Border line width, Cell padding, and Cell spacing work fine, and you can fine tune them later.

The table width and height options allow you to indent the table within the page. You can specify whether you want the table to occupy a certain percentage of the page or a specific number of pixels. If you leave the "Equal Column Widths" checkbox unchecked, column width is determined by the amount of information placed within the widest cell.

If you want the table to blend in with the rest of your page, use the same color or image file that you used for the page background. Otherwise, you may specify a different background for a more distinct look.

Once you press either **OK** or **Apply**, the editor gives you a blank table, as in Figure 9-11.

The Caption field is at the top, surrounded by dotted lines. Enter a caption here. You can place anything in the table cells; position your cursor and type away, adding whatever graphics, links, styles, etc., that you choose. Press the Tab key or use the mouse to move from cell to cell. The cells expand to fit whatever you put there, and the caption automatically remains centered.

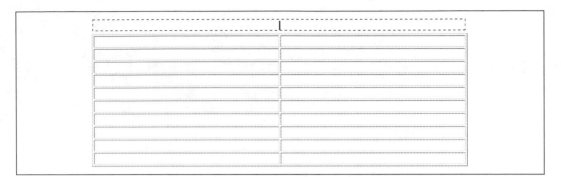

Figure 9-11. A skeletal table

Modifying Tables

You may want to make the top row of your table distinct from the rest. To do so, simply select the text and apply a style to it, as you would any other text. Tables may also have *header cells*. Text within is automatically bold and centered. To create a header cell, place the cursor in that cell and check the "**Header** style" box on the **Cell** tab of the Table properties dialog box (Composer) or check the "Header cell" box on the Cell properties dialog box in the **Table** menu (FrontPage Express).

Once you've started to input information into a table, you may realize you need additional rows or columns. To add a row, place the cursor in a cell in a row above the row you'd like to insert, then choose **Row** from the **Table** menu (Composer) or **Insert Rows or Columns**... from the **Table** menu (FrontPage Express). Add columns the same way.

Don't forget, however, that you might have strange needs. If you need a table that doesn't have simple rows and columns—that needs a top column cell to stretch across the two cells below it, for example—it's easy to merge and split table cells. Place the cursor within the cell you plan to alter. Then, select **Split Cells**... from the **Table** menu (FrontPage Express) or alter the Cells spans values on the **Cell** tab of the Table properties dialog box (Composer).

Note that you can use a combination of these options to create tables that aren't tables at all. A captionless, borderless table may be used to position information within various cells. The content of each cell then appears to be floating on the page. Thus, you can create complex layouts with additional layout options besides left, right, and center. A common way to format pages is to create a borderless table that has one row and two columns. Put a table of contents or list of links in the left column, and anything you want (including other tables) in the right column.

Specialized Images and Links

There are a few additional design elements that help with page organization and readability. They generally fall into three categories: icons, bullets, and rules.

Icons can symbolize well-known functions: a small picture of a house, for example, can serve as a link to your home page, or a mailbox could open a mail form to your email address.

You've already seen the black bullets in the list format, and bullets are just a dash of color indicating a new item in a list. You can choose small bullets of many different colors to place on the rest of your page—some of them even appear to be three-dimensional!

Finally, a rule is a horizontal bar, used to separate various areas on a page. A rule may be coded into HTML, in which case it will stretch to fit the page (select **Horizontal Line** from the **Insert** menu). Or, a rule may be an image you place on the page, which functions as any other image would. The advantage is that you can find it in various colors and styles. Unlike the horizontal rule under the **Element** menu, these rules are of a fixed length, and won't stretch to fit the margin of the page.

We'll also discuss other types of links: anchors, which allow links to specific locations on a page, mailto links, and links to sound files.

Graphical Icons, Rules, and Bullets

Icons, rules, and bullets are your basic images. Browse around the Web and find some rules, bullets, or icons that you like. There are plenty of web sites with free GIF files. If you find an item you'd like to include, select it, then drag or copy and paste it directly into your page. Images can be tricky to place, however. Try different locations, and preview the page frequently.

One way to add interesting design elements to a page is to turn images into links. Many pages use small images as clickable icons, and they're easy to create. You already know how to insert images. To make your icons "clickable," simply assign them a URL, as described earlier.

To create a bulleted list using custom bullets, find a bullet icon that you like, in a GIF file format. Place a copy of that image to the left of the first word in each bulleted paragraph, as in Figure 9-12.

Figure 9-12. Customized bullets

The text doesn't wrap as nicely as it does within HTML-generated lists. You also need to be careful to find (or create, see later in this chapter) GIF images with a transparent background, so that the bullets appear to be an organic part of the page. If these bullets didn't have transparent backgrounds, each one would appear to have a gray square around it. We'll discuss how to create your own transparent backgrounds later in this chapter.

Image Maps

Some webmasters use another method for turning images into links. An *image map* is an image that links to different URLs depending on where you click. Technically, any image that contains a link is an image map, so the images we described earlier are image maps, as well.

To create an image map that contains more than one link, you'll need an additional software tool. Any number of shareware applications exist for this purpose; take a look at any of the shareware sites described in the Resource Catalog to find one. MapEdit, from *http://www.boutell.com/mapedit/*, is a popular choice.

While image maps are interesting design tools, you don't want to use too many of them. Too many images are poor web form. You want to provide users with information, not ridiculously slow page loading.

Specialized Links

You already know how to create links to web pages. However, you should be aware of the different types of links: mailto links, and links to anchors and sound files.

An *anchor* is a placeholder that you put in a page so that links can jump directly to it. Certain pages can become very long, and you may want people to jump to different points without scrolling through all the information. Creating an anchor is very simple: select the text you want as an anchor, then click **Insert Target** on the toolbar (Composer); FrontPage Express doesn't support anchors, but it's easy to insert them into the HTML (see later in this chapter). To create a link to that anchor, select **Link...** from the **Insert** menu as you normally would. Composer displays the current named targets in the document; select the one you want from the list.

A *mailto* link doesn't actually link to anything: it spawns an email composition window with the address and subject that you indicate (see Figure 9-13). To create such a link, select the text you want to link, and click the **Insert/Edit** link button on the toolbar. In the Link To: box, enter the following string:

```
mailto:username@address
```

If you'd like to specify a subject for the email, add the string ?SUBJECT= immediately after the email address, with the desired subject following the equals sign.

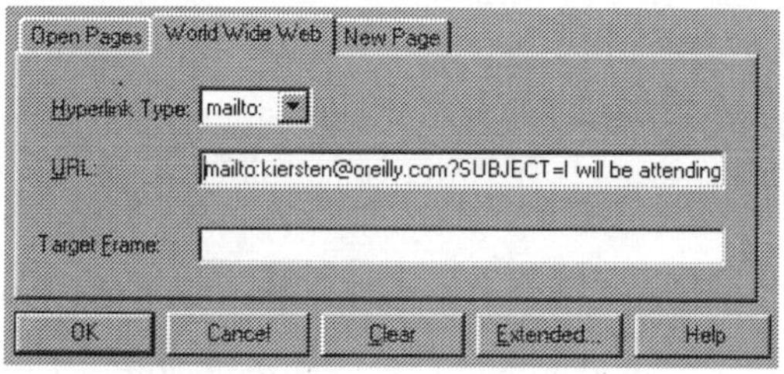

Figure 9-13. Creating mailto links

Links to sound files are normal URLs. Find a sound you like on the Web, and copy it to your hard drive. Create the link as you normally would, and upload the sound file to your server with your other files (see later in this chapter). When users click on that link, they'll hear the sound file (given that they have the proper software and hardware).

Creating Graphics

Graphical elements make web pages exciting, turning a page of text into something a little more personal. Photographic images add an even more personal touch. But how do you turn a photograph into a collection of ones and zeros? How do you create any graphic, for that matter?

In terms of creating graphics, the answer is: I don't know. I'm a graphic dunderhead. For actual information on creating Web graphics, see O'Reilly's *Designing for the Web*, by Jennifer Niederst and Edie Freedman. To learn how to pillage graphics and transmit photographs, see the rest of this section.

Photographic Images

Before, the only way to turn photographs into graphic images on your computer was to scan them in. Now, however, you have a few more options.* These options include creating digital images using a scanner, creating digital photographs with a digital camera, and commercially digitizing negatives (better known as photo disks).

Scanners

Using a scanner is a somewhat complicated business. First, you have to find one; copy shops (such as Kinko's) or computer cafés frequently have scanners connected to computers that you can rent by the half-hour. While I would like to provide a brief

---

* We won't discuss the wide world of photo enhancing here. For more information, see Donnie O'Quinn's *Photoshop in a Nutshell*, 2nd Edition (O'Reilly).

overview of how to use a scanner, the hardware and software used to drive them is too varied for such a description to be useful. Here, however, are a few tips:

- Ask for help. Copy shops frequently have clear instructions posted next to the scanner. If you don't find such instructions, ask an employee to show you how to use the scanner.

- Bring at least one floppy disk per two photographs you plan to scan.

- Edit as you scan. You may not want the entire content of the photograph you're scanning. If not, crop it to the correct size, which will save you a good deal of disk space.

- If the image doesn't look right, play with graphic options, and scan the image again if need be. If you're renting the scanner, you're usually charged for the amount of time at the machine, not the number of scans.

Digital cameras

A great means of transmitting photographic images onto a computer, digital cameras have finally fallen far enough in price to make them an option for many consumers. What's the advantage to using one, instead of using your usual camera and scanning in the images? Digital cameras let you snap away, then download the images directly to your computer; no developing is required.

Any camera you buy will come with instructions as to how to connect it to your computer and download images to it.

Picture disks

One nice hybrid option is to have your photographs digitized at the time you develop them. Kodak and other vendors offer a Picture Disk option, with which you receive floppy disks containing digital versions of your photos when you pick up the prints. Developing might take an extra day or two, but you drop off and pick up the film at the drug store or photo shop as you normally would. The pictures are compressed, and the quality varies, but you can export them to standard image formats.

Another interesting option, provided by Kodak, is to pick up your photos online. Instead of disks containing the images, you visit Kodak's site and select the images you want to download (see Figure 9-14). You can also select other options, such as making your pictures available for public viewing or turning individual images into jigsaw puzzles or coffee mugs. Take a look at *http://www.kodak.com* for details.

Public Domain Graphics

The primary means of finding images for Web pages, of course, is to look around the Web itself. Check the Resource Catalog for sites that provide images free for public use. You'll find everything from wildlife photographs to navigational buttons to

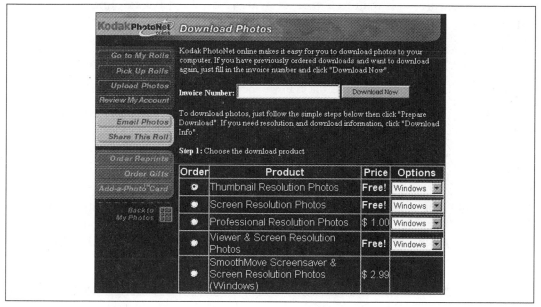

Figure 9-14. Downloading photographic images from Kodak

animated cartoons. When you find something you like at such a site, take it and use it—just be aware of any copyright issues that might be involved.

Copyright laws do apply on the Internet. If a web site doesn't state that its material is available for public use, don't consider it to be so. Contact a site administrator for permission.

Creating transparent backgrounds

Once you find an image you'd like to place on your page, there is one more issue you might want to think about: the background color. If you want to use an image as an icon on your page, it will look better if it looks like a line drawing on top of the background instead of a postage stamp. While most public-domain, icon-style images currently have transparent backgrounds, some still come postage-stamp style, as in Figure 9-15.

Figure 9-15. An icon that we'd like to have a transparent background

Getting rid of the background involves creating a transparent background, so that the background won't show up when you place the image on your page. To do so, download the desired image, and open it up in your favorite graphics program. Even the simplest shareware tools feature a way to create transparent backgrounds. Consult the application's help files for instructions. As an example, take a look at this tip from Paint Shop Pro:

> To select a transparent color for GIF files (e.g., for use on an Internet web page), use the eyedropper tool to select the background color, then, click on the Option button in the Save As dialog box and choose Set the Transparency Value to the BackgroundColor.

If we were to create a transparent background for the mailbox icon shown in Figure 9-15, the result would look like that shown in Figure 9-17.

HTML Coding: Don't Be Afraid

As you might guess from the term "HTML editor," you've been creating HTML code throughout the exercises we've described in this chapter. To see the source code, open a page you've been working on, then select **View** → **HTML** (FrontPage Express) or **View** → **Page Source** (Composer).* A window appears with a text file full of brackets and file names. If you look in between the bracketed instructions, however, you'll probably recognize the text you just created, and you'll get an idea of how HTML works (see Figure 9-16).

```
<p><font color="#FF6666">Q. Have you set a date?</font> <br>
<font color="#000000">A. Yes. Saturday, May 29th at 5:00 p.m.
This is one year and three days from the day that Floyd proposed.</font>
</p>

<h2><font face="Legends">Wedding Information</font></h2>

<p><font color="#FF6666">Q. Where will the wedding be held?</font>
<br>
<font color="#000000">A. Edgartown, Massachusetts, at the Harbor
View Hotel. Edgartown is located on Martha&#146;s Vineyard.</font>
</p>

<p><font color="#FF6666">Q. Can you afford that?</font> <br>
<font color="#000000">A. No.</font> </p>

<p><font color="#FF6666">Q. How can I reach Martha&#146;s
Vineyard?</font> <br>
<font color="#000000">A. Travel arrangements will be forthcoming.
However, if you haven&#146;t been invited, feel free to drive.</font>
</p>

<p><font color="#FF6666">Q. How many people will be there?</font>
<br>
<font color="#000000">A. Approximately 100. We are thus unable to
make any new friends at this time.</font> </p>
```

Figure 9-16. Displaying HTML code

---

* Unfortunately, this is where Composer really breaks down. While you can view the HTML, you can't edit it. To do so, you need to open the file in a text editor. Don't use Microsoft Word for this purpose, as it is very difficult to save the file with the correct *.htm* extension. Either Wordpad or Notepad, which ship with Windows, should work fine. If you'd like Composer to launch your text editor of choice for you, select **HTML source** from the **Edit** menu.

You're probably asking yourself, "Why should I care about how HTML works?" You should care, because there are certain neat features you can include in your pages that are only accessible through the code. These features include frames, Java applets, JavaScript elements, and more. More importantly, however, knowing how HTML works will guide the kind of web page you can create, even if you never work directly with HTML code itself.

The relationship between a browser and the HTML it displays is much different than what would seem to be an analogous relationship: that between a word processor and a file in that word-processor's file format. You should never have to look at the guts of a word-processing file—the program and the format are largely indistinguishable. They define each other. Microsoft is the only company that determines what constitutes a Microsoft Word file.

Web pages and HTML are completely different, because HTML is defined externally by groups of interested people and is designed to run on many different platforms and browsers. Microsoft, Netscape, and a group called the World Wide Web Consortium (or W3C) all determine what constitutes an HTML file. Therefore, it's possible for HTML to have features defined that aren't supported by your HTML editor—or by your browser. It's possible for your browser to have defined extensions (i.e., new HTML features) that aren't supported by other browsers or editors.

In fact, this is an important point: FrontPage Express certainly supports all of Microsoft's nonstandard features, and Composer certainly supports all of Netscape's. Both companies would just love to rope you into creating HTML pages that don't work right on the other vendor's browsers but are wonderful on their own.

What can you do about this? Test your pages in both Netscape and IE, and see if anything breaks. If something does, remove it, or create it differently. If there's a feature you'd like to include, but the editor doesn't support it, it's probably quite simple to insert that feature into the code manually.

The following pages provide an introduction to HTML. For a thorough discussion, see O'Reilly's *HTML: The Definitive Guide* by Chuck Musciano and Bill Kennedy.

Identification Tags

An HTML document consists of several tags that give information to the browser but don't affect the visible content. These tags give the title of the document, important keywords for search engines to note, when the header starts and ends, when the body of the document starts and ends, and so on.

Document identifier tag

The Wedding FAQ page opens with the <HTML> tag. <HTML> is the opening tag for all web documents. It tells the web browser that this is an HTML document, rather then a script, style sheet, or text file. </HTML> marks the end of the document. Note that everything else in the document is nested inside these two tags.

Header

<HEAD> and </HEAD>

Several important elements are contained in the header, including the title, key words, style specifications, and perhaps a JavaScript applet or two. These elements typically aren't displayed by the browser.

Title and meta tags

<TITLE> and </TITLE>

The title is the name of the document as it appears in the browser's title window, history list, and bookmarks page. The title tag is part of the header, thus it needs to be within the two header tags.

There are a few technical notes worth mentioning here:

- A document may have only one title.

- The title cannot contain anchors, links, paragraph marks, or text formatting.

- The title is normally not displayed within the text of the document itself, although the first heading frequently contains the same text as the title.

- Keep your title short, to 64 characters or fewer. Browsers may truncate the title in menus and hotlists.

The title should describe the page independently of its content. To select an appropriate title, imagine trying to find a page based on its title alone. If your page comes up on a search engine, you would much rather the title read "Mary Ann's home page" than "home page."

The <META> tag indicates additional information about your document, in the form of key-value pairs. This information may be used by web servers or document-indexing tools. Many people include a list of keywords for search engines to classify.

In the following example, the <META> and <TITLE> tags are nested within the <HEADER> tags, which in turn are nested within the document identifier tags. (We discussed adding META variables earlier.) The ellipsis represents the body of the document, which is itself nested within the <HTML> tags.

```
<HTML>
<HEAD>
<TITLE>Wedding FAQ</TITLE>
<META NAME="Author" CONTENT="Floyd Goodbody">
<meta name="KeyWords"
```

```
content="Floyd, Goodbody, Floyd Goodbody, Floydette, Trueheart, Floydette Trueheart,
wedding, information, party">
</HEAD>
...
</HTML>
```

Body identifier

<BODY> and </BODY>

We're almost ready to start writing the document, but there is one more technical item. The <BODY> tag indicates that we're ready to start the actual document.

Paragraph tags

The remainder of the tags (those within the <BODY> tags) will affect the visible content displayed in the user's browser. The paragraph tag, <P>, is the most common, and to a certain extent, is all you need. Your document could consist solely of <P> tags, followed by text:

```
<BODY>
<P>
My name is Fabio. Welcome to my home page!
<P>
Most people don't realize that I am a well-rounded intellectual. The fact is,
I am.
<P>
However, I don't have a whole lot to say.
</BODY>
```

Inserting Your Own Tags

Perhaps, while browsing the Web, you found a home page you really liked, with some features you don't know how to implement. You can cut and paste the section with these features into your page and then insert the text you want. Sometimes, however, it's actually easier to insert the tags yourself.

Flashing on the Web! (Or, how to use the blink tag)

Let's use the <BLINK> tag as an example. On a page with a blinking element, open an HTML window, and you'll see something like Figure 9-17.

```
<HR>
<P>
You can reach me at the e-mail address below.
<P>
<IMG SRC="mailbox1.gif" ALT="[mailbox]" HEIGHT=34 WIDTH=29>
E-mail:  <A HREF="mailto:ftrueheart@ora.com"> ftrueheart@ora.com </A>
<P>
<BLINK>This page is no longer under construction.</BLINK></CENTER>
```

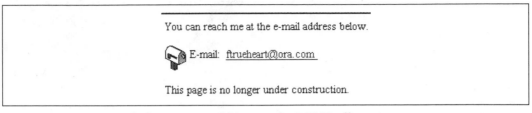

Figure 9-17. Open and close eyes quickly to see the BLINK effect

The selection starts with an <HR> tag, which draws the horizontal rule above the text. The paragraph tag, <P>, indicates the beginning of a new paragraph. The next tag <IMG>, which instructs the browser to load the named file as an image. The attributes SRC and ALT name the file and list alternate text, respectively. The other attributes of the <IMG> tag, HEIGHT and WIDTH, describe the image placement on the page. Finally, the <HREF> tag names a hyperlink reference; in this case, a mailto link, which we described earlier.

After starting another new paragraph, we finally get to <BLINK>. It tells the browser reading the HTML file, "Make the following text blink." It's followed by the text, "This page is no longer under construction," followed by the End Blink tag, or </BLINK>, which means, "The blinking is done."

If you'd like to make some of your own text blink, you could cut and paste this example into your page, and insert your own text in the blinking region. However, as you see in the code, my blinking "This page is under construction" is surrounded by formatting and line breaks you may not want. The easy way to make your text blink is to open an HTML window and scroll down to the text you want to blink. Place the cursor immediately before the first word you want to blink, and type "<BLINK>". Now place the cursor immediately after the last word you want to blink, and type "</BLINK>".

Close the window and save the page. If you're using Composer, it displays a host of annoying yellow tags to indicate that you're using very simple HTML that it nonetheless doesn't understand.

Load your page into a browser, however, and Voila! Your page has an annoying new feature.

You can use this technique to learn other design features you come across on the Web.

Links

To create a link by hand, you use the anchor tag, <A>, and the HREF attribute. The anchor tag tells the browser, "Make the following text a hypertext anchor," and HREF tells it, "Link the anchor to this file." Here's the syntax:

```
<A HREF="filename">Text that the user will click on
to link to the desired file</A>
```

If you are linking to another file in the same directory on the same server, you'll want to use a relative pathname:

```
<P>
You can take a look at my <A HREF="resume.htm">resume</A> or learn about
my <A HREF="wedding.htm">wedding</A>.
```

To link to a file on another server, however, you'll need to insert the full URL:

```
<P>
My friends Floyd and Floydette created a scary, yet thorough, page about
their <A HREF="http://members.theglobe.com/floydg/wedding/faq.htm">wedding</A>.
```

Anchor

Earlier, we described how to create anchor links within a document using Composer. The term "anchor" has a dual usage, unfortunately, both as the anchor tag, which is the basis for links, and as an anchor in a page, to create reference points within a document.

If you'd like to insert an anchor while using FrontPage Express, or by hand, place the following tags around the text to which you'd like to link:

```
<A NAME="anchor1">Seating Chart</A>
```

Note that this text won't be visibly differentiated in the viewer's browser—it's a place-holder for the browser to refer to, not for the viewer to click.

To link to that placeholder, you would insert a link to that reference, as follows:

```
<P>
Below, you'll find a <A HREF="#anchor1">seating chart</A> and other information.
```

Margins

We described how to create margins in a document using FrontPage Express. However, if you're using Composer and want to include margins in your document, include the TOPMARGIN and LEFTMARGIN attributes in your document's <BODY> tag, as follows:

```
<body bgcolor="#FFFFFF" topmargin="100" leftmargin="100">
```

Margin values are in pixels, which are quite small (about 75 per inch). The background color is a hexadecimal number that represents a color. #FFFFFF is white.

Paragraph breaks versus line breaks

HTML editors handle paragraph breaks poorly. The HTML standard for a new paragraph is for paragraphs to have whitespace in between them. If you want to break a line without starting a new paragraph, end a line with the break (<BR>) tag.

Some HTML editors function on the assumption that if you want whitespace, you should have to ask for it. Composer is especially bad about this: instead of placing paragraph (<P>) tags in the text when you press the Enter key for a new paragraph, Composer inserts two <BR> tags.

You might not care about this distinction, but a smattering of <BR> tags makes your code appear to be amateurish and difficult to read. More importantly, many <BR> tags can make layout difficult. So, just remember: <P> for paragraphs and <BR> for line breaks.

Whitespace

The other HTML paragraph standard is to provide only a single line of whitespace between paragraphs, no matter how many <P> tags you insert. To add additional whitespace, use the formatted style tag (<PRE> and </PRE>, for preformatted):

```
<PRE>
<P>
<P>
<P>
</PRE>
After a pause, Edmund looked at her soulfully.
```

Applets and Scripts

It's actually fairly easy to include some sophisticated elements, including Java applets and JavaScript programs, in your pages. It's much easier to paste them directly into the code, however, than to use the interfaces that Composer and FrontPage Express provide.

An *applet* is a small computer program that runs when a user loads a web page. There are many different kinds, with the most popular using the Java and JavaScript programming languages. FrontPage Express supports applets, but it doesn't support them very well.

That support comes in three forms: you can insert a Java applet, script, or "WebBot component" on a page via the **Insert** menu. When it comes to applets and scripts, however, you're better off inserting the code via an HTML window, as FrontPage Express's Insert windows are exceedingly confusing, when they work at all.

What's a WebBot component? In Microsoft's words, WebBot components are "built-in FrontPage objects that are evaluated and executed when an author saves a page or, in some cases, when a user browses to the page." In general, they appear to be prepackaged JavaScript functions. Three of them come with FrontPage Express: Include, Search, and Timestamp. Only Timestamp works, and it allows you to place a "last updated" message on your page that changes automatically.

Java

Java applets are small programs that you can download over the Web and then run on a user's computer. While creating your own applets would require extensive programming knowledge, it's actually quite easy to use Java applets on your web pages. You can download and paste them into a page, much like an image. Take a look at Gamelan (*http://www.gamelan.com*) or the Java Hermit (*http://www.celticedge.com/hermit/*) for tutorials and applets available for download.

JavaScript

JavaScript is a programming language designed to be executed from within HTML code. It's quite useful to the adept HTML user, as it allows you to control actions of the browser (the history list, location bar, and more). The Timestamp WebBot component, described previously, is actually a short JavaScript script.

While JavaScript is becoming more and more complex, there are some fairly simple functions that you can implement without a lot of programming knowledge. To learn about these functions, take a look at Cut-N-Paste JavaScript at *http://www.infohiway. com/javascript/indexf.htm* or the JavaScript Tip of the Week at *http://www. webreference.com/javascript/.*

Advanced Elements We Haven't Covered

This introduction to HTML has been quite brief. There are a number of important features that we haven't discussed at all. The major features that we've omitted are

- *Frames:* Powerful way of organizing the way sets of documents are displayed.

- *Style sheets:* Tool for defining how different kinds of text are displayed, rather than leaving the decision for the browser.

- *Forms:* Means of garnering user input. Not complicated in themselves, but you need to write software on the server to process the data.

To learn about these topics, see *HTML: The Definitive Guide* by Musciano and Kennedy (O'Reilly).

Publishing to the World Wide Web

Now that you've finally finished your web page, you're ready to upload it for public inspection. The first step is finding a *server,* a computer that answers requests from the Web for information. Then, you'll need to decide how to upload the page or pages that you've created. Using a *file transfer protocol* (FTP) application is usually the best choice, but you may also use the uploading tools that come installed with Composer or FrontPage Express.

File Management

When saving the page to the server, on which it's more difficult and dangerous to reorganize and delete files, practice sound file management.

Subdirectories

Keep in mind that organization is easier if you use subdirectories. You may want to provide a subdirectory for each linked page or to place all the images for your site in an */images* subdirectory. If you save images that way, you won't have to save multiple copies of frequently used images, such as backgrounds. Putting all your images i one directory will make your pages download more quickly; the browser will know that it doesn't have to download subsequent occurrences of images you use frequently.

Throughout this chapter, we've discussed the need (if you're using FrontPage Express) to place a copy of an image in the same directory to which you've saved your web page. You need to do so because when you upload the file to another server, FrontPage Express maintains the relative pathname it assigned when you first inserted the image (for example, *../Images/Gowns/joke.jpg*), rather than merely insert the image's filename (in this case, *joke.jpg*). By saving the image files to the same directory, FrontPage Express inserts only the filename. Composer does the right thing and converts the pathnames on the fly, depending on the option you choose while uploading (see later in this chapter).*

However, you may want to use your own subdirectories and not have the directory for each page be a mishmash of files. To do so, create a directory structure on your PC that mirrors the directory to which you'll be uploading. For example, I uploaded to a directory called *public_html* on a Unix server. On my PC, I save files to a directory called *webpages*. It's the subdirectories within these two directories that need to match. So, for example, if I save *faq.htm* to *C:\webpages*, I would then save images for that file to *C:\webpages\images*. I would then use my HTML editor's Insert Image command to browse for and insert those images into *faq.htm* from that directory. When I later uploaded *faq.htm* to my Unix server, in the directory *rusty/home/kiersten/public_html*, I'll upload the images separately, to *rusty/home/kiersten/public_html/images*, and the relative pathnames will be correct.

Using relative pathnames

You can now see why relative pathnames for images are vitally important. If you think you'll need to move your site, relative pathnames for links can save you a lot of trouble. Be sure to check your links and make sure that they work.

Absolute links are full-length URLs, such as *http://members.theglobe.com/username/home.htm*. However, if you are linking to a document within the same directory, it's

---

* Of course, if you're working on the computer that will be serving the files to the Internet, all of this is irrelevant. We're assuming, however, that you're working on the files on a PC, then uploading them to a Unix server.

better to use relative links; a relative link from your home page to, for example, an online résumé located in the same server directory would be *resume.htm*. The absolute link would be *http://members.theglobe.com/username/resume.htm*.

Relative links are easily portable, and therein lies their advantage. Some people prefer to create an entire web site on their personal computer before uploading it, and someday, you may want to move your pages to yet another server. With absolute links, you would have to change every URL with the *members.theglobe.com* directory in the filename; with relative links, you won't have to make any changes. Just upload the files according to the same directory structure.

Suffixes

Suffixes make management easier. It's a good idea to stick with *.htm* or *.html* for pages, and *.gif* or *.jpg* for images.

Filenames

Try to give your pages distinctive names: *home.htm*, *resume.htm*, and *projects.htm* are much more descriptive than *mary1.htm*, *mary2.htm*, and *mary3.htm*.

A special file, *index.html*, is the default file for a directory, and allows you to shorten the URL of your main entry point. For example, *http://www.oreilly.com* is equivalent to *http://www.oreilly.com/index.html*, and points to the file *index.html* in the top-level directory on the O'Reilly site.

Finding a Server

Once your web pages are in good working order, it's time to place them on a server. If you have access to a server already (via your company, college, or ISP), great. Find out from the system administrator about where to locate your pages, passwords, etc. If you don't currently have access to a server, it's actually easy to find one.

There are many sources that might be willing to host a web page. These include:

- Your place of business
- Your ISP
- Your college or university or alumni association
- A public domain server

What makes a server right for you depends on your needs. Do you need extensive system support? A lot of memory? A reliable, fast server?

In terms of the kind of web page we've described in this chapter, the most important server requirement will be good system support, in the form of clear instructions and FAQs. The Globe, described earlier, would be an excellent choice. If you'll be creating a more extensive or complicated site, you'll want to ask more questions. It's easy enough, however, to move a site to another server: you'll simply save the files to that new server and place a page at the old one linking to the new address.

Public domain server space

For a list of sites offering free web-page hosting, enter the term "Free Web page hosting" into any search engine, or visit Yahoo!'s listing of web services at *http://dir.yahoo. com/Business_and_Economy/Companies/Internet_Services/Web_Services/Hosting/ Complete_Listing/*.

Uploading Files

Let's look at the Globe (*http://www.theglobe.com*), the site at which we found Stevo's page. Registered members receive free server space. After filling out a brief registration form, a window pops up that directs us to build our own home page. The Globe's Homepage Builder directs you on uploading techniques, as shown in Figure 9-18.

HomePage Builder

CONSTRUCT YOUR WEB SPACE FOR ALL TO VISIT

FTP

FTP stands for File Transfer Protocol. It is a standard way of sending files from computer to computer across the Internet. Many Internet Service Providers bundle FTP programs in their connection software kits.

If you are familiar with using FTP software, use the following information:

1. Host: ftp.theglobe.com
2. Username: Use your member name for theglobe.com
3. Password: Use your password for theglobe.com

Download and learn how to use these FTP softwares:
Windows: WS-FTP, Cute FTP Mac: Fetch, Anarchie

Upload Files

This is where you can move files from your own computer or disk into your Globe directory.
Upload To: /kamic/

1. Type in the location and name of the file (e.g., C:\Windows\Desktop\thing.html), or choose the "Browse" button and find the file where you have it stored.
2. Hit the "Upload File" button, and the file will be moved into the directory in your Globe space that you're currently in.

Use the form below to "Browse" your local disk drive and pick a file to upload. Then select the directory in which you wish to place the file and press the "Upload file!" button. For more information, see the Help page.

Figure 9-18. Learning to place pages on a server

This information may seem a little confusing now, but it is actually all you'll need to publish your page on the Web. The Globe provides two options for uploading your page. First, via FTP, and second, via a very cute web-based form that uses your browser as an FTP client, as in Figure 9-19.

Click the **Browse** button to locate the page you just created on your hard drive. After you click **Upload File!** the page is transmitted to the Globe's server. You can upload not only HTML files in this manner, but any graphics files included in the page as

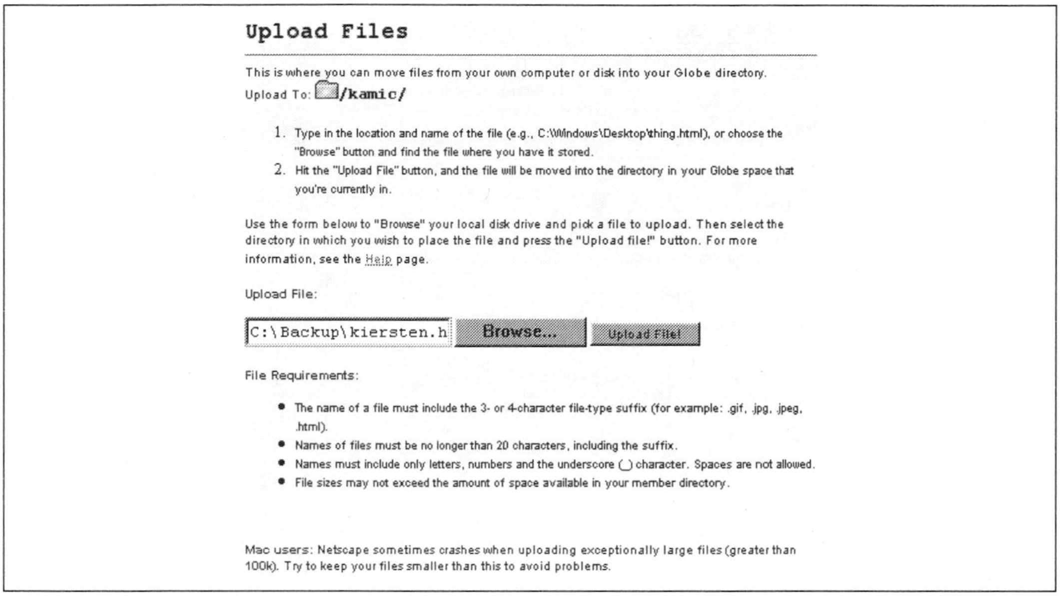

Figure 9-19. Uploading files

well. The next page you see tells you whether the upload was successful. If you click the **Continue** link, the resulting page provides a summary of your directory and the files in it, as in Figure 9-20.

From this screen, you can:

- Upload other files

- Create new subdirectories

- Move files within the directory

- Click the **Info** button to learn the page's URL, MIME type, and file size

- Click the **HTML** button to edit the page's HTML code directly

Uploading via FTP

Not all servers are as friendly as the Globe's, however. Additionally, you may want to transmit multiple files at once. To do so, open your FTP client. (For more information on using FTP, see the Appendix.) In the following example, the manner in which we upload files to The Globe's server isn't fundamentally different from the manner in which you would upload files to a corporate web site or any other ISP.

In this example, we're using FTPx, a client that emulates the Windows 95/98 and Windows NT operating system's Explorer application. Since this *isn't* anonymous FTP, as is frequently used elsewhere in this book, we'll need to enter connection and account information. That information was provided to us as described in Figure 9-21.

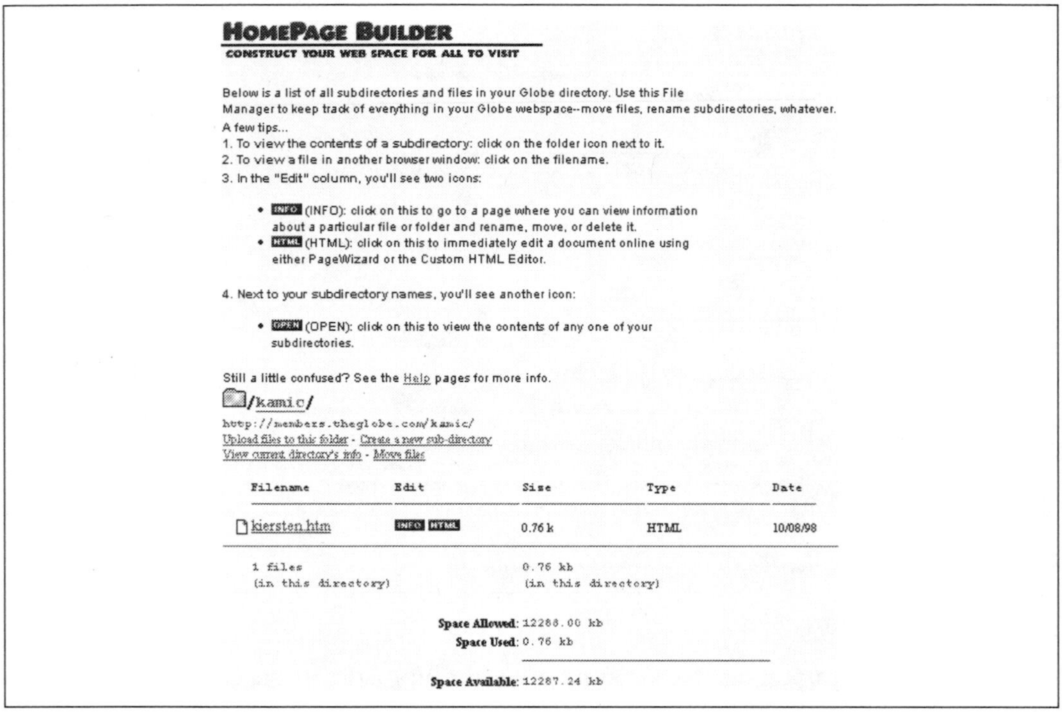

Figure 9-20. My directory on the Globe

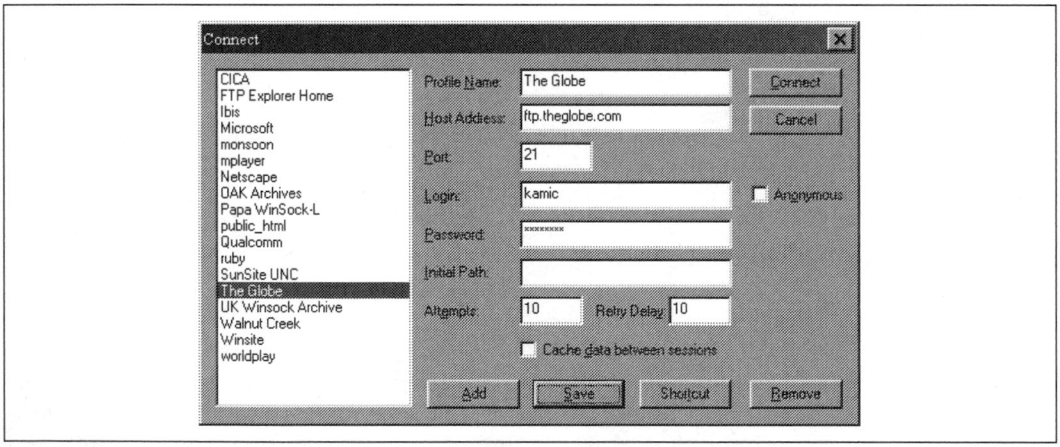

Figure 9-21. Connecting to the Globe's FTP server

Don't worry about the Port or Initial Path. Click the **Connect** button, and you'll see a screen like the one in Figure 9-22. As you can see from the information in the lower pane, the Globe's server transferred us directly to the correct user directory. The file we created and uploaded via a web browser is already there. To upload additional files, simply click the **Upload** button (the arrow, pointing up). Browse for the files on your system you want to upload. Holding down the Shift key allows you to select multiple files within a directory.

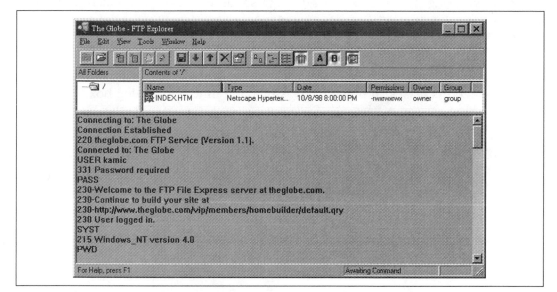

Figure 9-22. Uploading files

Any files you place in this directory will have essentially the same URL as the first—in this case, *http://members.theglobe.com/your_username/filename.htm.*

FTP is a great tool for uploading multiple files and for manipulating those files once they're on the server. You can also create subdirectories, move, rename, and delete files. How to do so depends on the FTP client you're using.

Creating subdirectories

With the mouse, click once on the icon for the directory where you want to add subdirectories. Select **New → Folder** from the **File** menu. To upload files to these directories, double click them, then click the **Upload** button and proceed as described previously.

Renaming files

Slowly click twice on the filename, enter a new filename, and press Enter.

Deleting files

Select the file you want to delete, and press the Delete key.

Uploading via an HTML Editor

Another option for uploading web sites is to use the functionality built in to the HTML editor you're using. I don't recommend doing so, as FTP gives you much more control over your directory structure. Some people, however, may not want to deal with the intricacy of FTP.

FrontPage Express

FrontPage Express makes an unfortunate assumption in its Save dialog box: it assumes you're working on the machine that's going to serve the page to the Web. Consequently, the uploading options are fairly inadequate.

If you've already saved the file, you'll need to use the Save As dialog box to access uploading options again. In the Page Location box, enter the URL of the server where the image should be placed, as in Figure 9-23.

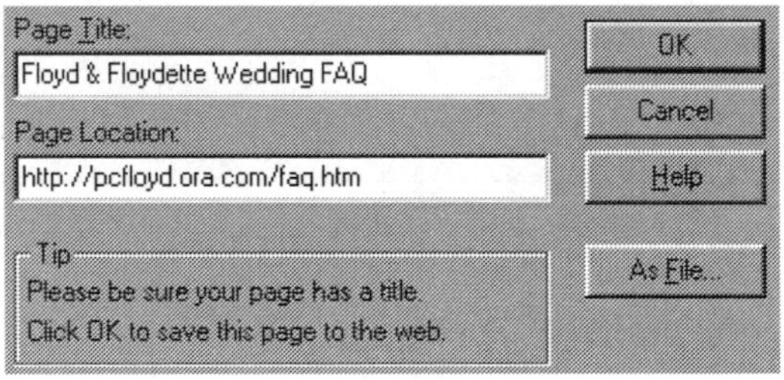

Figure 9-23. Saving to the server with FrontPage Express

In truth, I was unable to post pages to any remote server via FrontPage Express. This function is useful if you need to save a group of pages and images at one time (to the machine you're working on), but otherwise, it doesn't yet seem to be fully implemented. (It may work if the remote server you are using is the Microsoft server; as a rule, this is a poor assumption.)

Composer

Composer's upload function is much more useful than that of FrontPage Express. To access it, click the **Publish** button on the toolbar, as in Figure 9-24.

As you can see, the dialog box is fairly self-explanatory. Enter the URL or FTP address in the Location box, then your username and password, below. Composer saves the locations you upload to in the drop-down menu, which can be convenient if you save to different servers. Don't save your password if others have access to your computer. Composer gives you the option of uploading the other files in a page's directory along with it.

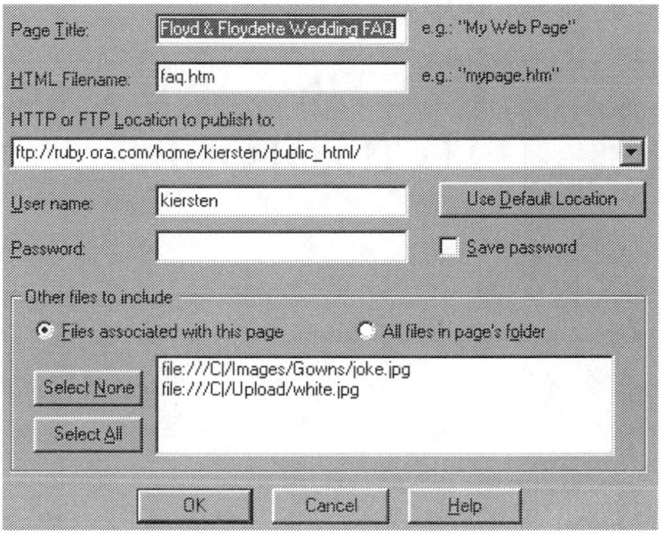

Figure 9-24. Using Composer to upload files

This is an important option. If you upload files associated with the page, Composer places the related files in the same directory and changes the code that denotes the location of those files accordingly. Thus, if you didn't upload the images with this file, the image source tags would look like this:

```
<img SRC="../Images/Gowns/joke.jpg>
<img SRC="../Upload/white.jpg>
```

whereas if you did upload the files, the tags would look like this:

```
<img SRC=joke.jpg>
<img SRC=white.jpg>
```

What does this mean? If you'd like to put your images in a subdirectory, create a sub-directory of the same name on your PC, and place images there. Then, upload those files to that subdirectory separately from the HTML page (that is, don't click the **Select All** button in the Other files to include dialog box).

Accessing your web page

Now that your page is on the Web, it's time to take a look at it. Open your web browser, and enter the URL of your page in the Location field. Admire your handi-work.

If you want to make changes to the page, go ahead. Either edit the copy saved locally on your PC, or download a new copy of the page by selecting **Save As...** from the browser's **File** menu. When you're done, upload the page to the server again. Press the **Reload** button on your browser to make the changes appear.

CHAPTER TEN

ESOTERIC AND EMERGING TECHNOLOGIES

The most misunderstood thing about the Internet is not what it does, but what it might be able to do. Most other computer networks were designed with a specific task in mind. They do that task, and do it well; but anything else they do with difficulty, if at all. In contrast, the Internet was designed as a general communication facility that allows computers located anywhere to become co-workers. What they work on is up to you and the imagination of software developers; there are few limits on what's possible. So, although the Internet does a great job of delivering email and moving files around, it can also be used for delivering live audio and video, software, and other things that we haven't thought of yet.

You already know about email, web browsing, and the like. In this chapter, we look at some applications that are distinctly different, like Internet telephone and desktop conferencing. Since we're talking about leading-edge applications, keep in mind that the future of any technology or product that we cover in this chapter is uncertain. For example, Internet telephony is currently popular because you can use the Internet to transfer a voice conversation cross-country (or around the world) without paying the long-distance charges associated with traditional telephone companies. If there's an increase in the price of Internet access or a drop in the price of long-distance telephone calls, you could see Internet telephony drop from view quickly. Other applications, like desktop conferencing, are useful and will continue to be developed—they'll undoubtedly play a big role in the next generation's Internet. Other applications don't have as clear a future.

Still other applications are being talked about, but haven't yet gotten out of the starting box. We'll show you some systems for delivering video over the Internet, but the dream (perhaps it's a nightmare) of delivering movies to the home via the Internet is still relatively far off. Some of the technology exists, but it's a lot more expensive than signing up for cable TV.

Interactive Communications

One of the earliest network-aware applications was the Unix *talk* program. This program let two people type at each other; in a sense, it was a predecessor to today's chat programs. The popularity of talk, followed by the popularity of multi party chat, has proved something important about the Internet. Surfing for cool sites or looking up forgotten lore is all well and good, but people really just want to talk to each other. Therefore, it shouldn't be any surprise that people developed ways of transmitting audio over the Net. And not just any audio—live audio, so that you can talk to friends in real time over the Internet. And it shouldn't be a surprise that people have gone even further, to multi party teleconferencing and video conferencing. What started out simple—talk is very primitive, by today's standards—ended up being quite sophisticated.

Unfortunately, these are all *isochronous* applications, and the Internet was never designed to support isochronous applications well. Isochronous means that the application requires timely delivery of a continuous stream of information. It can easily tolerate a bit of inaccuracy, but the information must keep flowing. Think of watching television: inaccuracy in the data your TV receives appears as static or snow in the picture. You can live with a little of it; in fact, you can live with quite a lot of it. But if the television network feed is cut for a short time the picture will freeze and jump. Or think of a telephone call. There can be quite a lot of static on the line before it becomes a real problem. But you've probably had calls when something has gone wrong with the phone company's equipment, and the voice periodically "dropped out" for a quarter second or so. Too much of that, and you hang up.

Why is this hard for the Internet? The TCP protocol, which most applications use, was designed for accuracy. It guarantees that information gets delivered 100% accurately. To do that, it frequently sacrifices timeliness. In Chapter 1, we talked about how the Internet splits data up into a bunch of packets, which are transmitted separately. But if any packet is damaged or doesn't get through, TCP tells the sender to send the packet again, and it waits until the new packet arrives. For voice, that would mean a nice quarter second gap while TCP is waiting for the replacement. Therefore, isochronous applications often don't use TCP; they use a simpler protocol called UDP, which doesn't bother with this replacement nonsense. If something doesn't get through, it's gone. That's a big improvement, because a momentary crackle or pop is better than a gap. But it still doesn't get to the root of the problem. The Internet was designed so that a nuclear warhead could vaporize a major network hub without disrupting communications. This means there are a lot of different ways to get from point A to point B. But all these routes take different times to get data between A and B—and you can't specify what path you want in advance. So there's still a problem: some of your voice data may reach your friend in half a second, other parts may take a tenth of a second, and still other bits may never get there at all. On top of that, throw in the congestion that every Internet user experiences from time to time, and you'll see why it is an uphill battle to make these kinds of applications work well. Frankly, it's a miracle they work at all.

Luckily, the communication lines used for the Internet are quite good, packets usually take the same route between two points, and congestion isn't often a problem. In other words, if you're lucky, you can use Internet phone and similar applications without trouble—and you'll be lucky more often than not. The applications themselves try to be as miserly as possible with network bandwidth and can do a surprising amount to compensate for congestion. But occasionally the communication will be choppy and the pictures jerky. Chalk it up to the load on the Internet. There is nothing that you or the application can do.

Of course, this also means that the more speed you can guarantee between the two ends of the connection, the more reliable and palatable these applications will be. If you are having an Internet phone conversation using your corporate intranet, which connects each office by large, fast, data communications lines, you will probably be quite satisfied. However, if your child is an exchange student in Pago Pago, you may save big on phone bills but only hear an occasional "Send money." Sometimes you get what you pay for.

There is hope for the future; the people who are worrying about where the Internet is going are fully aware of the problem. There are many proposals for the new replacement for the Internet protocol (known as IPv6) that will help alleviate the problem. There will probably be a way to connect to someone and inform the network that you need predictable delay for this connection, and the network will do what it can to guarantee that all your packets take the same amount of time to reach their destination. Of course, your Internet service provider will probably charge you more when you require special treatment, such as a predictable delay.

Internet Telephone

Internet Telephone was a concept (and a product) created by VocalTec Ltd. (*http://www.vocaltec.com*). This company is still the dominant player in this market. Its software package allows you to use your existing sound card to connect a PC to another across the Internet and send audio back and forth—in a sense, giving you a telephone connection but without any long-distance charges. In the early days, you had to put up with a lot of inconvenience to use this technology. One of the problems was that early sound cards were half-duplex devices, which means that they could only talk or listen at any given moment—not both. So early users had to adopt a style reminiscent of CB radio: "Hello Joe, Hello Joe, can you hear me, over."

In the past year, there have been many advances in the quality of Internet telephony, to the point that many users now consider it adequate for business calls. In addition, Internet telephony is becoming integrated with the rest of your existing communications services. For example, you don't even need a personal computer: you can buy an Internet telephone with a handset and an Ethernet jack. And you're not limited to calling people who have computers; gateways are in place that connect the Internet to the public telephone network, so you can call people who don't have computers. Furthermore, what started out as a fairly limited service, giving you the ability to call someone if he happened to be online and watching the computer, has caught up with modern telephone service: you can use Internet phone for paging, voice mail, teleconferencing, etc.

How Internet telephone works

First, let's talk a bit about how all of these services hang together, so that you understand some of the peculiarities of Internet telephony. Basically, you decide who you want to call. Then, you and your partner pick an Internet telephony package and install it on your computers. This software will cost $100 at most, and might even be free. The software knows how to encode and decode voice. All you have to do is tell your software the address of your partner's computer, and you are chattering away. Your telephony package handles functions like call hold, call waiting, and voice mail.

Simple as this sounds, it isn't completely trouble free. First, unless you are connected to the Internet via a LAN, you probably don't have a static IP address. Most dialup Internet services lend you an IP address only while you are connected, and they assign that address to someone else when you're no longer online. This could lead to some obvious (and potentially embarrassing) problems: imagine what would happen if telephone numbers were reassigned randomly among people in your town! The industry has two solutions to this problem. One is an *addressing service* that gives you a permanent "Internet phone number." When you come online, your computer goes to your chosen addressing service and tells it your Internet phone number and your current address. Someone who wants to call you can use this number instead of your IP address. The phone software then asks the addressing service to look up the address that's currently associated with your permanent phone number.

NOTE

There is no standard terminology for much of what we will be discussing here. One manufacturer may give you a unique Internet phone number, another may give you an ICQ#, and another something else. All of the services work in about the same way, so translating the concepts described here to the terms used by your provider shouldn't be difficult.

Addressing services are for long-term users. Some of them will not give you a unique number unless you buy Internet telephone software from them or else go through some sort of registration process. If you are a casual user of Internet phone, you may not want to go to the trouble. An alternative is a community bulletin board system. When you want to receive phone calls, you enter a "room" and say that you're ready and waiting. Other people using the bulletin board can then see that you're online, and give you a call. This kind of service is all you need if you're interested in meeting a lot of random people—which, historically, is one of the things people have done on the Internet. But the system also works for prearranged appointments.

Whether you use an addressing service or a bulletin board, be sure to use the descriptive information of your entry to the best advantage. If you go into a bar and hang around long enough, someone will come over and try to talk to you. In a bar you can make your intentions known through body language and other visual cues. On the addressing service, you only have about 30 characters to convey your intent. So, if you're only willing to accept calls from Mike L, say so. If you're interested in chatting with random people about your coin collection, say so. What you say will go a long way to determining who will call.

The next complication arises when you want to have a conference call. Your computer can barely compress a single packetized phone conversation over the typical home Internet connection. Sending all the audio data to each participant in a conference call would be hopeless. To support teleconferences, someone with a good Internet connection runs a conference server. The participants connect to the conference server instead of connecting to each other directly. The server retransmits what it hears from any of the connected parties to everyone in the conference. This service may also connect to the traditional telephone network, allowing people without access to the Internet to take part in a conference.

Finally, what if you have WebPhone by Netspeak, but you want to talk to someone who uses Tribal Voice's PowWow? Can you communicate? It depends. Some products only work if the same kind of software is used on each end of the call. (That's why you should decide who you want to talk to and then agree on a telephony package.) Other products know how to talk the competition's language. Still others use a standard called H.323. Theoretically, any products using H.323 should be able to communicate with one another. Ultimately, the product you choose depends on what you want to do. If you only want to use Internet telephony to save on calls to your daughter in college, you can probably get by with software that only talks to a similar product. If you want to use Internet telephony for business, pick a product that is H.323 capable.

VocalTec

Version 5.01 of Internet Telephone can be downloaded for free from the VocalTec web site. The version you get will work for two weeks; when the trial period expires, you'll be asked to register the program for $50. It can now compress an understandable phone conversation into a 7 Kbps/second datastream (easily within the capabilities of a 33.6 Kbps or 56 Kbps modem), so there is plenty of room to deal with congestion. If more speed is available (either because you have a faster connection or congestion is low), Internet Telephone takes advantage of the extra bandwidth to provide noticeably better quality. The most recent release requires at least a 75 MHz Pentium, and Windows 95/98 or Windows NT, so you won't have much luck if you're using an older PC. Sound cards are still a bit iffy. Some half-duplex cards are still around, so before you buy a sound card, you should check VocalTec's web site for recommendations.

Installing VocalTec Internet Phone is easy. The installation wizard asks you about your connection speed and where you would like the software to reside. It also asks you for a registration number. If you haven't paid your $50, leave this field blank. The wizard understands that this means a two-week trial installation. You click the **Next** button until you get to the screen shown in Figure 10-1.

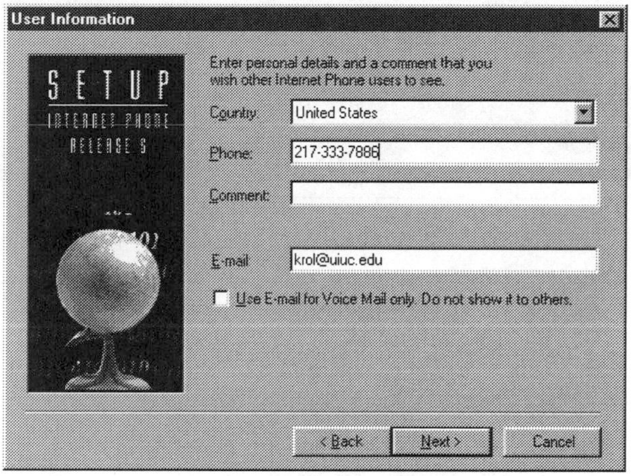

Figure 10-1. VocalTec installation

Here you are asked a few questions about yourself. The information you provide is placed in the directory for all to see, so think carefully about your answers. The "Use Email for voicemail only" checkbox determines whether you want to show your email address in the directory. If you check the box, people can send you voice mail but won't know what your address is—the program keeps it private. Keeping your email address private is probably a good idea, given that this kind of directory is a prime target for people sending junk email.

The first time you use Internet Telephone, it displays a screen for audio and video configuration.

Press **Start** and speak into the microphone. After a few words, press **Stop**; it will play back what you have spoken so that you can set the speaker volume (see Figure 10-2). When you are done, you are ready to make calls. Figure 10-3 shows Internet Phone's main screen. If you take a minute to examine the screen, it will be fairly obvious how to use the program.

To make a call, place an email address or an Internet phone address in the field at the top and press **Call**, or click on someone's name in the community browser. When a call is in progress, the **Hang Up** and **Hold** buttons become active and do the obvious functions. If someone decides to call you, the **Answer** button becomes active, and you'll hear a ringing sound. At this point, you can either ignore the caller by doing

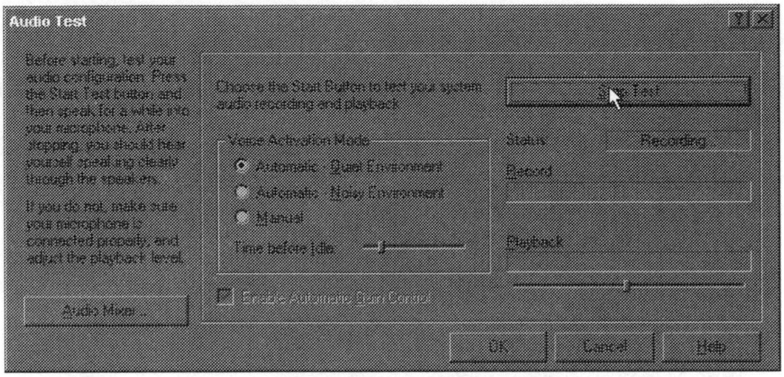

Figure 10-2. Setting audio levels

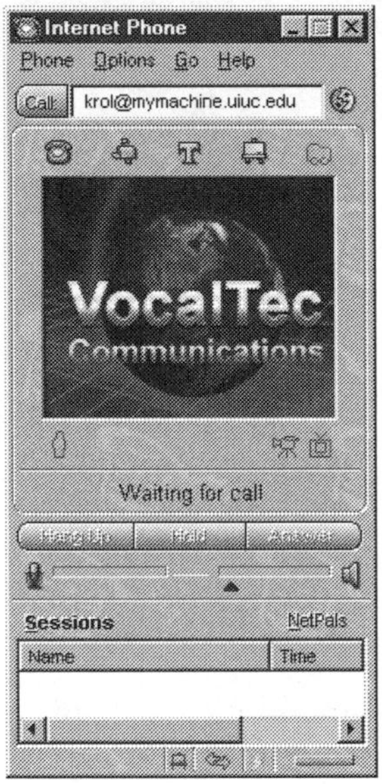

Figure 10-3. VocalTec Internet Phone

nothing or accept the call by clicking the **Answer** button. If you don't want to receive calls, select **Do not disturb** from the **Phone** menu.

The latest version of Internet Phone provides a wide range of features, including video (do you really want to see who you're talking to?), teleconferencing, voicemail and chat systems, and a community browser. The community browser is VocalTec's implementation of the bulletin board to find people who are willing to receive calls at that moment. One drawback of Internet telephony, at least on a PC-to-PC basis, is that your friends can only receive calls if their computer is on and connected to the Internet when you try to call. So most people arrange an approximate meeting time via email. At the appointed time, each participant checks the bulletin board. The first one to arrive just hangs around, waiting for the partner to arrive and place the call.

Figure 10-4 shows a snapshot of the community bulletin board. It looks just like a complicated web page. Internet Telephone uses either Internet Explorer or its own internal browser to display the page. In VocalTec's implementation, the board is broken up into areas and then categories within areas. Categories in the General area don't make much sense here, but if you go into the Hobbies or Leisure areas the categories are descriptive. In the General area, the categories merely segment a grouping that is too big to deal with otherwise. There is a scrollbar to the right of the categories in case there are more categories than will fit on one line.

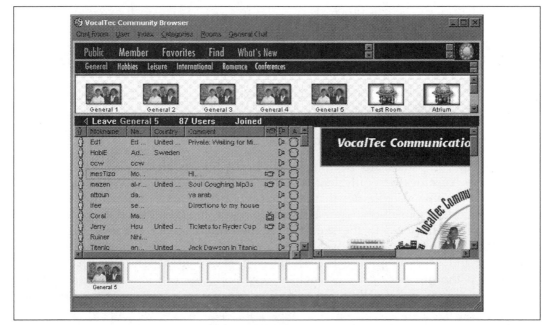

Figure 10-4. The community bulletin board

If you look at the entries in Figure 10-4, you notice that Ed is hanging out at the top of the list waiting for Mike to call. This should deter random people from calling just to chat—some people think "general" means sexual. There is no policing to make sure that people stay in the appropriate areas. To the right of the comments, you'll see icons. A camera means that this person can send and receive pictures; a television means that she can view only; no icon indicates that there is no video. Next is a speaker, which indicates that audio is available, and a telephone, which means that the user can speak. Just click on the person whom you want to contact and hope he answers.

You can view a category without being listed in it; your listing is only displayed to the world when you explicitly join a category. You remain joined until you explicitly leave. Even if you close the Community Browser window, you'll be listed as long as the phone software is running. To leave, click the left arrow next to Leave on the line below the categories.

Internet telephone service providers

One of the most interesting features of Internet Phone is the idea of an Internet telephone service provider (ITSP), which provides closer integration between Internet phone and traditional telephony. For a fee, an ITSP takes an Internet Telephone call and routes it into the traditional telephone system, allowing you to call a standard telephone from your computer. For example, your parents in Denver are technologically challenged and don't own a computer. You would like to call them regularly from New York, so you subscribe to an account with an ITSP in Denver and call them using Internet Telephone. The call proceeds over the Internet to Denver for free and then is transferred to the local phone company, which calls your parents phone, letting them talk to you. You pay only for the local-connection charge, and no long-distance charges. This service is currently available in about 50 cities worldwide; it makes sense to use it only if the person you want to call is a local call for your ITSP. See VocalTec's web site for information about where ITSPs are located. There are a surprising number overseas, particularly in southeast Asia.

Internet-based Private Business Exchanges (PBX)

A number of companies are beginning to market Internet telephony products that allow you to construct the equivalent of a PBX between multiple offices. You can buy normal-looking office telephones that plug into your office LAN, and various call managers (which map normal-looking telephone numbers into the IP world) and gateways that connect the IP world to the standard telephone world. For example, a company has a Chicago and a New York office and each office has a good Internet connection to its LAN and every employee has an Internet phone. If a person in the Chicago office dialed the number of a customer in New York, the call manager would know that the best route for that call would be to send it across the Internet to the New York office. There, the gateway would dial the local call and connect the IP telephone world to the standard telephone system, minimizing costs. Two of the leaders in this market are Cisco Systems (*http://www.cisco.com*) and Vienna Systems (*http://www. viennasys.com*).

Other vendors and add-ons

VocalTec is not the only game in town. It's in the middle of the road, both in terms of price and features. The other products range from free to roughly $100; in terms of features, the main variables are sound quality and fancy add-ons. Here is a short list of additional products:

PowWow (http://www.tribalvoice.com)
  The low end of the market is free. Sound quality and number of connections are limited. It has more of an "audio-chat-room" approach, as opposed to VocalTec's

"emulate-your-home-phone" approach, but can be used as a phone system. Pow Wow supports "white boards" (i.e., lets you draw) but doesn't support full video. It will work only with other PowWow-equipped computers.

Vienna Systems (http://www.viennasys.com)

This is a complete business systems provider. Vienna Systems can do anything from give you client software for a PC to sell you multiline Internet telephones, call distributors, gateways.

WebPhone (http://www.netspeak.com)

The high end of the market costs about $90. Web Phone's designed for business use; it has better quality and more advanced features (e.g., call forwarding, call waiting, voice mail, caller ID).

Voxphone (http://www.voxphone.com)

This is the most interoperable of the phones. It can talk to most of the network conferencing systems and many of the other Internet phone systems. Currently, its web site says that the company no longer sells to end users but it hasn't yet deleted the order form. So you can try to buy it. There's no free demo version.

One of the newest players in the Internet telephony business is AT&T, which has recently announced that it will become a long-distance company that uses the Internet as its network. In other words, in the future you'll be able to select AT&T's Internet service as your home phone's long-distance provider, rather than a traditional carrier like AT&T, Sprint, or MCI. Whenever you make any long distance call, AT&T will route the call across the Internet to another local phone company. You might not be able to hear a pin drop, but it will certainly be cheaper than almost anything else.

There is a fairly interesting market in PC-telephone accessories and add-on services. A number of devices connect your computer to standard telephones, letting you talk over a cordless phone to your computer, which in turn talks to another Internet phone user. This way, you can still cook and talk on the phone at the same time. Some of the interesting ancillary players are:

Pagoo (http://www.pagoo.com)

Pagoo is a traditional voice-mail site for Internet phone. Someone can leave you a message via Internet telephone at their site. You then pick up your voice messages at a later time using a web browser.

Compro Ezfone (http://www.ezfone.com)

Compro offers home adapters to connect traditional telephones to your computer or your computer to the telephone network to act as a gateway.

The Internet on your phone

We've talked about using your desktop computer as a telephone. The reverse is also possible: using your cell phone or some similar handheld devices as an Internet browser. This technology isn't as far along, but you should start seeing these devices in the next year or so. A lot of work is being done to minimize the amount of data that needs to be transmitted over wireless telephone connections. A specialized markup language called *Wireless Device Markup Language* (WML) is being developed for small screens available on handheld devices, and a special protocol called *Wireless Application Protocol* (WAP) is under development that's very stingy with the amount of data it sends, so it will work well over low-speed wireless links.

There are certainly other approaches to this problem that could win out; for example, 3Com, which makes the PalmPilot handheld computers, is certainly moving in the direction of phone capability—and as you've seen, browsers for the PalmPilot are already available. It may be too early to bet on WML, but something of this sort is bound to happen.

Desktop Conferencing and Collaboration

A lot of work is going into the area of desktop conferencing and collaboration through the Internet. Older technologies for conferencing and collaboration tended to be inefficient and expensive. The cost of a meeting could easily run to thousands of dollars if you had to fly participants in from different parts of the world. You could save some of the travel cost by video-conferencing, but this usually still required a trip to a special video conferencing center that was filled with special equipment, used private high-speed phone lines, and (in short) wasn't a whole lot cheaper than flying all the participants to a central location. Furthermore, although meetings helped you talk out issues face-to-face, you still left with a half dozen different sets of notes on how to update your project proposal. Wouldn't it be better to work together making changes to a single file? Wouldn't it be better to discuss what's needed, put the changes into the file at once, and have everybody agree? Wouldn't it be better to do this from the comfort of your office rather than travel around the world? That's what desktop conferencing is about: using the Internet (or some other network) so that your bits do the traveling, not you, and so that a team of people at different locations can work together effectively on one project.

Increases in computer and communication speed have spawned a new group of applications for desktop conferencing and collaboration. Although this sounds complicated, it's really just a clever application of tools we already have. Desktop conferencing facilities tend to be an integrated suite of applications for multiparty chat, electronic white board (a shared drawing board that your collaborators can scribble on), task sharing (for example, cooperatively editing a spreadsheet), audio, and video. They're set up so you can use all the applications at once conveniently. The trick is compressing the data streams from these many applications so that everything fits within the limits imposed by your modem and the Internet.

If you think this sounds like what you'd get from Internet Telephone, you are right. The latest version supports most of these applications, if not all of them. Unfortunately, most of the conferencing applications we have so far use proprietary protocols to talk among themselves, so if you have Internet Telephone, you can't have a conference call with Microsoft NetMeeting or your corporate compression labs videoconference facility. The whole industry is looking towards a standard way for electronic conferences to come together (Figure 10-5).

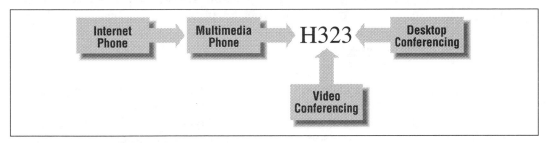

Figure 10-5. Merging of conference technologies

The big hope for interoperability between conferencing applications is an international telephony standard called H.323. Any software package that "talks" H.323 should be able to communicate with any other package. However, standards can take quite awhile to have any real effect. The tower of Babel is crumbling, but it has not fallen yet. For the immediate future, if you are working with a small group of people, you should all use the same software. If you want to live on the edge, you can try working cross-platform with products that support H.323; several of the Internet telephony products we mentioned do. Aside from the telephony products, Microsoft's NetMeeting and Netscape's Communicator support conferencing and collaboration.

Collaboration over the Internet sounds great, particularly for people with home offices, but it is severely taxing on even the fastest home Internet connections. Every application you add eats a bit more of your connection. Chats occupy the least bandwidth; video or task sharing require the most. This shouldn't scare you away; it just means you need to be careful about what you share. If you are discussing a spreadsheet, bringing up a shared window so everyone can look at (and edit) the same item can be the fastest solution. But if you want to share an application, plus reasonable quality voice, plus video, or if you are forever resizing or changing things in the window, the people at the other end of the connection will fall way behind because their screens won't be updated fast enough. The more you share, the more bandwidth you need. If you're working from home, bandwidth is almost certainly a limiting resource.

Microsoft NetMeeting

You can get NetMeeting from Microsoft's web site (*http://www.microsoft.com*) either as a product unto itself (about 3 MB of downloading) or as part of the full installation of Internet Explorer (26 MB). Either way, the product installs easily. An installation wizard checks your audio and video capabilities. You do need to enter some personal information in the **Call/Change My Information** menu, but after that you are ready to conference.

There are three ways to set up a conference. You can use one of the commercial directory servers (a bulletin board where you post your intentions), you can set up your own corporate directory server, or you can send your address to a few friends and have a private conversation. Of course, all of the problems we discussed about dynamic IP addresses in the section on Internet telephone applies here as well. You need to use a directory service unless you have a static IP address. By default, Net-Meeting uses one of the directory servers provided by Microsoft; this is where the adventure starts.

As part of the configuration process, you have to pick a directory server. (If you didn't, one was chosen for you.) When you start NetMeeting, it attempts to log into that directory server. If it is successful, your information is displayed on the directory server for all to see. The directory also gives some hints about your hardware capabilities; the little speaker indicates that you can handle audio, and the camera shows that you can handle video. The format of the directory listing will be self-explanatory after you have configured NetMeeting; every field that you filled in is shown on the screen somewhere, as shown in Figure 10-6.

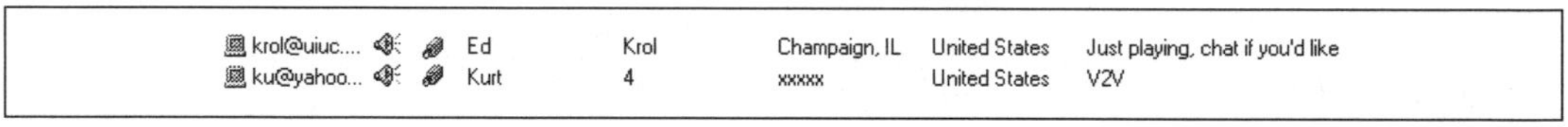

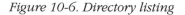

Figure 10-6. Directory listing

You aren't necessarily looking at the directory you are listed in. The directory you are logged into is listed in the bottom right corner of the screen. At the top right of the screen is a pull down list of all the directory servers configured into your NetMeeting client; the directory shown is the one that is currently displayed. You can display another directory just by selecting one from the pull-down list. This does not change the directory you are listed in; you must change your directory manually. Although this may seem odd, this is the way you want it to work. If you want to meet someone, you need to hang up your shingle in a single place; while you're waiting, you may want to check out other directories. You don't want your directory listing to move with you; you want it to stay in one place so people can find you.

You can restrict your display to certain categories. If you select Business use, NetMeeting won't display any categories intended for other kinds of use. The icon to the left of the names shows the current status of that person. If the icon has a little star on it, it denotes that the person is currently in the middle of a conference (see Figure 10-7). This doesn't mean you can call them, but it is up to them whether they have call waiting turned on.

Again, it's not hard to figure out what a lot of people want to do in their conferences. You can filter out most of the adult entries by telling NetMeeting to omit them. However, there's nothing to force people to put their conferences in the appropriate category, and it is amazing how many people think that live-sex shows qualify as business use.

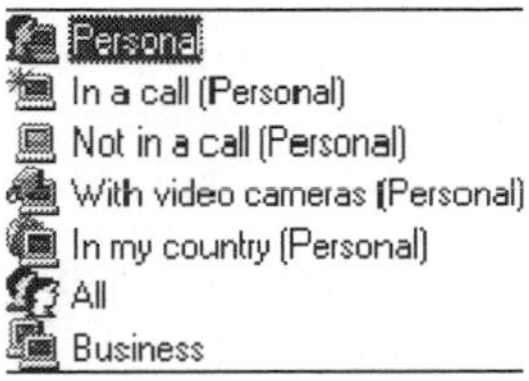

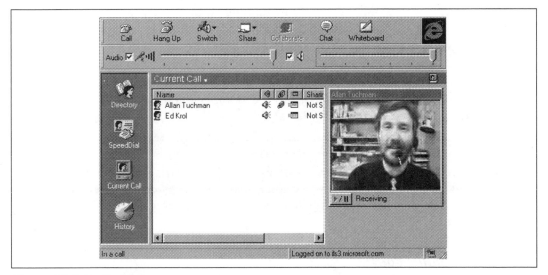

Figure 10-7. Connection categories

NetMeeting lets you meet with as many people as you want, but it only gives you two video channels. One of those channels is always the picture you are sending out. This sounds restrictive, but it really isn't bad. If you had more than two channels, the conference would be so slow and hard to manage that it would be useless.

Double-clicking on a directory entry places a call to that person. If he accepts, the screen changes to a window showing both your names; audio and video are enabled if they exist. Both audio and video can be disabled via a check box if you are feeling a bit sheepish about sharing too much. If I called my friend Allan and he accepted, I would see the screen in Figure 10-8. At this point, we could talk to each other.

Figure 10-8. In Conference

This is where collaboration gets interesting. In addition to chatting, we can use several other means of communication, listed in the **Tools** menu:

Chat
Chat in NetMeeting is very similar to IRC (Internet Relay Chat), Unix talk, or web chats you may have run into before. Whatever you type is displayed on the next line preceded by your name. Transmissions occur a line at a time. It is especially

useful to drop into a chat if you're having trouble with audio transmissions. If all you hear is bzzz, bzzzzz, bzzz from your speaker, you can use chat while you try to straighten out the problem.

White board

White board lets you scribble on the screen using the typical set of drawing tools you should be familiar with from PowerPoint or PaintShop Pro. Your scribbles are displayed for everyone in the conference to see. You can get some odd results if many people are trying to draw at the same time.

File Transfer

This does the obvious. Files sent to you are placed in a folder that is part of your configuration (normally the Received Files folder inside the NetMeeting folder). A submenu in the **File Transfer** menu allows you to get to the Received Files folder quickly.

Share Application

Sharing an application allows you to display any window on your computer so that other participants in your conference can see it. The display is view only. Start the application first and position it so that what you would like to display is visible. Next, pull down the **Tools** menu and stop on **Share Application**. You see a submenu that shows all the currently running applications. Select the one you want to share.

Start Collaborating

Once an application is being shared, you can allow others to make changes to it by selecting Start Collaborating. If you are all looking at a spreadsheet, rather than saying, "I think you ought to bump up the book budget by $1,000," you can just do it and say, "How about this?"

NOTE

If you start collaborating on your desktop (which is managed by a task called Explorer) all windows owned by Explorer may be accessed or executed. This includes virtually any file in an open window or on your taskbar. You need to really trust your collaborator.

Netscape Communicator

Netscape's Communicator at one time was in competition with NetMeeting for this business, but with the sale of Netscape it appears to have dropped support for online meetings from its browser. If the version you have still has these capabilities, then it is an old version. You won't find them in the newer ones.

Streaming

Streaming technologies try to deliver audio and video over the Net in approximately real time—meaning that you hear the music or see the video as it's being sent, without waiting for the whole thing to download. Doing this effectively, given the limited bandwidth available to most Internet users, requires data compression and buffering. Data compression simply means manipulating the data in some way so that it fits into as little space as possible. Buffering is the technology that portable CD players use to smooth out bumps. The player reads some of the song from the CD before any sound comes out. When it has read a reasonable amount, it starts playing the beginning of the piece from memory. Meanwhile, it continues reading the CD into the far end of memory. If there's a bump, the CD player can use data from the buffer, and you'll never know that the bump occurred. However, driving over a dirt road that's full of potholes will cause the music to stop or become jerky. The same thing happens on the Internet. Real-time media players buffer some portion of the stream—often a few minutes' worth—so that they have data in reserve should the Internet go through a slow period. If the Internet remains congested for long, or if there's some other problem that limits the speed at which you can get data, the player will use up the data in its buffer and stop while it waits for more to arrive.

Streaming is exciting because of its varied uses. When you visit an online record store, such as CDnow (*http://www.cdnow.com*), you can frequently listen to 30 seconds of each song on an album before you decide to buy it. Or stop by Fox (*http://www.fox. com*) and view the hot news items of the day as shown on the Fox Network news. Or listen to the netcast of your favorite college's basketball game (*http://www.broadcast. com*). Educational uses also abound. Restaurant management schools have video clips of napkin-folding techniques online, while musicology students no longer have to trek to the library to listen to recordings—the music is delivered to their dorm rooms on demand.

Preparing a video or audio program for distribution is not hard, but it is time consuming. The service provider must pass the raw data for the program into a high end personal computer (e.g., one with a 400 MHz Pentium) with enough disk space to hold several compressed versions. The computer encodes the data into a proprietary streaming format—usually creating several different output files to be used for users with different network bandwidth: one for users with 28 Kbps modems, one for users with 64 Kbps ISDN, another for users with a T1 connection, and so on. The encoded streams can either be stored in a disk file or passed to a streaming server on the Internet. Therefore, listening or viewing clients can get as much sound quality or video resolution as their network connection will support.

The Market

Streaming technology was a really hot market area for awhile, with RealNetworks and Vosaic attacking the middle of the road: medium bandwidth and medium resolution.

Real Networks created a separate client to play their recordings, and Vosaic built their player in Java so it automatically was downloaded with the stream. Another company, Vxtreme, created a client to go after the high-end market: high-quality sound and high-resolution video. This created the obvious problem: each vendor had different software, and one vendor's client wouldn't work with another vendor's server. As a result, streaming was more difficult to use than it had to be.

Netscape then included RealNetworks support in a browser release and war broke out. RealNetworks became the market leader. Vosaic became the Edsel: great technology, but it lost the market. Next Microsoft entered the fray. It gobbled up Vxtreme and included its technology into the Windows Media Player, which came out in the Internet Explorer package. It would play both RealNetworks' streams (as long as they weren't too new) and the Vxtreme format.

The latest salvo is RealNetworks version G2, which attempts to mitigate the problem of version changes. If you ask for a stream that your player does not know, it automatically goes to RealNetworks and downloads whatever modules are necessary to play it. Now, it's Bill Gates's turn to raise the bar once again.

RealNetworks

RealNetworks started out life as RealAudio and developed a product that distributed streaming audio over the Internet. Over the years the company has enhanced its product line to include both video distribution and an Internet service bureau to do distribution of netcasts. To listen to or view a RealNetworks stream, you must download and install the RealNetworks player. The basic software is free and available from *http://www.RealNetworks.com*. A deluxe version is available for $29 that includes more controls and the ability to save sound clips, but most people don't care about those things. We will look at the free version. (Another branch of their product line integrates streaming music with CD-quality MP3 capabilities. We will talk about that later in the chapter.)

The player installs easily using a wizard. The wizard informs your web browser to automatically start the player when you download RealNetworks files (ending in *.ra*, *.rm*, or *.ram*). The only critical bit of information is how you connect to the network. The choices range from corporate LAN through 14.4 Kbps modem; which one you pick determines both whether a program is available and how good it is once you get it. Make this selection based on actual expected capacity, not wishful thinking. If you have a 56 Kbps modem, but poor-quality phone lines force your Internet provider to connect at 9.6 Kbps, your modem will down-speed automatically and RealPlayer will think there is a much bigger pipe than there actually is. The result is that it will either complain while it is pre-reading the file, or perform poorly when it runs out of stream in the buffer.

Audio quality for typical modems is quite good; you can approach CD-ROM quality sound with a 28.8 Kbps modem. For audio, faster speeds won't increase quality as much as they will shorten the delay in buffering before the show starts. Video requires at least a 14.4 Kbps modem, and will be much happier at higher speeds. Most video source providers target 28.8 Kbps modems, because they are very common, and that's the lowest speed that gives reasonable quality. You'll get a picture that's about three inches square; it will be recognizable, but jerky if there is a lot of action.

The controls for the RealNetworks player are labeled much like a CD player. Figure 10-9 shows a RealNetworks program in mid-stream. From left to right, there is a **Play** button (arrow), the **Pause** button (double bar), and a **Stop** button. Next, there is a slider bar that allows you to move backward and forward in the content stream. The slider bar moves slowly to the right as playback proceeds. You can position yourself to a different part of the recording by dragging the slider bar with the mouse. The last button in that row allows you to hide everything but this control line. You may not want to show the whole RealNetworks window if you are in the middle of a stream that only contains audio.

Figure 10-9. Video stream in progress

In the Channels area, and in the **Presets** menu item, there are several built-in stream sources that you can choose. The ones on the main screen are mainly video streams; the menu bar has radio streams categorized by type of programming. You can listen or watch by clicking the one you want. The list of channels available on the main screen is dynamic, fetched from RealNetworks' Internet site. It is updated when you start the player. Should you want to see what is currently available, just click **Update** at the bottom of the section.

Between the Channels area and the viewing screen are some additional controls. The double arrows next to the word Channels causes the Channels area to disappear or reappear, making more room for the viewing area. Under that, the magnifying glass allows you to zoom the viewing area. Zooming makes the screen bigger but doesn't increase resolution; the more you zoom, the more pixelated the picture becomes. (The dots composing the picture become bigger and bigger until you can see them.) At the bottom of that column, you'll find a volume control and a **Mute** button.

At the very bottom, there is a status area that shows you how the network is doing. This example uses a 56 Kbps ISDN connection, so it chooses to use the 20.0 Kbps stream and to buffer 1 second worth of data. The icon next to the 20.0 Kbps shows an icon with the state of the connection. The right arrowhead shows that we are playing (it looks just like the **Play** button). It can also show that playback has stopped. A clock with spinning hands indicates that the player is waiting while it fills its buffer; a broken wire indicates network problems.

Finally, a link to the Excite Internet search engine helps you look for streams to watch or listen to. It works just like Excite's web search site and displays the results by firing up your browser. This collaboration was much touted in press releases, but it doesn't get you anything you couldn't have done before.

One bit of warning about both audio or video. Larger home computers are quite capable of playing a stream in background mode while doing other tasks. However, the nature of what you're doing can affect the quality. Editing a document may have some effect, but it should be minimal if your computer has sufficient horsepower. Downloading a big web page while you are playing a stream will obviously have an effect, because the player and your web browser will be competing for bandwidth. Most computers are designed to be very responsive to the mouse, so if you hold the mouse button down, the computer will be so intent on following the mouse it won't give other tasks the computing power they require. Playback may stop while the button is held—nothing bad, just an irritation. There is nothing you can do to fix this.

Serving RealNetworks content

RealNetworks makes its money from the server side. Servers are licensed according to the number of streams they can support concurrently. Basic 60-stream servers are free, but once you get addicted, the price goes up steeply: thousands of dollars for a few hundred streams, and tens of thousands of dollars for thousands of streams. There are some additional charges for management tools that allow you to allocate streams to particular programs or monitor your server. Other add-ons allow animated presentations for high-end distance-learning applications.

How many streams you need or can support is a really complicated question. The answer depends on your application and your willingness to let your clientele get a busy signal. If you have a hundred people in a German literature class and you want them to listen to a fifteen-minute poem before the next meeting, there is no reason to think you need a hundred-stream server. The odds are low that every student will connect during the same period, even the 15 minutes just prior to class. I would expect at most ten-active streams at any given time. On the other hand, if you are netcasting the

Rolling Stones concert in your town (remember to acquire the rights or you might get sued), you can expect every stream to be filled during the same two-hour period, regardless of how many streams you have.

Technically, there is no difference between the 60-stream server and the 1000-stream server except for a software lock. If you normally have a 60-stream application but occasionally require more, you can buy an *event key* from RealNetworks. For a couple hundred dollars, this key allows your server to provide a larger number of streams for 48 hours.

The real issue in capacity planning is not the software or the server; any reasonable Windows NT or Unix computer will do. The real limitation is the bandwidth of the server's network connection. RealNetworks' servers require a lot of network bandwidth. If two people in neighboring offices on Wall Street both want to listen to Allan Greenspan's speech in Washington, the server sends two identical streams from Washington to New York. If you do the multiplication, it's easy to see that it is easy to run out of bandwidth, even with a very fast connection. If you are distributing information streams within your company or campus, and you have few outside connections, this may not be a problem. If, however, you are providing coverage of a major news event, such as a presidential visit, you need a huge Internet pipe to your server. If your server has limited bandwidth, you can contract with RealNetworks to use its network. You provide the encoded stream to RealNetworks, usually over a dial-up ISDN connection, and it feeds the stream into its own server and worries about distribution bandwidth. So all these people who connect and waste bandwidth, waste theirs and not yours.

Microsoft Media Player

Microsoft's Media Player comes pre-installed with Internet Explorer on many PCs today. The Media Player plays a variety of stream formats, including RealNetworks and Vxtreme Web Theater. The player looks similar to RealNetworks' player, as Figure 10-10 shows.

Under the picture is a slider that allows you to position yourself in the stream. Under that are the familiar **Play**, **Pause**, and **Stop** buttons. Next to these are some buttons that allow you to fast forward and rewind, just like a VCR. On the far right are a **Mute** button and a volume control.

The bottom of the window shows some information about what is playing. It may be filled out, depending on how conscientious the provider has been. Here the clip name and copyright date are supplied. The last line is similar to the status line you have seen before. Here we see it is in the middle of buffering, and we are 11 seconds into a 29 minute 31 second clip.

Vxtreme Web Theater

Web Theater by Vxtreme is a high-end product that goes after as much resolution and fidelity as the connection allows. Vxtreme started out as a company of its own. If you

Figure 10-10. Microsoft's Media Player

look around the web, you will still see impressive sites that provide content in this format and give you a link to download the reader, but the actual reader is quite old. Most people use the Microsoft Media Player to view files of this format.

High-Quality Audio with MP3

As the technology of the Internet increases, the promise of making your computer a center of high-quality media that you can get online gets closer to fruition. Greater bandwidth will make downloading large video and audio files or receiving streaming media much more feasible for the average user. But as we wait for the promised broadband Internet access, the technology of encoding media that can be used on your computer continues to advance, giving us higher quality and using fewer bytes.

MP3—short for MPEG-1, audio layer 3—is a standard format for compressing audio into files that are vastly smaller than their uncompressed counterparts. The common suffix for these files is *.mp3*. MP3 files are small enough that they can be transferred easily over the average user's Internet connection. By turning raw sound data, such as Window's WAV files, into a compressed representation via a set of complex mathematical transformations, MP3 allows extremely high-quality audio to be transferred, stored, and categorized on almost any computer.

A five-minute song at standard CD quality expressed as raw data is:

44,100 (sampling rate)*2 (bytes per sample)*2 (channels)*60*5 = 52,920,000 bytes while a five-minute song compressed with MP3 with the usual encoding options is only:

128,000 (Kbps encoding rate, 2 channel)/8 bits per byte*60*5 = 4,800,000 bytes

The compressed version will sound nearly identical to the original, and subjectively, almost as good as a CD.

This is what makes MP3 so interesting. The ability to compress music into computer files that can be played back easily is neat but not very useful if they are too big to move from place to place easily, especially when CDs and tapes are both ubiquitous and portable. Three factors combine to make MP3 not just interesting, but important, at this moment in history:

- The computer is achieving ubiquity in American households, and most of them have sound output capability, as well as CD-ROM drives.

- The Internet is creating new, more decentralized models for commerce of all kinds.

- Consumers expect and get ever-increasing network bandwidth for a reasonable price.

MP3's compact nature coupled with networked computers in a rapidly increasing number of households makes MP3 a technology that will create a turning point in music distribution.

And this is exactly why the music industry, represented by the RIAA (Recording Industry Association of America), has focused its attention and legal resources on the MP3 format and the online community it has created. MP3 is just a file format, but as with almost any technology, it can be used in right and wrong ways. As you can imagine, it isn't very difficult to copy a song or two from one of your favorite CDs, encode it as MP3, and put it on a web site for free download or send it in email to twenty friends. Unless you have the permission of the copyright holder to reproduce and distribute her piece of music, you have violated copyright law.

You can understand that with the great power of the Internet to disseminate information widely and rapidly, the thought of music piracy via MP3s greatly worries record companies. In response, the RIAA has sought an injunction against the release of Diamond Multimedia's portable MP3 player, the RioPMP, and has aggressively moved to shut down web sites that offer illegal MP3s.

The primary complaint of the recording industry over MP3 is that it doesn't offer any protection against serial copying of copyrighted material. The same firestorm of complaint arose with the release of DAT tapes and CD recorders. From the recording industry's point of view, digital copying is a much more serious problem than copying analog tapes, because digital copies don't degrade. The industry was annoyed by people who copied audio cassettes and gave them to friends, but the problem was self-limiting: with analog technology, a copy wasn't as good as the original, even to a casual listener, and a copy of a copy was very low quality. Digital copies don't degrade and therefore can be handed down ad infinitum. A consortium of recording and technology companies has formed the Secure Digital Music Initiative (SDMI) to define a standard format that contains copyright information and a method to prevent copying. But it's doubtful whether such a format will be accepted by users who (legally or otherwise) are interested in trading music online.

MP3 threatens the music industry in other ways that are ultimately more interesting than bootleg reproductions of copyrighted material. Just as the Web allowed a profusion of online magazines, discussion forums, and other information outlets that weren't supported by the traditional print media, MP3 means that you no longer need a record contract to publish your band's CD. All you have to do is make the recording—at a commercial studio if you want, but you could do it at home—and distribute it via your web site. If you look at any of the MP3 sites listed at the end of this section, you'll see that most of the recordings come from first-rate artists who for one reason or another don't have a contract with a major record label. Now they don't need one.

MP3 is forcing the record industry to face the future of online digital music delivery. If you're interested in learning more about the potential of online delivery for changing the music industry, see *http://www.musicisum.com/learn.shtml*.

Playing MP3s

MP3s are obtained in a number of ways: downloaded from a web page, an FTP site, in an email attachment, on a disk, etc. Once you have the file on your computer, you need a program that can decode and play the file through your sound card.

MP3.com and other MP3 sites contain a long list of players that you can download and use. Many are shareware, while some are freeware. The most popular player is WinAmp (*http://www.winamp.com*). WinAmp, is easy to install and use, and it contains a number of advanced features, such as an equalizer, editable playlist, and a configurable interface (see Figure 10-11).

One of the most endearing qualities of WinAmp is the ability to use different *skins*— programmable, graphical interfaces that allow you to customize the look and feature display of the program. Many users in the MP3 community have created their own skins and make them available freely to others through the popular MP3 sites. Their are thousands of skins to choose from. For information on creating your own, see *http://www.winamp.com/skins/diy.html*.

Other media programs can play MP3s as well. Upcoming versions of Microsoft's Media Player and RealNetwork's RealPlayer support MP3 playback along with a multitude of other media formats (RealNetwork's offering is called RealJukebox). MP3 is also beginning to be used as a high-quality streaming format, although standard bandwidth is still a little small for this use.

Figure 10-11. WinAmp is one of the most popular MP3 players

Make Your Own MP3s

If you want to do more than just play MP3s, a variety of software allows you to make your own. At a minimum, you need an MP3 encoder. If you have created your own music, and it is stored on your computer as a WAV file or other format, an encoder program will convert it to an MP3 of the quality you desire (i.e., the sample rate).

You can also create MP3s from your CD collection (which is completely legal for personal use). Programs called CD "rippers" take tracks played by your computer's CD-ROM drive and store them in electronic form on your hard drive. The resulting files can be encoded as MP3.

Many software utilities combine ripping, encoding, playback, etc., all into one. Check out AudioCatalyst from Xing Technology (*http://audiocatalyst.com*) and MusicMatch Jukebox (*http://www.musicmatch.com*) for a few popular examples.

As the MP3 format gains wider acceptance, bigger software companies are stepping into the ring with their own MP3 applications. RealNetworks draws on its wide user base to support its upcoming RealJukebox.

Working in conjunction with RealPlayer, RealJukebox is a powerhouse application for doing all things MP3 on your computer. You can automatically MP3 encode your CDs as you listen to them, create playlists of MP3 tracks, and create an organized database of music on your PC (see Figure 10-12). It can also perform web searches for tracks, and in the future intends to be the primary application through which you can purchase online music.

MP3 on the Run

Digitally encoded music is great when you want to listen to music at your computer and create a database of your record collection, but you probably want to hear that

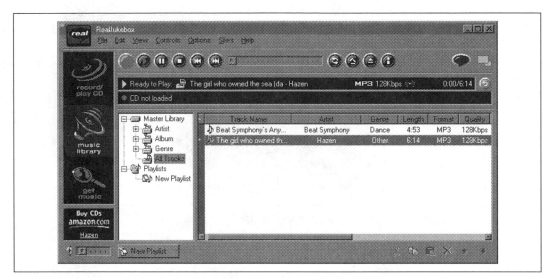

Figure 10-12. RealNetwork's RealJukebox can control the music on your computer

music elsewhere, don't you? At the end of 1998, Diamond Multimedia released the first portable MP3 player in the United States—the RioPMP.

The small (2.5 oz) device allows you to transfer MP3 files from your computer to the flash memory of the device, capable of storing up to 60 minutes of music. MP3 has been freed from your computer and is perfectly suited to headphone listening during your subway commute or morning run. Best of all, since the player doesn't use moving parts, motion-induced skipping doesn't occur.

Many other companies have released or plan to release portable MP3 players. Creative Labs has the Nomad; Eiger Labs the MPMan; RCA has announced the upcoming Lyra; portable music king Sony will undoubtedly make its offerings soon. In addition to portable devices, many other music components are being planned to support MP3 playback. There are already car stereo peripherals that can play MP3s from disks. Stereo components with MP3 support have also been planned.

MP3's Big Brother

At the beginning of this section, we noted that MP3 was really only a part of a larger format called MPEG-1. MPEG stands for the *Motion Picture Experts Group*; this group works on encoding formats for video and audio. A successor to the original MPEG format is used on DVDs and satellite transmission.

You can find MPEG players for just about any computing platform; many MP3 software sites have links to MPEG software. The results can be very impressive. Unfortunately, there aren't anywhere near as many MPEG files available as MP3 files and for a good reason. Although MPEG does a good job of compression (MPEG files are one third to one quarter the size of the equivalent QuickTime file, in my experience), the files are still huge—on the order of 3 to 4 MB per minute of running time. Therefore, an MPEG file that's more than a brief sample takes a long time to download, even with the fastest home connections available. And you couldn't save more than a few on even the largest disk drives.

There aren't many sites that collect MPEG files—probably because of the file size. The material you'd want to watch with MPEG also tends to be copyrighted. There are many garage bands with access to all the equipment you need to make an MP3 file, but making a video and converting it to MPEG requires a movie studio, plus digital video-editing equipment. These aren't toys that most of us have access to. For all of these reasons, MPEG remains an interesting curiosity. But with better compression algorithms, faster connections, and even larger disks than we have now, a future version of MPEG could become as commonplace as MP3.

Useful Sites

A sizable and excitable community has grown up around MP3 on the Web since the music format first became available.Musicians can have their music heard by posting it in MP3 format on web sites. Some web sites serve as a collection of MP3s made available by the artists. Many songs can be downloaded for free. If you like the music, links are provided to where you can purchase the artist's CD. Other sites have been created to provide technical resources for creating and playing MP3s, and still others provide powerful search engines to find the music you want on the Net. Check out the following links:

Music, News, and Software
http://www.mp3.com
http://www.mp3now.com

Search for MP3s
http://mp3.lycos.com
http://www.2look4.com

Software
http://www.winamp.com
http://www.real.com/realjukebox
http://www.xaudio.com
http://www.mpegtv.com

PortablePortals
http://www.rioport.com
http://www.nomadmusic.com

Push Technologies

Push technologies are so named because they reverse the normal method of accessing information. All the other Internet technologies let you select what you want and download (or pull) it to your computer. With push technologies, you tell the system where your interests lie, and the servers automatically push information matching your criteria to your computer. The theory is that most Internet connections are too slow to let you read something organized like a traditional newspaper comfortably. But most people only read the newspaper once a day, so why not configure your machine to download all the news that you might have an interest in its spare time? When you read the news later, it will have been pre-loaded.

There are two companies doing a lot in this area. They have distinctly different operating models. Pointcast's (*http://www.pointcast.com*) primary focus is to supply canned news items; these can be merged with corporate or group information. Castanet from Marimba (*http://www.marimba.com*) was designed to be a corporate intranet management tool. It combines the canned content sections of Pointcast with some system management and software-distribution features.

Pointcast

The Pointcast system is fairly complex technically, but it is easy to use. Think of Pointcast as a way to subscribe to magazines. Unlike printed magazines, you don't have to subscribe to the whole thing; you can subscribe to any portion you want and only get those parts. Pointcast's content is organized around a series of channels; each channel is like as a separate magazine. Within each channel are a series of subchannels, which can be viewed as the different sections of the magazine. For example, the CNN channel is divided into general categories, like news and features. Within news, you can subscribe to world news, U.S. news, or politics. Within features, you can subscribe to science and technology, travel, or health.

To start using Pointcast, you must download a 4.2 MB client from Pointcast's web site (*http://www.pointcast.com*). After the download, you start the installer, which creates the programs you need and starts a registration and configuration wizard. On the second and third pages of the configuration, you are asked a number of demographic and interest questions. This is the first step in deciding what kinds of content you would like to see. Each client can receive up to nine channels; your answers determine which channels you initially receive. During the installation process, you will be asked which browser you want to use. The articles in Pointcast are actually just web pages; you can use IE, Netscape, or a built-in browser to view the content. You can change your choice later, but you are probably better off using the internal browser if you are going to be reading a lot of news. It is well integrated into the product, and you won't have to pay the memory penalty from having so many applications running at the same time.

You will also be asked what kind of Internet connection you have. This is used to pick a good default for the automatic update interval. Push technologies try to download the content to your hard disk before you want it, minimizing network delays. If you have a LAN connection that's active all the time, Pointcast can set the download interval very frequently. If you are a dial-up user, it will update only upon demand. You can change the frequency whenever you want, but Pointcast tries to pick an appropriate update strategy based on your answers.

Now you have a Pointcast application running on your computer (Figure 10-13), a stock ticker-like display, and a screensaver install that all tell you, "No data is available. Click **Update All** button to get latest information."

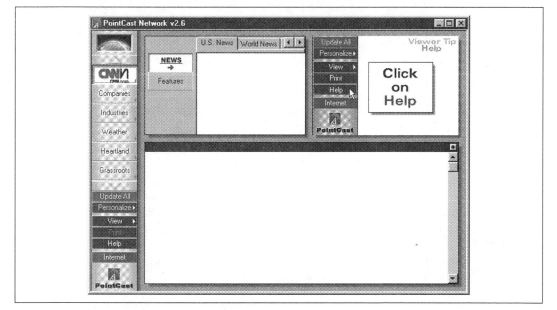

Figure 10-13. Running a Pointcast application

Don't do it! It will cause your client to contact a Pointcast server and start downloading news items out the wazoo (about 14 MB worth). On a 28.8 Kbps modem, the download will take forever. Fine-tune your content selection before starting the initial download. Don't worry after the initial download; the updates are far more reasonable in size. Only the first one is a killer.

The channels you are subscribed to as a result of the interests you expressed during the installation are listed on the left side of the screen. Figure 10-13 shows that we subscribed to CNN, Industries, Weather, Heartland, and Grassroots. There are actually ten channels in all, but to see the rest you must use the up and down scroll arrows on the top and bottom of the list. To modify this channel list, click the **Personalize** button and selectively add or remove channels, using the screen shown in Figure 10-14.

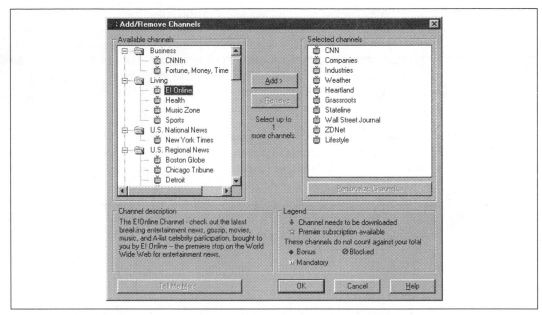

Figure 10-14. Channel selection

Most channels are associated with traditional media. For example, there are channels associated with the Wall Street Journal, E!, parenting, sports, and special events (Olympics, elections, etc.). You add a channel by selecting the channel in the left pane and pressing the **Add** button to move it to the right pane. Removing is just the opposite: select on the right and press **Remove**. Here we are about to add E! Online to those we already have. If you are not sure what a channel is, when you highlight it in the left pane, a synopsis appears in the lower-left corner of the window.

Notice the key in the lower-right corner. It gives you a clue to some of the other features of Pointcast. Premier channels (which I have never seen yet) are channels you must pay to view. Bonus channels are channels that are being promoted, so Pointcast has waived the channel number restriction for receiving them.

The rest of the key needs a longer explanation. When your Pointcast server starts initially, it goes to a pre-configured server. That initial server examines the IP address of your computer. If that address is under the control of an organization participating in the Pointcast network (e.g., your employer), it passes the connection off to the organization's local server. This does two things: it minimizes network utilization and gives that organization some control over what you can subscribe to. Your employer might decide that some channels (such as a your corporate channel) are mandatory; others (such as E! Online) might be restricted. There is nothing you can do to get around these limitations. After all, the organization is paying for the Internet connection you are using.

The content provider for each channel determines the channel's substructure. For example, the Wall Street Journal channel gives you the option of selecting or ignoring Front Page, Tech Center, Marketplace... articles. You select these subtopics in the **Personalize** menu; this time, select **Personalize channels**. There you will see a screen with a tab for each channel you selected. Click the tab of the channel you want to customize. It will show you the available subchannels as a series of checkboxes. Check the ones you want.

You should pick minimal content for the first go around. Until you get a feel for how you will use Pointcast, it's not worth downloading a lot of stuff you might never read. Adding a channel is easy, and adding them later will break the initial download up into more palatable chunks.

When you think that you've decided what you want to see, press the **Update All** button and wait for the news to start rolling in. The **Update All** button turns into a **Stop** button while the download proceeds. If you get tired of waiting or are called away and must disconnect, you can stop the download without losing the progress you have made. Pointcast knows what it has on your hard drive; when it resumes, it will start downloading only those stories that it needs.

Once the download is complete, you can read whatever you want. The basic Pointcast screen is shown in Figure 10-15. There are four areas. On the left are the buttons that control channels, updates, and personalization. The channel selectors are radio buttons; the button that is selected will have its textual label replaced by a cute icon.

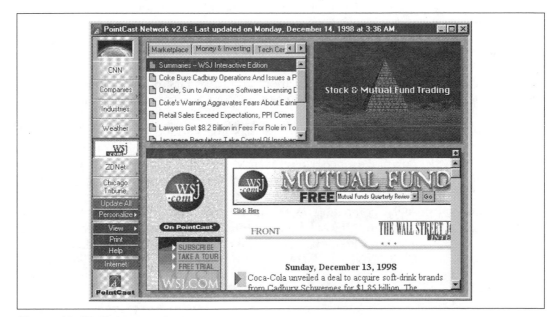

Figure 10-15. Pointcast viewing screen

In the top center of the screen top is the **Channel content** menu. It is very much like reading a newsgroup or discussion group. The tabs at the top of the screen determine which subchannel is selected. The number of tabs and their labels change depending on the channel and which subchannels you've decided to follow. As you click a tab, the headlines of the articles available in that subchannel appear below. If one of these piques your interest, you can select it by clicking on it. When you do, the content is displayed on the lower panel. Finally, the upper right displays Pointcast announcements and advertisements. It's the price you pay for using the system.

Those are the basics of using Pointcast, but you may still find it a bit intrusive without further personalizing. Go to the **Personalize** menu and select **Applications Settings**. The first thing you may want to change is the update schedule. If you are on a continuously connected computer, you can pick any schedule you would like; for dial-up connections, pick "on demand." This means it only updates when you click the **Update All** button. The last thing you need is for it to start an automatic update when you connect on another high-priority mission.

The Pointcast client comes with two other pieces. The first is a stock ticker that you can configure into your system. If you do, the headlines of the channels you have selected constantly scroll across the bottom of your screen. If you miss a headline, you can put your mouse over the ticker, hold down the button, and drag the ticker back to see what has gone off the screen. If a headline grabs your interest, you can double-click on it to see the story. The second utility is a screensaver that displays headlines of topics to which you have subscribed. It is a fairly complete screensaver that goes away with any keyclick, but if you click on one of the headlines with the mouse, it immediately displays the story. The screensaver is sometimes incompatible with energy-efficient auto-shutdown monitors, and saving your screen may demand a reboot.

There are a few final things to remember about Pointcast. First, information the screensaver or the ticker displays is only as recent as your update schedule. If you only download once a day, then you will be displaying the same stale news all day long. Second, each update downloads material that has been added or changed since the last update. The less often your schedule does downloads, the longer each download will take. If you do download once a day, it may take 20 minutes, but if you download hourly, each update may take only two minutes. It is up to you to determine what schedule is more convenient and better meets your needs. Finally, Pointcast channels are supposedly compatible with Internet Explorer's channels, which do approximately the same thing. If you select a Pointcast channel from within IE, you get a screen very similar to a Pointcast screen, but I found it to be less likely to perform well and very likely to abort. If you want the functionality of Pointcast, download its client.

Pointcast servers

If you think you'd like to create a Pointcast area server for your school or corporation, there are a couple of things you must consider. First, there can be only one corporate channel for any area. Areas are defined by IP addresses and aren't allowed to overlap. You can't decide to create a sales channel or a dormitory channel if your corporation or campus has claimed your address and is providing a channel already. However, if your administration is flexible, you should be able to lobby for a departmental subchannel on the corporate channel. It's easy to set up a subchannel; the server is capable of delegating authority for the subchannel. The server administrator enters a URL at the beginning of a channel; whoever can update that URL can create content on the subchannel. Not surprisingly, the content that Pointcast displays is in HTML, so if you are already creating web pages, creating the channel or subchannel may be all you need to do to distribute your pages through Pointcast. See Chapter 9 for more information.

The server allocated to Pointcast needs to be hefty enough to handle the load, which usually varies throughout the day. Problems can arise if you are providing Pointcast over a corporate network, because employees tend to share similar work habits. For example, let's say that everyone gets to work at 8 a.m. and turns on his or her PCs. Suddenly, every employee in the company is trying to download the company news, and the old machine that you managed to grab for the server is brought to its knees. As the administrator, you can control the users' download cycle and fix this, but it's just one more thing to worry about.

Castanet

To a subscriber, Castanet by Marimba appears to be very similar to Pointcast. You download a client; when you install it you can subscribe to various channels. The difference becomes apparent only when you examine the way channels work, and what their capabilities are. Pointcast is designed to distribute information and make it readily available. Castanet is designed to distribute applications and make them readily available. The confusion results because many Castanet applications merely distribute information.

Applications are written in Java using a toolkit called Bongo, which has all the requirements to provide a secure, distributed database application. Maybe a hypothetical example is in order. If your company used Castanet, it could create a channel for vacation and sick-leave reporting. If you want some time off, you could fire up the channel; it would prompt you for the request and forward it to a database at corporate headquarters. If the company decided to change the application, next time you used the channel it would automatically download the newer version.

There are certainly other ways to accomplish this. What Castanet really buys you is minimization of download time and application configuration management. The channels (i.e., the Java programs), reside on your computer permanently (or for as long as you subscribe). Therefore, if no changes have taken place, submitting a vacation request requires your starting a program on the local disk (fast) and uploading a few bytes (fast) to the server. Doing the same thing with a web page would require downloading the web page, possibly including a Java applet, images, and other things, before you could even start working.

When you download the client, it knows how to contact a Castanet directory channel that gives you lists of canned applications. These include channels for personal finance, business, distributing information, and game playing. Depending on the channel you pick, you may get a simple program or one that cooperates with other computers across the Internet. And they are all quite responsive because only the data needs to be transmitted. (Check out the classic games section; it allows you to play euchre, go, and chess against others across the world).

Futures

The future for the Internet is certainly bright. So many people are trying to develop new technologies, and new applications for current technologies, that predicting what might happen is certainly impossible. But that doesn't mean we can't try. Here are a few trends that are certain to continue into the future.

Connection Speed: Getting Faster and Slower

For the past 10 years, one goal of telecommunications has been to bring the communication speed available on a LAN to the user at home. This trend is driven by application developers who design their products to push the leading edge of what's available, assuming that the leading edge will be commonplace "real soon." If you access the Net over a modem from home you see this every day. Everything you want to do on the Web takes just long enough to be irritating. If the standard speed for a home modem is 28.8 Kbps, people design their applications to perform okay at 28.8 Kbps but wonderfully at 56 Kbps. When the standard moves to 56 Kbps, they start designing for people with 128 Kbps connections or higher. The human situation is meant to be frustrated by other humans controlling the technology.

At long last, the telephone companies and cable TV companies are bringing megabit speeds to the home—light at the end of the tunnel. For telephones, the technology is called ADSL, which stands for *Asymmetric Digital Subscriber Loop*; in telephone vernacular, this means a digital line to your home. This is a 1 megabit connection back to your Internet provider at prices far lower than ever seen before. Also, each major cable TV company is trying to provide high-speed Internet service over its cable network, using so-called *cable modems*. Cable modems usually offer higher speeds than ADSL, but that speed is shared with everyone else on the network. Both ADSL and cable modems are available in major metropolitan areas. However, if you are waiting for your mom-and-pop phone company to bring ADSL to Cass Lake, Minnesota, you've still got a long time to wait.

For the first time in a while, however, people are also worrying about the other end of the spectrum: low-speed communication. This is being pushed by palmtop devices and wireless communication. Wireless communication is nice because there are many frequencies to share and it doesn't require much infrastructure (no wire and cable to lay). However, it is hard to make shared wireless media go fast and be widely available. Think of cellular phones. They require communication speeds roughly similar to the speeds used by home modems in use today. Even in smaller cities, the cellular phone system is saturated. If you wanted to communicate faster, fewer people could use the system simultaneously.

Most of these wireless applications work fine at low speed. If you toss out large attachments and formatted content, email works fine on 2,400 baud modems, and so do most other palmtop applications. But why take a working system and leave it be? Now palmtops are coming ready to run Windows CE, a Microsoft operating system designed for small devices. So rather than being just email and a calendar, your pocket device will be able to get just as bogged down as your desktop computer.

One thing you may want from a wireless palmtop computer is the ability to control devices in your home. Companies are starting to produce device controllers that are accessible over the Internet. You'll be able to turn up the heat when you leave work, start the microwave when you are 10 minutes away from home, and start the dishwasher from the theater after your gourmet microwave dinner. The system will probably use your home computer as the Internet device and talk to the actual controllers at each appliance through an adapter that runs between the PC's serial port and the home power wiring. Your home computer is involved because you want a bit of authentication and security, so that your neighbor whom you have been feuding with over your property line doesn't turn up your heat to get you angry. You also may want to provide customization limiting what the controllers might do. This will place unprecedented demands for many small messages by many subscribers on the wireless system. And what we have now won't support it—yet.

XML and Tools for Interchanging Online Data

People who produce web pages today spend half of their time writing the content, and the other half trying to figure out how to trick HTML into doing what they want it to do. HTML was designed to have enough functionality to be useful, but simple enough for browsers on smaller home computers to interpret it. Now with the Web taking off and computers getting more powerful, people are clamoring for a more powerful way to define web pages: a new and improved markup language.

Purists say that we already have the be-all and end-all in markup languages: SGML, the *Standard Generalized Markup Language*. The problem is that with all of this generality comes an amazing amount of complexity. As a result, the number of people who have used SGML and have lived to tell about it remains small. Nevertheless, it's useful to think about the rationale behind SGML, because the creators of HTML were certainly familiar with their work.

SGML allows someone to define a group of tags for marking up text. This definition is called a DTD, a *Document Type Definition*. It turns out that HTML is just a particular DTD within the SGML family, and current browsers only know how to interpret this subset of the family. Think of trying to write a program to play card games. You could write a program that knows that there an arbitrary number of cards in the deck and allow the players to define the rules, including the nature of the deck (How many cards? How many suits?) for each game they want to play. Or you could write a game to play five-card stud poker. The first program would be very hard to write, slow, and hard to use. You would spend most of your time defining rules for games rather than playing the games. The second would be fast, and could be learned in a few minutes, but it's only useful if all you want to play is five-card stud.

XML, the *Extensible Markup Language*, tries to split the difference. It is SGML compliant, although it deletes many of SGML's more exotic features. As a result, it's much easier for a computer to process and for a human to understand. To continue our analogy, it is a program that allows all types of poker to be played.

What is nice about XML is that everything that already exists in HTML will still work. Someone has created a DTD for HTML, the definition of HTML, in XML. When the new XML-compliant browsers come out in the next year, they will know how to get that DTD. So, if you have an HTML page and don't care about no stinking extensions, it will work just fine. If you want to provide the latest and greatest in formatting, you can take the HTML DTD and add whatever bells and whistles you would like.

The real value of XML won't be in marking up text. People will probably stick with HTML for that task. What's interesting about XML is the added functionality it provides. One example of this is self-describing data. For example, you know you can get recipes from the Internet; you know that there are web sites that let you submit a shopping list and magically make the food appear at your doorstep. Why can't you select salad, main course, and dessert recipes from three different sites, tell your browser to compute a shopping list sufficient to make dinner for twelve, and submit the result to the grocery store automatically? The problem is that HTML doesn't tell you what the data means. An XML DTD can define tags that say things like "This is an ingredient; its units are ounces. This is the number of servings in one batch." When a recipe is coded using these tags, it becomes obvious what the information in the recipe means. An XML-compliant browser could download your recipes, analyze them, figure out what you need to buy, and generate a shopping list automatically.

One important extension to XML is the ability to digitally sign pages. It's easy to go to the Web and search for a price list for O'Reilly books. But how do you know that the price list really came from O'Reilly aside from the URL? After all, URLs aren't fool-proof. It's possible for someone to trick a browser into believing that a bogus page containing misleading data came from O'Reilly's URL. Digital signatures are a cryptographic means of locking a page so that no one but the author can make undetectable changes, even if the page moves to another URL. A digital signature allows you to ask, "Did O'Reilly really author this document?" and have complete confidence that the answer is correct. This comes out of a marriage of a technology called X.509 digital certificates and XML.

If you would like to track XML's progress, visit the World Wide Web Consortium's home page at *http://www.w3c.org.*

X.509 Certificates

In everyday life, how do you prove who you are? You pull out an ID: a passport, driver's license, corporate ID card, or something equivalent. Up until now, the Internet hasn't had any concept of an ID card. For the most part, Internet users believed that email addresses and web URLs were always trustworthy—even though we knew this wasn't really true. Five years ago, there wasn't much money changing hands over the Internet, so the consequences of a bogus email address or web site were limited: at worst, you might be the victim of a practical joke. But these days, with billions of dollars changing hands and credit card numbers flying back and forth, you really want some assurance that the people you're doing business with are who they say they are. The most likely solution to this problem is the X.509 certificate.

An X.509 certificate is an encrypted piece of data that says who you are and vouches for your identity. This is no different from the real world: my driver's license is nothing more than Illinois' Department of Motor Vehicles saying, "the person pictured here is Ed Krol." Most businesses have enough faith in this form of ID to allow me to write checks. A similar model applies on the Internet. There is no DMV, but a number of companies exist that issue certificates. You pay these companies some money, they verify who you are to their satisfaction, and they issue a certificate. (Two companies offering this service are VeriSign and Thawte; their URLs are *http://www.verisign.com* and *http://www.thawte.com.*) The worth of your certificate is only as good as the faith the recipient has in the issuing authority; there's nothing to stop you from issuing your own certificates. Of course, nobody is obliged to believe your certificate any more than they are obliged to believe a driver's license from the state of Krolconner. You can configure your browser to accept certificates automatically from a variety of sources.

The problem with a real driver's license is that it can be forged. To prevent forgery, states do things like add holograms to the license, so they can't be run through a copier. Similarly, if the license looks like it has been physically tampered with, you may find people who refuse to accept it as a valid ID. That's why digital certificates use cryptography. Without going into the technical details, cryptography guarantees that the certificate cannot be altered after it is issued. Software can easily detect alterations to the certificate and tell you that you're about to do business with a fraudulent entity.

Now that certificates exist, how do you use them? You probably have been using them already. Whenever you download software from Microsoft, your browser pops up a window that says, "This product has Microsoft's certificate attached, vouched for by

Microsoft." This prevents someone from releasing a pirate version of Internet Explorer that helps them to steal your credit card numbers or do something else hostile. You know that this file came from Microsoft and they say so; when you are big your word means something. (Whether you trust genuine Microsoft software not to do something hostile is another question.) Seriously, it would not be terribly difficult to create a self-signed certificate that appeared to be from Microsoft, but anyone stupid enough to do that should expect to spend a lot of money on highly paid lawyers. (Even more seriously, your old version of Internet Explorer knows what a certificate signed by Microsoft should look like. You could create a bogus self-signed Microsoft certificate, but it wouldn't be able to fool any software that had seen a real Microsoft certificate. Cryptography is wonderful.)

The Microsoft example demonstrates only half of the solution. Admittedly, it's an important half: you want to be sure that Internet vendors are who they say they are before making a purchase. But how do you prove your identity to a vendor? The same technology solves the problem. Although they're not common yet, you will soon start to see personal certificates. Once you have one, when you boot your machine and give the certificate's PIN (just to make sure someone else didn't just start using your machine), you can use the certificate to prove your identity.

Electronic Books

In 10 years, many of us will be sitting in our home-networked rocking chairs telling the younger generations, via a video phone call, how we used to buy music on compact discs, trade stocks by calling our brokers on a regular phone, and read books printed on paper. Maybe. A high-speed, universal Internet promises to change the way we do many things in our lives, and many of these promises are starting to be realized. Software is a natural product to be sold over a network. The MP3 craze has forced record companies to develop schemes to sell and distribute music online. For physical items, you can place an order and make a payment online. But your groceries can't be downloaded. The trend is that if a product can be digitized, why should it continue to cling to its physical medium? Get ready to curl up with an electronic book before you go to bed at night.

An electronic book, at its simplest, is just computer data containing the text of a book. More intricate encoding and markup tags may contain formatting information and ensure copyright protection as well. On this level, an *ebook* is really not such a technological achievement. Almost every document produced currently exists as computer data at some point in its existence, unless it is written by hand or on a typewriter.

What is new about electronic books is that they are sold and delivered via a network, and they require a new type of medium for pleasurable reading. Buying an electronic book saves you a trip to the bookstore and space on your bookshelf, but do you really want to read it on your computer screen? Probably not. Printed books are very comfortable to use and portable. A device that allows you to read electronic books will have to have the same qualities and some advantages to make it desirable to use.

One of these devices is the Rocket eBook. Slightly bigger than a handheld computer like the PalmPilot, the Rocket eBook downloads books from your computer so you can read them on its 5 x 3-inch LED screen. The Rocket eBook is capable of storing up to 4,000 pages of text, so instead of carrying around several books, this one device holds them all. You can page through books with buttons on the side of the screen. A stylus is included so you can use the menus on the touch screen, which provide capabilities such as bookmarking pages, annotating passages, searching, and adjusting the font size. At roughly the same size as a small paperback, you can read comfortably from any position. You can adjust the orientation of the page to accommodate you whether you are right- or left-handed or sitting at a desk.

The display can also be backlit so you can read without a nightlight. All in all, it is a very usable device—certainly a departure from paper-bound books, but it does have its own charm. Although the primary purpose of the Rocket eBook is book reading, you can also download and view web pages on it, along with other formatted documents. See *http://www.rocket-ebook.com*.

While the Rocket eBook is intended for leisurely electronic reading, other devices are geared towards for more professional electronic documentation. Glassbook, Inc. and SoftBook Press are two companies that look to provide technical and corporate information in electronic form via notebook PCs, handheld computers, and their own reading devices.

Glassbook (*http://www.glassbook.com*) is producing its own electronic reading devices much like the Rocket eBook. Additionally, it has formed the Open Electronic Book Exchange (*http://www.ebxwg.org*), which it is pushing as an industry standard for distribution and copyright protection of electronic books. Glassbook's software supports Adobe PDF documents, as well as Microsoft's HTML-based Open eBook specification, and it provides a structure for publishers to convert their products to electronic form and sell them online.

The SoftBook Electronic Book (*http://www.softbook.com*) is an LCD-screened device that is tablet-sized and provides its own built-in modem for downloading documentation from the SoftBookstore or another SoftBook server containing your particular organization's documents.

With the continuing popularity of handheld computing devices, a standard electronic format, and increased online commerce, ebooks could be the future of publishing.

Standard Ways of Doing Tasks

You wouldn't want to go out and buy a $200 electronic book reader that would only allow you to read O'Reilly books. You really would want a general electronic book player that accepts books from any publisher. For this to work, a standard format for the book must be agreed upon. As long as both ends are standards compliant, it won't matter who built them. This is what has made the Internet as powerful and useful as it is today: open interoperability standards.

In practice, the way this works is that one company produces a device (say, an Internet-accessible thermostat) that you control from any computer on the Internet, providing that it runs the company's software. Another company builds an oven controller that requires its oven control software package. The marketplace says these things are really neat, but it would be cheaper and more convenient for me to have one software package that controls everything. To make your computer, the oven controller, the thermostat controller, and other accessories work together, a home-device standards group springs up in the Internet Engineering Task Force (IETF). Here any companies developing products (all thinking their idea is God's gift to standards that will be adopted en masse) and any other interested parties get together and craft a standard that eventually gets adopted. Any manufacturer can then produce a product for either side of the communication path, and they should all work together.

I went through this scenario to illustrate that standards don't come automatically, certainly not at the beginning of a technology's life span. If you look at the standards that are being developed in the IETF today, you would probably say, "I would have thought those would have been standardized a long time ago." Standards are still being developed for network printing (wouldn't it be nice to be able to access a printer without having to add special print drivers?) and calendar interoperability (to allow you to access your company's Outlook server from a client you happen to like better). It takes demand and competition to initiate the standards process, and the process takes years to complete, so we actually aren't doing as badly as people think.

If you look at the standards under development now, you should realize that few of them are new communications facilities; most are repackaging of old ones: telephone to Internet telephone, television to streaming, and business meetings to net meetings. They are all 1998 remakes of the 1950s classics. The driving factor for these applications is not vision by the authors or some new technological discovery. The thing that made all of this possible is the lack of a time- and distance-based tariff for using the Internet. NetMeeting could easily have been produced to work over standard dial-up telephone calls. Some business folks would have used it, and the quality would be more predictable. Yet the motivation came from people wanting to connect to friends, family, and business associates cheaply. So if you want to predict what's next to make it on the Internet, try looking to the old.

CHAPTER ELEVEN

CONNECTION STRATEGIES

Throughout this book, we've described how the Internet works. By now, you've probably realized that the network is not infallible.

Eventually, when you send email, you'll see a message like the one in Figure 11-1.

Figure 11-1. What's up?

Now what?

You don't have to be an ace technician to deal with this situation, but you do need some guidance about networking in the face of adversity. First, we'll talk about what usually breaks, then about what you need to know to attack a problem. After that, we'll give you a reasonable approach to dealing with common network problems. It's not an exhaustive guide. We could easily construct scenarios that would lead you astray with this approach, but they would not be common in real life.

Some of the solutions we offer sound extremely simplistic. If you read this chapter when there is nothing wrong (and you should), you might think, "I'm not stupid. Of course I'd check the power cord." It's not that we think you're dumb. It's that we've all done the dumb things. When the pressure is on, people lose common sense, and often forget the most common-sense trouble spots. We've all wasted time trying to fix some non-existent exotic problem, when the real issue turned out to be amazingly simple.

We'll also discuss a different kind of problem: what to do when your Internet connection works but isn't up to snuff. This section is about entering the world of high-speed networking. This world used to be the exclusive province of universities and large corporations, but some new developments, like cable modem have opened it up to the home user. We obviously can't tell you how to order and install the equipment, but we can give you an introduction into the technologies that are available.

Finally, we'll discuss networking you can control: that within your own home. If you've got two or three computers, a printer, and a need for a high-speed Internet connection, you might save yourself a lot of time and aggravation by linking those computers together. It's easier and cheaper than you think.

The Ground Rules

When you're thinking about what's wrong with the network, there are two rules to keep in mind: the cheaper the component, the more likely it is to fail and the less likely it is to be noticed by someone who is able to fix it. You need to know what's right before you can figure out what's wrong

What do these rules mean? The Internet is frequently described as a cloud.* It's a vague, poorly defined thing (at least from your perspective—obviously, it's extremely well defined to the people responsible for making it work) that somehow takes data packets from your computer and carries them to some destination computer. You don't know (and usually don't care) how packets get from one part of the cloud to another. You don't even know what it's made of; you can assume that the cloud consists of many computers and high-speed telephone lines, but these days it also includes satellites, radio links, and even large parts of the cable TV network.

Think about this cloud in the context of the first rule (see Figure 11-2). As you move away from your computer, you know less and less about what happens to your data, and the data travels over more and more expensive equipment. The computer in your den probably cost less than $3,000; it's connected to a $150 modem that's connected to the telephone network by a cable that's worth $10 at the most. Your ISP, the point of contact between you and the cloud, probably uses modems that are similar to yours, servers that may have cost $10,000, and specialized phone lines that cost a few hundred dollars a month. If you looked into the workings of the cloud itself—that vague thing that makes up "the rest of the Internet"—you'd find routers and switches that cost hundreds of thousands of dollars, even more expensive phone lines, fiber-optic links, and exotic communications satellites that cost millions of dollars.

---

* The cloud is often called the Internet *backbone*, and that term may help you visualize it better. But no vertebrate ever had a backbone as complex or as subject to change as the Internet's. A backbone may be easier to visualize, but it's not a very good picture of what's actually out there.

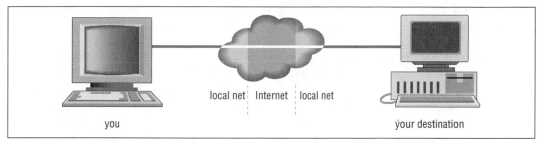

Figure 11-2. The Internet cloud

Now let's think about where failures occur and who's affected when problems occur. If your modem breaks, no one cares but you. Your ISP isn't going to call and say, "Gee, you haven't been online much lately. Is everything okay?" If you're in an office, it's conceivable that your system administrator will notice that your computer has gone offline and show up in your office to replace a faulty cable before you're even aware of the problem—but more likely, you have to track down the system administrator yourself, and get her to find time on her schedule to fix your problem.

If something breaks on your ISP's network, or if there's a more general failure on your local network, a reasonably large number of people will be affected. There's a good chance that some system administrator will notice the problem before you, particularly if it occurs during working hours. And it may even be fixed within two or three hours, particularly if it's not very serious.

Finally, what happens if something breaks in the cloud (i.e., the Internet backbone) itself? Although the cloud seems poorly defined to you, when it breaks, hundreds of thousands (if not millions) of people are inconvenienced, millions of dollars worth of equipment is sitting idle, and lots of businesses are losing real money. Therefore, the cloud is monitored extremely closely, 24 hours a day, 7 days a week. If some piece of equipment breaks, special monitoring software notices the problem and informs the engineer that's in charge of fixing it before you even know there's a problem. Routers automatically recompute the paths over which your data travels so that your data avoids the broken part of the network. In short, when something breaks in the cloud, you usually don't even notice it.

What does this mean when you sit down at your computer, try to browse the Rolling Stones web site, and nothing happens? Most unexpected network outages occur fairly close to the ends: either around your computer or the one you are trying to reach. It may be in your computer or between your computer and the wall, but the closer you get to the cloud, the less likely the problem is to occur. This doesn't mean that problems are always your fault. There is a destination computer sitting just as far from the cloud as you are, somewhere else in the world. The problem is just as likely to be on the other end. And, on rare occasions, there are problems with the Internet itself. But that should be your last assumption, not your first.

When something goes wrong, your major goal often won't be fixing the problem. If you can, great, but more often than not, the problem will be something you can't control. This is where the cloud starts: wherever the network gets beyond your control. In that case, your goal becomes figuring out when you can expect it to be fixed. Do you sit at your computer at midnight banging on the Enter key, or do you go into the living room (or go home, if you're at an office) and watch David Letterman? If it's 10 p. m. and you deduce that the problem's a bad cable, you can probably go watch Letterman; you probably will not be successful in finding a replacement cable before morning. If you're trying to access a web server that's temporarily offline until 11 p.m., you might stay at your computer and play some network chess.

Now we start getting into the second rule. You need to learn a little about the network while the network is running correctly. When things go wrong, a few simple tests will show you what's changed. You don't need anything special for these tests. You already have the tools you need: ping and tracert, both of which come with Windows 95/98.

Gathering Baseline Information

To do any reasonable amount of network troubleshooting, you need to push the cloud back a bit. You need some information on your local connection to the network and, if there is one, the router that connects you to the rest of the Internet. If you push back the cloud, every network in the world looks something like Figure 11-3. The precise character of the connection may vary, but in every case, some kind of wire connects your computer to something else. You need to find out a little about both yourself and the "something elses": who is responsible for them and how fast they respond. So right now, try to learn the following information:

- The IP address of your computer. These days, your IP address is often dynamically assigned at the beginning of each session, and therefore may not be the same from one session to the next. If that's the case, you're out of luck. Knowing your own IP address isn't absolutely essential, but it helps.

- If you're on a LAN (a Local Area Network, which is what you'll find in most offices), the IP address of another computer on the same network.

- If you're a dial-up user, the IP address of your service provider's terminal server. (Or, try the host that is listed on the **Gateway** tab in the TCP/IP configuration **Properties** menu.)

- The IP address of the router or gateway closest to your computer that is responsible for connecting you to something larger (the router in Figure 11-3). If you're a dial-up user, get the address of your service provider's router.

- Depending on your setup, a list of whom to call for particular problems at particular times. If you're a dial-up user who is connected to a commercial service provider, that's who you should call for problems that are not because of your

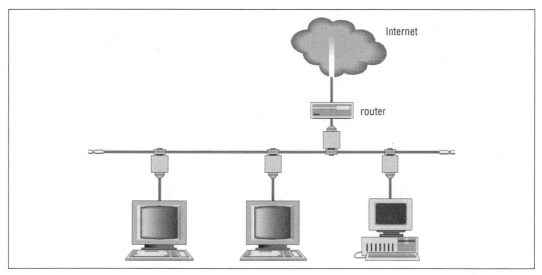

Figure 11-3. Network schematic

hardware. If you're in a more sophisticated network environment, there is probably a system administrator who can either deal with the problem for you or give you a good sense of whom to call for what kinds of problems.

- The state of the status lights on any networking equipment you have access to. If you're a dial-up user, you should know the state of the status indicators on your modem and the transitions they go through while you are making a connection.

In almost every case, the information you need is quite easy to get, but you need to modify the shopping list based on how your connection is made. For really large sites, the network infrastructure may be complicated but so is the support structure. The heartening thing is that the more complex your network is, the more help you are likely to find. A large network (either a large corporate network or one of the bigger nationwide ISPs) probably has a single phone number for customer support, answered 24 hours a day, 7 days a week.

Don't underestimate the importance of the first three items: the numeric Internet addresses of your system, the numeric Internet address of another computer on the same network, and the numeric Internet address of your service provider's terminal server. Elsewhere, we've always used computer names to contact things, rather than IP addresses. Troubleshooting is the exception to this rule. To use a name to make contact, your computer may automatically seek out a Domain Name Server to convert the name to an address. This requires a healthy network. If your network is in sad shape, it won't be able to do this; the tests you run using a name will be meaningless. An IP address is immediately usable, so it eliminates one source of error.

The Battle Plan

Let's get back to the task at hand. You go to your computer to work on the big project at 10 p.m., and you can't connect to the Yahoo! web site. So, let's look at the problem. Throughout this discussion, we need to assume that your connection has previously been working and just quit.

Knowing the Hours of Operation

The computers that provide network resources range from personal computers to gigantic mainframes. Network resources may include web sites, mail servers, gaming services, or other computing functions. Most of these, along with the network control computers, require some periodic maintenance. Most sites schedule maintenance during odd hours, like 2 a.m. Saturday, when the network load is usually light. However, scheduled down time varies from resource to resource. If you use a resource regularly, you should try to find out what its hours are supposed to be. You may save yourself a midnight attempt to access a resource that isn't available, anyway. (Unfortunately, most Internet sites don't post their maintenance schedule.) Also, remember that the Internet is worldwide. Friday business hours in the United States is 2 a.m. Saturday in Japan.

Did You Change Anything?

If you've ever used a computer, or helped others use computers, the following conversation should come as no surprise:

"It stopped working."

"Did you change anything?"

"No, it was working yesterday and then it just stopped."

"You're sure?"

"Well, I did change the screen color in my configuration file, but that wouldn't affect it." In many cases, your recent changes probably did cause the problem. If you have changed anything—a file or some hardware file—and your network connection hasn't worked correctly since, don't consider it unrelated, even if the relationship appears remote. Remember that Microsoft applications frequently make all sorts of changes to your configuration, especially when you're installing them. Before looking anywhere else, try to undo the change. Changing your screen color isn't likely to break anything, but it wouldn't be the first time someone installed a new sound card or CD-ROM drive and found that his network stopped working. These things shouldn't happen, but they do.

A good rule of thumb is to assume that the problem is at your end of the connection before you suspect problems at the other end. Make sure your end is working correctly before looking elsewhere. "Why?" you ask, "Didn't you say that the problem is equally likely to be at the far end?" Yes, that's true. But think about this: the far end is as likely to be in Japan as in Chicago and almost certainly isn't close to you. Before you make a long-distance phone call to Japan, make sure that the problem's not on your end.

Reading the Error Message

When some people get an error message, they become so flustered that they only see: ERROR—glitzfrick framus gobbledygook.

Relax, read the error message closely, and write it down. You need to write it down so that if you have to report it to someone, you have the exact text of the message. Nothing is more frustrating, for both the technical-support person and the network victim, than a message like, "It said 'error something something something.'" And if you take time to look at the error message carefully before you start calling out the troops, you might be able to fix your own problem. Even if you don't understand the whole message, you should be able to pick out a couple of words to help you along.

Windows error messages try to give helpful advice in plain English, but some of the suggestions can be misleading. The actual problem that produced the message in Figure 11-1 was a temporary network outage; the account information was fine. Don't focus too much on the possibilities suggested by the error messages; they may keep you from finding out what's really wrong.

Looking Around Your Computer

Now, assume that the finger of Murphy's law is pointing directly at you—or your computer. It's time to start looking around your home or office. In World War II, people blamed their problems on "gremlins": mythical beasts that caused bombs not to explode, engines to stop, etc., all for unknown causes. If you want to fix a computer, you'll have to take responsibility for finding the real cause, not blaming it on some creature. When computers stop working, the problem is usually people: if you're in an office, there are cleaning personnel, officemates, and you; if you're at home, there are you, your family, and your pets. It's amazing how many computer and networking problems are caused by damage to the cable between your computer and your modem or between your modem and the telephone. Janitors knock it out with a broom, or you roll over it a hundred times with a chair wheel and cut it. If you find something obviously wrong, fix it (or get someone to fix it).

Recognizing When Things Happen

To use the Internet, a number of things need to happen in sequence:

1. You initiate a dial-up connection.

2. Your machine connects, gets authorized, and negotiates a number of parameters.

3. You attempt to contact a site.

4. Your machine turns a name into an address.

5. It contacts that remote computer and works fine.

Along the way, the computer tells you things either via dialog boxes or on status lines near the top or bottom of the window. Get familiar with how and when these things change. If they change in unfamiliar ways, they offer clues as to where the problem lies. Certain messages occur at certain times and knowing when a message occurs in relation to others can be quite revealing.

For example, if you type "telnet ux1.cso.uiuc.edu" at your DOS prompt and your computer responds, "Trying 128.174.5.50," that tells you quite a bit. It tells you that your computer is connected to the Internet, and that you have successfully contacted the Domain Name System and converted the name into an address. So if you fail after that point, you probably should look more at problems with your application or the site you are trying to contact than at how your modem is configured.

Establishing Your Connection

First things first. You need to connect to your provider. (If you are not using PPP over a modem, this doesn't apply.) You will open your Dial-Up Networking match GUI icon and click on the icon that you have configured to call your Internet provider. You see a dialog box and you press **Connect**. Make sure you've configured Windows 95 to bring up a terminal window while dialing out (this was one of the options you had when configuring your Internet connection); you need to be able to see what's going on. The next thing that happens is that your modem should dial. This should be accompanied by a progress box that says the modem is dialing. If you don't hear it dial and the lights on the modem don't flash, there is a problem with how your modem is talking to your computer. Check the cables and whether the modem is connected to the port (COM1 or COM2) you thought it was. The COM ports should be labelled clearly on the back of the computer; if not, look at the manual that came with your computer. It doesn't say much, but it should tell you where the COM ports are.

If that was successful, eventually your provider should answer and the modem should start hissing and whistling. This is good. These noises represent the modems on each end trying to decide how fast they can talk to each other.

Once the modems are talking, account numbers and passwords are passed along. If something goes wrong here, check the documentation that is provided by your provider and make sure you got the upper- and lowercase correct; it does make a difference. If it all looks okay, but your account number and password still don't work, there is no recourse but to give your provider a call.

When that hurdle is crossed, your machine tries to negotiate a number of other issues with your provider. Usually, the biggest issue here is who is going to supply the IP address for your computer. Some providers provide you with a static IP address that you need to enter; the procedure is the same as if you had a LAN connection. Other providers send your machine a temporary IP address when you connect. If you get this wrong, you set an "Incompatible connection" error message.

Finally, if you made it this far, you are connected and see the dialog box shown in Figure 11-4. This dialog box gives a running total of how much time you have spent online.

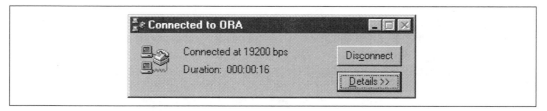

Figure 11-4. Connection status box

Some Hints About Dial-Ups

There are three common problems that occur when you try to dial in: the phone never answers, or it answers and doesn't talk, or it answers and talks but very slowly. Let's look at these problems in detail.

Ring, no answer

Check the number you dialed. Was it correct? If you dialed correctly and the remote system doesn't answer, that system may be down or its modem may be bad. Check the published hours of operation to make sure it should be up. If it should be working, try the same phone number a few times. Better yet, if you have any alternate numbers, try them. If you have two phone lines available, try dialing the number with a phone on the line that doesn't have the modem. While it is ringing, dial with your modem phone and see if it gets through. (Sometimes, if there are multiple phone lines through one number, one bad line will always answer the call. If you keep it busy with another phone, your modem call might get to a good one.) Even if you get through eventually, call your service provider and report the problem so it can be fixed.

Answer, then nothing

Here's one common scenario: the modem dials correctly, the remote system answers, and then everything goes dead. This usually points to a problem with your service provider's gear. Either the provider's modem is bad or the port on the computer it is connected to is bad. Either way, the only thing you can do is call in and report it. You might try again. If you have an alternate number, try it—getting a different modem to answer might bypass the problem.

There's one other possibility. There are certain modems that "don't like to talk to each other," particularly if they're made by different manufacturers (and particularly if they are 56 Kbps modems). However, we're assuming that you're troubleshooting a connection that has worked for you in the past. Unless you've just bought a new modem, incompatible modems probably aren't the problem.

Answers, but works slowly

Finally, you may find that the modem dials, the remote system answers, and everything works after a fashion, but nothing works well. The modem may drop the connection on its own, or everything may be painfully slow, with the modem's lights flashing erratically. There are many things that could cause this, but the most common would be noise on your telephone line. You can often hear the noise yourself. Many external modems have a built-in speaker and volume control. Turn up the volume a bit while the modem is dialing, and see if you can hear any hissing or crackling. It may be easier to plug a regular telephone into the jack and use it to make a few phone calls. Use the phone to dial your service provider (you'll have to listen to the nasty whistles that modems make), or try calling someone in the same telephone exchange as your service provider. If you can hear static in the background, you have problems.

If you have noise on the line, your phone company is the only one who can fix it. You may have trouble convincing them that there's really a problem. Persevere, and don't be afraid to make a jerk of yourself. You may be in for a long battle, particularly if the problem is intermittent.

Problems While Connected

It's possible for your computer to make a connection to your ISP successfully but still have problems accessing the Internet. Fortunately, there are some tools that will help you debug Internet problems. (In contrast, debugging connection problems requires a lot of trial and error, a lot of arguing with phone companies, and so on.) The error message in Figure 11-5 gives you a little more information to work with.

As the message says, you can try later. Or you can try a different site and see if you have better luck.

Figure 11-5. Feeling rejected

Remember that each application and each site uses a slightly different path through your computer and the Internet. So, if you click on *http://www.oreilly.com/* and it doesn't work, you might just try *http://whitehouse.gov/* (any of your favorite sites would do), or check your email. The odds are slim that all of these sites are down at the same time. If one works, it's not your problem.

Internet sites and web pages occasionally vanish or move to another location. While the Internet is more stable now than it was a few years ago, many resources are still maintained by students who eventually graduate. When this happens, the resource often disappears. That's life on the Net.

When something happens unexpectedly, several words and phrases often crop up in network error messages: "unknown," "unreachable," "refused," "not responding," and "timed out." Here's what each of these phrases means:

Unknown (or no such domain)
  In Chapter 1, we talked about the Domain Name System (DNS), which converts names like *www.yahoo.com* into numeric addresses like 204.71.200.68. This message means that DNS tried to convert a name into an address and failed. Either you misspecified the name (e.g., spelled it wrong), the name you're looking for really doesn't exist, or there is a problem with the Domain Name System. This last problem is almost certainly something you can't handle; get on the phone to your ISP. In a pinch, if someone can tell you the IP address you need, you can use it and bypass this problem.

Unreachable
  This is a real network problem. A portion of the network is down. The network is telling you, "I know where you want to go, but you can't get there from here." If this happens, there is nothing you can do but call your ISP.

Refused (or unavailable)
  The computer at the far end needs to accept connections for a particular service (e.g., anonymous FTP). Your computer successfully contacted the destination computer and asked to make the connection to a service, but the destination said, "No. " There are several possible reasons for this. The computer may be running but is not available for user access. This is frequently the case during maintenance periods or during filesystem dumps. It's also possible that the service has been

cancelled, i.e., the system's manager has decided not to provide it. For example, you might hear that a great game is available at *http://www.joesbaitshop.com:8018/ game.html*. When you try this, you get a "connection refused" message. This probably means that the computer's owner decided not to allow game playing anymore.

Timed out (or not responding)

When your computer sends a message to a remote computer, it expects a response in a reasonable amount of time, usually a few minutes. If it doesn't get a response, it gives up and sends you this message. Usually, that means the destination computer or a piece of the network is dead. This can happen in the middle of a conversation. Try again in about 10 minutes—long enough for most systems to recover from a crash automatically if they are going to. If it still doesn't work, investigate further. (You would get this message if the modem cable or the network cable suddenly fell off your computer.)

Trying to Reach a Local System

On the shopping list, we told you to try to get the IP address of another computer on the same local network—or the address of some machine on the provider's network (ideally, the terminal server you connect to) if you're a dial-up customer.

Here's where you use that information. The *ping* utility is shipped with Windows 95 and 98. It's a simple tool for finding out whether other computers are reachable. It's really easy to use. Just open a DOS shell, and then type "ping" followed by a hostname or a numeric Internet address. Here's how:

```
C:>ping www.uu.net
Pinging www.uu.net [208.229.230.133] with 32 bytes of data
Reply from 208.229.230.133: bytes=32 time<10ms TTL=255
...
```

This indicates that *www.uu.net* is alive and talking. It also gives us another important piece of information: the numeric address of *www.uu.net* is 208.229.230.133. Ping therefore is a good tool for looking up numeric addresses. It never hurts to save one or two numeric addresses in a file, so you can use them for testing when something is broken.

Here's what happens when the network is broken:

```
C:> ping 204.148.40.91
Pinging 204.148.40.91 with 32 bytes of data:
Destination host unreachable.
...
```

For some reason, data can't get through to the computer 204.148.40.91; it is "unreachable," one of the problems we discussed in the previous section. You might see other problems besides unreachable, but the big tip off is that you don't see a reply. Now let's talk about how to use ping to diagnose a network problem:

- If your computer is connected to a local network, start by trying to ping other systems on your network. (If you just connect to the Internet via a modem, skip this step.)

```
C:>ping 10.0.0.2
Pinging 10.0.0.2 with 32 bytes of data
Reply from 10.0.0.2: bytes=32 time<10ms TTL=255
...
```

If ping fails, your network is down. The problem may lie with your computer (Is your network cable plugged in where it should be? Cables often fall out.) or somewhere else on the local network. If you're in an office, contact the system administrator. If you've built a network at home, you're on your own. Start by checking the wiring. In this example, I was able to conclude that my local network was working properly.

- Try to ping your ISP's gateway or router. If you can't, you know that the connection to the Internet is down:

```
C:> ping 204.148.40.91
Pinging 204.148.40.91 with 32 bytes of data:
Destination host unreachable.
...
```

That's the situation we're in here: if I did more pings, I could prove that I couldn't access any sites outside of my own network. If you connect to the Internet through a modem, make sure that the modem is actually connecting to the ISP. Do its lights look normal? Is it getting a busy signal when it dials? Is the ISP answering? Again, the problem could be at your home: the modem cable may have fallen out of your computer, or your ISP could be having problems. Once you're reasonably sure that the problem isn't in your house, give your ISP's support desk a call.

- Try to ping some computers out on the Internet. If you can't ping the remote computer you need to reach, but you can ping another remote computer, the remote computer that you want to reach is down.

- If you can successfully ping the remote computer you've been trying to reach, the remote computer is working, though there may be problems elsewhere. If you continue to have difficulty connecting to it, the computer is temporarily busy or has no additional connections available. (If ping gives a large value for the time, the Internet may just be very busy. Or there may be noise on your local phone line, causing corruption in the data you're sending.)

If ping works when you give it numeric addresses but not when you give it hostnames, something is probably wrong with DNS; tell your service provider. The general rule, though, is to find out where things stop working by starting at home and testing sites farther and farther away: another computer on your local network (if you have one), your ISP's router, your ISP's web server, a site in another part of the world. Knowing exactly where the problem starts will be very useful when you talk to your ISP.

In the next section, we bring out the heavy artillery: traceroute, which analyzes the route data takes when it travels from point A to point B.

Looking at the Internet's Plumbing

There's a tool called *traceroute* (on Unix) or *tracert* (on Windows) that lets you watch the route your packets take between your computer and their destination. If you're really a nerd, you might do this for fun. If you're not a nerd, you probably don't care. But when you're looking at a problem, it's the most heavy-duty tool at your disposal. If you call your ISP and tell them you've been looking at a problem with traceroute, they'll be impressed, and it may help to convince them that you're someone to reckon with.

Traceroute uses a very clever technique to discover each router on the path between you and your destination. (The tricky part of this is that the path can change at any time, and there's no way to predict it in advance.) It sends three packets to each router and measures the round-trip time for each packet. So, if your packets get partway to the destination, and the round-trip times suddenly increase sharply, or packets start disappearing, you know roughly where the problem is.

Here's what traceroute looks like. I traced the route to Netscape's web server, *www. netscape.com*. (Actually, this is one of several servers that share that name, but for our purposes, it doesn't make a difference.)

```
tracert www.netscape.com
traceroute to www24.netscape.com (207.200.73.73), 30 hops max, 40 byte packets
 1  pnet-2 (204.213.233.2)  156 ms  139 ms  140 ms
 2  pnet-1 (204.213.233.1)  140 ms  139 ms  140 ms
 3  frame-gw-ds1.pcnet.net (204.213.235.1)  150 ms  266 ms  150 ms
 4  sl-gw6-pen-1-4-1544k.sprintlink.net (144.228.68.125) 160 ms 157 ms 160 ms
 5  144.228.60.17 (144.228.60.17)  160 ms  159 ms  150 ms
 6  sl-bb10-pen-0-2.sprintlink.net (144.232.5.13)  170 ms  157 ms  160 ms
 7  sl-bb10-stk-4-0-155M.sprintlink.net (144.232.8.58)  220 ms  219 ms 240 ms
 8  sl-bb10-stk-4-3-155M.sprintlink.net (144.232.4.45)  230 ms  219 ms 220 ms
 9  sl-gw10-stk-0-0-0-155M.sprintlink.net (144.232.4.77) 230 ms 229 ms 230 ms
10  sl-netscape-1--T3.sprintlink.net (144.228.146.26)  230 ms  219 ms  240 ms
11  h-207-200-69--74.netscape.com (207.200.69.74)  220 ms  239 ms  220 ms
12  h-207-200-69-69.netscape.com (207.200.69.69)  230 ms  219 ms  220 ms
13  h-207-200-73-73.netscape.com (207.200.73.73)  230 ms  229 ms  *
```

My packets bumble around *pcnet.net* (a local ISP), then get transferred to Sprintlink (a major Internet backbone component), and then find their way into Netscape, where they bounce around a little before finding their destination. On the left, you see the names and IP addresses of the routers en route to Netscape. The names are usually unintelligible, though you can sometimes glean some information from them. The numbers on the right show the round-trip times for each of the three packets that went to each router. A star indicates that a packet was sent to the router, but that it didn't make its way back. A few stars here and there are nothing to worry about. In this trace, the last packet we sent didn't make its way back, but I wouldn't worry. If a lot of stars show up part way through, something may well be wrong. The point where the stars start appearing is likely to be a trouble spot.

The round-trip times also look pretty healthy. Obviously, they tend to be longer toward the end of the trace than they are at the start, but there are no sudden jumps. If I suddenly saw the round-trip times jump from the 200 ms range to 500 or 600 ms, I'd be pretty concerned. Again, the point where the jumps start is likely to be the trouble spot. If round-trip times are uniformly bad, unfortunately there's probably nothing to worry about. The Internet just has bad days, usually when somebody like Netscape releases a new browser.

If the packets never reach their destination, you definitely have trouble. *traceroute* quits after 30 hops or so, figuring that a path that long is bound to be bad.

There's a lot you can't tell from traceroute, so you definitely should be humble when mailing around its results. In particular, don't worry if you see a line like this:

```
10 * * *
```

This probably means that you've run into a router that has been configured not to respond to traceroute packets. That's fairly common. If everything else looks normal, you can ignore a few lines like this. Many other factors can make traceroute output look really strange. But if you're experiencing problems, traceroute is the first tool to use for diagnosis. I guarantee that it's the first tool your ISP will use when investigating your trouble report. If you've already done the ground work, you'll get better service.

Talking to Operations Personnel

Sooner or later, you'll have to talk to someone at your service provider. Knowing a few ground rules will help. Airplane pilots are taught that, whenever they talk on the radio to air traffic controllers, every message should say:

- Who you are
- Where you are
- What you want to do

These same guidelines apply to calling your service provider's support staff. First, they need to know who you are—otherwise, they can't ask you for more information or tell you that they've solved the problem. Where you are (the name of your computer and possibly its IP address) and what you want to do (the name of the remote computer and the service you want to get) allow operators to figure out the path your communications should take. This is the essential data necessary to diagnose and solve a problem. However, it is only the minimum. In addition, keep in mind why you've called the network operators. If you've followed our short procedure earlier, remember what you've done, why you did it, and what the results were. Why are you convinced that the problem isn't on your desktop? The answer to this question contains very important clues about the nature of the problem. If you've done any probing with ping or traceroute, be sure to tell them what you discovered.

The operator you call should be the one running the network closest to you. Your local network operators are the only ones who monitor connections to your campus or building. It isn't like calling up the president of GM to get action on your car. In the network world, a national operator only knows about his network's connection to regional networks. Once he determines that MCI, or Sprint, or whatever isn't at fault, they will call the regional network responsible for your connection. In turn, the regional network will call your campus, corporate networking center or Internet service provider. Very likely, they will then call you. Save yourself some time: start at the bottom.

Some Consolation

It may sound like there's not much you can do. In some sense, that's true. Think of your washer, dryer, or VCR. If they break, you can make sure all the plugs and hoses are tight, or maybe pull out a jammed cassette. There are a few things you can fix. But, much of the time, there is nothing you can do but call up the Maytag repairman and talk about the problem knowledgeably. Even if you can't solve the problem yourself, the more information you can gather, the better service you'll get. The people who run networks are besieged by people whining about problems who haven't a clue what they're talking about. If you can prove that you do have a clue what you're talking about, you're making it much easier for them to solve your problem—and that may help to move you to the top of the list. If nothing else, the network engineers would much rather spend their time talking to people who have done some research and understand something about the Net, than people who are just saying, "It doesn't work and I don't know why."

Upgrading Your Connection

As I'm sure you know, sometimes the Internet is less like a superhighway and more like the parking lot after a football game. If you're just surfing for fun, this is when you go and watch television, or do something that indicates that you have a life. But if your business depends on it, or if you're naturally a tense person, you call your ISP and complain. That's the equivalent of honking your horn. Unfortunately, it often does about as much good as honking your horn.

Don't get the wrong idea: most service providers do a good job under poor conditions. They have a lot of people complaining, most of whom don't know what they're talking about, and many Internet problems are truly out of their control. But a time comes when you have to say, "Take this modem and shove it. I'm taking my business elsewhere."

A less drastic solution may be upgrading to a better connection technology. Let's face it: 28.8 Kbps modems are marginal for a number of the services we've talked about in this book. 56 Kbps modems are better, but if you're upgrading, you might as well look at all your options. In the last few years, a number of interesting high-speed alternatives have become available. Upgrading to a faster technology may require changing service providers, but it may not. If you're basically happy with your service provider, ask what options they provide.

We'll spend a few pages discussing what to do when you're really frustrated: how to go about picking service providers and how to think about some of the newer connection technologies.

Evaluating Service Providers

If you have an Internet connection already, you're probably familiar with the major pieces that connect you to the Internet. Of course, the major player is your Internet service provider, which is the company that sells you a connection to the Internet. Your ISP usually buys its own Internet connection from a larger ISP. ISPs come in all sizes, from tiny companies working out of someone's basement to monsters like America Online. The phone and cable TV companies are starting to get into the act too. The ISP you choose, and the type of service you buy, has a lot to do with whether your Internet experience is pleasant or painful. If you're currently shopping for an ISP, you've probably found that out the hard way. It's important to shop carefully.

If you're evaluating an ISP, the most important thing to find out is how often you'll hear a busy signal when you dial them. This has everything to do with the ratio of customers to modems, which can be as bad as 30 to 1. Fifteen customers per modem is pretty typical, but you'll be hearing busy signals often at peak hours. Under 10 customers per modem is very good; if the ratio gets as low as 4 customers per modem, you'll rarely, if ever, hear a busy signal. It shouldn't be surprising that few ISPs will tell you their customer-to-modem ratio; it's never as good as you'd like. But they usually organize their pricing policies around these ratios, so you can have some control over your fate. There's usually a bargain basement "unlimited access" service priced at around $10/month; stay away from this unless you like busy signals. The next step is usually priced at $30–$40/month and has some kind of access limitation (for example, 100 hours/month) beyond which you get additional charges. Don't let the limited hours scare you; this is where you want to be. Most ISPs will sell you an expensive account where they dedicate a phone line for your private use, but you don't need that. Just make sure they have enough lines to serve their customers and are committed to adding more lines as they grow. You'll pay a bit more than for a bar-gain-basement service, but you'll be much happier.

It's also worth asking how your ISP is connected to the rest of the Internet: who do they buy their connection from? Do they have a single connection or several? At what speeds do these connections operate? Most good ISPs these days have two or more T1 connections (dedicated phone lines that carry 1.5 megabits per second). Multiple con-nections are a good thing; that means the service provider will stay online if some-thing goes wrong with one of the connections. If the ISP specializes in high-speed technologies, we'd hope to see that it uses T3 (45 megabits per second) rather than T1.

It may be worth asking how your IP address is assigned. You can either be given a permanent address that's yours forever, or an address that's assigned dynamically each time you make a connection to the Internet. For the ISP, dynamic addressing is better. It doesn't need as many addresses, and addresses are getting expensive. But the real question is what's right for you. If you're a typical home user, a dynamically assigned address is just fine. In fact, it may even be better, because it shields you from some kinds of configuration changes your ISP might make. Absolutely all of the Internet's services work with a dynamically assigned address. The one thing you can't do is run any kind of server (like a web server) for the outside world. But you don't want to; running a server is a hassle, and you'd have to buy an Internet connection that's up all the time, which is very expensive. If you want your own web page, your ISP can cer-tainly set one up for you on their server. That way, he gets the headaches.

If you have a home office and telecommute, the question is a bit more complicated. You still don't want to be running your own server unless you can justify a full-time, dedicated connection. But some companies use packet-filtering firewalls to keep Inter-net intruders out. That basically means that they restrict access to their network to a few specific IP addresses. If your employer does this, you probably need a fixed IP address to make it through the filters. Some ISPs charge more for a fixed address; some don't; some just won't give you a fixed address.

The best place to start looking for an ISP is on the Internet. (That shouldn't be a sur-prise.) Two excellent resources listing ISPs all over the United States and internation-ally are *http://www.boardwatch.com/isp/* and *http://thelist.internet.com/*. Check both—there are significant differences between the two lists.

The Connection Itself: Modems and Beyond

Now let's move away from the ISP, and look at some of the hardware and software pieces that make the connection. The software that makes the connection between you and your ISP is called PPP. To be precise, PPP is the name of the protocol that the software implements; the software itself probably has some fancy name that some marketing department chose. These days, the PPP protocol is used by virtually any type of connection, whether you're using a modem or a high-speed dedicated connection. You may also have heard of SLIP, which is an older piece of software that serves a similar purpose. Some people still use SLIP and claim it's more efficient, but they're sadly deluded. SLIP is actually about 1% more efficient but is nowhere near as flexible, isn't as good at maintaining connections under poor conditions, and doesn't have the security features that have been added to PPP in recent years. That's an awful lot to pay for 1%. You probably don't have a choice between PPP and SLIP, but if you do, choose PPP. (If you're software doesn't support PPP, upgrade it. If your ISP doesn't support PPP, go somewhere else. Now.)

I'm sure you already know what a modem is: it's a small box that connects one of your computer's serial ports to a telephone line. Modems are quite well standardized, so you usually don't have to worry about compatibility between different modem vendors. However, it never hurts to use a modem by the same vendor that your ISP uses or recommends. Incompatibilities aren't unknown.

A router is a piece of hardware that connects one network to another. Routers are the glue that ISPs use to stick their own networks together and connect their network to the rest of the Internet. When you get a "host unreachable" message, it's probably because a router screwed up somewhere.

You'll probably never see a router unless you build a network in your home or business. If you do build a network in your home (and that's becoming common, now that Ethernet cards are cheap and many homes have two or more computers), you might consider using a simple router to connect to the Internet. A low-end router designed for home use runs $500 to $700. That's more expensive than a modem, but it can be cheaper than buying a separate modem, phone line, and Internet account for every computer you want to connect. (Most low-end routers have a modem or an ISDN interface built in.)

Connection Technologies

Now we're getting to the more interesting part: the different technologies that carry data between you and your ISP. Your choices here have a lot to do with how much you pay and how fast your data moves. Measuring how fast your data moves is trickier than it sounds. Most modems have a label that tells you a *baud rate* (28.8 Kbaud, etc.). The use of the word "baud" here is actually incorrect; it really is "bits per second." Higher speed technologies like ISDN and cable modem quote speeds in terms of kilobits or megabits per second. These numbers are, for the most part, directly comparable. To get an idea what this means in terms of real data, I use the following rule of thumb: a 28.8 Kbps modem working under almost perfect conditions moves data at about 10 MB per hour. Under really, really perfect conditions, you might see 12 MB per hour, but that's making a lot of assumptions: your telephone line is particularly noise free, the Internet itself is lightly loaded, and a lot of equipment spread out all over the country is working perfectly. If you see 10 MB/hour, consider yourself adequately blessed. Likewise, 57.6 Kbps should get you 20 MB/hour, and so on.

Of course, all megabytes are not created equal. Therefore, you can get apparent performance much better than 10 MB/hour out of your 28.8 Kbps modem. That's because modems have built-in compression software that squeezes extra space out of the files you transfer to make things go quicker. This is a great feature—but it does get in the way if you're trying to test performance. If you want to experiment with transfer rates, take a large file and compress it with WinZip, gzip, or some other compression utility before downloading it. Compressing a file effectively disables the modem's compression: the modem can't compress the file any further, so the transfer rate you see is the actual time it took to transfer all the bits. If you can't get at the file to compress it (for example, you want to test downloading a file from someone else's web server), do your experiments with JPEG or GIF images; these file formats have compression built-in.

With that in mind, let's talk about different connection technologies:

28.8/33.6 Kbps modems
These can move data simultaneously in both directions at their full-rated speed. The only trick is that you'll probably never see the full-rated speed. That has nothing to do with the modem, and everything to do with your phone line. The modem starts out by making a lot of horrible whistling noises that it uses to test various connection speeds. It chooses the one that will work best depending on the conditions on your phone line. I've never seen my modem connect at 33.6 Kbps, and I've only rarely seen it connect at 28.8 Kbps. Of course, if you're in an area with good phone lines, you might do better.

57.6 Kbps modems
This is the current, state-of-the-art modem technology. (You'll often hear 57.6 rounded to 56.) It's probably as fast as modems can go; to go faster, you'll have to use some more exotic technology, like ISDN. Like 28.8 Kbps modems, these start by testing the waters and picking an actual communication rate that's appropriate for the condition of your phone lines. There's one important difference between 57.6 Kbps modems and the slower ones: 57.6 Kbps modems only give you really high speed for downloading. They are made with the assumption that most people download a lot more than they upload. For the most part, that's true. But if you want to run your own web server, or frequently upload data from your home office, this may be a consideration. The maximum upload speed isn't *too* shabby: 28.8 Kbps.

ISDN (Integrated Services Digital Network)
Traditional phone lines carry analog data between your phone or modem and the phone company's central office. ISDN is a newer all-digital technology. At long last, it's finally available in most of North America; it's been available in Europe for some time. One ISDN line provides two 64 kbit/second channels, called B channels. There's also a 16 kbit/second D channel that's used for signaling. When you're sending data, you can use one or both of the B channels for a 64 Kbps or 128 Kbps connection. You get full speed in both directions. Some ISDN equipment will automatically drop one of the B channels if you pick up a phone, letting you

talk and send data at the lower 64 Kbps rate at the same time. With some services, the D channel can be used as a continual low-speed data connection for stock or news tickers and things like that. One of the nicest things about ISDN is that everything is digital, including the dialing. So, rather than waiting for your modem to dial the ISP's number, and the ISP's modem to pick up and answer, an ISDN connection can be up and running within seconds.

ISDN used to be quite expensive (and unavailable). Lately, the prices have become fairly reasonable, though startup costs are still painful: $300–$800 for your own equipment (ISDN modem on the low end, a router on the high end), $100 or so for phone company installation (fortunately, you can use the same phone lines), another $100 or so startup fee from your ISP, $40–$100 per month for your ISP account (depending on what kind of service you buy), and probably $40 per month for the phone company. As with traditional modem connections, a lot of ISPs would love to sell you a dedicated phone line for your ISDN connection, but you don't need it, unless you're a serious business user. Most telephone companies charge you one cent per minute per B channel (or something in that neighborhood) for the time you're transferring data. In some states, there's a loophole that lets you get around this per-minute charge: if you set up your equipment to send voice rather than data, it will use a somewhat lower 57.6 Kbps rate per channel, but the per-minute charge won't apply. The newsgroup *comp.dcom.isdn* is a good place to look for helpful information and advice.

Cable modem

Yes, the cable TV companies are getting into the act. Cable Internet service is currently available in most major cities, but should become much more widely available in the near future. It is very high-speed service, claiming peak rates of 28 megabits/second for downloads, and 128 kilobits/second for uploads. (The actual maximum rates depend a lot on the equipment your cable company uses.) The service normally costs between $30 and $50 per month, including rental of the cable modem itself. Availability depends on your cable TV company. See *http:// www.home.com/* to check whether your cable provider offers the service.

This sounds great, but there are a few caveats. First, you should be aware that the extremely high data rate is shared by everyone connected to the same cable. This could easily be 500 to 1,000 households. When you're the only one on the block who's signed up, service will be fantastic. But when everybody on the block has signed up, it may be a different matter. 10 megabits sounds like a lot, but split it many ways and add inefficiencies, and you're talking a much different situation. Second, do you trust your cable company as an ISP? How quickly will it fix problems? Does it know how to fix problems? Keep in mind that selling Internet connections is an entirely new business for them, and it's not one they know much about yet. However, if you're satisfied with your cable TV service, it's a reasonable bet you'd be satisfied with cable modem service. (In one bad storm when I had lost power, I actually saw a cable truck out in the street supplying power to a repeater so they could maintain service to the rest of the town. That's a pretty impressive standard for service.)

Satellite

If cable TV companies are involved, it shouldn't surprise you that satellite companies are also looking at the Internet. They provide high speeds of 200 to 400 kilobits per second to your home, but use a standard modem link for data sent back to the Internet. To use these services, you first need to buy a standard DSS dish with a special card for Internet service. The package costs about $300. Monthly costs begin at $20 for lower speed, 6 p.m. to 6 a.m. service; the sky's the limit for faster, continuous service. This service is still coming of age. Current customers complain that the download speed is good, but not as good as advertised, and there are outages. Some of this may be solved when the suppliers gain experience; some problems, such as signal fade during storms, are endemic to the technology. This technology is most appropriate in an area where the other connection technologies are unavailable.

ADSL (Asymmetric Digital Subscriber Line)

ADSL is the phone companies' answer to cable modems. Like cable modems, ADSL provides very fast downloads and moderate-speed uploads. Download speeds for ADSL are roughly the same as for cable modems; ADSL's upload speeds are higher (640 kbits/second). As with cable modem, the actual speed supported depends a lot on the equipment your phone company uses. The big difference is that an ADSL connection isn't shared: you get all the bandwidth to yourself. And, like ISDN, it works over the standard phone lines that are running into your house now.

This sounds great—where do I sign up? Well, you probably can't. ADSL is available only in major cities and you must be within 10,000 feet of cable from a telephone company node that is ADSL-ready. So even if you're in a city, if you are in a residential area you might be too far away from a node with the equipment installed (telephone companies tend not to believe that people want high-speed services to their homes). It is certainly more expensive than most of the other solutions, but if you need the speed, it is cost effective. On the plus side, many PC manufacturers are including a modem that handles ADSL as well as traditional analog phone lines. You may already have the equipment you need.

Those are most of the options for home users or small businesses. We didn't say anything about leased lines, frame relay, ATM, and other things you may have heard about. Those are all much more expensive technologies that cost hundreds of dollars per month and up; they're designed for connecting medium to large offices. If you want to connect your company to the Internet, those are the technologies to look at. But, with very few exceptions, they're not for most Internet users.

Home Internetworking

A few years ago, if you had a computer and an Internet connection, you were satisfied. If you were a "professional," you might even have had a dedicated phone line for your computer. But more likely, you just let people get busy signals while you were on the Net.

That model really doesn't work very well anymore. An increasing number of home users have two or three computers, all of which may be in use at the same time: the kids may be doing homework, while you're doing banking or working on your stock portfolio. And a lot of people have home offices with two or more computers, printers, and other equipment. Do you get three phone lines, three modems, and three Internet connections? It could get pricey, not to mention inconvenient.

The Internet is all about networking—why not take the next logical step, and bring the network into your home? That way, all your computers can share one Internet connection. Furthermore, they can share other resources, like printers. Building a computer network in your home isn't fundamentally difficult. However, there are a lot of details involved. In this section, I'll get you pointed in the right direction, but I won't try to cover the entire territory.

What a Network Looks Like

Figure 11-6 shows a simple network, like the one you might set up in your home. You've got a connection to an ISP, a strange box called a *router*, another strange box called a *hub* (explained later in this section), a couple of computers and printers, and some wires connecting everything.

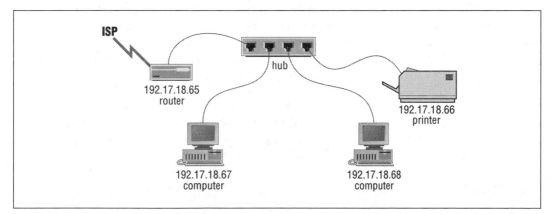

Figure 11-6. A simple network

Let's talk briefly about the two strange boxes. A router forwards messages between two or more networks. In this case, the router allows messages on your ISP's network (hence the rest of the Internet) to be forwarded to your home network and vice versa. Routers are usually special-purpose computers—sort of like a modem, but much smarter. The simplest routers have two network interfaces: one is a phone jack (or a cable TV jack) that connects to the outside world, and the other connects to your network. You can buy the router, or, in some cases, rent one from your ISP. (Renting is particularly common with cable-modem service, where the router usually comes with the connection.) If you buy the router, I strongly recommend that you buy the brand of router* that your ISP recommends. Routers can cost as little as $300, but you're more likely to pay around $600.

The care and feeding of a small router suitable for home use isn't rocket science, but it does require a reasonable understanding of how the Internet works—more than would fit in this book. Fortunately, many ISPs will set up the router for you (particularly if you buy it from them). Not only is this easier for you, but it keeps the people who know just enough to be dangerous from screwing up the ISP's network. It also eliminates finger-pointing when things break: if your ISP bought and configured your router, you can call them and say, "It doesn't work, fix it." If you're doing it on your own, you're likely to hear, "Oh, brand X routers don't do Y correctly, and you probably set up Z wrong. We're not doing anything; the trouble is your fault."

There's one other routing option that you should be aware of. It's possible to use a general purpose computer as a router. That computer has to run Windows NT or some version of Unix (Linux is an excellent choice)—Windows 95 or 98 won't do. You can still use the computer to do regular work, provided that you don't turn it off when you're done. Configuring a computer to act as a router is not particularly difficult, and something you may want to look into if you're a real power user, but it's still beyond the scope of this book.

The other mysterious box is a hub. A hub is basically a box where you plug in the wires from all the computers. Anything that comes in on one of the wires is automatically sent out over the others. Hubs sound like they ought to be expensive, but they cost as little as $30. These days, some routers have built-in hubs. The price depends on whether the hub is switched (a feature you almost certainly don't need), the speed at which it handles data (which I'll discuss later), and the number of ports (the number of wires you can plug in). My diagram shows a four-port hub—and that's about the smallest size that's useful. Hubs are pretty robust pieces of equipment that will be in service for a long time, so buy one a bit oversized. Get a six- or eight-port model. You may want to plug in your furnace and oven in a few years.

Ethernets

Finally, let's talk about the wiring. The internal network that you're using is called an *Ethernet*. There are two common kinds of Ethernet these days—10BaseT and

---

* The most common brands are Cisco, Ascend, and Bay.

100BaseT. The difference is basically the speed at which they carry data: 10BaseT gets you 10 megabits per second, or about 350 times what you get with a 28.8 Kbps modem. 100BaseT gets you 100 megabits per second (surprise). Unless you have fantasies about live video distribution within your household, 10BaseT is enough. 100BaseT hubs are more expensive (another surprise), and not worth paying for unless you have a real need for it.

The actual wiring that you use looks a lot like modern phone wire—and in fact, it is. Wire is rated by category that tells how good it is at both sending the signal and rejecting signals that may be induced in it by neighboring wires. Most normal wiring is Category 3, which is good enough for 10BaseT, and can be abused in almost any way imaginable: you can leave the wire on the floor, run it through heating ducts, whatever you want. You're not allowed to have any single wire more than 300 feet long— unless you're Bill Gates, I'm betting that's enough. There's a higher grade of wire called Category 5. (There's also a Category 4, which is a little hard to find.) Category 5 wire is just fine for 10BaseT Ethernet. It's designed for higher-speed networks, like 100BaseT. As long as you're only interested in 10BaseT, you can use what's cheapest or most convenient.

Higher-speed networks, like 100BaseT, are a more tricky proposition. You definitely don't need 100BaseT now, but if you want to do a full-blown installation and install the wiring in your walls, you should think about it. Who knows what new network applications we'll be working with in five years? You don't want to be ripping wires out of the wall because they won't support high-definition video phone or some other new toy. However, installing a 100BaseT network means more than Category 5 wire. There are a lot of restrictions on how the wire is installed that 10BaseT users can ignore. So, if you want to wire your house for 100BaseT, consider hiring a professional network installer.* (Although it looks like telephone wire, it isn't, and telephone installers are known for taking shortcuts that won't work for networks.)

You can get either Category 3 or Category 5 wire at any decent computer store. They can sell you patch cables with connectors already attached in a variety of lengths (the most convenient), or spools of cable with separate connectors that you attach yourself (which you'd need if you are wiring your house permanently). If you buy the cable in bulk, you may need to borrow or buy a crimping tool to put connectors on the wire. The connectors themselves look just like modern phone jacks, only larger. The technical name for the connectors is RJ45.

Ethernets used to be built out of coaxial cable, which is like the cable used for cable TV. If somebody suggests that you start messing around with coax, ignore him. It's more expensive and harder to deal with. (The coaxial technology is called 10Base2 or

---

* If you want to install 100BaseT yourself, buy any of the books available on network installation. There are lots of restrictions—like how sharply you can bend the wire, how close it can be to other wires, and more. It's not that you can't do it yourself, and professional installers aren't cheap. But if you really want 100 MB networking, either for your own use or as a feature when you sell the house, you have to make sure it's done right.

10Base5, depending on the kind of wire.) If you find some old equipment that uses coaxial cable, you should be able to find a converter from the coax connector (BNC) to twisted pair (RJ45). But network interfaces, hubs, and everything else are so cheap these days that I'd spend the money on up-to-date equipment.

Network Interfaces

So far, we've discussed the plumbing of Ethernet connections. You also need something to connect—we're not yet at the stage where the standard PC comes with a network interface built-in. Every computer or printer you want to connect to your network must have an Ethernet card. Installing an Ethernet card isn't fundamentally difficult, provided you are comfortable poking around inside your computer. If you're not, you can certainly find a shop to install the card for you. If you are comfortable working under the hood, I'll tell you how to install an Ethernet card in a relatively recent computer running Windows 95 or 98.

Picking a card

There are many vendors who make Ethernet cards, and for the most part, you can use any vendor's product in any computer. You need to pick a card that matches your computer's bus architecture and the kind of wiring you've chosen for your Net. Bus types are listed in your computer's documentation. Busses common on newer machines are PCMCIA, PCI, and Microchannel. As long as the card you buy matches your computer's bus type, you are in good shape. The bus architecture determines the shape of the connector that the card plugs into, so if you have the wrong type of card, you won't be able to install it. Some computers have two or more kinds of busses, usually so that you can use cards from older systems you may have lying around. I don't recommend using older Ethernet cards. They work fine, but they are harder to configure.* Assuming that you're using 10BaseT wiring, you should buy a card that has an RJ45 jack on the back (the kind that looks like a big telephone jack). There are other possibilities and adapters to fix things if you pick the wrong type or want to use an older board, but why bother with them if you don't have to?

Ethernet cards also vary in how you configure them. Cards labeled "plug and play" may cost a bit more, but they automatically try to fit into your computer along with any other devices that you may have. They are the easiest to install. The extra money is well worth it.

The next thing you need to worry about is getting a driver for the card. This is software that Windows uses to talk to the card. Suitable software sometimes comes with the card on a diskette; sometimes manufacturers will have it available on their web site. To avoid having to worry about drivers, many people buy cards that are NE2000

---

* Then again, if you are comfortable moving around jumpers to set IRQs and other hardware parameters, there's no reason not to use the older boards. But if you can do that, you probably don't need to read this section.

compatible. NE2000 was a brand of card whose way of communicating became fairly common. Many operating systems can use these Ethernet cards fairly easily, and Windows 95 and 98 should have a built-in driver for the card. All in all, if you shop around you should be able to get a decent Ethernet card for about $40.

Installing the card

Installing a modern plug-and-play Ethernet card requires four steps:

1. Plugging the card into the computer.

2. Telling the system how to access the card.

3. Telling the system to use this card when it wants to talk TCP/IP.

4. Configuring TCP/IP to be appropriate to your ISP.

If you get a plug-and-play card, you can install it into your computer, boot it up, and look at the Control Panel in the **Start** menu's **Settings** selection. On Windows 98, select **System Properties** and the **Device Manager** tab. If it worked you should see a selection in the menu called **Network Adapters**. If you double-click **Network Adapters**, you should see the name of your card. Double-click that name, and you should see the screen shown in Figure 11-7. (For Windows 95, the procedure is pretty much the same, though the names of some of the menus have changed.)

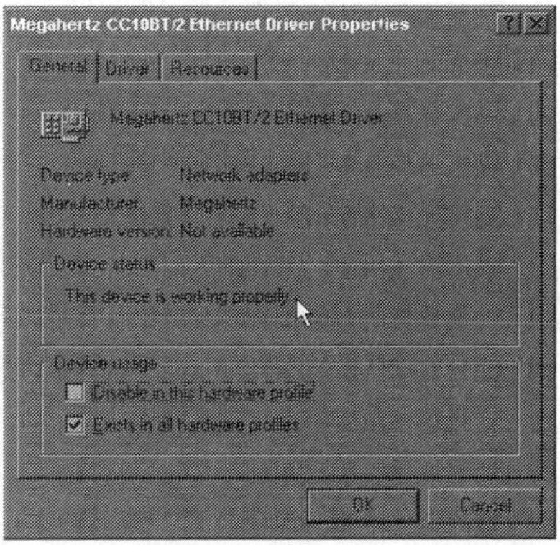

Figure 11-7. Modifying network adaptors

If a dialog box that says "The device is working properly" pops up, your system knows how to access the card and you can skip to the section on configuring TCP/IP.

If you don't see the name of your card (or something compatible with your card), click **Add** on the Network control panel.

You will be asked whether you want to add a client, a protocol, a service or an adapter. Pick Adapter and press **Add** again. Your system may go through some effort to build an adapter database; it will eventually come up with a screen that lists a whole slew of adapter manufacturers. Click on the manufacturer of your card in the left pane, and hopefully the model you have will be listed in the right. If you find it, click on that and you are done. If you can't find the appropriate make and model, you should have a diskette with appropriate software on it that came from the card manufacturer. (Or you could have downloaded the software from the manufacturer's web site.) Click **Have Disk** and proceed. After you've finished, you should find the card type in the system's list of adapters; click on it to finish the process.

Configuring TCP/IP

Now that you've got all the hardware installed, it's time to configure the Internet protocols so that they can do their job. There are a number of approaches to take. I'm going to describe the easiest (but not the cheapest), and then do some hand-waving about how, with some technical skill, you can get the cost down.

First, I'm assuming that you took my recommendation and had your ISP configure your router. That's most of the work. Now all you've got to do is configure TCP/IP on each of the computers on your network. And that's a lot easier than configuring a dial-up connection.

Internet communications is based on the concept of an IP address, which is a bunch of numbers looking something like this: 204.135.23.7. In the past, when you dialed in over a modem, your ISP lent your computer an IP address while it was connected. The address wasn't necessarily the same every time. That won't work when you're connecting a network: you need a separate Internet address for each computer you want to add on your network. Your ISP will have given you an IP address for each computer, an IP address for your router, a network mask (the same for every computer), the IP address of a gateway (also the same for every computer), and the IP address of one or more DNS servers. The gateway is probably your router, and therefore has the same address. (There are ways of setting things up where the gateway would be some machine at the ISP's office—so don't worry if the addresses are different.) Write this information down in a table, like Table 11-1.

Table 11-1. Address Assignments for My Home Network

Computer	IP Address	Net Mask	Gateway	DNS Server
Mike's computer	192.17.18.67	255.255.255.248	192.17.18.65	192.17.1.1, 204.15.28.9
Judy's computer	192.17.18.68	255.255.255.248	192.17.18.65	192.17.1.1, 204.15.28.9
Printer	192.17.18.66	255.255.255.248	192.17.18.65	192.17.1.1, 204.15.28.9
Router	192.17.18.65	255.255.255.248	Don't care	Don't care

It's a good idea to include the router in the table for completeness, but you really don't care about its configuration: you just assume that the ISP set things up right.

Once you've installed an Ethernet card on your computers, you need to tell the system what to do with it: in particular, you need to enter the information from the table above. So go back to the Network control panel. Now you should see your Ethernet card in the list (mine is an SMC EtherEZ…). Click on the card and click **Properties**. You should see a configuration window that has two tabs: **Driver Type** and **Bindings**. Go to the **Driver Type** tab and click on the driver type specified in the card's manual; most of the more modern cards use the NDIS32 driver, so pick this unless the card manufacturer says otherwise. Then go to the **Bindings** tab. Check "TCP/IP" and press **OK**. You've told the system that when it wants to talk TCP/IP, it can use this card.

Finally, go back to the Network control panel, select "TCP/IP," and click **Properties** again. Go to the **IP Address** tab. Check "Specify an IP address" and enter one of the addresses that your ISP has given you, and the subnet mask.

Next, click the **Gateway** tab and enter the address of the gateway your ISP told you to use. It is likely to be the address of the router on your home network. And finally, click the **DNS configuration** tab. Make sure DNS enable is checked and enter as many DNS servers as your ISP provided. You do this by specifying them in the field next to the **Add** button and then pressing **Add**. They will then be added to the list shown below it. Press **OK** and reboot for good measure. Go through the same process with every computer on your network, and you're ready to go.

Cost-Effective Printing

Most people begin with a single computer connected to a printer through its parallel port and a modem connection to the Internet. Now that you're setting up a home network so several computers can share an Internet connection, it would also be a good idea to share your printer. After all, that's what networks are for. The straightforward approach would be to implement it exactly as shown in Figure 11-6: connect every device by its own Ethernet cable back to the hub. This solution is attractive because of its simplicity: every device talks to another directly over the Ethernet. However, this simple approach will cost you more than necessary. You would have to buy an Ethernet card for the printer, and might also have to upgrade its software and add memory. At best, this might cost $100. At worst, you might find out that you need a whole new printer.

But there are other solutions. Remember that any Windows 95/98 or Windows NT computer with a printer connected to it can share the printer with other computers on the same network. The network wiring for this configuration is shown in Figure 11-8.

You don't have to buy any new hardware or upgrades to the printer, but you do have to change the configuration of the computer that's connected to the printer. Go to your Control Panel area and double-click **Network**. Then click on **File and Print**

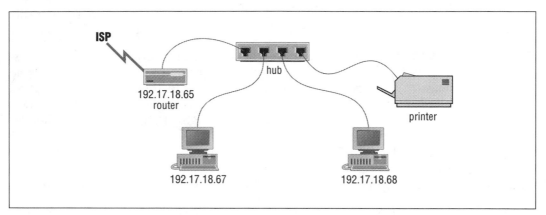

Figure 11-8. The print server network

Sharing. You see a dialog box that allows you to check I want to allow others to print to my printers and then click **OK**. You may be asked to reboot at this point.

Now you have enabled print sharing, but you need to say which printers you would like to share. Go to the **Printers** area of your computer, click on the printer you would like to share and then select **Properties** in the **File** menu. When you get that printer's configuration window, select the **Sharing** tab, shown in Figure 11-9.

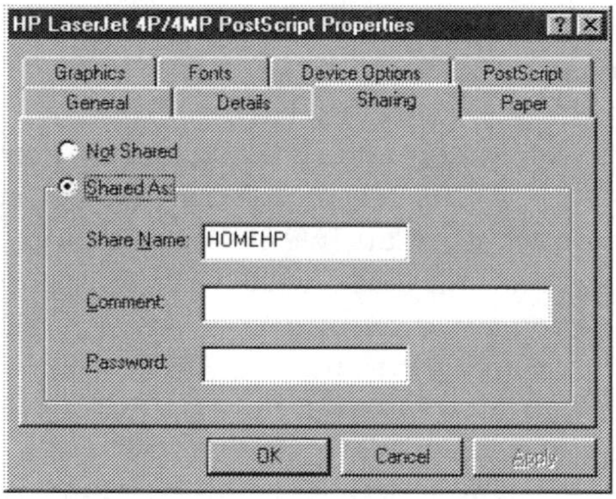

Figure 11-9. Exporting a printer

Click the **Shared As** button and fill in a name in Shared Name. You can ignore the other fields, unless you want to force your kids to type a password before they can use the printer. Seriously, the password might be necessary in an office, but it's overkill in a home. Click **OK** when you're done.

Now you need to tell your other computers that they can use this printer. On each of those machines, go to the Printers page and double-click **Add Printer**. This starts the printer configuration wizard, which walks you through adding a printer. First, you have to say that you are installing a Network Printer. You then have to tell it how to find the printer by filling in the box "Network path or queue name." Here you enter:

        *ipaddress**sharedname*

where *ipaddress* is the IP Internet address of the computer directly connected to the computer, and *sharedname* is the name you gave to the printer. In the network we've been setting up, you would type

        \\192.17.18.68\\HOMEHP

From here on, the questions in the setup are straightforward. When you get to the end, you'll be ready to print. Make sure that the computer connected to the printer is turned on whenever you want to print, or nothing will happen. You may want to leave it on all the time.

If you want to connect your printer directly to your Ethernet, it's not hard. You'll just have to consult your printer manual to find out how to enter its IP address and net mask. It probably won't care about the DNS server. Be forewarned: configuring printers isn't hard, but you tend to spend a lot of time pushing silly buttons on the printer's front panel.

Saving IP Addresses

Now for the hand-waving. You may have fallen on the floor when your ISP told you how much a block of IP addresses would cost. However, you don't really need to buy a block of addresses from your ISP. You only need one address, and it can even be dynamically assigned—in other words, just exactly the same situation you had before you built a network, costing not a penny more. The name of this trick is network address translation, and it's understood by virtually every router you can buy.

Your router gets the one address that your ISP provides. You then make up private addresses for all the computers on your network. Without explaining private addresses, they look like this: 10.0.1.1, 10.0.1.2, and so on. Make up as many as you need by changing the last number in the set; it can be anything from 1 to 254. Remember to assign a number to your router, too. In this configuration, your router gets two addresses: one that your ISP knows about, and one that the computers on your network know about. Your net mask is 255.255.255.0.

The problem with private addresses is that your router isn't allowed to forward any packets coming from these addresses to the Internet, and your ISP certainly isn't going to forward any packets with private addresses to you. So how do you communicate with the world? The router performs a massive fake-out by rewriting all of the outgoing packets to look like they came from it—and remember, the router has a legitimate IP address assigned by your ISP. When responses come back, it figures out which of the machines on your private network they should be sent to and revises them accordingly. One benefit of address translation and private addressing is additional security:

nobody can find out what you have inside your network, so it's more difficult for them to attack you.

Any ISP that is used to dealing with small networks should be able to set up your router to use address translation. Although it sounds like it's dishonest—after all, you're getting a huge number of addresses for the price of one—using up addresses too fast is a big problem for ISPs. It's in their interest to help you conserve addresses.

Does address translation change the configuration of your internal machines? Not at all—you'll still have to enter IP addresses, net masks, the address of one or more DNS servers, and so on. The only difference is that you can make up your own IP addresses—as many as you like. Table 11-2 presents a revised version of our table, showing how you might assign addresses in this scenario.

Table 11-2. Address Assignments for My Home Network

Computer	IP Address	Net Mask	Gateway	DNS Server
Mike's computer	10.0.1.2	255.255.255.0	10.0.1.1	192.17.1.1, 204.15.28.9
Judy's computer	10.0.1.3	255.255.255.0	10.0.1.1	192.17.1.1, 204.15.28.9
Printer	10.0.1.4	255.255.255.0	10.0.1.1	192.17.1.1, 204.15.28.9
Router	10.0.1.1	255.255.255.0	Don't care	Don't care

Non-Ethernet Solutions

There are two new technologies making their way into home networking that don't depend on the old tried-and-true Ethernet. These use existing telephone wiring and spread spectrum radio rather than special, dedicated cable. Both of these are so new in the home consumer market that we couldn't evaluate them. We can, however, tell you what to expect. If you think these are appropriate solutions, wait until they become available and look at the trade journals.

Telephone Wiring Solutions

You are probably saying, "Wait a minute, you talked about Ethernet on telephone wiring before. How is this different?" When we discussed 10BaseT Ethernet, we were talking about using the same kind of wire that is used for telephones. Now we are talking about using the wiring already installed in your home—the wires that your telephone is plugged into. Intel (*http://www.intel.com/anypoint/*) and Diamond Multimedia (*http://www.thedigitaldreamhome.com/*) are both marketing products of this sort. They offer a special interface card which costs about $90 that you plug into your telephone jack. It can then network with any other computers similarly configured at 1 megabit/second. The frequency it uses to signal is different from the frequencies used by the telephone, so your telephone supposedly can be working at the same time over the same wires.

They also give you software that allows one computer to act as a router over an existing Internet connection. The implication is that if you have that one modem, ISDN connection, or cable TV connection in your home, you can share it among all the computers you have connected to the telephone system. This would not be a bad solution, especially if you have a connection that will automatically come up when you use it. The only real worry is that, historically, Windows computers do a really poor job acting as a router. If your best modem is on your best Pentium, you may find that it feels like a much slower computer because it's wasting all its time doing the networking for the house.

Spread Spectrum Radio Solutions

Spread spectrum radio has been around for a long time; it is used for voice, military, and data applications. It is noted both for its security and its ability to coexist with other radio applications, preventing the need to assign frequencies. It works by having a synchronized receiver and a transmitter that jump around to different frequencies at high speed. The trick lies in synchronization. If the receiver and transmitter aren't synchronized, you only hear a little static. You can even use the same frequencies without trouble. When the receiver and transmitter are synchronized, they can communicate without interference from other sources.

Home networking products that use spread spectrum radio are available from Diamond Multimedia (*http://www.thedigitaldreamhome.com*) and Apple (*http://www. apple.com/airport/*). The products are similar to each other. You buy a base station (less than $200) and install it in the computer that has the Internet connection. Next, you install a card ($50) in every other computer you want networked. As long as the computers are within 150 feet of the base station, they can all communicate.

CHAPTER TWELVE

SEARCHING AND FINDING

There's a wealth of information on the Web. Most of it's worthless.

That's the way it may feel, anyway, when you're looking for a specific fact, file, or application. And if you're searching for information about a person, you may find a simultaneous lack and overabundance of information.

Finding information can be difficult, especially since search engines use somewhat differing syntax and methods to produce results. First, you'll need to know where to look: on the Web, in a Usenet newsgroup, or in a reference source. Then, you'll need to know how to look efficiently, via one search mechanism, or many, and using a search technology suitable to your target. You may even need to search for a search engine that searches for information on a particular topic.

Finding a person on the Internet is becoming easier and easier. And I don't mean just finding information about a person. Some people-finding sites on the Web will search on an individual's name and state, and return an email address, postal address, phone number, and map of the neighborhood. Some even return a list of the neighbor's names and phone numbers.[*]

Searching for Geniuses

How do you find tickets to Carnegie Hall on the Web? Practice, practice, practice.

---

[*] Feel threatened by this? I sure do. See Chapter 5 to learn how to remove your personal information from such services.

Please excuse the bad joke. One not entirely ineffective means of finding things on the Internet is to flail around until you find what you're looking for. For example, entering the terms "Carnegie Hall tickets" into Infoseek yielded the results in Figure 12-1.

Infoseek found 984,225 pages containing at least one of these words: **Carnegie Hall tickets** (click for tips or Advanced search)

    ⦿ New Search   ○ Search only **within** these 984,225 pages

   [   ]   **seek**

Search results 1 - 10, grouped by site

Hide summaries | Ungroup these results | next 10

Simon Fraser University Pipe Band - 1998 Highland Arts Festival
Update on Simon Fraser University Pipe Band 1998 Highland Arts Festival & Concert at Carnegie Hall. Concert at Carnegie Hall: February 20, 1998 Highland Arts Festival ...
79% http://home.istar.ca/~rmm/haf98upd.htm   (Size 10.8K) Document date: 7 Mar 1998

Carnegie Hall
New York, NY Great Singers in Recital Dmitri Hvorostovsky, Baritone Mikhael Arkadiev, piano $17/28/35/45/65 A limited number of student/senior citizen discount tickets, priced at ...
71% http://www.culturefinder.com/output.htm/Carnegie_Hall_EVENT1.htm   (Size 3.0K)
Document date: 28 Apr 1998
Grouped results from http://www.culturefinder.com

American Composers Orchestra - Scope of Activities
Carnegie Hall Subscription Season: . The ACO season features five subscription concerts at Carnegie Hall. Programs typically represent a diverse range of American music, including a ...
71% http://www.artswire.org/aco/scope.htm   (Size 6.1K) Document date: 17 Jan 1998
Grouped results from http://www.artswire.org

Figure 12-1. Practice, practice, practice

It turns out that the second resource, aptly titled Carnegie Hall, has a link to a ticket butler, from which I may procure tickets. Easy enough, right?

Well, there are a few subtleties to note. After all, I do this as a living:

- I chose Infoseek for the search. This very popular search engine frequently scores highly in articles about search engines, including reviews by c|net and Ziff-Davis.

- The search terms were very specific. I didn't enter just "Carnegie" or "tickets," but "Carnegie Hall tickets." Even better results could have been returned had we further refined the terms.

- The search terms were capitalized. Infoseek knows that "Carnegie Hall" is different than "carnegie hall"—meaning that it recognizes that the capitalization reflects this is a *specific* entity we're looking for and so searches for the *phrase* "Carnegie Hall" and the term "tickets," instead of the three terms "carnegie," "hall," and "tickets."

- Notice, too, that the first result on the list is entirely unsuitable to our purposes. For some reason, the first result is almost never the one you want.

Search Engines

Which search engine should you use? That depends on what you're looking for. The technology, database, and style of the various search engines varies widely. Since technology changes quickly, which one is best, and how each works, can change from day to day. For general searches, I've found HotBot and Infoseek produce the best results. Yahoo! is also an excellent tool, though it's a directory, rather than a search engine. Search.com is something of a hybrid: a directory of search engines. For specialized searches, this is a good place to start.

Here is a list of popular search engines and their URLs:

- AltaVista: *http://altavista.digital.com*
- AOL NetFind: *http://www.aol.com/netfind*
- Ask Jeeves: *http://www.askjeeves.com*
- Dea.com: *http://www.deja.com*
- Excite: *http://www.excite.com*
- Google: *http://www.google.com*
- HotBot: *http://www.hotbot.com*
- Infoseek: *http://www.infoseek.com*
- LookSmart: *http://www.looksmart.com*
- Lycos: *http://www.lycos.com*
- Northern Light: *http://www.nlsearch.com*
- Search.com: *http://www.search.com*
- Yahoo!: *http://www.yahoo.com*

All-Purpose Searching

The most popular search engines on the Web sometimes use differing syntax, but they generally search the same way. Most importantly, you should be specific. As in the query we discussed previously, "Carnegie Hall tickets" got us farther than "tickets," and the natural-language query "Where can I buy tickets to Carnegie Hall?" would have gotten us even farther. And, while simply typing "www.carnegiehall.com" doesn't work in this case, you'd be surprised how often it does. If you're looking for a specific company's web site, try *www.whatever.com* first.*

---

* The *.com* extension works even when it shouldn't, as the commercial designation has become the extension of choice on the Web. Consequently, even enterprises that should use *.gov* or *.org* (such as Boston's public transit system, the MBTA, for example), use *.com*.

Here are some general tips to keep in mind:

- Be precise, and enter as many search terms as possible; enter "Easter egg dye," for example, rather than "Easter eggs."

- Remember that singular search terms work better than plurals. "Easter egg" will return as many, and better, hits than "Easter eggs."

- Wildcard characters can be a big help. The asterisk (*) is a common symbol for zero or more characters. If you were searching for a department store and didn't know how to spell the name, entering "Bl*mingdales" should yield links to a range of Bloomindales, Blümingdales, and Blommingdales on the Web.

- Use operators to trim your results. We'll further discuss operators later; but the plus and minus signs are the most basic. For example, "+Easter+egg+dye" would return only sites that contained all three search terms, while "+Easter+egg -dye" would return sites that included "Easter" and "egg" but not "dye."

- Search twice. Perform a search on "+Easter+egg+dye," then search the results for "blue." Some search engines, including Infoseek and HotBot, allow you to perform a search on the results, from the results page (see Figure 12-2).

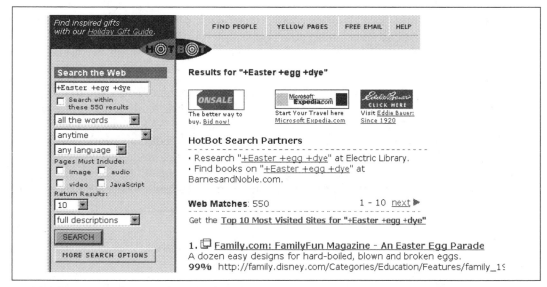

Figure 12-2. Searching within results

Operators

Search engine operators are just like the mathematical operators you learned about in Algebra in high school.* These operators specify the kind of documents you want to

---

* Okay, yes, *fine*, Mr. Grewell, I'm using what I learned in Advanced Algebra in "real life."

search for and how the terms entered should relate to one another. Although there may be a few exceptions, these operators should work as described at any search engine you come across.

And (or +)

Searches for documents containing each of the search terms. For example, "Crate AND Barrel AND flatware."

Or

Searches for documents containing any of the search terms. Consequently, this is a really useless operator when used on its own (see Nesting later in this list). An example would be "State OR Federal."

Not (or -)

Excludes any document containing the search term after the NOT. For example, "State NOT Federal" would return documents with the term "State," but would reject documents containing both the terms "State" and "Federal."

Near (N) and Within (W)

You'll have to invest a lot of thought, prior to your search, to use these operators. NEAR defines how many words may come between your search terms. So, "O'Reilly N2 Perl" indicates that you want to view only documents that contain the terms "O'Reilly" and "Perl" within two words of each other. WITHIN is similar, but the second search term must come after the first; to continue the example, "O'Reilly W2 Perl" indicates that "Perl" would have to follow "O'Reilly" within two words.

Nesting (parentheses ( ))

Use parentheses to control the order in which your searches are executed, again, just as in high school math. This is where the OR operator really shines. For example, a search on "(State OR Federal) AND (constitution AND rights)" would first find all the documents containing the terms "State" and "Federal," and then search them for the terms "constitution" and "rights." The search engine would then return documents that contained the terms "State," "constitution," and "rights," along with documents that contained the terms "Federal," "constitution," and "rights." Got that?

Zero or more characters (*)

An asterisk will stand in for zero or more characters in a search.

One character (?)

A question mark stands in for one character in a search. I can't think of an example where this would be useful ("I want to search for dogs, dots, or DOS. I know just what to do!"), but should one arise, you know how to handle it.

Quotation marks ("")

Quotation marks are my most frequently used operator. Put them around words you want to search for as a phrase. For example, ""Boston Market"" will return documents about the food chain, while "Boston market" will return documents about markets in Boston.

Capitalization

Many search engines recognize proper nouns, so capitalize away.

Meta words and keywords

Meta words (also called keywords) allow you to search very specific HTML fields when you follow them with a colon and your search term (don't insert a space). For example, the query "title:Pekinese" searches for documents with the term Pekinese contained in the HTML title tags of the document. Table 12-1 presents a summary of meta words, their functions, and their usage.

Table 12-1. Meta Words

Meta Word	Example	Usage
domain:keyword	*domain:oreilly.com*	Searches only the selected domain.
feature:keyword	*feature:video*	Searches for pages containing the specified feature. Other valid feature values include acrobat, shockwave, frame, and image.
linkdomain:keyword	*linkdomain:oreilly.com*	Finds all the pages linking to the specified domain; in this case, all the pages that link to *oreilly.com*.
linkext: extension	*linkext:pl*	Searches for pages with embedded files with the specified extension. linkext:pl would result in pages with embedded perl scripts.
newsgroup:newsgroupname	*newsgroup:ne.forsale*	Searches for articles posted to that newsgroup.
scriptlanguage:language	scriptlanguage:javascript	Searches for pages that use JavaScript or VBScript.
title:keyword	*title:Floyd*	Searches for pages with the specified word in the title.
url:keyword	url:entertainment	Searches URLs for the specified term.
after:day/month/year	*after:10/25/70*	Searches for documents created or modified after the specified date.
before:day/month/year	*before:01/02/72*	Searches for documents created or modified before the specified date.
within:number/unit	*within:6/years*	Searches for documents created or modified within the specified time period. Units may be days, months, or years.

Natural language searching

All of the information I've given you feels like a lot to process. If you don't want to learn a wealth of commands before performing your next search, try a search engine that utilizes natural-language queries.

Natural-language queries is a fancy term for asking a question the way that you normally would, in plain English. Just type in your query, with a question mark at the end, and let the search engine sort out the keywords, operators, and concepts behind what you mean. See Table 12-2 for a listing of search engines that support natural-language queries. Ask Jeeves, at *http://www.askjeeves.com*, may be a good choice; its software is backed up by a group of actual human beings who analyze the queries.

Searching without visiting the search engine

Want to search directly from the address bar at the top of your screen? It's easy, if you're using Explorer 5.0 or Navigator 4.5.

If you're using Internet Explorer, entering a term in the Address bar causes Explorer to search for the term using the Microsoft Network's Autosearch feature. The page most likely to be the one you want is displayed in the main browser window, while a list of search results is displayed in the left-hand pane. (You can customize this feature; to change the defaults, access **Tools → Internet Options → Advanced → Browsing**.)

If you're using Netscape Navigator, entering two or more words into the address bar causes Navigator to choose a search engine and return the results. (If you enter one word, Navigator appends "www." and ".com" around the term and tries to connect to the site.)

Meta Searches

Table 12-2 lists web sites that allow you to search more than one search engine at a time. The best sort through the results and eliminate duplicates.

Table 12-2. Meta Search Engines

Name	URL	Number of Engines Searched	Eliminates Duplicates?
Dogpile	*http://www.dogpile.com*	13	No
Highway 61	*http://www.highway61.com*	5	Yes
Mamma	*http://www.mamma.com*	6	Yes
MetaCrawler	*http://www.metacrawler.com*	5	Yes
Savvy Search	*http://guaraldi.cs.colostate.edu:2000/form*	24	Yes

Deja.com

One search engine deserves special mention: Deja.com. Why? Because, unlike the rest of the search engines we discuss, it doesn't search the Internet. It searches Usenet newsgroups and does so in a remarkably thorough fashion. You can search by subject, forum, author, date, or keyword (see Figure 12-3).

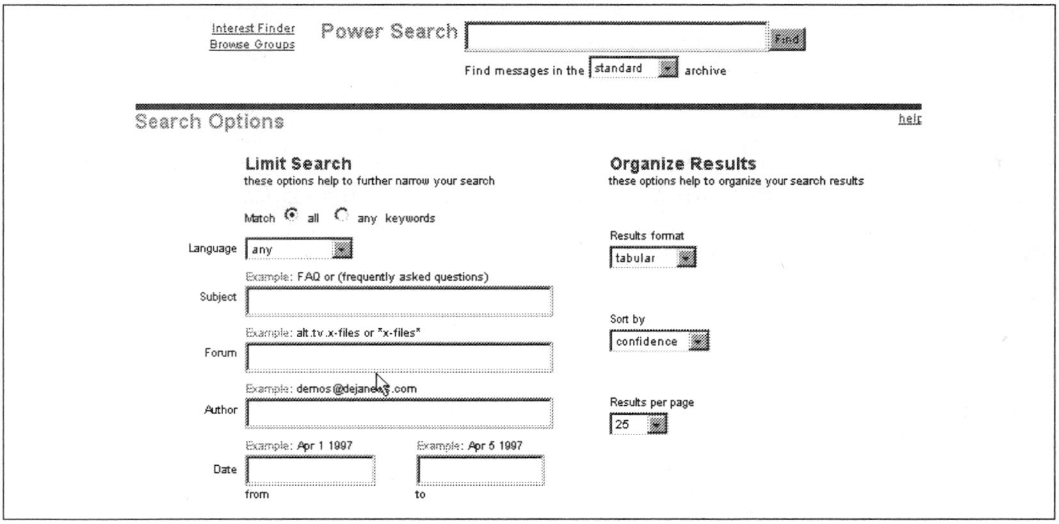

Figure 12-3. Using Deja.com's power-search feature

Choosing the archive you want to search is helpful, as well. Your choices, Complete, Standard, Adult, Jobs, and For Sale, can make searching a much quicker process.

As you can see, by using the power-search feature, you can narrow your search options sufficiently that Deja.com is much more likely to return the information you're looking for on the first pass.

Search Utilities

A number of shareware and freeware applications exist to search multiple search engines at once. The free applications generally support banner advertising (which is innocuous enough, except for the animated variety). You probably don't need an application like this, but if you frequently perform complex or repetitive searches, these utilities do provide the ability to:

- Save searches

- Search multiple search engines at once

- Verify that links exist and remove duplicates

The following applications may be found by searching for the company name, or visiting a shareware archive listed in the Resource Catalog.

BeeLine

TransCom Software created this excellent standalone client. BeeLine searches a number of different sources—search engines, people finders, news sources, software archives, and newsgroups—for the words or phrase of your choice. It then verifies and condenses the results, making them easier to browse.

infoGIST Biz infoFINDER

Another standalone client that searches web search engines, news, and Usenet, but with a business focus. You may also search categories such as "Company Info" and "Biz Topics." The format is convenient, listing found links in a left-hand pane. Clicking on a link brings up information about it in the main window, while double-clicking loads the desired page in a browser.

KDS Concept Explorer

This unusual client uses *knowledge bases* to perform concept searches. Users save documents related to queries to a directory, then use Concept Explorer to analyze the data. Future searches are then "smarter." Previously created knowledge bases may be purchased from KDS.

Copernic

A standalone client that features channel-based searching (Games, Movies, Travel, etc.) and tight integration with Internet Explorer in a three-pane format. While the channels make searching quicker, they aren't any more thorough than using a standard search engine and may actually miss some results by not searching the Web at large.

CyberAge Raider

This browser plug-in uses animated planets, spinning past in a particularly migraine-inducing fashion, to display a collection of web links on various topics. If you really want to use this product, right-clicking on the animation presents a list of the links spinning past you, which open in a second window.

Express by Infoseek

Infoseek's free browser plug-in sits to the right of the browser's location bar. Access it, and a channel listing appears on the left of your browser window, incorporating both a channel guide and a multiple engine search that let's you query AltaVista, Excite, HotBot, Infoseek, Lycos, WebCrawler, and Yahoo!, either by speed or relevance. Searches may be saved, and the results viewed in an interesting, no-need-for-the-Back-button (hey, they were excited about it) format.

WebFerret

A standalone client that searches AltaVista, AOL NetFind, EuroSeek, Excite, Infoseek, Looksmart, Lycos, Search.com, and Yahoo! Very quick, with a single pane interface.

Inforian Quest 98

Another standalone client with different channels for Usenet, entertainment, news, FTP, technology, and major search engines.

IQBoX

This handy little application sits in the taskbar until you double-click it, when it pops up a dialog box. Right-click on the listed search engine to choose from 10 of the most popular, enter your query, and click **Go!** The results appear in your browser window.

Finding People

Looking for someone?

The Web is a lost-lover's dream. Using it, you can search for an old friend's email address, phone number, or even directions to her house.

Even if stalking isn't your bag, the Web is a great resource for keeping in touch; looking up phone numbers, area codes, Zip Codes; and acquiring door-to-door directions.

Finding Someone

If you're trying to look up an old friend, various web sites allow you to search for the email addresses, phone number, and street address of an individual. All you need is a name, although providing a state or city will streamline your search. Keep in mind that finding people on the Web is still an inexact science.

Here are some of the better people finders that you may want to try:

- Switchboard: *http://www.switchboard.com*

- Infoseek People Finder: *http://www2.infoseek.com/Facts?pg=email.html*

- InfoSpace: *http://in-105.infospace.com/info/email1.htm*

- Yahoo! People Search: *http://people.yahoo.com*

- MESA: *http://mesa.rrzn.uni-hannover.de*

- WhoWhere?: *http://www.whowhere.lycos.com*

As an example, let's say we wanted to find an old friend named Jennifer Friedman. We could open up Yahoo!'s People search, and enter the information we know about her, as in Figure 12-4.

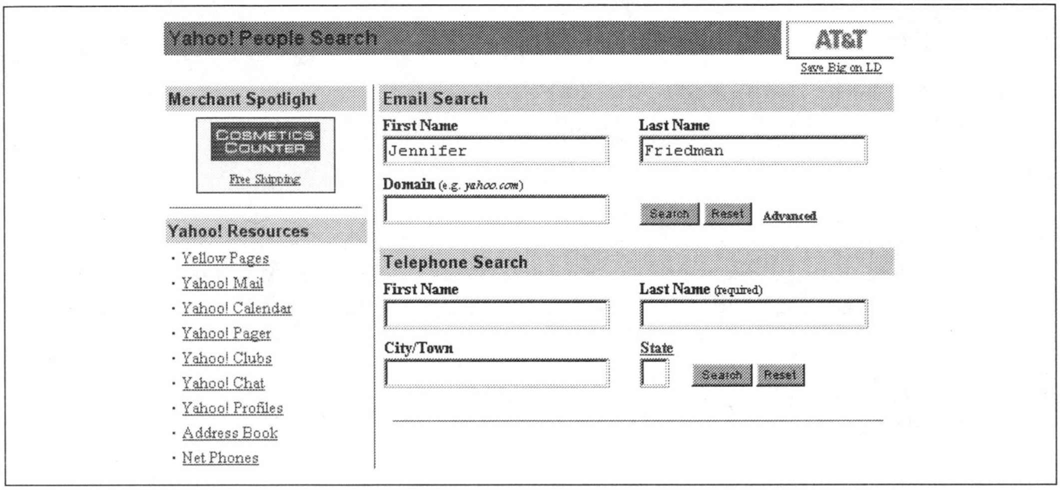

Figure 12-4. Finding Jennifer Friedman

Click the **Search** button, and Yahoo! returns 17 potential matches, shown in Figure 12-5.

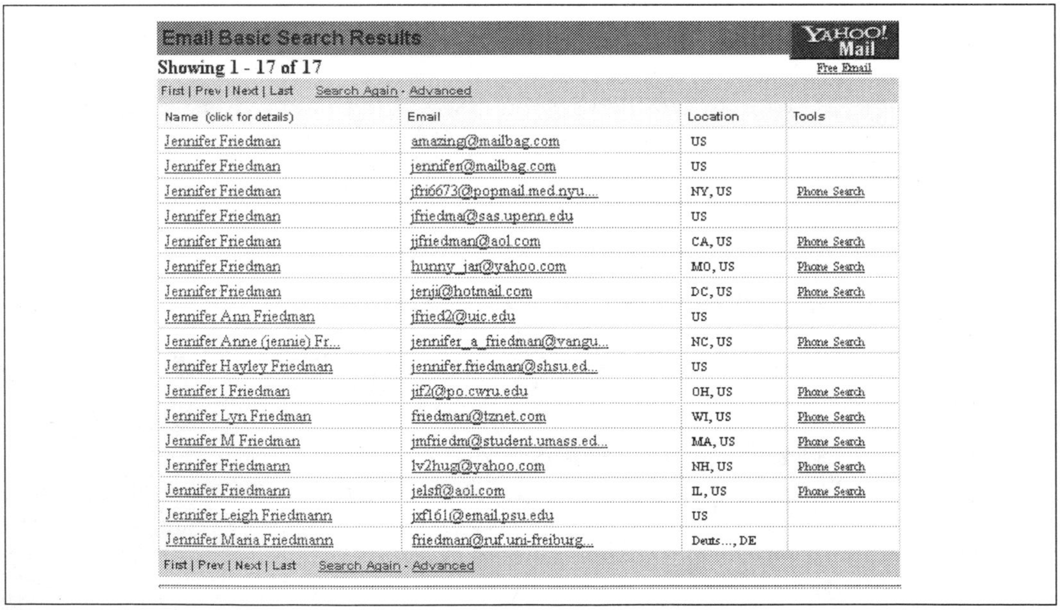

Name (click for details)	Email	Location	Tools
Jennifer Friedman	amazing@mailbag.com	US	
Jennifer Friedman	jennifer@mailbag.com	US	
Jennifer Friedman	jfri6673@popmail.med.nyu....	NY, US	Phone Search
Jennifer Friedman	jfriedma@sas.upenn.edu	US	
Jennifer Friedman	jjfriedman@aol.com	CA, US	Phone Search
Jennifer Friedman	hunny_jan@yahoo.com	MO, US	Phone Search
Jennifer Friedman	jenji@hotmail.com	DC, US	Phone Search
Jennifer Ann Friedman	jfried2@uic.edu	US	
Jennifer Anne (jennie) Fr...	jennifer_a_friedman@vangu...	NC, US	Phone Search
Jennifer Hayley Friedman	jennifer.friedman@shsu.ed...	US	
Jennifer I Friedman	jif2@po.cwru.edu	OH, US	Phone Search
Jennifer Lyn Friedman	friedman@tznet.com	WI, US	Phone Search
Jennifer M Friedman	jmfriedm@student.umass.ed...	MA, US	Phone Search
Jennifer Friedmann	lv2hug@yahoo.com	NH, US	Phone Search
Jennifer Friedmann	jelsfi@aol.com	IL, US	Phone Search
Jennifer Leigh Friedmann	jxf161@email.psu.edu	US	
Jennifer Maria Friedmann	friedman@ruf.uni-freiburg...	Deuts..., DE	

Figure 12-5. But which one is our long-lost friend?

As you can see, Jennifer Friedman is a fairly common name. Determining which address is the correct one, if any, is not an easy task. From the list, however, we could eliminate all the entries that spell "Friedman" with two "n's" instead of one. Since Jennifer's middle name is "Candice," we can also eliminate Jennifer Ann through Jennifer M. This leaves us with seven potential matches.

Now what?

If you know more about your friend than the one in our example—the city she lives in, an old email address, or an old organization—try the advanced search.

Filling in additional information (Figure 12-6) narrows down our choices. The Smart-Names feature acts as a sort of wildcard, searching for variations on popular names.

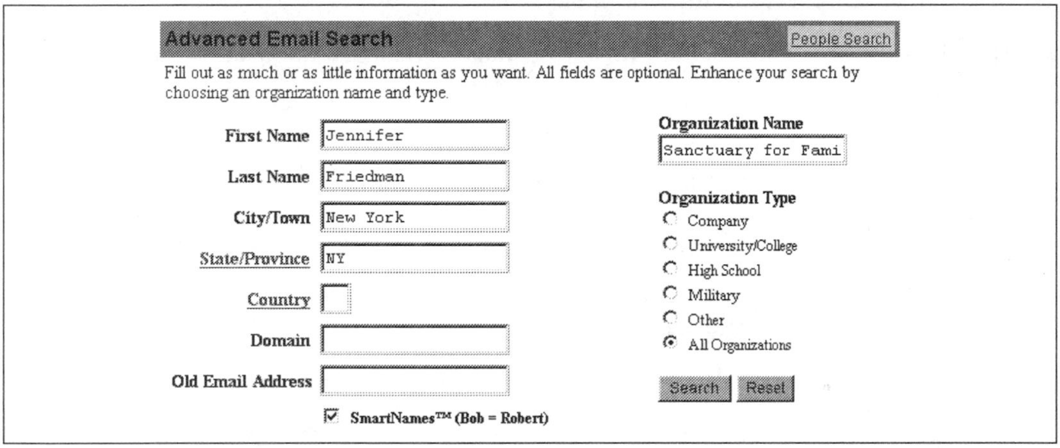

Figure 12-6. Searching with additional information

Unfortunately, in our case, the advanced search didn't turn up any matches.

Let's go back to the earlier list, then. There's one more sneaky method we could use to try to find Jen: a Usenet archive search.

If you're looking for an email address, try searching for an author name at a Usenet archive site—I found it turned up more reliable results than most of the people finders. Context helps, as well—if you know that Jennifer Friedman likes horror novels, and you find a posting from a Jennifer Friedman at *alt.books.stephen-king*, you know you've probably found your girl.

If a Usenet archive doesn't turn anything up, however, and you really wanted to find her, you could now try a (polite) mass-mailing to the seven remaining potential matches. Or, you could try another people finder, or call mutual friends and try to find her the old-fashioned way.

Here are some general tips for finding a person's vital information:

- If you're getting too few returns, try searching using the person's last name and only the first letter of the first name.

- By the same token, try nicknames.

- Try wildcards. For example, we could have entered "Jen* Friedman" to get hits on Jen, Jenni, or Jennifer Friedman.

Finding Phone Numbers

We've already covered how to find an individual's phone number. But there are all sorts of phone numbers available on the Web, from white pages and yellow pages to toll-free listings to reverse-number lookups.

- White pages directories search for individuals or businesses based on a name.

- Yellow pages directories look for businesses and can be useful for finding a list of businesses in a town or Zip Code.

- Sites that provide reverse-lookup features allow you to learn an individual's name and address from a phone number. Enter the number, click **Search**, and the site provides the name of the individual connected with that number.

- Toll-free directories provide listings of 800 or 888 numbers, which are usually national and may be otherwise hard to find.

The following listings provide links to popular phone-number lookups.

Area codes

AmeriCom Long Distance Area Decoder: *http://decoder.americom.com*

555-1212.com Area Code Lookup: *http://www.555-1212.com/aclookup.html*

ACR's International Calling Codes: *http://www.the-acr.com/codes/cntrycd.htm*

White pages

US West Directory Expert: *http://yp.uswest.com/cgi/search.fcg?form=QuickSearch*

WorldPages: *http://www.worldpages.com*

Yellow pages

Ameritech Internet Yellow Pages: *http://yp.ameritech.net*

Anywho Business Search: *http://www.tollfree.att.net/bgq.html*

At Hand Network Yellow Pages: *http://athand.com*

Big Yellow: *http://www.bigyellow.com*

WhoWhere? Yellow Pages: *http://www.whowhere.lycos.com/redirects/yp_index.rdct*

BigBook: *http://www.bigbook.com*

Reverse Lookup

Anywho Reverse Telephone Number Search: *http://www.tollfree.att.net/telq.html*

InfoSpace Reverse Lookup: *http://in-142.infospace.com/info/reverse.htm*

Toll-Free Numbers

Internet 800 Directory: *http://inter800.com*

Anywho Toll-Free Directory Search: *http://www.tollfree.att.net/tf.html*

Finding Places

The Web has always been a great reference tool, but now it's becoming the first truly interactive reference tool. I don't know anyone who enjoys deciphering maps while driving. Now, you can use the Web to create maps just for you.

Create a map to tell you how to get from your city to a city in another state. Or, create a map to tell you how to get from your front door to the museum downtown. You can even create a map to tell you where to find museums in a given neighborhood—or bus stops, or pet stores, or pharmacies.

Finding Directions

One of my favorite web applications is MapQuest, a site that provides detailed driving directions. Such web sites provide city-to-city, and sometimes even door-to-door directions for traveling from place to place. Instead of scouring a map, or waiting for a Triptik from AAA, you can punch in a few locations and receive detailed driving instructions.

These web sites are still relatively new and don't always provide the most direct routes. Unfortunately, none currently allow you to specify portions of your route—for example, telling the application you'd like directions from Boston to New York City, via I-95 instead of the Mass Pike. As with search engines, which one is right for you will be a matter of what you're looking for: MapBlast! tends to provide quicker routes, while MapQuest provides more detailed local maps.

In compiling this list, I left out a few sites that advised me to take a left turn onto a one-way street going the wrong way.

- MapQuest: *http://www.tripquest.com*

- Yahoo! Maps: *http://maps.yahoo.com/py/maps.py*

- MapBlast! Driving Directions: *http://www.mapblast.com/mapblast/path.hm*

- euroShell Route Planner: *http://www.euroshell.com/base_routeue.html*

Using one of these applications is easy. Access the correct site, and click the link to **Driving Directions**. Figure 12-7 shows the opening screen for MapQuest's driving directions feature.

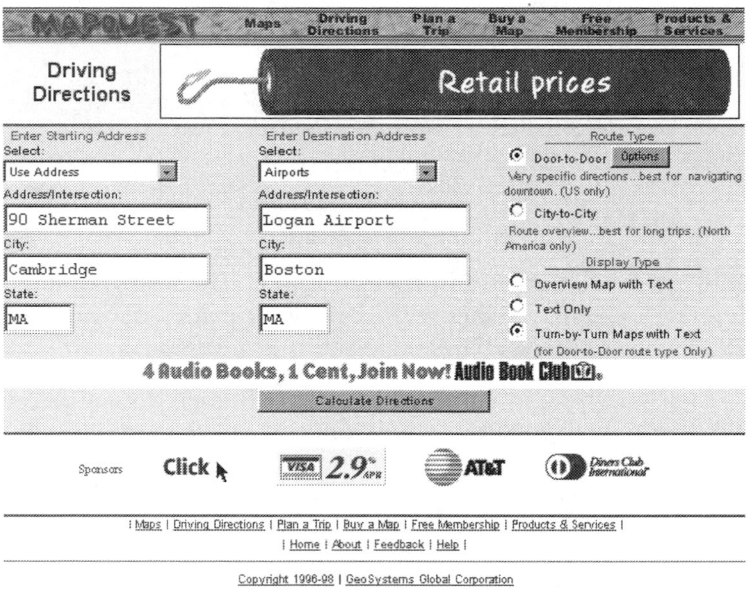

Figure 12-7. Learning how to reach the airport

In general, you'll probably use a street address as a starting point. However, MapQuest provides a number of starting and destination options: amusement parks, city halls, historical monuments, hospitals, and sports complexes all appear on the **Starting/Destination Address** drop-down menus (see Figure 12-8). If you use this feature, MapQuest asks you to confirm the location on the screen.

Now, you need to confirm your route and display type or the style in which MapQuest will return directions. As you can see in Figure 12-9, we probably want door-to-door directions to be able to reach the airport. When it comes to the Display Type, you have three options:

- Overview Map with Text: MapQuest provides two detail maps (of your starting and end points), and text describing each turn in your trip.

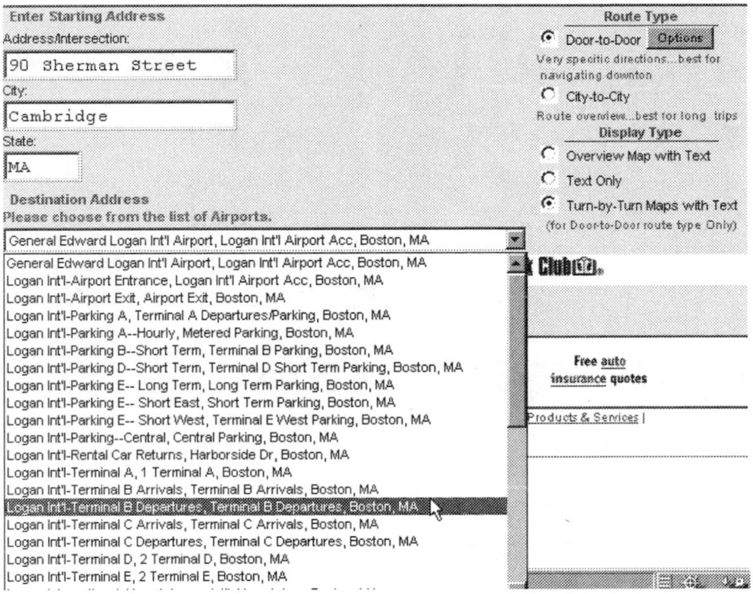

Figure 12-8. You can even choose to receive directions to a specific airport terminal

- Text Only: MapQuest provides only the text description of your journey.
- Turn-by-Turn Maps with Text: MapQuest provides small maps detailing each turn in your trip.

Which option should you choose? That depends on how confusing your trip is and how much ink you have in your printer. The maps print beautifully on a color printer, but they also eat ink for breakfast.

In our case, let's say that we go with the detailed turn-by-turn maps with text. Figure 12-9 shows a portion of the detailed map that MapQuest provides.

Creating Maps

Sometimes you may actually want to get out of your car and look around. If you're visiting an unfamiliar area or scouting out a neighborhood you're thinking about moving into, online maps can help, too.

MapQuest, Yahoo! Maps, and MapBlast! each allow you to enter a street address—even an intersection will do—city, and state. It then produces a map of the neighborhood for you, as in Figure 12-10.

Each of these applications allows you to zoom in or out to examine the area in the detail you prefer. You can also click a link to get driving directions to this location.

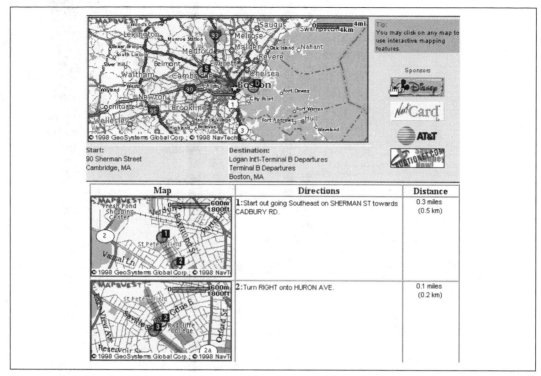

Figure 12-9. Finding the airport

Figure 12-10. MapBlast! map of Manhattan

Perhaps more interestingly, however, you can use MapQuest and Yahoo! Maps to learn about the services in a particular area. Say we wanted to find an Italian restaurant near 59th Street and 5th Avenue in Manhattan. Enter the address into MapQuest, then click the **Dining** link on the resulting map. Over a dozen kinds of foods are listed. Check the box next to Italian, and click the **Update Map** button to see a map like the one in Figure 12-11.

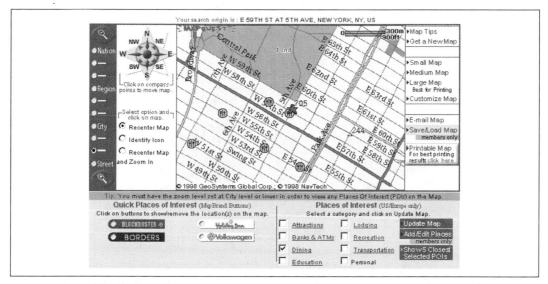

Figure 12-11. The fork-and-spoon icon represents Italian restaurants in the neighborhood

As you can see, you can also use the Places of Interest dialog box to find attractions (landmarks, parks, tourist information, etc.), ATMs, lodging, and more. The **Transportation** link, in particular, may be helpful, since it lists bus stops, train stations, and other important information.

Yahoo! Maps provides a similar feature. After creating a map of an area, click the **Find Nearby Businesses** link. The next screen you see looks like the standard Yahoo! directory tree; you'll find categories on everything from Automotive to Education to Real Estate to Travel. Once you find the business or service you're interested in, Yahoo! puts it back on the map for you and provides links to related services. In Figure 12-12, we've pinpointed an Italian restaurant.

Since Yahoo! Maps provides phone numbers, you wouldn't even need to dine at the Italian restaurant—just order takeout, instead.

PalmPilot Mapping

Maps on your PalmPilot are certainly more convenient than paper maps, although they are more difficult to fold. A program called Quo Vadis, available from *http://www. marcosoft.com/quovadis/default.stm*, allows you to scroll through grayscale maps as you travel. The searchable maps feature landmarks including intersections, shopping malls, and airports, and you can save your last position. Fifty-six maps of U.S. states and territories are available for download to registered users. Quo Vadis is compatible

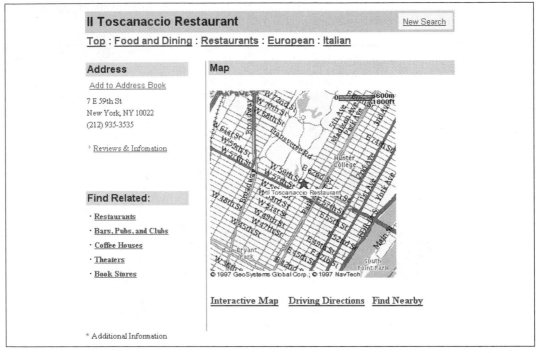

Figure 12-12. Finding restaurants via Yahoo! Maps

with the Global Positioning System, which, if you want to shell out for the fancy gadget, will locate your position to within 10 feet.

Archaic Search Technologies

Before this chapter comes to a close, we'll have a brief vocabulary lesson. Without it, you may think that there's some knowledge that I've failed to impart.

Before the Web came along, people needed a way to archive, find, and download files. Of the text-based tools that were used for these purposes—FTP, Gopher, Archie, and Veronica—only FTP really survives today. The rest are really obsolete. You may hear them mentioned, however, or find them to be of use for certain esoteric purposes.

Gopher

Gopher's relation to the Web is rather like that of the Neanderthals to *homo sapiens:* they evolved at similar times, shared a common ancestry, and even superficially resembled each other. One, however, was much better suited to survival than the other.

Gopher is a text-based document-retrieval system. Documents are displayed in a hierarchical, tree-based format on gopher servers, and gopher clients can search Internet servers for keywords or subjects.

Web browsers have always included the ability to view information on gopher clients. In fact, a few years ago, one frequently came across URLs such as this one: *gopher://gopher.micro.umn.edu*. Most people didn't even realize it when they were looking at a gopher server. Figure 12-13 shows the gopher server at the University of Minnesota, where gopher originated.

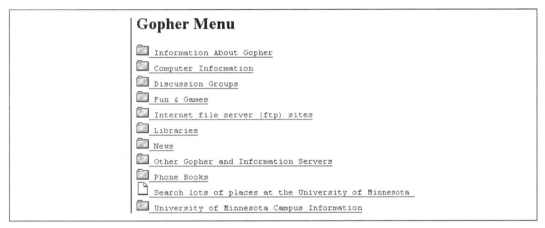

Figure 12-13. A gopher server

While gopher is named after the University of Minnesota's mascot, the Golden Gopher, it seems likely that gopher will continue to go the way of the Neanderthal, quietly heading toward extinction.

Archie

Archie is something of a protosearch engine, creating and searching a database of files available at anonymous FTP sites. In the past, you used either an Archie client connected to the Internet to search for files, or sent in an email query and awaited a reply. Once presented with a list of hits, you downloaded files via an FTP client.

Today, most Archie searches are performed via an online form like the one at *http://archie.rutgers.edu/archie.html*. The system is buggy, and the results you find are often dated. Ironically, however, one of the reasons Archie survives is its difficulty: the notorious WAREZ servers, where people make pirated software available for FTP, utilize Archie as their search mechanism of choice—the esoteric technology makes the files difficult to reach except for those in the know.

Veronica

Veronica stands for Very Easy Rodent-Oriented Netwide Index to Computerized Archives, which was really just a way to have Veronica join Archie on the Net; an even less widely known service was called Jughead. In any event, Veronica was a way to search gopher sites much as Archie searches FTP servers. It's rather hard to find a Veronica interface anymore; one of the few remaining, *http://galaxy.einet.net/gopher/ gopher.html*, doesn't even bill itself as such.

CHAPTER THIRTEEN

DOWNLOADING AND INSTALLING FILES

So far, we've explained how to browse the Web, read Usenet, and search for all sorts of things. When it comes to downloading and installing files, however, you may still feel a little nervous. Is it safe to download programs from the Internet? And how exactly do you download and install files to your computer, anyway? Are special tools involved?

These are good questions, but the answers aren't as hard as you might think. You should always have good virus protection software installed on your computer, run it regularly, and update it periodically. Once you've taken these precautions, you're fairly safe downloading shareware applications from established shareware archives, such as those mentioned later in this chapter and in the Resource Catalog of this book.

You don't need any special tools to download or install files, but there are a few that make the process a little easier. A web browser may not always be the best tool for mining the resources of the Web—an FTP client frequently downloads files more efficiently and easily. And a decompression utility called WinZip allows you to access files that have been compressed for easier Internet transmission.

Downloading Files with a Web Browser

Using a web browser to download files is quite simple. Once you find the file you're looking for—a shareware application, text file, multimedia file, etc.—you'll probably find downloading instructions along with it. Download the file according to those instructions. Usually, these instructions are as simple as clicking a link and saving the file to your hard drive, an in Figure 13-1.

Save the file to a download or temp directory. Odds are that you want to leave the filename as specified. You definitely want to leave the file extension as specified, or

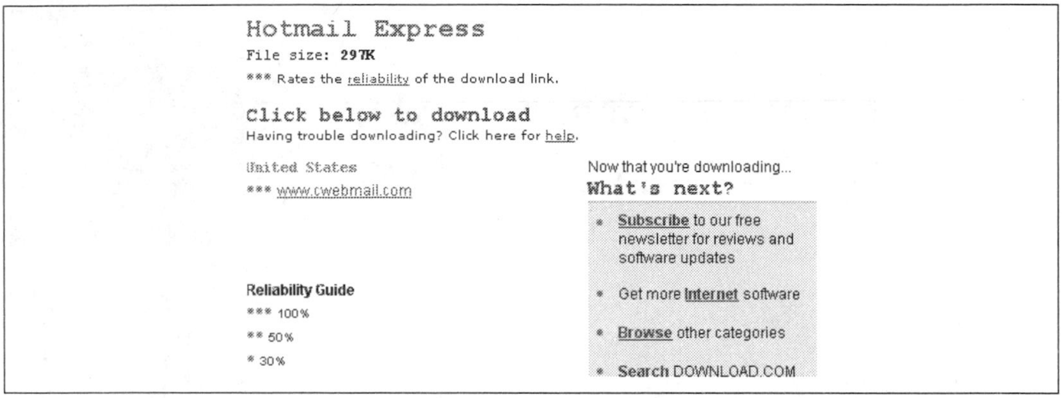

Figure 13-1. Downloading a mailer plug-in from Download.com

the file may not open correctly. See the section on Installing Files, later in this chapter, for more information.

File Transfer Protocol Is Your Friend

Once you've found a file you're looking for, you need to download it. Using your browser may not always be your best bet.

FTP is the acronym for File Transfer Protocol. As the name implies, the protocol's job is to move files from one computer to another. It doesn't matter where the computers are located, how they are connected, or even whether they use the same operating system. Provided that both computers can talk the FTP protocol and have access to the Internet, you can use the FTP application to transfer files. Some of the nuances of its use do change with each operating system, but the basic command structure is the same from machine to machine.

Sound familiar? It should. World Wide Web browsers have incorporated FTP technology from the get-go. Why, then, would you want to use such an archaic tool?

Because it's a better tool. FTP lets you perform the following functions that you can't perform with a standard web browser:

■   Resume interrupted downloads in midstream. If you lose your connection, or need to stop the transfer for any reason, simply start the download again later. If you download the file to the same directory, the download picks up where it left off.

■   Download multiple files with fewer commands. Instead of downloading a single file at a time, you can download multiple files, saving the repetition of the initial steps.

■   Download large files. A web browser generally can't deal with a file that's larger than its cache. Thus, browsers sometimes fail completely for large file transfers.

- Download from directories that aren't available on the Web. These "hidden" directories are placed on FTP servers that don't allow web access. Even if you knew the directory and filename, you couldn't download a file there with a web browser.

- Upload files to servers. If you connect to an office from home or want to display a web page, you'll need to upload files (and download them, too).

In general, an FTP client will perform all of these actions more quickly, efficiently, and intuitively than a web browser.

Using FTP used to be hard—you had to type actual *commands*—but it isn't anymore. Download an FTP client with a Windows Explorer-like interface, and you'll already know how to use it. FTP Explorer (*http://www.ftpx.com*, free for non-commercial use), CuteFTP (*http://www.cuteftp.com*), and FTP Voyager (*http://www.ftpvoyager.com*) are a few highly regarded examples.

Using FTP to Download Files from the Web

But, wait! You might be thinking, Where am I going to *find* these files to download efficiently? Why, on the Web.

Say you'd like to download the latest behemoth release of Netscape Communicator. If you were at c|net's *download.com* site, you might reach the screen in Figure 13-2 and feel some trepidation at the 10.5 MB file size.

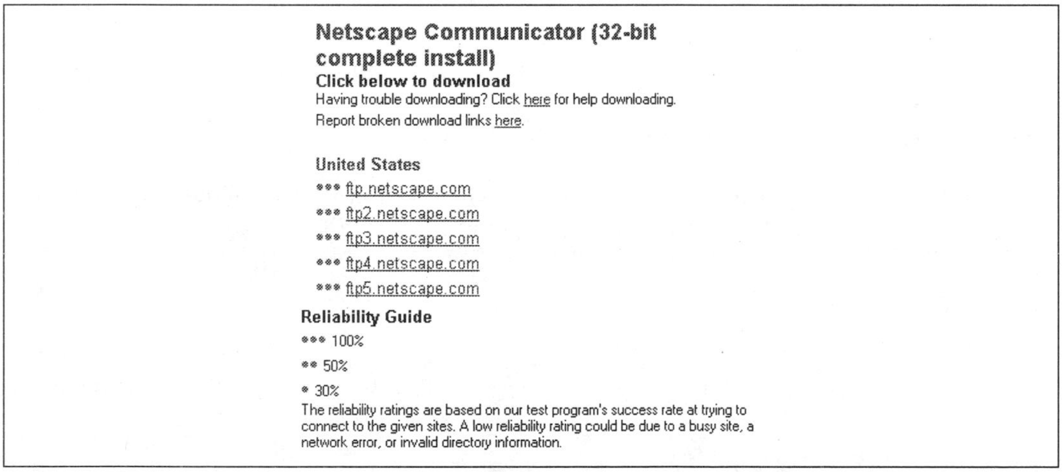

Netscape Communicator (32-bit complete install)
Click below to download
Having trouble downloading? Click here for help downloading.
Report broken download links here.

United States
*** ftp.netscape.com
*** ftp2.netscape.com
*** ftp3.netscape.com
*** ftp4.netscape.com
*** ftp5.netscape.com
Reliability Guide
*** 100%
** 50%
* 30%
The reliability ratings are based on our test program's success rate at trying to connect to the given sites. A low reliability rating could be due to a busy site, a network error, or invalid directory information.

Figure 13-2. Sites from which you may download Netscape Communicator

Instead of clicking on one of the listed links and beginning the download process, open your FTP client.

We've copied the link listed at *download.com* and pasted it into the Host Address field (see Figure 13-3). We also named the profile "Netscape," but we could have called it anything we wanted. Many servers allow the public to log in anonymously; it's considered polite to leave your email address as the password, so that administrators can track visitors. Checking the Anonymous box fills in this information for you.

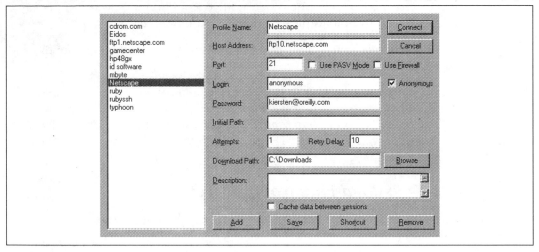

Figure 13-3. Logging in to Netscape's public server

When we first log in, we're greeted with five folders: *bin, dev, etc, pub*, and *usr*. Pub stands for public, so double-click that folder to go deeper into the directory. As you can see from the contents listing just below the toolbar in Figure 13-4, we'll have to wade through a number of directories until we find the file we want. Once you do, double-click on the filename and download it to your computer.

ASCII Versus Binary Mode

FTP downloads files in one of two modes: ASCII or binary. As a general rule, move text or HTML files in ASCII mode and all others in binary mode.

Installing Files

Once you've found a file you're looking for, you may not know how to install it on your computer.

First, find the file you want, and download it according to the instructions on the download site. Save it to a download or temp directory, leaving the filename as specified.

Now, close any open applications on your computer. You may need to perform a manual close (by pressing Ctrl-Alt-Del at the same time) to shut down any background or taskbar applications. As a general rule, you need to do this only when the

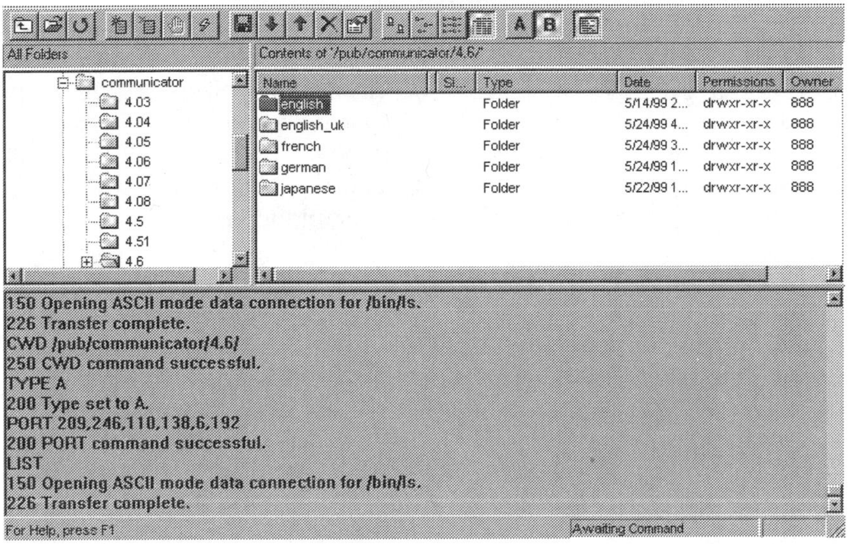

Figure 13-4. The results of our search

file you've downloaded is an application similar to one that's currently running. For example, you probably want to close the RealPlayer application if you've downloaded a newer version of it, or another media player.

Odds are that the file you found has been compressed for download. If so, you need to decompress it before it can be installed. Doing so is pretty simple, since for the most part, files are compressed in one of two ways: in a self-extracting archive that decompresses when you double-click it, or as a ZIP file, for which you need a decompression utility called WinZip.*

How do you know which file is which? The downloaded file will probably have an icon that looks like one of those in Figure 13-5.

setupex.exe   q2-314-demo...   Dllshow.zip   winzip70.exe   pipedrm.zip

Figure 13-5. Various types of downloaded files

If the file extension is *.exe*, the file is a self-extracting archive. If the file extension is *.zip*, it's a ZIP file. Two of the files don't quite fit these rules: *q2-314-demo...*, which is

---

* There are, of course, a number of other compression schemes, including StuffIt files for the Mac. WinZip is by far the most prevalent, and it handles several other compression schemes and is thus the only one we'll describe here. StuffIt works in a manner analogous to WinZip, however, so if you're using a Mac, download StuffIt and proceed.

the demo for Quake II, and *winzip70.exe*, which is the WinZip self-extracting archive (that installs WinZip itself). Even though *winzip70.exe* is a self-extracting archive, the icon looks like a ZIP file. Why? Because WinZip is trying to be cute. This example illustrates an important point, however, which is that self-extracting archives will sometimes feature icons that represent the application they contain, rather than the standard setup/installation icons. The Quake II demo file is actually a similar example: in this case, id software, the makers of Quake II, didn't bother with an icon at all, leaving the user with the standard Windows executable icon.

Installing Self-Extracting Archives

Self-extracting archives are generally quite easy to install. Close any open applications and double-click the file. Follow the prompts.

Installing WinZip Files

To install a WinZip file, you first need to install the WinZip application itself. Download it from *http://www.winzip.com/ddchome.htm* or from one of the Windows shareware archives listed in the Resource Catalog, and follow the instructions for installing a self-extracting archive.

Now, double-click the icon for the archive that you've downloaded. WinZip launches and displays the archive's contents, shown in Figure 13-6.

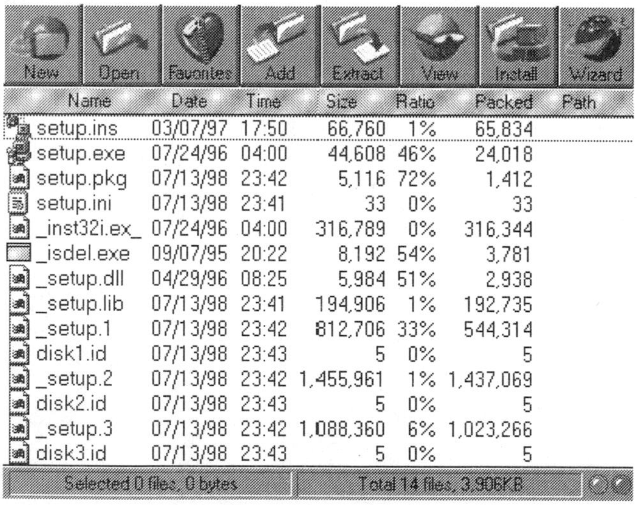

Figure 13-6. Contents of a ZIP archive

Now that we've opened the file, we have three options:

- Examine the files—WinZip actually allows you to run some files from *within* the archive. You can read text files to check out the contents of the archive, and sometimes even run an executable (depending on the complexity of the installation). It's a good way of deciding whether you'd like to install software you've downloaded.

- Extract files—extract all the files to a directory, then double-click the setup icon.

- Install—click the **Install** button, and follow the prompts to install the file as you would with a self-extracting archive.

Not every archive will enable WinZip's Install feature. If an archive does, use it; once the file is installed, you can simply delete the archive.

If an archive doesn't enable the Install feature, extract the files to a temp directory, or a directory you've created for this purpose. Either the files should be self-explanatory—for example, the archive consists of a single, compressed application—or a readme file should explain how to proceed.

Running Installed Applications

Once you've installed an application, you probably have a good idea of what to do next: double-click it. However, you may need a little more guidance.

Many downloaded archives come with readme files. A *readme* file is a text file that is frequently included in an archive or download to provide information about it: instructions, purposes, help files, known issues, bugs, registration information, etc. If a readme file exists, read it.

Other applications come with standard help files that you can look to for guidance.

Removing Downloaded Files

If you decide you don't want the files you've just downloaded, remove them. First, look for an uninstall utility in the program's directory. If you don't find one, use Windows' Add/Remove programs utility. Follow the prompts to remove the file.

CHAPTER FOURTEEN

RESOURCE CATALOG: BEST OF THE WEB

After thirteen chapters of talking about how to do various things, we thought we'd show you what you can do. The next two chapters are a brief catalog of Internet resources: web sites that we found particularly interesting or important.

The Internet is so huge, it's impossible to catalog all of it, and we never entertained the thought of trying. Yahoo! does a reasonable job of organizing and listing hundreds of thousands of web sites, and the search engines that we discussed in Chapter 12 will get you to good sites for any topic that you're interested in. So why bother writing a catalog at all?

For one, it's fun. But it also serves a purpose. If your first exposure to the Internet is through a search engine, you might find it frustrating. Or you might think, "All I ever wanted to know about plastic surgery on elephants is here; this is great." But in neither case would you get a feeling for the true breadth of what's out there: resources and sites discussing every imaginable topic, often by people who are passionately interested and well informed about their specialty.

That's what we're trying to do here. We list a relatively small number of resources that cross a huge number of categories, trying to give you a sense of the possibilities. We really have not tried to be exhaustive in any category—we picked the sites that looked most interesting and that we thought were the most stable (i.e., the sites that were most likely to be in existence a year or two from now). The catalog isn't just for computer nerds; as you can imagine, there's no shortage of web sites that discuss computing. We've included as few of these as we could justify. It's not hard to find *www. microsoft.com*; if you're seriously interested in computing, you shouldn't have any trouble compiling a list of sites as long as you like.

We have tried to include at least one *meta-site* in each category. A meta-site is one that doesn't contain much information of its own, but it consists primarily of a list of other sites that are relevant to the topic. Good meta-sites are the rare gems of the Internet world; when you find one on a topic that interests you, add it to your hotlist immediately.

We've used five icons to identify sites that are of particular interest:

⊕   A site with good links to other related sites

✦   A site that requires registration (but no fee) in order to use it.

✎   A site that provides a way for you to search its contents.

♨   A site that uses Java, and which therefore might take a while to download.

$ A site that requires you to pay a fee in order to access to the full range of services.

We've also found it necessary to split the catalog into two parts:

Chapter 14
    This is the Resource Catalog proper. It's where you'll find all the fun and interesting stuff. Web sites listed in this section range from the useful to the inane.

Chapter 15
    This section covers the web sites and resources that support various chapters in this book. Curious about auction sites or alternatives to Amazon.com? Check here.

One word about what is not in this catalog: no one got into the catalog by paying us. There is no advertising, and inclusion is subject entirely to the whim of the authors. If you would like to get into the next edition, send mail to *webresources@oreilly.com*, but please be aware that:

ı   We won't reply. You'll find out if you got in when the next edition comes out.

ı   No whining or multiple submissions. We reserve the right to be prejudiced against whiners and stalkers.

ı   The rules for inclusion aren't going to change: sites must be interesting, informative, or tickle our fancy in some way. So please don't submit boring sites. (And yes, all personal home pages are boring by definition.)

ı   We aren't likely to include sites that consist mostly of advertising (either for your products or others) or sites that charge a fee to access information. We will make exceptions for particularly valuable sites, so if you fall into this category, don't give up hope—just build a site that's so interesting we have to include it.

Finally, another word about what's not in this catalog. You wouldn't know it to listen to a lot of self-appointed experts, but the Internet is a lot more than the Web. This catalog only reflects the Web, and it omits very valuable resources like Usenet newsgroups, mailing lists, chat servers, and other things. Frankly, the only reason we didn't include resources like these is that we couldn't figure out how to evaluate them. Omitting mailing lists is really unfortunate but the only way to maintain our sanity.

After all, about the only way to figure out whether a mailing list discussing baroque music is useful is to subscribe to it and participate in it for a while, and that was clearly impossible given the thousands of lists that exist. But don't ignore these other resources. Although the Web gets all the press, there's nothing more useful than a good mailing list focused on a topic you care about.

We shouldn't have to say this, but we will. The Web changes very quickly, and some of these sites may have vanished before the book is in your hands. If you find any broken links, send email to *webresources@oreilly.com*. We'll try to maintain a list of changes on the book's errata page, at *http://www.oreilly.com/catalog/twi3/errata*.

AERONAUTICS & ASTRONAUTICS

NASA Spacelink

Spacelink celebrates its tenth anniversary in 1998, making it an Internet ancient. Provided by NASA's Education Division, the site links to educational services, instructional materials, NASA projects, NASA news and a NASA overview.

http://spacelink.msfc.nasa.gov

Shuttle and Satellite Images

The following sites make available photographs and other images taken aboard the space shuttle, during the Magellan, Viking, or later missions, or via the Hubble telescope. Data formats vary.

Space shuttle photographs

http://www.nasm.edu/ceps/RPIF/SSPR.html

NSSDC photo gallery

http://nssdc.gsfc.nasa.gov/photo_gallery/photogallery.html

Space radar images of Earth from SIR-C/X-SAR

http://www.jpl.nasa.gov/radar/sircxsar/

Atlas of Mars and Viking Orbiter image-finder

http://ic.arc.nasa.gov/ic/projects/bayes-group/Atlas/Mars/

AGRICULTURE

AGLINKS—Links for the Agriculture Industry

The agriculture enthusiast will find a wide variety of Internet resources clearly organized under several headings using basic alphabetized lists to help simplify your search; choose from general agriculture, farms and companies, markets, magazines and newsletters, government, research and education, and weather. This one's fast and easy because it foregoes the complex web graphics and instead uses a very simple format. ⊕

http://www.gennis.com/aglinks.html

Agriculture (Engineering and Technology)

References galore, including academic organizations and books. Under some of the specific headings (in total, agronomy, animal husbandry, fisheries, forestry, horticulture, industrial applications, range management, wildlife management) resources are sparse but others list related collections, events and government/nonprofit organizations to connect to for probably the most current information on the subject. ⊕

http://www.galaxy.com/galaxy/Science/Agriculture/Engineering.html

Agriculture and Food Industry Resources

The old U.S. Department of Agriculture master gopher index has become this collection of agriculture resources. Domestic and international links to business directories, resources, newsgroups, universities and colleges, and government departments can all be found here.

http://www.oneglobe.com/agriculture/

AgriGator Agriculture Information Index

A rich collection of Internet sites and sources related to agriculture, maintained at the University of Florida. Don't be deceived by the simple-looking home page, which actually organizes information remarkably well. If you click on one of the 12 categories listed, you'll be rewarded with a wealth of links. You also might want to check out the AgriForum for a chat on agricultural topics. ⊕

http://gnv.ifas.ufl.edu/WWW/AGATOR/HTM/AG.HTM

Not Just Cows

Not Just Cows continues its role as Internet innovator. Wilfred (Bill) Drew's guide to resources on the Internet that cover agriculture and related subjects was one of the first of its kind on the Net. Now, it contains links to two separate agriculture web rings, noncommercial World Wide Web links, and the Moooo sound file.

http://www.snymor.edu/~drewwe/njc/

World Wide Web Virtual Library: Agriculture

Out of North Carolina State University, this index has a broad spectrum of links from agriculture sites around the world to databases and software in addition to the U.S. sites and universities found on other web pages. It's fancy, but well organized and thorough. ⊕

http://ipmwww.ncsu.edu/cernag/cern.html

ARCHAEOLOGY

Archaeological Fieldwork Opportunities

A service for those seeking archaeological fieldwork opportunities, this server offers detailed descriptions of planned research trips. Also listed are archaeological contractors and links to other Internet resources that pertain to archaeology. The Archaeological Fieldwork server is maintained by Ken Stuart of Cornell University.

http://www.sscnet.ucla.edu/ioa/afs/testpit.html

Archaeology from the Air

A collection of 20 photographs made up of aerial views of significant excavation sites in Israel. These pictures represent a lot of Roman and Byzantine architecture, are good sized, and each has a description next to it. Credit goes to photographer Duby Tal and pilot Moni Haramati for these interesting and historical views.

http://www.israel-mfa.gov.il/mfa/go.asp?.MFAH00qs0

ArchNet

ArchNet, at the University of Connecticut's Department of Anthropology, provides links to archaeology sites worldwide. You'll find listings according to region or subject, as well as links to news, museums, academic departments, and journals and publishers. A text-only version is available as are mirror sites in Catalan, Dutch, French, German, Italian, and Spanish ⊕

http://archnet.uconn.edu

Classics & Mediterranean Archaeology

An index to archaeology resources on the Net, sponsored by the Department of Classical Studies, University of Michigan. The table of contents includes texts, projects, journals, bibliographies, indexes of links, exhibits on the Web, course material and teaching resources, departmental descriptions, and more information. ⊕

http://rome.classics.lsa.umich.edu/welcome.html

Peabody Museum of Archaeology and Ethnology

Harvard's Peabody Museum has created a web site of exhibitions, archival collections, special projects, and events. If you want to learn more about Archaeology, a specific exhibit, or the people behind an exhibit, this is a good place for the beginner to start.

http://www.peabody.harvard.edu

ART HISTORY

Art Market Index by ADEC

Curious about the selling price for a piece of art? This site catalogs over 1,300,000 auction sales since 1987. 60 responses cost $50. $

http://www.auctionrecords.com

ArtServe

An art history server at Australian National University, created by professor Michael Greenhalgh. ArtServe springs from Greenhalgh's interest in discovering computing applications for students of the humanities. The site features 70,000 images of art and architecture, mainly from around the Mediterranean. You'll find images of everything from "some of the world's great typefaces" to stills from Leni Riefenstahl. ✦

http://rubens.anu.edu.au

Asian Arts

A large collection of images from exhibits of Asian art at museums and galleries worldwide. You'll find links to associations, exhibitions, articles, and galleries related to Asian art worldwide. An index of links to other Asian art sites and a calendar of events are also available.

http://www.webart.com/asianart/index.html

Broadacre All-Wright Site

The best Frank Lloyd Wright site we could find contains essays on the life and work of the twentieth century's premier architect. It also contains links to everything from quotations to Wright properties for sale.

http://geocities.com/SoHo/1469/flw.html

Leonet

A site dedicated to Da Vinci, not Dicaprio. Visit the Leonardo Da Vinci museum, the Italian leather directory, or explore the art, culture, and museums of Vinci.

http://www.leonet.it

Mexican Painters and Muralists

Image files of paintings and murals by 15 renowned Mexican artists, including Rufino Tamayo, Diego Rivera, and Jose Clemente Orozco. Each artist is represented by two or more works. The exhibit is presented by the University of Guadalajara.

http://mexico.udg.mx/Ingles/Arte/Pintura/pintores.html

National Museum of American Art

The online home of the Smithsonian Institution's National Museum of American Art is everything a museum web site should be. Twelve online exhibitions, including "The White House Collection of American Crafts" and "Secrets of the Dark Chamber: The Art of the American Daguerreotype " present rich multimedia tours of dozens of works by American artists. You'll find scores of images, videos, and sound files in a thoughtfully organized format that miraculously doesn't take hours to download.

http://www.nmaa.si.edu

Vatican City and the Sistine Chapel

A rich visual tour of Vatican City, from San Pietro Basilica to the Pontifical Palaces. Images are in JPEG format. The tour was created by Christus Rex, a "nonprofit organization dedicated to the dissemination of information on works of art preserved in churches, cathedrals and monasteries all over the world." A jump up one level to the Christus Rex home page (overview) provides access to tours of the Sistine Chapel and the Vatican museums. Especially noteworthy are the breathtaking images from the Sistine Chapel featured here. This site, developed by Michael Olteanu at the Christus Rex web site, features a well-organized archive of 325 JPEG images, including full representations of Michelangelo's chapel ceiling and his Last Judgment mural. Although it would be nice to

have more descriptions and background information on the works, they speak nicely for themselves.

http://www.christusrex.org

Vatican Exhibit

Images and text from an exhibition at the Library of Congress, including manuscripts from the Vatican Library in all areas of historical interest. Explore the site via the object index, or visit different "rooms" on topics including archaeology, humanism, mathematics, music, medicine and biology, "Nature Described," Orient to Rome, and Rome to China. Images are large, but provided in JPEG format.

http://metalab.unc.edu/expo/vatican.exhibit/exhibit/Main_Hall.html

World Arts Resources

An impressive site and the best index to arts resources on the Net. Organized by the Ohio State University (at Newark) Art Gallery, World Arts Resources features links to hundreds of museums, publications, institutions, and commercial resources. ⊕

http://www.wwar.com

ASTRONOMY

AstroWeb: Astronomy/Astrophysics on the Internet

A searchable web site maintained by the AstroWeb Consortium, a group of nine individuals at seven institutions. The wealth of resources are "tested 3x a day to verify aliveness." You'll find links to observing resources (i.e., telescopes), archives, publications, software, and research. ⊕

http://www.stsci.edu/astroweb/astronomy.html

National Space Science Data Center

This site features links to a wide variety of astrophysics, space physics, solar physics, and lunar and planetary data garnered during NASA space missions.

http://nssdc.gsfc.nasa.gov

The Nine Planets: A Multimedia Tour of the Solar System

An exciting and comprehensive tour of our solar system written in nontechnical language. The Nine Planets site is loaded with interesting information, including history, current theories, mythology, and data garnered by spacecraft. The Nine Planets is well organized and easy to navigate and includes lots of images, some animation and sound files, and a glossary of terms. This is an excellent resource for general statistical research as well as casual browsing. Take the express tour, or work your way systematically through the hierarchically organized data.

http://seds.lpl.arizona.edu/nineplanets/nineplanets/nineplanets.html

Space Telescope Science Institute

If you want the latest news from or about the Hubble Space Telescope, this is the place to look. The site features other telescopes as well, along with images and news releases, educational activities, and information about the Space Telescope Science Institute itself.

http://www.stsci.edu/top.html

Views of the Solar System

Use your mouse to explore space. You can travel to each of the planets, where you can visit asteroids, comets, meteors, and moons. The site offers fine graphics and a wealth of information, often presented in a fairly technical manner. Compiled by Calvin J. Hamilton of Los Alamos National Laboratory, Views also offers dozens of links to other space-related sites.

http://www.hawastsoc.org/solar/eng/homepage.htm

The Web Nebulae

Stunning images of gaseous nebulae, from the Pleiades to Supernova 1987a. Each image is accompanied by a brief information file. In the words of creator Bill Arnett, "If you look up at the night sky with your naked eye all you see is a black void with a few points of white light. But with a camera and a telescope an entirely different view unfolds in brilliant color and amazing detail. The pages that follow introduce a few of these spectacular objects. The study of the physics of many of these objects is of considerable scientific importance but their simple beauty can be enjoyed by all."

http://seds.lpl.arizona.edu/billa/twn/

AUTOMOBILES

CarInfo.com

Mark Eskeldson, the author of *What Car Dealers Don't Want You to Know* and *What Auto Mechanics Don't Want You to Know* presents this site dedicated to consumer information related to cars. You'll find sections on current news reports, leasing secrets, buying secrets, auto repair secrets, and more. ⊕

http://www.carinfo.com

Cars@Cost

This car-buying service describes itself as being like "an HMO for car buyers." The site offers to sell certain makes and models of cars to consumers at or below MSRP. Placing an order requires a $75 retainer; if you actually buy a car through the service, the buying service fee ranges between $275 and $499. $

http://www.carscost.com

Car Talk

A tremendously rich automotive site from Tom and Ray Magliozzi, National Public Radio's Car Talk guys. Features include puzzlers, pictures of Tom and Ray, and audio excerpts from the radio program, but the real resource is the car information. You'll find model reports, answers to questions directly from manufacturers, lemon laws, a listing of quality mechanics (called the Mechan-X Files), and much, much more.

http://cartalk.cars.com

eAuto: Everything Automotive

eAuto is the site for auto enthusiasts of all stripes. Features include a car-buying service, automotive classifieds, news, industry headlines, chat, and automotive web site, newsgroup, and mailing list reviews.

http://www.eauto.com

Edmund's Automobile Buyer's Guide

Edmund's provides a wealth of information on prices, reviews, and safety for both new and used cars. You'll also find consumer information, road tests, and a nice section listing current rebates and factory incentives.

http://edmund.com/edweb/

AVIATION

Aviation Enthusiast Corner

An extensive reference guide to aircraft types and specifications, museums and displays, and air shows, maintained by volunteers at Brooklyn College. The site doesn't quite live up to its overproduced look, but if you're trying to find an air show, aircraft, or museum, this is the place to start.

http://www.aero-web.org/air.htmll

Aviation Internet Resources

This compendium of aviation-related links will guide you to web sites related to everything from airlines to airports to reservations to stock quotes. You'll also find multimedia files and news regarding aviation. Updates, including links to hundreds of new sites, are provided regularly. ⚲ 🌐

http://AIR-online.com/AIRwelcome.shtml

DTC DUAT

Pilot flight services via the Internet. This site provides pilots with weather briefings, flight-planning services, and software to use the FAA's Direct User Access Terminal Service (DUAT). You must be a pilot to use this resource.

http://www.duat.com

Landings

An elegantly arranged collection of aviation news, editorials, searchable databases, and web links can be found here. Scroll down to the bottom of the page for an easy-to-use directory that includes links to soaring, air shows, ballooning, hang gliding, helicopters, aerobatics, and skydiving. 🌐

http://www.landings.com/aviation.html

Soaring Server

Links to articles, contests, records, badges, related to gliding and soaring, sponsored by the Soaring Society of America (SSA).

http://acro.harvard.edu/SSA/ssa_homepg.html

BASEBALL

Baseball America

The online version of the popular fan magazine.

http://www.baseballamerica.com

Baseball Weekly

The online version of *USA Today's* up-to-the-minute baseball newspaper.

http://www.usatoday.com/bbwfront.htm

Fastball.com

An independent baseball news site that can keep pace with the big boys.

http://www.fastball.com

Major League Baseball @Bat

The official site of Major League Baseball.

http://www.majorleaguebaseball.com

Skilton's Baseball Links

John Skilton's insanely comprehensive collection of links to baseball resources on the Net, including major league teams, minor league teams, defunct leagues, ballparks, people, products, scores, stats, team pages, archives, and baseball newsgroups. A Java applet on the home page runs down current scores. ☕ 🌐

http://www.baseball-links.com/index.html

BASKETBALL

Basketball America

News, information, and statistics about NBA, ABL, CBA, and NCAA basketball.

http://www.basketballamerica.com/xfiles/

Coach's Edge

Coach's Edge is the place to look behind the scenes of basketball at the strategies and plays from NBA and NCAA programs.

http://www.coachesedge.com

Fox Sports: Pro Basketball

Pro basketball scores, highlights, standings, and videos, in NetShow format.

http://www.foxsports.com/probask/

NBA.com

The official web site of the NBA, complete with a Java-based scoreboard, live player chats, and news on games and players. ☞

http://www.nba.com

WNBA.com

News and information about the Women's NBA, including audio and video files, scores, and schedules.

http://www.wnba.com

BIOLOGY

Harvard Herbaria Databases

Harvard University's Herbaria web site features all the information you could possibly want about its herbaria stuff, including links to libraries, collections, and searchable databases.

http://www.herbaria.harvard.edu

Human Genome Project Information

Begun in 1990, the Human Genome Project was created to increase our understanding of human genetics and biology by determining the genetic code for the human genome. If this scares you as much as it does me, check in with this site often to keep an eye on things. Resources are organized so as to be of use to both scientists and the lay person.

http://www.ornl.gov/TechResources/Human_Genome/home.html

Johns Hopkins Bioinformatics Web Server

This creative WWW server provides a collection of interconnected protein sequence, structure, and enzyme function databases. These protein databases also include links to other information, including bibliographic citations from MED-LINE and pictures of three-dimensional crystal structures from the Brookhaven structural database. Electronic publications for biology include the Primer on Molecular Genetics, genomic information databases, such as the Mouse Locus catalog (with a fetching portrait of its subject), and links to other resources.

http://www.bis.med.jhmi.edu

National Center for Biotechnology Information

This site gives you access and includes information about the NCBI's DNA databases. You'll also find links to such topics as Clusters of Orthologous Groups and Online Mendelian Inheritance in Man.

http://www.ncbi.nlm.nih.gov

Virtual FlyLab

Budding research geneticists and mad scientists will be equally drawn to this site, which allows users to virtually "breed" fruit flies in search of the secrets of genetic inheritance. The FlyLab is well documented and illustrated, making it a pleasure to use for those who aren't squeamish about drawings of forked fruit fly bristles. This virtual application was designed by the Electronic Desktop Project at California State University, Los Angeles.

http://vearthquake.calstatela.edu/edesktop/VirtApps/VflyLab/IntroVflyLab.html

WWW Virtual Library: Biosciences

This massive index to the bioscience resources on the Net is maintained by Keith Robison of the Harvard University Biological Laboratories. Subjects covered include biological molecules, biotechnology, genetics, immunology, plant biology, and many, many more. ⊕

http://www.vlib.org/Biosciences.html

BUSINESS

American Stock Exchange

The American Stock Exchange is a source for daily market summaries, equity and option information, and exchange-related news clips. You can also get a list of the day's most active stocks (delayed by 20 minutes), search for a company listed on the exchange, or read extensive introductions to the Exchange's Options & Derivatives or SPDRs & WEBs. You'll also find news and information geared toward a professional audience in both text and RealPlayer formats.

http://www.amex.com

Business Resource Center

This center contains information about starting a new business, managing that business, building a web site, and marketing products and services. You'll also find news, products, and chat rooms. The information, in the form of articles, is probably most useful to those starting a small business.

http://www.morebusiness.com

CheckFree Investment Services Quote Server

Fifteen-minute-delayed stock quotes without the fuss: just type in the ticker symbol (actually, up to five at a time), and click the Get Quotes button. Clicking the Market Watch banner takes you to a concise summary of action on the Dow Jones, Standard & Poor's, NASDAQ, NYSE, and other exchanges.

http://www.secapl.com/cgi-bin/qs

Chicago Mercantile Exchange

The Chicago Mercantile Exchange (CME) is a trillion-dollar marketplace for commodity, stock index, currency, and interest rate futures. Its web page provides a wealth of information for anyone interested in commodities trading. Check out the Electronic Trading and Order Routing section for the latest quotes and trades. The Education Center contains an informative introduction to the futures market, under the heading Web Instant Lessons.

http://www.cme.com

Internet Advertising Resource Guide

If you're thinking about advertising on the Net, or if you're just curious about what advertisers are up to, the Internet Advertising Resource Guide is worth a visit. The site is principally made up of links to other sites around the Net, arranged by subject. The subjects covered include Print Publications on Advertising on the Internet, Business Presence on the Internet, and "Acceptable Advertising Practices on the Internet." The Internet Advertising Resource Guide is maintained by Hairong Li of the Missouri School of Journalism.

http://www.admedia.org

The NASDAQ Stock Market

This page includes news of all things NASDAQ. Get quotes, learn about companies on the NASDAQ exchange, read market news, and track your portfolio.

http://www.nasdaq.com

National Technology Transfer Center

This is the hub of a national network that links U.S. companies with federal laboratories to turn government research results into practical, commercially relevant technology. The center operates the Gateway Service, a free telephone service that provides contacts between the private sector and various branches of the federal laboratory system. The center also runs Business Gold, a bulletin board for activities and information relating to technology-transfer opportunities.

http://iridium.nttc.edu/nttc.html

Publishers' Catalogs Home Page

An international directory of links to publishing companies on the Web, created by Northern Lights Internet Solutions. Companies are listed by country. The 300-plus links in the directory range from Nedbook International in the Netherlands to the Knopf Publishing Group in the United States.

http://www.lights.com/publisher/

Small Business Administration Web Server

Online help for small businesses, including lists of SBA offices and the Service Corps of Retired

Executives (SCORE), training aids, information on government contracting, and an explanation of loan programs. The site also features links to disaster assistance, property for sale, and local SBA resources. ✆

http://www.sbaonline.sba.gov

Thomas Register of American Manufacturers

The Thomas Register is America's preeminent directory of commercial products and services. Online, there's no need to worry about back strain or paper cuts. If you need supplies, click the gargantuan yellow Search button, register (if you haven't already), and you're on your way. Access to the online directory is via a search engine; type in "chicken wire" or "plastic pipe," for example, and you're directed to a list of suppliers. ⚲ ✏

http://www2.thomasregister.com

CAREER INFORMATION

Note that fees here are generally for posting ads, not for searching ads.

100 Careers in Wall Street

This site markets itself as a place for individuals to search for their "dream careers." If *you* want to work on Wall Street, this is the site for you. A three-month ad costs as little as $40 for an advertiser to place. ⚲ $

http://www.globalvillager.com/villager/WSC.html

A+ On-line Resumes

A+ On-line Resumes will convert your resume to HTML and post it on the Web for three months for $40. Employers may post job listings for $25 per month. ⚲ $

http://ol-resume.com

Airline Employment Assistance Corps

If you become a member of the Airline Employment Assistance Corps, you can post your resume on its site, free of charge. Membership is only $10. Employers, however, may post openings for free. ⚲ $

http://www.avjobs.com

American Agricultural Economics Association

This very straightforward site lists positions wanted for $10 per line and positions available for $20 per line. ⚲ $

http://www.aaea.org/employment2.html

Aviation Employee Placement Service

This site advertises itself as the only searchable aviation employment database, making your résumé available to thousands of employers worldwide. Enrollment is free for ten days. ⚲ $

http://www.aeps.com/aeps/aepspart.html

Broadcast Employment Service

This job bank gears itself toward jobs in television. Submitting a résumé costs between $25 and $75 per year. Employers may post openings for free. ⚲ $

http://www.tvjobs.com

Career Magazine Resume Bank

A well-organized site with a wealth of resources, Career Magazine offers a range of services and requests that employers contact them regarding pricing. ⚲ $

http://www.careermag.com/resumes/resumebank.html

CareerMosaic

CareerMosaic is an employment information service operated by Bernard Hodes Advertising. The main site is broken up into eight sections: Jobs, Employers, ResumeCM, Online Job Fairs, the Career Network, International Gateway, Career Resource Center, and College Connection. CareerMosaic also sponsors industry-specific sites and alliances with organizations like Women in Technology. ⚲

http://www.careermosaic.com

CareerPath.com

CareerPath's defining feature is its job database: it includes both the current week's and previous Sunday's Help Wanted classifieds from more than 50 major U.S. newspapers, including the *Boston Globe, Chicago Tribune, Los Angeles Times, New York Times, San Jose Mercury News, Washington Post*, and *Wichita Eagle*. It also allows you to search the job listings from the web sites of major employers. ⚲ ✎

http://www.careerpath.com

CareerWeb

Another resource for people who are recruiting employees or looking for jobs. The site features a strong international section and a good search function that lets you search for jobs by keyword. You can also search by category, location, or employer. The site features a strong Career Bookstore page. ⚲ ✎

http://www.cweb.com

Community Career Center

A gathering place where not-for-profit employers and management personnel can meet. Annual membership fees vary; non-members pay $125 for each 60-day job posting. ⚲ $

http://www.nonprofitjobs.org

GeoWeb Electronic Job News

GeoWeb maintains a job bank for positions in the geo sciences and information technologies. Posting a résumé currently costs $49.99 for six months. Employers can advertise job openings for $195 per month. ⚲ $

http://www.ggrweb.com/job.html

INFOMINE/Careermine

Careermine calls itself the "most extensive and comprehensive mining employment site on the Internet." Contact *ksmythe@info-mine.com* for rates. ⚲ $

http://www.infomine.com/careermine/

JobCenter

JobCenter provides a clear, nicely organized site. Posting your résumé online costs $20 for six months, with the extra benefit of automatic matching and email updates. Posting jobs costs $20 for two weeks. ⚲ $

http://www.jobcenter.com

JobLink

An excellent resource for job-hunting journalists. Employers may post positions for free for five weeks. ⚲ $

http://ajf.newslink.org/joblink.html

Job-Source, Inc.

Employment and job placement in the medical field. The employer registration fee is as low as $150 annually. ⚲ $ ✎

http://www.Job-Source.com

The Monster Board

While I've never been able to figure out why it's called the Monster Board, this is really the premier job-search site on the Net. The job search agent feature is top notch. You'll find a resume builder, events listing, and apartment locator in the career center, and a number of rotating career fairs and recruitment seminars. Employers wishing to post a job or search the resume database should call 1-800-MONSTER to speak with an account representative; posting can cost as little as $175. If that seems pricey, take a look at the site. ⚲ ✎

http://www.monster.com

NJ Jobs: New Jersey Employment Opportunities

Posting your résumé at NJ Jobs costs $20 for one month. Job listings cost $25 per week. ⚲ $

http://www.njjobs.com/resume_post.html

Résumé-Net

Résumé-Net caters to Silicon Valley's computer industry. Posting a resume here costs $10 per month; the site doesn't post job listings and is free to employers who want to browse the résumé database. ⚲ $

http://www.resume-net.com

ResumeXPRESS

This site promises "the most powerful résumé-matching system in the employment industry today" and charges commensurately. A "full-year's subscription" costs $89.95; updates within that year cost an additional $45. Employers (or "hiring agents" as called here) may search the database for free. ⚲ $

http://resumeXPRESS.com

SearchBase Executive & Recruiter Gateway

SearchBase is designed to connect junior- and senior-level executives with recruiters. A one year resume listing costs $98. ⚲ $

http://www.searchbase.com

Shawn's Internet Resume Center

This site has few frills, but seems quite functional. Posting your résumé here requires a one-time fee of $30. Posting a job costs $5 per listing. ⚲ $

http://www.inpursuit.com/sirc/seeker.html

Show Biz Jobs

This site is a fantastic resource for the job seeker in the entertainment fields. Well organized and clear, you can search for jobs by company, job category, city, or posting date. ⚲

http://www.showbizjobs.com/jobserch.cfm

CHEMISTRY

ChemCenter

The American Chemical Society provides access to databases and online chemistry news, along with fun features like "This Week in Chemical History ..." and "Live from Dallas—Your ACS National Meeting Online Guide." You'll also find sections on professional services, conferences, publications databases, education, shopping, and resources. ⊕

http://www.acs.org

ChemLinks

The ChemLinks site is really an upper-level directory to other collections of chemistry-related links. You'll also find some nice links about New Jersey. ⊕

http://www2.cybernex.net/~jsauer/index.html

WebElements

WebElements is a hypertext periodic table. The symbol for each element links to a page containing general information on the element and data on radii, valence, electronegativities, effective nuclear charge, phase-change temperatures, etc.

http://www.shef.ac.uk/uni/academic/A-C/chem/web-elements/

CHILDREN & PARENTING

AdoptionNetwork

AdoptionNetwork is an online volunteer effort to help serve the information needs of everyone involved in the adoption process, from adoptive parents, to adoptees, to birthparents. No political agenda is apparent at the site. Resources available include directories of support groups and adoption agencies, various FAQs, chat groups, classified ads, and a collection of links to other adoption-related web sites. ☕ ⚲ ⊕

http://www.adoption.org

Berit's Best Sites for Children

This is what every "best sites" page should be like. Berit Erickson, who works for Cochran Interactive Inc., has organized dozens of sites by category, provided good descriptions about them, and rated each on a scale of one to five. There are well over 700 sites reviewed here, from science and history sites to kids' magazines and home pages. ⊕

http://db.cochran.com/li_toc:theoPage.db

Family.com

Disney's family-focused web site isn't just a shill promoting the benefits of a family vacation to a theme park in Florida. In fact, this remarkably comprehensive and well-organized site features interesting articles, surveys, recipes, activities, advice, local events, and bulletin boards. If you're looking for advice about parenting, something to do with your kids, or what to make for dinner tonight, take a look at Family.com.

http://family.go.com

Kidlink

Kidlink describes itself as a grass-roots organization that strives to involve children under age 15 in a global dialog. The site serves as a coordinating center for conferencing via public mailing lists, chats, and online art exhibits. Participants have included approximately 100,000 kids from 117 countries. Kidlink sponsors activities in English, French, German, Hebrew, Icelandic, Japanese, Norwegian, Portuguese, Spanish, Italian, Danish, Makedonian, Turkish, and Nordic languages. Visit the site to find out how to set up or join a Kidlink project.

http://www.kidlink.org

Kids' Space

A marvelous site for kids to share their artwork, music, and stories. Be sure to take a look at the Story Book, where kids are presented with a collection of five small images and invited to write and submit a story incorporating the images. The stories that have been collected so far include *The Big Tomato* from Kyle Owen (age 7), which begins, "One day a big red tomato came to my front door wearing a big yellow hat. My family opened the door and was surprised that a tomato was wearing a hat." Kids' Space was created by Sachiko Oba, a doctoral student at Teachers College, Columbia University.

http://www.kids-space.org

CLASSICAL LANGUAGES & LITERATURE

Bryn Mawr Classical Review

This review of classical subjects has been published since 1990 and has all its articles online. The web page is a front door to an easily navigable gopher index; there is also a search feature.

http://ccat.sas.upenn.edu/jod/bmr.html

Electronic Resources for Classicists: The Second Generation

A very concise, remarkably well-organized directory of classics links, including information gateways, electronic texts, bibliographies, classics department home pages, fonts, software, and professional organizations. ⊕

http://www.tlg.uci.edu/~tlg/index/resources.html

Gesamtverzeichnis der griechischen Papyrusurkunden Aegyptens

This is an index of dated Greek papyri from Egypt, arranged by century. The contents of the documents are not included, but standard papyrological abbreviations point to the printed literature in German.

http://www.ub.uni-heidelberg.de

The Internet Classics Archive

This is a superb presentation using modern technology to access the wisdom of the classics. The site includes masterpieces such as Plato's *Republic*, Virgil's *Aeneid*, and Homer's *Iliad* and *Odyssey*, classics that have shaped Western thought, literature, politics, and society. The archive has a brilliant search engine that locates key words or phrases and cites where in the text they appear. In a search, you can browse through the works of any or all of the 17 authors cataloged. The site, compiled by Dan Stevenson, contains translations of hundreds works. ⊕

http://classics.mit.edu

MiamiLINK Classical Languages: Greek and Latin

Miami University's collection of resources for students of Classical languages.

http://www.lib.muohio.edu/inet/subj/litlan/clas.html

Selected Internet Resources for Classical and Medieval Studies

This is a helpful directory with several pointers to classical studies web sites and projects, from the University of Michigan. ⊕

http://www.lib.umich.edu/libhome/rrs/classes/classmed.html

COMICS

Comic Art and Grafix Gallery Virtual Museum and Encyclopedia

A dynamic undertaking by "Museum Director" Richard Halegua, who incorporates some nifty graphics of his own, such as the Clark Kent-to-Superman morph. On its way to becoming an excellent resource by providing history, biographies, current happenings, and information on collecting.

http://www.comic-art.com

Comic Book Resources

According to site creator Jonah Weiland's description, this is "one of the largest collections of comic book links … and the only place on the Internet where you can HEAR the interviews with comic book creators." The site does feature a substantial collection of comic book links, message boards, chat rooms, weekly polls, news, etc. ⊕

http://www.comicbookresources.com

ComicsPage.com

ComicsPage.com provides daily links to a number of comic strips and panels. Most of these are second-tier (Broom Hilda, Dick Tracey, Gasoline Alley, etc.), but the site shines with its selection of editorial cartoons. You'll find archives and a daily cartoon from such artists as Jeff MacNelly, Steve Sack, Jack Ohman, and more.

http://www.comicspage.com

The Dilbert Zone

The exploits of everybody's favorite nerd … available on a one-week delay at the Dilbert Zone. Scott Adams, the cartoonist, provides some hilarious background on the strip, from early rejections to photos of how he creates the characters. You'll also find a four-week archive, the Daily Mental Workout, and the Center for Duhcision Making.

http://www.unitedmedia.com/comics/dilbert

This Modern World

Tom Tomorrow is an editorial cartoonist featured in *Salon*, the *Nation*, and other publications. This web site, in the voice of the author, features discussions of his work, links to articles by and about him, and an archive of cartoons.

http://www.well.com/user/tomorrow/

WebComics Daily

Here's a clever site that grabs the actual cartoons from more than 40 daily and weekly comics sites on the Web and publishes them together in newspaper funny-page format. The only drawbacks are the long wait for images to be downloaded and the poor scans of some of the comics. Not a mere collection of links to other comics sites, David de Vitry's WebComics brings actual comics from around the Web together in one place.

http://www.webcomics.com

COMPUTING

ACM SIGGRAPH Online!

Even though the title of the page sports an exclamation point, this is an excellent site for anyone interested in computer graphics. The Special Interest Group on Computer Graphics provides links to calendars, publications, conferences and work shops, and education, career, and art and design resources.

http://www.siggraph.org

ActiveX Journal

The ActiveX Journal for HTML Writers is a webzine that publishes online articles with lots of sample code and illustrations. A limited-time guest license allows you to explore the site before you subscribe. Unfortunately, you'll need a number of ActiveX controls even to read the site. $

http://www.folkarts.com/journals/activex/

CERT* Coordination Center

CERT, the Computer Emergency Response Team, is a federally funded group charged with dealing with computer and network security problems. Its server has papers about security concerns, tools to evaluate security, and an archive of alerts about current break-in attempts.

It also provides resources to help report, and recover from, incidents.

http://www.cert.org

Compression FAQ

A collection of frequently asked questions to the comp.compression Usenet newsgroups. The most useful questions here may be, "What is this .xxx file type?" or "Where can I find the corresponding compression program?"

http://www.cis.ohio-state.edu/hypertext/faq/usenet/ compression-faq/top.html

Directory of Computer and Communication Companies

A user-friendly collection of links to computer and communications businesses on the Net with a search feature to help locate them. The Computer and Communication Companies directory is maintained by staff at the University of California's Lawrence Livermore National Laboratory.

http://www.cmpcmm.com/cc/companies.html

Free Online Dictionary of Computing

A searchable glossary of programming languages, architectures, networks, domain theory, mathematics, and other information relating to computing. This site also contains links to several other computing-oriented glossaries, lists, and compilations.

http://wombat.doc.ic.ac.uk/foldoc/

LAN Magazine

Network Magazine Online features a rich collection of articles and product reviews related to local area networks. Major departments include the current issue, news & analysis, free stuff!, and a collection of tutorials on topics ranging from dynamic ISDN to Ethernet frame types.

http://www.networkmagazine.com

Visual Basic Home Page

Carl 'n Gary's Visual Basic Home Page is a resource courtesy of Carl Franklin and Gary Wisniewski. As the guys will tell you, "Our ongoing mission is to create a virtual gathering place for Visual Basic programmers throughout the world.

... This page is dedicated to the free exchange of software, ideas, and information." You'll also find a beginner's page, links to books, electronic magazines and articles, and games and graphics programming.

http://www.cgvb.com

VRML Repository

A clearinghouse for information related to Virtual Reality Modeling Language (VRML), "a developing standard for describing interactive three-dimensional scenes delivered across the Internet." Materials available include specifications and a keyword search, along with links to example applications, software projects, and other sources of VRML information. The VRML repository is maintained by the San Diego Supercomputer Center.

http://www.web3d.org/vrml/vrml.htm

COOKING & FOOD

EDIBILIA

This remarkable site, part of the rec.food.cooking ring, is replete with recipes. Most are in the "Meal Master" format, which allows you to file them in the Meal Master recipe database, available as shareware from *http://ourworld. compuserve.com/homepages/S_Welliver/*. Recipes are grouped by ethnic cuisine (European, African, Subcontinental, etc.), cooking method (baking), and ingredients (chocolate). The site also features links to just about every other recipe or food-related site on the net. Although EDIBILIA lacks a much-needed search engine, the wealth of resources here is a tremendous resource. ⊕

http://www.ibmpcug.co.uk/~owls/edibilia.html

Epicurious Food: Recipe File

You'll find more than 7,600 recipes from *Bon Apetit* and *Gourmet* magazines at Epicurious. The excellent search feature lets you combine keywords and categories to find only the dishes you're looking for. Epicurious also sponsors a dictionary of food terms (to simmer is "To cook food gently in liquid at a temperature (about 185°F) low enough that tiny bubbles just begin to break the surface"), and links to the magazines. 🔍

http://food.epicurious.com/e_eating/e02_recipes/recipes.html

Over the Coffee

Tim Nemec's impressive collection of coffee resources, including information on preparation, drinking, and vendors. Especially fun is the reference desk, where one will find a table of contents with links to books and authors, general coffee information, and even "personal coffee pages," among other things.

http://www.cappuccino.com

Ragu Presents—Mama's Cucina

Don't miss this creative site, which features the witty Mama. In Mama's Kitchen, you'll find *Mama's Cookbook*, with "recipes galore!," Mama's Secrets, and Cooking 101. In the Dining Room, you can learn to speak Italian with Professore Antonio, who provides helpful example phrases, including, "One day, maybe you'll grow up to be a Pope!" as a sound file. There are even Goodies from Mama, including coupons for Ragu products and a Ragu t-shirt.

http://www.eat.com

The Real Beer Page

The Real Beer site promises "Everything you could ever want to know about craft-beer," and more. Features include a brew tour to locate breweries in North America; brew travels, to facilitate using public transportation while drinking beer; and games, events, and links involving beer. Avoid the Burp Me section unless you're a fan of, well, burping.

http://www.realbeer.com

Top Secret Recipes on the Web

Want to know how to make Crab Bisque the way the Soup Nazi did on *Seinfeld*? Then check out Todd Wilbur's hysterical site. Wilbur features "cloned" recipes of your favorite fast-food and brand-name recipes, from Mrs. Field's cookies to the McDonald's® Arch Deluxe®. Check out the rest of the site, too—Wilbur's a funny guy.

http://www.topsecretrecipes.com

Vegetarian Resource Group

The Vegetarian Resource Group has plenty of links, recipes, cookbooks, journals, and research papers on why eating animals is bad and why you should be ever vigilant about where seemingly innocuous ingredients come from. There's even a vegetarian game, which rates you as a vegetarian.

http://www.vrg.org

DATING

BGLAD.com: Personals for Gays and Bisexuals

This free dating site is geared toward gays and bisexuals. Interested participants post personal ads and search for a loved one of his or her own. Photos may be uploaded along with the ad. You'll also find a lengthy listing of other dating sites geared toward gays and lesbians. 🔍 🌐

http://www.bglad.com/personals/

Date.com

Though some services are free to all, joining date.com will give you access to this singles site's chat rooms, classifieds, member profiles, email sending and receiving privileges, and other offerings geared toward finding a partner. There seems to be three tiers of membership: nonmembers, partial members, and full members, with benefits to each. Rates are listed as $9.95 for one month, $28.50 for three months, $49.95 for six months, and $79.95 for one year, but it is unclear for which membership these prices are for. Starting your own personal single's profile seems to be free as well. 🔍 $

http://www.date.com

Introducing.com

Value Memberships: $9.95 per month; Red Memberships: $29 per month; Platinum Memberships: $59 per month. Audio and video clips may be included with your profile for an additional fee. 🔍 $

http://www.introducing.com

Match.Com

One of the biggest dating services on the Net offers a seven-day free trial membership. A one-month membership is $12.95; longer membership commitments scale the fee back. Thus, if you need a one-year membership, the rate drops to $7.95 per month. Other site features include an event calendar, an online magazine dedicated to relationships, columnists providing advice, tips on sex, and a column on the gay dating scene. ⚲ $

http://www.match.com

singlesearch

Range of prices, starting at $30 for two "local" searches; posting a profile is free. ⚲ $

http://www.singlesearch.com

ECONOMICS

The Dismal Scientist

A fascinating site that's filled with economic information, articles, forecasts, and indicators. Articles are updated daily, and you'll find a helpful section on Economic Releases over the last week, including Housing Starts, Jobless Claims, and Industrial Production.

http://www.dismal.com

Dr. Ed Yardeni's Economics Network

Ed Yardeni is the Chief Economist of Deutsche Morgan Grenfell in New York, and he's put together a well-organized site that's chock full of current economic information. Features include online chat rooms, topical studies, a weekly analysis, and weekly briefing. ✏ ☕

http://www.yardeni.com

Economics Departments, Institutes and Research Centers in the World

An extensive and searchable listing of the 3,280 institutions in 148 countries that focus on Economics. Site creator Christian Zimmerman, of the University of Québec at Montréal, verifies the links regularly. ⚲

http://ideas.uqam.ca/EDRIC/

FINWeb

FINWeb is a financial economics web site managed by James R. Garven, Ph.D, from Louisiana State University. Garven's stated primary objective is to list Internet resources providing substantive information concerning economics and finance-related topics, and he's put together a substantial list of links to resources on electronic publishing, working papers, databases and research tools, and general Economics links. ⊕ ⚲

http://www.finweb.com

The Information Economy

The definitive site for information about the economics of the Internet, compiled by Hal Varian, one of the first to take the Internet seriously as an economic force. ⊕

http://www.sims.berkeley.edu/resources/infoecon/

Resources for Economists on the Internet

A guide to over 700 resources of interest to professional and amateur economists. Bill Goffe, of the University of Southern Mississippi's Department of Economics and International Business, created the guide and tried to select resources that "either offer a substantial amount of information, or are specialized to a specific area." ⊕

http://econwpa.wustl.edu/EconFAQ/EconFAQ.html

EDUCATION

Adolescence Directory Online

A large and well-structured collection of links to Internet resources related to adolescence and secondary education. Subject areas include mental issues, conflict and violence, teens only, and health issues. The adolescence directory is maintained by the Center for Adolescent Studies at Indiana University. An archive of its publication *Teacher Talk* is also available at the site. ⊕

http://education.indiana.edu/cas/adol/adol.html

American Financial Network

For a $245 fee, the American Financial Network guarantees to show you how to qualify for at least $1000 in financial aid, or your money back.

The site is largely an interface to interacting with the company. ☕ $

http://www.moneyadvice.com

The Berkman Center for Internet & Society

One of the best, most innovative educational resources on the Net. Harvard University's School of Law presents "cybercourses," free to the public. The first two, Intellectual Property in Cyberspace, taught by William Fisher, and Privacy in Cyberspace, taught by Arthur Miller, were a rousing success.

http://cyber.harvard.edu

Chinook College Funding Service

This Web-based service allows you to perform a preliminary free assessment to determine how many scholarships you may be eligible for. Receive results online for $15, or via Express Mail for $44. The service will request pertinent applications for you for an additional small fee. $

http://www.chinook.com

The Chronicle of Higher Education

The full text of the weekly tabloid that covers all aspects of the college and university business. Each week's issue features a well-organized listing of hundreds of teaching, research, and administrative jobs in higher education. ✎ ✐

http://chronicle.merit.edu

CyberItalian

If you'd like to learn about the Italian language and culture, start here. The first three lessons are free. To continue with lessons 4 through 11 you'll need to pay the $14.95 membership, which also entitles you to CyberItalian updates, use of the message board, and access to chat with Pinocchio, a great tool for enhancing conversation skills. $

http://www.cyberitalian.com

Developing Educational Standards: Overview

The site describes itself as "a repository for as much information about educational standards and curriculum frameworks from all sources (national, state, local, and other) as can be

found on the Internet." You can examine standards by state, subject area, or department. ⊕

http://putwest.boces.org/Standards.html

Educause

Educause helps educational institutions stay on the cutting edge of information technology by showing them how to integrate information technology into classrooms, curricula, and research. Among other resources, visitors who click the Publications link will find current and past issues of *EduPage*, an information technology newsletter published three times per week. *EduPage* summarizes printed news coverage of interest to the leaders and citizens of the Internet.

http://educause.edu

EdWeb: The Online K–12 Resource Guide

EdWeb is a site dedicated to exploring technology and school reform, maintained by Andy Carvin of the Corporation for Public Broadcasting. Carvin states that users can use the site to "hunt down online educational resources around the world, learn about trends in education policy and information infrastructure development, examine success stories of computers in the classroom," and more. The site provides access to many useful resources for K–12 teachers—some interactive—including discussion groups, lesson plans, and stories about firsthand teaching experience. The interface is simple to use and offers access to an online technical dictionary on every page.

http://edweb.cnidr.org

Embark.com

Looking to go to college or professional school? Embark.com offers a great set of resources for those about to make the change. You'll find information about careers, majors, individual schools, financial aid, and more. ✎

http://www.embark.com

English as a Second Language

This site uses the World Wide Web as an environment to help people learn to speak English. There are a variety of resources for students and teachers of ESL. Sections include listening and speaking, reading with understanding, grammar and writing, ESL-related information, and English language schools. ⊕

http://www.lang.uiuc.edu/r-li5/esl/

FinAid: The Financial Aid Information Page

Mark Kantrowitz, co-author of *The Prentice Hall Guide to Scholarships and Fellowships for Math and Science Students*, has compiled this collection of WWW links to financial aid information resources on the Internet. The Financial Aid Information page directs visitors to more than 50 general and school-specific financial aid resources. The resources are relevant to graduate and undergraduate students, and cover science and liberal arts disciplines. This is an invaluable, free resource for anyone starting college or graduate school. ⌕

http://www.finaid.org

Grolier Multimedia Encyclopedia Online

$65 gives you a one-year subscription to the popular encyclopedia. Features include over 35,000 articles from the Academic American Encyclopedia, multimedia features, and Grolier's own list of web links. $

http://gme.grolier.com

Human Languages Page

An impressive archive of language resources on the Net, compiled by Tyler Chambers, a student at Willamette University. Some of the resources, like the Glossary of Computer Terms in Vietnamese, are links to simple lists of words and their translations. Others, like the Russian and Eastern European Studies home page, offer general cultural information but little in the way of language primers or lessons. Versions of the Human Languages Page are also available in nine other languages, including Spanish, German, Russian, and French. ⌕

http://www.june29.com/HLP/

The JASON Project

Teachers often wonder, "Where should we go for our next field trip?" How about Hawaii? Or the Galapagos Islands? Perhaps the Mediterranean Sea. Each year the JASON Project takes a select group of students and teachers to a remote area on a two-week scientific expedi-

tion. The trip, held from late February to early March, is broadcast in real time, using state-of-the-art technology, to a network of educational, research, and cultural institutions. The results of the trips are cataloged at this site, so classes can visit them anytime. The JASON Project was founded by Dr. Robert Ballard, who discovered the location of the sunken *R.M.S. Titanic*.

http://www.jasonproject.org

Literature Online

This searchable library contains over 250,000 works of English and American literature. Rates are available from a Chadwyck-Healey representative at 800-752-0515; free trials are available. $

http://lion.chadwyck.com

Math Archives

A collection of software and other resources to aid in the teaching of mathematics at the college and university levels. Also includes newsletters, reprints, and other material of interest in the area. Software is available for both Mac and Windows 95 formats.

http://archives.math.utk.edu

Miranda Educational Consultants

Miranda boasts of being more than a scholarship-search service. Features include matching funding sources to your interests, a guide to colleges that provide the best combination of education and funding, a career database, month-by-month schedule, and assistance in preparation for scholarship and financial aid applications including searching, writing, mailing and reviewing. $

http://www.kern.com/miranda/

National PTA Online Subscriptions

This site actually allows for subscription to two related services: Advocates for Children and the PTA. An Advocates for Children subscription costs $75 per year and provides advocacy news, articles, and information, an online discussion group, and the electronic versions of *Our Children* and *What's Happening in Washington* magazines. A PTA subscription requires an active PTA ID number and costs $25 per year; a discussion group, PTA clip art and logos, and electronic versions of *Money Matters*, hand-book, and bylaws are included. $

http://www.pta.org/Subscr/submaint.asp

Pathways to School Improvement

A collaboration between educators, researchers, and community leaders, Pathways to School Improvement seeks to address critical issues in education. You'll find good ideas and resources for teachers and communities, particularly in the Topics section. ⚲

http://www.ncrel.org/sdrs/

Peterson's Education Center

The online door to summer jobs, summer programs for teens, and college knowledge is open. Peterson's now provides online information on undergraduate colleges, graduate study, distance learning, study abroad, applying to college, special schools, summer programs for kids, and summer camp jobs.

http://www.petersons.com

Quest: NASA's K–12 Internet Initiative

An ideal starting point for K–12 teachers who want to use the Internet as an educational tool. Quest, sponsored by NASA, offers tips for bringing the Net into your school, training and technical hints, and links to other education resources. Through this site, students can get in touch with NASA scientists and "volunteer" on NASA projects. Topics include the neurolab online, space team online, and Aero design team online. ⚲

http://quest.arc.nasa.gov

The Student Guide: Financial Aid from the U.S. Department of Education

The U.S. Department of Education's Student Guide was written to help parents and potential students make sense of U.S. Government financial aid. The guide covers everything from financial need to applications to deadlines. Specific information is available on programs like Pell Grants, Direct and FFEL Program Loans, Federal Work-Study, and Federal Perkins Loans. If you don't like reading online, a 126 K compressed

ASCII version of the guide is available for down-loading.

http://www.ed.gov/prog_info/SFA/StudentGuide/

Student Services

You'll have to fill out a detailed form before you can enter this site, but it's quite popular. What they actually do won't seem clear until you receive the snail mail brochure. $

http://www.studentservices.com

Test Prep Sites (SAT, GRE, LSAT, etc.)

Who'd a thunk it? Useful information, canny advice, even genuine words of wisdom can be found at the Kaplan and Princeton review sites. Both sites offer basic information on preparing for standardized tests, including the SAT, ACT, GMAT, GRE, LSAT, MCAT and TOEFL. The sites go beyond trying to lure students to enroll in their courses—they offer helpful guidance to aspiring college students, from tips to getting financial aid to thoughtful career advice. The Ontario School Counselors' Association's links to U.S. Testing information provides an up-to-date listing of various web sites on the subject of standardized testing.

http://www1.kaplan.com
http://www.review.com/index.cfm

Virtual Schoolhouse

A large but somewhat jumbled collection of links to K–12 Internet sites compiled by the Cisco Educational Archive. Subject areas include schools and universities on the Internet, the art room, virtual field trips, the techie's corner, and the principal's office.

http://metalab.unc.edu/cisco/schoolhouse/

Web66: International School Web Site Registry

A collection of links to U.S. primary and secondary schools with web sites. Schools are listed by continent, country, or special category (arts, charter, gifted & talented, etc.). You'll also find links to public libraries on the Internet and post-secondary institutions.

http://web66.coled.umn.edu/schools.html

Yamada Language Guides

A large index to the language resources of the Net, compiled by the Yamada Language Center at the University of Oregon. Each of the 75+ languages covered by the index has its own page of links. A collection of non-English fonts is also available here.

http://babel.uoregon.edu/yamada/guides.html

ELECTRONIC MAGAZINES (EZINES)

eZines Ultimate Magazine Dabase

This comprehensive listing of electronic magazines on the Web is presented in a searchable, hierarchical catalog format. Magazines are submitted and reviewed by readers. ⊕ ⚲

http://www.dominis.com/Zines/

FEED

An online magazine with a focus on arts, politics, and technoculture. The well-written articles are interesting and elegantly formatted. Recent topics include "Viagra," "J. Crew," and "the School of the Americas." You'll find intelligent discussions in the Feedline section, and an elegant use of hypertext links to other sources throughout the site.

http://www.feedmag.com

Fine Art Forum

A monthly magazine of arts announcements from people and organizations in the United States and Europe. One of the oldest network services for the arts, the magazine just celebrated its 11th birthday—which makes it 107 in non-Internet years. Visitors will find reviews, events, and art "spaces" on the Web.

http://www.msstate.edu/Fineart_Online/home.html

Lockergnome's Free Windows 95/98/NT Newsletter

Don't let the moronic title throw you off. This ezine is a great resource for anyone using a Windows PC. Filled with advice, downloads,

links, and witticisms from Christopher Pirillo, Lockergnome is a well-organized treat.

http://www.lockergnome.com

Netsurfer Digest

Interested in the latest happenings on and about the WWW? *Netsurfer Digest* maintains an extensive, unorthodox collection of links offered in a weekly ezine from Netsurfer Communications, Inc. The collection of articles and links for a recent week ranged from discussion of the face on Mars to the entire contents of Willie Nelson's new album being available online. Categories include "Breaking Surf," "Online Culture," "Arts Online," "Books and E-Zines," and "Surfing Science." ⊕

http://www.netsurf.com/nsd/index.html

Psychic Chicken Network

Wondering about your fate? Ask Gary Piland's psychic chicken. This site also contains an excellent archive of "Why did the chicken cross the road?" jokes, including my favorite by Ernest Hemingway.

http://www.ruprecht.com

The Red Hot Chili Paper

This irreverent webzine is dedicated to cooking and the wacky personalities who like to cook. The design is compelling and easy to navigate, the writers are hysterical, and the recipes look delicious. Be sure to check out Caroline Elizabeth's Drunken Stinky Chicken in a Pick-Up.

http://chilipaper.com/index.html

Salon Magazine

Far and away the best general interest magazine on the Net. Salon features daily and weekly stories, book, movie, and television reviews, and regular columnists and comics including Camille Paglia, Anne Lamott, and David Horowitz. The Table Talk section is one of the more sophisticated forums going. Overall, this is the *New Yorker* of the Web. ✐

http://www.salon1999.com

The Smoking Gun

This innovative site makes a practice of chasing "paper trails," by publishing public domain documents of interest. Like the traffic ticket David Duchovny received while riding his bicycle in New York.

http://www.thesmokinggun.com

ENGINEERING

American Society for Engineering Education (ASEE)

In addition to general information about the ASEE, this site features an extraordinarily comprehensive list of resources useful to engineers and others. Included at the site are links to corporate home pages, university engineering departments, and research and development facilities, such as national and corporate labs. ASEE is a nonprofit organization dedicated to improving engineering education. ⊕ ⚲

http://www.asee.org

Galaxy's Engineering and Technology Resources

The Galaxy web catalog's list of resources for many types of engineering and for industry-related subjects like nondestructive testing and technical reports. The site goes on to include other areas of potential interest, including academic organizations, events, commercial organizations and discussion groups. ⊕

http://galaxy.einet.net/galaxy/Engineering-and-Technology. html

Internet Connections for Engineering

An extensive index to the engineering resources of the Internet, compiled by the Engineering Library of Cornell University. The index is organized alphabetically, according to discipline. ⊕

http://www.englib.cornell.edu/ice/

The Semiconductor Subway

A collection of links to semiconductor- and Microsystems-related information, featuring a cool subway-layout imagemap to take you to the sites; they're also grouped and discussed by discipline. The Semiconductor Subway is kept on schedule by Duane Boning of MIT.

http://www-mtl.mit.edu/semisubway.html

Society of Women Engineers

The SWE created this web site to further their mission of stimulating women to achieve full potential in careers as engineers and leaders, expanding the image of the engineering profession as a positive force in improving the quality of life, and demonstrating the value of diversity. Sections include career guidance, the president's newsletter, awards, conventions, regions, and student services.

http://www.swe.org

ENVIRONMENTAL ISSUES

CIESIN Global Change Information Gateway

The Consortium for International Earth Science Information Network (CIESIN) provides information from the Socioeconomic Data and Application Center, CIESIN's gateway to the NASA Earth Observation System Data and Information System, and the Global Change Research Information Office, CIESIN's gateway to the U.S. Global Change Research Program. ⚲ ✎

http://www.ciesin.org

EnviroLink

A comprehensive online environmental information service provided by the EnviroLink Network, a nonprofit organization based in Pittsburgh, Pennsylvania. The beautifully layed-out page features links to sections on education, events, government, enviroarts, and sustainable business networks. A recent highlight featured a live Internet chat with Koko, a female gorilla who understands sign language. ⚲

http://envirolink.org

Environmental Working Group

This group of researchers, computer experts and writers based in Washington, D.C. "provides information and policy analysis to the general public, environmental organizations and other public interest groups, journalists and policy makers." You'll find separate pages for each topic, including tap water, pesticides, farm subsidies, air pollution, and transportation policy. One feature that's certain to keep you up at night is the Where You Live section, which allows a search of EWG's online databases for environmental dangers to your specific state, county, or town. ⚲

http://www.ewg.org

Garbage

Want to find out what actually happened to that half-eaten Twinkie you threw away last year? Take a look at Garbage, an exhibit from the Annenberg/CPB Project Exhibits collection, which demonstrates just what happens to the solid waste that individuals and corporations generate each year.

http://www.learner.org/exhibits/garbage/intro.html

Links to Information Sources for Hydrogeology, Hydrology, and Environmental Sciences

Alphabetically organized index of environmental resources, color coded by offering institution. ⊕

http://www.us.net/adept/links.html

National Renewable Energy Laboratory

Part of the U.S. Department of Energy, the NREL's mission is to conduct and coordinate "renewable energy research and technology development that private industry cannot reasonably be expected to undertake." Check up on its alternative fuel, solar, and wind technology research at this well-organized site. ☕

http://www.nrel.gov

FOOTBALL

CNN/SI: Pro Football

Indepth news coverage of the NFL, along with pages covering Arena, CFL, and WLAF football. From CNN and *Sports Illustrated*.

http://www.cnnsi.com/football/

Dick Butkus Football Network

The famous announcer covers everything football, from the NFL to Pop Warner. You'll also find profiles, contests, chats with football

stars, and weekly thoughts from Dick Butkus himself. ⊕

http://www.dickbutkus.com/dbfn/

NFL Teams Web Ring

A directory of fan pages on NFL teams. ☕

http://www.knowitallclub.com/htmdocs/nflteamswr.html

NFL.com

This clearly-organized site provides links to a site for each of the NFL teams, features on players, statistics, schedules, and more. The TV and Radio Index pages provides listings of game schedules and times.

http://www.nfl.com

Totally Football Links

A splendid index of football resources of all kinds, listing more than 2,000 links. ⊕ ☕

http://www.3sports.com

GARDENING

4Gardening.com

All the gardening links and information you could need, organized into sections: helpful hints, products, and guides and Magazines. Sponsored by the 4Internet Network. ⊕

http://www.4garden.com

The Garden Gate

Eventually every fanatical gardener has to face the age-old question: What to do when it's too dark or too cold outside to garden? Why not pull up a chair, grab your mouse, and stroll through the Garden Gate. From the Gardener's reading room to an excellent collection of links to Internet resources for gardeners, this page could keep you busy for hours. The Garden Gate's pages are created and maintained by Karen Fletcher.

http://garden-gate.prarienet.org

The Gardener's Source List

"A select source list of plants, seeds, growing supplies and books for the garden and greenhouse." Choose from 23 topics, with 4 to almost 40 references in each. Mostly composed of names, addresses and phone numbers of garden providers around the country, some of which also have web pages you can jump over to. ⊕

http://fmweb.aces.uiuc.edu/pef/sources

Henrietta's Herbal Home Page

If you're interested in the medicinal or culinary uses of herbs, Henrietta's is the place to start. You'll find loads of medicinal and gastronomical information that ranges from newsgroups and noteworthy sites to pictures and shareware programs.

http://metalab.unc.edu/herbmed/

Seeds of Hope ... Harvest of Pride!

This unfortunately named site is a resource for community vegetable gardeners. Dennis Rinehart, editor, of Ohio State University Extension takes an in depth look at urban gardening programs in Ohio. Anyone interested in gardening as a potential community project will find all the reasons and resources they need to start one.

http://www.bright.net/~gardens/index.html#contents

GEOGRAPHY

3D Atlas Online

The 3D Atlas was created by *Compton's Encyclopedia* to support their CD-ROM on the topic, but you don't need the CD to appreciate this comprehensive site. Features include the view from space, maps and mapping, cultural world, geological Earth, the natural world, climactic conditions, and human impact. You'll also find geography related software and a geographic glossary. ⚲ ⊕

http://www.3datlas.com

Color Landform Atlas of the United States

Ray Sterner has created a veritable geographer's delight. Click on a state link, and then choose to view that state as a shaded relief map, satellite image, or by county. You can also view a black-and-white image or download the map as a PostScript file. Some historical maps are pro-

vided as well, along with a number of external links related to the particular geography of each state.

http://fermi.jhuapl.edu/states/states.html

Geographic Information Server

An interface to data supplied by the U.S. Geodetic Survey and the U.S. Postal Service. Make requests by name (Sebastopol, for all cities named Sebastopol, or Sebastopol, CA, for all cities named Sebastopol within California); the server returns latitude, longitude, population, Zip Code, elevation, etc.

http://mapping.usgs.gov/www/gnis/gnisform.html

MapQuest

If you need to plan a trip, plan a move, or get driving directions, MapQuest is the place to start. Use the TripQuest link to create door-to-door driving directions, complete with overview map, or TravelPlan USA to get lodging, dining, and city information from the Mobil travel guide. The Interactive Atlas uses Java to zoom in on maps, providing details down to the street level about everything from local attractions to recreation, shopping, and transportation. ✦ ☛

http://www.mapquest.com

Perry-Castaneda Library Map Collection

Housed at the University of Texas at Austin, this is a huge collection of country, city, and regional maps, most of which were created by the CIA. If you like to keep apprised of current events, be sure to check out the electronic maps of current interest section, where you will find maps for parts of the world that are currently in the news.

http://www.lib.utexas.edu/Libs/PCL/Map_collection/Map_collection.html

Xerox PARC MapViewer

MapViewer is an application that dynamically renders a map based on user input. Click on a region and MapViewer will zoom in on it. You can also use a link to the geographic name server at the University of Buffalo to locate a particular location. Typing in "San Jose, California," we find that it is the county seat, and had a population of 629,442 in 1980. We can click on its location to display a map of the United States and a map of Northern California, showing where San Jose is.

http://pubweb.parc.xerox.com/map

GEOLOGY

Earthquake Image Information System

The Earthquake Image Information System (EqIIS) provides web access to thousands of photos of quake damage. The EqIIS database can be queried and browsed by date and location of quake or by name of photographer. More than 80 quakes are covered, ranging around the world from the 1923 quake in Tokyo, Japan, to the Whittier Narrows, California earthquake of 1987. EqIIS was developed with support from the Federal Emergency Management Agency in cooperation with the University of California Museum Informatics Project.

http://nisee.ce.berkeley.edu

Geology Link Page

This extensive list of World Wide Web links related to geology is maintained by Bret C. Rediker. Resources are organized by GeoSocieties, government geologic surveys, specific fields of study, and general resources. ⊕

http://www.realtime.net/~revenant/geo.html

Hydrology-related Internet Resources

An impressive collection of links, maintained by Tim Scheibe of the Earth and Environmental Sciences Center at the Pacific Northwest Laboratory. What is hydrology? "The occurrence, distribution, movement and properties of the waters of the Earth and their relationship with the environment."

http://terrassa.pnl.gov:2080/EESC/resourcelist/hydrology.html

U.S. Geological Survey

A service provided by the United States Geological Survey. You'll find news releases, information about the survey, resources, software, and other services related to geology, hydrology, and cartography. Organized by topic, it includes

audio and animated material as well as text and pictures.

http://www.usgs.gov

VolcanoWorld

VolcanoWorld is a growing site that was created to educate students and others by delivering data, including high-quality remote-sensing images, near real-time volcano information, and interactive experiments. The site includes links to current and recent eruptions, images of volcanoes, and a volcano slide show. You can also ask questions of volcano experts who will email you a response. VolcanoWorld is the production of a team of 12 experts, primarily from the University of North Dakota. ⊕

http://volcano.und.nodak.edu

HISTORY OF CIVILIZATION

American Memory

Online archival collections presented by the Library of Congress. A search through the collection of 1,609 color photographs from the Farm Security Administration and the Office of War Information, ca. 1938–1944, turned up digital images of a 1940s "juke joint" in Belle Glade, Florida, a Ferris wheel at the 1941 Vermont state fair, and women assembling a bomber plane at a Douglas Aircraft factory in Long Beach, California. Other notable collections include Early Motion Pictures, 1897–1916, and Life History Manuscripts from the Folklore Project, WPA Federal Writers' Project, 1936–1940. ✎

http://rs6.loc.gov/amhome.html

Anne Frank Online

The web site dedicated to the German-Jewish teenager forced into hiding during the holocaust. The site includes a biography, excerpts from and discussions of her infamous diary, information on education and a traveling exhibit, and goings on at the Anne Frank Center USA. ✎

http://www.annefrank.com

A Cybrary of the Holocaust

Compelling and comprehensive, this site lucidly conveys the horror of the Holocaust. The exhibit presents history, survivors' tales, images, and artwork to a devastating yet mindful effect. Visitors will also find forums and mailing lists for survivors and their families. A Cybrary of the Holocaust was developed by an international team of educators and historians, and is available to teachers on CD-ROM. ⚲

http://remember.org

Information Servers at the Smithsonian Institution

A collection of links to servers maintained by the Smithsonian Institution in Washington, D.C. Among the resources available from the information servers at the Smithsonian Institution page are the Center for Earth and Planetary Studies, the Natural History Web, and the Smithsonian Institution Photo Server. ⚲

http://www.si.edu

Native Web: Resource Center

Index, by subject, of web links relating to native peoples and their cultures. ⊕ ⚲

http://www.nativeweb.org/resources

Oneida Indian Nation of New York

Resources and documents that explain the history of the Oneida Indian tribe. Of particular interest is the Treaties link, which details important documents relating to the relationship between sovereign tribes and the United States Government. Be sure to read the little known historical facts.

http://www.oneida-nation.net

Slave Narratives

Narratives from former slaves in the United States, including Moses Roper, Solomon Northup, and William Wells Brown.

http://metalab.unc.edu/docsouth/neh/about.html

Soviet Archives

The Library of Congress has an exhibit of materials from the opened Soviet archives. There is information about life under the Soviet system,

Chernobyl, the Cold War, Cuban missile crisis, and many other topics. Anyone interested in understanding cold war history should know about this archive.

http://metalab.unc.edu/expo/soviet.exhibit/soviet.archive.html

HOBBIES

Amateur Radio—Best of the Web

A guide to Internet resources related to Ham radio and instructional information regarding how to get into the hobby. Sections include getting into amateur radio, directories: callsign, QSL, repeater, and amateur radio news.

http://ourworld.compuserve.com/homepages/emayer/

Cyberspace World Railroad

A rich online resource for train buffs, maintained by Daniel Dawdy. In addition to a collection of weekly news reports from the Association of American Railroads, there are longer stories in the lounge car, old railroad advertisements, a huge collection of links in the switch track area, and a nifty collection of railroad clip art.

http://www.mcs.com/~dsdawdy/cyberoad.html

Internet Chess Library

The Internet Chess Library is an excellent resource, featuring an archive of world championship games, a help desk, a collection of FAQs, ratings information, and a comprehensive list of Internet chess resources.

http://caissa.onenet.net/chess/

Joseph Wu's Origami Page

Joseph Wu's Origami Page provides some extraordinary examples of origami, the ancient art of paper folding. Learn when and where the art originated (no, not Japan) and where the name "origami" comes from. This site would be more engaging if it had more instructions, particularly for beginners; however, it does have links to other origami sites. ⚲

http://www.origami.vancouver.bc.ca/

Money Origami

Some people grow orchids, others fold money. Sherwood Clay Randall Jr. will teach you how to turn bills into a spider, a picture frame, a Valentine, and more.

http://www.umva.com/~clay/money/

Moto Directory

As of our last check, the Moto Directory listed 4,383 links relating to the best gift to get for your last birthday. Many are personal home pages, others are produced by motorcycle companies, and some, like rider training/safety, are a public service. Personal pages are organized alphabetically, with separate categories for commercial links, road racing/competition, and offroad/motocross. ⚲

http://www.moto-directory.com/welcome.htm

Sapphire Swan Dance Directory

A thorough and easy-to-use index to dance resources of the Internet. Browse links by dance style, from Balkan to Zydeco.

http://www.SapphireSwan.com/dance/

Shortwave Radio Catalog

A large amount of information and links to servers related to radio, including shortwave, ham, broadcast AM/FM, and satellite. This site has links to home pages of broadcast stations, news organizations like the BBC and Voice of America, and technical information about operating transmitters.

http://itre.ncsu.edu/radio/

Textiles.Org

From knitting and crocheting to rug hooking, Textiles.Org presents links to other textiles sites on the Net. The server also features two excellent local resources: a kid's link and a message bulletin board.

http://www.textiles.org

World Wide Quilting Page

Just about everything you ever wanted to know about quilting. The World Wide Quilting Page offers how-to advice, a history of quilting around the world, and info on where to find

fabric and supplies. At the design board, you can see what fellow quilters are doing; another site lists computer software for quilt designing. The site includes a FAQ page and links to other textile information on the Web, not to mention the "Third and Final WORST Quilt In The World Contest." ⚲

http://ttsw.com/MainQuiltingPage.html

Your Flyfishing Resource Guide

Links to information about equipment, videos, magazines, fisheries, photo albums, lodges, software, guides, and more, all related to fly fishing. The site also sponsors forums on gear, travel, and tying, as well as "For Sale by Flyfisher" and "Hatch and Fishing Reports." ⚲

http://flyfish.com

HOCKEY

In the Crease Professional Hockey Journal

News, scores, and reports on multiple hockey leagues, including the NHL, IHL, AHL, ECHL, and WPHL. ☕ ⊕

http://www.inthecrease.com

Le Coq Sportif Guide to Hockey

News, scores, and features about ice hockey and the NHL. ☕ ⚲

http://www.lcshockey.com/index/

The National Hockey League

The official site of the NHL.

http://www.nhl.com

USA Hockey

Information about amateur hockey in the United States. ☕

http://www.usahockey.com

Zamboni

Want to know about those hulking machines that clean the ice at the hockey rink at halftime? This is the site for you. It also sports an elegant layout and a great graphic on the opening page.

http://www.charged.com/issue_0/frost/stories/zamboni/

INTEREST GROUPS

Africa Connector

The Africa Connector provides links to just about every Africa-related resource on the Web, whether it relates to weather, news, or the Internet on the continent. This site is organized in catalog format.

http://old.law.columbia.edu/africa/conn.htm

AltSex: Alternative Sexuality

An index to documents, newsgroups, mailing lists, and web sites related to alternative sexuality and sexual politics. Specific subject areas include BDSM, polyamory, sex and health, transgender issues, and gay and lesbian resources. A well-organized, frank, open-minded and intelligent site.

http://www.altsex.org

disinformation: the subculture search engine

With subcategories including propaganda, revolutionaries, censorship, counterculture, counterintelligence and newspeak, you know this is a site for the Fox Mulder in all of us. The stated purpose of the site is to "provide a portal to the emerging radical intellectual movement flourishing in the World Wide Web community and point users of the service toward the highest quality, most powerful and culturally important information the Internet has to offer. There is a thriving counter culture living in cyberspace, a place bearing scant resemblance to AOL's 'Mayberry RFD'... ." Subjects raised for discussion are followed by recommended web sites. ⊕ ⚲

http://www.disinfo.com

Femina: Web Search for Women

A collection of links geared toward women, in a Yahoo!-style catalog format. ⚲

http://www.femina.com

Queer Resources Directory

A good resource for the gay, lesbian, bisexual, and transgendered community. It has sections concerned with AIDS facts and treatments; resources and contact information for various support and activist groups; bibliography of publications, movies, radio, and other media of interest to the community; civil rights; and domestic partnerships. Also, has portions of the *GLAAD* Newsletter online. ⚲

http://www.qrd.org/qrd/

Vietnam Veterans Home Page

The Vietnam Veterans Home Page provides an interactive onlinen forum for Vietnam Veterans and their families and friends to exchange information, stories, poems, songs, art, pictures, and experiences. The page presents views of the war through the eyes of those who served in it. The page also includes a listing of veterans organizations and support groups. The Vietnam Veterans Home Page is maintained by Bill McBride, a Vietnam veteran who served in the Marine Corps.

http://grunt.space.swri.edu/index.htm

INTERNATIONAL GOVERNMENT

Charter of the United Nations

View this historic 1945 document online. Includes the ability to search, look at treaties, and find related links. ⚲

http://www.umn.edu/humanrts/instree/aunchart.htm

The Commission on Global Governance

Learn about this group of 28 leaders from around the world who are seeking U.N. reform to enhance the global community. Get recent updates, and read the Commission's report entitled *Our Global Neighborhood*.

http://www.cgg.ch

EUROPA (European Union)

A large collection of information about the European Union's "goals, institutions, and policies" in 10 different languages. Among interesting resources here are a "European Consumer Guide to the Single Market" (beneath the ABC link) and a delineation of the different institutions that will guide the Union (beneath the Institutions link). ⚲

http://europa.eu.int/index.htm

International Constitutional Law

Listing of constitutional documents, in English, including those from the following countries: Albania, Angola, Australia, Austria, Belgium, Belarus, Bosnia, Brazil, Bulgaria, Cambodia, Canada, Chechnya, China, Congo, Croatia, Czech Republic, Denmark, Eritrea, Estonia, Europe, Finland, France, Germany, Greece, Hawaii, Hong Kong, Hungary, India, Iran, Iraq, Ireland, Israel, Italy, Japan, Kuwait, Latvia, Lithuania, Libya, Luxembourg, Macedonia, Madagascar, Malta, Mauritania, Mongolia, Morocco, Namibia, Nepal, Netherlands, New Zealand, Oman, Paraguay, Poland, Portugal, Romania, Russia, Rwanda, Saudi Arabia, Serbia and Montenegro, Singapore, Slovakia, Slovenia, South Africa, South Korea, Spain, Sweden, Switzerland, Syria, Taiwan, Tibet, Tunisia, United Kingdom, United States of America, Yemen, and Zambia.

http://www.uni-wuerzburg.de/law/home.html

The Library of Congress Research Tools

Strange as it may seem, the U.S. Library of Congress hosts a number of excellent resources on International affairs. In particular, take a look at the Country Studies/Area Handbook Program for more information. ⚲

http://lcweb.loc.gov/rr/tools.html

NATO

The North Atlantic Treaty Organization's home page is presented in French and English. You'll find a description of the organization itself, and an archive of texts, fact sheets, press releases, speeches and other materials.

http://www.nato.int

United Nations News

Compiled five days a week and digested monthly, the U.N. News covers areas of the globe and events that involve this international body. Mostly this means trouble areas, but the site also contains updates for other parts of the world in which the U.N. has been involved, but which are now relatively stable. Information appears in English, French, and Spanish.

http://www.undp.org/toppages/news/newframe.htm

THE INTERNET

The Argus Clearinghouse

The Clearinghouse provides one-stop access to over 150 subject guides to Internet resources. Most of the guides have been compiled by academics, lending them authority that many Net guides lack. Subjects covered include futurology, theater, Tibetan studies, philosophy, and aerospace engineering. ⚲ ⊕

http://www.clearinghouse.net

checkdomain.com

Want to know whether the brilliant domain name you've come up with is available? Take a look at this site, which has a remarkably easy interface for searching InterNIC's database.

http://www.checkdomain.com

Electronic Frontier Foundation

The EFF exists to promote existing academic and personal freedoms in the new worldwide computer society. It fights against network censorship, and for freely available information, privacy, and democracy. Included on this server is information about the foundation (in the EFF directory) and the Computer and Academic Freedom Archives. ⚲

http://www.eff.org

Internet Oracle Resource Index

The Internet Oracle is a fascinating, collective humor effort. While it's silly, it's one of the best uses of the Net I've seen. Users mail questions to the Oracle (in the form of other Oracle users), which then provides a witty answer to the question. The Oracular "priesthood" chooses the best, funniest answers for inclusion in the Oracularities in the Usenet newsgroup *rec.humor.oracle*. The web page serves as a gateway, and includes help files, FAQ's, and a form for submissions.

http://www.pcnet.com/~stenor/oracle/index.html

Internet Society

The Internet Society is an international professional organization established to encourage the evolution, standardization, and dissemination of techniques and technologies that allow diverse information systems to communicate. The Society publishes newsletters, organizes conferences, and manages email distribution lists to educate the worldwide community about the Internet. The Society sponsors the Internet Architecture Board and its Internet Engineering and Research Task Forces, and maintains liaisons with other international organizations and standards bodies as part of its effort to assist in the evolution and growth of the Internet. ✐ ⚲

http://info.isoc.org

Life on the Internet

PBS Online presents this site. It not only provides a handy beginner's guide, but an impressive array of subjects covered in 26 stories, from understanding the Internet's role in education to finding someone you know. These stories are based on the PBS TV series, and if you desire to see more than text and photos, videos of each episode can be ordered here. Fun features include trivia and a timeline.

http://www.pbs.org/internet/

The List

An invaluable directory of Internet service providers in the United States and around the world. Maintained by Mecklermedia, the directory can be accessed by country name, country code, or U.S. telephone area code. Clicking on an area code generates an alphabetical list of all the companies providing Internet connectivity for that area. The record for each company includes the URL for the company web page and the kinds of dial-up and dedicated services they provide. ⚲

http://thelist.com

Netiquette Home Page

A concise guide to good citizenship on the Internet, as adapted from Virginia Shea's book.

http://www.albion.com/netiquette/index.html

Pete Beim's [Unofficial] Eudora FAQs & Links

Everything you wanted to know about the Eudora email program but were afraid to ask. Includes information on customizing Eudora and dealing with spam.

http://www.cs.nwu.edu/%7Ebeim/eudora/index.html

Publicly Accessible Mailing Lists

An index of email lists available on the Internet, maintained by Stephanie da Silva. Among the hundreds of groups indexed here, you'll find phonecard collectors and hockey-goalies. You can browse the index by name and subject. ⚲

http://www.NeoSoft.com/internet/paml/

World Wide Web Consortium

This international industry consortium was established in 1994 to develop common web protocols. If you are into architecture and interfaces, this is the place for you. History and issues of the Web are put forth here, but information is generally geared toward developers and high-end users. The Consortium is led by Tim Berners-Lee, director and creator of the World Wide Web, and chairman Jean-Francois Abramatic. ✐

http://www.w3.org

JAVA

Cafe au Lait Java FAQs, News, and Resources

A resource geared toward learning Java from Elliot Rusty Harold, author of O'Reilly's *Java Network Programming*.

http://metalab.unc.edu/javafaq/

Gamelan

A substantial archive of free software and pointers to resources related to Java. ⚲ 🌐

http://www.gamelan.com

Java Home Page

The official web site from Sun, the creators of the Java language. ☕ ⚲ 🌐

http://java.sun.com

JavaReport Online

An online magazine about the development of the Java language.

http://www.javareport.com

JavaWorld

IDG presents an online magazine about the programming language. 🖥 ✎

http://www.javaworld.com

LAW

ACLU: American Civil Liberties Union

This well-designed site features news releases, special collections, and links to the text of legislation and decisions pertaining to ACLU-related cases. Nicely organized according to 15 issue-focus pages (including church and state, immigrant rights, and workplace rights). ✎

http://www.aclu.org

Counsel Connect: The Online Service for Lawyers

For $120 per year Counsel Connect subscribers have access to any 12 online CLE seminars in a year or one of Counsel Connect's case-law services, which include daily email digests of all state and federal appellate decisions in California, Texas and Illinois. Newsletter services covering corporate counsel, small-firm management and technology, Internet and intellectual property law, and Internet legal research topics will be offered soon. All subscribers receive access to moderated discussion groups on all legal and management topics, member-controlled private discussions and libraries, archives of public documents from prominent cases, and an email account. $

http://www.counsel.com

The Cyberlaw Encyclopedia

The Cyberlaw Encyclopedia organizes resources according to topics of interest in the computer field, allowing you to read news articles, legislation, and court decisions on the various subjects. Topics include confidentiality obligations, EDI and electronic commerce, and censorship and free speech.

http://gahtan.com/cyberlaw/

Internet Law Library

Sponsored by the U.S. House of Representatives, the Internet Law Library serves two important purposes. First, it provides a full-text, searchable copy of the United States Code, free of charge. Second, the site has organized thousands of links to Internet law resources by subject or jurisdiction. You'll also find links to U.S. treaties and the laws of other nations. ✎

http://law.house.gov

Law Journal Extra!

For $100 per year, you get both print and online subscriptions, including a searchable archive of back issues. $

http://www.ljx.com/reg/registra.html

Lexis-Nexis

The GC Advantage software provides a smooth interface to a wealth of legal and news sources. They're very cagey about their rates; go to the subscription page at *http://www.lexis-nexis.com/lncc/general/subscribe.html* to find the telephone number or email address to contact. $

http://www.lexis-nexis.com/lncc/

The Police Officer's Internet

The self-proclaimed "world's foremost law enforcement web site" recently added links to 500 new sites in one month alone. You'll find a catalog-style directory with links related to criminal justice law, law enforcement agencies, memorials, specials ops, training events, and law enforcers' personal home pages. ⊕

http://www.officer.com

Supreme Court Rulings

Project Hermes makes the U.S. Supreme Court's opinions and rulings publicly available via the Internet. The information is posted worldwide electronically within 15 minutes of the Court's announcement in Washington, D.C. Opinions and decisions from the 1989 term to the present are available, mainly in Adobe Acrobat format. You'll also find a collection of 580 other historically important rulings. ✎ ⊕

http://www.law.cornell.edu/supct/

Tenant Net

Information for renters, organized by state.

http://tenant.net/main.html

U.S. Constitution

The text of the *U.S. Constitution,* in full or divided by article and amendment.

http://www.law.cornell.edu/constitution/constitution.overview. html

West's Legal Directory

West's Legal Directory is a "comprehensive directory of law firms, government offices, corporate law offices, and lawyers" published by West Publishing Company of Eagan, Minnesota. You can run searches on any keyword or combination of keywords—read the search methods file for more information. Moreover, the company promises to soon "enable secure communications for clients and lawyers on the Internet" via Verisign certificates. ⚲

http://www.lawoffice.com

LITERATURE

Acses, Universum's Smartest Bookfinder

Many people don't realize that Amazon.com isn't the only bookstore online. Acses will search through dozens of sites to find the best price for your book. The advanced search option will even find the lowest price on bundles of books, so that you can save on shipping. ⚲

http://www.acses.com

British Poetry 1780–1910: A Hypertext Achive of Scholarly Editions

An archive of poems from Coleridge, Keats, Shelley, Wilde, and other greats. This collection is hosted by the University of Virginia's Electronic Text Center.

http://etext.lib.virginia.edu/britpo.html

Complete Works of William Shakespeare

The web of our life is of a mingled yarn, good and ill together: our virtues would be proud, if our faults whipped them not; and our crimes would despair, if they were not cherished by our virtues. —*All's Well That Ends Well*

An online collection of Shakespeare's plays and poetry created by Jeremy Hylton, a graduate student with the Library 2000 project at MIT. Aside from allowing visitors to browse through Shakespeare's works, the site features a keyword search tool that lets users search for words or phrases in the database (like "web," for example). There's also a hypertext glossary built into each work. ⚲

http://the-tech.mit.edu/Shakespeare/works.html

The Electronic Journalist

The Society of Professional Journalist's site includes an online version of *Quill* (SPJ's monthly magazine), a code of journalistic ethics, and a list of resources on Freedom of Information issues. The site also includes pointers to journalism publications and news media online. ⚲

http://www.spj.org

Electronic Poetry Center

A collection of links to Internet poetry resources, compiled by Kenneth Sherwood and Loss Glazier of the University of Buffalo. Local resources include the RIF/T poetry journal, "An Electronic Space for Poetry, Prose, and Poetics." Poetry enthusiasts should check out the sound room, an archive of sound art, spoken word poetry, audio hypermedia, and arts radio broadcasts, some in RealPlayer format. ⚲

http://wings.buffalo.edu/epc/

Elements of Style

The original 1918 edition of William Strunk's classic guide to effective writing, brought to the Web by Columbia University's Project Bartleby. Strunk focuses on the basics; the heart of the book consists of the chapters "Elementary Rules of Usage" and "Elementary Principles of Composition."

http://www.columbia.edu/acis/bartleby/strunk/

Indigenous Peoples' Literature

A site that brings to life the traditions and philosophies of native peoples through stories, poetry, prayers, and quotations of tribal leaders. Indigenous Peoples' Literature is edited by computer programmer Glenn H. Welker of Virginia, who also maintains the Indigenous Peoples of Mexico home page.

http://www.indians.org/welker/natht2a.htm

Letters from an Iowa Soldier in the Civil War

An affecting and unusual resource, this site maintains a collection of letters written by Newton Scott, a private in the 36th Infantry, Iowa Volunteers, during the Civil War. During the three years he served, Scott wrote letters to his sweetheart and parents. Here the letters are transcribed as written, without changes to the spelling or punctuation. Also included are Scott's service record, his obituary, and links to other Civil War information on the Net. This simple site is well designed and adds a very personal note to the many Civil War resources already available. Congratulations to William Scott Proudfoot, a librarian at West Valley College in Saratoga, California, who says he developed the project just "to see if I could do it!"

http://www.civilwarletters.com

Octavo

An ambitious effort to sell online digital reproductions of rare books in Adobe's PDF format. The books aren't cheap, but the samples are spectacular, and worth looking at just to see what's possible. The digitized books may include transcriptions, translations, and other commentary.

http://www.octavo.com

The Online Books Page

John Mark Ockerbloom, in conjunction with the Universal Library Project at Carnegie Mellon University, maintains this excellent resource of more than 6,000 English works, available free of charge. Texts that appear here are either free of copyright restrictions or have been permitted by the copyright holder to appear for noncommercial use. Browse by author, subject, or title. Links are provided to books in progress and the Internet Public Library. ⚲ ⊕

http://www.cs.cmu.edu/books.html

Project Gutenberg

Project Gutenberg is an ambitious nonprofit and volunteer effort to get as much literature as possible into machine-readable form. Its holdings include the works of Shakespeare, lots of Lewis Carroll, Moby Dick, and a rapidly growing number of classic texts, speeches, and reference materials. ⚲

http://promo.net/pg/

Science Fiction Resource Guide

From the Philip K.Dick FAQ to William Gibson's Alien 3 script, this is a gigantic collection of links to science fiction resources on the Net. The site is maintained by Chaz Boston Baden. ⚲

http://sflovers.rutgers.edu/Web/SFRG/

Voice of the Shuttle

A far-reaching listing of scholarly resources for all kinds of literature and other fields in the humanities. ⚲ ⊕

http://humanitas.ucsb.edu

Writers' Resources on the Web

The site describes itself as "a comprehensive writing resource full of market information, tips on improving your writing, articles, interviews with professional authors and editors, networking opportunities, and a guide to the best resources for writers on the Net." Topics covered include a searchable library of writers' guidelines and resources and links dedicated to the craft of writing. ⚲

http://www.inkspot.com

MACINTOSH

Cult of Macintosh

An almost frighteningly comprehensive site about all things Macintosh. The games section, for example, links to pages related to DOOM and 7th Guest, since they're available on the Macintosh platform. Sections include Apple, games, newsgroups, persons, software archives, top 20, FAQs, indices, MUGs, periodicals, powerbook, propaganda, software pages, and vendors. You'll find mirror sites in Colorado, South Dakota, Florida, South Africa, Singapore, Hong Kong, Japan, and Australia. ⊕ ⚲

http://cult-of-mac.utu.fi

iMac2Day

Everything iMac and then some. The site is updated daily, and provides a retail price scanner, tech support, articles, reader reports, how-to guides, and more. You'll also find news, software, recommended books, and links to other Macintosh and iMac sites. ⊕ ⚲

http://www.imac2day.com

Info-Mac Home Page

The self-proclaimed largest collection of Macintosh software in the world. Beautifully organized. ⚲

http://www.info-mac.com

MacWEEK Online

Ziff-Davis presents the online version of the popular magazine. ⚲

http://macweek.zdnet.com

TidBITS

An up-to-date email and web newsletter covering the Macintosh Internet community.

http://www.tidbits.com.

MATHEMATICS

e-MATH

e-MATH is an Internet node that provides mathematicians with an expanding list of services that can be accessed electronically. e-MATH is intended as an electronic clearinghouse for timely research information in the mathematical sciences. You'll also find sections dedicated to Employment and careers, authors and reviewers, meetings and conferences, and what's new in mathematics. ⚲

http://e-math.ams.org

GAMS (Guide to Available Mathematical Software)

The National Institute of Standards and Technology created this online cross-index of available mathematical software in order to provide scientists and engineers with improved access to reusable computer software. You can search for

software by what problem it solves, the package name, module name, or text in module abstracts. ⚲

http://gams.nist.gov

The Geometry Center

Fascinating for both the mathematically inclined and the mathematically inept, this site is a gathering of geometry information funded by the National Science Foundation and located at the University of Minnesota. The Center's mission is to stimulate research in geometry and promote the development of computer tools for visualizing all those squares and parallelograms. This well-constructed site lists current projects, multimedia documents, video productions, course materials, and geometry software. A quick peek at the design-rich Geometry Picture Archive confirmed that there have been big-time changes in geometry lately—this stuff looks interesting! ⚲

http://www.geom.umn.edu/welcome.html

History of Mathematics Archive

A concise history of the study of mathematics, consisting of biographies of seventeenth and eighteenth century mathematicians, mathematical papers, and a directory of web sites related to the topic.

http://www.maths.tcd.ie/pub/HistMath/HistMath.html

Mathematics Web Sites Around the World

This large collection of mathematics related links is broken down by categories: societies and associations, institutes and centers, commercial pages, mathematics journals, mathematics preprints, subject area pages, other archived materials, and mathematics software. It's maintained by Penn State University. ⚲

http://www.math.psu.edu/MathLists/Contents.html

MEDICINE

Achoo Healthcare Online

Catalog-style directory to healthcare resources on the Web. ⊕ ⚲

http://www.achoo.com

Aesclepian Chronicles

Aesclepian Chronicles is a holistic medicine journal published monthly by the Synergistic Medicine Center of Chapel Hill, North Carolina. Articles are written for a general audience and tend to focus on the spiritual and psychological side of health and healing.

http://www.forthrt.com/%7Echronicl/homepage.html

AL-ANON and ALATEEN

This site is a straightforward presentation of information from the AL-ANON and ALATEEN organizations, which are devoted to helping families and friends of alcoholics. The 12 steps and 12 traditions of AL-ANONare listed, as are the telephone numbers and addresses for AL-ANON offices all around the world. Probably the most useful document offered on this site is the 20-question questionnaire entitled "Are You Troubled by Someone's Drinking?," which is designed to help people decide if they need the services of AL-ANON. Links are provided to mirror sites in 12 languages, including French, Spanish, and German. ⚲

http://www.Al-Anon-Alateen.org

The Arc

This site maintains a compendium of resources and information for people with mental retardation and those concerned about them. The organization publishes fact sheets on key topics, explains how to be an effective legislative advocate, and discusses the Americans with Disabilities Act. You'll also find links to Arc offices across the nation. The Q&A page offers options for employment, education, and community living. ⚲

http://TheArc.org/welcome.html

BirthQuest

This international searchable database is dedicated to searching out adoptees, birth parents, adoptive parents and siblings. A $20 registration fee is required. ⚲ $

http://www.birthquest.org

Blindness Resource Center

A large collection of links to Internet sites related to blindness. Among the resources listed in the collection are Raised Dot Computing, the New York Institute for Special Education, and a biography of Louis Braille.

http://www.nyise.org/blind.htm

CancerGuide: Steve Dunn's Cancer Information Page

"I am convinced that researching my options has been an important factor in my survival. Naturally then, I am a strong advocate of patients doing their own research, including delving into the most recent technical literature on their disease. Helping you do that is what CancerGuide is all about."—Steve Dunn, on the pros of researching your cancer. A guide for cancer patients who want to understand more about the disease and their treatment options. The author is a cancer survivor himself.

http://cancerguide.org

CISTI, The Canada Institute for Scientific and Technical Information

CISTI offers a wide range of services for varying prices. Services include document delivery for information in its library, information alerts that deliver filtered content to your desktop, searches and tables of content from any of 14,000 journals, and more. ⚲ $

http://www.nrc.ca/cisti/cisti.html

Computer-Related Repetitive Strain Injury

"Use a light touch when typing. Don't tightly squeeze the mouse. Take frequent breaks." These are among the tips found at this site for avoiding repetitive strain injury, which also offers diagrams of proper typing position and descriptions of the first warning signs of injuries. The author of the page is Paul Marxhausen, an engineering electronics technician who suffers from RSI.

http://engr-www.unl.edu/ee/eeshop/rsi.html

Deaf World Web

Deaf and hearing people alike can click into the world of the deaf at this expanding site, the self-proclaimed "Central Deaf Point on the Internet." Visitors will find resources organized by category: the sign of the day, general resources, talks, nations, "Deafulture," and an information desk. ⌕

http://dww.deafworldweb.org

Depression.com

This well-organized, well-designed site contains a wealth of information about depression as a treatable illness. Topics include sex and depression, living with a depressed person, antidepressant therapies, and more; this isn't a site designed to push Prozac. It's sponsored by Bristol-Myers Squibb, under the editorial direction of Michael Castleman and a staff of professional medical writers. ⌕

http://avocado.pc.helsinki.fi/~janne/asdfaq

DisABILITY Information and Resources

It's not fancy, but this straightforward listing of links is both remarkably comprehensive and updated frequently. Topics include politics, databases, and even—gasp!—resources not on the net. ⌕

http://www.eskimo.com/~jlubin/disabled.html

Facts for Families

Presented by the American Academy of Child and Adolescent Psychiatry, Facts for Families is a collection of almost 60 fact sheets covering the mental health issues faced by children and teens today. Among the topics covered in the collection are children and divorce, teenagers with eating disorders, and responses to child sexual abuse. Each fact sheet is written in an even and accessible style that explains the nature of each malady, its likely causes, and recommendations for treatment. Several fact sheets have been translated into French or Spanish. ⌕

http://www.aacap.org/web/aacap/info_families/

FDA Center for Food Safety and Applied Nutrition

"Some people are convinced that in children, sweets are a major culprit in causing hyperactivity and other behavior and cognitive (learning) problems. Recent evidence suggests that it's unlikely."—from *Candy: How Sweet It Is!*

The Center for Food Safety and Applied Nutrition (CFSAN) is a department of the FDA with the mission "to promote and protect the public

health and economic interest by ensuring that the food supply is safe, nutritious, wholesome, and honest, and that cosmetics are safe and properly labeled." The CFSAN WWW site provides access to a variety of FDA publications, covering such areas as food additives, biotechnology, food labeling, and foodborne illnesses. ⌕

http://vm.cfsan.fda.gov/list.html

A Forum for Women's Health

Health information for women, organized by lifecycle or by subject. You may also search the site, or submit questions to a female doctor. ⌕

http://www.womenshealth.org

HabitSmart

HabitSmart is a web site created by the California-based outpatient facility of the same name. The web site features thoughtful articles on a variety of issues related to substance abuse. Titles include "The Codependency Idea: A Disease of Caring," "HabitSmart: A Practical Approach to Changing Addictive Behavior," "Moderation Training," and "Smoking Reduction."

http://www.cts.com/crash/habtsmrt/

International Food Information Council (IFIC)

According to the IFIC, this site is "the source on food-related issues." These people don't mess around; the site is packed with information about health and nutrition, most of it in the form of the online versions of IFIC pamphlets. The pamphlets are organized according to audience (parents, educators, consumers, etc.), and cover such subjects as caffeine, food coloring, biotechnology, pregnancy, hyperactivity, and aspartame. ☕ ⌕

http://ificinfo.health.org

Just Say Yes: Sex Ed for Teens

A healthy, nonjudgmental look at sex from the Coalition for Positive Sexuality. Originally published in pamphlet form for Chicago high school students, Just Say Yes covers sex myths, respect, safe sex, birth control, STDs, and pregnancy.

http://www.webcom.com/~cps/JustSayYes/index.html

The Medicare and Medicaid Agency

Although the documents here are often frustratingly dense, this is a good place to learn about the more intricate aspects of Medicare and Medicaid. Visitors to the Medicare and Medicaid site will find such resources as news updates, HCFA employment opportunities, and a listing of upcoming events and meetings. ⚲

http://www.hcfa.gov

The National Alliance of Breast Cancer Organizations

The NABCO web site serves as a central clearinghouse for information about breast cancer from NABCO's network of more than 370 organizations. The site provides current information about breast cancer, updates on events and activities, and links to other Internet sites related to the topic.

http://www.nabco.org

National Institute of Allergy and Infectious Diseases

This division of the National Institutes of Health provides major support for scientists conducting research aimed at developing better ways to diagnose, treat, and prevent the many infectious, immunologic and allergic diseases that afflict people worldwide. The web site is notable for its sections on AIDS, asthma, transplants, and emerging diseases. ⚲

http://www.niaid.nih.gov

National Institutes of Health (NIH)

Information on and links to biomedical data, activities and grants of the NIH, and the NIH library. You'll also find a link to specific institutes and centers within the NIH. ⚲

http://www.nih.gov

National Multiple Sclerosis Society

The web site of the National MS Society provides a resource for information about the disease in English, French, Hungarian, Italian, and Japanese. You'll also find listings of local resources and an array of World Wide Web links related to the topic.

http://www.nmss.org

NicNet—Arizona Program for Nicotine and Tobacco Research

A catalog of the anti-smoking resources on the Net. Among sites in the index are the University of Pennsylvania's collection of smoking, tobacco, and cancer documents and a U.S. Department of Health and Human Services pamphlet called Check Your Smoking I.Q. There's also a nifty set of links to general and health sciences indexes with material on smoking. ⚲

http://www.nicnet.org

Online Birth Center

If you, or someone you know, is considering home birth or using a midwife to assist in a birth, this page could prove to be a valuable resource. Donna Dolezal Zelzer, who put this page together, has done a thoughtful job of compiling information on home birth, midwives (including a history of midwifery), and other related topics, including breastfeeding, nutrition, and high-risk pregnancies. ⚲

http://www.efn.org/~djz/birth/birthindex.html

PDIC: Parkinson's Disease Information Center

Jeffrey Kaye's up-to-date list of Parkinson's-related information on the Internet. Of particular interest is the legal center, where visitors may read about current legislative issues and laws of concern to those with the disease; includes full-text copies of the Udall Bill and the Americans With Disabilities Act.

http://pdic.jeffreyskaye.com

Pediatric Points of Interest

An index of links for pediatric physicians as well as for parents of young children. Categories include hospitals, parenting resources, and "fun stuff" on the Web for kids. ⚲

http://www.med.jhu.edu/peds/neonatology/poi.html

University of Connecticut Health Center

Librarians will conduct searches of the biomedical literature to support the patient care, educational, and research programs of the University of Connecticut Health Center. Fees start at $25 plus applicable charges. ⚲ $

http://www3.uchc.edu/~uchclib/departm/infserv/fee.

U.S. National Library of Medicine (NLM)

The NLM holds more than 4.5 million records, including books, journals, reports, manuscripts, and audio-visual items, and offers online information on a variety of medical topics. The MED-LINE database covers the fields of medicine, nursing, dentistry, veterinary medicine, the health care system, and the pre-clinical sciences, and contains bibliographic citations and author abstracts from more than 3,800 biomedical journals. ✍

http://www.nlm.nih.gov

World Health Organization

A WWW service offering information on the WHO's major health programs, as well as press releases, email/phone contacts, and general information about the organization in French and English. ✍

http://www.who.ch

MOVIES

Ain't It Cool News

If you're looking for gossip about movies, this is the place to go. Webmaster Harry Jay Knowles has scouts that report on early screenings of both Hollywood and independent films, not to mention juicy tidbits about behind the scenes goings-on. It's not the most professional site, but it's packed with information. ☕

http://www.aint-it-cool-news.com

The Greatest Films

Original reviews and synopses of the "best" Hollywood classic films. The content is fairly commercial—they go out on a limb and really like *Casablanca*—but still interesting. You'll find sections on film genres, great scenes, film posters, quizzes, and more.

http://www.filmsite.org

Internet Movie Database

A fantastic site that features information on thousands of movies. All cast and production information is hypertext linked, meaning you can identify a director you like and quickly discover the names of her other films. Most films are also accompanied by a rating (on a scale of 1 to 10), created by averaging the votes of users of the site. ⊕

http://us.imdb.com

Moviefone.com

Need to know what movies are playing in your area, and when? Punch up this site. You'll find information, comprehensive schedules, and streaming video clips, and can even purchase tickets online. ✍

http://www.moviefone.com

Mr. Cranky's Guide to Movies

A man after my own heart, Mr. Cranky reviews both recent releases and video rentals in a cranky manner. A recent review of *Godzilla* ran, "The story is paper-thin, the dialogue could have been scripted by an ESL student, and the character development makes one pine for the complexity of an Emilio Estevez tour de force."

http://www.mrcranky.com

MUSIC

Annotated Grateful Dead Lyrics

This web server is for the Deadhead in all of us. Maintained by David Dodd, the site provides lyrics, by permission, with links to footnotes for words or phrases that might benefit from elucidation. It's definitely worth adding to any Deadhead's hotlist.

http://arts.ucsc.edu/gdead/agdl/

The Blue Highway

From Robert Johnson to John Lee Hooker, the Blue Highway leads you on a stroll through the lives and music of the blues masters. More than 20 great musicians are profiled in these pages, and although the profiles are brief, they are well written and complemented by pictures and sound samples (.WAV format). The Blue Highway was created by Curtis Hewston, who has also put together a Blues news area and a collection of links to other Blues sites on the Net.

http://thebluehighway.com

Concert Schedules from POLLSTAR

Where is Pearl Jam playing this summer? Who's booked for your local theater? Who's coming to Akron this fall? Find out from POLLSTAR, a vast database of concert schedules. Searches can be run for bands, venues, and cities directly from the home page. Other services available at the POLLSTAR site include a list of the 40 most-requested tour schedules and a selection of tour gossip. ⚲

http://www.pollstar.com

Folkmusic.org

FolkBook offers a rich collection of information about folk music. Fans can find bios, discographies, and tour information for artists like the Indigo Girls and Mary Chapin Carpenter. Aspiring folk musicians will find links to the singer-songwriters' sites on the Net. FolkBook also has a comprehensive list of links to other music sites on the Web. Overall, this is a great place for the folkaholic to browse through: tons of information and a lot of fun.

http://www.folkmusic.org

JazzWeb

The complete Internet jazz resource. Visitors will find discographies, FAQs, and links to dozens of other jazz sites on the Net. This web site is maintained by the staff of WNUR-FM of Evanston, Illinois. ⚲

http://www.acns.nwu.edu/jazz/

Love 4 One Another

This offering, from the Artist Formerly Known as Prince, is eclectic and the use of nonstandard English is extremely irritating. Even so, the Artist makes remarkably good use of the multimedia format. ☕

http://www.love4oneanother.com

The Original Unofficial Elvis Home Page

Andrea Berman's Elvis home page brings together images of Graceland, classic photos of Elvis, sound clips from his music, and even a link to a hysterical Ouiji board seance. The home page states that its intention is to honor Elvis's musical and cultural legacy, not to belittle or defame him. There are, nonetheless, sec-tions on Elvis and aliens, Is Elvis alive?, and the space Elvis chronicles.

http://metalab.unc.edu/elvis/elvishom.html

Worldwide Internet Music Resources

This mind-boggling site contains links to every music site imaginable (and a few you wouldn't have imagined). Meticulously maintained by some very cool people at the Indiana University Music Library, Music Resources on the Internet contains links to everything from the Pearl Jam home page to the Fractal Music Project. Artist-specific, occasion-specific, local-music, and record-label sites: they're all here. Set aside a few hours and check it out. ⊕

http://www.music.indiana.edu/music_resources/

NEWS AND MAGAZINES

AJR NewsLink

NewsLink, from the *American Journalism Review*, has created excellent indexes to newspaper, magazine, and radio and TV station sites on the Web. You'll find both national and international offerings. Links to the indexes are found at the top of NewsLink's home page. ⊕ ⚲

http://www.newslink.org/menu.html

Computer Magazine Archive

$4.95 per month gives you searchable access to the top 87 computer and computer-related publications. $

http://cma.zdnet.com

Electronic Newsstand

The Electronic Newsstand is a free service that publishes summaries of recent magazine and journal articles with links to magazine web sites. You can subscribe directly from this page or just decide which magazine you might want to buy this month after reading descriptions about topics of interest. ⚲ ⊕

http://www.enews.com

Epicurious Travel

From the Condé Nast magazine group comes this interactive travel magazine. You'll find weather reports, maps, a bed-and-breakfast finder, and directories of hotels and locations. You'll also find articles and content from *Condé Nast Traveler magazine.* ⚲

http://travel.epicurious.com

Fairfax Research

This Australia-based firm delivers filtered news content, business information or research directly to you. Rates vary. $

http://www.theage.com.au

The Financial Times

This venerable international newspaper goes online with a daily summary of top news stories as well as articles on the Americas, Europe, and the Asia/Pacific region. A 30-minute-delayed list of world stock market indices provides a nice complement to FT's solid reporting. ☕ ✎

http://www.ft.com

The Gate

The online service of the big San Francisco newspapers, the *Chronicle* and the *Examiner*, and KRON-TV. The Gate features a daily online edition of each paper, with news, sports, columnists, reviews, classifieds, health, business, and weather. You'll also find video clips on some stories. The excellent search feature searches articles and photos from both papers for free, back to 1995. Visitors will find plenty of interesting information to keep them busy. ⚲

http://sfgate.com

HotWired

HotWired is *Wired* magazine's home on the Internet. Although it takes a few minutes to get your bearings, HotWired is full of thought-provoking articles and engaging interactive resources for anyone interested in computers or the computer industry. While HotWired is extremely image-intensive, it does feature a Stop button that turns that sunningly annoying animated graphic into a static image.

http://www.hotwired.com

The Irish Times on the Web

World Wide Web home of Dublin's *Irish Times*. The site presents news in eight sections: today's

paper, sports extra, teanga b bheo (the paper's Irish language section), appointments (employment), Dublin live, crosswords, business2000, and a searchable archive. ☕ ⚲

http://www.irish-times.ie

Jupiter Communications

Jupiter Communications offers a number of different research services and newsletters, including Internet Games, Interactive Content, and Digital Kids. Strategic planning and web libraries are also available; prices vary. $

http://www.jup.com/tracks/content/

Lexis-Nexis ReQUESTer

Search through newspaper archives dating back twenty years. The cost? A pricey $169 per month. That's a flat rate, however. Lexis-Nexis' InfoTailor, a daily news delivery service, is an additional $5 per month. Call 1-800-227-4908 to sign up. $

http://support.lexis-nexis.com/reQUESTer/

MoJo Wire

Mother Jones magazine brings us this interactive offering. It's still carrying the torch of "progressive" politics, updated daily. ⚲

http://www.motherjones.com

The NandO Times

A great source for U.S. and international news. Most articles come from either Reuters or the Associated Press, with access to A.P. articles requiring a free registration. Major sections of the *NandO Times* include global, nation, sports, politics, health/science, opinions, business, and entertainment. Each section features a news summary and links to longer stories. Published by the New Media Division of the News & Observer Publishing Co. in Raleigh, N.C. ⚲

http://www2.nando.net

NewsEdge NewsPage

This "awareness news service" provides articles from more than 2,000 information sources. The archives stretch back only five days, however. Premium service is $6.95 per month; basic service is free. $

http://www.newspage.com

The Onion

The online edition of the hysterical satirical newspaper.

http://www.theonion.com/index.html

Pathfinder

Pathfinder is home on the Net for the Time Warner publishing empire. Visitors to Pathfinder will find scores of articles and reviews from *LIFE, Sports Illustrated, Money, People, Time, Entertainment Weekly*, and *Vibe*, as well as special features like daily news reports, chat bulletin boards, and Ask Dr. Weil, an extensive collection of articles and advice from the health guru. The Pathfinder interface is attractive and easy to use, although browsing can be frustrating due to the time it takes to load its large image maps. Overall, this is an excellent site, well worth a visit. ⚲ 🍵

http://www.pathfinder.com/welcome/

Profound

This business information service covers news, reports, articles, and studies for a $19.95 monthly fee plus $6.95 per hour online. Profound uses Adobe's Acrobat technology, so you may view documents in their original format. $

http://www.profound.com/info/products/profound/index.html

TechWeb

CMP Publications' publishes computer and online magazines like *Communications Week, Information Week*, and *NetGuide*. TechWeb presents selected articles from each publication, but its shining star is the full-text searching capability. The search engine lets you select any single publication or all of them, specify a range of dates, and search for specific titles, authors, sections, and columns. After your initial search, you can widen your inquiry by adding all of the words in one or more articles to your request. ⚲

http://www.techweb.com

UMI

UMI supplies eight different newspapers, serials in microform, and dissertation archives, including ProQuest Direct, IntellX, and DataTimes.

Many different options and price plans are available for each. $

http://www.umi.com/hp/WhatWeDo.html

Wall Street Journal Interactive Edition

Signing up for the Wall Street Journal online gives you access to three publications: the *Wall Street Journal, Barron's*, and *SmartMoney Interactive*, each with a two-week searchable archive. During the two-week free trial, you also have access to the Dow Jones Publications library, which later becomes an additional premium service. Rates are about $50 per year, though discounts are available if you subscribe to one of the print publications. The secure site is well organized and allows for easy cancellation or modification. $

http://www.wsj.com

OCEANOGRAPHY

National Oceanographic Data Center (NODC)

The NODC's global holdings of physical, chemical, and biological oceanographic data currently total over 60 gigabytes, making it the world's largest publicly available ocean data archive. This server provides access to those holdings, as well as other products and services.

http://www.nodc.noaa.gov

NOAA Fisheries

From the U.S. National Oceanic and Atmospheric Administration Service comes a great server chock full of marine (ocean, not military) data. Coverage includes domestic and international marine fisheries programs, reports, graphics, sea temperature maps, audio clips of whale songs, assorted marine videos, and the obligatory links to related online information. This is a well-designed server, with an active What's New page and regular updates. ⚲

http://www.nmfs.gov

Ocean Information Center (OCEANIC)

The Ocean Information Center Bulletin Board is provided by the University of Delaware. The site features technical and organizational material about various oceanographic experiments, field trials, and meetings.

http://diu.cms.udel.edu

Ocean Planet

A fascinating, if time-consuming, tour. Presented by the Smithsonian Institution, Ocean Planet uses images, text, and walk-through environments to educate people about the environmental issues affecting the world's oceans. While intriguing and well presented, the viewer has to navigate through many links, which can be tedious. ✒

http://seawifs.gsfc.nasa.gov/ocean_planet.html

Woods Hole Oceanographic Institution

No pictures of humpbacks breaching or sea otters swimming here. However, for the more scientifically minded, especially those interested in oceanography, this site provides extremely detailed information on myriad seminars, research projects, and educational programs at WHOI. Links to other oceanographic resources are included as well. The weekly calendar section lists all upcoming activities, many of which are geared toward the general public.

http://www.whoi.edu/index.html

PALEONTOLOGY

The Age of Dinosaurs Lives On

The Carnegie Museum of Natural History presents this wonderful online tour of the Mesozoic era. Elegantly laid out and nicely cross-referenced.

http://www.clpgh.org/cmnh/doe/dino/index.htm

The Field Museum of Natural History

A tour through the prehistoric world of dinosaurs. With text and images, the Field Museum of Natural History offers a taste of its "Life Over Time" exhibit. Find out where dinosaurs lived, what they ate, and how they moved. You'll also find a teacher's guide with sample activities, and a few interesting animations.

http://www.fmnh.org/exhibits/web_exhibits.htm

Honolulu Community College Dinosaur Exhibit

A fun, well-designed tour of the permanent dinosaur exhibit at Honolulu Community College, complete with photographs, illustrations, movies, and even (rather slow-loading) audio narration. The exhibits themselves are actually replicas from the originals at the American Museum of Natural History in New York City.

http://www.hcc.hawaii.edu/dinos/dinos.1.html

Paleontology Without Walls

The University of California Museum of Paleontology server is an interactive natural history museum available over the Internet. This museum without walls is well organized and makes interesting use of large graphics. You can learn about phylogeny, the "Tree of Life," or examine photographs of great white sharks off the California coast, which proves that paleontologists study living things as well as fossils.

http://www.ucmp.berkeley.edu/exhibit/exhibits.html

Paper Dinosaurs

A collection by the Linda Hall Library in Kansas City, Missouri that presents an extensive visual history of dinosaur discovery with indepth narrative. Composed mainly of drawings and other original publications rather than photographs. You'll find many of the classic papers of chronicling the discovery of the dinosaurs, including the original publications of Gideon Mantell and Othniel Marsh.

http://www.lhl.lib.mo.us/pubserv/hos/dino/welcome.htm

PERL

The Perl Journal

The web site for, you guessed it, The Perl Journal. You'll find a wealth of information here, including the full contents of the magazine, contests, FAQs, job search information, and more. ⚲

http://www.itknowledge.com/tpj/

Perl Mongers

This site describes itself as "a coordinating and communication center to connect people, information, ideas and resources" related to making Perl more useful. Sections include about the institute, what's can new, current events, what you can do, benefits of joining TPI, sign me up!, the oasis, what is Perl?, what is Perl 5?, the Perl Journal, Perl mailing lists, acquiring perl software, CPAN, Perl support, the Perl wish list, and the oft-hilarious Perl humor, Perl poetry, and match your wits. ⊕

http://www.perl.org

www.perl.com

O'Reilly's own Perl page, edited by Tom Christiansen. The site contains just about everything you need to know about the Perl language, including news, software, journals, institutes, and a who's who.

http://www.perl.com

PERSONAL COMPUTING

4Shareware

This comprehensive shareware site includes links to major shareware archives, quick listings of valuable shareware for immediate download, and guides to help you learn about shareware in general. ✎ ⊕

http://www.4shareware.com

c | net, The Computer Network

Find useful and up-to-date information about the Net and personal computing, such as tips for getting the most out of your browser, articles on selling online, email protection, and technical news. You'll find features, reviews, and personalities as sections of the site. c | net's subsites include news.com, computers.com, builder.com, gamecenter.com, download.com, shareware.com, browsers.com, search.com, and snap! online. ✎ ✐

http://www.cnet.com

Cryptography: The Study of Encryption

Part of the WWW Virtual Library, this site contains a remarkable collection of links to informa-

tion on the practical and philosophical aspects of encryption.

http://world.std.com/~franl/crypto/

DaveCentral Shareware Archive

This clearly organized site provides software, shareware, freeware, demos, and betas for the Windows and Linux platforms. The Recent Additions/Updates columns on the home page are a handy and interesting resource. ✎

http://www.davecentral.com

Games Domain

The Games Domain features links to thousands of gaming resources, including FAQs, walk-throughs, information lists, charts, FTP sites, a huge games home-page catalog, and much more. Visitors will find everything from Doom to Darts, MUDs to Mortal Kombat, PBMs to PiD, EA to Epic. There are also links to more than 5,000 games and demos for immediate downloading, and a magazine called *GD Review* that features news, previews, and reviews for the gaming community. ✎

http://www.gamesdomain.com

Shareware.com

Have you ever wanted to find a shareware program, but weren't quite sure of its name? This database will help you search the major Internet shareware archives for program descriptions that match the words you supply. If the search is successful, you get a list of links to all known mirror sites that archive that program. At the time of this writing, users could search 11 different archives, containing software for Unix, Macintosh, Windows, DOS, OS/2, Amiga, and other platforms. ✎ ✐

http://www.shareware.com

ZDNet Software Library

The site is a bit hectic, but you'll find a wealth of resources here, including links to software and articles about downloading and the Internet. Windows 95/98/NT only, however. ✎

http://www.zdnet.com/swlib/

PERSONAL FINANCE

Bank-CD Rate Scanner

Want to be sure to get the best rate on your certificate of deposit? This site scans more than 3,000 banks daily and presents the results in an easy-to-read format.

http://bankcd.com

BigCharts

This free site provides a valuable tool for investors: charts of stock prices. The site provides interactive charts, quotes, reports and indicators on more than 50,000 stocks, mutual funds and market indexes. You can even customize the charts to your liking. ⚲

http://www.bigcharts.com

CommerceNet

CommerceNet bills itself as "the premier industry consortium for companies using, promoting, and building electronic commerce solutions on the Internet." The not-for-profit group's information network is designed to promote electronic commerce. Nearly 500 companies now participate, but anyone interested in online commerce can examine the news sections or buy logo clothing (just in case the "geek" tattoo on your forehead didn't take). ✦

http://www.commerce.net

Consumer Information Center

Don't let the innocuous name fool you: This is one of the best sites on the Internet for basic personal finance information. The CIC is a U.S. Government organization that distributes pamphlets on consumer issues. The publications are arranged by subject; visitors to the money section of the site will find information on credit cards, investment fraud, and financial planning. Accessing the online publications is free, despite the costs listed below the links. Other useful sections within the CIC site include housing, employment, cars, and small business.

http://www.gsa.gov/staff/pa/cic/

Doh! Stock Picks

Despite it's association with Homer Simpson, this is an award-winning financial site designed to help make investing in stocks less confusing. Aside from stock picks, there is advice from expert investors, company information, and links to other financial pages. The format is clear and straightforward.

http://www.doh.com

FinanCenter's Home Department

If you're looking for a new home, FinanCenter's Home Department is a great place to start. Use the pull-down menus to calculate everything from how much you can borrow to how much the payments will be. The SmartDeals and SmartFacts sections will help you find the loan you need and understand the terms you'll read. The Java Relocalc applet even lets you compare cost of living and other important factors between the city you live in versus the city you're moving to. It takes a little while to load, but it's well worth it.

http://www.financenter.com/homes.html

GetSmart

GetSmart provides free information about all types of borrowing. Use this site to learn about options regarding home loans, debt consolidation, credit cards, student loans, and auto financing.

http://www.getsmart.com

Morningstar

A great personal finance site for tracking stocks and getting investment advice. ✦ ☕

http://www.morningstar.net

The Motley Fool: Finance and Folly

The folks at the Motley Fool bring you personal investment advice with a touch of whimsy. You'll find buying guides, tax FAQs, guides to investing, and more. ✦ ⚲

http://www.fool.com

PETS

Cat Fanciers' Home Page

Maintained with care by two ailurophiles, Marie Lamb and Orca Starbuck, this site is packed with feline lore. There are many FAQs on exotic breeds—from Ragdolls (bred from a female Persian and male Birman) to Chartreux (known as the "blue cats of France"). You'll find more practical information here, too, on such subjects as feline leukemia virus and the overpopulation crisis. There are links to veterinary resources as well as to cat home pages; this is a site any cat lover should check out.

http://www.fanciers.com

Dogs

Your Mining Company Guide to dogs and pets brings a comprehensive guide to dog-related sites on the Web. You will find everything from veterinary and adoption databases to pictures of lost and found pets and those available to be adopted.

http://dogs.about.com

The Electronic Zoo

This site for animal lovers (compiled and maintained by veterinarian/computer nut Ken Boschert) is truly without peer. From amphibians to ruminants, catfish farming to Ferret Central, the Electronic Zoo has easy-to-navigate, comprehensive collections of Internet animal resources, grouped both by subject (animals, veterinary) and resource type (mailing lists, gopher and web sites). Sponsored by NetVet, the Zoo is a well-maintained site with a search facility, what's new list, and continual updates.

http://netvet.wustl.edu/e-zoo.htm

FINS: Fish Information Service

An archive of information about aquariums, including general information about fishkeeping, discussion archives, images, and aquarium plans. You'll also find a glossary of terms used among aquarists, software, images, and MPEG and QuickTime movies. ✑

http://www.actwin.com/fish/index.cgi

NetVet World Wide Web Server

NetVet Veterinary Resources is a comprehensive collection of online veterinary information. Among its offerings are the Missouri Association for Agriculture, Biomedical Research Education, the Animal Welfare Information Center, and American Academy of Veterinary Informatics. There are also general pointers to major Internet resources in veterinary medicine, agriculture, biology, environment and ecology, and medicine, as well as animal-related files, databases, FTP archive sites, and electronic publications. ✑

http://netvet.wustl.edu/vet.htm

Sherlock Bones

Did your new puppy escape from the yard? Don't despair. John Keane, a self-proclaimed "leading authority in the field of pet retrieval," has created this site as an introduction to his service.

http://www.sherlockbones.com

TravelDog

Can't hit the road without Fido in tow? Check out TravelDog for the latest in pet-friendly accommodations, products, tips, and even daycare.

http://www.traveldog.com

PHILOSOPHY

American Philosophical Association

The APA is "the main professional organization for philosophers in the United States." Its web site serves to promote the APA's mission to promote the exchange of ideas among philosophers, encourage creative and scholarly activity, to facilitate the professional work and teaching of philosophers, and to represent philosophy as a discipline. It has serious information on serious subjects and contains addresses, information on upcoming events, grants, fellowships and academic positions, bibliographies, and calls for papers.

http://www.udel.edu/apa

Chinese Philosophy Page

Steven A. Brown's page covers a wide range of philosophies, including Confucianism, Daoism, Legalism, Mohism, Ming Jia, and Yin Yang. You'll also find a link to mailing lists related to Chinese philosophy.

http://www-personal.monash.edu.au/~sab/index.html

Guide to Philosophy on the Internet

Peter Suber, of Earlham College, created this remarkably comprehensive site documenting the philosophy resources on the Internet. The table of contents links to sections on guides, philosophers, topics, associations, journals, teaching/ learning, etexts, bibliographies, mailing lists, newsgroups, projects, preprints, jobs, dictionaries, quotations, and miscellany. Or, you can browse through the catalog of links or search by keyword. 🔍 🌐

http://www.earlham.edu/~peters/philinks.htm

Journal of Buddhist Ethics

An online publication dedicated to scholarly papers and discussion of ethical considerations in Buddhism, with a focus on how Buddhism approaches modern ethical issues. The first issue was released in the Fall of 1994, and if it maintains its current level of clarity this journal will be worth the time for interested philosophers and students of Buddhism. The site also accepts submissions, links to a list of scholarly resources, and includes a list of related net resources.

http://jbe.la.psu.edu

Philosophy

Links to canonical philosophic texts and scholarly philosophic organizations on the Internet. Presented by the English Server, a cooperative publishing humanities texts online since 1990.

http://eserver.org/philosophy/

PHOTOGRAPHY

California Museum of Photography

This museum of photography, sponsored by the University of California at Riverside, presents a number of fascinating exhibits in its "Webworks" section. You'll find interesting photo essays with titles such as "Glass Houses," "Scanner as Camera," and "Imaginary Places."

http://www.cmp.ucr.edu

Covington's Homeless: A Documentary

Proof that the Web can be used for creative expression, John Decker's documentary on drifters in Covington, Kentucky is an original and moving work, complete unto itself and wholly satisfying. There are four groupings: Backpack Bill, Patty and Art, Living in the Streets, and DJ's New Apartment. You can experience the photographs one at a time; there's just enough narrative to tie them together. In one photograph, homeless men are sitting in a line underneath a bridge overpass, each with a bottle in hand and wearing a baseball cap—as if they were sitting in a dugout, watching a ballgame. You forget about being on the Net and find yourself drifting away, staring into these faces. Be sure to use the Next button to move through the dozen or so photos in each grouping.

http://www.intac.com/~jdeck/cov/index.html

Digital Camera Resource Page

An excellent resource for those interested in digital photography. The news and reviews are extremely up to date, and the sale/special offer announcements are invaluable. The site is conscientiously maintained by Jeff Keller and Delane Barrus, two computer designers.

http://www.dcresource.com

The Digital Photography Exhibit

Bradley University and the Peoria Art Guild bring the Web this annual, international-juried exhibit of images created by artists working with cameras and computers. The 1998 exhibit is entitled "Land Escapes."

http://www.bradley.edu/exhibit/index.html

photo.net

If you're interested in photography, dogs, or travel writing, take a look at Philip Greenspun's marvelous site. You'll find discussion forums, photo exhibits, extensive equipment reviews, and technique and how-to hints. You'll also find Greenspun's self-published web memoir, *Trav-*

els with Samantha, about his cross-country trip following the death of his beloved Samoyed, George. Don't read chapter 1 if stories about sick dogs make you cry.

http://photo.net/philg/photo/

PHYSICS

The American Physical Society

The home page of the editorial offices of the society. Contains sections on members of the organization, meetings, topical groups, careers and employment, contacts and governance, prizes, awards, and fellowships, research journals, the APS E-print Server, news about physics and the APS, education and outreach, related scientific societies, Internet resources related to physics, and information about meetings and conferences. ✎

http://www.aps.org

CERN Experiments

The European Laboratory for Particle Physics lets you look into a long list of approved experiments and research projects. The lab also provides links to research projects and experiments under study.

http://www1.cern.ch/CERN/Experiments.html

The Internet Pilot to Physics

A gigantic collection of links to the physics resources of the Internet. The site is maintained by Mikko Karttunen of the McGill University Department of Physics, and Gunther Nowotny of the Technical University of Vienna. Visitors will find links to pre-print archives, labs, physics departments, and job listings. ⊕ ✎

http://www.physicsweb.org/TIPTOP/

Los Alamos Physics Information Service

This server, maintained by the Los Alamos National Laboratory, contains links to archives for everything from high-energy physics to quantum cosmology to superconductivity.

http://xxx.lanl.gov

Physics News Update Newsletter

News and information related to physics, from Phillip F. Schewe of the Physics Publication Information Department of the American Institute of Physics. The site also contains archives and a search feature. ✎

http://www.hep.net/documents/newsletters/pnu/pnu.html

POLITICS

Abortion Rights Activist Home Page

A news and information resource devoted to the struggle to preserve abortion rights in the United States. Material is available in six categories: information about abortion, clinic violence, tools for activists, reference library, and feedback. The Abortion Rights Activist home page is maintained by Adam Guasch-Melendez. ✎

http://www.cais.com/agm/main/index.html

Amnesty International Online

An excellent archive and research center for anyone interested in exploring or promoting the topic of human rights. You'll find news about Amnesty International and its current campaigns, an archive of information about previous campaigns, a library of the organization's reports on human rights conditions worldwide, downloadable software, and an extensive catalog of links to resources on politics on the World Wide Web. ✎ ⊕

http://www.amnesty.org

National Organization for Women

Find out what topics are on the forefront of NOW's agenda and learn how to become involved in the largest U.S. feminist organization. This site lists information about upcoming rallies, abortion rights, global feminism, and violence against women. Some of the most touching points are the personal stories, including the accounts of a rape survivor and a welfare mother. Also included are updates on legislation, information on reaching local chapters and joining NOW, and the latest issue of the *National NOW Times*. Links to resources for feminists are included. ✎

http://www.now.org

Peace and Conflict

A solid collection of links relating to the study of peace and conflict. While it's somewhat over-animated, you'll find a useful calendar of events and a directory of programs, course lists, and syllabi related to the field.

http://csf.colorado.edu/peace/

The Right Side of the Web

Right-wing attitude and Internet savvy. Though infrequently updated, the Right Side of the Web presents both original material and links to other sources of information on the Net (under the pop-up list index). Local resources include comics, cartoons, audio clips, jokes, and more. There is a list of related books with ordering info, and a whole section devoted to Whitewater called the W-Files, with links. Also includes live chats, debates, and polls along with current topics. ☕

http://www.rtside.com

PSYCHOLOGY

American Psychological Society (APS)

Information about the APS—membership, job postings, conferences, and research.

http://www.psychologicalscience.org

Cognitive and Psychological Sciences on the Internet

A library of links to psych resources on the Net, maintained by Ruediger Oehlmann of the University of Essex, England. The collection presents over 100 links in the areas of academic programs, conferences, journals, discussion groups, publishers, and software. ⊕

http://matia.stanford.edu/cogsci/

FreudNet

Visitors will find news, network resources, a whole page of links related to Sigmund Freud, and information on the American Psychoanalytic Association regarding meetings and fellowships. Published by the Abraham A. Brill Library of the New York Psychoanalytic Institute.

http://plaza.interport.net/nypsan/index.html

Guide for Writing Research Papers

Help is close by for anyone who needs to properly format a psychology paper. Revised and maintained by Charles Darling, Professor of English at Capital Community-Technical College (Hartford, CT), this is a good resource for students who need to submit work that prescribes to the American Psychological Association.

http://webster.commnet.edu/apa/apa_index.htm

MentalHealth Net

A well-rounded information service sponsored by CMHC Systems. This award-winning site has a polished look and covers myriad topics, including anxiety, bipolar, depression, eating disorders, and personality disorders. The main page displays weekly news updates, and the index links to sections on disorders and treatments, professional information, a reading room, and managed care and administration. Choose from books, services, articles, discussion forums, and more.

http://www.mentalhelp.net

Psycoloquy

An online academic journal about psychology published by the American Psychological Association.

http://www.princeton.edu/~harnad/psyc.html

RECREATION

GolfWeb

If golf is your bag, this is the place for you. CBS Sportsline sponsors this very comprehensive and well-crafted site with a number of extensive sections, including a library, listings of places to stay, instruction, equipment, ProShop, and Tour Action sections. Within these are a surprising number of articles and reviews (from antiquities to equipment), courses, schools, tournaments, and much more.

http://www.golfweb.com

GORP: Great Outdoor Recreation Pages

A well-designed and growing site made up of original documents and links to all manner of information for the outdoor enthusiast. Included are some descriptions of National Parks within the United States, all sorts of outdoor activities (mountain biking, boating, hiking, fishing, skiing) and information on how to find out more about them on the Internet. There is a general listing for other Internet locations, and sections for gear, food, health, and more.

http://www.gorp.com

Grand Canyon National Park

A superb experience for anyone interested in this most popular of National Parks. We especially like this site because it is nothing like some of the glossy and numbingly official tourist guides that appear on the Net. This site is authored by a private individual who knows and loves the park and who has organized that knowledge and passion into an archive that is useful and a pleasure to navigate. If you go here, you'll get a quick history (check out the visitation figures), detailed maps, descriptions of trails, a listing of park services, a list of other sites worth visiting in the Grand Canyon area, and a short reminder of things to consider to make your trip there a green one.

http://www.grand-canyon.az.us/grand.htm

iSKI.com

If you're planning your next snow excursion, this is the place to start. You'll find information on resorts, news, shopping, weather, equipment, and the Olympics. There's also a chat feature and message boards, contests, and a retailer directory.

http://www.iski.com

The Running Page

The Running Page lists running clubs, shows you where to run in 130 U.S. cities, and lists local races and marathons. The site also links to recent race results, cross country analysis, the rec.running FAQ, and others. The Running Page is maintained by Dennis G. Rears, a computer engineer at the U.S. Army Armaments Research and Development Center in New Jersey.

http://metalab.unc.edu/drears/running/running.html

The Sailing Page

A big page of pointers to Net sailing resources, including links to the Tall Ships FAQ, the International Lightning Page, and the Guide to Historic Wrecks of the United Kingdom. The Sailing Page is captained by Mark Rosenstein, who pilots a desk at Bellcore when he's not out on the open waters.

http://www.apparent-wind.com/sailing-page.html

REFERENCE

Acronym Dictionary

A searchable index of 6,000 acronyms.

http://www.ucc.ie/acronyms/

American Library Association (ALA)

A large directory of information from the American Library Association. Much of the material here deals with the organization of the ALA, its bylines, and its publications. A collection of documents on intellectual freedom and regular editions of the *ALA Washington Office Newsline* is also available.

http://www.ala.org

AT&T 800 Directory

Let your mouse do the walking. You can find 800-numbers online using this AT&T-produced directory. Browse by category (like the yellow pages) or by name (white pages). This directory goes beyond printed versions with a string search that lets you find a listing even if you know only part of the company's name; check out the advanced search for even more options.

http://tollfree.att.net/tf.html

Bartlett's Familiar Quotations

Tap into the wisdom of great thinkers through Bartlett's Familiar Quotations. This site includes a search engine for words and authors and a chronological list of primary authors. Don't expect to find any of your 20th century favorites here—the collection ends with the 19th century.

http://www.columbia.edu/acis/bartleby/bartlett

CIA World Factbook

The CIA maintains a detailed, encyclopedic dossier on every country, recognized island group, and certain regions. Each entry contains information about population, economic condition, trade, conflicts, and politics. There's lots of stuff you won't find here—such as the number of nuclear warheads aimed at the Pentagon. But there is information important to travelers, like weather, natural hazards, and severe weather seasons. There is also a good weights and measures table, a list of United Nations bodies, and a list of international organizations and groups.

http://www.odci.gov/cia/publications/factbook/index.html

Dead People Server

Need to know whether some famous person is alive or recently kicked off? Check out this server, dedicated to "a list of interesting celebrities who are, or might plausibly be dead." Search for a specific celebrity, or browse by first letter of last name. ⚲

http://www.dpsinfo.com

Online English Grammar

Need to learn more about conjunctions, and can't remember the School House Rock song? Check out Anthony Hughes handy online reference. The table of contents provides a useful subject index, but the site unfortunately lacks a search feature.

http://www.edunet.com/english/grammar/index.html

Roget's Thesaurus

Enter a word, find the synonyms. A hooligan is both an evil doer and a blusterer.

http://www.thesaurus.com

Telephone Area Codes

Where is telephone area code 203? What's the area code for Nashville, Tennessee? If you ever have questions like these, the Long Distance Area Decoder belongs on your hotlist. Using an online form, you enter the location or area code you're interested in—the decoder responds by filling in the blanks. The Long Distance Area Decoder is provided as a promotion by AmeriCom, Inc. ⚲

http://decoder.AmeriCom.com

Virtual Reference Desk

A great collection of links to the reference sources of the Internet, compiled by Carl E. Snow of the Purdue University Library. Among the plums available here are the AT&T 800 number directory, a list of Internet country codes, and the College Slang dictionary. 🌐 ⚲

http://thorplus.lib.purdue.edu/reference/

Webster English Dictionary

A hypertext interface to the Webster English dictionary. All roots and words are linked to their definitions. "Hooligan," perhaps from Patrick Hooligan, an Irish hoodlum in Southwark, London, is a noun meaning ruffian or hoodlum.

http://www.m-w.com/dictionary/

RELIGION AND BELIEF

About Al-Islam and Muslims

An informational site regarding the practices of Islam.

http://www.unn.acc.uk/societies/islamic/about/

Book of Mormon

The Book of Mormon. Just when you thought Jesus had done it all, here he comes with another testament. ⚲

http://www.new-jerusalem.com/scripture/bom/contents.htm

Catholic Resources on the Net

A comprehensive collection of pointers maintained by John Ockerbloom of Carnegie-Mellon University.

http://www.cs.cmu.edu/Web/People/spok/catholic.html

I Ching

The I Ching (*Book of Changes*) is an ancient Chinese system of divination. An oracle is cast by flipping coins or, more traditionally, by manipulating yarrow stalks. With this online version, there's no need to throw sticks or open the book. You'll also find links to readings of Tarot cards and Runes and biorhythms.

http://www.facade.com/Occult/iching/

Maven

An excellent index of links related to Judaism and Israel in catalog format. This remarkably comprehensive site claims to link to more than 5,600 well-described resources and presents a menu of related subjects on the left side of the screen after you select from the opening menu. Topics range from the arts to companies and employment to communities and synagogues to entertainment, computers and Internet and more. ✦

http://www.maven.co.il

Not Just Bibles: A Guide to Christian Resources on the Internet

A comprehensive hypertext file of mailing lists, archive sites, gopher and web servers, bulletin boards, newsgroups, and other publications regarding Christianity, both historic and current.

http://www.iclnet.org/pub/resources/christian-resources.html

Sikhism

"Any human being who faithfully believes in: (i) One Immortal Being, (ii) Ten Gurus, from Guru Nanak Dev to Guru Gobind Singh, (iii) the Guru Granth Sahib, (iv) the utterances and teachings of the ten Gurus and, (v) the baptism bequeathed by the tenth Guru, and who does not owe allegiance to any other religion is a Sikh."—Sikh Code of Conduct

A large and well-designed collection of resources devoted to Sikhism, maintained by Sandeep Singh Brar.

http://www.sikhs.org/topics.htm

SPIRIT-WWW

A truly eclectic compilation of spiritual resources on the Net, from ancient Vedic wisdom to the latest theories on free energy and interdimensional travel. This site is maintained by Rene K. Muller, a noted contributor in this field, and it's rumored that simply focusing on the site's brilliant golden mastheads can raise you to a higher state of being. ✦ ✎

http://www.spiritweb.org

Virtual Christianity: Bibles

The Bible is a versatile text, available in many different languages and translations. This site provides links to multiple translations and versions of this popular text, including some that are searchable. The site purports to be "maintained in conjunction with Truth and Reason," so how can you go wrong?

http://www.internetdynamics.com/pub/vc/bibles.html

Zen Page

"When the screen is rolled up the great sky opens,/ Yet the sky is not attuned to Zen. / It is best to forget the great sky/And to retire from every wind."—from *The Gateless Gate*.

The focus of Ben Walters' Zen@Sunsite is on the Gateless Gate, a famous collection of Zen koans. In addition to browsing the Gateless Gate via its index page, visitors can choose to generate a random koan. Other resources available at this site include the alt.zen FAQ and a collection of links to other Zen sites on the Net.

http://metalab.unc.edu/zen/

SEARCH TOOLS

About.com

People with expertise in various areas put together subject guides and keep them up to date. You'll find more than 500 guides here, including computing, the arts, literature, travel—almost anything you might want to know.

http://www.about.com

ALL-IN-ONE Search Page

A page configured to run remote searches on hundreds of Internet resource databases. From the page, you can search WWW indexes, software repositories, email addresses, and dictionaries.

http://www.allonesearch.com

Ask Jeeves

This site, unlike other search engines, allows users to enter queries in plain English. The site then returns a list of "matched questions," in the form of drop-down menus. The knowledge base is built by humans—the site's staff actually does the research, instead of web robots—so answers are more likely to be on target. If the site can't propose a suitable answer for your question, a meta-search of major search engines is provided as a backup.

http://www.askjeeves.com

Due Diligence Data of Boston

A private investigator has compiled a database of over 50,000 names from public sources. If you want to run a background check to find out whether an individual has links to organized crime, white collar crime, corruption, or fraud, you can conduct a confidential inquiry here. A $25 fee is charged for successful searches. ⚲ $

http://world.std.com/~mmoore

Essential Links

A concise page of top-level directories on a wide variety of topics. ⚲ ⊕

http://www.el.com

Four11

If you have a hunch someone you know is rolling down the Infobahn, but you can't locate that person, you might try Four11 directory services. Now under the Yahoo! umbrella, Four11 has a fast, custom database engine for searching email or telephone listings, gleaned from voluntary registrations, Usenet, and ISPs. New listings are incorporated daily. You can search the directory by any combination of first name, last name, location, old email address, affiliation, and more.

http://people.yahoo.com

The Internet Sleuth

Want to search more than one search engine at a time? If you know your subject, the Internet Sleuth can help you find the information you need. The Sleuth links visitors to searchable net resources in dozens of subject areas, from agriculture to veterinary science. The home page lets you search up to six databases at once, including AltaVista, Excite, Lycos, Infoseek, and more.

http://www.thebighub.com

PriceScan

Prices for computers and computer equipment fluctuate wildly. PriceScan searches through a wide database of stores to find the lowest price for the information you specify and even provides dynamic charts of prices over the past year. ⚲

http://www.pricescan.com

The WWW Virtual Library

An amazing example of the collaborative power of the Net, the WWW Virtual Library consists of more than 50 independently maintained subject indexes to net resources. Although the WWW Virtual Library home page resides on the CERN server in Switzerland, most of the individual indexes are available from the home servers of their maintainers: the Anthropology index comes from USC, Cognitive Science from Brown University, Engineering from NASA. This is a terrific resource that will only get better as it grows with the Internet.

http://www.w3.org/hypertext/DataSources/bySubject/ Overview.html

Yahoo!

The Yahoo Guide is the Net's largest—and clearly the most excited!— subject index of WWW resources. Site creators David Filo and Jerry Yang created an index structure that is both easy and fun to browse and is now the most widely copied on the Net. Aside from its subject listings, Yahoo features a search function and hotlists of what's cool and what's popular. Seeming to grow every day, Yahoo! also offers freemail accounts, stock updates, news coverage, personalization options, a credit card, loan center, and more. ⚲ ⊕

http://www.yahoo.com

SPORTS

CBS SportsLine's Member Club House

CBS promises that membership entitles you to everything a sports fan could want, and while I doubt that my forking over $4.95 per month or even $39.95 per year will result in a lot of personal time with Michael Jordan, it does include real-time scores, late breaking news, exclusive interviews, live radio archives, electronic lines, trivia, contests, and more. $

http://cbs.sportsline.com/u/clubhouse/

ESPN SportsZone

One of the premier sources of sports news, this site, connected to the popular all-sports cable channel, with up to the minute updates and content on pretty much every sport, sporting event, and athlete, offers professional-style quality and articles freely. ESPN Insider accounts (offered at $39.95/year or $4.95/month) offer added content, such as weekly columns and special articles, from this site's expert staff of writers. $

http://espnet.go.com

Fantasy Golf

Everything you could ever possibly want to know about fantasy golf, or golf in general. The site includes magazines, links, features, and more. ⚲

http://www.fansportsnetwork.com/gsg.htm

FIFA On-Line (Federation Internationale de Football Association)

News and information about soccer and the FIFA World Cup. You'll also find publications, press releases, and information about youth events.

http://www.fifa.com/index.html

NandO Sports Server

Daily sports news from the New Media Division of the News & Observer Publishing Company. You'll find vast stores of information on college and professional baseball, basketball, football, and hockey, not to mention golf, boxing, the Olympics, and more. Stories and stats come from either Reuters or the Associated Press. This is a site worth returning to again and again. ⊕

http://www2.nando.net/SportServer/

RotoNews Fantasy Sports

If you play a rotisserie sport, take a look at this site for free fantasy sports league information. ⚲

http://www.rotonews.com

Statistics Services

What would sports be without statistics? Many sites provide statistics services—for a fee. $

http://www.customstat.com
http://www.expressstats.com
http://www.jasperstats.com
http://www.msstats.com
http://www.usastats.com
http://www.stadiumstats.com
http://www.msen.com/~tqstats

Tennis Server

The Tennis Server, from the Racquet Workshop and the Tenagra Corporation, serves up a healthy slice of tennis information to the Internet. There are current and back issues of *Tennis News*, equipment and player tips of the month from tennis pros, rules and codes, and links to other online tennis news and tips.

http://www.tennisserver.com/Tennis.html

Ultimate Fantasy Sports

Football, baseball, basketball, hockey. Approximately $200 to become the "lifetime owner" of a team. head-to-head games that include live drafts, weekly free agent pickups and real trades. $

http://www.ultimatefs.com

Women's Sports Page

The Women's Sports Page, put together by a grad student at the University of Texas, is a remarkably comprehensive collection of women's sports resources on the Net that ranges from archery to wrestling. Category pages include entries on athletes, general women's and girls' sports pages, issues in women's and girls' sports, organizations and associations, other index and listings pages, product and service businesses, and publishing and broadcast media.

http://fiat.gslis.utexas.edu/~lewisa/womsprt.html

TELEVISION AND RADIO

Audiences Unlimited, Inc.

Want to watch your favorite television show being taped? Take a look at the Audiences Unlimited site, which serves up free tickets.

http://www.audiencesunlimited.com

GIST TV

More television content than you can shake a stick at. You'll also find games, gossip, soap opera updates, television schedules and listings, contests and RealPlayer interviews. ☕ ✦ ✧

http://www.gist.com

National Public Radio Home Page

A fun site for NPR fans, including information on programming, member stations, and transcripts. RealPlayer users will benefit from online editions of *Morning Edition*, *Talk of the Nation*, and *All Things Considered*. The site also provides summaries, in text form, of the day's news. ☕

http://www.npr.org

TV-Free America

According to TV-Free America, a nonprofit group dedicated to encouraging Americans to reduce the amount of television they watch, a television is on for 6 hours and 47 minutes each day in an average U.S. home. This web site provides news and support in the fight against the machine.

http://www.tvfa.org

Ultimate TV

Ultimate TV has grown from merely a massive collection of links to TV-show sites on the Internet into a repository for all things television related. You'll find original reporting on television around the world, schedules and listings, soap opera updates and summaries, a "promo lounge" where you can view scenes from upcoming shows in RealPlayer format, a chat area, and, yes, a huge list of links to television web sites. There's even an employment section, TV Jobline, underneath the Biz link. ✧ ⊕

http://www.ultimatetv.com

Variety.com

The venerable entertainment magazine comes to the Web. You'll find indepth reporting on the television industry, along with movies, music, business, high-tech, and more, in a newspaper-style format. ✦ ✧

http://www.variety.com

THEATER

American Association of Community Theatre

The AACT is a national organization of community theaters, representing some 7,000 theater groups. The web site provides information about benefits, a yearly calendar of state, regional and national events, a listing of member companies by state, job listings, advocacy information, and links to web resources of interest to those in the theater. ✦ ✧

http://aact.org

The Costume Page

This site has over 2,000 unique links for the study or making of costumes, divided into areas such as supplies, schools/instruction, organizations and events, historical, ethnic/folk, and theatrical costume, as well as Halloween.

http://users.aol.com/nebula5/costume.html

On Broadway

Heading to New York and looking to catch a show? The bright marquee of On Broadway offers listings on current and upcoming Broadway shows, gleaned from magazines that are in the know: *New York*, *the New Yorker*, and *Theatre Week*. These online playbills are bare bones—just text listings of the show title, theater address, play dates, and ticket prices. Two nice features are the links to related online listings of the shows and links to soundtracks for musicals.

http://www.on-broadway.com

Opera America

Want to know when Rigoletto will play in Peoria? Opera America's web site can help. This Washington, D.C.–based organization hosts a web site full of searchable opera information, including sections on publications, arts education leadership, and professional development. ✐ ✎

http://www.operaam.org

Playbill Online

An informative, well-designed site that features remarkably comprehensive theater listings for New York, London, and regional touring companies, along with theater news, job listings, and trivia. You'll also find RealPlayer audio updates on theater news and a link to buy tickets online.

http://www.playbill.com

Storytelling, Drama, Creative Dramatics, Puppetry, & Reader's Theater for Children & Young Adults

A remarkable listing of links related to theater for kids. ⊕

http://falcon.jmu.edu/~ramseyil/drama.html

TRAVEL

American Odyssey

Wherever I go in the world, people I meet say they dream of doing the ultimate road trip—a drive through the United States of America. Whether you'd like to set off on your own and need a few good suggestions or just want to read about someone else's experiences, Brett Leveridge's four-month American Odyssey is an excellent place to begin. It's well written, entertaining, funny—Brett has a way of exposing himself to local cultures that reveals as much about them as it reveals about him.

http://www.brettnews.com/amod/

CDC Travel Information

The Center for Disease Control offers reams of official information on diseases from around the world. The traveler's health section lists countries and the diseases you may encounter there, prevention, symptoms, and remedies. Also listed are vaccine requirements, areas where outbreaks are occurring, as well as information on

established diseases like malaria, dengue and yellow fevers, AIDS, cholera, rabies, and others.

http://www.cdc.gov/travel/travel.html

Council on International Educational Exchange

From the people who offer those handy International Student Identity Cards comes this web site, where you can explore the possibilities of working, volunteering, and studying abroad. If you've got the time and an adventurous spirit, check this site out. ✎

http://www.ciee.org

Healthy Flying

Diana Fairechild knows the importance of flying healthfully. She flew 10 million miles as an international flight attendant before being grounded because of the damaging effects caused by the cabin environment. To help others avoid the stresses of international flying, she wrote *Jet Smart*, a welcome addition to any traveler's bookshelf. Diana has now put much of her collected wisdom online. You can learn about special meals, packing, jet lag, dehydration, sleeping, and adjusting to a new time zone. You can even ask Diana questions of your own. The site also serves as "the forefront of a networking and lobbying campaign to improve conditions for airline passengers."

http://www.flyana.com

International Travelers Clinic

After years of working with travelers and answering their health and medical questions, Gary P. Barnas, M.D., of the Medical College of Wisconsin, decided to create a web page. You will find some excellent information here, including what to pack in a medicine kit, advice on traveling while pregnant, a list of common diseases and how to avoid getting them, and advice on avoiding altitude sickness, motion sickness, and auto accidents.

http://www.intmed.mcw.edu/travel.html

Internet Guide to Hostelling

A very thorough and well-maintained WWW/FTP site that includes a hostels FAQ, worldwide hostel directory, the backpackers guide to budget guidebooks, and information about the creator of this site, Darren K. Overby, an avid hosteller and hostel owner in San Francisco.

http://www.hostels.com/hostels/

Lonely Planet Travel Guides

The Lonely Planet site offers text and tips for anyone thinking of venturing into the world. One of the best features of this site is the health area, an archive of preventions, remedies, and cures for exotic and common maladies that lurk in the shadows. ✎ ⊕

http://www.lonelyplanet.com.au

Rec.Travel Library

From the newsgroup rec.travel comes this remarkable archive of travel information and personal travelogues. You'll find information about travel modalities, destinations, and the like, along with pointers to other travel information resources. ⊕

http://www.Travel-Library.com

Shoestring Travel E-Zine

Composed of readers' email submissions and good posts to various rec.travel newsgroups, Shoestring Travel is dedicated to helping budget travelers find the best cheap food, lodging, and transportation tips on the Net. At the time of this review, there were tips from netizens who had recently visited Hawaii, Mexico, and a range of other intriguing destinations. There were also listings of cheap hotels in New York, San Francisco, and Boston, plus links to railroad timetable info, currency exchange rates, home exchange clubs, and other resources of interest to those traveling on the cheap. ⊕

http://www.stratpub.com

Travel Warnings and Consular Information Sheets

The latest U.S. State Department travel advisories for just about any country you're interested in visiting. The advisories provide background information about current U.S. relations with a particular country. There is also information about medical facilities, crime, currency regulations, drug penalties, and embassy locations. This resource is a good one to check first—a

recent fact sheet had details about the Anthrax vaccine.

http://travel.state.gov/travel_warnings.html

USA CityLink

Links to state and city pages across the United States. Some are fairly dull, others contain funky local information worthy of intensive surfing.

http://usacitylink.com

A Visit to Nepal

A superb visit to Nepal is in store for anyone who makes the trip to this site. Scott A. Yost's six-week trekking journey is meticulously recorded in text, annotated photos, and interactive maps. At the bottom of the main page are links to a variety of other sites that contain information on Nepal.

http://www.vic.com/nepal/

The WWW Speedtrap Registry

Andrew Warner maintains a list of speed traps by state, along with pages discussing police use of radar, a Lidar FAQ, and a driver's chart describing whether detectors and scanners are legal in a particular state. You'll also find links to Reasonable Drivers Unanimous and the National Motorists Association.

http://www.speedtrap.com

U.S. GOVERNMENT

The Capitol Steps

If you're in the mood for political satire, take a look at this site, created by a troupe of current and former Congressional staffers. New content appears each week.

http://www.capsteps.com

Congressional Email Directory

A remarkably well-organized directory of email addresses for U.S. Senators and Congressional Representatives, compiled by Jeffrey Hoffman. The directory is organized alphabetically by state; addresses are interactive, so you can send a message directly from your browser. Many links are to the representative's own home page.

http://www.webslingerz.com/jhoffman/congress-email.html

Environmental Protection Agency

The official information server of the EPA, containing listings of projects and programs, press releases, speeches, and newsletters, environmental data and software, and more. You may also search for environmental information by Zip code, or check out the concerned citizens section to learn more about how to think globally and act locally. ✎

http://www.epa.gov

Federal Bureau of Investigation

Everything that could possibly be investigated about the Federal Bureau of Investigation. Well, almost. You'll find an intriguing collection of information from the FBI, including a current top-ten most wanted list and material on current cases, including the Centennial Park bombing, TWA flight 800, and the robbery of the Isabella Stewart Gardner Museum. There's also a convenient link to FBI field offices by city. ✎

http://www.fbi.gov

Federal Web Locator

A hotlist of links to U.S. Government WWW resources, compiled by the Villanova Center for Information Law and Policy. While the search engine was somewhat buggy (performing the same search on Infoseek returned better results), this is a good place to start if you're not sure which agency you're looking for. ✎

http://www.vcilp.org/fed-agency/fedwebloc.html

FedWorld Information Network Home Page

If you want to search for a topic on a federally hosted server, start at FedWorld. Search for reports, information services, or via keyword from the convenient drop-down menus. ✎ ⊕

http://www.fedworld.gov/#usgovt

Internal Revenue Service

Perhaps the friendliest thing about the IRS is this web site. The *Digital Daily* supplies a complete set of tax forms in a variety of formats, and valuable information on where to file and where to

get help. You'll also find links to electronic filing information, tax statistics, help, and a calendar for problem-solving day, when the IRS provides free assistance to those with longstanding tax problems. ✎

http://www.irs.ustreas.gov

Peace Corps

The Peace Corps, that venerable U.S. organization started by President Kennedy, is online with information on how U.S. citizens can join and serve abroad or domestically. Along with getting a feel for the organization and its goals, you can find out which occupational categories need filling, which countries need volunteers, how the interview process works, and where to get additional information. There is also an email form for sending mail to the district office nearest you.

http://www.peacecorps.gov

Social Security Online

This site is a treasure trove of information about social security, from estimating your benefits (request the information online and the SSA will mail you the result), to cost of living information, handbooks, and guides for employers. You'll also find forms, information in Spanish, a link to the locations of local offices, and news about the SSA. The kids' pages provide a vaguely frightening explanation of how social security *will* be there when today's toddlers retire. ✎

http://www.ssa.gov/SSA_Home.html/

THOMAS: U.S. Congress on the Internet

If you're curious about the doings of Congress, past or present, this is the place to start. Created "in the spirit of Thomas Jefferson," THOMAS is a Library of Congress server devoted to information on the U.S. Congress. Among other resources, visitors to THOMAS will find links to news about current legislation, the latest floor actions, the text of bills currently up for debate (including a search feature), directories of members of the House and Senate, congressional Internet services, committee information, historical documents, and more. ✎ ⊕

http://thomas.loc.gov

U.S. Army Home Page

While the opening image of armed men wearing gas masks is perhaps not in the best taste, this is a comprehensive and well-organized site for anyone interested in anything about the U.S. Army. Use the site as a jumping-off point to more than 60 U.S. Army web sites, including the Pentagon's Artificial Intelligence Center, the Tank-Automotive Research, Development and Engineering Center, and Syracuse University ROTC. ⚲

http://www.army.mil

U.S. Census Information Server

The self-proclaimed "Factfinder for the Nation," the Census Bureau's web site organizes information so that citizens can make their own use of it. You can get financial data on state and local governments, as well as schools. Although the actual census data is not available due to privacy laws, the Data Extraction System (also known as SIPP-On-Call) summarizes recent census data based on criteria you supply. Through a somewhat cumbersome interface, you can perform a search based on a huge number of variables and receive the results in your Telnet window, by email, or by a temporary file stored at the Census FTP site. The Bureau's statistical briefs are PostScript documents describing poverty in the United States, analyzing housing changes from 1981–1991, or profiling people of Asian and Pacific Islander heritage in the American population. This is a tremendous resource. ⚲ ⊕

http://www.census.gov

U.S. Department of Education

Provides information about the Department of Education's programs and staff. You'll find links to funding opportunities, financial aid, research and statistics, publications, news, and office locations. ⚲

http://www.ed.gov

U.S. Navy

The official starting point for people interested in finding online resources provided by the U.S. Department of the Navy. This service provides an index of links to all the Navy's online servers. To use the search engine, click the site index button, under the S section in the alphabetical listing. The link to the FAQ on sending email to sailors will be particularly useful to those with friends or relatives at sea. ⚲

http://www.navy.mil

Welcome to the White House

On October 20, 1994, the Clinton Administration continued its march into the 21st century by unveiling the new White House web server, dubbed "Welcome to the White House: An Electronic Citizen's Handbook." Today, the server features news, press releases, email links for the President and First Lady, Vice President Al Gore's favorite political cartoons, and a search-by-subject database of all the government information on the Internet (under the Virtual Library icon). Unfortunately (but perhaps understandably), the what's hot link doesn't include information about Monica Lewinsky. ⚲ ⊕

http://www.whitehouse.gov

UNIX

Computer Security Information

An excellent library of links to Unix, the Internet, and WWW security-related sites. The collection is maintained by Jessica Kelley of the National Institutes of Health Distributed Systems Section.

http://www.alw.nih.gov/Security/security.html

The Linux Documentation Project

Web site of a group dedicated to "developing good, reliable documentation for the Linux operating system. The overall goal of the LDP is to collaborate in taking care of all of the issues of Linux documentation, ranging from online documentation (man pages, HTML, and so on) to printed manuals covering topics such as installing, using, and running Linux."

http://www.ssc.com/mirrors/LDP/

The Linux Journal

Resources here include an explanation of what Linux is, a Linux FAQ, a comprehensive list of Usenet groups, the Linux manual pages, a list of other Linux web servers, and a searchable Linux software map. The site was created by the Linux Organization, a not-for-profit group of Linux users. The server is maintained by Specialized Systems Consultants, Inc. publishers of *Linux Journal.*

http://linuxjournal.com:8080/cgi-bin/frames.pl/about_linux.html

UNIXhelp for Users

A hypertext guide to the Unix operating system, intended for beginning users of Unix. Includes descriptions of how to use common commands, manage jobs, and use email, and longer descriptions of common tools. You'll also find explanations of concepts that may be difficult for beginning users to grasp, such as what constitutes an operating system and commands and processes.

http://www.teleport.com/support/unixhelp/

Virtual Computer Library

This electronic library provides links to information sources on computers and computing. Subjects indexed include academic computing, FAQs, Internet information, publishers, and WWW information. The what's new section lists recent additions to the site. This resource is maintained by the University of Texas Computation Center. ⚲

http://www.utexas.edu/computer/vcl/

USENET

Deja.com

A fantastic tool that allows users to search a vast archive of Usenet news postings by keyword, author, and date. You can even read and post to Usenet news groups directly from the site, and make use of handy search and email functions that it provides. The archive is updated frequently to cover the past month's postings for hundreds of newsgroups. Read the Help documents to make full use of the search and retrieval functions. ⚲

http://www.deja.com

FAQs by Category

Need the answers to some frequently asked questions, but don't know where to look? Try this listing of Usenet FAQs, by category. The list is utilitarian in form, but provides a treasure trove of information.

http://www.lib.ox.ac.uk/internet/news/faq/by_category.index.html

RemarQ

Currently, RemarQ is the web-based Usenet archive that's easiest to navigate. They won't try to steer you into a proprietary community, but send you straight to the newsgroups. The format is clear and straightforward, and the site provides additional handy features, such as My RemarQ (for personalization) and email. ⚲

http://www.remarq.com

Talkway

A Usenet archive that's much like Deja.com. You'll need to work a little harder to get the site to admit that it's accessing Usenet newsgroups—the site administrators want you to think that you're accessing their "communities." Nonetheless, you'll find lots of groups and lots of messages at the site. ⚲ ✐

http://www.talkway.com

USENET Info Center Launch Pad

Formerly called "The Bible of Usenet," this is a comprehensive list of answers to FAQs about Usenet. The site includes documents for new users and the Newsgroup Info Center where you can browse the groups by category, or view the master list of Usenet groups. There's also a handy collection of text versions of the USENET FAQs.

http://metalab.unc.edu/usenet-b/home.html

WEATHER

Cyberspace Snow and Avalanche Center

Jim Frankenfield produces this specialized site, which provides avalanche bulletins for many states and countries, professional and educational resources and two fun sections: other cool stuff, which has pictures, news, discussions and first hand accounts to peruse; and an online avalanche store if you're interested in ordering books, videos or safety equipment.

http://www.csac.org

Intellicast USA Weather

With its big and colorful national weather outlook map, the Intellicast weather page will make you feel like the meteorologist on your local TV station. Once you've finished with the outlook, you can call up a few satellite and radar images and then check the forecast for the metro area nearest you. For international weather conditions, select the Around the World link at the top of the page.

http://www.intellicast.com/LocalWeather/World/ UnitedStates/Navigation/

NCAR Data Support Section Server

The National Center for Atmospheric Research has a wide variety of data and programs available to aid meteorological research. ⊕

http://www.ucar.edu/rs.html

Unisys Weather Processor (WXP)

WXP, with sleek weather map graphics, is a general-purpose weather visualization tool for current and archived meteorological data. Developed at Purdue University, it includes satellite imagery, surface and upper-air data, and radar info. There are forecast models and links to Earth and atmospheric home pages.

http://weather.unisys.com

The Weather Channel

Online version of the familiar TV channel. Complete with travel conditions, continuously updated maps of current national and local weather, international forecasts, and corresponding seasonal information. Additional sections include a golfer's guide, health and allergies, gardening, aviation, and the school day forecast. Of course, you can search for your city's forecast and select the type of map you want to see. ⚲ ⊕

http://www.weather.com/homepage.twc

Weather Information Superhighway

Compiled by the National Weather Service, the Weather Information Superhighway lists dozens of sites for weather updates and climate prediction. The weather underground section lists university weather services—another area offers regional climate centers and gives information on droughts, heat waves, hurricanes, and blizzards. You'll also find international weather, satellite images, and weather maps and movies. ⊕

http://www.nws.fsu.edu/wxhwy.html

WINDOWS

The All Windows Information Page

This old-style, non-corporate Windows site is a tremendous resource for Windows users, and covers operating systems including 3.x, NT, 95, and 98. You'll find articles, lots of links to other windows sites, tips and tricks, and lots of free software and shareware. The Freebies software section is updated monthly and includes all sorts of helpful windows applications. ⊕

http://www.plazaone.com/allwindows/

Internet Resources for Windows Developers

Robert Mashlan's collection of links to Net resources useful to Windows product developers. Resource areas covered include FTP sites, FAQs, developer magazines, and mailing lists.

http://www.r2m.com/windev/

PC World Online

An impressive site from the publisher of *PC World* magazine. PC World Online brings together feature articles, news, columns, and product reviews from the magazine, along with a terrific hot software download area. Another great feature is a searchable database of back issues of the magazine. The buyer's guide is tremendously helpful for anyone shopping for a new PC.

http://www.pcworld.com

WinFiles.com

Everything Windows you could possibly want. You'll find the usual shareware, drivers, and tips and tricks. But you'll also find bug fixes, software reviews, channel subscriptions, and price comparisons. ⚲

http://www.winfiles.com

Winsite Archive

A huge Windows shareware archive. Barebones but comprehensive, with one-line text descriptions of the files. ⚲

http://www.winsite.com

WORLD WIDE WEB

A Beginner's Guide to HTML

Tap into "A Beginner's Guide to HTML" and learn everything you wanted to know and more about hypertext markup language, the tool you need to write web documents. Well-organized and cogent, the guide uses concise language to explain how to create HTML documents. Especially valuable for beginners are links to The Minimal HTML Document and Links to Specific Sections. Other sections include troubleshooting, inline images, and character formatting.

http://www.ncsa.uiuc.edu/General/Internet/WWW/ HTMLPrimerAll.html

EarthCam

One of the most famous, early World Wide Web sites featured a camera aimed at a coffee pot, so that researchers down the hall could check whether it was full. Today a broad range of cameras are aimed at weird things, including coffee houses and llama ranches. EarthCam can direct you to them, from the scenic to the weather to the weird. ⚲

http://www.earthcam.com

The HTML Goodies

There's more to publishing on the Web than simply knowing how to code HTML. You must also think about interface design, consistency,

differences between various web browsers, and the type of information you're presenting. This site provides links to tutorials and primers on HTML, links to free images, Java goodies and more.

http://www.htmlgoodies.com

Project Cool: Anyone Can Build a Great Web Site!

California's Project Cool has made this information about web page creation available on the Web since January 1996. The stunning opening page, with its image of Saturn, links to five different forums: DeveloperZone, with web page building information for beginning and amateur programmers; DevSEARCH; Sightings; Peoplesphere; and Future Focus.

http://www.projectcool.com

Refdesk.com

This site bills itself as "Your single best source for facts on the Net," and they just might be right. A single, well-organized page provides search boxes for a dictionary, thesaurus, and encyclopedia, the Web, the weather, and stock market quotes. The Research Tools column provides links to everything from telephone rates to the atomic clock to email addresses and the 'Lectric Law Library. Favorite Destinations showcases the most popular sites on the Web for business, comimcs, entertainment, shopping, financial matters, health, magazines, search engines, jobs, online banking, radio, video, sports, travel, weather, and more. It's the best of the Web at your fingertips. ⚲ 🌐

http://www.refdesk.com

Ultimate Chatlist

Want to know who's chatting about what? Take a look at this comprehensive chat site, which includes chat listings broken down by "categories," software, awards, and message boards.

http://www.chatlist.com

CHAPTER FIFTEEN

COMMERCIAL AND FINANCIAL RESOURCES

While writing this book, I realized that certain sections—Chapters 6 and 7 in particular—needed to be supported by long lists of web addresses. It seemed unwieldy to include them in the body of a chapter, what with all the examples already listed there. And they also didn't fit into the Resource Catalog, because there wasn't much to say about them. There's nothing really distinctive about any of the resources for buying and selling cars that you can't discover from the URL. (What did you think you were going to find at the Luxury Car Network?) But what use is a book about the Internet that doesn't tell you where to shop?

Buying Stuff

Buying Books and Music

Amazon
http://www.amazon.com

Barnes & Noble
http://www.bn.com

Borders
http://www.borders.com

Bibliofind (rare and used books)
http://www.bibliofind.com

Acses
http://www.acses.com

Tower Records
http://www.towerrecords.com

CDNOW
http://www.cdnow.com

Real Media
http://www.real.com

Liquid Audio
http://www.liquidaudio.com

MP3.com
http://www.mp3.com

Buying Tickets

MovieLink
http://www.movielink.com

TicketMaster
http://www.ticketmaster.com

American Airlines
http://www.americanair.com

U.S. Airways
http://www.usairways.com

Expedia
http://expedia.msn.com

Priceline
http://www.priceline.com

Commercial Resources

Buying Cars

Consumer Reports | Cars & Trucks
http://www.ConsumerReports.org/Categories/CarsTrucks/index.html

FinanCenter —Autos
http://www.financenter.com/autos.htm

Luxury Car Network
http://www.luxcarnet.com

Auto-By-Tel
http://www.autobytel.com

AutoWeb
http://www.autoweb.com

CarFinance.com
http://www.CarFinance.com

Microsoft CarPoint
http://carpoint.msn.com

Car Talk Classifieds
http://cartalk.com/Classifieds/

Trader Online
http://www.traderonline.com

Clair Motors
http://www.clair.com

World Wide Wheels
http://wwwheels.com

Renting Cars

Auto Europe
http://www.autoeurope.com

BreezeNet's Guide to Airport Rental Cars
http://www.bnm.com

Alamo Rent-A-Car
http://www.goalamo.com

Avis Rent-A-Car
http://www.avis.com

Budget Rent-A-Car
http://www.budgetrentacar.com

Hertz Rent-A-Car
http://www.hertz.com

National Car Rental
http://www.nationalcar.com/index.html

Thrifty Car Rental
http://www.thrifty.com

Houses

Mortgage Quotes by Microsurf
  http://www.mortgagequotes.com/info.html

The Abele Owners' Network of Homes for Sale by Owner
  http://owners.com

Homescout
  http://www.homescout.com

Yahoo! Real Estate
  http://realestate.yahoo.com

HomePath
  http://www.homepath.com

E-Loan
  http://www.eloan.com

Apartments

Spring Street
  http://www.springstreet.com

Rent.net
  http://www.rent.net/

Yahoo Classifieds: Rentals and Roommates
  http://classifieds.yahoo.com/rentals.html

Computer Equipment

While the web sites listed here all had typical prices that fell within acceptable ranges, prices vary wildly. I used the game "Carmageddon" as a test package. Prices for this popular game ranged between $20 and $55.

Outpost.com
  http://outpost.com

The Dell Store
  http://www.dell.com/store/index.htm

PCs for Everyone
  http://www.pcsforeveryone.com

Micron
  http://www.micron.com

Insight
  http://www.insight.com

CDW
http://www.cdw.com

NECX Home and Office Computer Center
http://necxdirect.necx.com

CompUSA Direct
http://www.compusa.com

Gateway
http://www.gw2k.com/home/

beyond.com
http://www.beyond.com/index.htm

TechShopper
http://www.techweb.com/infoseek/shopper

Apple Computer
http://www.apple.com/buy/

BUYCOMP.COM
http://www.buycomp.com

Price Watch
http://www.pricewatch.com

The Adrenaline Vault—Hardware and Software Price $earch
http://www.avault.com

General Shopping

The BizRate Guide
http://www.bizrate.com

Compare Net—The Interactive Buyer's Guide
http://www.compare.net

Price Watch™—Street Price Search Engine
http://www.pricewatch.com

The Shopping 100
http://www.shopping100.com

@ShopSafeMall.com
http://www.ashoppingguide.com

Internet Bridal Gown Ordering Center
http://www.internetbride.com

Benchmark BeHOME
http://www.behome.com/cgi-bin/shop/index.tam

Speigel
http://www.speigel.com

Online Shopping
http://onlineshopping.about.com

Perfect Present Picker
http://presentpicker.com/ppp/

coolshopping.com
http://www.coolshopping.com/index.phtml

MuseumShop@Home
http://www.museumshop.com

Wedding Registry

Ross-Simons
http://www.ross-simons.com

Selling Stuff

Classified Ads

Yahoo! Classifieds
http://merchandise.classifieds.yahoo.com

Classifieds 2000
http://www.classifieds2000.com

FreeClassifiedAds.com
http://freeclassifiedads.com

Online Auctions

BidFind World Wide Web Auction Search
http://www.vsn.net/af/

eBay Auction Classifieds
http://pages.ebay.com/aw/index.html

AuctionPort
http://onlineshopping.miningco.com/index.htm

OnSale Auction Super Site
http://onlineshopping.miningco.com/index.htm

Auction Universe
  http://www.auctionuniverse.com

Kruse International
  http://www.KruseInternational.com

Priceline.Com
  http://www.priceline.com

CD Compilations

CDuctive
  http://digital.cductive.com

CustomDisc.com
  http://www.customdisc.com

HitBOX.com
  http://www.hitbox.com

MusicMaker
  http://www.musicmaker.com

Radio Nostalgia
  http://www.lofcom.com/nostalgia/

SuperSonic Boom
  http://knowledgeway.org/cgi-bin/resource?Display=2095

Online Banks

Table 15-1 lists online banks, the financial software they support, and whether you can log in directly through the Internet.

See *http://www.intuit.com/banking/participating.html* for the most recent list of Quicken-friendly banks, or the Online Banking Report at *http://www.onlinebankingreport.com/top100banks2.shtml* for the top 100 banks with Internet service, or *http://www.yahoo.com/Business_and_Economy/Companies/Financial_Services/Banking/Internet_Banking/* for the most current list of Internet banks. For some reason, a disproportionate number are in Texas.

Note: I've tried to list every bank which supports Intuit's Quicken, Meca's Managing Your Money, and Microsoft's Money programs, the big three of personal finance software.[*]

---

[*] Since I was unable to access Microsoft's page of Money features, there may be some I've missed and it's not because I'm trying to ignore the big money-hungry conglomerate that simply does not need any more free advertising.

Table 15-1 . Online Banks

Bank Name	URL	Other Access	Applications
American Express	*http://www.aeb-eg.com*	AOL	BankNOW, Quicken
American National Bank	*http://www.amnat.com*		Quicken
BancOne	*http://www.bankone.com*		Managing Your Money, Money, Quicken, Browser
BankBoston	*http://www.bankboston.com*		Money, Quicken
BankAtlantic	*http://www.bankatlantic.com/online.htm*	AOL	BankNOW, Quicken
Bank of Stockton	*http://www.bankofstockton.com*		BankNOW, Quicken
Bank of America	*http://www.bankofamerica.com/ index.cfm*	AOL	Managing Your Money, Money, Quicken, Browser
Bank of New York	*http://www.bankofny.com*		
Banque CIBC	*http://www.cibc.com/francais/*		Quicken
Banque Nationale du Canada	*http://www.bnc.ca*		Quicken
Canada Trust	*http://www.canadatrust.com*		Quicken
Centura Bank	*http://www.centura.com*		BankNOW, Quicken
Chase	*http://www.chase.com*		Quicken
CIBC	*http://www.cibc.com/index.html*		Quicken
Citibank	*http://www.citibank.com*		Quicken, Browser
Comerica	*http://www.comerica.com*		Quicken
Commerce Bank	*http://www.commercebank.com*	AOL	Money, Quicken, Browser,
Commercial Federal Bank	*http://206.154.102.72/quickenlite/04801/*		BankNOW, Quicken
Compass Bank	*http://www.compasspa.com*		BankNOW, Quicken
Confederation Desjardins	*http://www.desjardins.com*		Quicken
CoreStates Bank	*http://www.corestates.com*	AOL	BankNOW, Money, Quicken
Crestar Bank	*http://www.crestar.com*	AOL	BankNOW, Quicken, Browser
Eastern Bank	*http://www.easternbank.com*		Quicken

Table 15-1 . Online Banks (continued)

Bank Name	URL	Other Access	Applications
First American National Bank	*http://www.fanb.com*		Money, Quicken, Browser
Firstar	*http://www.firstar.com/myfin/ myfin-enroll-fr.html*		
First Chicago	*http://www.fctc.com*	AOL	BankNOW, Money, Quicken
First Citizens Direct	*http://www.fcbcf.com*		Managing Your Money, Money, Quicken, Simply Money
First Hawaiian Bank	*http://www.fhb.com*	AOL	BankNOW, Quicken
First National Bank of Anson	*http://www.fnbanson.com/pands.htm*		Browser
First Tennessee	*http://www.ftb.com*		Managing Your Money, Money, Quicken, Browser
First Union	*http://firstunion.com*	AOL	BankNOW, Money, Quicken, Browser
First Virginia	*http://www.Firstvirginia.com*		Browser
Fleet	*http://www.Fleet.com*		Managing Your Money
Great Western Bank	*http://www.greatwesternbank.com*		
Harris Bank	*http://www.HarrisBank.com*		
Huntington Banks	*http://www.huntington.com*		Managing Your Money, Money, Quicken, Browser
KeyBank	*http://www.keybank.com*		Money, Quicken, Browser
LaBanque TD	*http://www.tdbank.ca*		Quicken
Laredo National Bank	*http://www.lnb-online.com*		Quicken
LaSalle Banks	*http://www.lasallebanks.com*		Quicken
M&T Bank	*http://www.mandtbank.com*	AOL	BankNOW, Quicken, Browser
Marquette Banks	*http://www.marquette.com*		Quicken
Marshall & Ils-ley	*http://www.mibank.com*		Browser

Table 15-1 . Online Banks (continued)

Bank Name	URL	Other Access	Applications
Mbanx (English and French)	*http://www.mbanx.com/index2.html*		Quicken
Mellon Bank	*https://www.mellon.com/personal/direct/ bankbyweb/*	AOL	BankNOW, Money, Quicken
Michigan National Bank	*http://www.michigannational.com*		Quicken
National Bank of Canada	*http://www.bank-banque-canada.ca*		Quicken
National Penn Bank	*http://www.natpennbank.com*		Quicken
NationsBank	*http://www.nationsbank.com*		Managing Your Money, Money, Quicken, Browser
NBD Bank	*http://www.nbd.com*	AOL	BankNOW, Money, Quicken, Browser
Nevada State	*http://www.nsbank.com/nevada_state_ bank.html*		Quicken
Norwest Banks	*http://www.norwest.com*		Money, Quicken
PNC Bank	*http://www.pncbank.com*	AOL	BankNOW, Managing Your Money, Quicken
Regions Bank	*http://www.regionsbank.com*		BankNOW, Quicken
Republic National Bank of New York	*http://www.rnb.com*	AOL	BankNOW, Money, Quicken
Sanwa Bank California	*http://www.sanwa-bank-ca.com*	AOL	BankNOW, Quicken
Schwertner State Bank	*http://www.txloanstar.com*		Browser
Star Bank	*http://www.starbank.com*		Browser
State National Bank	*http://www.statenb.com*		Browser
SunTrust	*http://www.suntrust.com*	AOL	BankNOW, Money, Quicken
Texas Commerce Bank	*http://www.gblocker.com/FlagCard.html*		Quicken
TD Bank	*http://www.tdbank.ca*		Quicken
Union Bank of California	*http://www.uboc.com*	AOL	BankNOW, Quicken

Table 15-1 . Online Banks (continued)

Bank Name	URL	Other Access	Applications
U.S. Bank	*http://www.usbank.com/cgi/cfm/ home.cfm*	AOL	BankNOW, Money, Quicken, Browser
Wachovia	*http://www.wachovia.com*		Money, Quicken, Browser
Wells Fargo Bank	*http://wellsfargo.com/per/*	AOL, Prodigy, WebTV	Money, Quicken, Browser
Zions Bank	*http://www.zionsbank.com*		Quicken, Browser

Brokerage Companies

There are many companies with an Internet presence that would love to represent you on the floors of the major stock exchanges. Table 15-2 lists a sampling of the most popular Internet brokerages:

Table 15-2. Online Brokerages (as of 10/9/98)

Company	Minimum Opening Balance	Realtime Quotes	Commission (Market and Limit)	Maximum Execution Time
Ameritrade	$2000	100 opening account; 100 free per order, else $20 monthly	$8 Market < 10,000 shares; $13 Limit < 10,000 shares	1 min < 2,000 shares (advertised thru 3/1/99)
DLJ Direct	$0	100 opening account; 100 free per order, else 500 per $20	$20 Market/Limit < 1,000 shares; $.02 per share over 1,000	None
Datek Online	$3000	Free	$9.99 Market < 5,000 shares; $9.99 Limit < 5,000 shares	1 min < 5,000 shares
E-Schwab	$2500	100 opening account; 100 free per order	$29.95 Market/Limit < 1,000 shares; $.03 per share over 1,000	None
E-Trade	$1000	Free	$14.95 Market < 5,000 NYSE/AMEX; $19.95 Market < 5,000 NASDAQ; $19.95 Limit < 5000; $.01 per share over 5,000	None

Table 15-2. Online Brokerages (as of 10/9/98) (continued)

Company	Minimum Opening Balance	Realtime Quotes	Commission (Market and Limit)	Maximum Execution Time
Fidelity.com	$5000	Free	$25.00 Market < 1000 ($14.95 after 12 trades); $30.00 Limit orders < 1,000; $.02 per share over 1,000	None
Suretrade	None	100 per day	$7.95 Market, Limit < 5,000; $.01 per share over 1,000	None
WellsTrade	$1000	100 opening account; 100 per order	$29.95 Market/Limit < 1,000 shares; $.03 per share over 1,000	None

Digital Cash

For more information, or to open an account, see the following:

Cybank
> *http://www.cybank.net*

CyberCash Wallet
> *http://www.cybercash.com/cybercash/consumers/wallet.html*

eCash
> *http://www.digicash.com/index_e.html*

VeriFone Personal ATM Family of Appliances
> *http://www.verifone.com/solutions/consumer/html/patm.html*

The PC Pay System
> *http://www.innovonics.com/pcpay/pcpayhome.html*

Virtual Pay
> *http://www.virtualpay.com*

THE PREVIOUS
GENERATION

Network applications have come a long way in the past few years; now you can usually do just about anything with a simple click of the mouse. However, while the first generation Internet applications aren't pretty, they are effective. Two of the best of these are Telnet and FTP, both of which have been around since the beginning of Internet time. Telnet allows your computer to act like a terminal connected to a computer somewhere else in the world. If you are a valid user of that remote computer, you can log on, issue commands, and receive results on a 24-row by 80-column display. There isn't anything but text, but often that's all you need. FTP is a way for you to manipulate and transfer files on a remote computer.

Sometimes these older tools are the only way to get the job done. There are prettier versions of Telnet and FTP than the ones that are shipped with Windows; we've described a nicer version of FTP earlier in the book. But if you're at a friend's computer trying to download some files, and Internet Explorer won't work for some reason, it's not a good time to go out and download WS_FTP. Likewise, if you're in a friend's dorm room and want to read your mail from someone else's server, you don't want to download and install QVTnet first. Somewhere in the back of your mind, you should reserve a few brain cells for the old and nasty FTP and Telnet clients that you can count on anywhere. The Internet isn't all that different from other activities, like woodworking: just because there are power saws and electric screwdrivers doesn't mean that you can forget how to use old fashioned hand tools.

Telnet

Telnet allows your computer to act as a terminal to another computer. It was once the predominant tool for doing remote computing, but it has been supplanted by the World Wide Web. Still, old-fashioned 24-line terminals are able to accomplish a lot, and they still serve as a least common denominator when more complicated services don't work. Telnet is particularly common in communities that really care about universal access and aren't willing to assume that everyone is using the latest software and hardware. In particular, libraries and government agencies still frequently provide Telnet servers.

To use Telnet, connect to the Internet as you normally would and then run the Telnet program on your computer. You can do this either by selecting **Run** from the **Start** menu of your computer and typing "Telnet" in the dialog box or by going to the Windows folder on your hard drive and clicking on the **Telnet** application. This opens a window that mimics the old-style terminal. To connect, pull down the **Connect** menu and select **Remote System** (see Figure A-1).

Figure A-1. Connecting with Telnet

When you open a new connection, you see a small dialog box, as shown in Figure A-2.

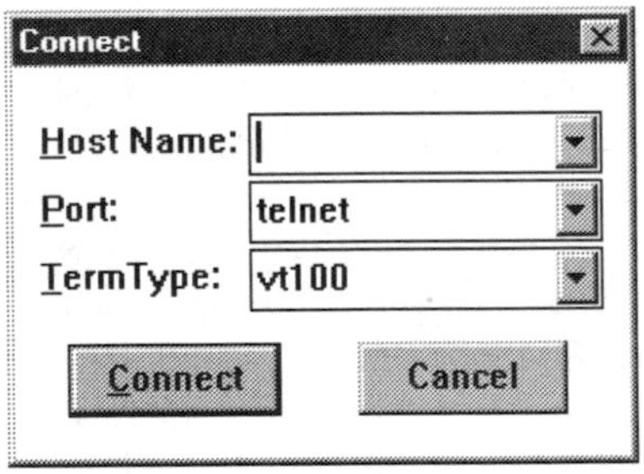

Figure A-2. Connection dialog box

Enter the name of the computer you want to connect to in the Host Name field and press **Connect**. Your computer connects to the remote one as a timesharing terminal; whatever you type is transmitted to the remote machine. You can then type any commands appropriate for that computer. Remember, the remote computer, not yours, determines what you can and can't do. You may have to give a login name and a password.

You should keep your eyes peeled for hints about how to use the computer to which you are connected. Especially keep track of information about how to disconnect—

you will probably need to use a command at the end of the session. When you enter the logout sequence (the actual command depends on the remote computer's software, but logout is a good guess), your computer should respond with the message box you see in Figure A-3.

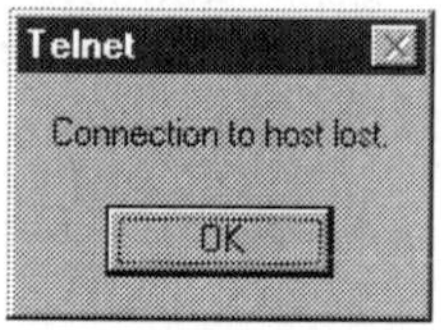

Figure A-3. Logout Successful

Although this sounds like an error message, it really means everything has shut down normally.

It is always better to issue the appropriate logout command rather than just "hanging up the phone" by quitting Telnet. However, if you forget the appropriate command, or if something goes wrong with the Telnet session, simply quitting will do the job.

There are many other options for Telnet. Telnet can mimic other terminals and perform other functions; for a more complete discussion of Telnet, see *Internet in a Nutshell* by Valerie Quercia (O'Reilly).

File Transfer Protocol (FTP)

FTP is a fully functional tool for manipulating files on a remote computer. This makes the program very complex in all its glory, but don't be scared away. What most people do with it is move files to and from their personal computers. If this is all you need to do, you only need to know about seven commands.

To demonstrate, let's look at one of the tasks we were trying to accomplish in Chapter 9. At the end of that chapter, we showed you how to upload files to a web server, using three techniques: a fancy web page provided by the server (a neat feature, but the exception, rather than the rule), tools built into Composer and FrontPage, and a nice graphical FTP client. Now let's see how to use FTP classic. You have been given the task of updating the web pages of a local chapter of your service club because of your computer prowess. You've viewed the web site and want to retrieve the old version of the home page and spruce it up. The file you want is *index.html* in directory chapter 1236 of *www.rotaryoptimistsexchange.org*. The login name is "rox" and the password is "charity." What do you do next?

First, realize that *www.rotaryoptimistsexchange.org* is the name of a computer on the Internet. There's nothing special about the www. If that computer happens to be running an FTP server, your FTP client can reach it. Most web servers do run FTP servers, primarily to allow people like you to update the files on them.* Your strategy is to suck the HTML page down to your computer, where you can use Netscape Composer to change it. Then you want to upload the modified file to the server along with a picture that you would like to add.

Connect to the Internet as you normally would and then run the FTP program on your computer. You can do this either by selecting **Run** from the **Start** menu of your computer and typing FTP in the dialog box, or by going to the Windows directory on your hard drive and clicking on the FTP application. Either of these will open a new window with a single line in it:

```
ftp>
```

This is the FTP program waiting for you to connect to the remote computer. You ask it to connect with the *open* command, followed by the name of the computer:

```
ftp> open www.rotaryoptimistsexchange.org
```

FTP responds with some information about the connection, and asks for your login name and password. Enter those when they are requested:

```
220 www.rotaryoptimistsexchange.org FTP server (Version wu-2.4.2-academ[BETA 18-VR
13](1) Mon Feb 15 10:38:18 CST 1999) ready.
530 Please login with USER and PASS.
Name (ux1.cso.uiuc.edu:(none)): rox
331 Password required for rox.
Password:
230 User rox logged in.
FTP>
```

Your password did not echo, but you are connected. Time to get the file you want. First, you need to move to the folder where the file resides. You use the change directory command, *cd foldername*, to do this. Once you have moved, you can check whether the files are there with the command *dir*:

```
FTP> dir
150 Opening data connection for /bin/ls.
total 8
drwxr-xr-x   2 rox      system       512 May  4 09:09 chapter1236
226 Transfer complete.
FTP> cd chapter1236
250 CWD command successful.
ftp> dir
150 Opening data connection for /bin/ls.
total 8
-rw-r--r--   1 rox      system      1063 May  4 09:09 index.html
226 Transfer complete.
```

---

* What about Telnet? Could you Telnet to this site? In principle, yes: *www.rotaryoptimistsexhange.org* is just the name of a computer, and there's no reason it couldn't be running a Telnet server. However, in most cases, there isn't a good reason for a web server to allow Telnet access, so Telnetting to this address probably wouldn't work.

The first *dir* showed us that the directory we are interested in actually exists. We changed to that directory and gave the *dir* command again, which showed us the file we wanted to fetch. The format of the file listing is determined by the server. It may vary as you move from remote computer to remote computer.

To move a file from a remote machine to your computer, you must "get" it. In the simplest case, all you would need to do is issue the command *get index.html* to move the file to your computer. The problem with this is that the server expects HTML files to end in *.html* and Windows really wants them to end in *.htm*. The *get* command allows you to rename the file as you get it; just type the new name after the original name:

```
ftp>get index.html index.htm
1094 bytes received in 0.0069 seconds (1.5e+02 Kbytes/s)
FTP> quit
221 Goodbye.
```

Now that you have the file on your computer, you can shut down the FTP program with the command *quit*. The file now resides on your desktop; it's time to make your modifications. When you are done, it's time to move the file back to the server. Connect as before and change to the appropriate directory. Now you need to *put* the file back:

```
ftp> put index.htm index.html
150 Opening data connection for index.html.
226 Transfer complete.
2314 bytes sent in 0.0055 seconds (2e+02 Kbytes/s)
```

In addition to modifying *index.html*, you wanted to add the club logo to the web page. Therefore, you also need to move the file *logo.jpg* from your My Documents folder up to the server. The *cd* command changes the directory on the remote computer. To change the directory on your local computer, you use the command *lcd*. To move into the My Documents folder, issue the command:

```
FTP> lcd c:/MYDOCU~1
Local directory now C:\My Documents
```

There are two things to notice. First, FTP always uses the forward slash (/) to denote directories, even on Microsoft computers. It is interpreted correctly as the backslash (\ ) on these computers. Second, the version of FTP that comes with Windows is quite old and doesn't understand modern Windows filenames and directory names, which can include spaces. There are two solutions to this problem. The solution we chose here was to use the MS-DOS name for files. To get this name, find the file in your Windows explorer and request its properties. You can also enclose the filename or directory name within quotes; for example *lcd "c:/My Documents"* will work just fine.

Finally, we are ready to move the logo up to the server, but there is another twist to worry about. FTP likes to know if a file is just text (i.e., a file that can be displayed with Notepad) or contains some kind of binary data. Text files frequently need some conversion when they are moved and may be modified by the FTP program to make them appear the same on either end. These days, almost anything you want to transfer (Word files, pictures in any format, Excel spreadsheets, etc.) should be moved in binary mode. HTML files and email messages are about the only things that qualify as "just text"; they can be transferred in ASCII mode. Therefore, uploading the logo requires you to switch to binary mode:

```
ftp> binary
200 Type set to I.
ftp> put logo.jpg
150 Opening data connection for logo.jpg.
226 Transfer complete.
4532 bytes sent in 0.00064 seconds (3.8e+03 Kbytes/s)
```

Issue the *quit* command and go to your club meeting to collect your kudos.

Frankly, it's a real pain to worry about what files should be transferred in which mode. On modern computers, transferring text files in binary mode will almost certainly work correctly. But transferring binary files in ASCII mode will almost always damage them. So I recommend using binary mode for everything; just get used to typing binary as soon as you've logged onto the server.

FTP is a powerful program with many other esoteric options. You might be able to get away with ? at a command prompt to get a list of commands or *help commandname* to get a one line explanation of its use. If you want more, consult *Internet in a Nutshell* by Valerie Quercia (O'Reilly).

Anonymous FTP

Some FTP servers permit a special kind of FTP access called *anonymous FTP*. Anonymous FTP allows public access to a set of files. To use anonymous FTP, enter "anonymous" as the name, and your email address as the password. Otherwise, it's the same, with a few quirks:

- Some anonymous FTP servers won't let you list the files that are in their directories. In other words, you have to know what you want in advance; you can't poke around and hope you'll find something interesting. (Servers like this tend to confuse Internet Explorer and Netscape, forcing you to use an FTP program.)

- Most servers that allow anonymous access do not allow you to upload files. If they do, there will probably be a directory called Incoming where you can place the files.

- If an anonymous FTP server allows you to upload files, it almost certainly will not allow you to delete or replace files that are already there. This means that if you are uploading a file and get the name wrong, you can't fix it.

INDEX

Symbols

.doc (Microsoft Word), 85
.exe (file extension), 437
.ini files (see initialization files)
.mpg (MPEG video player), 85
.pdf (Adobe Acrobat reader), 85
.ps (Postscript reader), 85
.sit (Stuffit), 84
.tar (GZIP), 84
<A> anchor tags, 328
<BLINK> and </BLINK>, 327
<BODY> and </BODY>, 327
<HEAD> and </HEAD>, 326
<HREF> tag, 328
<HTML> and </HTML>, 325
<IMG> and </IMG>, 328
<META> and </META>, 326
<P>, 327
<TITLE> and </TITLE>, 326

Numbers

3Com, 350
5Star Communications, 96

A

abbreviations (email), 35
absolute links, 332
accessibility
    and remote computing, 516
    and web page design, 306
Acrobat, 125
acronyms, email, 35
Acrophobia (game), 254
Acropolis Casinos (web site), 256
Acses, Universum's Smartest Bookfinder
        (web site), 186, 187
activation order (stock market), 238
active channels (see channels)
active desktop items (see desktop items)

ActiveX controls (see plug-ins)
address book, 23, 82
    PalmPilot, 47
addresses, email (structure), 22
addresses, Internet, 14, 15
    names, 17–19
    numeric, 14, 390–392
    permanent telephone numbers, 343
    (see also IP addresses)
addressing services, 343
admin mailing list, 49
ADSL (Asymmetric Digital Subscriber
        Line), 372, 400
advertising, online, 212–220
    classified, 209
    Usenet, 55
    want ads, 177
    web classifieds, 214
Advocacy groups (Usenet), 56
aggregators, content, 129
AIFF (Audio Interchange File Format)
    email, 84
airline tickets, 192
Alexa, 130
aliases (email), 21–23, 42
AltaVista, 153
Amazon.com, 184, 187
America Online (see AOL)
American Stock Exchange (see AMEX)
Americans with Disabilities Act, 306
AMEX (American Stock Exchange), 232
anchors, 320, 329
animations and games within web browser
        window, 125
anonymizers, 172
Anonymous Cookie, 152
anonymous FTP, 520
anonymous remailers, 102, 159, 170
antiques, buying online, 207
Anti-Spam Network, 104

AOL (America Online)
   archiving of email and Usenet posts
      (privacy issues), 153
   email package, 31
   email, returned, 43
   games, 256, 275–279
   history of, 8
   and junk mail, 103
   legal issues, 9–11
   shopping, online, 180
applets (see Java applets)
application configuration management
      (Castanet), 371
applications
   downloaded and installed
      (running), 439
   NetMeeting (sharing and changing), 354
Arachne (DOS web browser), 133
Archie, 431
archiving
   email messages (privacy issues), 153
   newsgroups, and online shopping, 213
   World Wide web, 130
ARPAnet (Defense Department network)
      and Internet history, 4
artificial intelligence, 251
ASCII
   character set (email), 36
   and remote computing, 520
   (see also formatting)
ASCII mode (FTP downloads), 436
Ask Jeeves (web site), 418
Asymmetric Digital Subscriber Line, 372,
      400
AT&T and Internet telephony, 349
ATT WorldNet (games), 276
attachments (see email attachments)
auctions, online, 207, 215
   reserve, 215
   reverse, 194
audio
   alerts (email), 39, 70
   high quality (MP3), 360–365
   Liquid Audio, 189, 190
   real time (see real time)
Audio Interchange File Format (see AIFF)
AudioCatalyst (Xing Technology), 363

authentication
   mailing list subscriptions, 51
   PPP, 10
Auto-By-Tel, 203
automated mailing lists, 49
automobiles
   buying, 200–204
   loans, 200, 202
   rentals, 203
      reservations, 193
   used, buying online, 203
   web sites, 200, 202
AutoSurf crawler, 131
AvantGo, 141
avatar, 98
AVI, 84

B

backbone, 380–382
background mode (streaming), 358
Badtimes virus, 179
bandwidth, 351, 359
Bank Rate Monitor (web site), 202
banking, online, 221–230
   banks, 222, 508
   check writing, 222
   choosing a bank, 224
   example, 226
   fees, 222
   security issues, 223, 227
   software packages, 225
BankNOW, 225
Barnes & Noble (web site), 186
baud rate, 397
BCC, 24
BeeLine, 420
bellwether stocks, 231
Berners-Lee, Tim, 5, 107
Best Places Finder (search engine), 204
Better Business Bureau (web site), 184
Bezerk Online Entertainment Network
      (web site), 254
Bezos, Jeff, 184
Bigfoot, 95
bill paying, online, 222
binary mode and FTP, 436, 519
BinHex encoding (email), 83
Black Widow, 134
blind carbon copy (see BCC)

blink tags (HTML), 327
Blizzard, 282
BMP (bitmap), and email, 84
body tag (HTML), 327
bonus channels (Pointcast), 368
Bonusmail, 96
bookmarks, 113–117
  folders for, 114
  framed documents, 112
  online investing, 235
  PalmPilot, 139
  privacy issues, 150
books
  buying online, 184–189
  electronic, 376
    compatibility issues, 377
  reviews, online, 185, 187
bootlegged recordings, 191
boot-sector viruses, 156
Borders (web site), 186
brokerages, online, 231–244
  opening an account, 233
  security issues, 234
  web sites, 512
brokers, ticket, 192
browsers and browsing (see web browsers,
    web browsing)
buffering (real-time audio and video
    transmission), 355
bulletin boards
  Internet Phone, 346, 347
  and Internet telephony, 343
bus architecture and Ethernet cards, 404
business, history of Internet use, 5, 7–11
BuyDirect (web site), 199

C

c|net privacy test, 145
CA (Certificate Authority) (see certificates)
cable (TV) modems, 372, 397
  Internet service, 399
cable, coaxial, 403
cache
  folders (clearing), 94
  optimizing, 129
  privacy issues, 150
  size (PalmPilot), 141
cameras, digital, 322

capacity planning (streaming), 359
capital gains tax, 244
Car Talk (test drive notebook), 202
carbon copies (see CC)
CarFinance (web site), 200
carpal tunnel syndrome (see repetitive
    strain injuries)
CarPoint (web site), 200, 202
cash, digital, 249
Castanet (Marimba), 366, 371
Castle Wolfenstein, 254
CC, 24
CDs (music)
  compiling, 190
  and MP3s, 363
  web sites, 361
censorship, 171
  of Internet content, 12
  (see also filters)
CERN (European Organization for Nuclear
    Research), 5, 108
certificates, 125, 375
  Certificate Authority, 123
cgi (Common Gateway Interface), 111
channels, 112, 135–138
  adding (Pointcast), 368
  PalmPilot, 141
  subscribing to, 136
  using with a modem, 137
chat, 96, 98
  groups, 56
  Internet Phone, 346
  NetMeeting, 353
  privacy issues, 155
cheats (online gaming), 257, 258
check writing, online, 222
checking for new mail, 38
ChiBrow, 134
child pornography, 174
children, 154
  browsers, web, 134
  data collection from, 147
  monitoring and controlling Internet
    use, 117, 171
  and online games, 252, 267
  privacy issues, 154
circuit-switching, 13
Civilization II (online game), 288
  scenario tutorial, 261–264

classified advertising (see advertising)
client-side prediction, 282
coaxial cable, 403
collaboration
    NetMeeting (features), 353
    security issues, 354
    (see also conferencing)
collectibles, buying online, 184, 207, 208
colleges and universities
    choosing online, 118
    and Internet history, 5
COM ports, 386
Command & Conquer: Red Alert, 289
commercial software and viruses, 158
common carriers and censorship, 12
Common Gateway Interface (see cgi)
communications software, choosing, 26–31
Communicator, 30, 351
    and NetMeeting, 354
community bulletin boards (see bulletin
       boards)
compatibility
    chat and instant messaging, 97
    email and attachments, 29, 83, 84
    and HTML, 6
    Internet (history), 5
    Mosaic (web browser), 6
complaints (online shopping), 184
Composer
    colors and background tab, 308
    directories, 332
    entering text, 309
    features, 299
    formatting, 311
    and HTML, 324, 325, 328
    image options, 314
    images, 312, 332
    lists, 316
    margins, 329
    meta variables, 304
    paragraphs, 311
        tags and whitespace, 330
    pathnames, 332
    uploading, 331–339
    whitespace, 314
compression (see data compression)
CompuServe, 8, 12
Computer Virus Myths (web site), 165

computers and computing
    equipment, buying online, 196
    handheld computers (see handheld
        computers; PalmPilot; palmtop
        devices)
    remote computing, 515–520
        access to files, 520
        manipulating files, 517
concept searches, 420
conferencing
    and collaboration, 350–354
    conference calls, 344
        NetMeeting, 352
    facilities (white board), 350
    security issues, 374–376
    servers, 344
configuration
    and email, 40, 71
    and viruses, 166
confirmation (mailing list subscriptions), 51
connecting to the Internet (sequence of
       events), 386
consumer information web sites, 184
consumer rights (privacy issues), 149
content aggregators, 129
content-filtering software and children (see
       nanny software)
conventions (shopping) (see shopping
       online)
cookies, 110
    accepting, rejecting, and deleting, 151
    access to, 151
    and online shopping, 177
    privacy issues, 149, 150, 152
    security issues, 123
Copernic (search utility), 420
copyright
    books, 376
    images for online use, 322
    music, 361
country codes (domains), 18
crafts, buying and selling online, 208
crashes (stock market), 242
credit cards
    and online shopping, 179–180, 183
    special, for web use, 155
    (see also security)
crime, 173
    (see also law and legal issues)

Crowds, 172
cryptographic software (see encryption; PGP)
Curb Market (see AMEX)
customization of mailers (see configuration)
CyberAge Raider, 420
CyberBookies (web site), 257
Cyberchefs (web site), 195
cybercrime, 173
Cyberdog, 134
Cybermeals (web site), 195
cyberstalking, 8, 145
Cypherpunk remailers, 169

D

data compression
    .zip (PKZIP), and email, 84
    decompressing downloaded files, 437
    Macintosh files, 437
    and real-time audio and video transmission, 355, 360
data lines, ownership of, 8
data transmission speed, 397
Defense Department, and early Internet, 4
Deja.com, 63–65
    and availability of newsgroups, 54
    and online shopping, 212, 213
    privacy issues, 153
    as search engine, 419
deletion of email, 41
delivery, local (online shopping), 184, 195
desktop items, active, 136, 138
    (see also channels)
device controllers, 373, 378
dialog boxes (troubleshooting), 386
dial-ups (troubleshooting), 387
digests of mailing list mail, 52
digital cameras, 322
digital cash, 249
direct dial-up (online banking), 222
directions, 425–430
directory servers (NetMeeting), 352
DirectX, 286
discounts (online shopping)
    airline tickets, 192
    AOL, 182
    books, 185
    groceries, 194

discussions, distributed, 21
Display Doctor, 286
distributed discussions, 21
DJIA (Dow Jones Industrial Average), 231
document identifier tag (HTML), 325
document management (PalmPilot), 143
Document Type Definition in SGML, 374
domain, 18
    Domain Name System, 17–19
        and troubleshooting, 389
    (see also host)
Doom, 254
DOS, with Kali, 266
Dow Jones Industrial Average (see DJIA)
downloaded software, and viruses, 158
downloading
    AOL games, 276
    as background process, 129
    files, 433–439
    from hidden directories, 435
    high speed, 399, 400
    interrupted, 369, 434
    minimizing download time, 371, 372
    software, 199
    speed, 126–129, 397
    web files with FTP, 435
    (see also material to be downloaded, e.g., music)
DTD (Document Type Definition) (in SGML), 374
DWANGO, 279

E

Earthlink (games), 276
ebooks (see books, electronic)
editing, 121
Edmund's Automobile Buyer's Guide, 203
education, opportunies on the Internet, 154
electronic books (see books, electronic)
Electronic Communications Privacy Act, 148
email, 20–53
    abuse of, 184
    address book (converting from one mailer to another), 82
    addresses (structure), 22
    attachments, 26
        security issues, 159

email, attachments (continued)
 sending, 83, 84
 viruses, 156, 157
 audio alerts, 70
 automatic response, 88
 checking for new mail, 38
 compatibility issues, 10, 29, 83, 84
 composing messages, 23–26
 configuring, 40, 71–82
 deleted, 41
 early business use, 5
 file attachments, 82–85
 file extensions, 85
 file transfer capabilities (Internet
  history), 5
 filters, 39, 67–71
 folders, 38
 forgery, 158
 forwarding accounts, 93–96
 free accounts, 92–96
 games, 251, 287
 graphics, 84
 graphics formats, 84
 HTML, 93
 large files, sending, 84
 mailboxes, 38
 Mail Delivery Subsystem, 41
 mailing lists, 47–53
 mainframe-based, 28
 messages
  archiving (privacy issues), 153
  copies of, 24
  encryption, 159, 161
  formatted (receiving), 40
  formatting, 33, 36
  forwarding, 25
  including, 25
  incoming, 38–41
  redirecting, 25
  remote storage, 28
  replying to, 25
  returned, 41–44
  signing, 162
  sorting, 67
  storing, 27
  unwanted, 67
 notification, 39, 70
 on more than one computer, 85–92
 organizing, 67

PalmPilot, 44–47
passwords, 158
permanent addresses, 92
Pine and MIME, 31
plug-ins (categories), 81
POP servers (message storage and
  deletion), 87
privacy issues, 93, 145–152, 158
 workplace email, 149
security issues, 158
 plug-ins, 168
signature files, 35
signatures, verifying, 162
software, 27
 choosing, 26–31
 configuring, 31
 upgrades, 40
travel use, 85–92
user profiles, and junk mail, 102
vacation programs, 88
web-based accounts, 93–96
workplace privacy issues, 159
embedded graphics and HTML (Internet
  history), 6
employers (see workplace Internet use)
Encapsulated PostScript (see EPS)
encapsulation, packet, 16
encryption
 email, 159, 161
 encrypted information, 155
 encrypted web sites, 123
 legal issues, 233
 software, export of, 12, 159
 web browsers, 223, 233
 (see also security; PGP)
Environmental Protection Agency (Zip
  Code web site), 205
EPS (Encapsulated PostScript) (email), 84
error messages, 385, 389
 (see also troubleshooting)
Ethernets, 402–410
 cards, 404–406
  drivers, 404
  installing, 405
 (see also networks)
etiquette, Internet, 32–34
Eudora
 configuring, 71–74
 coordinating with Netscape, 74

creating stationery, 37
message storage and deletion, 87
plug-ins (categories), 81
vacation filter, 88
with PGP, 161
Eudora Pro/Lite (email package), 29
European Particle Physics Laboratory (see
CERN)
event keys (RealNetworks), 359
Excite (search engine)
privacy issues, 153
and RealNetworks, 358
executable files and viruses (see program
viruses)
Expedia (web site), 193
Explorer
and anonymous FTP servers, 520
bookmarks (Favorites), 113
control buttons, 120
encryption techniques, 223, 233
and Eudora, 29
Favorites folder, 114
free distribution of, 10
history list, 117
history of, 108
home pages, 109, 110
IEv5, 150
IE version 4.0+, 150
and Internet Phone, 347
and Java, 9, 128
keyboard control, 132
Multimedia settings, 126
and NetMeeting, 351
pop-up menus, accessing, 121
saving and printing documents, 120
searching with, 418
searching within documents, 120
and Secure Sockets Layer, 223
shortcuts, 122
URLs
entering manually, 111
smart, 129
user interface for Windows 98, 10
wallpaper option, 122
web pages, 121
Express by Infoseek, 420
Extensible Markup Language (see XML)
extensions (see file extensons)

F

Fair Credit Billing Act, 183
fan paraphernalia, buying online, 184
Fannie Mae (HomePath web site), 206
FAQs (frequently asked questions), 54, 57
FASTore, 129
FBI, 173
Federal Trade Commission (web site), 184
File Transfer Protocol (see FTP)
files
attachments (handling), 82–85
compression (see data compression)
extensions, 85
installing, 433–439
procedure, 436
large
downloading, 434
email, 84
multiple (see multiple files)
transfer (NetMeeting), 354
transfer capabilities (Internet history), 5
filters
content-filtering software, 171
email, 39, 67–71
junk mail, 103
NetMeeting, 352
news, 62
order (email), 70
packet, and permanent IP
addresses, 396
financing (see automobiles; mortgages)
flames, 54
folders, email, 38, 67
font and image size, changing, 132
food (buying online), 194–196
forgery, email, 158
formatting
email, 33, 36, 40
formatted files on the web, 125
web pages, 311
forwarding accounts and web-based
accounts, 93–96
forwarding email messages, 25
Fourth Amendment and privacy and
security issues, 148
frames, 111
fraud, 8, 174, 179
(see also shopping online, complaints)

free email accounts, 92–96
free merchandise, 183
free speech, 12
   (see also censorship)
frequently asked questions (see FAQs)
FrontPage Express
   anchors, 329
   applets, 330
   background (colors), 308
   directories, 332
   entering text, 309
   features, 298
   formatting, 311
   and HTML, 325
   images, 312, 332
   lists, 316
   margins, 308
   meta variables, 304
   paragraphs, 311
   pathnames, 332
   sound, background, 308
   templates, 300
   uploading, 331–339
      options, 338
FTP
   anonymous, 520
   anonymous FTP client (using browser
      as), 111
   ASCII and binary modes, 519
   downloading with, 433, 434
   FTPx, 335
   options, 520
   and remote computing, 517–520
   and Telnet, 515
   text files, 519
   and Windows, 519
funding of Internet (see Internet
   funding and ownership)

G

Gamblers' Anonymous, 257
gambling
   legal issues, 12, 253, 256
   offline, 256
   online, 253, 256
Game Center (c|net game site), 258
GameGirlz (web site), 259
GamePower (CMP web site), 258

games
   board games, 256
   card games, 256
   Castanet, 372
   chat clients, 282
   configurations, 286
   customing, 261–264
   direct TCP/IP or modem
      connections, 264
   email, 251, 287
   finding online, 264
   finding players online, 282
   hardware, 265
   help, 257, 258
   multiplayer, 256
      local networks, 254
      network options, 251
      real-time, 265
      traditional computer games, 281
   online environment, 252, 276
   real-time, 265, 269
   servers (choosing), 267
   services and networks, 251, 265–281
   shooter games, first person, 254
   standalone applications, 281
   support, 260
   web sites (see World Wide web, games)
   (see also gambling)
Games Domain (web site), 260
GameSpot (ZDNet web site), 259
GameSpy (customizing), 284
gateway (home networks), 406
GIF (email), 84
The Gift (web site), 207
Glassbook, 377
the Globe (web server), 334
GNN, 8
Golden Palace Online Casino (web
   site), 257
good traders lists, 183, 210
Goodtimes virus, 157
Gopher, 430
GoPlay, 95
government funding for Internet use in
   schools, 8
Grab-A-Site, 134
Graphic Interchange Format (see GIF)
graphics
   email, 84
   embedded in text (Internet history), 6

text descriptions, 307
(see also photographs; images)
Gravity (newsreader), 58
groceries, buying online, 194
group discussions, 21
GZIP, 84

H

H.323 (Internet standard), 344, 351
hack codes (online gaming), 258
hackers, 173
half-duplex sound cards, 342
handheld computers, 350
handheld devices, 377
(see also PalmPilot)
Handweb, 141
Happy Puppy (web site), 258
Happy99 virus, 157, 165
hardware, 396–400
buying online, 197
Internet, 14, 380–382
used, buying online, 198
hate speech, 171
HateWatch, 171
header tag (HTML), 326
headines (Pointcast), 370
Heckler's Arcade (web site), 276
helper applications (see plug-ins)
hijacking of newsgroups, 54
hints (online gaming), 258
history file, 117
privacy issues, 150
history of Internet, 3–13
hit counter (web page), 315
hoaxes (viruses), 156, 157
home networks (see networks, home)
home pages, 109–110, 129
creating, 299
personalizing, 110
HomePath (Fannie Mae web site), 206
host
addresses and system names, 17
hostnames (email), 22
portion of Internet address, 15
web pages (see web servers)
(see also domain)
hotel reservations, 193
HotJava, 133
Hotmail, 95

hours of operation (network
resources), 384
HREF attribute, 328
HTML, 298
coding, 324–325
compatibility issues, 6, 325
editors, 298
and email, 36, 40, 93
files (features), 325
formatting, 302
image tags, 328
origin, 6
paragraph and line breaks, 329
searching specific fields, 417
tables, 316–318
tags, 325–330
cutting, pasting, and copying, 327
whitespace, 330
and word processors, 309
(see also links; web page design)
HTTP (Hypertext Transfer Protocol), 4
hubs (home networks), 401, 402
hypertext
anchors, 328
links (see links)
and World Wide web, 107
Hypertext Markup Language (see HTML)
Hypertext Transfer Protocol (see HTTP)

I

identification tags (HTML), 325–330
identification, personal (online), 375
identity snatching, 145
IE (see Explorer)
IEMMC (Internet Email Marketing
Council), 101
IETF (Internet Engineering Task Force), 7,
378
iMAC (Apple compter), 11
images, 321
automatic loading, 126
finding online, 322
image tags (HTML), 328
and pathnames (web pages), 332
from photographs, 321
IMAP (Internet Message Access
Protocol), 28
using with Pine, 79
including email messages, 25

incoming email, 38–41
I-Net Casino (web site), 257
infoGIST Biz infoFINDER, 420
Inforian Quest 98, 421
information mining, 145
Infoseek, 413, 420
initialization files (Eudora), 72
insider trading (stock market), 244
instant messaging, 96
    clients, 100
Integrated Services Digital Network (see
        ISDN)
intellectual property, theft, 174
Intercasino (web site), 257
interface, email, 28
International Salary Calculator, 204
International Standard Book Number (see
        ISBN)
Internet
    addresses (see addresses, Internet)
    applications, first generation, 515–520
    buying and selling (see shopping,
        online)
    children's use of (see children)
    cloud, 380–382
    communications
        email and news, 20–65
        interactive, 341–360
        tools, 96
    connection hardware and
        technologies, 396–400
    control of, 7
    definition, 3–4
    etiquette, 32–34
    fraudulent use (see fraud)
    funding and ownership, 9
    games (non-web), 264–287
    gaming (history and culture), 251–254
    hardware, 14, 380–382
    history, 3–13
    home use of, 8
    lags, 265
    law and legal issues, 9–13, 173
    misuse of, 8
    operation of, 13–19
    origins, 4–7
    personal information, 149–153
        removing, 152
        (see also privacy)

protocols
    (see names of specific protocols)
reliability, 7
selling (see selling, online)
standards, 84
    development, 377
    encoding (email attachments), 83
    H.323, 344, 351
    history, 4
    responsibility for defining, 7
telephony, 340
    and standard telephones (see
        telephones, standard)
    arranging calls, 346
    compatibility issues, 344, 350
    hardware, 349
    software, 348
trademark use on, 19
workplace use (see workplace Internet
    use)
Internet Angel (offline browser), 135
Internet Engineering Task Force (see IETF)
Internet Explorer (see Explorer)
Internet Gaming Zone, 279
Internet Phone (VocalTec), 342, 344–348
    features, 346
Internet Protocol (see IP)
Internet Relay Chat (IRC), 99, 282
Internet ScamBusters (web site), 184
Internet Service Provider (see ISP)
Internet Telephone (see Internet Phone)
interrupted downloads, 369, 434
Intuit's TurboTax, 246
invalid return address (email), 43
investing, online, 231–244
    security issues, 233, 234
investments (online sources of
        information), 243
IP (Internet Protocol)
    addresses
        and filters, 396
        home networks, 406, 409
        numerical, 14
        static and dynamic, 343, 396
        and troubleshooting, 382–383, 387
IPv6, 342
packets (Internet history), 4
packet-switching, 13–16

IPX/SPX, 265
   IPX networks, and games, 268
IQBoX, 421
IRAs, 233
IRC (see Internet Relay Chat)
IRS, 245
ISBN (International Standard Book
      Number), 188
ISDN (Integrated Services Digital
      Network), 397, 398
isochronous applications, 341–360
ISPs (Internet Service Providers)
   evaluating and choosing, 395
   hardware used by, 380
   and home networks, 401
   lists of, 396
   and troubleshooting, 386, 393, 396

J

Jack (game), 254
Java
   applets, 330
   disabling Java or JavaScript to increase
      downloading speed, 127
   and operating systems, 9
   and web page design, 330
JavaScript, 331
Jeopardy (game), 255
JPEG (Joint Photographic Experts
      Group), 84
junk mail, 8, 31, 96, 100–106
   avoiding (software), 106
   filtering, 70, 103
      Outlook, 78
   and free email, 93
   Internet Email Marketing Council (see
      IEMMC)
   and Internet telephony, 345
   law and legal issues, 103
   and online shopping, 179
Juno, 96
jurisdiction over Internet, 12, 253, 256
   (see also law and legal issues)

K

Kali, 265–269
KDS Concept Explorer, 420
Kelley Blue Book, 203
key pair (PBP), 160

keyboard entry, 132, 178
key-value pairs (HTML), 326
keywords, 417
kill files (news), 62
Kiplinger's TaxCut, 246

L

lags (Internet), 265
LAN (see networks, local)
law and legal issues, 9–13, 154, 253, 256
   copyright, 322
   IETF, 8
   privacy, 148–149
   (see also specific area, e.g., gambling)
law enforcement, 173
layers of service (networking), 13
links
   absolute, 302, 332
   anchor, 329
   AOL, and online shopping, 182
   between web documents, 107
   creating, 302, 328
   depth, and AvantGo (Palm Pilot), 142
   distinguishing from plain text, 109
   hyperlink reference, 328
   and image maps, 320
   PalmPilot, 140
   relative, 302, 332
   specialized, 320
   (see also HTML)
Liquid Audio, 189, 190
list servers, 49
list-management programs, 48
listproc
   mail digest, 52
   removal from mailing list, 53
   subscription to mailing lists run by, 51
listserv
   mail digest, 52
   removal from mailing list, 53
   subscription to mailing lists run by, 51
   suspending mailing lists, 91
loan balancing (online brokerages), 235
loans, auto (see automobiles, loans)
lobbies (games), 282
local area networks (see networks, local)
logical operators, 415
login name (email), 22
Lynx, 133

M

Macintosh
    file compression, 437
    Internet history, 7
    with Kali, 266
macro viruses, 156, 157, 167
magazines, subscribing online, 366–371
MailCity, 96
Mail Delivery Subsystem, 41
mailing lists, 21, 47–53
    administrative (admin) mailing
        address, 49
    automated, 49
    choosing, 48
    digests of mail, 52
    lists of, 48
    management programs, 48
    owner or moderater, 48
    sending and receiving mail, 51
    source of junk mail, 102
    subscribing, 48, 49–51
    suspending, 91
    syntax, 50
    web pages, 49
Mail Notification, automatic
        (Messenger), 74
mailto links, 320
mainframe-based email, 28
majordomo
    mail digests, 52
    removal from mailing list, 53
    subscription to mailing list run by, 51
    suspending service, 92
Managing Your Money (personal finance
        software), 226
MapQuest!, 425–429
maps and directions, 425–430
margin (investments), 236, 241
markup languages, 373
McVeigh, Timothy, 153
Media Player, 125, 359
    and MP3s, 362
    privacy issues, 150
medical privacy, 147
Melissa virus, 30, 156, 167
Messenger, 30, 57
    configuring, 74
    configuring news, 62

email and news, 21, 25
    filtering news, 62
    reading, 59
    threaded discussion, 61
    and vacation email programs, 90
meta searches, 418
meta tags (HTML), 326
meta variables, 304
meta words, 417
Microsoft
    compatibility issues, 9
    installation problems involving Microsoft
        applications, 384
    legal issues, 9–11, 125
    and streaming technology, 356
    (see also names of specific products)
MIME (Multipurpose Internet Mail
        Extensions)
    attachments, and returned email, 42
    encoding (email), 83
    and Pine email package, 31
misc.forsale (newsgroup), 175
misuse of Internet, 8
Mixmaster remailers, 169
modems
    28.8/33.6 Kbps, 395, 398
    57.6 Kbps, 398
    cable, 397, 399
    channels and active desktop items
        with, 137
    compatibility issues, 388, 397
    establishing connections, 386
moderators of newsgroups, 54
Money (personal finance software), 226
money laundering, 174
mortgage rates, comparing online, 206
Mosaic, 6, 131
Motion Picture Experts Group (see MPEG)
Motley-Fool Investment Guide, 244
MovieLink (web site), 192
Moving Cost Calculator, 204
MP3, 360–365
MPEG (Motion Picture Experts Group), 84
MPEG-1, audio layer 3 (see MP3)
Mplayer, 272–275
    games (listed), 273
MS Word and viruses, 156, 157, 167
MS-DOS and FTP, 519

MSIE (Microsoft Internet Explorer) (see Explorer)
MSN Gaming Zone, 279–281
MUD (Multiple User Dungeon), 251
Mulberry, 30
multiplayer games (see games)
Multiplayer Online Games (MPOG), 258
multiple files (downloading), 434
music
    buying online, 189–192
    copying, digital, 362
    distribution, 361
    downloading, 189
    legal issues, 361
    MP3 encoding, 363
    music industry, 361
    publishing, online, 362
      web sites, 365
    recordings, bootlegged, 191
    sellers, online, 189
    trading, 191
    web sites, 190
    (see also audio; CDs)
MusicMatch Jukebox, 363

N

NAGS (Netizens Against Gratuitous Spamming), 103
names as Internet addresses, 17–19
nanny software, 171
NASDAQ (National Associates of Securities Dealers), 232
National Center for Supercomputing Applications, 6, 108
National Consumer Complaint Center (web site), 184
National Science Foundation (see NSF)
natural language, 418
Navigator
    and anonymous FTP servers, 520
    bookmarks, 113
    control buttons, 120
    encryption techniques, 223, 233
    history file, 117
    history of, 108
    and Java, 128
    keyboard control, 132
    origin, 6
    Personal Toolbar, 115

    personalizing home pages, 110
    pop-up menus, accessing, 121
    Preferences dialog box, 126
    saving and printing documents, 120
    searching with, 418
    searching within documents, 120
    and Secure Sockets Layer, 223
    Send Page option, 122
    templates, 300
    URLs
      entering manually, 111
      smart, 129
    wallpaper option, 122
    web pages (editing), 121
NCSA (see National Center for Supercomputing Applications)
NE2000 compatible Ethernet cards, 404
NeoPlanet, 129, 131
Net Grocer (web site), 194
Netaddress, 96
Netcenter, 95
NetForward, 95
NetMeeting, 351, 351–354
    collaboration features, 353
    and Communicator, 354
    directories, 352
Netscape
    anti-trust suit against Microsoft, 10
    and streaming technology, 356
    (see also names of specific products, e.g., Messenger)
networks, 7
    address translation, 409
    cards, 404–406
    error messages, 389
    and games, 251
    hardware, 402–410
    high speed, 403
    history of Internet, 8
    home, 397, 401, 402–410
      printing, 407–409
      security, 409
    hours of operation, 384
    installing, 403
    interfaces, 404–406
    layers of service, 13
    local, 14
      games, 254, 265
      troubleshooting, 382, 390–392

networks (continued)
    net mask, 409
    proprietary, 4
    routing and addressing, 14, 15
    unreliability, 4, 7
New York Stock Exchange (see NYSE)
New York Times crossword puzzles, 255
news, 366–371
    servers, publicly accessible, 62
newsgroups
    advertising, 55
    archiving, and online shopping, 213
    availability through news servers, 54
    discuss groups and binary groups, 57
    finding for buying and selling, 212
    naming scheme, 55–56
    participation in, 53
    reading, 61, 65
    subscribing to, 58, 63
    types, 55
    (see also Usenet)
newsreaders, 57, 59, 62
nicknames (see aliases)
notification (email), 39, 70
NSF (National Science Foundation) and
        Internet history, 5
NYSE (New York Stock Exchange), 231

O

Oasis Casino, 257
OECD (Organization for Economic Co-
        operation and Development), 146
offline browsing, 129, 131, 134
    PalmPilot, 141–143
omnibus laws, 146
one-click ordering, 177, 178, 189
    AOL, 182
ONElist, 48
Online Banking Report, 226
online browsers, alternative, 131–134
online profiles, 149
    privacy issues, 153
Open Electronic Book Exchange, 377
Opera (web browser), 131, 132–133
operating systems, and home
        networks, 402
opt-out lists, 101
orderid number (privacy issues), 150
orders (stocks), 237

Organization for Economic Co-operation
        and Development (see OECD)
origins of the Internet, 4–7
The Other Browser-Emailer (TOBE), 133
Outlook, 57
    BCC field, 24
    changing the format of forwarded
        messages and Usenet posts, 78
    configuration, 75–79
    configuring news, 62
    email
        attachments, 25
        and news, 21
    filtering news, 62
    message storage and deletion, 87
    Outlook 98 and email attachments, 26
    Outlook 98 and Outlook Express (email
        package), 29
    plug-ins (categories), 81
    reading, 59
    stationery, 37
    with PGP, 161
Over the Air Equipment, Inc., 103
ownership of Internet (see Internet
    funding and ownership)

P

package, 344
packets, 16
    encapsulation, 16
    packet-filtering firewalls, 396
    packet-switching and IP, 13–16
Pagoo, 349
PalmPilot
    address book, 47
    document management, 143
    email, 44–47
    interfacing with PC, 44
    maps and directions, 429
    PalmPilot Mail, 44
        deleting, 46
        new message, 46
        reading and answering, 45
        Setup program, 45
    Palmscape, 141
    saving web pages, 141
    web browsing, 134, 138–143
    (see also handheld computers)

palmtop devices, 361, 364, 373
  (see also handheld computers)
PAML (see Publicly Accessible Mailing
      Lists)
paragraph tags (HTML), 327
passwords
  email, 158
  online banking, 223
  and online shopping, 179
  (see also security)
patch (online gaming), 258
pathnames for images (web pages), 332
payload (viruses), 156
PC and Macintosh (Internet history), 7
Peapod (web site), 194
people
  finding on the Internet, 412, 421–424
    privacy issues, 152
permanent internet addresses (see IP
      addresses, static and dynamic)
personal finance software, 222, 225
personal identification (online), 375
Personal Information Manager (PIM), with
      Outlook 98, 29
personal information on the Internet, 149–
      153
  collection from children, 154
  removing, 152
  (see also privacy)
Personal Toolbar (Netscape
      Navigator), 115
PGL (Professional Gamer's League), 269,
      289, 293, 294
PGP (Pretty Good Privacy), 159
  export of, 12
  using with Unix, 162
  with unsupported mailers, 163
photographs, 321
  scanning to produce graphic
      images, 321
photographs, digitalized, 322
Picture Disks, 322
pictures (Internet history), 6
pictures (see also graphics; images)
PIM (see Personal Information Manager)
Pine, 30, 79, 86
ping utility, 390–392
  ping rate, 267
  ping rate and QuakeWorld, 285
pixels, and web page design, 308

PKZIP and email, 84
plain-text (see ASCII)
Play by Mail (PBM) Games (web sites), 287
plug-ins
  email (categories), 81
  web browsers, 124
Pointcast, 134, 366–371
  downloading and installing, 366
  initial download, 367
  personalizing, 367, 370
  servers, 371
  update schedule, 367, 370
police, local (computer crime units), 174
POP (Post Office Protocol)
  access, and web-based email
      accounts, 94
  clients (email), 38
    security issues, 158
  POP3 mailers, 27
  travel use, 86
pornography
  child, 174
  and junk mail, 103
  legal issues, 12
portfolio (investments), 236
Post Office Protocol (see POP)
postmarks, 104
Pow Wow (Internet telephony
      software), 349
PPP (Point to Point Protocol), 4, 10, 17,
      396
  and games (Kali), 266
preferences (web pages), and downloading
      speed, 126–129
Preferred Mail (AOL), 103
  (see also filters, junk mail)
premail (Unix freemail frontend), 170
premier channels (Pointcast), 368
Pretty Good Privacy (see PGP)
Priceline (web site), 194
prices
  auction, 207
  books, 187
  cars, 200
  comparing online, 203
  computers and computer
      equipment, 197
  stocks, 236–237
  (see also discounts)
PriceWatch (search engine), 197

print size (see font and image size)
printers
    home networks, 407–409
        configuring, 407
privacy, 145–152
    consumer rights, 149
    right to, 148
    software, 159–169, 171–173
    web-based email accounts, 93
    (see also security; archiving)
privacy test, 145
Private Idaho (freemail frontend for
       Windows), 170
Prodigy, 8
Professional Gamer's League (see PGL)
profiles, online, 149
program viruses, 156
proprietary networks, 4
protocols (see names of specific protocols)
Proxiweb, 139–141
pseudo-anonymous remailers, 169
Publicly Accessible Mailing Lists, 48
publicly accessible news servers, 62
push channels and technologies, 366–372
    and offline browsing, 134

Q

Qspy, 282
Quake, 254, 265, 289, 291, 295
    MSN Gaming Zone, 279
QuakeSpy, 254, 265
    (see also GameSpy)
QuakeWorld, 254
    games, 282
Quicken (personal finance software), 226
QuickTime, 84
quotes (stock), 236–237

R

rare domains, 19
real time
    audio and video transmission, 355–360
    communication, 98
    games, 265, 269
    stock quotes, 242
RealAudio (see RealNetworks)
RealAudio format, 190

RealNetworks, 356–359
    controls, 357–358
    installing, 356
    streaming technology, 355
    version G2, 356
RealPlayer, 124, 125
    compatibility issues, 10
    and MP3s, 362
recipient unknown (returned email), 43
Recording Industry Association of
       America, 361
recurring payments, 222
Red Alert, 289, 291, 295
redirecting email messages, 25
references (see research (online shopping))
relative links, 332
reliability of the Internet, 7
remailers, anonymous, 102
remote computing
    access
    email, 28
    (see also computers and computing)
rentals, car, 203
repetitive strain injuries, 288
    (see also keyboard entry)
reply attribution (Outlook), 75–78
replying to email messages, 25
research (online shopping)
    books, 185
    cars, 200–203
    computers and computer
       equipment, 196
    homes and neighborhoods, 204–206
    on individual buyers and sellers, 209
research and engineering, and Internet
       history, 7
ResellerRatings (web site), 198
reserve auctions, 215
restaurants (buying from online), 195
retributive action (junk mail), 101
returned email, 41–44
returns (merchandise purchased
       online), 179
reverse auctions, 194
reverse-lookup features (telephone
       numbers), 424
RIAA (Recording Industry Association of
       America), 361
Rich Text Format (see RTF)

Riddler (web site), 253
right to privacy, 148
right-angle brackets (email), 25
RingWorld: The webRing Directory, 218
RioPMP, 361, 364
rippers, 363
Rocket eBook, 377
Rocketmail, 95
routers, 14
    home networks, 397, 401
    tracing, 392
routing and addressing between
        networks, 15
RTF (email), 84
running installed applications, 439

S

S&P 500 (Standard and Poor's 500), 232
scanners (see viruses, checkers)
scanning photographs to produce graphic
        images, 321
scenario file (games), tutorial, 261–264
scenarios (online gaming), installing, 262
schools (Internet use), 8
Scrabble, 290
SDMI, 362
searching and search engines
    concept searches, 420
    logical operators, 415
    multiple (meta searches), 418, 419
    natural-language queries, 418
    search engines, 414
        and Usenet newsgroups, 419
        web browsers as search engines, 418
    standalone clients, 419
    terms, 413, 414–417
    tools, text-based, 430
    Usenet posts, archiving of (privacy
        issues), 153
    utilities, 419
    (see also specific search engines, e.g.,
        Infoseek)
Secure Digital Music Initiative (SDMI), 362
Secure Sockets Layer (see SSL)
SecureTax (web site), 247
Securities and Exchanges Commission, 243
security, 144–174
    and banking, online, 223
    communication and collaboration, 354

conferencing and communication, 374–
        376
    email, 158
    and online investing, 233, 234
    and shopping, online, 175, 182–184
    taxes, 247
    web browser settings, 123
    (see also privacy)
self-describing data (XML), 374
self-extracting archives, 437
self-regulation (business), privacy
        issues, 147
selling, online, 211–220
sendmail, 103
SGML (Standard Generalized Markup
        Language), 373
shared files, and viruses, 158
shareware, 199
shipping and handling charges (online
        shopping), 179
Shockwave, 125
shopping, online, 175–220
    advantages and disadvantages, 178–179
    auctions (see auctions, online)
    buying, 184–210
    buying and selling between
        individuals, 207
    complaints, 184
    computers and computer
        equipment, 196
    conventions, 207
    delivery charges, 194
    general merchandise, 206
        web sites, 207
    major purchases, 199–206
    payment, 188
    privacy issues, 150
    security issues, 155, 175
    selling (see selling, online)
    shopping cart (see stores, online)
signatures (email messages), 35, 162
skins (WinAmp feature), 362
SLIP, 397
slow downs, and viruses, 165
smart agent technology (offline web
        browsing), 135
smart cards (digital cash), 249
smileys, 34
SMSN, 279

smuggling, 174
SoftBook Electronic Book, 377
software
   buying online, 199
   downloadable, 199
     (see also shareware)
   privacy, 159–169
   viruses, 158
Solram, 349
SonicNet, 189
sound
   cards, and Internet telephony, 344
   formats, 125
   and web page design, 308, 321
   (see also audio)
spam (see junk mail)
specifications, public (World Wide
      web), 107
SSL (Secure Sockets Layer), 223, 233
stalking, electronic, 8, 145
Standard and Poor's 500 (see S&P 500)
Standard Generalized Markup Language
      (see SGML)
Star Trek (game), 252
Starluck Casino (web site), 256
start page (see home page)
Station (web site), 255
stationery (email), 37
status line, and troubleshooting, 386
stocks
   orders, 237
   prices, 231
   quotes, 236–237, 242
   sales commissions, 231
   shorting, 241
   stock exchange, 231
     regulation, 243
     (see also brokerages)
   stock exchanges
     AMEX, 232
     NASDAQ, 232
     NYSE, 231
   stock market
     monitoring online, 241
     web sites, 242
   stock ticker (Pointcast), 370
   stop orders, 238, 239
   trading and prices, 235–242
     example, 239
   (see also investing)

stores, online, 176, 177
storing email messages, 27
streaming, 355–360
   hardware requirements, 356
   servers, 358
student loans, 249
StuffIt, 84, 437
subnet mask, 15
subscribing
   mailing lists, 48
   web sites, 116
Surf Express, 129
suspending mailing lists, 91
syntax
   mailing lists, 50
   search terms, 413
system names and host addresses, 17

T

T1 connections, 396
tags, HTML (see HTML tags)
Tax Cut (tax preparation software), 246
taxes
   capital gains, 244
   filing online, 244–247
     security issues, 247
   and stock transactions, 236
   tax preparation software, 222, 245, 246
   web-based preparation and filing, 246
Tax Systems (web site), 247
TCP, 16, 341
   and real-time communications, 341
TCP/IP, 265
   configuring for home networks, 406
telecommunications
   hardware, 372
   teleconferencing (Internet Phone), 346
   (see also Internet
     telephony)
teleconferencing, 344
   (see also conferencing
     conference calls)
telephone lines
   digital, 372
   noise, 388, 391
telephone numbers (finding), 424
telephones, standard
   and Internet telephony, 342, 348, 349

Telnet
  access to web servers, 518
  and remote computing, 515–517
  and Unix mail accounts, 86
  with Pine, 79
templates
  template file viruses (see macro viruses)
  web page design, 299–301
TEN (Total Entertainment Network), 269–272
  and Professional Computer Gamer's
    League, 289
  games, 270
terrorists, 173
test-drive notebook (Car Talk), 202
text files
  FTP, 515, 519
  Telnet, 515
text-based browsers, 133
text-based games, 251
Thawte, 375
threads, 53, 61
TicketMaster, 192
tickets
  airline, 192
  electronic, 194
  events, 192
Timestamp (FrontPage Express), 330
tips (online gaming), 258
title tags (HTML), 326
TOBE (The Other Browser-Emailer), 133
Top Gun Wingman (see Proxiweb)
Total Entertainment Network (see TEN)
traceroute (Unix), 392
tracert (Windows), 392
Trade-direct (web site), 183
trademark, use of on Internet, 19
trading
  investments (online), 232
  on margin (stock market), 241
  online shopping, 208
transaction history (online
    investments), 236
Transmission Control Protocol (see TCP)
Trash directory (email), 41
travel, 193
  and email, 85–92
  online ticket ordering, 193
  (see also tickets; automobiles)

Trojan horses, 157
troubleshooting, 379–394
  baseline information, 382–383
  dialog boxes and status lines, 386
  tools, 388
Turbo Tax, 246

U

U.S. Customs, 174
U.S. Defense Department, and early
    Internet, 4
U.S. government
  funding of Internet, 8
  and privacy laws, 148
U.S. Secret Service, 174
UDP, 341
uniform resource locator (see URL)
uninstalling files, 439
Unix
  and early web browsers, 6
  and Internet standards (Internet
    history), 4
  mail accounts (reading from a PC), 86
  Unix talk, 97, 341
  and vacation programs, 90
unknown host or recipient (return of
    email), 42, 43
unreliability (networks), 4, 7
unsubscribe (mailing list) (see mailing lists)
Up4Sale (auction web site), 215
upgrades to email software, 40
uploading
  Composer, 338
  and directory structure, 332
  files, 435
    and anonymous FTP, 520
  FrontPage Express, 338
  and FTP, 335, 517
  multiple files, 335
  via HTML editor, 338
  web pages, 331–339
    example, 334–335
URLs, 108
  entering manually, 110
  smart, 129
U.S. National Science Foundation (see NSF)
used cars, 203

used computers and equipment (buying
    online), 198
Usenet, 47, 53–63
  information for new users, 56, 60
  Newsgroups (Internet history), 5
  and online shopping, 212–220
  postings
    and junk mail, 102
    privacy issues, 153
user profiles and junk mail, 102
User's Networks (see Usenet)
username (concealing), 155
uuencode (email), 83

V

vacation programs, 88
verifying email signatures, 162
VeriSign, 159, 375
video
  encoding, 364
  real-time (see real time)
Vienna Systems (Internet telephony
    software), 349
viruses, 156–158
  Badtimes, 179
  checkers, 164–165
  and downloaded software, 158
  Goodtimes, 157
  Happy99, 157, 165
  how to determine whether you have a
    virus, 164
  Melissa, 30, 156, 167
  myths, 165
  and online games, 264
  removing, 165
  virus shields, 165
    configuration, 166
VirusScan, 165
VocalTec Ltd (see Internet Phone)
voice mail
  Internet Phone, 346
  and Internet telephony, 349
Vosaic (streaming technology), 355
Voxphone (Internet telephony
    software), 349
Vxtreme (streaming technology), 355
Vxtreme web Theater, 359

W

walk-through (online gaming), 258
Wall Street (investing), 231
Wall Street Journal, 244
want ads, online, 177
WAP (Wireless Application Protocol), 350
WAV (Microsoft file format), 84
web browsers, 4, 108
  alternative, 130–138
  banking, 225
  browser windows (Opera), 132
  control buttons, 120
  downloading with, 433
  encryption, 223, 227, 233
  history file, 117
  plug-ins, 124
  standard telephone as, 349
  text-based, 133
  XML-compliant, 374
web browsing, 108–113
  Browsing Companions and content
    aggregators, 130
  increasing speed, 126–129
  offline (see offline browsing)
  PalmPilot, 138
  privacy and security (software
    tools), 171
  with PalmPilot, 138–143
web classifieds, 214
web directories (privacy issues), 152
web guide (see channel)
web page design
  alignment of text and images, 313
  borders and margins, 329
  bullets, 316, 319
  captions (tables), 317
  color, 308
  compatability issues, 306
  converting image compression
    formats, 314
  formatting, 311
  graphics, 321–324
  headings, 310
  hit counter, 315
  icons, 318
  image maps, 320
  images, 312, 332
    as links, 314, 319
    photographic, 321

sources, 303
  text descriptions, 307, 313
  transparent background, 323
indentation, 317, 329
Java applets and JavaScript
    programs, 330
keywords, 326
last updated message, 330
lists, 316
margins, 308
page properties, 304–308
paragraphs, 311, 329
rule (horizontal bar), 319
sound
  background, 308
  files, links to, 321
tables, 316–318
text, 309–312
whitespace, 314, 317, 329
(see also HTML; links)
web pages
  bookmarking, 113–117
  changing on the server, 339
  channels, 112
  copying information from, 121
  creating using templates, 299–301
  downloading older versions, 517
  emailing from (mailto link), 320
  file management, 332–333
    on server, 337
  frames, 111
  moving, 332
  photographs, 322
  saving and printing, 120
  searching, 120
  shopping cart, 177
  storefront, for selling, 217
  suffixes for pages and images, 333
  titles, 326
  unavailable (accessing), 130
  uploading, 331–339
  (see also World Wide web
    document management)
web Phone (Internet telephony
    software), 349
web rings, 218
  for selling, 218
web servers, 4, 333

web sites
  addresses (see URLs)
  children's, 154
    (see also nanny software), 154
  consumer information, 184
  games (see World Wide web
    games)
  subscribing to, 116
web stores (see stores, online)
web styles, standard, 311
web Turbo, 135
web-based email accounts, 93–96
  privacy issues, 93
webBot components (FrontPage
    Express), 330
webFerret, 421
webMail, 95
The Wedding Network (web site), 207
wedding registries, 206
Westwood Studios, 282
What's the Big Idea? (game), 254
Wheel of Fortune (game), 255
white board (NetMeeting), 354
whitespace, HTML, 330
  (see also web page design)
WinAmp, 362
Windows
  Active Channels, 135–138
  active desktop, 134
  and DirectX, 287
  and FTP, 519
  with Kali, 267
  Windows 98
    Internet Explorer as user interface, 10
  Windows CE, 373
windows, browser (see browser windows)
Windows, Media Player (see Media Player)
WinZip, 438, 439
Wireless Application Protocol (see
    WAP), 350
wireless communication, 373
wiring (home networks), 403
WML (Wireless Device Markup
    Language), 350
women and online gaming, 259
Word (see MS Word)
workplace Internet use, 396
  privacy issues, 148, 159, 172

World Wide Web
  advertising (see advertising, online)
  animation and games, 125
  and archiving, 130
  browsers and browsing (see web
      browsers; web browsing)
  clearing cache folders, 94
  cookies, 110
  document management, 113–122
  formatted files, 125
  fraudulent use (see fraud)
  game-related sites, 257–260
  games, 253–264
      (see also names of individual games)
  information for new users, 108–113
  invention of, 5
  newsgroups available on, 54
  pop-up menus, accessing, 121
  privacy issues, 145–152
  security, 123
  specifications, 107
  and Telnet, 515
World Wide web Consortium (W3C), 325
WorldPlay games (AOL), 276
worms, 157
wrapping lines (email), 37

X

X.509 certificates, 375
XML (Extensible Markup Language), 373
  digital signatures, 374

Y

Yahoo!
  games (web site), 258
  pager, 100
  publicly accessible news services (web
      site), 62
  web rings, 218
You Don't Know Jack the Netshow
      (game), 254
You Don't Know Jack the Sports Netshow
      (game), 254

Z

Zimmerman, Paul, 12
Zip Code web site (EPA), 205
zone (see channel)
zoom feature (Opera), 132

About the Authors

Kiersten Conner-Sax is a freelance writer, focusing on computer and film topics. Her short story "Spinning" appeared in the *Lowell Pearl*; she has also written a screenplay, entitled "Putt Putt." Her film reviews have appeared in the *Boston Phoenix* and at NewEnglandFilm.com.

Kiersten grew up in California and attended college in New York City. In 1996, she further reduced her marketable skills with a Master's degree in creative writing from Emerson College. She currently lives in Manhattan with her husband, Adam, and their dog, Mugsy.

Raised in the Chicago area, **Ed Krol** went to the University of Illinois, got a degree in computer science, and never left.

In 1985 Krol became part of a networking group at the University of Illinois where he became the network manager at the time the National Center for Supercomputer Applications was formed. It was there that he managed the installation of the original NSFnet. During the same period, he also wrote the *Hitchhiker's Guide to the Internet* because he had so much trouble getting information and was sick of telling the same story to everyone.

In 1989 Krol opted to leave the fast lane and returned to pastoral life on campus, where he remains to this day assistant director for Network Information Services, Computing and Communications Service Office, University of Illinois, Urbana. He also writes a monthly column for *Network World*.

He has a wife and daughter (who is in the *Hacker's Dictionary* as the toddler responsible for "Mollyguards"). In his spare time Krol is a pilot and plays hockey.

Colophon

Our look is the result of reader comments, our own experimentation, and feedback from distribution channels. Distinctive covers complement our distinctive approach to technical topics, breathing personality and life into potentially dry subjects.

The image on the cover of *The Whole Internet: The Next Generation* is adapted from a 19th-century engraving from the Dover Pictorial Archive. The image is entitled, simply, "World." Depicted in this image are a globe, a telesope, books, and a quill. The image symbolizes humankind's curiosity about the world and desire to explore it.

Jane Ellin was the production editor for *The Whole Internet: The Next Generation*. Maureen Dempsey was the proofreader; Nancy Kotary provided quality control; and Kimo Carter, Colleen Gorman, and Abby Myers provided production support. Mike Sierra provided FrameMaker technical support. Christine Stone wrote the index.

Hanna Dyer designed the cover of this book, based on a series design by Edie Freedman. The image is adapted from a 19th-century engraving from the Dover Pictorial Archive. The cover layout was produced by Kathleen Wilson using QuarkXPress 3.3 and the ITC Garamond font. Whenever possible, our books use RepKover™, a durable and flexible lay-flat binding. If the page count exceeds RepKover's limit, perfect binding is used.

Alicia Cech designed the inside layout, based on a series design by Nancy Priest and implemented in FrameMaker 5.5.6 by Mike Sierra. The text and heading fonts are ITC Garamond Light and Garamond Book. The illustrations that appear in the book were produced by Robert Romano and Rhon Porter using Macromedia Free-Hand 8 and Adobe Photoshop 5. This colophon was written by Clairemarie Fisher O'Leary.

How to stay in touch with O'Reilly

1. Visit Our Award-Winning Web Site

http://www.oreilly.com/

★ "Top 100 Sites on the Web" —*PC Magazine*
★ "Top 5% Web sites" —*Point Communications*
★ "3-Star site" —*The McKinley Group*

Our web site contains a library of comprehensive product information (including book excerpts and tables of contents), downloadable software, background articles, interviews with technology leaders, links to relevant sites, book cover art, and more. File us in your Bookmarks or Hotlist!

2. Join Our Email Mailing Lists

New Product Releases

To receive automatic email with brief descriptions of all new O'Reilly products as they are released, send email to:
listproc@online.oreilly.com
Put the following information in the first line of your message (*not* in the Subject field):
subscribe oreilly-news

O'Reilly Events

If you'd also like us to send information about trade show events, special promotions, and other O'Reilly events, send email to:
listproc@online.oreilly.com
Put the following information in the first line of your message (*not* in the Subject field):
subscribe oreilly-events

3. Get Examples from Our Books via FTP

There are two ways to access an archive of example files from our books:

Regular FTP

- ftp to:
  ftp.oreilly.com
  (login: anonymous
  password: your email address)
- Point your web browser to:
  ftp://ftp.oreilly.com/

FTPMAIL

- Send an email message to:
  ftpmail@online.oreilly.com
  (Write "help" in the message body)

4. Contact Us via Email

order@oreilly.com
To place a book or software order online. Good for North American and international customers.

subscriptions@oreilly.com
To place an order for any of our newsletters or periodicals.

books@oreilly.com
General questions about any of our books.

software@oreilly.com
For general questions and product information about our software. Check out O'Reilly Software Online at **http://software.oreilly.com/** for software and technical support information. Registered O'Reilly software users send your questions to: **website-support@oreilly.com**

cs@oreilly.com
For answers to problems regarding your order or our products.

booktech@oreilly.com
For book content technical questions or corrections.

proposals@oreilly.com
To submit new book or software proposals to our editors and product managers.

international@oreilly.com
For information about our international distributors or translation queries. For a list of our distributors outside of North America check out:
http://www.oreilly.com/www/order/country.html

O'Reilly & Associates, Inc.
101 Morris Street, Sebastopol, CA 95472 USA
TEL 707-829-0515 or 800-998-9938
     (6am to 5pm PST)
FAX 707-829-0104

International Distributors

UK, EUROPE, MIDDLE EAST AND AFRICA (EXCEPT FRANCE, GERMANY, AUSTRIA, SWITZERLAND, LUXEMBOURG, LIECHTENSTEIN, AND EASTERN EUROPE)

INQUIRIES
O'Reilly UK Limited
4 Castle Street
Farnham
Surrey, GU9 7HS
United Kingdom
Telephone: 44-1252-711776
Fax: 44-1252-734211
Email: josette@oreilly.com

ORDERS
Wiley Distribution Services Ltd.
1 Oldlands Way
Bognor Regis
West Sussex PO22 9SA
United Kingdom
Telephone: 44-1243-779777
Fax: 44-1243-820250
Email: cs-books@wiley.co.uk

FRANCE

ORDERS
GEODIF
61, Bd Saint-Germain
75240 Paris Cedex 05, France
Tel: 33-1-44-41-46-16 (French books)
Tel: 33-1-44-41-11-87 (English books)
Fax: 33-1-44-41-11-44
Email: distribution@eyrolles.com

INQUIRIES
Éditions O'Reilly
18 rue Séguier
75006 Paris, France
Tel: 33-1-40-51-52-30
Fax: 33-1-40-51-52-31
Email: france@editions-oreilly.fr

GERMANY, SWITZERLAND, AUSTRIA, EASTERN EUROPE, LUXEMBOURG, AND LIECHTENSTEIN

INQUIRIES & ORDERS
O'Reilly Verlag
Balthasarstr. 81
D-50670 Köln
Germany
Telephone: 49-221-973160-91
Fax: 49-221-973160-8
Email: anfragen@oreilly.de (inquiries)
Email: order@oreilly.de (orders)

CANADA (FRENCH LANGUAGE BOOKS)

Les Éditions Flammarion ltée
375, Avenue Laurier Ouest
Montréal (Québec) H2V 2K3
Tel: 00-1-514-277-8807
Fax: 00-1-514-278-2085
Email: info@flammarion.qc.ca

HONG KONG

City Discount Subscription Service, Ltd.
Unit D, 3rd Floor, Yan's Tower
27 Wong Chuk Hang Road
Aberdeen, Hong Kong
Tel: 852-2580-3539
Fax: 852-2580-6463
Email: citydis@ppn.com.hk

KOREA

Hanbit Media, Inc.
Sonyoung Bldg. 202
Yeksam-dong 736-36
Kangnam-ku
Seoul, Korea
Tel: 822-554-9610
Fax: 822-556-0363
Email: hant93@chollian.dacom.co.kr

PHILIPPINES

Mutual Books, Inc.
429-D Shaw Boulevard
Mandaluyong City, Metro
Manila, Philippines
Tel: 632-725-7538
Fax: 632-721-3056
Email: mbikikog@mnl.sequel.net

TAIWAN

O'Reilly Taiwan
No. 3, Lane 131
Hang-Chow South Road
Section 1, Taipei, Taiwan
Tel: 886-2-23968990
Fax: 886-2-23968916
Email: taiwan@oreilly.com

CHINA

O'Reilly Beijing
Room 2410
160, FuXingMenNeiDaJie
XiCheng District
Beijing, China PR 100031
Tel: 86-10-86631006
Fax: 86-10-86631007
Email: beijing@oreilly.com

INDIA

Computer Bookshop (India) Pvt. Ltd.
190 Dr. D.N. Road, Fort
Bombay 400 001 India
Tel: 91-22-207-0989
Fax: 91-22-262-3551
Email: cbsbom@giasbm01.vsnl.net.in

JAPAN

O'Reilly Japan, Inc.
Kiyoshige Building 2F
12-Bancho, Sanei-cho
Shinjuku-ku
Tokyo 160-0008 Japan
Tel: 81-3-3356-5227
Fax: 81-3-3356-5261
Email: japan@oreilly.com

ALL OTHER ASIAN COUNTRIES

O'Reilly & Associates, Inc.
101 Morris Street
Sebastopol, CA 95472 USA
Tel: 707-829-0515
Fax: 707-829-0104
Email: order@oreilly.com

AUSTRALIA

WoodsLane Pty., Ltd.
7/5 Vuko Place
Warriewood NSW 2102
Australia
Tel: 61-2-9970-5111
Fax: 61-2-9970-5002
Email: info@woodslane.com.au

NEW ZEALAND

Woodslane New Zealand, Ltd.
21 Cooks Street (P.O. Box 575)
Waganui, New Zealand
Tel: 64-6-347-6543
Fax: 64-6-345-4840
Email: info@woodslane.com.au

LATIN AMERICA

McGraw-Hill Interamericana
Editores, S.A. de C.V.
Cedro No. 512
Col. Atlampa
06450, Mexico, D.F.
Tel: 52-5-547-6777
Fax: 52-5-547-3336
Email: mcgraw-hill@infosel.net.mx

O'REILLY®

TO ORDER: **800-998-9938** • **order@oreilly.com** • **http://www.oreilly.com/**
OUR PRODUCTS ARE AVAILABLE AT A BOOKSTORE OR SOFTWARE STORE NEAR YOU.
FOR INFORMATION: **800-998-9938** • **707-829-0515** • **info@oreilly.com**

O'REILLY™

O'Reilly & Associates, Inc.
101 Morris Street
Sebastopol, CA 95472-9902
1-800-998-9938

Visit us online at:
http://www.ora.com/
orders@ora.com

O'REILLY WOULD LIKE TO HEAR FROM YOU

Which book did this card come from?

_____

Where did you buy this book?
- ❏ Bookstore
- ❏ Direct from O'Reilly
- ❏ Bundled with hardware/software
- ❏ Computer Store
- ❏ Class/seminar
- ❏ Other _____

What operating system do you use?
- ❏ UNIX
- ❏ Windows NT
- ❏ Macintosh
- ❏ PC(Windows/DOS)
- ❏ Other _____

What is your job description?
- ❏ System Administrator
- ❏ Network Administrator
- ❏ Web Developer
- ❏ Programmer
- ❏ Educator/Teacher
- ❏ Other _____

❏ Please send me O'Reilly's catalog, containing a complete listing of O'Reilly books and software.

Name _____   Company/Organization _____

Address _____

City _____   State _____   Zip/Postal Code _____   Country _____

Telephone _____   Internet or other email address (specify network) _____

Nineteenth century wood engraving
of a bear from the O'Reilly &
Associates Nutshell Handbook®
Using & Managing UUCP.

POST CARD

BUSINESS REPLY MAIL

FIRST CLASS MAIL   PERMIT NO. 80   SEBASTOPOL, CA

Postage will be paid by addressee

O'Reilly & Associates, Inc.
101 Morris Street
Sebastopol, CA 95472-9902